Dearest Bubushkin

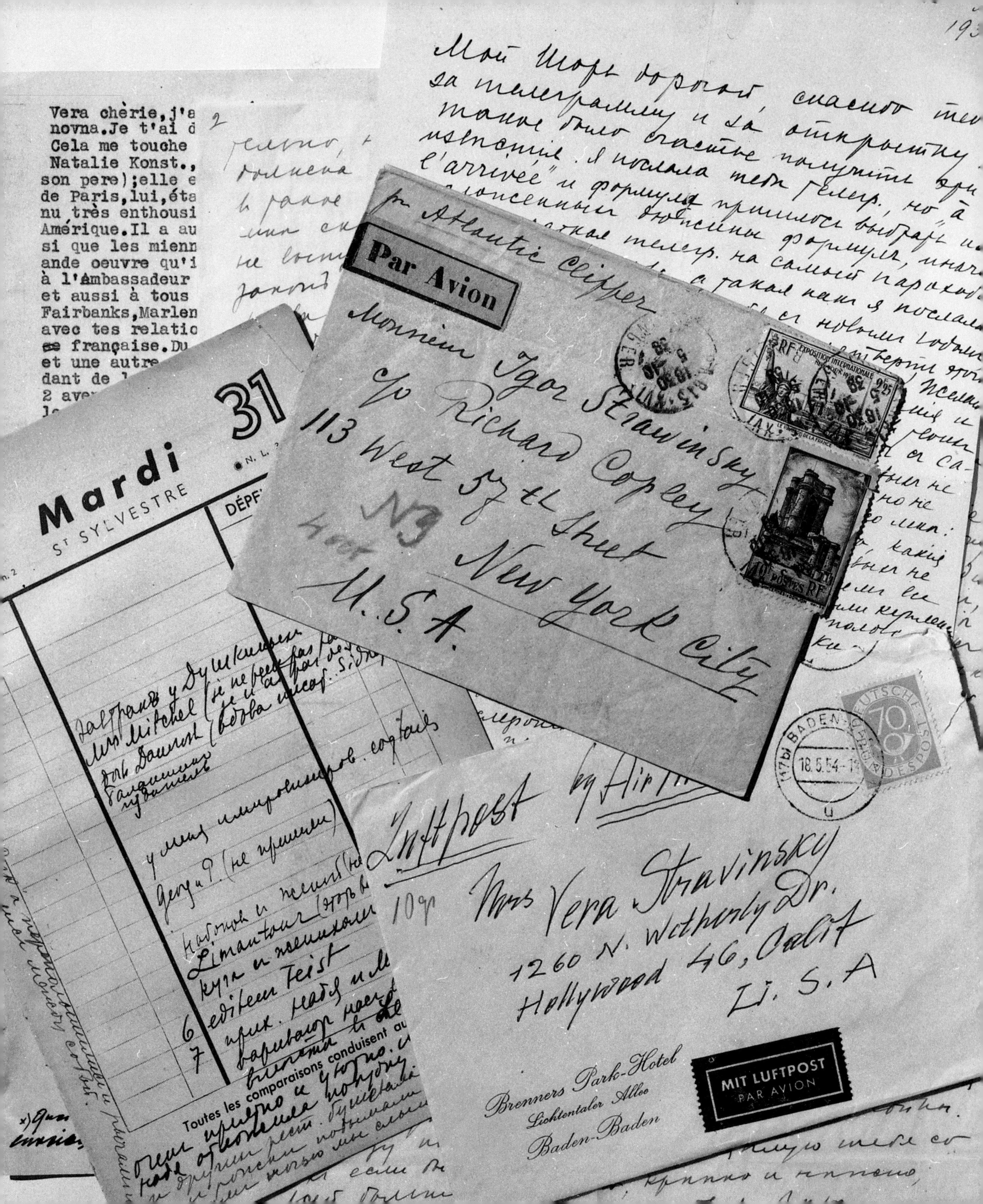

193

Vera chérie, j'a
novna. Je t'ai d
Cela me touche
Natalie Konst.,
son père); elle e
de Paris, lui, éta
nu très enthousi
Amérique. Il a au
si que les mienn
ande oeuvre qu'i
à l'Ambassadeur
et aussi à tous
Fairbanks, Marlen
avec tes relatio
se française. Du
et une autre
dant de l
2 aven
lo

Mardi
St SYLVESTRE

31

Toutes les comparaisons conduisent au

Atlantic Clipper

Par Avion

Monsieur Igor Strawinsky
c/o Richard Copley
113 West 57th Street
New York City
U.S.A.

Luftpost   by Air

Mrs Vera Stravinsky
1260 N. Wetherly Dr.
Hollywood 46, Calif.
U.S.A.

Brenners Park-Hotel
Lichtentaler Allee
Baden-Baden

MIT LUFTPOST
PAR AVION

Edited by Robert Craft

Dearest Bubushkin

The correspondence of Vera and Igor Stravinsky, 1921–1954,

with excerpts from Vera Stravinsky's diaries, 1922–1971

Translated from the Russian by Lucia Davidova

With 183 illustrations

Thames and Hudson

TO THE MEMORY OF VERA AND IGOR STRAVINSKY

Lady, you are the cruell'st she alive,
If you will lead these graces to the grave
And leave the world no copy.

Endpapers: Letter from Igor to Vera, May 18, 1954.

Designed by Pauline Baines

© 1985 Robert Craft

First published in the USA in 1985
by Thames and Hudson Inc.,
500 Fifth Avenue,
New York, New York 10110

Library of Congress Catalog Card Number
85-50350

Printed and bound in Great Britain

Preface

Readers will not require any introductory data on the life of Igor Stravinsky, this being already well known or available elsewhere. They should be provided with a résumé of Vera Arturovna de Bosset's life, however, at least until February 21, 1921, when Serge de Diaghilev introduced her to Stravinsky. From that year until the composer's death in April 1971, Vera and Igor were separated only during the periods, 1921 to 1933, that he spent with his family in residences in Biarritz, Nice, Grenoble (La Vironnière), and while he was on four transatlantic concert tours and two short tours to the Baltic.

Vera de Bosset, an only child, was born at Aptekarsky Ostrov, 3 Troizkaya Ulitsa, St. Petersburg, on Christmas day, 1888.[1] Her mother, Henriette Fyodorovna Malmgren, of Swedish ancestry, born in 1870 (also on Christmas day), died near Moscow during World War II. Henriette's brother Eugene Malmgren, the cellist, had once employed the eighteen-year-old Igor Stravinsky as piano accompanist, and another relative was the Arctic explorer Finn Malmgren (a statue of whom stands in Stockholm). Vera's father, Artur Efimovich de Bosset, descended from a family of Huguenots (one of them the Prefect of Paris under Napoleon), was a wealthy manufacturer of electrical equipment in Kudinovo, near Moscow. He, too, had a famous brother, the tenor, Bosse, of the Maryinsky Theater in St. Petersburg, while a cousin, the Admiral Marquis Theodore de Bosset, hero of the Russo-Japanese War, was the confidant of Tsar Nicholas II. (Vera preserved photographs of Theodore de Bosset as well as obituaries from Lima newspapers, sent to her by her father's second wife—from 1917—Irena Emilovna Mella.) Artur de Bosset died in Santiago, Chile, in August 1937.

From 1898, Vera was brought up at her family's country estate at Gorky, between St. Petersburg and Moscow, on the Nizhni Novgorod line. Educated by French and German governesses, Vera spent her summers in Switzerland, France, and Germany. At age thirteen she entered the Pussell boarding school in Moscow, graduating cum laude four years later, certified to teach mathematics. During her adolescent years in Moscow she studied music and became an accomplished pianist, but after seeing the productions of Stanislavsky and the performances of Bernhardt, Duse, and Isadora Duncan, Vera realized that her vocation was the theater. She also matriculated at the famous ballet school of Lydia Mikhailovna Nelidova where, still a young girl, she met Diaghilev and Fokine on one of their talent-scouting expeditions.

Until World War I intervened, Vera studied science (chemistry) and arts (painting) at the University of Berlin. She married a Mr. Lury in c. 1910,[2] but her parents had the union dissolved. Her second husband, Robert Shilling, was a fellow student in Berlin, and in a note written in 1962, after a trip to Moscow, Vera recalled that "Ekaterina Furtseva, Soviet Minister of Culture, had the same apartment in which I lived when I was married to Shilling. I remember that Tairov, the director of the Kamerny Theater company, came to see me there—and told me very frankly that he knew I was rich, as well as talented and beautiful, and that his theater needed money." Vera became a member of the company and, at the same time, a well-known film actress as Helen in Protozanov's War and Peace (1915), and as the star, opposite the son of the choreographer Marius Petipa, in a number of comedies.

Yet the chronology of this period in Vera's life remains puzzling for the reason that she was definitely in Belgium (and probably in Paris) in the spring of 1913 with Sergei Yurievich Sudeikin (1882–1946), who had been engaged by Diaghilev as a scene painter for the forthcoming production of Le Sacre du printemps. Ironically, Sudeikin's name is better known in the history of poetry than in that of painting, his first wife, Olga Glebova Sudeikina having been the inamorata of Anna Akhmatova. Sudeikin had painted murals for the famous "Stray Dog" cabaret, where Akhmatova recited her poems, and where Olga danced, sometimes scantily clad (in photographs of her that the Stravinskys preserved from a decade later, in France, she is altogether naked), and acted in such productions as Belayev's Blundering Psyche. The handsome young dragoon officer, Vsevelod Knyazev, also in love with Olga, shot himself when he discovered that his successful male rival was Alexander Blok.

At this time, Olga and Akhmatova shared an apartment. In an unpublished autobiographical note written in the 1970s, Vera remembers "the trouble Olechka had leaving Petrograd to go to Paris and that Igor helped her with visas. . . . She was always unlucky in love. In Paris she lived in poverty, in a maid's room, making a little money by breeding small birds and making artificial flowers. Once, when someone asked me who she was, I answered: 'The first wife of my second husband.'"

Sudeikin and Olga had separated in March 1916, and he and Vera moved from Moscow to St. Petersburg, living at first in a flat above another renowned artists' café, "Prival Komediantov,"

The initials R.C. in the footnotes refer to the present editor.

[1] Her American passport gives the year as 1892, but Mrs. Stravinsky always admitted that Sudeikin had induced her to become four years younger when she applied for a Georgian passport in Tiflis during the Russian Revolution to replace her Tsarist passport. Confirmation that she was born in 1888 is found in a letter to her from her younger stepmother, Irena Mella, January 20, 1970: "I greatly admire you for keeping so young at 82."

[2] See Literary Georgia, Nos. 10–11, Tbilisi, 1967. R.C. has been unable to discover any other reference to Vera's first husband, but the letters of her life-long friend, Olga Sallard (see Vera's diary, August 13, 1923) refer to "your three marriages" before Stravinsky, and reveal that husband number three, Sudeikin, was referred to as "The Prisoner of the Caucasus" (an allusion to Lermontov).

where their closest friends included the poet Kusmin[1] and the composer Arthur Lourié (1892–1966).[2] (It was here that Vera had to be hidden from the violent womanizer Mayakovsky.)

In the autumn of 1916, Vera and Sergei had taken another apartment, this one on the Ekaterinsky canal, where they were living at the time of the assassination of Rasputin. In February 1917, they went to Moscow, where Sudeikin met with Shilling, after which Vera was able to obtain a legal separation from him. Back in St. Petersburg, she was injured during the March 1917 riots that resulted—after the police fired on a crowd—in the abdication of the Tsar. (The Russian government cabled Stravinsky, in Rome, asking him to compose a new national anthem, which was performed there at the next presentation of the Ballets Russes.)

Vera and Sudeikin returned to Moscow, and from there joined the exodus of "White Russians" to the Crimea. Her mother came to the Crimea, too, but returned to Moscow. In February 1918, in Meshor, near Yalta, Vera and Sergei were married (common law, proofs of divorce on both sides being unobtainable during the Revolution). In the spring of 1919, they fled on a schooner from Yalta to Baku. Then, in Tiflis [Tbilisi], Vera became a citizen of the Republic of Georgia. The magazine *Literary Georgia*, Nos. 10–11, op. cit., contains the Georgian poet Titian Tabidze's memoirs of Serge Sudeikin and Vera de Bosset when they lived in Griboyedova Street in Tiflis.

While in the Crimea and the Caucasus, Vera became known as a painter; her career as an artist is rarely mentioned in the present book, however, partly for the reason that she painted more vigorously and consistently in the decade after Stravinsky's death than ever before.[3] Also in the Crimea, in the Caucasus, and during her first year in Paris (May 1920 to June 1921), Vera kept a scrapbook in which Osip Mandelstamm and other poets of her acquaintance wrote verses in her honor, musicians composed pieces, and artists drew and painted her portrait—a treasure of Russian culture eventually to be published in facsimile, together with her diaries of this pre-Stravinsky period.

At the beginning of the correspondence in the present volume, the reader should remember that Vera knew Diaghilev before she knew Stravinsky, and that Sudeikin knew Diaghilev even before Diaghilev knew Stravinsky. (As an entry in Vera's Crimean diary reveals, Sudeikin had not met the composer before 1921.) In September 1921, Diaghilev engaged Vera for the role of the Queen in his revival of *The Sleeping Beauty*. Later he commissioned her to design and execute costumes, including some of those for Matisse's *Chant du Rossignol* (1925), Goncharova's *Firebird* (1926), and Rouault's *Prodigal Son* (1929).

After a quarrel at the end of May 1922, Vera left Sudeikin. In August he moved to America permanently, and Vera moved to an apartment with Gabrielle Buffet, who had separated from her husband Francis Picabia. Also in 1922, Vera and Tula Danilova, a refugee friend from Moscow, opened a fashion and theater accessories shop, Tulavera, at 92, rue de la Boëtie. The two women made the curtains for Henry Bernstein's play *Judith*, for which Léon Bakst had designed the costumes and Sudeikin the decors. This partly explains Vera's claim, in one of her first letters to Stravinsky, to knowledge of the theatrical world. In 1923, in Monte Carlo, she rehearsed for the role of the bride in *Les Noces*, but withdrew because she was so much taller than her stage fiancé.

In 1924 Vera created the costumes for the Paris premiere of *Histoire du soldat*. In the 1930s, she studied cosmetology

professionally and developed an elite clientele; her letters refer to this and also to some of her work as a couturier. But her main occupation in the French years was helping Stravinsky, accompanying him on his concert tours and dealing with the demands of the press, society, and his family. She wrote many of his letters for him in Russian and French, and almost all of those in German. She was a sounding board for his compositions in progress, praising and encouraging him, and she played a critical role in influencing his choice of music for his concert programs, effectively countering his tendency to favor his least popular creations.

*

"Dearest Bubushkin"—the etymology seems to be connected with Vera's word for Stravinsky in a pouty, complaining (of bubus) mood—begins with the earliest surviving correspondence, from the summer of 1921. When Igor and Vera met on February 21, 1921, it was love at first sight, but since he was married, had only recently broken off an affair with Gabrielle Chanel, and even at the moment was involved with a female member of the Baliev dance company, the romance with Vera did not blossom until his return from Madrid in May. By July 14, the relationship between Vera and Igor had become torrid; every year on that date he sent her a gift or other reminder (in 1966, for instance, a note: "1921 to 1966 = 45 years"). In late July 1921, Stravinsky rejoined his family at Anglet, a village about 10 kilometers north of Biarritz. He saw her during his subsequent trips to Paris and was alone with her in London in late October and early November.

Most of the letters in the present volume were sent to Stravinsky in America in 1935, 1936, 1937, and 1939. No letters from either correspondent survive of his first visit to the United States in 1925. The only other letters between the couple date from 1952, 1953, and 1954 during very brief concert tours when Mrs. Stravinsky did not accompany her husband. Only four letters survive from the period between the brief flirtatious exchanges of 1921 and the longer series of Vera's 1935, 1937, and 1939 letters: a 1927 note from Igor to Vera; Vera's letter to Igor on the death of Diaghilev; her greeting to Igor on his fiftieth birthday (June 1932); and a 1933 report from Vera to Igor at home (La Vironnière). All four are included here, since, unlike the three volumes of Stravinsky's correspondence,[4] the letters in the present book are not selected but, with reasonable certainty, complete.

Shortly before Vera's departure for America at the beginning of 1940, Igor requested that she destroy all of his communications to her. With the exception of one note from 1921, which had special significance for her, and two letters containing verses that he had written for her, she complied. Fortunately, he kept carbon copies of some of his letters and telegrams to her from the autumn of 1939, and he preserved almost all her letters to him, giving them to her in 1955, when she planned to write her autobiography.

In 1965, while moving from 1260 to 1218 North Wetherly Drive, Hollywood, Stravinsky placed his first wife's letters to him in a brown paper bag on which he wrote: "To be destroyed after my death." A New York Surrogate Court ruled, however, that since he was eighty-three at the time and did not destroy them himself, and made no mention of them in his subsequent wills, the letters should be preserved and made available to scholars. The collection is now in the Paul Sacher Foundation in Basel. In the 1970s Vera made packets of her letters to Stravinsky, tied them with colored ribbons, and placed them in a box with her handwritten statement, signed by three attorneys as witnesses:

---

[1] For a translation of Kusmin's poems about Vera and Sudeikin, see *Stravinsky in Pictures and Documents*, New York, 1978. The original manuscripts of this and of other poems by Kusmin were in Mrs. Stravinsky's possession at the time of her death.

[2] Stravinsky's musical assistant from 1924 to 1931. He became a refugee in America soon after Stravinsky, but the two men never met again. Answering a letter from Vera announcing Lourié's death (1966), Ira Belline (see Vera's diary,

January 19, 1923) expresses surprise that he died in poverty, or, at any rate, left no money for his wife, Ella, since "their daughter Mary has a husband as well as a rich protector, Paul Louis Weiler" (April 26, 1967).

[3] See *Fantastic Cities and Other Paintings* by Vera Stravinsky, Boston, 1979.

[4] *Stravinsky: Selected Correspondence*, London, Vol. I (1983), Vol. II (1984), Vol. III (1985).

1 January 1913. London. Photo by Saul Bransburg.

2 1913. London. Photo by Saul Bransburg.

2

1

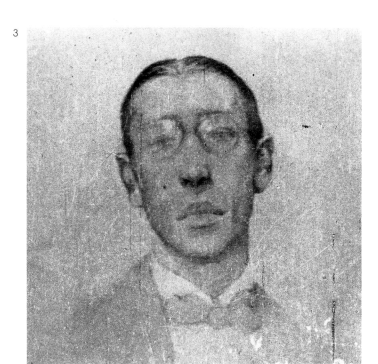

3 May 1913. Paris. Drawing by Ivan Thiele.

4 1916. Moscow. Vera's costume designed by Serge Sudeikin.

5 1916. St. Petersburg. Photograph of a portrait of Osip Mandelstamm by Lev Bruny. The inscription reads: "To Vera Arturovna from Nina Balmont" (daughter of the poet Konstantin Balmont).

5

Вере Артуровне

от Нины Брут Балмонт

фотография с портрета

поэта Мандельштама

работы Льва Бруни

Петербург, 1916 г.

6 1920. Zurich.

"To be published by Robert Craft after my death." I did not open the box until February 1983.

Despite the gaps in time between the groups of letters, the history of Igor and Vera is not difficult to follow. The 1935, 1936, and 1937 sequences introduce the reader to Stravinsky's family and to some of his and Vera's closest friends. The September to December 1939 letters reveal a deepening maturity in the relationship, and, incidentally, offer descriptions of life in Paris during the first months of World War II that are of independent historical interest.

*

Vera kept diaries in her childhood, resumed them during the Russian Revolution (1917–19), again from 1922 to 1931 (the volume for 1925 appears to have been lost),[1] during 1938, and from 1940 through to Stravinsky's death in 1971. These books comprise the only record of Stravinsky's personal life from January 1940 to April 1948. (My own diaries during the 1950s are much more extensive than Mrs. Stravinsky's, but the material in hers and mine seldom overlaps.) As published here, her diaries have been drastically cut. Only one day out of five or six has been included, and then the entry has been reduced to a line or two, mentioning people met, places seen, and some activity of Stravinsky's. Almost all of the record of Vera's life without Stravinsky has been omitted. I have also avoided duplication of Stravinsky's own medical diaries published in *A Stravinsky Scrapbook*,[2] but included his diary entries in 1941 and 1942 (in square brackets after her entries); these consist mainly of the calendar of his lessons in composition to a pupil, Ernest Anderson. If Vera's complete diaries were to be published, the result would be a book or books of great bulk containing a more detailed account of her life than of Stravinsky's.

Even in capsule form, the diaries reveal a scarcely believable schedule of travels and social life, which, together with the extremely full agenda of business and medical appointments, makes one wonder when Stravinsky found time in which to compose. The editorial cutting has not distorted the picture of the Stravinskys in transit, but much of their social activity, including a few thousand lunches and dinners at which they were hosts or guests, had to be eliminated. Even so, some readers might be disconcerted by the glitter of famous names that remains; but Vera Stravinsky was the least star-struck resident of Hollywood, being in awe only of her husband. The companionship and care that she gave him, shielding him and attending to his health, are the highlight of the book.

The diaries establish that the Stravinskys' closest Hollywood friends, the Bolms, Sokolovs, Eugene Lourié and Berman, were predominantly Russians or Russian-speaking, and that until 1948 almost everyone else was French or French-speaking (Mr. and Mrs. Arthur Sachs,[3] the Forbeses,[4] the Blisses,[5] *et al.*). The Stravinskys' happiness in California is another feature of the diaries, as is the discovery that the main hobbies of the composer and his wife were gardening and movie-going, and that they were fond of Santa Barbara to the extent of wanting to move there (see the entries for October 1943).

The originals of the diaries until 1950, and of all the letters (except for a few in French written in 1939), are in Russian; the 1950–71 diaries are almost entirely in English. All translations from the Russian are by Mme Lucia Davidova, who had known Vera and Sudeikin in Paris in 1920 and who was a close friend of Igor and Vera Stravinsky from the late 1940s until their deaths. Mme Davidova is familiar with the characteristics and idiosyncrasies of the Stravinskys' Russian, English, and French usages. (For only one example, Stravinsky used to say that something or other "does not arrange me," meaning "suit me," but an initial attempt to preserve the flavor of his English by retaining "arrange" as the translation of the Russian or French word resulted in too many puzzles.)

I am responsible for the translations from the French and for editing the text of the entire book. I am also responsible for failing to identify many names, but I decided to leave them "unglossed," irritating as this may be for the reader, in the hope that others may be able to provide information about them for a future, fuller edition. I am also responsible for choosing not to use ellipses to indicate cuts, and to forego brackets for readings of problematical and difficult-to-decipher words. The "scholarly" apparatus that could be, perhaps should have been, attached to Vera Stravinsky's uncomplicated narrative would sink it.

Acknowledgments

On the Hudson side, my gratitude to Mme Lucia Davidova for her translations of innumerable pages of difficult-to-decipher Russian script; to Brett Shapiro, who not only winnowed the illustrations from many hundreds more, but who also typed and retyped the manuscript; and to Elbert Lenrow and Lawrence Morton, who read and corrected the text.

On the Thames side, my deepest appreciation for Pauline Baines's presentation of photography and texts, which has managed to satisfy the often contradictory claims of art and historical importance; and for Gill Paul's intelligent copy editing and fine eye for detail. My profound thanks to Ronald Davidson-Houston, meticulous editor and skillful coordinator, and to Stanley Baron, whom Vera Stravinsky knew as a good friend and who has made this book possible.

R.C.

---

[1] Olga Sallard, in Illats (Gironde), wrote to Vera in Venice, September 1951, saying that "several of your journals are in my possession, but I have not sent them because of the expense." Undoubtedly this refers to the 1925 and 1932–37 diaries. Vera was extremely occupied at the time—the letter also refers to the burden on Stravinsky, still weakened by pneumonia, of the presence of his children in Venice during rehearsals and performances of *The Rake's Progress*—and forgot and never returned to the matter.

[2] London, 1983.

[3] Arthur Sachs, of Goldman and Sachs, had first visited Stravinsky in Biarritz in 1924. The two men became close friends during World War II when Sachs lived in Santa Barbara. He commissioned the Symphony in Three Movements and gave the manuscript to the New York Public Library.

[4] Edward Forbes, of Cambridge, Massachusetts, invited Stravinsky to give the Charles Eliot Norton Lectures at Harvard in 1939–40.

[5] Robert Woods Bliss was United States Ambassador to Argentina. Mrs. (Mildred) Bliss had commissioned Stravinsky's Concerto in E flat.

Delaunay, Kochno, Moi Sonia Delaunay Diaghi=lew Falla L'italien Bazocchi

Espagne Avril 1921

7 April 1921. Madrid. The identifications are in Stravinsky's hand.

8 1921. Paris. Drawing of Vera by Sudeikin.

Letters and Diaries

1921

Vera to Igor

Monsieur Igor Stravinsky
Anglet
near Bayonne
Cottage l'Argenté

7, av. Frémiet
Paris 16
[July] 1921

Dear Igor Fyodorovich, Your postcard, like all of your news, gave us great pleasure. I am glad that you remember us and love us, even in the whirlwind of resort life. Our own lives seem to be settling, and we are not as unhappy as we were before you left. The season has not yet started, but Seriozha[1] has a few fairly good commissions, one of them for America.

On your return, we will invite you to a good dinner and also pay back the 100 francs that we owe you. During the monster's stay in Paris (Seriozha does not refer to Diaghilev otherwise), we had several visits from Kochno,[2] who brought news of you and how you were spending your time.[3] Come back soon, for we are envious. Seriozha is in a good mood (I hope I do not speak too soon!), and he very much wants to see you, though exactly *what* he wants I do not know; perhaps it is to go on a spree with you. At this moment he is shouting to me from a distance of seven rooms (a large apartment, isn't it?) that he loves you, misses you, and that it is time for you to return to Paris and to rest from your rest. Inwardly we have not changed and are as nice and charming as we used to be, especially towards you. Outwardly, a slight change is noticeable: I have plucked my eyebrows to a thin line and am told that it is becoming. I also have a new black dress in which I look like a young widow out of a play by Ostrovsky. Seriozha will order a dinner-coat in London when he goes in September to attend to important business!

We were in Versailles for a few days' rest from Paris, which is completely empty in this season. Everyone traveling in the direction of Biarritz asks for your address, which I give to some and refuse to others. Among the former is Fatima Hanum[4] (you will remember going to her house), who insisted on "seeing Stravinsky and having a drink with him." Since you seem to have a reputation, I gave her your address in order that she can convince herself to the contrary.

Dear friend, I conclude this letter with a tender kiss. Both of us love you and are looking forward to your return. Our greetings to your family. Please write to me. And remember when you return that I want to see you very much. Vera Sudeikina.

Vera to Igor

Monsieur Igor Stravinsky
Anglet
near Bayonne
Cottage l'Argenté

7, av. Frémiet
Paris 16
July 27, 1921

Dear Igor Fyodorovich, The trousers are ordered, and you will have them by the first of August. You did not say anything about sending them, but I am certain you do not expect to sport them in Paris in winter. They cost 100 francs, at least until you have worn

---

[1] The painter Serge Sudeikin, Vera's husband. (The name is spelled Sergei when not followed by the surname.)

[2] The poet Boris Kochno (b. 1904) had known Vera during the Russian Revolution. In October 1969, she wrote the following memoir of him: "Boris Kochno was a young poet. I liked his young romantic appearance, his enthusiasm for the same things: we recited Russian poems to each other, and he copied a whole book of Anna Akhmatova's poems for me. One day we talked about the Ballets Russes and he said, 'How I would like to meet him [Diaghilev]. I saw him once in the foyer in the Théâtre des Champs-Elysées and almost fainted. Such an appearance!' Kochno told me about his former love affairs and said that he was free at present and looking for a 'higher attachment.' Some weeks later, I telephoned him and invited him to come at four to our hotel, saying that Diaghilev was coming for tea. It was a Sunday and all of the barbers were closed; Kochno said he could not shave himself; he came at three and I tried to shave him with a Gillette. Diaghilev arrived an hour later but was not especially impressed. Finally, he invited Kochno for lunch the next day, and the romance started then. It did not last long, but the friendship continued until Diaghilev's death. He greatly appreciated Kochno's devotion, cleverness, and literary knowledge. Diaghilev's passion for book collecting was developed by Kochno, and the two of them went regularly to Warsaw to buy old Russian books. . . . Not long after Kochno had returned with Diaghilev from Spain, in the spring of 1921, Diaghilev asked me to have tea with him alone. I wondered why, since he was always so busy, and guessed correctly that something had happened between him and Kochno. 'Yes; and I have to confess that I met a young dancer [Anton Dolin] with whom I am in love. I want to tell you about it first. Are you shocked? Do you feel like criticizing me?' I said something banal about the difficulties of analyzing the experience of love, love is love, etc., which I mention only because some years later Diaghilev was critical of me for a time in my love affair with Stravinsky, moody with me when he saw me coming to Stravinsky's studio, and when I asked him what had happened, he responded with exactly the same banalities."

[3] Kochno had just returned from Anglet, where he had been working with Stravinsky on the libretto of *Mavra*. Since little has been published concerning the relationship between the two men, the following note, from the librettist to the composer, sent from London, on July 1, 1927, indicates the tone that prevailed between them in the Diaghilev period: "Dear Igor Fyodorovich, I am writing to you in order to continue the nice habit of talking to you every day. I received your postcard at the very minute that I was counting on my fingers how many days are left between the 1st and the 24th of July, the date of our departure. Unfortunately, I could not make the total come to less than 24. Tell Vera that I am prepared to face any seasickness if this would reduce the time of my stay in England, but no one has offered me any such exchange. This mood of mine is enhanced by the continuation of the solar eclipse: the days are dark. Furthermore, it is pouring. I dream about the hot summer in Paris when one wants to get into a cool bath. I would be glad to hear from you that it is not like that there and I would be glad to hear from you anyway. I kiss Vera, and kiss your hand. Your Boris." Kochno came to the premiere of *The Rake's Progress* in Venice in 1951, and, in June 1979, to the exhibition of Vera's paintings in Paris.

[4] Fatima Hanum, a Russian refugee friend of Vera's, became an art dealer in Paris. During, and for seven years after, World War II, she lived in Vera's rue de l'Assomption apartment.

them, after which they will acquire historic value! (What an attempt at humor!)

We have been in the new flat for two weeks now. The first week was very difficult, the second somewhat easier. I don't advise anybody to try to decorate an apartment. Hotel life is my ideal, and I often think nostalgically about our hotel.

The heat in Paris is frightful. If only we can straighten out our finances—and we do have hopes—we will go away somewhere for about two weeks.

I will be more than happy if you write. Most heartfelt greetings to Ekaterina Gavrilovna.[1] We kiss you tenderly. Vera Sudeikina.

Vera to Igor

Monsieur Igor Stravinsky   7, av. Frémiet
Anglet   Paris 16
near Bayonne   August 8, 1921
Cottage l'Argenté

Dear Igor Fyodorovich, Please give me errands, even every day; I will be glad to do them. I did not answer immediately, for the reason that I could not find Zederbaum.[2] He emerged only yesterday, and this is what he says: the teacher in question (his name is Tronadaro) will be lecturing all winter at the University and therefore cannot leave Paris. If you wish, I could put an advertisement in the newspapers, interview the teachers myself, and, if I find a suitable one, send you the details and await your decision. But I must know your terms: How soon do you want him, what is the salary, and is he required to be with the children all day or only during the hours of lessons? I think we can easily find one.

I went to Deauville recently to sell Seriozha's paintings to some Americans. Now, for a while at least, we are more settled financially. You see how businesslike I am. You can entrust me with the most complicated financial matters. How are your trousers, your steamer trunks, and our "friends in common" faring? I kiss you tenderly. S[ergei] kisses you also. Vera Sudeikina.

Igor to Vera

Mme Sudeikina   Anglet
7, av. Frémiet   Cottage l'Argenté
Paris 16   August 21, 1921

Answering your nice letter, in which you describe so well the sultry days of your Paris sojourn, I send you this poem with my portrait and music (which, this time, I hope you will learn by heart for my arrival). My self-confidence as a poet has been stung by the competition with A. Pushkin's wonderful poem, "The Autumn," which you quote in your letter.[3] If you wrote it from memory, then please take the trouble to memorize mine also, in order to be able to recite it at Christmas (in the German fashion) as a present to me. I embrace you with love and longing. I miss you. Your I.

Vera to Igor

Monsieur Igor Stravinsky   7, av. Frémiet
Anglet   [Early September] 1921
near Bayonne
Cottage l'Argenté

Dear Igor Fyodorovich, This letter will tell you all that I know about Diaghilev. On receiving your wire, I telephoned the Hôtel Continental and was informed that he had left for London the same morning. But I already knew this from Boris [Kochno], who has seen us quite frequently this time during his Paris visit, and who had told us the day before that they were leaving for London. He also said that they have business here and would definitely be back soon. The ballerina Balasheva called on us this afternoon and said that in a few days she had to give Diaghilev an answer about *The Sleeping Beauty*; she expects him to return from London Monday the 12th.

Now I have a business proposition for you. If your finances are not in a very brilliant state, would you be interested in writing music for a play by a French writer who is subsidized by a Rothschild? The people concerned are dying to have you. If you are not opposed to the idea in principle, let me know and I'll ask them to write to you directly and formally. My role is simply to find out if you are interested. When conversations in Paris turn to you, someone always says that you work only with Diaghilev and are unlikely to go with anyone else. I hope for a quick reply. Forgive this sloppy letter: I am in a terrible hurry. With a hearty kiss, Vera Sudeikina.

Vera to Igor

Monsieur Igor Stravinsky   7, av. Frémiet
Anglet   Paris 16
near Bayonne   September 19, 1921
Cottage l'Argenté

Dear Igor Fyodorovich, I hope that you have settled your differences with Diaghilev since he is planning to come to see you tomorrow. I had a very useful conversation with Boris and hope that it will do some good. Now about my proposition: Francis Picabia has written a play[4] which he hopes to put on next winter, not for one performance but for a run of about two months. He talked about you to Vermel,[5] saying that if you agreed to write music for it, you would be very well paid. A Rothschild (I am not sure which one) will finance it. Tell me whether this interests you and what you would like me to do about it. If you are not interested, please do not blame me, since in that case I would hesitate to propose anything again. I am in touch with all sorts of theatrical and musical enterprises, and something else may come up in the future.

I received your letter about the writing paper and your portrait and was delighted with your suggestion about the latter. I have ordered my photograph to send to you in exchange, but I could not order the writing paper: I looked through the whole telephone book without finding that particular shop, so I will have

---

[1] Igor's wife and first cousin (1881–March 2, 1939), also referred to as Katya and Katik. Apparently he had not yet told her of his liaison with Vera, who had also not revealed to Sudeikin the nature of her attachment to Stravinsky. When Igor confessed to his wife, late in 1921 or early in 1922, a tearful, "Dostoevskyan scene" ensued, as Igor described it in a letter (lost or destroyed) to Vera. About two and a half months after the London premiere (November 2, 1921) of *The Sleeping Princess* (*The Sleeping Beauty*), Sudeikin, finally aware of the relationship between Vera and Igor, wrote to Diaghilev asking him to send Vera back.

[2] Dr. Vladimir Zederbaum, secretary to Serge Koussevitzky.

[3] Neither Igor's poem and music, nor Vera's letter has survived.

[4] *Les Yeux chauds*. Picabia sent the text to Stravinsky on May 26, 1922. (An English translation is given in *Stravinsky: Selected Correspondence*, Vol. II, op. cit.) From the summer of 1922 until 1926, Vera shared an apartment with Picabia's ex-wife, Gabrielle Buffet, at 82, rue des Petits-Champs. Mme Picabia became Stravinsky's representative for stage performances of *Histoire du soldat*. After his death (April 6, 1971), she wrote to Vera from Azay-le-Rideau: "I am deeply touched by the ending of Igor's life. He takes with him so many distant but still lively memories. I knew that he wanted to be buried in Venice and naturally you will accompany him on this last journey. How I would love to see you. If you go through Paris, call me. I think of you from the bottom of my heart and embrace you."

[5] Director of the Chauve-Souris dance company.

9 December 1921. Biarritz.

10 1921. Biarritz.

to go elsewhere. As for the portrait,[1] you look perky and not at all angry, as you seem to be in some of your other photographs.

I want to ask you a favor. We would like to rent a piano. Could you ask Pleyel to reduce the price for us? Would that be a nuisance for you? Perhaps you could tell them that when you come to Paris you might be using it in our house. Forgive me, and if this is inconvenient, do not bother about it.

Sergei is leaving for London at the end of this month. I would love to go to the premier of *The Sleeping Beauty*, but I do not know whether I can manage it.[2] Both of us kiss you tenderly. Our heartfelt greetings to Ekaterina Gavrilovna. Vera Sudeikina.

1922

January

4 Sorin[3] at the theater. **5** Sergei [Sudeikin] at the theater at 4:30 p.m. Sorin comes in the evening. **6** At the Vieux-Colombier[4] at 2 p.m. Sergei goes to a meeting at Kuznetzova's.[5] **7** We go to a play-reading at Butkovskaya's. Evening—Balasheva. **8** Visit from Henrietta Hirshman.[6] **9** Lunch with Henry Bernstein. **10** Copeau at 2 p.m., Borovsky at 3. **12** Bakst dines with us. **15** Peshkov[7] dines with us. **17** George Schlee[8] in the evening. **21** Sergei to 2, rue d'Artois. Schlee here. **27** To Sorin's, to pose for the portrait. Vermel here. **28** Sorin at 1. At Bakst's at 6. **29** Meeting at Kuznetzova's. **31** Boris [Kochno].

February

1 Boris. **2** Svetlov for dinner. **4** Sorin. **11** To Copeau's rehearsal at the Salle Drouot, with Boris and Sorin. **12** Maris Kugulskaya.[9] We go to Diaghilev's. Boris. **13** Vieux-Colombier. Drouot. **14** Boris and Sorin. **22** We move. [Stravinsky writes to Diaghilev from Biarritz, remarking on a sadness in the tone of Diaghilev's last letter and adding: "If I cannot help you with my music, what can I help you with? Despite my admiration for my male member I am not willing to offer you consolation with it. . . ."] **27** Sorin's birthday.

March

2 Diaghilev comes here. **4** Schlee and Peshkov **5** Meeting at Kuznetzova's **6** Coco [Chanel] and Achenia [Melikov]. To the Salon d'Automne. **7** With Diaghilev and Nouvel to the Vieux-Colombier opening. **8** Rehearsal at the Vieux-Colombier. **9** Tea here with

Americans. **10** Last package to Igor Fyodorovich. **16** Exhibition at the American [Paul] Rosenberg's. **18** At Henry Bernstein's. **19** Photographer at 2. Dinner with Stravinsky. **22** To the Femina Theater with Tula Danilova. **24** With Rosenberg to Sorin's. **26** Dinner at the Côte d'Or Restaurant.

April

3 At the Vieux-Colombier. **10** Yakovlev.[10] **14** Kugulskaya. **16** To a lecture by Zdanevich.[11] **22** Leave for Monte Carlo. **23** Visit with [Vera] Nemchinova [the ballerina]. **25** Menton. See Dubrovskaya [the ballerina]. **27** Nice. **29** To the museum and the ballet in the evening.

May

1 Sergei Pavlovich [Diaghilev] leaves. **2** Visit with Tamara [Lourié]. **4** To Villefranche. **10** A visit from Zdanevich. **11** Visit with Koussevitzky. **12** I pose for Sorin. To Zdanevich's lecture. **13** At Tula Danilova's at 4. **14** Visit from Zederbaum. **18** Sergei goes to Henry Bernstein's. In the evening to the Diaghilev Ballet. **20** Sergei at Bernstein's. **21** I pose for Sorin. **23** I pose for Bakst. **25** 3 p.m.: I pose for Bakst. **26** To the Gudashvili exhibition. **29** In the evening: Diaghilev. **31** Tula Danilova and Zdanevich.

June

1 Pose for Bakst. Kugulskaya. To Pigalle. **2** I design a carpet. **4** I pose for Seriozha. **5** Bakst. **14** Photographs. **15** Today is the opening of our business.[12] Bogoyavlenskaya, Errazuriz,[13] Trubetzkaya, Vershinina. **21** Sashenka, Man Ray,[14] Chomiakova, Reinach. **23** Pitoëff.[15]

July

14 Visit from [Alice] Nikitina. **30** To the Villa Mercedes to see the Princess Lieven.

August

2 To Deauville. **12** Take costumes to Deauville. Visit there from the King of Spain.[16] **19** Sergei sails for New York.

October

11 Photographs of me at Lipnitzky's. Dress rehearsal for *Judith*. **15** Give tickets for *Judith* to Salomeya.[17]

---

[1] See *Igor and Vera Stravinsky: A Photograph Album*, Thames and Hudson, London and New York, 1982.

[2] Soon after this letter was written, Diaghilev invited Vera to play the role of the Queen in the Tchaikovsky ballet. During rehearsals for the part in London, October 27, 1921, Kochno warned her in the following verse that her flirtation with Stravinsky was threatening her marriage to Sudeikin. (Lydia Lopokova, later the wife of economist John Maynard [Lord] Keynes, had been Stravinsky's mistress intermittently from 1916 to 1920.)

> *V.S.*
> Dear Friends of my childhood
> What is new in the company [The Ballets Russes]?
> What about Lyda [*sic*], Lyda Lopokova?
> And Igor—the old friends?
> But I find things out by chance.
> I was blessed with a gift of omniscience.
> And, for you, what could be nicer than a family of
> Friends, like Vera, from childhood.

[3] The painter, Savely Sorin, had been one of the Sudeikins' closest friends in the Crimea in 1917–19. He painted Vera's portrait there and again in Paris in 1922.

[4] The theater, of which Jacques Copeau was director.

[5] She introduced the Blue Bird Theater to the United States.

[6] Friend of Igor's in St. Petersburg before World War I, and friend of Vera's in Paris from 1921. She was Koussevitzky's secretary in Boston, but is better known as the sister of Paul Léon (alias Noel), James Joyce's secretary in Paris in the late 1930s.

[7] Maxim Gorky's illegitimate son.

[8] Valentina's husband, later the constant companion of Greta Garbo.

[9] One of Vera's closest Russian refugee friends until her death in the mid-1950s. After World War II, when Baron Osten-Saken (see Vera's letter to Igor, January 11, 1933) left Vera's rue de l'Assomption apartment and moved to Mexico, Kugulskaya lived there for about eight years.

[10] Alexander Yakovlev, uncle of Tatiana Liebermann, painted Vera's portrait.

[11] Ilya Zdanevich, futurist writer. He inscribed one of his books in verse to Vera, describing himself as "under the shoe of Vera Venus Sudeikina." His book *Yanko, King of Albania*, contains a dedication to Serge Yurievich Sudeikin in hand-painted letters scrambled on the flyleaf.

[12] Tulavera. See the Preface, page 6.

[13] Eugenia Errazuriz, patroness to both Stravinsky and Picasso. Her collection of Stravinsky manuscripts, given to her by the composer in 1920 and including the holograph full score of the *Ragtime* for eleven instruments and sketches for *Histoire du soldat*, was sold at auction in New York in December 1983, and is now in the Sacher Collection in Basel.

[14] 1890–1976. Artist and photographer.

[15] Probably Lyudmila Pitoëff, who had danced the part of the Princess in the first *Histoire du soldat*, Lausanne, September 28, 1918.

[16] Alfonso XIII was one of Diaghilev's and Stravinsky's greatest admirers and patrons.

[17] The Princess Andronikov. A friend of Vera's from 1919, in Tiflis, to 1978, in London.

11 1922. Paris.

1923

January

9 Igor arrives. **12** Achenia [Melikov]. **14** To the flea market, and with Ira[1] to see *Eugénie Grandet*. **15** To a German film. Lunch in an Italian restaurant with Diaghilev, who feels ill. **18** With Igor to Grand Guignol. **19** With Igor to Rouen. **20** Storm and lightning over Rouen cathedral. **21** Wonderful, wonderful! **22** At the Opéra, we see Maurice Ravel and Gabriel Pierné. **23** Igor leaves. Supper at Liarsky's. **26** Supper with Bogoyavlensky. **27** Igor arrives. **29** Concert Jean Wiéner[2] at the Salle Pleyel.

February

6 With Igor to *Philémon and Baucis*. **7** To see *Aux armes, citoyens*. **8** With Igor to Cimarosa's *Il matrimonio segreto*. **10** To the Cirque Médrano. **11** Tea at the Hôtel des Réservoirs. **13** See Dora Katorza in *Agnes*. **19** To the exhibition at the Salle des Indépendants. **20** To the exhibition of Princess Vrussov. **23** To the Bal Bullier.

March

6 To [Charles] Le Cocq's *Giroflé*. **9** To *Phèdre*. **12** Boris and Nikitina. **15** With Salomeya and Ira. **16** A banquet for the Kamerny Theater in exile. **17** Tula's birthday. **19** At 8 to *Adrienne Lecouvreur*. **22** Again to *Giroflé*.

April

9 Arrive in Monte Carlo. **13** Rehearsal of *Noces* with the Princess present. **14** Ansermet arrives. **17** Opening of the Ballets Russes season.

May

12 Tula's wedding.

June

10 Evening with Igor at Princesse de Polignac's.[3] **13** Gala performance of *Noces*. Dr. Poulard. **24** Jean de la Fontaine. **25** Falla. Evening at Princesse de Polignac's.[4] **30** Versailles Festival.

July

1 Supper on Murphy's boat.[5] **3** Dinner with Igor at the Princesse de Polignac's. **4** Dinner with Igor at Prince Argutinsky's.[6] **5** With Igor at Crémaillère with Darius Milhaud and Paul Morand.[7] **6** Lunch with Igor at Prince Argutinsky's with Princess Bassiano.[8] Evening at Montmartre. **7** With Igor to Pierrefonds by Compiègne. **8** With Igor to Chantilly. **9** Igor leaves.

August

3 To the Prefecture and the German Consulate.[9] **10** Igor arrives. **11** To Château-Thierry with Igor and Argutinsky. **12** Château-Thierry. **13** Telegram to Picabia. At 6 p.m., Olga Sallard.[10] **15** We arrive at Wiesbaden, and, at 10:40 p.m., Griesheim, where we spend a bad night at the railroad station. **16** Leave for Weimar at 7 a.m. Ballet in the evening. **17** Weimar, the Bauhaus. **19** Bauhaus. *Histoire du soldat*. Mme Busoni [the wife of Ferruccio Busoni] weeps. Evening with Wassily and Nina Kandinsky and Scherchen.[11] Leave for Frankfurt at 1 a.m. **20** Spend the night in Wiesbaden. **21** Leave for Paris at midnight. **26** With Igor, Argutinsky, and Alexandre Benois at Magny-en-Vexin. **27** Parc Mont-Souris. Restaurant du Lac. **28** Enghien. **30** Igor leaves at 8:15 p.m.

September

10 I begin a cure at Enghien.[12] Weight 80 kilos.

October

4 Lunch with Argutinsky. **10** Igor arrives. **11** At Koussevitzky's: two Americans play Mozart. **13** To the Salon d'Automne. **18** Premiere of Igor's Octet at Koussevitzky's concert.[13] **22** Igor writes constantly now about Ekaterina Gavrilovna's jealousy. He is trying to protect her in every way. If we go to Spain, those two weeks will be unbearable for her, since she imagines us together all the time. I wonder whether he shouldn't tell her that he will come later. There is no need to worry about my feelings.[14] **25** Koussevitzky conducts the *Sacre*.

November

5 Jacket to Marie Laurençin. Phone Picabia. **12** Write to Sudeikin.

---

[1] Ira Belline (Irina Beliankina), 1903 (Kiev)–1971 (Marrakesh), the daughter of Lyudmila Beliankina, Stravinsky's first wife's sister, was a model, a painter, an actress, a set and costume designer, and a couturier. In the early 1920s she was employed by Chanel and Molyneux, and from 1925 she designed costumes for the theater and cinema. At Diaghilev's request, she appeared in Nicolas Nabokov's ballet *Ode* (1928). She began to paint during World War II, but did not exhibit until the 1950s, notably in Tangier (her residence from 1947), Madrid, and Rabat. Her letters to Vera in the 1950s, 1960s, and 1970–71 contain interesting observations about the Stravinsky family and the Russian background. Thus a hard rain in Marrakesh reminds her of "the big puddles in Ustilug" (November 16, 1967), and the litigation between the Stravinsky children and Vera provokes the comment: "If my father were alive he would have said that the moral traits in the children come from the Kholodovsky side"—i.e., from the family of Stravinsky's mother. "How is it that all of uncle Igor's children turned out to be so stupid?" (December 21, 1970). In 1962, Barbara Hutton, a long-time friend, gave Ira a home in Marrakesh. On December 28, 1967, Ira reported to Vera that Hutton had eloped with a very young Italian but was having difficulties in shedding her Indonesian. In order to buy her freedom, "she sold her emeralds—Catherine the Great's emeralds—for 45 millions." By this time, however, Ira was much closer to the sons of Paul Getty, one of whom had purchased a castle in Morocco. Vera visited Ira in Marrakesh in April 1971, and in August of that year Ira died of a kidney ailment.

[2] Pianist (1896–1982), partner of Clément Doucet in a famous duo-piano team. Wiéner founded a Paris concert series for modern music.

[3] Winnaretta de Polignac (1865–1943), daughter of Isaac Singer, the sewing machine manufacturer, presided over the most important music salon in Paris. On December 15, 1893, Winnaretta married the impoverished aristocrat Prince Edmond de Polignac. The prince was a well-known homosexual, which allowed Winnaretta the freedom to pursue her own sexual preferences. In 1916, she commissioned Stravinsky's *Renard*. He gave preview performances of many of his new works in her home.

[4] The private premiere of Manuel de Falla's *El Retablo de Maese Pedro*.

[5] Gerald and Sara Murphy's houseboat on the Seine. See *Living Well is the Best Revenge* by Calvin Trillin.

[6] Prince Vladimir Argutinsky-Dolgurokov (1874–1941) of the Imperial Russian

Embassy in Paris. A close friend of Diaghilev's and of Stravinsky's before the Russian Revolution, he continued, after it, to live in France.

[7] The novelist, best known in English for his stories, *Fancy Goods* and *Open All Night*, introduced by Marcel Proust and translated by Ezra Pound.

[8] Marguerite Caetani (née Chapin) founded the review *Botteghe Oscure*, named for the street of her palace in Rome.

[9] Igor and Vera were going to Weimar for the Bauhaus performance of *Histoire du soldat*.

[10] One of Vera's closest friends, Olga Ilinishna Sallard suffered from tuberculosis, and in the 1930s was obliged to live in a sanatorium in Davos. Vera bore the expenses of the treatment and visited her there several times. As Vera's principal confidante in France immediately after World War II, Olga, in her letters, is both a mirror of life in the American branch of the Stravinsky family and the chief source of information about Soulima Stravinsky's life in occupied France from 1942, when she shared an apartment in Paris with him and his future wife. As a friend of Vera's in Russia, Olga also reveals something of Vera's relatives—as in a letter of September 15, 1947, mentioning Vera's uncle Bosset, his factory near the Don, and his sons, who had managed to emigrate to Germany at the end of the war, but were living under terrible conditions. Olga died in an automobile accident on March 30, 1961.

[11] Herman Scherchen (1891–1966), conductor. During this visit to Weimar the Stravinskys also met Paul Klee and Carl Ebert (1886–1980), the narrator in the *Soldat*.

[12] On September 20, Stravinsky, in Biarritz, sent a fifteen-page sketchbook titled *The Little House at Kolomna [Mavra]*, to "Madame Vera Sudeikina, chez Mme Leder, 15, Boulevard Cotte, Enghien-les-Bains (S. & O.)."

[13] Stravinsky conducted his Octet, Koussevitzky the *Eroica* Symphony and Prokofiev's First Violin Concerto (premiere).

[14] This entry is on a separate piece of paper.

12

12 1923. Valley of the Seine. Photo by Vera.

13 April 1924. Serge Sudeikin.

13

Picabia. Barbette.[1]   **13** Picabia at 10:30 a.m.   **16** Lunch at Picabia's in Saint-Cloud with Stravinsky, Cocteau, and Tristan Tzara.   **27** Theater: *La Dame aux camélias.*   **30** St. Laurent. Molyneux. Marcelle Meyer.[2]

December

14 Igor and I go to Raymond Radiguet's funeral.[3] I finish my costumes for Diaghilev.   **26** Igor leaves at 8 a.m.   **28** Tula takes my costumes to Diaghilev in Monte Carlo.

January

1 In the daytime, Janacopulos.[4] Dinner with Valechka[5] and Trubnik. Afterward, in the evening, I design ten things.   **2** At 2:15 Igor and I take the train to Brussels. Paul Collaer[6] meets us with his wife and Piron. The Grand Hotel. Dinner at Piron's.   **3** Afternoon and evening with Collaer in his house on the canal in Malines.   **4** While Igor is in Antwerp I spend the afternoon with Piron and Jean. On Igor's return the four of us dine together.   **5** Igor is up at 6. At 2:30 we go to a concert of his music. He says that the performance of the *Symphonies of Wind Instruments* is ''too soft.'' Many people for tea at the hotel.   **6** We leave for Antwerp by car. After a rehearsal there, lunch at M. Franck's. Tremendous elegance: flowers, vintage wines, waiters, lots of paintings, Chinese antiques, African sculpture—the host wants to be up-to-date. Back to Brussels for a 6 p.m. rehearsal of *Mavra*. Later at Piron's.   **7** My birthday. Sleep late. Igor and I lunch at the Louvain restaurant. The performance is a great success. The conductor tells me how great it must be to be loved by a genius.   **8** In Brussels by 12 p.m.   **9** Back in Paris. Worries about the financial situation.   **10** Dine with Gaby Picabia.   **11** I borrow money where I can. At 6:45 p.m. I return to Brussels and am received at the hotel with champagne.   **12** Igor lunches at Baron Buffin's. Dinner at Collaer's: Brélia.   **13** Rehearsal at the Conservatory. We send a letter to Poulenc.[7] Lunch at Piron. Dinner at the hotel and early to bed.   **14** I arrive late at the rehearsal and run into Arthur Lourié. Lunch with him and P. Katzenthal.[8] Lourié is very happy to see and to talk with Igor. Gaby Picabia arrives. Later Igor and I have tea. The concert is a colossal success. Supper and dancing afterward.   **15** Antwerp.   **18** I receive 21,000 [francs] from the lawsuit.   **22** Paris. Dinner with Benois and Argutinsky.   **23** Igor leaves.   **24** Dinner with Gaby, Ogilvie, and Tula at the Boeuf sur le Toit.   **26** Go to St. Cloud with Marie Laurençin and Gaby Picabia.

February

1 Helena Rubinstein.   **3** Poulenc dines with me.[9]   **7** Visit from Cocteau.[10] He is looking for people from Paradise.[11]   **23** Helena Rubinstein and Léon Bakst at 8.   **25** Tomashevsky at 10 a.m.

March

6 We leave for Barcelona in a wagon-lit.   **7** We are very nervous at the frontier but all goes well.[12] I think my bracelets made an impression on the border guards. At 8 p.m. we move into a beautiful apartment at the

Barcelona Ritz.   **8** Drive to the beach. Juan Mestres[13] and Pena come to see Igor. In the evening we attend a performance of Pergolesi's *La Serva Padrona.*   **9** At midnight we go to a cabaret where gypsies dance. Watch a Russian gypsy woman Sagarino Antonovna Tiomkina. We drink a lot of Jerez [sherry] and feel ill.   **11** Visit to Madame de Picabia.   **12** Visit to the Baroness dell'Aguila.   **13** Igor's concert.   **16** Visit the Cathedral. Watch a *sardana* [street dance] and go to a bullfight. Dinner with a minister of state, Rodez, at the Excelsior.   **20** To Montserrat with Rodez. Banquet at the Ritz.   **21** Farewells with flowers and applause.   **22** The Madrid Palace Hotel.   **24** Reception at Bauer's.   **25** Igor's concert.   **27** We leave Madrid.

April

9 To the Jean Wiéner concert.   **15** Helena Rubinstein.   **17** H. Rubinstein.   **18** At 11:30 a.m. Lyudmila Pitoëff comes for a fitting.   **28** H. Rubinstein.

May

1 At Princess Bassiano's.   **9** Ball at the Marquise de Polignac's.   **14** Evening at Polignac's, where Igor's Octet and Concerto are performed.   **22** Stravinsky gala at the Opéra: Koussevitzky conducts and Igor plays the first performance of Igor's Concerto.   **26** Ballets Russes gala: *Les Biches*, *Noces*, *Tentations*.

June

5, 6, and 7 The Tulavera Exhibition.   **8** To Samois for two days.   **10** To the theater to see *La Mort tragique de Rasputin*.   **11** Ballets Russes (*Biches*).   **13** Ballets Russes: *Le Sacre du printemps*.   **14** To the Nightmare[14] at La Cigalle.   **24** Garden party at Bassiano's in Versailles.[15]

July

12 Presents for July 14. To Montmartre with Ira and Valechka.   **13** We leave for Copenhagen at 8 a.m. Igor is detained at the Belgian frontier because of a faulty visa and we are sent back to France, where Igor hires a car and we enter at another border station.   **14** Brussels. Lunch at the Louvain with Piron and Jean.   **15** Cologne, Hamburg, Warnemunde, and Copenhagen.   **16** At Hansen's[16] villa.   **18** Igor's Tivoli concert.   **21** We return to Paris.   **28** Igor goes to Nice, then to Biarritz.

August

3 Igor returns from Biarritz.

September

1 Sign a contract with Lichine.   **4** Igor here.   **18** Igor leaves.

October

27 The Tulavera Exhibition opens.   **29** Igor arrives from Nice at 8 a.m.   **30** Igor and I leave for Warsaw.

[1] American transvestite trapeze artist, friend of Cocteau's, real name Vander Clyde. See Francis Steegmuller's *Cocteau* for an account of Barbette in Austin, Texas in 1966.

[2] 1897–1958. A close friend of Igor's and Vera's, Marcelle Meyer played one of the piano parts in the premiere of *Les Noces*.

[3] The death of the novelist and poet at the age of twenty had shocked Igor and Vera—and all literary France.

[4] Vera Janacopulos, the soprano, was married to M. Staal.

[5] Walter Nouvel, Diaghilev's life-long friend.

[6] The Belgian musicologist, author of the first monograph on Stravinsky.

[7] Igor and Vera signed a group letter to Francis Poulenc on stationery of the Louvain restaurant.

[8] Russian musician, emigrated from Petrograd to Paris with Lourié. Lourié and Katzenthal helped Stravinsky's mother obtain permission to leave the USSR in 1922.

[9] In December 1924 Poulenc wrote to Vera: ''What is happening with you? I embrace you for the New Year and wish you happiness in proportion to my affection, which is to say a lot. I will be at Touraine during the month of January. I am told that you are following Igor to America. You must be a happy woman. In any case, I hope to see you soon. Much affection, Francis.''

[10] On this occasion Cocteau drew two portraits of Auric in Vera's autograph album.

[11] Cocteau had been taking opium since the death of Radiguet.

[12] Igor and Vera, as stateless persons, had been turned back at borders more than once.

[13] Manager of the Barcelona orchestra.

[14] Name of a nightclub.

[15] In Washington DC, January 1962, Saint-John Perse reminded Stravinsky that they had met more than once at Bassiano's in Versailles.

[16] Publisher of Stravinsky's Concertino for String Quartet.

14 Summer 1924. Copenhagen.
Photo by Vera.

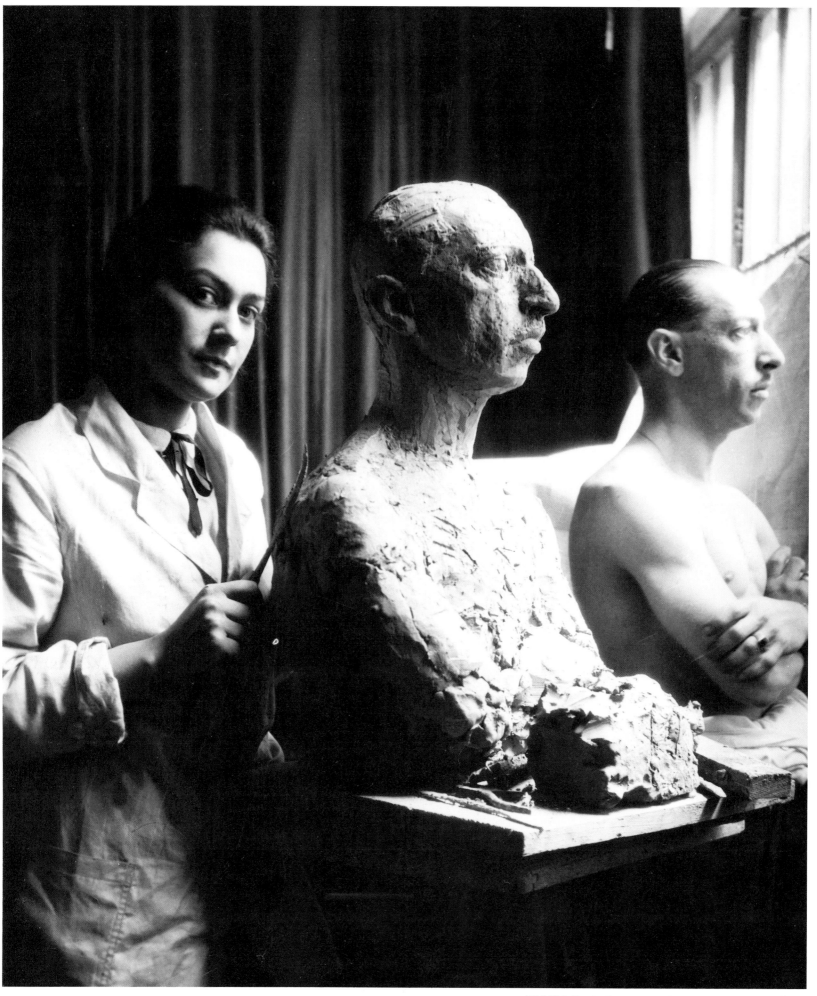

15 1924. Paris. Posing for Tatiana Alalou-Jonquières.

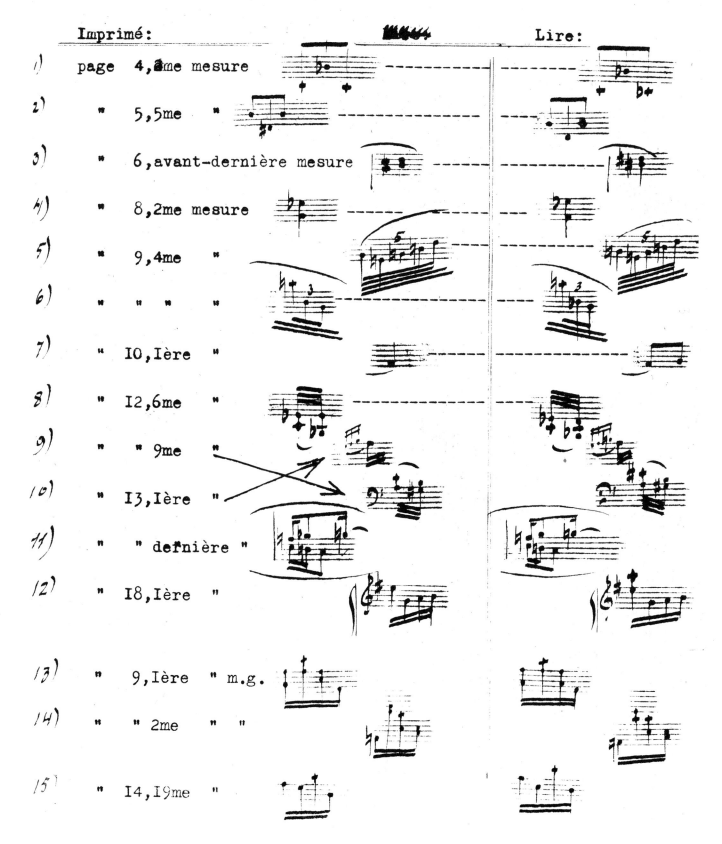

ERRATA

16 Stravinsky's *errata* for his Piano Sonata, 1924.

17

17 1924. Biarritz.

18 October 1924. Nice. With Catherine.

19 November 1924. Warsaw.

18

19

November

1 We arrive in Warsaw. Rehearsal at 11 a.m. Meet Fitelberg[1] and lunch with him. In the evening, Hainatzki, the conductor of the Philharmonic. We go to the operetta *Maritza* and dine afterward in the Hotel Europe. **2** Rehearsal, then lunch with the Meyers. **3** A possible contract for Germany. Dinner at Mme Grossman's. **4** Igor's concert, then supper at the Warszawa Club. **5** Grand dinner at Mme Grossman's with Polish aristocrats. Igor's second concert with the Warsaw Philharmonic. Supper at Meyers'. **6** A gathering at which Igor plays his Sonata.[2] Lunch in an old restaurant. Walk around Warsaw, then, in the evening, to the circus. **8** Leave for Prague. At the Warsaw station, flowers, candy, presents, and photographers. **9** No one meets us at Prague and our rooms at the hotel are terrible. Igor is furious. **13** Igor's concert. 4,000 people in the audience. Spend the evening at Götze's. **14** We leave for Amsterdam. **15** Amsterdam: a charming hotel, the Doelen, and wonderful accommodations. **17** A wire from Tula summoning me: she has broken her leg. **18** Lunch at Willem Mengelberg's: impressive collection of paintings. **19** Well-planned lunch in honor of Stravinsky at Sam Bottenheim's.[3] **23** Igor conducts his Amsterdam concert. **24** Winterthur. **26** Igor plays his Concerto in a concert in Winterthur. **29** Geneva. **30** Igor goes to Lausanne and I go directly to Leipzig.[4]

December

1 I arrive in Leipzig at 9 a.m., Igor at 2 p.m. **2** Lunch at Wilhelm Furtwängler's. **3** According to Igor's contract, he must stay until the 15th. **4** Rehearsal at the Gewandhaus, and concert there in the evening. **5** Igor and I arrive in Berlin. **7** Rehearsal. Lunch at Thyssen's. **8** Igor's Berlin chamber music concert in the evening. **27** Le Havre. Igor sails on the S.S. *Paris* to America. I return from Le Havre to Paris at 12 p.m.

Vera to Catherine

167, blvd. Carnot
Nice

82, rue des Petits-Champs
December 28, 1924

Without any unnecessary words, Ekaterina Gavrilovna, I would like to express my gratitude to you for giving me the opportunity of writing to you, which will be a great relief in this sad and troublesome time; I am happy that this has happened. It is difficult to talk about all those moments that trouble or touch us and that also give meaning to everything. But you will understand, since we have a common language. To whom, if not to you, should I write about what is dear to me? And from whom but you can I receive news that is dear to me?

I went to Le Havre on Saturday to see Igor off. Although it had been decided from the beginning that I was not going, in the last few hours before his departure he seemed so unhappy that I stayed with him until he left. Robert Lyon[5] came with us, and it was in his name that I sent you the telegram saying that Igor had left in good spirits.

We were in Le Havre from eight to ten o'clock and were allowed to visit the ship and to have dinner on board. Igor's cabin is the best one, in the exact center, and with all conveniences. A piano had been installed. Sabline[6] was allowed to come from third class to help Igor unpack and to dress him. I fear that Sabline will not be much help: he seems to be slow, sleepy, and not very intelligent.

When we reached Le Havre, a great storm was raging at sea and everything was shaking and tearing. This made life on the ship seem very strange. As soon as the passengers had gone aboard, music started playing, the restaurant and the bar were opened, and the vessel looked like a large first-class hotel—all of this so that the passengers would not think of the stormy night and of the possible dangers awaiting them. This was my impression, at any rate, but most of the American passengers did not seem to be bothered, and they certainly looked calm, almost too calm. The ship was supposed to sail at ten but was delayed because of the storm. Visitors were asked to leave at ten, however, and we did. Igor stayed below in his cabin and did not come up on deck. He must have felt depressed. The experience of leaving like that can only be balanced by the joy of returning. Robert Lyon left with the night train, but I spent the night in Le Havre, listening for the whistles in order to hear when Igor's boat left, but I could not distinguish them from the whistles of other boats.

December 29

On my way back from Le Havre, I saw newspapers that reported a terrible storm near the English coast of the Channel lasting forty-eight hours. Today I went to the steamship office and learned that the *Paris* sailed at 1 a.m. and is proceeding normally. Igor must be traveling peacefully now. Robert Lyon will send him a radiogram today saying: "All is well."

1925

Vera and Catherine to Igor[7]

[Cable]
Igor Stravinsky
Detroit, USA

Nice
March 1, [1925]

We are together today and embrace you. Vera and Catherine. [Original in French.]

[Returning to Paris from the United States in the last week of March 1925,[8] Stravinsky met Vera and went with her directly to Barcelona for concerts before joining his family in Nice, where he began the composition of the Serenade on April 11. He interrupted this work to take his family for a brief trip to Rome (photographs with Berners at the Janicolo, the Baths of Caracalla, etc.). Back in Nice, he completed the Serenade movement on May 19. He then went to Paris, bought a Renault, and returned to the Côte d'Azur with Vera. The Hymne in the Serenade was composed between July 18 and August 3. Vera Nossenko and A. Poliakov visited him that month and he accompanied them on excursions to Gairant, Grasse, Cagnes-sur-Mer. Work was resumed on the Serenade on August 14, but he interrupted it to go with Vera to Venice and Florence. After returning to Nice he made a trip to Antibes, Aix-en-Provence, and Toulon, then completed the Serenade, and set out on a concert tour with Vera. (He was photographed in Basel with the composer Suter, November 14, 1925.)]

---

[1] Gregor Fitelberg, the conductor. He had led the first performance of Stravinsky's *Mavra*.

[2] See the photograph on p.61, *Igor and Vera Stravinsky*, op. cit.

[3] Manager of the Concertgebouw Orchestra in Amsterdam.

[4] Stravinsky did not want his wife's relatives in Lausanne to know that he had a traveling companion, fearing this information would reach his mother.

[5] Director of Pleyel et Cie, Paris.

[6] Alexis Sabline, valet and translator to Stravinsky during his 1925 American tour. See *Stravinsky: Selected Correspondence*, Vol. II, op. cit.

[7] On March 1, at Stravinsky's request, Vera met his wife in the Stravinsky home in Nice. After the encounter, the two women sent a cable to him at the Hotel Statler, Detroit. Vera kept this cable, which Stravinsky gave to her, to the end of her life, together with a photograph of her in his home taken by Catherine.

[8] Appendix F in *Stravinsky: Selected Correspondence*, Vol. II, op. cit. wrongly states that Stravinsky recorded six of *Les Cinq Doigts* on March 14, just before leaving New York. He recorded all eight of the pieces.

Groupe du jubilé Steinway à New-York
1925

20 January 11, 1925. Steinway Hall, New York. Walter Damrosch is seated at Stravinsky's right. To the composer's left are Wilhelm Furtwängler, Joseph Steinway, Josef Hofmann. Serge Rachmaninov is seated behind Hofmann, Fritz Kreisler to Rachmaninov's right. Nikolai Medtner is behind Stravinsky, Alexander Ziloti (white tie) in the third row. Sixteen years earlier, in St. Petersburg, Ziloti, the pupil of Liszt and the friend of Tchaikovsky, had conducted the first performance of the young Stravinsky's *Fireworks*.

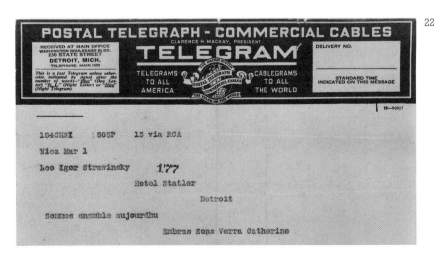

22

21 January 1925. New York. Aeolian Hall.

22 March 1, 1925. Cablegram from Vera Sudeikina and Catherine Stravinsky, sent from Nice to Stravinsky in Detroit: ''We are together today and embrace you. Vera and Catherine.''

23 1925. Paris. In his Pleyel studio, rue Rochechouart.

24 September 1925. En route to Venice. Photo by Vera.

25 September 1925. Venice. Palazzo Contarini dal Zaffo. With the Princesse de Polignac and Artur Rubinstein.

København
2 Dec 1925
Restaurant Nimb
après mon concert
organisé par Mme H. Hauch
du Nationaltidende
Igor Strawinsky

Friis-Petersen   Hoff Ding   Felsing   Haakon Nilson   Hemme   Lunged

26 December 2, 1925. Copenhagen. The identifications are in Stravinsky's hand.

January

3 Tea at Arthur Lourié's. **6** I move to the Hôtel des Acacias. **7** Spend my birthday at Guy de Matharel's.[1] **13** To the cinema. **14** Dinner at the Renaissance Restaurant with Rosette and Guy de Matharel, Jonquières,[2] and Bob [Robert Lyon]. **15** Passed my driver's license examination. **16** To the theater with Tula. **19** To the theater: *La Femme silencieuse*. **20** Igor arrives for three days. **21** Very nice evening with Igor at Lourié's. **22** Igor gives me a Renault. **23** Lunch and walk with Igor in St. Cloud. **25** At Tula's. **26** At Lourié's. **27** Festival Stravinsky. **28** Dinner with Tatiana and Jonquières. **30** To Versailles and St. Germain. **31** My first drive through Paris in my own car.

February

3 With Suvchinsky[3] at Lourié's. **6** Visit from Marina Tsvetaeva. **7** To St. Cloud and Versailles. **9** At Dmitrenko with Maria Lange.[4] At Lourié's. **10** To Arthur Lourié's concert. **13** To the Moulin Rouge. **14** Drive to Rambouillet. Dinner at the Empire. **15** At noon: Dmitrenko and Tomashevskaya. **16** To the cinema with Ira. **17** Igor arrives.[5] **18** Lunch with Bottenheim. **20** Lunch with Marcelle Meyer and Gaby Picabia. Dinner at Guy's. **21** Igor and I leave for Amsterdam. **24** Igor's concert in Rotterdam. **25** Igor's concert in Amsterdam. **27** Igor's chamber music concert in Amsterdam. **28** *Sacre*.[6]

March

2 Haarlem. Igor's concert. Reception afterward at Baron Roell's. **3** Leave Amsterdam at 2:05 p.m., arrive in Brussels at 6:30. **4** Back to Paris. Met at the station by Guy. **7** Drive with Guy. Lourié in the evening. **8** Farewell party at Matharel's. Bob. **11** Dinner at the Grand Vefour. Igor and I leave for Budapest. **13** Budapest, the Hotel Hungaria. **14** Dinner at Gustave Barczy's. **15** Igor's concert. Supper at Parr's. **16** To Vienna. **17** Lunch at Menten's, the Dutch Minister of State. **18** Lunch at Kugel's. Evening at Menten's. **19** Lunch with the French Minister, de Beaumarchais. Igor's Vienna concert. Enormous success. **20** Lunch with Dirk Fock.[7] **21** Visit the Kinsky Palace, and see a performance of *Fledermaus*. **22** Leave for Zagreb. **23** Igor's concert in Zagreb. **24** Train from Zagreb to Milan. **25** Milan, the Hotel Cavour. **26** Nice. **29** To Cannes with Igor. **31** With Igor to La Lanterne.

April

3 I return by train from Nice to Paris. **4** Spend most of the day with Lourié. **17** Lunch at Arthur Lourié's. **18** To Versailles and Ville d'Avrey with Valechka Nouvel. **19** To Chantilly with Kaminska. **21** Second injection. Meeting with Zdanevich at Maria Lange's. **22** Ira at 8:30 p.m. **28** Meeting at Lange's.

May

6 Leave on the Orient Express for Milan. **7** Milan. **8** Visit Smirnov and Romanov.[8] **9** Igor conducts the premiere of *Petrushka*. **12** The second

Petrushka. Supper with Smirnov, Obouchov, Romanov. **23** Paris. A drive in the country. **31** I sell my Renault.

June

1 I buy a new Renault for 17,000 [francs]. **3** To Koussevitzky's concert (loge). **6** Drive to Versailles with Argutinsky. **7** Lunch at Paul Kochanski's.[9] Meeting at Lourié's. **9** Dinner at Kochanski's. **10** Dinner at Jacques Maritain's. **13** Dinner at Mme Errazuriz's. **14** Lunch at Tony Gandarillas'.[10] **15** Madeleine Lyon at 3 p.m. Lourié for dinner. **15** We go to Cocteau's rehearsal. **17** 6:30 p.m. François Xavier. Gaby Picabia at 10:30 p.m. **18** At Dr. Carton's with Argutinsky. **20** Maritain. Marcelle Meyer's concert. **21** 1 p.m. Argutinsky. **26** Go to Vladimir Horowitz's concert. **27** To Villènes-sur-Seine with Tamara and Olga. **29** Salomeya and Ilya Zdanevich. **30** Lipnitzky at 1:30.

July

2 Igor returns from Italy.[11] With him to Villènes-sur-Seine, La Nourée. **5** Lunch at the Ermitage in Meudon. **6** Lunch with Gabriel Païchadze[12] and his wife. **7** Lunch at Tula's. At 4 p.m., Igor at Pleyel. **8** Dinner at the Pergola in Villènes. **9** Masson 10 a.m. Ira and the Louriés. **10** Igor comes at 3 p.m. **11** With Igor to the Vallée de Chevreuse. **12** With Igor to Rambouillet. **13** With Igor to the Hostellerie de la Garonne. Cerney-la-Ville. **15** Dinner at Kochanski's. **16** Dinner with Igor, Ira, Guy, Jonquières. **17** Dinner at the Select, at Billancourt, with Igor and Guy. **18** Dinner with Igor, Suvchinsky, Arthur Lourié, Guy, at St. Germain. **21** Sobachkin[13] is very sad today. **22** Sobachkin is very merry today. **24** The Ramponneau Restaurant with Igor, Guy, Jonquières. **25** Lunch at Corbeil. At 4 p.m., Louis Aragon. Dinner at Pleyel. **26** With Igor to the cinema. **27** To Boislève, with Igor, Arthur Honegger and his wife, and Guy. **28** Lunch with Païchadze at Café de Madrid. **29** To the cinema with Igor. *Force et beauté*. **30** Lunch with Igor and Cocteau. Dinner at the Café Weber. **31** Lunch with Igor and Diaghilev. Leave Pleyel at 7:40 p.m., reach Moulin at 4 a.m.[14]

August

1 Leave Moulin at noon. Lunch at Lapalisse. Dinner at Beaurepaire. Grenoble: the Hôtel Majestic. **2** Cocteau gives me a present, gloves trimmed with panther fur. We leave Grenoble at 1:20 p.m. Lunch at Mure, dinner at Dignes. Arrive in Nice at 2:30 a.m. **3** To Juan-les-Pins for dinner. **4** From 9 to 12 a.m., swim at Juan-les-Pins. To Cannes with Guy. Return to Paris at 9:10 p.m. **12** Raymond Roussel [the writer]. Lunch with M. Lyon. Dinner at Fontainebleau with Robert Lyon, Jacques, and Guy. **14** At Pougues-les-Eaux, Grand Hôtel du Parc. **18** Return to Paris.

September

2 I move from Pleyel. **11** 12 noon Zinaida Dmitrievna. 3 p.m. Smirnova. Leave for Villiers. **12** Villiers: Mme de Petit Thouars. **17** Move to the little house. **21** Igor arrives. **22** Housewarming (blessing) of the little house.[15] **24** We go to Olga Ivanovna's in Montmorency. **26** To the flea market.

---

[1] From the mid-1920s, Count de Matharel and his wife Rosette were among Igor's and Vera's closest friends. The references to Isthmia and Toulon in Vera's diary are to the Matharel's Villa Isthmia at Cap Brun (Toulon). Vera became the godmother of one of the Matharel sons. Guy de Matharel died after World War II and his widow remarried. She visited Vera's exposition of her paintings in Paris, June 12, 1979, as Rosette d'Overschie.

[2] Husband of Tatiana Alalou-Tann (1902–1969), sculptress who in 1924 made a head of Stravinsky. She later changed her name to Alalou-Jonquières.

[3] Pierre Suvchinsky had heard the first performance of Stravinsky's *Fireworks* in 1908, and had met the composer in Berlin in 1922. In 1939 Suvchinsky ghosted the chapter on Russian music in Stravinsky's *Poetics of Music*.

[4] The film actress and friend of Vera's since childhood. See Vera's letter to Igor, March 15, 1937.

[5] Stravinsky had completed the major revisions in *Le Sacre du printemps* in the early part of the month, then worked with Cocteau on *Oedipus Rex* in Villefranche-sur-Mer, and gone with him to Marseilles and Toulon.

[6] This was the first time that Stravinsky conducted *Le Sacre du printemps*.

[7] Conductor of the concert in which Stravinsky played his Concerto. Vera does not

say that Alban Berg and Anton Webern came to see Stravinsky at one of the receptions.

[8] The choreographer. He composed the dances for Stravinsky's *Nightingale* in 1914.

[9] Violinist, introduced to Stravinsky by Artur Rubinstein in London in June 1914. Igor and Vera were very fond of him and his wife Zosia. Stravinsky's first violin and piano arrangements were made for Kochanski.

[10] Eugenia Errazuriz's nephew, a member of the Chilean diplomatic service.

[11] In June, Stravinsky had played his Piano Concerto in Milan (La Scala, and Sala del Popolo) under Scherchen, then taken his wife to Florence. The photos of Stravinsky at the Certosa di Pavia date from this stay in Milan.

[12] Director, since January 1926, of the Edition Russe de Musique, Stravinsky's publisher.

[13] Vera's nickname for herself ("dog").

[14] Igor, Vera, and Cocteau went by car from Paris to Nice, with Vera driving.

[15] Vera's new apartment at 22, rue Ranelagh.

27 1926. Biarritz.

28 1926. Marseilles. With Jean Cocteau.

29 1926. With Cocteau. Photo by Vera.

28

29

30 February 15, 1926.
Budapest.

31 1927. Paris.

October

10 Igor leaves for Nice.   **30** I finish my *Firebird* costumes for Diaghilev.

November

2 Work with Diaghilev begins.   **16** I deliver my *Firebird* costumes.
18 More costumes delivered.   **29** I have a new car, a Mathis.

December

1 Igor arrives.   **3** To a Viennese operetta.   **10** Dinner at Matharel's. Cinema.   **11** To a concert by Claudio Arrau with Nouvel.   **12** Lunch at Staal's.   **16** 13 baskets of costumes arrive for *The Sleeping Beauty*.
18 Igor departs, not feeling well.   **20–27** Mad rush of work over *The Sleeping Beauty* costumes.

January

4 Dinner at Ramponneau with Valechka and Argutinsky.   **5** Send Igor's suits to Milan.   **7** Russian Christmas.   **8** Lunch at Lourié's.   **19** I sell the Renault for 14,000 francs. Evening at Staal's.   **23** Tea party here for the Louriés.   **26** Tea at the Café du Dôme. Dinner at Mme de Petit Thouar's.
31 Mme Mengelberg at Staal's.

February

13 To the cinema with Ira.   **18** Igor arrives.   **19** Lunch with Igor at Mme Errazuriz's with Tony Gandarillas and Princess Violette Murat.[1] Dinner here.   **20** Lunch with Igor and Guy de Matharel at Ramuntcho.   **21** We leave Paris by car and lunch at Meaux. At 7 p.m. we are in Châlons-sur-Marne.   **22** To Nancy, Hôtel Thiers. [Vera and Igor jointly sent a card to Diaghilev from Nancy, giving news of their journey.]   **23** To Strasbourg, the Maison Rouge. Cinema.   **24** Help Igor to write business letters. Cinema.   **25** To Lunéville, the Hôtel des Halles.   **26** Lunch at Nancy, Place Stanislas. Dinner at Châlons.   **27** Arrive in Meaux in time for dinner.

March

2 Igor and I have migraine headaches.   **3** Dinner at Valechka's.   **4** Guy for lunch here. Arthur Lourié for dinner.   **5** Arthur for lunch.   **6** Lunch at the restaurant Miretta.   **7** Dinner at Staal's.   **8** Dinner at Lourié's.   **9** *Blini* here. Valechka. Dinner at Robert Lyon's.   **10** Igor leaves at 7:30 p.m.
11 With Nathalie Goncharova at Claridge's. Dinner at Samoilenko's.[2]
12 Evening with Ira.   **14** Cercle Russe with Arthur Lourié.   **21** Lunch with Nouvel at La Biche. Tea at the Cascade.   **24** Lunch at Lourié's. For tea here: Prince Obolensky[3] (Quai d'Orsay).   **25** Tea at Maria Lange's.
26 Lunch at Mme Borovsky's. Go to Joseph Szigeti's concert.   **29** I deliver three costumes to Diaghilev.

[1] Stravinsky's patroness since 1916.

[2] Husband of Fatima Hanum.

[3] Vera knew Obolensky in Russia during the Revolution, and the Stravinskys often saw him in the 1950s, when he was manager of the restaurant in the Drake Hotel, New York City.

[4] George Balanchine danced the part of Kastchei.

[5] Protégé of Gustav Mahler and one of the few conductors held in esteem by Stravinsky.

[6] Stravinsky accompanied the singers and choruses at the piano in a preview of the opera-oratorio presented by the Princesse de Polignac. Prokofiev and Otto Klemperer were present.

[7] The absence of any comment on this occasion probably means that Vera did not want Stravinsky to read her diary and knew that if he asked to see it she could not refuse. She used to describe the first performance of *Oedipus* in considerable detail, as well as Stravinsky's foul mood following the poor audience reception of the work. According to Peter Heyworth's *Otto Klemperer*, the consensus is that Stravinsky's conducting was not clear.

[8] See *Stravinsky in Pictures and Documents*, op. cit.

[9] Friend of Igor's and Vera's. See her 1940 diary.

April

8 For tea here: Prince Obolensky. Dinner and the film *Ivan the Terrible*.
17 To Billancourt.   **18** To Coucy-le-château in Soissons.   **19** To Beauvais. [On April 23, Stravinsky, in Nice, sent Diaghilev an Easter letter thanking him for a payment.]   **24** Russian Easter.   **25** Lunch at Lourié's. Tea at Mme Borovsky's.

May

3 Igor arrives.   **4** Lunch with Igor and Diaghilev in the restaurant de Gouffres.   **5** Small errands, including buttons, for Igor.   **7** Rosette gives birth to a daughter. I go with Igor to Janacopulos's concert.   **9** Evening with Igor at Staal's.   **10** Igor finishes the orchestra score of *Oedipus Rex* at 4 a.m. in my apartment.   **15** Dinner with Igor at Père Avril's.   **17** With Igor to a chorus rehearsal for *Oedipus*.   **18** To the funeral service for Grey's father. Dinner at the Bois.   **19** Rehearsal of *Firebird*.[4]   **20** Dr. Lavezzari.   **24** Dr. Lavezzari. *Oedipus* rehearsal.   **26** To a rehearsal of *Firebird* and *Sacre*, conducted by Oskar Fried.[5]   **27** At 11 a.m., Kviatkovsky. To the performance of *Firebird*.   **28** At 9 a.m. *Oedipus* rehearsal. Tea with Sam Bottenheim. Dinner at Lourié's.   **29** At 9 a.m. *Oedipus* rehearsal. Evening at Polignac's.[6]   **30** 9 a.m. rehearsal. 3 p.m. Dr. Lavezzari. The premiere of *Oedipus*.[7]   **31** Dr. Vannier.

June

1 The second performance of *Oedipus*.   **3** The third performance of *Oedipus*.   **11** We go to the Radziwill exhibition, then to the last performance of the Ballets Russes season.   **14** To a "Concert Mécanique."[8]   **17** I go with Igor to London and stay at the Felix Hotel in Jermyn Street.   **19** Radio concert from 4:30 to 5:30. At 7, Hoity Wyborg.[9]
20 Lunch at Lord Berners'.[10] To the London Zoo.   **22** To Falla's concert. Evening at Miss Wyborg's.   **25** Lunch at a Russian restaurant. To the cinema with Edward Clark and Kettner.   **27** Igor's festival. The King of Spain comes.   **28** Buy presents at Asprey's. A visit to the Russian Patriarch. Dinner at Wyborg's.   **29** Arrive in Paris. Dinner with Valechka.   **30** Igor is at Paul Morand's with Edouard Herriot [the President of France]. In the afternoon, we leave for Villènes.

July

9 Païchadze for dinner here with Igor.   **10** To the movies with Igor: Buster Keaton.   **11** Igor leaves for Nice.[11]   **21** I go to visit Olga Mietens[12] at Chaville.   **23** Leave for Biarritz with the Matharels, and stay at the Hôtel du Palais in Poitiers.   **25** Biarritz.[13]   **30** To the premiere of *Volcano*.   **31** Lunch at Orlov's in Saint-Jean-de-Luz.

August

2 Tea in Saint-Jean-de-Luz and dinner at Cabouz.   **6** To the premiere of *Blue Bird*.   **8** We drive to La Hendaye.[14]   **14** Guy arrives with Grigory Pavlovich.   **20** Arrive at 6 p.m. at Pasredon.

[10] Lord Berners (Gerald Tyrwhitt), composer and writer. See *Stravinsky: Selected Correspondence*, Vol. II, op. cit.

[11] Stravinsky spent August and part of September at Echarvines and Lac d'Annecy. He inscribed a photograph taken at that time, "Convalescence de Catherine. Dr. Sloussarev," and another photograph, "Excursion in the Hotchkiss to Beauvezer." In September he was with Picasso at Juan-les-Pins, the time of the often misdated snapshot of Pablo and Olga Picasso, Stravinsky, and Cocteau.

[12] Vera's father's brother married a Mietens (or, in Russian, Mitene). Vera knew Mietenses in France in the 1920s: a 1971 letter from Olga Mietens, whatever her relationship to Artur de Bosset, mentions Vera's rue Ranelagh apartment and family reunions at Chaville. Vera was in correspondence with Olga from 1946 until her death in 1972, and during a visit to Paris after that date, Vera visited Vera Mietens and her grandson Arnaud Faure at 163, rue de Sèvres.

[13] For Stravinsky's involvement with the Biarritz restaurant of Grigory Pavlovich Beliankin, 1925–30, see *Selected Correspondence*, Vol. II, op. cit.

[14] On August 12, Igor wrote from Nice to Vera in Biarritz: "Here is a photo from *Vanity Fair* which I have had copied to send you. I will rephotograph still another picture and also send it to you. Isn't this one good? I ask you not to go on a trip alone. Please wait for Guy, even after the 17th. I sent you the money registered, and you should have it by the 15th. I hope you will be able to cash the check immediately. I received your letter of Thursday in which you write about a walk with Ira and Ganya [in Biarritz; Ganya, Ira's younger brother and Stravinsky's godson suffered from petit mal]. I kiss you warmly. Your Igor."

32 1927. Paris.

September

29 Paris. Igor arrives. Lunch at the Francis restaurant with Guy and Arthur Lourié. **30** Valechka for lunch. Evening at Lourié's.

October

1 Evening with Igor at Païchadze's. **2** We leave for London. **3** With Igor in London to October 14. **15** Return from London. Dinner with Païchadze. **17** Igor's rehearsal. **18** Igor's rehearsal and concert, the inauguration of the new Salle Pleyel.[1] **19** Igor and I go to the cinema. **21** We lunch at Staal's and go to the cinema in the evening. **22** With Igor to the cinema. **27** Dinner at Matharel's. **29** Igor and I leave Paris in my Mathis and spend the night in Valence. **30** We arrive in Nice. **31** Dinner at Isthmia.

November

1 I leave Isthmia for Paris. **8** Ira and Coco Chanel here. **12** Lunch at Achim-Khan's **21** At Alexandre Benois's. **24** Igor arrives unexpectedly. **26** At Staal's.

December

1 Igor leaves for Nice. **3** At Trubetzkoy's.[2] **13** To the grande duchesse ball at the Ritz. **17** To the cinema: Emil Jannings. **21** To Marie Picabia's wedding. Dinner at Marcelle Meyer's. **22** Dinner at Lourié's. **27** To the Diaghilev Ballets Russes. **28** To Horowitz's concert with Tulia. **29** To the Ballets Russes.

January

1 For dinner here: Ira, the Louriés. **7** Russian Christmas. **26** Coquetail [sic] party here. **29** Igor arrives. Lunch at Achim-Khan's. Versailles. **30** Versailles.

February

1 Versailles. **7** Dinner with Igor at the restaurant Cochon au Lait. **10** Stravinsky's concert. **11** Ansermet arrives. **13** Dinner with Igor at Benois's. **15** At 11 a.m. we go to the German Ambassador's. Dinner at Lourié's. **16** With Igor to the cinema. **18** Stravinsky's second concert. **19** With Igor at Rambouillet. **22** We leave for Berlin. **23** Berlin. We go to Klemperer's rehearsal from 11 a.m. to 3. **24** 11 to 2 p.m.: again to Klemperer's rehearsal. **25** Robert Lyon arrives. In the evening: *Oedipus Rex*, *Mavra*, *Petrushka* at the Staatsoper with Klemperer. **26** To Strasbourg. **27** Arrive in Paris.

March

2 At Lourié's. Papa [Vera's father]. Tea at Corne-biche. Cinema with Igor. **10** Leave Paris. Lunch at Sens. Dinner and the night at Châlons. **11** Lunch at Vienne. Guy comes with Montélimar. Spend the night at Avignon. **12** Igor leaves Rome. I lunch in Marseilles with the Admiral.[3] **14** Igor and I to Bichon. **15** Igor and I leave for Barcelona. **16** Igor's first Barcelona rehearsal. **17** [On March 17, Vera's mother wrote to her from Moscow: "Hurrah, hurrah, hurrah! At last I have a letter from my darling daughter! I cried for joy and rushed downstairs to share my happiness with my friends the Stepanovs. I bought some sweets and gave them to all of my neighbors, who rejoiced with me. The telephone worked overtime, too, since I had to spread the news to everybody. I

---

[1] Ravel conducted, as well as Stravinsky.

[2] In a letter to Vera, August 16, 1939, Suvchinsky mentions the *Memoirs* of Evgeny Trubetzkoy, adding that "he was a man of great culture."

[3] Vera's uncle, Theodore de Bosset. This entry, and those of the 14th and 16th, are in Stravinsky's hand.

[4] To Paris in November/December 1925.

[5] Possibly Robert Shilling, Vera's classmate at the University of Berlin before World War I, and her husband, briefly, before she met Sudeikin.

---

received many congratulations, and you can imagine how very, very happy I am.

"I had been wondering why my letters did not reach you. Not having any other address, I was sending them in care of Lourié and to the Hôtel Pretty. Very disturbed by the absence of news from you, I consoled myself with the thought that you had too much work and no time to write. But you did not forget me, and you still love me. Isn't this true?

"I live on memories of my trip.[4] It was so nice to see everyone, but I did not see as much of you as I would have liked. Now I do not know when we will be with each other again. At that time the passport was 35 roubles. Now it costs 225, a lot of money for me.

"Perhaps you will come here with Igor Fyodorovich. How marvelous it would be to see you here. Last Sunday, in a concert in the large hall of the Conservatory, Oskar Fried conducted *Le Sacre du printemps*. The hall was sold out and I could not get a ticket, but last year I heard the *Sacre* conducted by this same Fried, at which time I had the feeling that you were listening to it with me; this may sound strange to you, but understandable. I have been going to concerts more frequently now, less often to the theaters. Robert[5] used to get theater tickets for me, but he no longer works at the Moscow Theater. He gives German lessons instead because he can make more money. He visits me regularly and asks about you each time.

"I wrote to you how much I enjoyed visiting Olechka on her estate. She has very nice children and is a good housekeeper. Aunt Olga and Aunt Margot still live together. I had a very good time with them, but they have aged considerably. In Revel, I stayed with Katya Mitene, who seems to be doing quite well as a manicurist; in any case, Nadiusha is helping her out. Nikolai Semenovich is as thoughtful and courteous as ever.

"On returning to my work, I was greeted very warmly with a tea party (pastries, candy, and flowers). The director, Mr. A. Bach, touched me very much when he said: 'You see how the chemists like you; they are as happy as I am to have you back.' Evidently many people expected that I would remain in Paris.

"I conclude my letter because I want to mail it immediately. Tell me when you receive it. I will number all of my letters to you and I suggest that you do the same. Uncle Edr. [?], father's[6] brother, died last year on Olechka's estate. Write to me: Henriette Fyodorovna Bosset, Karpov Chemical Institute, Voronzovo Pole, Moscow, USSR. My darling Vierochka, I kiss you with all my heart. Give my best regards to Igor Fyodorovich.

"*P.S.* I am enclosing father's letter. He has asked for your address several times. Please write to him. He will be very happy."] **21** Igor's Barcelona rehearsal. **22** Igor's first Barcelona concert. **23** Tea at the painter Junient's. Dinner at the Maison Dorée with Mme Barentzer. **24** Banquet at the Ritz. Mr. and Mrs. Bosch and the composer Paisa. **25** Igor's matinée concert (5 p.m.). Dinner with Rodez. **26** We leave Barcelona at 3:10 p.m. **27** Stay at Châlet Lisette (terrible!).

April

1 Move to the Hôtel du Dauphin. **16** Igor leaves Nice for Paris.[7] **17** Premiere of *Le Train bleu*. **19** With Igor to Amsterdam. **20** Lunch with Bottenheim and Paul Kronheim. **21** Igor's rehearsal. Supper with Bottenheim and Kronheim. **22** We listen to Ansermet's concert on the radio from Amsterdam. **23** Rehearsal with Ansermet. **24** Rehearsal. The Amsterdam concert. **25** I return to Paris. **29** Ansermet arrives from London.

May

7 I leave with Igor for London on the Golden Arrow. **12** To the London Zoo with Edward Clark. Igor's BBC concert at 9:30. Supper with Morales. **13** Igor's 4 p.m. BBC concert. Dinner at the Berkeley Hotel.

---

[6] In *c*. 1979, Vera wrote: "I saw my mother crying in the Summer Garden in St. Petersburg. We were sitting next to the statue of Krilov, and I had to explain to her that my father wanted to divorce her in order to marry someone else. I told her over and over that her life would be better this way. My poor, poor mother looked at me with her blue eyes, not understanding why this should happen to her after thirty years of marriage. My father assumed that I would understand because I was divorcing my first husband at the time."

[7] Earlier in the month, Stravinsky had taken his family to Rome: photographs survive of him at the Quirinale, Piazza Colonna, Palazzo Barbarini, and, with Nicola Benois, Tivoli.

33

33 1927. Nice.

34 February 1928. Berlin.

35 1928. Strasbourg.

34

35

36–38 1928. Amsterdam.
Rehearsing *Histoire du soldat*.

39 April 1928.
Washington, D.C.
Adolph Bolm in
Apollon Musagète.

14 We return to Paris.   **19** Igor plays his Concerto with Bruno Walter.[1]
21 Dr. Vannier.   **22** Stravinsky's concert.   **29** Flowers from Gregory
Ratov.   **31** Evening at the Cercle Interallié.[2]

June

1 7 p.m.: Princess Trubetzkoy.   **12** The premiere of *Apollon* at the Ballets
Russes.   **17** With Igor at Ida Rubinstein's.[3]   **19** Stravinsky festival.
22 Meudon. Ermitage.   **23** Supper at Chanel's.   **24** Igor leaves for
London.   **25** Valechka, Pavka,[4] and Ira for dinner.   **27** Igor records for
Columbia in London.   **28** Igor records for Columbia.   **29** Igor arrives
from London.   **30** Farewell dinner: Igor, Valechka, Pavka, Païchadze, Ira.

July

1 Igor leaves Paris.[5]   **18** We go swimming in the Seine.   **24** Biarritz.
29 To Saint-Jean-de-Luz with Ira, Lenia, Mary.

August

4 Guy comes for three days.   **10** Visit the Bayonne Museum.   **19** Leave
Bordeaux for Paris.

September

1 Paris. Igor arrives from Annecy.   **2** We go to Scheveningen and the
Kurhaus.   **3** Igor's rehearsal.   **5** The costumes are chosen for *Carmen*.[6]
Igor's concert at 8:15 p.m.   **6** To Paris.   **15** With Alexandre Benois at
Verame.

November

7 Igor arrives from Zurich.   **13** I go to Amsterdam with Rosette.   **15** The
premiere of *Carmen*.   **16** Igor's concert at Pleyel.   **18** Igor's second
Pleyel concert.   **19** Rehearsal at the Opéra.[7]   **22** Rehearsal.
23 Rehearsal.   **24** Rehearsal. The premiere. Afterwards at Ida
Rubinstein's.

December

4 The second performance with Ida Rubinstein.   **20** To the Ballets Russes,
also at the Opéra.   **22** I deliver the costumes to Diaghilev.   **30** To Dijon
and Besançon.   **31** To Basel.

January

1 I arrive in Davos.[8]   **8** Leave Davos for Paris.   **26** To Geneva, the Hôtel
Suisse.   **27** Igor arrives at 11:18 a.m., and we leave for Dresden.
28 Dresden, the Hotel Bellevue.   **29** Igor's morning rehearsal of *Oedipus*.
Walk in the town. 6–8 p.m. a chorus rehearsal of *Oedipus*.   **30** We go to
a performance of Richard Strauss's *Egyptian Helen*.   **31** Attend a
performance of *Pique Dame* conducted by Fritz Busch. Reception for Igor
at the Hotel Bellevue.

February

1 Rehearsal of *Oedipus Rex*. Igor's concert at 7:30 p.m. After the concert
at Sommers's.   **2** To the museum. Lunch at Ebhardt's, the general
director. A nice dinner, the three of us, with Païchadze.   **3** Dresden to
Leipzig, Frankfurt, and Strasbourg.   **4** To Lyons.   **5** The museum. Go to a
performance of *Tosca* in Lyons.   **6** I leave for Paris.   **15** Kviatkovskaya
for lunch. To Ansermet's concert: *Baiser* and *Noces*.   **16** To *Prince Igor*.
17 Lunch at Lourié's.   **18** The presentation of my spring collection at our
Maison Verame. Germaine Lyon.   **26** Igor arrives. We go to the Jannings
film *The Patriot*.   **27** Igor's rehearsal.

March

5 Igor's concert. In the evening: Suvchinsky and Lourié.   **7** We go to see
The Trial of Mary Dugan. An accident with my Mathis.   **14** With Igor for
lunch and dinner, and to a performance of Bach's *St. John Passion* at the
Salle Gaveau.   **16** Igor leaves. I find a dog.

April

1 In Biarritz to the 9th.   **10** Leave Biarritz for Paris.   **11** Arrive in Paris.
With Diaghilev at 5 p.m. at his hotel.   **22** With Gabrielle Picabia.
26 Dinner with Irène Dana.[9]   **28** I leave for Monte Carlo.   **29** Monte
Carlo, the Hôtel de Paris.

May

5 Russian Easter.   **6** Paris.   **8** Igor records *Firebird* for Columbia.
10 Igor records for Columbia.   **11** Igor's Columbia recording of
Renard.[10]   **13** I organize a business enterprise with Ira.   **14** Igor is in
London.   **15** The Ballets Russes arrives. *Renard* rehearsal.   **17** Igor
returns from London. Prokofiev's orchestra rehearsal of *Prodigal Son*.
18 Dress rehearsal.   **19** Rehearsal of *Prodigal Son*. A lot of work![11]
20 We go to the preview of *Prodigal Son* at Princesse de Polignac's.
21 To the Ballets Russes: *Renard*.   **27** Opening of Fedya's[12] exhibition at
38, rue de la Boétie.   **31** Stravinsky festival conducted by Monteux.

June

1 Tchelichev's[13] exhibition.   **11** Igor leaves for London with Svetik.[14]
19 Igor returns from London: his name-day lunch.   **24** I leave for London
with Igor.   **25** Rehearsals at 10 and 2.   **26** Rehearsal. We visit Hampton
Court Palace.   **27** Rehearsal at 10 a.m. Igor's concert.   **28** We leave for
Paris.

July

2 Igor goes to Nice.

August

14 Ira goes to Biarritz, I go to Pasredon.   **20** Paris. [On this date Vera
wrote to Igor, Chalet des Echarvines, Talloires: "The death of Diaghilev
has shaken me terribly. I have not been able to pull myself together since
this morning, and I can think of nothing else. I am distraught and sad.

---

[1] See the Appendix, "The Fermin Gémier Affair," in *Stravinsky: Selected Correspondence*, Vol. II, op. cit.

[2] A well-known Paris club.

[3] Stravinsky was about to begin the composition of *Le Baiser de la fée* for Mme Rubinstein.

[4] Pavka Koribut, Diaghilev's uncle.

[5] Stravinsky spent the summer in Echarvines. Arthur Lourié stayed with him for a time during this period, and Alexis Yellachich.

[6] Vera designed the costumes and decors for a production of *Carmen* in Amsterdam, conducted by Pierre Monteux.

[7] For the premiere of *Le Baiser de la fée*.

[8] To see Olga Sallard, who was a patient in a tuberculosis sanatorium.

[9] Irène Dana, the Countess Heiden, a well-known couturier, who renewed her friendship with Vera in the 1960s in Hollywood.

[10] *Renard* was not recorded, as scheduled, on the 11th. The piece had been rehearsed by Roger Desormière for the performances by the Ballets Russes.

[11] Vera had made costumes designed by Georges Rouault for this ballet.

[12] Theodore (Fedya, Fedik) Stravinsky (b. 1907), the composer's elder son, a painter.

[13] Pavel Tchelichev (1898–1957), the leading Russian painter of his generation. Stravinsky had first met him in Berlin in October 1922.

[14] Sviatoslav Soulima (Nini, Svetik) Stravinsky (b. 1910), the composer's younger son, a pianist. The origin of the name Soulima is not, as has been suggested, the character Zulima in Novalis's *Heinrich von Ofterdingen*.

41

40

42

40 1929. In the country near Paris.

41 1929. Nice.

42 1929. Paris.

43

Wondering whether you might not have heard, I sent you a telegram. I learned about it myself from the newspapers. Then Argutinsky telephoned. He did not know any details but he gave me Pavka's address, and I sent him a telegram (Koribut, Grand Hôtel des Bains, Venice). Lately Pavka has been receiving the most tender letters from Diaghilev, more tender than ever before, and on Saturday, feeling very ill, Diaghilev sent for him. According to the newspapers, the cause of death was blood poisoning. Pavka sent a telegram to Argutinsky saying that Diaghilev had died without suffering. All of his friends are there now, Misia [Edwards Sert], Chanel, and others, so he was not alone among the young, who probably lost their heads.

"My friendship with you is linked to my friendship with Diaghilev. I cannot separate our relationship from that period. All morning I cried and cried.

"What will happen to the Ballets Russes now? Does this mean that everything is finished, all of the Russian seasons? Will there be no more performances?

"I feel sorry for the old fellows, Valechka, who was Diaghilev's oldest friend, and Pavka—who will now be thrown out into the street. All this is terribly sad. Farewell, my dearest, Your V."] [On August 26, Stravinsky, in Talloires, wrote to Walter Nouvel: "I prefer silence to a letter which expresses so inadequately what I feel. But I have summoned the courage to try to express my feelings . . . the sharp pain in my heart as a result of the sudden disappearance of Seriozha whom I loved so much. Let this letter be a witness of this. . . . Today, the 9th day after his death, Vera will offer a *panikhida*[1] service for the death."]

September

24 Igor arrives. **29** Ira arrives. We go to Chartres. **30** My name day.

October

5 At the Théâtre Antoine. **7** Igor's rehearsal. **8** General dress rehearsal. **9** With Igor to *The Merry Wives of Windsor*. **13** For lunch: Grigory Pavlovich, Ira, Arthur [Lourié], Svetik, Igor, and I. Igor leaves. **17** Lunch with Svetik. **18** Dinner at Lourié's.

November

1 For lunch here: Svetik and Arthur. **2** Leave for Davos. **6** To Szymanowski's[2] at Guardaval.

December

4 Paris. Igor and I give a cocktail party in our house. **6** Igor's concert.[3]

January

7 Cocktail party in our house: Alice Nikitina, R. Lefebure, *et al.* **8** Salomeya and Achenia. **12** To Saint-Germain with Nikitina and Lifar. **17** Ira's mother arrives. Tea with Lifar. **18** Igor and I leave for Berlin at 8:15 a.m., arrive in Basel at 4:18 p.m., and depart from there at 5:40. **19** Arrive in Berlin at 9 a.m. Go to the performance of *The Magic Flute* at the Kroll Opera. **20** To the aquarium and the theater: *Menschen im Hotel*. **21** To an Emil Jannings film. **22** Lunch with Passavant. We see *Palmengarten im Vaterland*. **23** Igor's concert. Supper at Fürstenhof's. **24** To the cabaret *Kü-Ka* with Hans Curjel.[4] **25** We visit the Berlin Zoo,

then Igor's rehearsal at the radio. **26** Igor's radio concert. To *The Threepenny Opera*. To a skating rink with Païchadze. **27** Passavant and Hirsch. Take the 6:40 train to Leipzig, the Kaiserhof Hotel. **28** Party at Jalowitz's with Klemperer. **29** To Wagner's *Rienzi*: boring. **30** Igor's rehearsal. Lunch at Brecher's. The Leipzig concert. **31** At the zoo, a newly born leopard. Elephants amid the palms. Buy books. Igor gives me a lesson about modulations.

February

1 We visit the Breitkopf and Härtel archives and see manuscripts by Bach, Beethoven, and Chopin. **2** Düsseldorf, the Palast Hotel. **3** Lunch with Weisbach. We go to the cinema. **4** To the zoo, where we feed wild animals. **5** Igor's rehearsal. Cinema. **6** Rehearsal. Lunch with Weisbach. Igor's concert, after which we take the Orient Express to Bucharest. **7** Kugel is at the station in Vienna. **8** Bucharest, the Athénée Palace Hotel, a good dinner. **10** Dinner in a Rumanian restaurant, the Petrovici. At the theater, a play by Oscar Wilde—in Rumanian! **11** A drive with Paganiy. **12** Igor's concert. Champagne at the Athénée afterward. **13** Wonderful lunch for Igor at Feder's. We go to tea at Madame Procupiu's, with the Queen of Yugoslavia and the Queen of Greece. **14** We buy icons, then have a terrible dinner with Michonzniki. **15** Shop with Mme Michonzniki. Lunch with Georgesco.[5] A very good dinner with Georgesco and Feder. **16** Lunch with Paganiy (Columbia). Igor goes to visit Queen Marie. Igor's concert. We leave Bucharest at 10:15 p.m. **17** On the train, Bucharest to Budapest to Prague. **18** Arrive in Prague, Hotel Ambassador. **19** Lunch at the French Legation with Talich,[6] Jacques Thibaut, Ysaye. **21** Museum. Lunch at the hotel. Poliakov. **22** Lunch and dinner with Vanek at the Czech musicians' club in Hopjanova. **23** Drive through the surroundings of Prague. Nice dinner at Vanek's. **24** Lunch at Böcker's. Evening, with caviar, at Reiser's. The Fata Morgana Club. **25** Igor's rehearsal. To the theater: *Sokols* (*Ecole des moniteurs*). Igor's concert. Supper afterward. **27** We leave for Paris. Presents from Böcher, Löwenbach, Kepl. **28** Arrive in Paris at 1:45 p.m. Twelve guests for dinner.

March

1 Lunch at Roger Martin du Gard's.[7] **2** Caviar *blini*. Igor leaves for Nice. I go to see Olga Sudeikina.[8] **5** At Mme Mumm's.[9] **7** Ira leaves for Biarritz. **8** Mme Errazuriz. Dinner with Fedya. **16** Tea here for Svetik and Fedya and their girlfriends. **20** For lunch here: the Matharels, and Jack Hylton.[10]

April

13 Valenciennes. I go to Soulima's concert.[11]

May

23 [On this date, Stravinsky wrote to his wife from Amsterdam: "Katik dear, I am very tired—I get only six hours of sleep a night, but I feel good and am in excellent spirits. . . . At the moment we [Vera and I] are sitting down to dinner. The newspapers were brought to us and one of them had the enclosed picture of me at the station. I think we'll go out for a walk and then go to bed early: I have two rehearsals tomorrow."]

July

18 To Avignon with Igor. **20** To Fontaine-Vaucluse with Igor. **21** To Marseilles with Igor. **22** In Marseilles with Igor. **23** I return to Paris.

---

[1] Russian Orthodox memorial service, normally conducted on the anniversary of a death.

[2] Karol Szymanowski, the Polish composer, a tubercular patient at Davos.

[3] The premiere of *Capriccio*, Stravinsky at the piano, Ansermet conducting.

[4] Stage director of the Kroll Opera.

[5] Conductor of the orchestra in Bucharest.

[6] Conductor of the orchestra in Prague.

[7] The 1937 Nobel Prize winner for *Les Thibaults*, his most widely read work. Friend of the Stravinskys, Roger Martin du Gard's *Souvenirs du colonel* was widely acclaimed in the 1980s as one of the pinnacles of the twentieth-century French novel.

[8] Olga Glebova Sudeikina, the painter's first wife, best known today for her association with Anna Akhmatova. See the Preface, page 5.

[9] The mother [?] of Olga Mumm. Née Struve, the daughter of a high-ranking Russian diplomat, Olga Mumm married into the champagne family. Her daughter Elena (née Hélène-Marthe von Mumm, 1906), Vera's closest friend in the family, married Edmund Wilson in the late 1940s, after his divorce from Mary McCarthy. More than once, Vera and Igor stayed with the Mumm family in their home in Johannisberg (near Frankfurt), overlooking the Rhine. One of Elena's brothers had tuberculosis and once when his family visited him in Davos, Vera saw them there.

[10] Conductor of a jazz band. See *Stravinsky: Selected Correspondence*, Vol. II, op. cit.

[11] Stravinsky did not go. Soulima played his father's Sonata there, and on December 22 in Lausanne.

43 1930. Ira Belline in her costume for the ballet *Ode* (1928).

44 February 1930. Düsseldorf.

45 February 1930. Leipzig. With Otto Klemperer.

45

46

47

46 January 31, 1930. Leipzig Zoo. Photo by Vera.

47 May 26, 1930. Haarlem. Posing for a film. Stravinsky had just returned from a visit to Peter the Great's Holland residence.

48 August 27, 1930. Locarno.

48

49 August 11, 1930. Charavines-les-Bains. With his mother on her birthday.

50

51

50 November 1930. Wiesbaden. Photo by Igor.

51 November 3, 1930. Bremen. Hillmanns Hotel.

52 November 1930. Munich

August

20 Le Touquet.   **26** Take the St. Gothard Express to Bellinzona and Locarno.   **29** Ascona.

September

6 To Stresa with Guy, via the Simplon and Domodossola.   **8** Dijon to Paris.   **21** At Zosia Kochanska's.   **28** I leave for Geneva. Igor arrives in Basel.   **29** With Igor and Ansermet in Basel, the Hotel Three Kings. To the cinema.   **30** Lunch in Ticino. The zoo. Dinner at van der Mühle.

October

1 Igor's rehearsal. Visit to the Kunsthalle.   **2** Igor's concert in Basel.
6 Paris.   **7** Igor leaves for Nice.   **21** Leave with Igor for Mainz.
22 Holland.   **23** See a performance of *Mahagonny*.[1]   **24** Lunch at the parents of Willy Strecker.   **25** To Kloster Eberbach. Igor's concert in Mainz.   **26** Dinner at the Streckers', who have many Picassos.   **27** Drive to Koblenz, Bad Ems, Bad Schwalbach.   **28** Lunch in Johannisberg at Mumm's.   **29** To a rehearsal of *Urfaust*. Dinner at Ludwig Strecker's.
30 Igor's rehearsal.   **31** Igor's concert in Wiesbaden.

November

1 We go to the Paul Klee exhibition.   **2** Mainz to Cologne and Bremen.
3 Bremen: public dress rehearsal. Wendel.[2]   **4** Lunch at Wendel's. Supper at Ahrens'.   **5** From Bremen to Berlin. Ansermet.   **6** To Klemperer's concert, which includes Schoenberg's arrangements of Bach. Igor plays his Sonata on the Berlin Radio.   **7** Berlin. Igor's rehearsal.   **8** At 11 a.m., *Histoire du soldat*. Tea at von Benda's (nice atmosphere; she is Finnish). Supper at Fürstenhof's.   **9** A walk. *Histoire du soldat* again at 12 noon. Lunch at the zoo. Cinema.   **10** To the Berlin Museum, which is opened especially for us. Lunch at Klemperer's. At 8:25 p.m. we leave Berlin for Munich.   **11** We walk but, still feeling cold, go to the cinema to warm up.   **12** Munich. To the Frauenkirche, the Alte Pinakothek, and book shops.   **13** After Igor's rehearsal we go to the Bayerisches Museum. Lunch at the Vier Jahreszeiten with Wetzelberger.[3] Dinner at the hotel.   **14** To the Deutsches Museum. We buy a camera.
15 To Nymphenburg and to the zoo. *Bonbonnière*, a stupid cabaret.
16 Back to the Alte Pinakothek. To Hofbräuhaus. Eric Schaal[4] comes for champagne and dinner.   **17** We photograph churches and the Englischer Garten. Lunch at the Vier Jahreszeiten.   **18** Frankfurt. Weisbach meets our train. We go to Goethe House.   **19** At 3 p.m. we see *Der blaue Engel*. Igor works with Hans Rosbaud.   **20** To the museum of sculpture. Igor talks on the radio. Dinner with the Hirsches.   **21** Walk to the zoo. Igor's rehearsal. With Strecker to *Fledermaus*. [Stravinsky wrote to his wife on November 21: "Katik, my dear, just a few words, not to leave you without any news, even though at the moment I have absolutely no news to tell you. . . . I have received your letter (the one containing the misunderstanding about the train that I would be taking to Frankfurt) and was surprised that you did not mention the letter I wrote to the girls, in which I said that I was leaving Munich on the evening of the 17th (i.e., on an overnight train) and consequently would be arriving in Frankfurt early on the morning of the 18th. I leave for Vienna on Wednesday afternoon and arrive at 7:00 in the morning on Thursday. I said a few words on the radio yesterday about my compositions *Baiser de la fée* and *Capriccio*. I had been asked to do that in light of my concert here in the Funkstunde, since it is not a simple concert, but one with Radio Übertragung, as in Berlin."]   **22** Igor's rehearsal. Lunch at Henkel's. We go to a performance for children of Hindemith's *We Build a City*. Dinner with the Streckers. [Stravinsky wrote to his wife on November 22: "Katik, my darling, I witnessed our final rehearsal with great satisfaction. Rosbaud is a very good conductor and musician and has this new orchestra, put together only a year ago, well in hand.

"French passports do not require Belgian visas; yours has been renewed, has it not? Bring me the large score of the Symphony which I left at home, not wanting to drag it about."]⁵   **23** Igor practices the piano while I paste in the scrapbook.   **24** Supper with the Hirsches.   **26** Train to Vienna.   **28** We shop at Klein Graben. Party at Kugel. Supper with Korngold.⁶ [Stravinsky wrote to his wife from Vienna on November 28: "These hands, which you ought to recognize, were photographed while I was still in Munich.⁷ The other photos, on which I am writing you this letter, my Katik, were also taken there. . . . Evidently Spanjaard is no conductor *at all*, and, judging from what I have seen of him at our short lunch and at the rehearsal, he is the most uncivilized man I have ever met. What is more, he has never played any of my compositions, and openly admits it.

"Yesterday I witnessed the first rehearsal. I do not foresee any particular difficulties with him for the moment (I'll be watching out again today), but there is no cause for optimism either! I have a rehearsal at 2:30. It's 10:30 in the morning now.

"The sky here is covered by clouds. I have not seen the sun since I left Munich.

"I had a nice letter from Fedya. He complains about money, but I gave him enough to last him until my arrival in Brussels and our meeting there, as well as for acquisitions. I do not understand why he did not have enough!

"That is all for today, Katik; I must get dressed and run so that I will have some time, if only 10 minutes, to warm up my fingers.

"I kiss all of you dear ones, but you more affectionately than anyone else. Your Gima.

"P.S. From Nuremberg I go to Mainz, where I am to spend the night of the 5th. On the 6th, Strecker has invited me to a formal dinner with Her Majesty's brother. From there, on the morning of the 7th, I go to Mannheim, straight to the rehearsal. These places are far apart from each other."]   **29** Museum. Concert with Spanjaard. Supper at the Imperial.
30 Museum. Drive through the Prater. With the Kugels to Hitzing. We leave at 11 p.m. for Nuremberg.

December

2 Museum. Walk. Supper at the Grand Hotel.   **3** Lovely weather. To the Tiergarten and to *Fidelio* in the evening.   **4** Nuremberg. In bed resting and reading.   **5** Dinner with Strecker and Samuel Dushkin.⁸   **6** Lunch with Strecker and Dushkin. Dinner with Prince von Hessen.   **7** Mainz. Ludwigshafen. The Museum. In the evening to *Ariadne auf Naxos*. Supper with Dr. Kahn.   **8** Walking. Resting. Dinner at Dr. Kahn's.   **9** Mannheim, the Palast Hotel.   **10** Ludwigshafen. Train to Paris.   **14** Brussels.
18 Amsterdam.   **20** Igor's Paris concert.

1931

January

1 Walk in the forest at Fontainebleau. Go with Païchadze and Prokofiev to see *The Blue Angel*.   **2** To *Le Roi Candaule* with Nikitina and Ira.
10 The Prokofievs come for tea.   **12** Ira rents an apartment at 9, rue Marboeuf.   **26** Igor and I go to London. Evening with Ansermet and Guy.   **27** To the British Museum.   **28** Igor's concert at Queen's Hall.
29 Rehearsal with Jack Hylton. To the Persian exhibition.   **30** To Mengelberg's rehearsal. Dinner at Courtauld's to meet Klemperer.
31 Lunch with Edward Clark. Igor's rehearsal. Dinner at Lord Berners'.

February

1 Lunch at Lord Berners'. Tea with Asquith. Concert and dinner afterward with Mengelberg and Clark.   **2** A good crossing. Arrive in

---

¹ Not to be confused with the expansion of the Brecht-Weill *Der Aufsteig und Fall der Stadt Mahagonny*.

² Conductor of the orchestra in Bremen. He performed *Le Sacre du printemps* and Stravinsky played his *Capriccio*

³ Conductor of the orchestra.

⁴ Photographer, continued to correspond with Stravinsky in later years from Jackson Heights, New York.

⁵ Stravinsky invited his family to attend the premiere of the *Symphony of Psalms*, Brussels, December 14.

⁶ Erich Wolfgang Korngold (1897–1957), composer of *Die tote Stadt* (1920).

⁷ The photograph was taken by Eric Schall.

⁸ Violinist. See the chapter "Dear Samsky" in *Stravinsky: Selected Correspondence*, Vol. II, op. cit.

53 1930. Vienna. Hotel Bristol. Photo by Vera.

Paris at 5 p.m. Our house is cold. **3** To Ira's, for the first time at 9, rue Marboeuf. Igor leaves. I dine at Païchadze's. **15** Igor arrives. Lunch at Païchadze's. Tea at Ira's. Igor's rehearsal at 8 p.m. **16** Ansermet here for lunch. Igor's rehearsal at 2 p.m. Dinner with Ansermet. Lifar's premiere at the Opéra. **17** Rehearsals with Jack Hylton and Dushkin. Igor records *Symphony of Psalms*. Jack Hylton at the Opéra. **19** Lunch at Dushkin's. Igor's concert at Walter Straram's. **20** Igor's rehearsal (2 hours). Play chess. The Ansermet-Stravinsky concert. Reception at Mme Errazuriz's. **21** *Blini* with sturgeon. Contract with Straram. For dinner here: Robert Lyon, Ansermet, Clark. **22** Lunch here. Choral rehearsal 2–4 p.m. **24** Concert Ansermet-Stravinsky, a colossal success. **25** Dinner at the Francis restaurant with Ansermet and Straram. Dushkin's concert. **26** We walk in the Bois. Lunch at Francis'. Dinner at Nadia Boulanger's. **27** Igor leaves for London. Dinner at La Rue's with Mme Mumm.

March

5 With Strecker and Courtauld. **6** Lunch at the Rivière restaurant with Paul Léon.[1] **7** We go to Prokofiev's concert at the Châtelet. Supper for 11 people at l'Esturgeon. **8** Lunch for Dushkin at Strecker's. Later, at my house: Nouvel. **11** Igor leaves. **25** To Gieseking's concert in the evening.

April

16 See Chaplin's *City Lights*. **17** To René Clair's *Million*. **18** To the Toulouse-Lautrec exhibition. **19** Paris to Milan, Milan to Trieste. **20** Trieste. Igor has an evening rehearsal. **21** Cathedral San Giusto. **22** Museo Civico del Arti and Lapidarium. **24** Meet a charming Norman: René Baton.[2] Igor's concert is successful. **25** By hydroplane to Venice. Evening songs of gondolieri in Venice. **26** To the Accademia and the Palazzo Ducale. Vaporetto to the Giardini Pappadopoli. Walk to the Frari and then to Florian's. Dinner at Martini's. **27** Museo Correr. San Marco. Venice to Padua, Hotel Storione. **28** Santa Giustina. St. Anthony. Giotto's frescoes. Padua to Verona. **29** Verona to Lago di Garda and Milan. **30** Milan to Nice to Cannes to Toulon (Hôtel du Pont), in a pullman.

May

1 Isthmia. **3** Toulon to Pasredon (at 11:30 p.m.). **5** Paris. **6** *Countess Maritza* rehearsal until 3 a.m. Ira's costumes. **7** Tea with Maria Lange, Svetik's concert in the Ecole Normale. **9** Lunch with Nouvel at Quai Voltaire. **20** English lesson in the evening.[3] **21** Feast of the Ascension. English lesson 4–5 p.m. **22** Opéra. **23** English lesson 10–11 a.m. **26** English lesson. **28** English lesson. Picnic in Meudon forest. **29** Lunch here with Ira, Fedya. 5 p.m. Antal Dorati, Ira, Picabia, Guy. **30** English lesson.

June

1 English lesson. **2** English lesson. Tchelichev's exhibition. Gabrielle Picabia here. **4** English lesson. **5** English lesson. **8** English lesson. **9** Boris Kochno at 10 a.m. Exhibition. **10** English lesson. **11** English lesson. At Roosevelt's.[?] **13** English lesson. Gabrielle. **15** English lesson. **16** English lesson.[4] **19** Biarritz. **23** Limoges to Paris. English lesson. **24** English lesson. **25** The boys dine with me.[5] Prokofiev for tea. **26** English lesson. **29** English lesson.

July

1 English lesson. **3** English lesson. **4** [?] With Igor to Starissy. **7** English lesson. **11** To Nadia Boulanger's at Gargenville. **14** Our tenth anniversary.[6] **15** *Symphony* at Nadia Boulanger's.[7] **23** Stravinsky makes the decision to move to Paris permanently. **30** Igor arrives. **31** With Lyudmila Gavrilovna[8] to Meudon.

August

2 Explanations with Igor. **3** Drive with Lourié to look at country houses. **4** Valechka here. **5** Lunch at the Casino Enghien. Igor leaves for Voreppe.

October

14 Dinner at Dushkin's. **15** Dinner at Païchadze's. **18** With Ira all day. Cinema. **20** Leave Paris with Igor. **21** Berlin. Igor's 2 rehearsals. **22** Two rehearsals. Dinner with Carl Flesch and Hindemith. **23** Berlin concert, premiere of Violin Concerto. Dinner with Fürstenbergs, Milstein, and Meyrovitz. **24** 5 p.m. At Strecker's. Rathaus with Friedenau. To the theater: *Du Barry*. **25** At Hindemith's. **26** To the revue *Tingle-Tangle*. **27** We go to the cinema. **28** Leave for Halle. **29** Halle. **30** Wiesbaden, the Hotel Rose. **31** Walk in the forest. Dinner at Strecker's.

November

1 Walk in the forest. **3** Cinema. **4** Supper at Henkel's. **5** Rehearsal at Frankfurt. **6** Walk with Mme Rosbaud. Rehearsal. Dinner at Strecker's. **7** Two rehearsals. Dinner at Hirsch's. **8** Rehearsal and concert at Frankfurt. Pleasant supper in restaurant Falstaff. **9** Igor's Frankfurt concert. **11** Concert with Dushkin. **12** With Igor to London (Ostend to Dover), the Langham Hotel. **13** Rehearsal. **15** Rehearsal. Dinner at Ice Club (Courtauld). **16** At Paganiy's. At Rettner's. **17** Shopping. Courtauld's. **18** London to Dover to Brussels to Cologne. **19** Cologne to Darmstadt (Trederhorn). **20** Darmstadt. Rehearsal. Cinema. **21** Rehearsal. We go to see *The Sleeping Beauty*. **22** To *La Forza del Destino*. **24** Wiesbaden. Dinner with Streckers. **25** Mainz. Dinner with Ludwig Strecker. **26** Lunch at Mumms'. Cinema and dinner with Mr. Carlos. **27** Rehearsal. Dinner with the Streckers. Cinema. **28** To Hindemith's *Das Unaufhörliche*. **29** Rheingold and Reinhart. Cologne, the Dom Hotel. Dinner with Alma Moodie[9] and Spengler. **30** Cologne. 11 to 1 p.m. at Stackelberg's. Concert, then supper at Wiesel.

December

1 At Stackelberg's 4 to 6 p.m. Concert. Supper at the Dom Hotel. **2** Wiesbaden. Cinema. **5** Igor works with Dushkin. Strecker brings the recordings. **7** Hanover. Lunch at the Mumms'. Strecker. **8** A photograph showing Igor in full dress listening to recordings. Dinner at Hummel's. **9** Wiesbaden to Hanover. **10** Cinema—Pallenberg. Dinner with Dushkin. **12** Museum. Walk. Von Müller and wife. **13** Hanover. Rehearsal. Zoo. **14** Hanover. **15** The Nord Express to Paris. Concert at the Salle Gaveau; ''all Paris'' is there. **17** Stravinsky concert. Reception at Fairchild's.[10] **18** Katya is here.[11] **19** To Ira's with Alice Nikitina. With Igor to the Beliankins. **20** Lunch at Païchadze's. Suvchinsky and Arthur here. Igor is with Maritain. **21** To Yehudi Menuhin's concert. **22** Igor leaves. I go to a René Clair film.

---

[1] See Vera's diary, January 8, 1922.

[2] René Baton [Rhené-Baton], director of the Trieste Orchestra, had conducted *Le Sacre du printemps* in London in 1913.

[3] Vera preserved the notebooks for her English lessons with Serge Nabokov in May 1931, November 1934, and October 1939.

[4] On this date Stravinsky went from Nice to Voreppe (Grenoble) to look for a house. (He found one and moved there July 18.) On his return to Nice from Voreppe he did not compose but worked on the proofs of the Violin Concerto. His mother's doctor had put him on a strict diet because of liver and gall-bladder upsets apparently resulting from a medication that he had been taking for his migraines. He went from Nice to Paris, June 27, and from Paris directly to Voreppe.

[5] Stravinsky's sons were in Paris. They returned to Nice on July 3.

[6] Igor and Vera dated their union from July 14. In 1931 Stravinsky spent the day at Vera's apartment in the rue Ranelagh, as a photo caption reveals. (The photo is not in the present book.)

[7] Stravinsky played his new recording of the *Psalms* there.

[8] Stravinsky's sister-in-law.

[9] Australian violinist, protégée of Werner Reinhart, Miss Moodie gave the first performance of Stravinsky's *Suite italienne*.

[10] Blair Fairchild. See *Stravinsky: Selected Correspondence*, Vol. II, op. cit.

[11] Stravinsky's wife was momentarily in Paris.

54

55

54 1931. Darmstadt.

55 April 1931. Trieste. Photo by Igor.

56 1931. Versailles. Photo by Igor.

Berlin, 23 oct. 1931
worn die ...te
ausführung

J Strawinsky

57 October 23, 1931. Berlin.

58

58 March 1932. Venice. Photo by Igor.

59 April 1932. At Villa d'Este, Cernobbio. Photo by Igor.

59

60

60 1932. Grenoble. The composer with his mother and wife listening to a broadcast of Soulima Stravinsky giving a piano recital.

61 June 1932. Voreppe. With his daughters, Milene and Lyudmila.

62 June 1932. Voreppe. With his sons, Theodore and Soulima.

63 June 18, 1932 (fiftieth birthday). Voreppe.

61

62

63

64 June 1932.

65 September 1932. Vera and Blaise Cendrars en route from Biarritz to Paris. Photo by Igor.

66 1932. Davos.

1932 — 1933

Vera to Igor

Monsieur Igor Stravinsky
La Vironnière
Voreppe (Isère)

22, rue Ranelagh
Paris
June 17, 1932

I congratulate you,[1]
My Matushkin
    Sobachkin
      Bubushkin
My Dearest
    beloved
      golden one.
I am very happy about your fiftieth birthday and I send you all my love and best wishes for us both, for a long and loving union. May God keep you, my beloved, and may all the coming years be under His protection. I send you the tenderest kisses. Until Sunday at 22:17 in Chalon-sur-Saône. Your Vera.

Vera to Igor

Monsieur Igor Stravinsky
La Vironnière
Voreppe (Isère)

22, rue Ranelagh
Paris
Monday, January 11, 1933

My dear Matushkin, Thank you ever so much for the gloves. They fit me marvelously and are very attractive. [Original in German.] Thank Katya for me for the chocolates; and the children for having remembered and congratulated me and for their kind wishes.[2]

I am enclosing a few photographs, just received: lunch with Lur-Saluce,[3] and me with you on the Potsdammerplatz in Berlin. How strange to look at photographs taken only a few months earlier. I am not going to wear any more summer linen dresses. They do not look neat on me, but mussed up and as if I were wearing a crumpled sheet.

Suddenly I have begun to feel wonderful: my face has turned rosy-red, I look well-rested, and my appetite resembles a wolf's. Could it be that [Dr.] Lavezzari has helped me that much?

On my birthday I made a buffet with *zakuski*, vodka, and champagne. (Imagine, I found a wonderful still champagne at Henriot's for 12 francs a bottle, and I can get a dozen of them.) Then I spent the whole day seeing well-wishers. In the evening I did some hard drinking with Ira and the entire Osten-Saken

family. Fred Osten-Saken[4] arrived very recently, finally having obtained an 8-day permit (!). But he has already succeeded in boring everyone; moreover, since he is here, he will probably get permission to remain. I drove him to Versailles today and was rewarded with a wonderful lunch.

On my birthday, Ira roasted a lamb, then drank herself silly; but she was very funny and happy. The poor dear looks terrible now (she has no clients) and is taking many medications. I try to go out with her for daily walks in the Bois de Boulogne, but she is yellowish and has become anemic.

I enclose a postcard that I received from little Peter Balashov, Olga Mumm's nephew, to whom I introduced you at the concert. He sent me another letter but, not knowing my address, he asked his Babushka to send it to me, ''Because that woman really caught my eye.'' [Original in French.] Imagine, a nine-year-old boy!

Sam [Dushkin] called and asked whether you would still be here on the evening of the 18th. We are leaving on the 19th, aren't we? If you are here, he will refuse an invitation to some American soirée. Dushkin has had a terrible tragedy in his house: Gar [the dog] caught a fatal disease and must be put to sleep. Sam and Beveridge[5] go around weeping from morning until night about it. I advised them to buy another dog immediately.

Well, my little one, that is all for today. I am looking forward to being together with you again soon, and I send you a million loving and tender kisses. Your little pet, V.

1934 — 1935

Vera to Igor

Monsieur Igor Stravinsky
''REX''
Départ le 27 dec. 1934

22, rue Ranelagh
Paris 16[6]
December 28, 1934

Bon voyage dear Bubushkin and don't forget your little ''doggie.''

Vera to Igor

Monsieur Igor Stravinsky
c/o Musical Art Management Corporation
30 Rockefeller Plaza
New York City[7]

December 28, 1934[8]

My dear, my beloved, I wonder how you feel, rocking on the sea,[9] but I hope that it is calm and that you are surrounded by

---

[1] June 18, 1932 was Stravinsky's fiftieth birthday. Stravinsky had been with Vera during most of March, some of April and the beginning of May. They were in Belgium (Antwerp and Brussels) for concerts on March 14 and 15, in Venice from the 16th (for a concert on the 19th) until the last day of the month: the Princesse de Polignac arrived in the city on the S.S. *Rotterdam* during the visit. After going to Florence, Igor and Vera were in the Villa d'Este at Cernobbio at the beginning of April. On May 4 they drove from Mâcon to Paris. During the Paris sojourn, their Citroën was stolen while they were lunching at Fontainebleau, but later retrieved. They also dined with Arthur Lourié and his wife in a restaurant near St. Cyr. On the 19th, Stravinsky took the train to Chalon-sur-Saône, where he was met by Vera and Walter Nouvel. On the 20th, Igor and Vera were in Dôle and Besançon. On the 21st they dined in Karlsruhe and spent the night in the Frankfurter Hof. On the 23rd they heard Hans Rosbaud's performance of *Mavra* in Frankfurt. On the 24th they were with the Streckers in Wiesbaden, and on the 26th at the Schlosshotel in Heidelberg. On the 27th they saw Grünewald's triptych in Colmar, staying at the Maison Rouge in Strasbourg. They were in Dijon on the 28th, and on the 29th in Paris, where they attended Artur Rubinstein's wedding at the beginning of July. Stravinsky then returned to Voreppe where, at the beginning of August, he received visits from Fernand Auberjonois, Lourié, and Dushkin—an excursion with him to Sassenage. On August 16, Stravinsky met Vera at Valence, and the next day they drove to Arles. On the 19th, en route to Montpellier, they encountered a gypsy caravan and took many photographs of it. Then, via Les Baux and Carcassonne, they drove to Biarritz. From Biarritz they went to Arcangue to see the Arcangue family. On August 27 and 28, Igor and Vera, and Monsieur and Madame Mensepekie (to Stravinsky's left in photo 133, *Igor and Vera Stravinsky* op. cit.) drove to Gavarny and St. Bertrand de Comminges.

[2] January 7 was Vera's birthday, Old Style (Julian) calendar, December 25, in the New Style (Gregorian) calendar. She celebrated on both days.

[3] Lur-Saluce, proprietor of Château Yquem. See photo 53 in *Igor and Vera Stravinsky*, op. cit.

[4] Baron Fred Osten-Saken (1888–March 19, 1974) friend of Vera's since December 3, 1908 (as his letters remind her). Vera also knew his sister, Baroness Illa Osten-Saken, who lived in Baden-Baden, and his mistress, Erika, who, according to Vera's photograph albums, seems to have had a propensity for nude sunbathing. Impoverished by the Russian Revolution, Baron Fred earned a modest living from Marcel Boussac as an expert on racehorses, in France, Ireland, and, after World War II, in Lexington, Kentucky. As an old man, in the 1970s, Baron Fred used to conclude his letters to Vera: ''Ne quitte pas ce monde avant moi.''

[5] Beveridge Webster, American pianist. Two years later he played Stravinsky's *Concerto per due pianoforti soli* with the composer and, with Stravinsky conducting the New York Philharmonic, Mozart's Concerto in G, K453.

[6] All of Vera's letters until December 1936 were sent from this address.

[7] All of Vera's letters to Stravinsky in America were sent to this address, to be forwarded.

[8] On December 28, 1934, Stravinsky's wife wrote to him: ''The boys are going to Polignac's for New Year's Eve and the girls are going with Suvchinsky to the movies.''

[9] Stravinsky and Dushkin had sailed on the S.S. *Rex*, from Villefranche-sur-Mer, December 27, 1934. The boat docked in New York, January 3, 1935.

luxury. I am glad you received my flowers. I was afraid that Georgette[1] would forget, and though I asked her to send pink ones I am not sure that they were available. I cannot tell you how sad the rest of the evening was for me. My face was still swollen the next day, and now I feel ill and have a lot of pain.

I was very touched by Katya's telephone call that same evening; she said she wanted to kiss me and to let me know that she was thinking of me. How extraordinary! Such thoughtfulness is not easy to find in the present-day world. I am truly and deeply touched by her.

The whole of yesterday passed in eating and drinking in the "Cercle International des Arts" where Kirsta[2] dragged us all, Ira, myself, Fred, and your sons. We have now formed an impression of that enterprise, and instead of the anticipated political atmosphere or gambling, found the place very proper. Champagne, *pirozhki*, and candles were passed around. But I do not see what advantage this has for the hostess of the club. She is a modest-looking pregnant woman whose husband has a strange appearance, a type like Stavisky.[3] I asked Wolf [Georgette's husband] to inquire about him at the Stock Exchange. I saw many people I knew, and Kirsta was right when she said that people would be there who could be useful for business. Among others, I saw Sadoven,[4] but since she was all dressed up and looking like a parrot, I did not recognize her even after talking to her for a while. Later I asked Kirsta the identity of the parrot, and she answered, "[Maria] Kurenko, a famous singer." I really put my foot in it by asking her about *Mavra*. I do not know whether she realized that I took her for someone else. I have the impression that this club could be useful in procuring orders for costumes, or arranging an exhibition or concert.

Last night Tula had a big party. A hostess of genius, she had thirty well-dressed guests for supper in her small apartment. Small tables were put up, and my housekeeper Hélène, in a white apron, passed champagne around—turkey with truffles, and jellied fish, all first-rate. A Hindu princess was expected but did not come. Downstairs, the concierge, taking advantage of the occasion, put up a poster: "Check-room for the first floor," and was delighted to make some money. Please tell Dushkin that I saw Tania at Tula's. Tania wanted to write to Beveridge, to ask him to bring her a radio, but she did not know his address. I gave her Meyrovich's.[5]

After your departure, beautiful weather set in; I hope you also had it at sea. I so want you to have a good trip and a good rest. Send me interesting postcards. May God be with you. I am with you in all my heart all the time, and I am watching over you in my thoughts. I kiss you with all my great love. Your Vera.

Vera to Igor

December 30, 1934

My dearest Bubushkin, In my thoughts I continue to follow you on your trip,[6] but I want so much to know how everything is going in reality. You should write something down every day, a sort of diary. After all, you are a writer now.[7] You may have thought of this yourself, however, so it's a little late to be giving you advice.

I am indisposed and spending the day in bed with a hot-water bottle. For two hours I listened on the radio to a very good recording of Bach's *St. John Passion*. Then Fred and Wolf came to see me, interrupting the music so that I did not hear it to the end. I had let Wolf borrow my car to go out of town, and I could smell the woods when the car came back. The weather is wonderful.

Yesterday I dined with Ira. A friend had sent her some grouse, and Kirsta had brought three pounds of lobster that Kurt Jooss[8] gave her for Christmas. The whole meal was beautifully prepared. I surprised myself by gorging. When Lyudmila Gavrilovna said that the brothers Osten-Saken are a "classical combination," Kirsta remarked that Ira and I are another one.

On the way back from Ira's, one of the tires on my car blew out. We spent an hour and a half changing it, all of my tools being completely rusty; we had to borrow a jack from a neighboring garage. I was so out of patience that if I had found dynamite, I would have blown the whole thing up. With all that trouble, my feet were so cold that when I returned home I had to take a hot footbath.

Yesterday I went to the Louvre library to make some sketches of the jewelry. I'll try to create something based on an idea that I have for some interesting bracelets, but I am not sure how to do it. Yesterday I dreamed that I found a bracelet in a corner behind a chest of drawers, a long-lost bracelet which then gave birth to several small bracelets. And what kind of dreams do you have, Matushkin?

Three days ago Wolf invited me to a wonderful lunch. I expected him to divulge some "confidences" or to discuss business, but the purpose was to suggest that we *tutoyer* each other and to celebrate the occasion. Georgette always complained that he never so much as brought her a flower, but he always brings me and Ira some little sign of his attention. One has to know how to treat men!

I still do not know where I will spend New Year's Eve—perhaps nowhere. Ira is unexpectedly invited to Mantashev, Kirsta is going elsewhere, and I am left with two barons. To you, my dearest, I wish a colossal success in America and all other satisfactions. Especially I want you to be healthy, to be without colitis, and to return with stuffed suitcases. My best wishes and a kiss to Dushkin for the New Year. I embrace you tenderly and kiss you countless times. Your Sobachkina.

P.S. I saw Katya on Friday. She gave me money for two months.[9] Many thanks, Matushkin.

[1] Georgette, née Princess Mestchersky, was one of Vera's close friends in the 1930s. By 1935 Georgette had separated from her husband, Wolf, and married Dr. Pearce Bailey (1903–1976), president of the American Academy of Neurology. Bailey had studied with Freud, Jung, and Adler, and, together with Otto Rank, founded the Psychological Center in Paris. In 1936, the Baileys moved from France to America—New York City, then Charleston, SC, where Vera stayed with them in February 1940.

[2] The diaries mention two Kirstas, one of whom Vera refers to as her "niece," though being an only child, she had none. R.C. has not been able to find a family name for either Kirsta.

[3] Serge Alexandre Stavisky, whose sales of worthless bonds incriminated high French officials, discredited the Radical Socialist government, and forced the resignation of Edouard Daladier. Stavisky's murder in January 1934 is thought to have been masterminded by the French police.

[4] Russian contralto, she sang the role of Jocasta in Stravinsky's *Oedipus Rex*.

[5] Stravinsky's New York concert agent.

[6] Stravinsky's wife wrote to him December 31: "I read that there are heavy storms on the Atlantic but perhaps not where the *Rex* is crossing. . . . If your intestines are in order, perhaps you are eating well. . . . Today I entertained Lyudmila Sergeevna Chekhova and her sons Mitya and Alya. Alya, your godson, liked you a lot and the quantity of your gloves made a big impression on him."

[7] A reference to the *Chroniques de ma vie*.

[8] Choreographer. He staged the dances in Stravinsky's *Perséphone*. Best known for his ballet, *The Green Table*.

[9] Catherine wrote to Igor on December 29: "I gave Vera 300 francs yesterday, as you requested. I asked her to come to the bank and we sat in the car for a while and talked. In a day or two we will set a time for me to go and visit her. . . . May God, the Blessed Virgin, and the prayers of St. Nikolai Chudotvorets and St. Christopher keep you safe."

FRÈRES
TOUJOURS A MIEUX

UN GRAND MUSICIEN RUSSE SE FAIT NATURALISER FRANÇAIS. — Le célèbre compositeur Stravinsky, l'auteur de l' « Oiseau de Feu » et de « Petrouchka », qui réside en France depuis de nombreuses années, vient d'opter en faveur de sa patrie adoptive...

67 June 4, 1934. Clipping from *L'Intransigeant.* "What can be the connection between my French naturalization and this photograph with Furtwängler, made in 1924 in Berlin?" Stravinsky's marginalia says. The composer's habit of adding comments to newspaper clippings was inherited from his father, so it would seem. When the Moscow Theater Museum acquired Stravinsky's father's archives from his years in Kiev and St. Petersburg, 1876–1901, the newspaper *Vechernaya Moskva* (*Moscow Nightly*) reported that he had written on most of the items. Thus an announcement that a performance had been cancelled because of the illness of the tenor, N.N. Figner, is inscribed by Stravinsky *père*, as it would have been by Stravinsky *fils*, "Not due to illness but to caprice."

68

69

68 July 1934. London. With Victoria Ocampo.

69 September 1934. With Nadia Boulanger at her Gargenville home.

70 1930s. Poem by Stravinsky, "Chanel dite 'Coco.'"

71 1930s. Vera's poem reads: "I am moved and feel moved looking at your face. How wonderful that you are with me!" Stravinsky set his answer, "I don't want any dog," to music, the joke being that Vera often signed her notes to Igor,"Sobachkin" (doggie).

Vera to Igor

January 2, 1935

Igor, my dearest, Thank you for the cable and the card. Receiving those two communications gave me such happiness. I sent you a cable marked "on arrival" and had to choose the message from twelve samples. If I had sent it directly to the boat, the cost would have been seventy, instead of only twenty-four, francs. Happy New Year, Bubushkin–Matushkin. What a pity that I will not be seeing you for a whole quarter of this year. I send you all my wishes for a permanent cure of your colitis. I also wish you great success and satisfaction in your travels.

I wanted to start the New Year with the best intentions—not to spend much money, not to drink, etc.—but this is impossible. Kirsta was the first to say: "But if you do not want to celebrate, what *do* you want to do?" When I answered that I did not want to spend money, she said that they will provide everything. In the end we had food, vodka, and champagne—for which I had to pay half because Kirsta had no money and Wolf had paid half. She got very drunk and started to telephone everybody, saying unbelievable things, even calling Svetik, who was dining with Mme Polignac, and overwhelming him with congratulations, among which figured the most outrageous specimens of Russian swear words (including references to masturbation). Fred telephoned Mme Hurtado.[1] When she asked who was calling, he said "Ansermet."[2] The next day she actually went to Switzerland to visit Ansermet. The whole scene was very stupid. Fortunately everyone left immediately after midnight. I resolved to spend the next day in my own way and to my own liking. In fact, I spent the whole morning at the Louvre, the rest of the day with Argutinsky and Hambourg, seeing Hambourg's private collection. He has a good clientele, so I hope for some sales.

Tomorrow Katya and Mika[3] are coming to tea. I must also pay obligatory visits to old lady Matharel and to the little Thouars. This last will cost some money, since I must bring a present to my godchild, as well as candy for the other children, all of which is a bore. On the whole I spend very few days in the way I would wish, because I must cook and clean and do chores for other people—my constant complaint. I will be glad when the holidays are over. I am feeling well, except that I broke a tooth, and my dentist is away. Ira will talk to her dentist; I hope, but doubt, that he will give me a special price. The 100 francs that you gave me will be spent either on the dentist or on the identity card, for I intend to go for it tomorrow, as well.

The weather has changed. The rains come every day but luckily not the cold, and I am economizing on the heat. Bubushkin, my dearest, I am so impatient for news about your arrival. How were you met? What is your hotel like, and how is the weather? When will I receive your first long letter? You won't have much time to write. I send you all my love. May God keep you. I kiss you with all my strength but also very tenderly. Your Vera.

Vera to Igor

January 8, 1935

My precious Bubushkin, Your cable was the greatest joy for Christmas and the day of my birthday. I was so sound asleep that I actually fell out of bed when the postman knocked on the door at seven-thirty a.m. Trying to get up, I caught my foot in a torn sheet and fell head first, feet in the air. A good start for the day, as you see. The thought of my precipitous fall kept me laughing. Last Sunday I received Holy Communion and felt happy all day. As always, Father Vasily was kind and understanding during confession, which touched me deeply. Your children brought a lovely azalea plant from Katya and then stayed for tea. Svetik made me a present of Schweitzer's book on Bach.

On Christmas Eve we had a traditional dinner at Ira's with borsch made of sturgeon, *kasha*, and a pie. Wolf, Fred, and Kirsta were there, and I received many gifts. Kirsta got drunk again and annoyed Grigory Pavlovich, who talks about her now with disgust. Ira and I do not know what to do about her. When she is drunk she bothers the men, who run away from her. Last night the same people came to dinner, also Valechka and Hurtado. We were afraid that Valechka would be Kirsta's victim this time, but she did not drink, was very sad, and talked only about exorcising her devils. This time Elena Hurtado got drunk on two glasses of vodka, threw herself on the sofa and laughed hysterically. Valechka said to me, "The next time you invite me, I hope that you have fewer people. I do not care for the hysterical laughter of drunken females." Elena is particularly nervous. It seems that Ansermet asked her to come to Geneva, and that Mme Ansermet found out about it and tried to commit suicide by taking veronal and opening the gas jets in the kitchen. Mme Ansermet had taken the precaution of asking her sister to come, however, and of calling the police, who quickly broke down the doors. Now Mme Ansermet is in the hospital crying: "Ernest, please come, I adore you!" But in spite of this, Ansermet insists on divorce.

Last night was my final reception. I am glad the holidays are over. Now the expenses will be less and I can live modestly, doing what I like. Constant harassment seems to be my fate, and only when I am traveling with you do I feel peaceful and cozy.

I visited Olga Sallard recently. She has terrible pains in her back and will probably have to go to Davos again or else have an operation here. She thinks I have neglected her and is hurt. I telephoned a Russian doctor who will see me tonight to discuss her condition; then, tomorrow, I will have to take her to him. This means that I will miss hearing Svetik on the radio tonight. Wolf telephoned today asking me to bring him some food: he is alone and has the flu. Ira will go there in the daytime and I in the evening.

When will I receive your first letter? I want to know all the details. What a shame that you did not write a few lines every day on the boat, which could have been sent on your arrival in New York. Igor dearest, I think of you every hour and would love to be kissing you. May God bless you. All yours, Vera.

Vera to Igor

January 13, 1935

My precious Bubushkin, I miss you so much, and it is still too soon for me to start counting days. I am very sad, at times very bored with everyone here. I feel like rebelling. But instead, I continue cooking, washing dishes, and doing all sorts of chores for other people. I have not read a good book lately, made any drawings, or created anything with my hands.

Katya must have written you that at Glicklikh's[4] request Ira's father went to Warsaw. This could mean good business, but just how good would be difficult to say. Ira told no one except me and your family, since if he were to bring back any money, everyone would pounce on it. I had to be told because Grigory Pavlovich's passport had expired and my help was needed to have it renewed at the police department—which caused a lot of trouble.

I also had to take Olga to laboratories and doctors, who decided that she must go to Davos for two or three months. Now I will have to help her buy what she needs for the trip. The doctor

[1] Elena Hurtado, an Argentine singer, was Ansermet's mistress and the cause of his wife's attempted suicide. See Vera's letter to Igor, January 8, 1935.

[2] Ernest Ansermet had first conducted in Buenos Aires in 1917, with the Diaghilev Ballets Russes. He returned to form a symphony orchestra in 1924, and visited the city as a guest conductor during several subsequent seasons.

[3] Lyudmila (Mika, Mikusha, Mikushka) Igorievna Stravinsky (1908–1938), Stravinsky's elder daughter.

[4] A lawyer in Warsaw attempting to sell land owned by Stravinsky in Poland.

who operated on her, and his wife, too, are very friendly with Olga, and therefore will help in the arrangements for her without charging much.

I received your first letter, written before your arrival in New York, and Katya and I telephoned each other. I did not expect that the ocean would have been so stormy. I am so sorry for you, Matushkin. Since you probably could not work, how did you spend your time?

Yesterday I saw Victoria Ocampo.[1] She is returning to Buenos Aires very unwillingly and hopes to be in Paris again as soon as possible. When I gave her your photograph, she was more than flattered—as she should be—and very pleased with your inscription.

I am always seeing the same people who do not bring anything new or fresh into my life, but only take too much of my time. Since women seem to want to confide in me, I have to see them all separately. Now I must talk to Elena Hurtado, then Mika, then Georgette, then my niece. Even Ira announced yesterday: "I have to talk to you without witnesses." I dream of going south to see my relatives,[2] but for the present they have no room for me.

The cold has suddenly come and the first snow has fallen—with an adverse effect on my budget. Today Ira will bring a friend who spent eight years in Indo-China. I had lunch with her a few days ago and she described so many interesting things that life in Paris seems very dull in comparison. To her, France is so boring and so decadent that she is returning to the Orient, which, she says, has so many more opportunities and is so much livelier and more colorful.

I want to follow your travels, but I do not know exactly where you are. Is it possible that you will fly across the whole of America? I wonder when you will receive my fourth letter. I took it at night to the Gare St. Lazare, but since the doors were closed, I had to mail it in the ordinary way, which is never very safe. I did not receive your postcard from Villefranche-sur-Mer until the fourth of January. So much for the French postal service! I close my letter with tender kisses. I wish you all the best and greatest success. Your little sobachkina misses you. Best wishes to Sam.

Vera to Igor

January 18, 1935

Igor, my beloved, Thank you for your letter of the 9th. Your phrase, "To tell you the truth, my life is quite lonely," made my heart ache. Poor Bubushkin. Probably you are not very busy yet, and free time is weighing on you. To be rushing madly about and not have time to think is almost preferable. But you do not write about receptions, interviews with journalists, and so on.[3]

I telephoned Katya, but since she was in church, I spoke with Mika and Svetik. I did not hear his concert at the Russian Conservatory last night because Fedya called to say that the hall is very small and that your mother would be there. He also said that I should not sit next to Ira and should not talk to them or even to mutual friends because your mother noticed me in church and has been asking everyone who I am.[4] Under the circumstances, I decided not to go. I hear that Svetik played well, and though the audience seemed cool in the beginning, he was received quite well toward the end, *Petrushka* being particularly successful.

I felt very ill this week with a terrible migraine and nausea. No doubt my liver was overloaded; I am now on a diet. Strange that this happened after the Russian New Year. No one would believe that I did not indulge on that occasion, but, in truth, I did not have even a drop of wine and went to bed at ten.

This week I have apportioned my time so that on at least one day I will not use my car but stay home, work, paint, and read, using the rest of the time for errands and for friends—more for them, as always, than for myself. In the past I drove the car for my own pleasure, but now, most of the time it is at the service of others. Yesterday, for instance, I went with Olga to buy the ticket to Davos and a few other things that she needed, then took her to Ira, who gave her some old clothes. Thus the whole day was spent with Olga. Dinner was at Georgette's, with Fred and Wolf, but it was so boring that we yawned all evening, Georgette looking at us with sad eyes. Wolf is always lively when he is alone with me or Ira, inviting us to restaurants, giving us presents, but with Georgette, he complains all the time. Today I invited my niece, Kirsta, and Fred to lunch.

Two days ago Mika came to see me. She said that Lifar's brother is courting her, and she asked my advice. We decided to go to a class drawing from the nude in an art academy in Montparnasse. Mika has been doing this before, to the horror of your mother.

I continue to make sketches for jewelry. Elena Hurtado saw them and was very encouraging. I myself am not convinced. Ansermet asked me for your address. I think he is getting a good engagement in Mexico, as well as concerts in New York. I have heard nothing further about his wife, but he is determined to leave Switzerland. The Minister of Fine Arts in Mexico is a good friend of his, and a move there seems possible. Kirsta complains that she misses German intellectuality, and that life in Paris is not conducive to concentration. I agree, and now I try to stay home every other day and concentrate. I continue to derive much pleasure from my radio, and on the day of the plebiscite in the Saar, I listened to triumphant marches, church bells, and flamboyant speeches; it must have been difficult to resist being profoundly moved. The Germans certainly know how to organize such victorious, sentimental celebrations.

The cold is intense now, and electricity is needed in order to read in the daytime. Was your warm overcoat useful? Tomorrow Grigory Pavlovich returns from Poland, I wonder with what results. Katya just telephoned, so I read part of your letter to her.

How can I send all my loving kisses, Matushkin, so that you would feel them at such a long distance? I think of you endlessly, my dearest. God bless you. Take care of yourself. Your Vera.

P.S. Did you receive my cable on arrival? Did you see Sudeikin yet?

Vera to Igor

January 23, 1935

My little one, Where are you now and what are you thinking? I received your letter of the 7th (Katya sent it to me) four days later than the one of the 9th, immediately telephoned Païchadze about Ida [Rubinstein], and he sent you a cable.

Everything these days revolves around Grigory Pavlovich's return from Warsaw with the money. This is very good luck for

[1] Victoria Ocampo, founder of the review *Sur* and discoverer of Jorge Luis Borges, met Igor and Vera in London in July 1934. Mme Ocampo narrated the title part in Stravinsky's *Perséphone* in Buenos Aires (1936), Rio de Janeiro (1936), and Florence (1939), with the composer conducting.

[2] Vera's father and his second wife were living on the Riviera.

[3] On January 19, 1935, René Auberjonois, in Lausanne, had written his son Fernand, in New York, asking him, if he saw Stravinsky there, to talk to him about the generally negative opinion of his recent music in "advanced" circles in Paris. Fernand made notes on his father's letter, describing the "great friendliness" with

which the composer received him in his hotel—"style Louis-Philippe for export, adapted to the taste of the steel magnates of the first decade of the century. Stravinsky asked me to accompany him to his publishers where, all morning, he was obliged to sign scores and record jackets for a large number of admirers, which he did attentively but with bad grace. We lunched afterward in Manhattan's Italian *quartier* on an excellent pheasant with wild rice and a very good Burgundy. He was enthusiastic about the red-skinned rice, and the wine erased the impression left by the painful autographing session. I did not ask my father's questions and the conversation was about buffalo hunting."

[4] Stravinsky's mother never discovered his liaison with Mme Sudeikina.

them, and perhaps Ira will be rid of her worries for a while. I don't know how much it amounted to, but only that there is some for you as well. Your lawsuit of two years ago—when I had to go for you to lawyers and translators—has also been successfully resolved, and you will receive some 25,000 francs. (I have my eye on the 10% that you promised me for my efforts.) After paying her debts, Ira wants to find a larger apartment. They have had troubles enough in their small one, for which reason we are looking around. She is keeping the true source of the money a secret, even from such friends as Kirsta, and has put out the story that she won it in the National Lottery. Ira is also pretending that Madeleine Kennan is contributing some money. She will be a saleslady in Ira's shop.

Grigory Pavlovich returned wearing a new overcoat. He looks ten years younger and is paying attention again to his "Boyard-Boroda."[1] Business has subsequently picked up there, which is a good recommendation for him and which will be good for his position. On this streak of good luck we purchased some lottery tickets but won nothing. Katya must already have written you about the money from Warsaw.

On Monday I went to the funeral service for Svetlov in the Russian church on the rue Daru. The poor old man died after several months in the American Hospital. During his last days, only Trefilova [the ballerina] was with him. Many ballet people were in the church, as well as Valechka, Zeretelli,[2] Tcherepnin,[3] and others. Valechka must have been thinking that his turn might be next. Only Trefilova and Lifar who, in Valechka's words, "has to get in on everything," went to the cemetery. Valechka is a real cynic.

I continue to rush around and curse everybody who takes up my free time. My one interest at the moment is in helping Ira arrange her new apartment with the minimum of expense and still make it attractive. I fear that Kirsta's club will take too much of my time; probably it will mean only lots of trouble for me, the expense of gasoline, and perhaps a few connections. I attended a meeting there yesterday and was asked to come again today.

I saw Olga Ilinishna off to Davos yesterday. I would not mind leaving Paris myself, but I will have to "stick around." You, no doubt, dream of staying in one place and of *not* flying from one city to another. If you were here, I would not wish to go anywhere. I wait impatiently to hear about your concerts and the people you meet. I am going with Ira tonight to see Spinelli in *Ecole des cocottes*. Do you remember when we saw Spinelli in the Palais Royale? That memory is my real reason for going there. I conclude by kissing you very hard. I miss you so much, so much! Your Vera.

Vera to Igor

January 30, 1935

Igor my dearest, I do not receive news from you very frequently, although your Chicago letter took only nine days, which is prompt compared to that postcard from Villefranche. The freezing American weather has struck us here. Since Sunday, Paris is cold and snowy, and everyone is fighting flu. In your family, the boys were sick first, then Katya, and who knows whether or not the girls will follow. I fight it off by taking hot baths, resting in bed, and swallowing aspirin. The dampness in my house is unbelievable and the cold quite exceptional. I will be grateful if I can get through the winter without succumbing and thankful for

the gift of such good health. To fall ill now would be most inconvenient, the Beliankins being in such a turmoil of moving into their new flat, and Ira so busy preparing a new collection of clothes: naturally I must help them. They have exchanged their small apartment for a much larger one—quite reasonable, in my opinion—in the same building. The new one is on the corner of the rue Marbeuf and Clément-Marot, over a restaurant, Rivière, where you and I once had lunch and also dined with Dushkin. The flat had to be thoroughly cleaned, lighting fixtures had to be bought, and electricity installed. Armchairs must also be purchased for the sitting room. I nearly did this for them, at an auction (four chairs and a large sofa for 320 francs) but did not want to risk it (for other people). And good that I didn't because Grigory Pavlovich is now saying that they have too many other expenses and that he has decided to re-upholster the old furniture and make it do for the present. I also found curtains and lamps for them.

Lyudmila Gavrilovna is exhausted, and no wonder, for she has to look after the dress-making business as well as take care of the apartment. She criticizes all of Ira's decisions—and mine—but does what we want in the end. Since a lot of nervous energy is expended in this shouting all day long, Ira came to me on Sunday night simply to rest. I was alone during the day and enjoyed it, sewing, reading, and just walking around like a lady instead of my usual Sunday occupation of making sandwiches, cooking, and washing dishes.

Yesterday Fatima Hanum asked me to drive her to Montmorency, where we inspected a new clinic for Samoilenko who, to our great surprise, recovered. I had to do it, since I felt guilty that I did not visit them often enough while he was ill. In any case, we found a good sanatorium where she will take him in a few days.

I saw Vera Vasilievna.[4] She has left her apartment and is looking for another, less expensive one, staying meanwhile with the Koussevitzkys in Meudon. I have the address of a German gymnastics teacher (I must get rid of the rheumatism in my joints) who lives two steps from me on the Quai d'Auteuil. Starting February 1, I will go there twice a week and have private, instead of group, lessons, for which she will charge me only 100 francs a month.

It is exactly a month since you left, Bubushkin. I miss you very much, my little one; it will be a long time before you return. Moreover, the time does not pass quickly, though I hustle and run around a lot. I embrace you with all my heart and wish you all good fortune. Keep well. Greet Dushkin. Please write more often. I kiss you very, very lovingly, my beloved. Your sobachkina.

On Sunday, Monteux conducted excerpts from the Diaghilev repertory—*Apollo* among your pieces—and Lifar danced. But I did not go, fearing it would be wretched and sad. Bronia Nijinska is in Hollywood working on something. Perhaps you will see her. Victoria Ocampo left for Buenos Aires but did not telephone to say good-bye.

Vera to Igor

February 1, 1935

My little one, Having just learned—a telephone call from Fedya—that you will be in New York for ten days, I am rushing off a few words to you. I am so happy about your great success and that your abilities as a conductor have finally been recognized. If you

[1] The department of Russian cuisine in the Café de la Paix. René Auberjonois, in a letter to his son Fernand, describes a lunch there with Stravinsky, April 24, 1935: "We decided to risk the Café de la Paix, where Beliankin, an ex-engineer whose acquaintance I had made years ago in Morges, is in charge of the Russian cuisine. Everything was Russian: the waiters, dressed like muzhiks; the dishes, ultra-Old Russia; and Beliankin himself, more than six feet tall, beard to the bottom of his stomach. He speaks *nègre* ('Voé' instead of 'Oui'; 'la potache hollandesse' for

'potage hollandais'), and he kisses the hands of the ladies."

[2] Prince Alexis Zeretelli was one of Stravinsky's concert agents in the late 1920s.

[3] Alexander Tcherepnin, the composer.

[4] The wife of Gabriel Païchadze.

have any clippings, I would love to see them: I want to look at the American Bubushkin.

So much has to be done for Ira's new flat that I scarcely have time to breathe. I have been out all morning trying to find a three-way mirror, and now I am looking for a working table and a Moroccan carpet, which Katya has offered as a housewarming present. Katya, like everyone else here, is in bed with flu: not a soul has escaped illness.

I was to have had my first gymnastics lesson today and was looking forward to it, but just received a note saying that the teacher is in bed with flu. At Nicolo's restaurant yesterday, I had *blini* with the Osten-Saken brothers and Ira: this is the modest sum total of our distractions in Paris! And how are you managing with food and wines? I have not had any wine for two weeks and longer—in fact, since you left—and as a result I am not invited anymore.

The last time I had people here was on my birthday. Since then I have led a very quiet life. I do not even have anything to write about, no theater, no cinema. Well, not quite. I went with Ira to the Palais Royale to see Edmond Guy in a stupid French play. (We did *not* see Spinelli; it was completely sold out.) What a dull letter this is, partly because I am writing between two errands and because it is freezing cold, but I wanted to congratulate you immediately on your successes. I kiss you from the heart. May your successes continue, but write to me more often. God bless you. Your Vera.

Vera to Igor

February 5, 1935

Dearest Igor, Today I have been longing to be away with you in some small town. I was walking in the evening, inhaling a barely perceptible aroma of spring, and I felt a great longing for you. You will say, "Only now?" But now the feeling is particularly sharp, and moments come when I feel as if I were at the end of my endurance. Then, after a while, the ordinary duties take over: telephone calls, washing dishes, and sundry household problems, which help to distract a little. This week passed quietly. I did not use my car much—and, by the way, it is slowly beginning to fall apart, getting old like all of us; I try not to abuse it. I had to drive Ira out of town on Sunday, but that was unavoidable.

The other day Ira went to Mme de Polignac's musical evening. What a queer old lady! She invited Ira, but not Fedya and certain other people close to you, and this even though Nadia Boulanger was conducting some of your works (Ira could not say exactly which ones). Since Fedya was very eager to go, Ira tried to arrange an invitation for him through Sonia[1] but did not succeed. Ira is becoming a very fashionable dressmaker, and because of her beauty is invited everywhere and mentioned in the press. Now Strecker, the artist, is painting her portrait. She is very pleased, though none of this success is reflected in her business affairs. I am dining at her house today, her housewarming dinner, with Valechka and the Osten-Saken brothers.

Fred is still very much around, gloomy and green in the face; his affairs are worse than ever and he considers his future as very black. The last blow was a deal that almost went through, then crashed at the last moment. But everybody seems to complain and not to enjoy anything. Then I began to worry and started to make artificial flowers again as I used to do. I thought about taking this

[1] The Princesse de Polignac's secretary.

[2] Stravinsky's younger daughter (b. 1914).

[3] One of Stravinsky's lawyers.

[4] Advance for *Chroniques de ma vie*, Spanish-language rights.

[5] Advance from Victor Gollancz for *Chroniques de ma vie*.

up again as a business, even though it only brings in pennies and will never amount to much more.

I made peace with Hurtado the other day. She has been neglecting me and, tired of telephoning her, I snubbed her in turn. (Milene[2] and Ira have complained about her also.) She phoned me the other day saying she was in bed and very depressed. After seeing her I understood some of the reasons, such as the sight and smell of her apartment, which is full of red plush and pompoms and reeks of boiled leeks. Her face was gray, and she was reclining in a gray dressing gown on grayish sheets. Her doctor had ordered her to bed to lose weight. She said that she does not sing any more, but I think she is losing her mind, since she has an *idée fixe* about being young and beautiful and starting life over again. Ansermet was supposed to pass by here for a few hours on his way from Oslo. I hear that he is in a desperate state.

I woke up today with a terrible headache and a swollen face, which two pills and some hot compresses relieved a little, but I staggered like a drunk. Outside in the street some poor unemployed man was singing. I intended to throw some money out of the window but could not find any change. Then I went to my bathroom and forgot about the beggar. Suddenly I heard a violin and, remembering Dushkin, decided to throw one whole franc, which I wrapped in a piece of paper. Then the playing became so beautiful that I thought a franc was not enough, and that such extraordinary music deserved more. At this point I realized that Fritz Kreisler was playing on my radio! I forgot that I had left my radio on, and while I was looking for the money, the Kreisler recording started. As a result neither the beggar nor Kreisler got the franc.

Well, my Bubushkin, I must close this letter. I embrace you with love and tenderness. May God protect you in all your traveling and send you much luck and success. Your Vera.

Vera to Igor

[Enclosure: a review from *Marianne*, February 6, 1935, of the Stravinsky-Dushkin Columbia recording (LFX 335) of the "Nightingale's Aria and Chinese March."]

February 7, 1935

My dear, my beloved Bubushkin, Many thanks for your long letter and the enclosed postcards. Your news gives me so much happiness that I glow with it the whole day. Thank you again. Do my letters reach you regularly? How was it in New York, and where are you now?

Life here is the same as ever except that I have had my hands full helping Ira to arrange her apartment, even making deliveries and buying buttons for her—which is not exactly part of furnishing an apartment. It is beautiful though, I must admit, and the salon is so attractive (and was so inexpensive) that she cannot believe it is really hers. Our greatest difficulty was in moving all the furniture, for though the big pieces had to be left to professionals, we carried the innumerable small ones ourselves. The Beliankins, Ira, and I, and even Fred, helped, and all of the work, the painting, the installing of electricity and telephones, was accomplished in one week. Ira is now showing her collection of dresses, with the assistance of a salesgirl and model.

The exertion was good for my circulation. At any rate, I was at the doctor's yesterday. He said that the swelling around my eyes could have been from bad circulation or from my liver. He prescribed two medicines and a strict diet, no bread and no salt for three weeks; he insists that I lose weight. He is a very nice man, talks a lot about music, and, so far, he has not taken any money. We will see about the results.

I went to see Soulié[3] yesterday and he filled out all of the applications for me. I conveyed your instructions to Fedya; everything has been done, and the money has been received, both from Ocampo[4] and from England.[5] Ocampo sent me a card on the way to Buenos Aires "*à bientôt*," which seemed somewhat odd considering that Argentina is so far away; but everything is relative. Beveridge phoned to relay your greetings.[1] He is in Warsaw now, so I will send him a letter there that he can mail to my mother when he is in Moscow. For some reason he did not want to take it with him from here.

The weather is lovely, as if spring were coming, but everyone has flu. I am trying not to give in to it, and at the very thought I take a hot bath and go to bed: immediately it seems to disappear. Since Georgette complains that I do not see her often enough, I expect to see her today. It is true that everyone seems to neglect her, even Fred, who used to be so attentive. She looks thin and unwell and has hinted that her husband is too much influenced by Ira. Stupid! Wolf has gone to Belgium to look for work.

Since Kirsta also wants to see me, I probably will be obliged to have a reception this Sunday. She is trying to get me to work for her club, an idea that does not appeal to me, nor do I see any benefit in it for me. I have hardly any time in which to read and am unable to concentrate. Dearest, I send you all of my tenderest thoughts. Please write more often. I miss you so much. Loving kisses, my beloved. Your Vera.

Vera to Igor

February 12, 1935

My dear little one, I am again waiting to hear the rustle of a letter from you being slipped under the door. Quite a long time has passed since the last one, and I am eager to know what you are doing in your spare time. Perhaps you are courting Greta Garbo, Marlene,[2] or some other seductive woman, and have forgotten your little Sobachkina. But the Sobachkina is more congenial and no one could love you more than she does. What is more, she has grown younger lately, in spite of her respectable age, because she has started to exercise. I am really enchanted with my German gymnastics teacher, even though she frightened me when I first saw her: she looks like Goering, has gray-haired bangs, and one leg is shorter than the other. Nevertheless, she is a remarkable and cultured woman and she quickly understood my needs. She gives me the same exercises as Dr. Lavezzari did, but she charges me 100 francs for eight lessons a month (as compared with 150 francs a visit to Lavezzari). She spent the first lesson straightening out my vertebrae and my spine, perspiring the while more profusely than I did. She lifted me by the head, then by the feet, found me very rusty and promised to make me pliable and well-shaped in a few months. These lessons are the only fun I have had in recent weeks. The rest seems gray, dull, and monotonous, even though I seem to rush about a lot.

On Saturday I had Valechka, Fred, and Argutinsky for dinner. It was lively and amusing, not at all like the other day, when I had so many people. Some played bridge, and the others drank vodka, ate everything in the house, and smoked so much that in two days I could not clear the place of the reek of tobacco. Incidentally, your sons also came. (The girls want to come tomorrow for tea.) Today Ira gives a big reception. She has invited 50 people to view her collection and is nervous that it will not show off to advantage in the apartment. Now a lady has asked me to decorate her apartment when she moves, and I am tempted, for it would be wonderful to make some money! I ordered carpets for Ira, a gift from Katya; a certain shop makes them to order, all in one color. We chose pale blue ones, which look Moroccan but are not quite so thick.

Today I took my radio to be repaired. I hope nothing is seriously wrong with it as I'm accustomed to listening to music all day and educating myself.

I accompanied Fatima Hanum to visit her husband. He is recovering miraculously. It seems that Samoilenko did not go to church, and that they did not have any icons in their house. When he became ill, the doctor who visited him, a Russian, asked: "Why is there no icon near your bed? You should buy an image of St. Nicholas the Miraculous." Thinking he meant that Samoilenko must really be dying, Fatima bought the icon and he recovered. Then when he left the hospital, he forgot to take the icon along. Fatima spent 100 francs in tips trying to recover it, but without success, and she could not find a similar one. Returning home, I found that I had one very like it and took it over right away. She was so happy; she had been afraid that Samoilenko would get sick again.

Now, my Bubushkin, I must finish as I have to go to Ira's. I cover you with tender kisses and pray that among your triumphs and flirtations you will not forget your little Sobachkina and will also write more often. Yours with all heart and soul, Vera.

Vera to Igor

February 19, 1935

My little one, dearest, beloved, This is the third day that I have tried to write to you, but I am interrupted all the time, and every morning and evening has been busy. Ira came at nine yesterday, remarked on the beautiful weather, and asked me to go to Versailles with her for breakfast. The weather really is lovely, the sun is actually beginning to get hot, and the air was so fresh and transparent that we returned quite drunk with it. I fear that this will end up with frosts in June, but for the moment, one feels like a kitten squinting in the sun. I would like to put on a straw hat and set out in search of a green pasture.

Your long letter gave me tremendous joy. You described the meeting with Sudeikin so well. He must be completely without work to come to you for help and connections. In my opinion Tchelichev is not right at all for *Firebird*, but then, I find his painting "untidy." Perhaps he has changed, however, and, anyway, you can always indicate to him what you want him to do. What was decided? I am especially pleased that you conducted other compositions besides your own, and that you had success in doing so. Mika brought me your postcard with the description of your radio concert. I phoned Païchadze and learned that Ida does not want to go to America, and that the cable he sent was not to you but to Koussevitzky. I saw him only yesterday, since, like most people here, he has been in bed with flu.

Poor Katya is still weak after her flu and, fearing complications, she is very careful and stays in bed most of the time; I have not seen her recently. Milene came the other day to have tea with me. The conversation was exclusively about Alberti [her singing teacher]: she can talk about nothing else, but perhaps it is good to be so engrossed in her work. Maybe I will start singing also. My gymnastics teacher says that I talk, breathe, and laugh through my throat, whereas I should emit sounds from my chest. It is true that my neck and glands feel strained and that I am tired when I move much or even talk. This is a consequence of incorrect breathing, so now I do my exercises and sing at the same time, which amuses me. I persuaded Georgette to join me in my gymnastics lessons; they will do her good and divert her from grieving over life without Wolf. She was so hysterical at Ira's the other day that we gave her valerian drops and got Wolf on the phone, whereupon I lambasted him in Russian. His only response was, "You are the only woman who knows how to talk to me," and he did not change toward Georgette after this conversation. She still hopes to continue her life with him and has decided not to give him a divorce. Why can't the fool see that the whole thing is over?

Recently Ira gave a very successful party. So many people

[1] Beveridge Webster had just played Mozart's Piano Concerto K453 with the New York Philharmonic, Stravinsky conducting.

[2] Vera does not write "Dietrich" because Igor and Marlene had been friends since Berlin in the 1920s.

came that she had to bring out the stools and benches from the kitchen, and Ganya had to take a taxi and fetch some chairs from your house. Even the entrance hall was mobbed. Food was brought over from a restaurant. Yet so far, very few orders have been received, so I don't see the profit in it. The explanation may be in the season: many people are out of town for winter sports.

Last night a new hall was inaugurated at the Club. I dislike so many things in that organization that I did not want to go, but Mme Kochura sent me a complimentary ticket, and I could not refuse. It was so boring that I began to yawn and left after the intermission. Mme Sadoven sang in Spanish, and a young woman from one of the embassies danced an unexciting Brazilian number that looked more like a Norwegian one. I had seen some of the performers before, at one of the ethnological lectures that I attended with Fred. I suppose I would have had a better time if I had been with friends, but, being alone, I did not even laugh. The Club behaved badly toward Kirsta, and they speak badly about her, though she worked hard there and treated everyone well. Arthur Lourié, touring in France, sent me a letter asking about you and wanting to know your address. I sent it to him.

[February 24, 1935][1]

Everyone is outraged and shaken by the execution—decapitation—of two women in Germany. Did you read about it? The French newspapers published descriptions of this barbarism on their front pages. The women were friends of Fred, and he was in a terrible state, reading the details.

I have a swelling around my eyes and am going to an oculist today, a Russian who is not expensive. I've also found a new dentist who lives near me and was recommended by Argutinsky. As you see, I am taking good care of my health, which makes my friends laugh: they consider me to be very healthy.

Where will your next news come from? I am so impatient to know how you liked Los Angeles, and to have your impressions of it. Did Dushkin lose his heart there? Please write, my dearest Bubushkin. I embrace you with all my loving heart and send you millions of the tenderest kisses. May God be with you. Your Vera.

Vera to Igor

February 27, 1935

My dearest Bubushkin, Thank you for your letter of February 12. I cannot tell you how happy I am to receive your letters and to learn all the details. Each time I receive your news, I telephone Katya immediately, and she does the same for me. She feels much better now, her temperature is normal, and she has been up for several days. Mika and Milene are coming to have tea with me today, and perhaps Fedya as well. He has painted several very successful portraits and is doing one of Arlette Marchal at the moment.

I am leading a very strict life, getting up and going to bed early, taking my gymnastics lessons—which last longer and longer: yesterday I was there from 5 to 8 p.m. After the lesson we talked art and philosophy. My teacher is an amusing woman, but she is influenced by German modernism, which shocks me at times. In a few days we will get together at her house, someone will read a chapter from a book, and each of us will illustrate it according to his imagination, which is more play than a lesson but can be quite entertaining. The results often look like paintings by Henri Rousseau.

My new life also includes walking and a diet. After my visit to the oculist, I even stopped smoking; he said that the swelling around my eyes is a first warning and if not taken care of, other symptoms of blood thickening would follow. Eventually a stroke

could result. How pleasant! I told him that I was very healthy, and he said: "This can also happen to healthy people." Perhaps he is right. My eyesight is excellent, and after my first week on the diet, the swelling disappeared. The diet forbids all fats and even everything grilled. Red wine, which seems to congest me, is also forbidden. A little cognac or vodka, but no red wine. He wants me to walk a lot, and he approves of my gymnastics. If I do not feel better in two or three weeks, he will give me injections—I do not know what kind—but I have improved already and doubt that they will be necessary.

The weather is not conducive to walking. You may have read about the storms in France. Trees and fences were uprooted in Paris, and in the provinces people were killed and injured. Some days I had to hold on to the chairs and I thought that the roof would blow off. An airplane flew from Paris to Cologne, a distance of 350 kilometers, in only an hour. The winds are not calm yet, and my shutters still rattle, but the sun has finally appeared and it is getting warmer. On Sunday, disregarding a light rain, a group of us went for a walk in the forest, where the approach of spring is visible. Soon the trees will be green and the flowers in bloom.

I have not used the car, partly for economy but mainly in order to walk more. Kirsta spent the whole day with me yesterday, lunch, tea, and a walk. With company every day, I have to cook quite a lot.

Almost nobody entertains any more, the rich for reasons I do not know, and our friends because they do not have the money; they sit at home. Only occasionally, about twice a month, Mme de Frey asks me to a modest lunch. Even Ira does not invite me often. Fred comes here almost every day, however, and since his affairs are in a bad state, I have to feed him a little. He is deeply disturbed by events in Berlin but does not admit it. He looks very thin and gray in the face. That infamous evening when everyone was arrested, followed by those horrible executions, was just a year ago.

I have learned to typewrite, which amuses me. I will type my next letter to you, though I can do it only in French. Now when you need to write a business letter in a hurry, you can take the machine along and I will type.

It is two months since you left. I wanted to learn many things during your absence, to study English, to embroider the carpet, and much more, but the time passes so quickly. Probably I lack organization, but I am active all day, shopping, cleaning the house, walking, and by the end of the day I am dead tired and asleep by 11.

I impatiently await your description of the concert in Los Angeles. Were any movie stars present? What do they look like? Who seduced you and how?

I conclude with tenderest kisses, my beloved. I so want to embrace you in person. Do you know the date of your departure? May I come to Cherbourg to meet you? Now that spring approaches, I especially dream of it. I embrace you, Bubushkin. Yours in heart, body, and soul. Sobachkina.

Vera to Igor

March 13, 1935

Bubushkin my dearest, I am in despair, having so little news from you. Of course I get some by way of your letters to the Faubourg Saint-Honoré, but I am without a word from you in God knows how long. If I hear any little noise by the door I rush to see whether it is your letter, only to find an annoying bill or a note from Olga Ilinishna in Davos. This is sad.

Lent has begun. I am going to church and working hard to make artificial flowers. Though I do not eat meat, I cook a lot, for the many "hungry" people I have to feed. Today Pearce Bailey called, Georgette's American friend. He is giving a cocktail party to which I will take your sons, since Svetik must circulate and go

[1] On February 25, 1935, Stravinsky met with forty composers in Culver City and made a speech to them in German which was recorded and has been preserved.

out a little before his concert. Poor Katya is still suffering from after-effects of the flu but has a very good doctor now, a specialist in lung and throat diseases fast becoming famous in Paris. I pray to God that she will get well soon.[1]

We have had so much cold weather and snow of late that no amount of heat did any good. God only knows why I am still on my feet and did not get flu. Several times my automobile was in for repairs; it was in such bad condition that the mechanic trying it out almost crashed into a wall. Today at last the sun came out. I pray that spring arrives soon.

I expect Elena Hurtado for tea. I almost quarreled with her on the phone because she lost a very expensive book on Cézanne that does not belong to me and that I let her borrow. Now she claims that it was stolen from her. Her career as a singer is ended, she says, and she wants to leave for Italy or Spain, but the truth is that Alberti gave her up—Milene told me—and that is why she became crazy and impossible.

Bubushkin, tell me something amusing about yourself. You must be seeing many interesting people. I know so little about it, and in comparison with you I feel so provincial. Only once have I even been to the cinema—an entertaining film about capturing animals for zoos, especially interesting about monkeys. It seems that when they get hold of something good to eat they do not let go, no matter what. Thus some succulent edible is placed in a coconut, secured with a rope, and the monkey who does not let go is caught.

I spent an evening with Maria Lange. The poor woman had a heart attack, was more than a month in bed, and is without money. On all sides people are ill or starving.

Did you see Nijinska? Kirsta, who is also starving, is impatiently expecting her and hoping that she will give her some work. I embrace you from a loving but slightly sad heart. I cannot believe that you forgot your little Sobachkina and blame it on your being very busy. Yours with all my soul, Vera.

Vera to Igor

March 18, 1935

Dearest Igor, Your letter brought me great joy, though now the sad news about Katya's illness and its complications overshadows everything. I can imagine how worried you are and how difficult it is for you to be working so far away and at the same time anxious to return home. That Katya will be in a sanatorium when you return is especially sad, but I am confident that she will get well there. Lyudmila Gavrilovna said that ever since the new doctor told Katya to keep her window open day and night, she feels better, her temperature is lower, and her mood is brighter. Now at least she knows what is wrong and what to do about it, and she has accepted everything with her usual courage. Oh those stupid doctors, especially Lipshitz, who kept saying that nothing was wrong with her! Having been accustomed to lung trouble all her life, she has developed a certain immunity, which will help her to recover from this episode as from so many others. It is really regrettable that x-rays were not taken earlier so that she could be well for your arrival. Now she will probably stay in the sanatorium for three months. My poor Matushkin! I am so sorry that you will have to live with this worry during your travels, but it is at least fortunate that Katya could go to the mountains immediately and to such a good sanatorium.

Do you expect to return for Easter, or before? I have just come back from the Trocadéro, hoping to see the rehearsal of Les Noces, but I could not get in and I did not see anyone who could help me. Then with the onset of terrible menstrual pains, I came home and took aspirin. Now I am cooking lunch for a "starving" niece of mine.

Again yesterday I had many guests. I cannot say that I enjoyed it, but I also cannot chase everybody out. If only one of them had come with a happy expression or some good news, but they are all in terrible circumstances, expecting only catastrophes; especially Fred, who talks about death all the time. What a cheerful crowd! The only good sign is that if they all come to me for consolation, it must mean that my *élan vital* is intact.

I sell the flowers that I make, but even though flowers are fashionable now, business is slow. Bubushkin, darling, my nearest one, how I would love to embrace you. I hope that your next letter contains news about the date of your arrival. This dreadful time of loneliness, longing, and sadness must come to an end at last. I embrace you with all my loving heart. God be with you, my dearest. Yours with all my soul, Vera.

Vera to Igor

March 25, 1935

My beloved darling, Soon I will be able to start a letter to you, "This will be the last one," and my heart rejoices at this thought. I am sitting in front of an open window making flowers, and one could think that I represent spring: I love this work. I also sell flowers, once for 10 francs, another time for 15—all of which helps. I think I will be selling better soon.

I meant to write immediately after Svetik's concert, but the days pass so quickly: this must be old age. Time did not fly so fast when I was younger. There were not many people at the concert, perhaps three to four hundred. He played well but was terribly nervous in the beginning, in the Bach and Beethoven. He improved and played quite splendidly toward the end. The Weber, the Debussy, and, of course, *Petrushka*, were the best, this last provoking a veritable shower of applause. He behaved like a modest and nice boy and won all hearts. The public, of course, consisted almost entirely of friends and acquaintances. After the concert some of us went to Marignan for coffee. Svetik lost some money on the concert, which is too bad. The next day, Uninsky played in the same Salle Gaveau. His performances were dreadful, it seems, but the hall was packed, including the stage.

On Saturday I went to the funeral of Nadia Boulanger's mother, a very deluxe one, with a million candles and 2000 people. The music was wonderful, with a chorus and soloists, as well as an orchestra that included horns and timpani. Nadia was the most impressive person in that opulent crowd. Her face transfigured with grief, she stood against a black grille, accepting expressions of sympathy; but she looked so changed that I hardly recognized her and thought for a moment that I had strayed into the wrong funeral by mistake.

On Sunday I had many guests again, even though I told everyone that I did not expect to be home. By six o'clock a crowd was here. One woman arrived with an enormous dog that upset one of my tables and smashed everything on it, including my only good lamp. She will buy me a new lamp, but at that moment I was about to throw everyone out.

I saw your children in church this morning (Fedya's birthday) and heard encouraging news about Katya. It seems that she is doing well and will be out of the sanatorium sooner than expected. Lyudmila just telephoned to say that she had a good report from the nurse. The only problem is the terrible weather there, foggy days and nights. God, I hope that Katya gets well soon. It would be such a pity if she weren't in Paris for your return! Bubushkin dear, thank you for your last two letters, and also thank Sam for his nice one. (By the way, I am lunching tomorrow at Beveridge's.) I embrace you with all my loving heart and kiss you a million times in thought. Your Sobachkina.

---

[1] Stravinsky had just learned from his wife's sister that Katya was seriously ill and would have to go to the sanatorium at Sancellemoz.

72–76 February 1935. Los Angeles. Photos by Edward Weston.

72

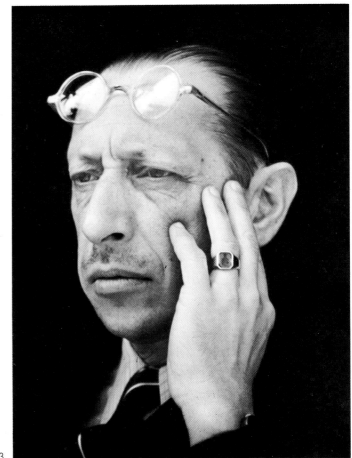

73

74

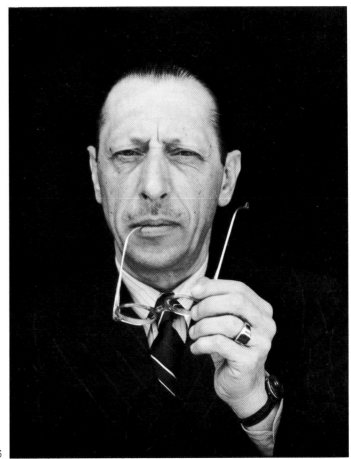

75

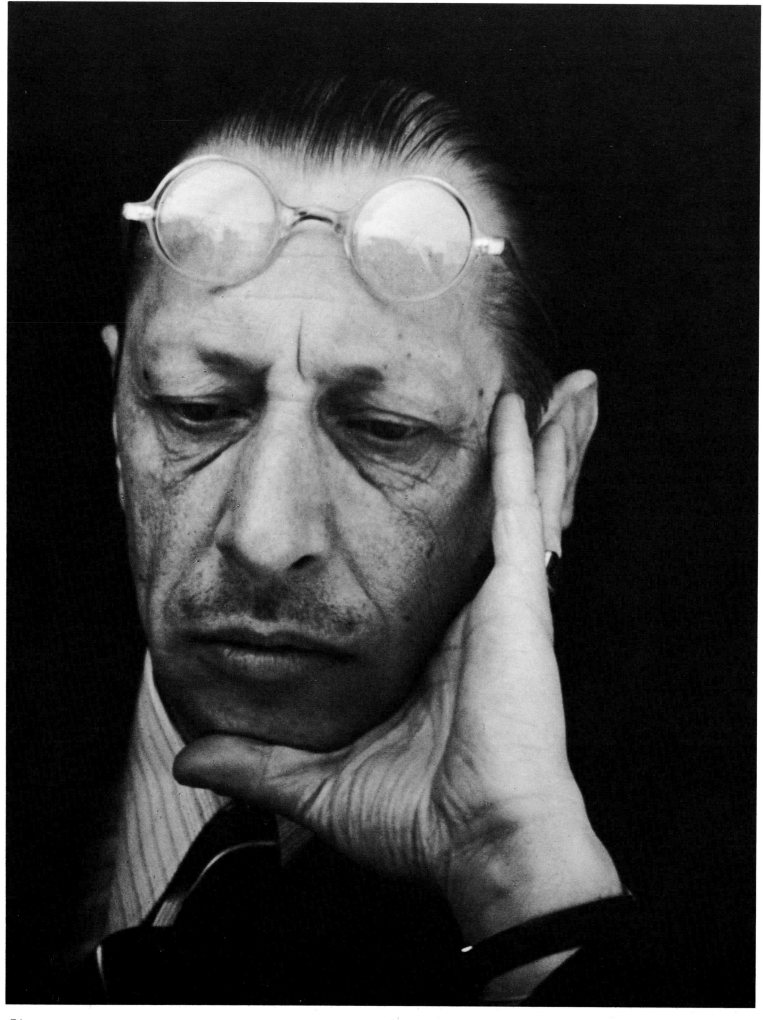

Vera to Igor

April 2, 1935

My precious Igor, Is it possible that this is my last letter? If you leave around the 14th it would be useless to write again. I imagine how tired you must be and how glad to finish this exhausting trip—to "cry for joy," as Artur Rubinstein used to say on boarding the ship.

I suppose you heard the good news from Katya. She is feeling much better now and, I am sure, will recover quickly. Dearest, how worried you must have been, and to be so far away and not to know all the details must be torture. I saw all of your children yesterday at Ira's. It was her thirty-second birthday, and she received a lot of flowers and served us tea and cake. Her father presented her with a dog. Now they will have two dogs, hers and Ganya's, and many difficulties. Both are young and not yet housebroken; they leave messes and tear everything to pieces. Moreover, they have to be walked or taken to the Bois de Boulogne for a run, which can only be done by driving them there in my car, not an amusing prospect for me.

I am very busy at the moment making flowers (yesterday I sold 150 francs' worth), which means that I can only take time to see my customers and that I have none left for anything else. Yesterday I worked until midnight and had to be up at six to be able to deliver an order by evening. The chaos in my room resembles that in Argutinsky's apartment. Since my housekeeper has been ill for a week, unwashed dishes have accumulated in the bathroom, and the carpets are strewn with cuttings of artificial flowers. But I am pleased that my business has developed so quickly. Artificial flowers are very fashionable at the moment, which is a great advantage.

Your book was published a few days ago. I bought it and am reading it, even though you already described the contents to me. Like all French books, it is printed on terrible paper. But it looks good and will surely sell out.

I am keeping up with my gymnastics and now, after two months, I can see the good results. I feel better in general and am thinner and more supple.

Georgette phoned me last night in hysterics. She cannot bear her life and wants to commit suicide. I will have a talk with her today. I seem to specialize in giving advice, which often takes a lot of my time. Mika has stopped relying on me, but perhaps her problems have straightened out. Surprises await you.[1]

What is the political outlook in America? (How foolish to ask, since you have no time to answer.) We have had some bad moments, with much talk about war. The owner of my garage told me that many people fear a German invasion and have left Paris. I personally believe that everything will be settled because no one wants war.

I have been strong throughout these sad days of separation, but now I feel like crying. Au revoir, my dearest. How wonderful it is to say "until soon." I can scarcely believe that I will see you soon. I send you a million caresses and kisses. Your Vera.

Vera to Igor

Monsieur Igor Stravinsky
Oslo[2]
Friday morning, October [?], 1935

My own Bubushkin, How I envy you up there in Scandinavia, and in autumn—the northern lakes, the distant skies. The weather here is wretched, though warm. Yesterday was bright and sunny, but by mid-afternoon a dirty, dusty fog had rolled in.

Katya telephoned me in the morning; either her voice was tired or it has become generally lower. She gave me news of Denise, who is better. No doubt Katya has already told you about this.

I spent the day driving my niece [Kirsta], Olga (Ilinishna), and Olga's cousin around Paris, taking them to lunch, driving them again afterward, and then inviting them to a café. The results are that I spent a lot of money, tired myself out, and was scolded by Olga for not looking very well. Probably this is because I have not spent much time in the fresh air recently, or simply because I tire very easily and days like that one exhaust me.

Last night I dined at the Colisée with Georgette, on oysters, champagne, and green beans. She ate large quantities of other things as well, but I gave up.

Olga Ilinishna gave me the *Excelsior*, which I am forwarding to you. I do not know whether to send this letter to Oslo or to Stockholm, and I must go to the post office to find out when it would reach Oslo by air mail. I have been at home all day today. . . .

I have just called to find out about Denise. The poor girl is definitely better, but she has the beginnings of pleurisy. The Beliankins have just seen Dr. Karasik, who says that she will certainly recover but will have to spend at least a month in bed. Her heart is strong, and her youth will be an advantage. Fedya does not leave her side; he is suffering greatly. Denise's mother has arrived.

Now I am off to the post office and will finish this note. My little one, I kiss you tenderly, tenderly, and I wish you success. Please write to your little Sobachkina, and send me a sample of Scandinavian earth. This is my Swedish blood manifesting itself: I want terribly to lose myself in that countryside. With all my heart and soul, Your V. Warm regards to Sam.

Vera to Igor

Monsieur Igor Stravinsky
c/o Göteborg Palace Hotel
Göteborg, Sweden
Wednesday, October 9, 1935

My dear little one, Thank you for your letters and postcard. What a splendid country, and how jealous I am of you, living in such a beautiful hotel: what a view, what a situation, and, if the weather is also good, that is wonderful. Here the weather changes in accordance with political developments: first it is wretched, then comes a strong wind that tears everything to pieces, so that I do not know whether the roof on my little house will hold. On such days any semblance of coziness is blown out of the house and to hell. The fireplace, the radio, and even my sewing offer no consolation. These past few days I have tried to spend most of my time indoors.

Nevertheless, I have had to make frequent automobile trips to Olga Ilinishna's and to take dinner to Valechka. He has had a cold and is as helpless as are all bachelors, but I was flattered that he turned first to me for help. (He is quite lost in Dushkin's large apartment.) Now I must drive Lyudmila Gavrilovna to the hospital to visit Denise, so great a distance to Neuilly that Lyudmila Gavrilovna is at least grateful to me. I myself have not yet been to see Denise.[3] Visits exhaust her, and no one is allowed to stay with her for more than ten minutes. She still has a very high

---

[1] On April 13 Stravinsky left New York on the S.S. *Ile de France*, which docked at Le Havre on the 26th. Vera was waiting for him in Le Havre, and between there and the Gare St. Lazare, she broke the news of his daughter Mika's engagement to Yuri Mandelstamm, a poet (not related to Osip) employed by a Russian émigré newspaper in Paris. Vera often uses the affectionate form of his first name, Yura.

[2] Stravinsky and Vera were together in August and September 1935, driving, in their Mathis, from Voreppe to Venice, via Turin, then from Venice to Bologna via Padua. This pleasure trip is difficult to account for, since Stravinsky was behind schedule on the composition of the *Concerto per due pianoforti soli*, and on his return to Paris had only two weeks before going to Scandinavia for concerts. But he had done the same thing the year before—interrupted work on *Perséphone*, also behind schedule, to give concerts in Copenhagen and Kaunas (with Dushkin, March 25; they stayed in the Hotel Metropol). Dushkin and Stravinsky traveled from Copenhagen to Warnemunde, March 23, by boat, and from Berlin to Kaunas (to Paris) by train.

[3] Denise Guerzoni (b. 1914) married Theodore Stravinsky in 1936.

temperature. The doctors were right when they said that she would not be released before three or four more weeks. Let us hope that no complications develop.

Ira has a wonderful two-month-old poodle. Picture a little black lamb, but with a lovely puppy's face and covered with fine, silky-haired curls. Everyone who sees it is enchanted. Ira is making a marquis's evening coat for it.

The wind is truly tempestuous, for which reason I sleep poorly, with a sinking feeling in my heart and a variety of apprehensions. Several people called this morning to say that the wind has made them ill; Tula went so far as to have a "heart attack" and stay in bed all day. I cannot afford to do that: I have "courses" to attend in addition to a small order to fulfill, so small as not to be worth mentioning. If I can manage to visit the coiffeur, fill the car with gas, and pay the tax on the radio—the government has become very strict and will fine everyone who does not pay—then I will be satisfied.

On the 22nd, I will be going to a big wedding: André Widhof is marrying a wealthy and pretty girl, and Ira and I are invited to the ceremony and lunch.

When will you return? I was about to send this letter to Stockholm when Katya telephoned and said that your next address is the Göteborg Palace Hotel.

Bubushkin, my dear, I wish you great success and I hope that you are feeling well. How is your health? I kiss you with all my love and await you impatiently. It is very dull here without you. With all my heart, your little Sobachkina.

Vera to Igor

Monsieur Igor Stravinsky
Hotel Angleterre
Copenhagen   Friday, October [?], 1935

My dear Bubushkin, Thank you for your letter from Sweden. (This is my third letter.) I also received your postcard. Yesterday I heard *Histoire du soldat* on the radio. Obviously Rivière has a certain influence there, because the programs are much better now, on the whole, and they do not come exclusively from abroad, but also from the PTT itself.

I have been sitting at home for three days. Finally the battery has been changed. Today, for the first time in what seems like a long while, I took the car out, which was not only nice but also necessary because of rain. I had to stop at Georgette's, since she is leaving for England tomorrow. They are taking their car and, while the weather is still good, will spend their time walking through the English countryside. Being fed up with Paris, I very much wanted to go with them. I have never been here so long at one time. Finally we have had some autumn weather, so I have used the fireplace. Today I had Isabelle Dato for tea; she had called and wanted to have a small dinner party for you and me. Now she has gone to Rome for a wedding; then, after two weeks back here, she will go to Spain or to Argentina. She also finds Paris dull and boring, but at the moment everyone is down on Paris.

I read a great deal during the three days that I spent at home, taking walks but only within the *quartier*. Arthur recommended an English novel, Charles Morgan's *The Fountain*. It is really refreshing, or, at any rate, I have not enjoyed a book and been so absorbed in my reading in a long time. All that one can do in Paris these days is to lock oneself away and read.

I have no new information about Denise. She is a little better, but only a little. To cure such different illnesses as anemia and kidney trouble at the same time is difficult, for two completely different diets must be followed. The doctor believes that the illnesses will linger. I hope that she is better by the time that you are here.

Mimi Godebska's mother died. I was astonished by Mimi's cheery mood when I saw her yesterday. I had been preparing a few words of condolence for her, but she put me at a loss, prattling on in such a lively mood about some piece of gossip.

People are coming to Ira now, and she has a few orders. Her collection is not very good this year, however, at least not to my taste. Her originality has always been her strong point, but this year her new things are less interesting. The other couturiers have worked hard to find an amusing style and a richness in the color scheme.

I want to send this letter by airmail and will close now so that I can go to the post office in good time. Farewell, Matushkin. I embrace you warmly and kiss you with all my love. Your V.

Vera to Igor

October, 1935

Bubushkin, my beloved, Count Babashkin-Scandinavsky, Thank you for the letter, which, though late for my name day, was postmarked yesterday in Paris. I did not really celebrate. Olga Ilinishna came at 7:30 a.m. and stayed until afternoon. Then I went to Ira's, and went to dinner with her and Sonya at the Greeks'.

I expect Mika and her fiancé today and possibly Svetik, Milene, and Fedya as well, except that Fedya spends all of his time at Denise's. She is better but there are complications: the pleurisy is over but she is anemic and also has liver trouble. She is too young to be so ill.

On Sunday I had unexpected guests, Wolf, Ira, and Elena, who talked continually about her successes and her intention of taking singing lessons from Alberti again. Kirsta came, too—uninvited—and brought with her the unpleasant atmosphere of the society in which she now revolves and which I make such an effort to escape. Her closest friends, it seems, are Lady Abdy and Marie-Laure de Noailles. Ida Godebska died suddenly, from an embolism. So many deaths this year!

I am going out now to send a wire to Mimi Godebska. I was at Misia's on Saturday. Lifar was there, but rushing off to see Marie-Laure, for he has taken Markevich's place. One would think that these people must be tired of each other!

The weather is autumnal and, opening my window in the morning, I half expect to see snow. I ordered some wood, lighted a fire, and now my little house feels cozy.

Bubushkin, Sweden is famous for its knives, as you know, so bring me something from Sweden made of steel—and do not misinterpret this as an *esprit mal tourné*. Or perhaps you can bring me a brush—a nailbrush or even a toothbrush. I have a weakness for brushes, which I must look up in Freud. I see that you have made great progress in your English. Bravo! I cannot say the same for myself.

I kiss you, my little one, with all the tenderness of my heart, and I am looking forward to more letters. Don't be lazy! Yours with all my being, V.

Vera to Igor

Monsieur Igor Stravinsky
Hotel Angleterre   Saturday, October [after the
Copenhagen, Denmark   9th], 1935

My dear, I have no idea where to send this final letter. You left only one Stockholm address, and everything is confused.[1] Nobody is certain of the Copenhagen address, but I spoke with my grandfather[2] today and, like me, he assumes it must be the Angleterre. To find out from any member of your family on the telephone is impossible: either everyone is ill or no one is home. Svetik has a boil; Milene is in bed, apparently with a cold; Mika is

[1] After Norway, Stravinsky's schedule of Scandinavian concerts was revised en route.

[2] Vera's maternal grandmother and grandfather lived in Paris in the 1930s.

busy with preparations for her wedding; Fedya spends all of his time in the hospital with Denise; Katya can come to the phone only rarely. So you will be arriving on Wednesday, evidently in the afternoon. Wednesday evening I have guests, my unsuccessful clients, the ones I had had tea with (Vinogradov), and my gymnastics teacher. I had been putting it off constantly but finally had to invite them, and now we have made arrangements for Wednesday. I hope that your train does not arrive at night. For some unexpected and almost unbelievable reason, the weather is splendid today, but it may turn bad at any moment, which has been the pattern recently.

I had been thinking of working quietly at home when I received an urgent letter from Georgette, in London, asking me to fetch her dog from the veterinarian and to deliver it to the house of her former cook in a suburb. Now Tula is ill and I have to visit her. Tomorrow I go to Denise, then, in another nearby hospital, to Ira's leading saleslady, who has had an operation. What a lot of people are ill! Today I received postcards from Mexico [Ansermet], Positano [Semenov], and Berlin [Fred Osten-Saken], letters from London and Italy, and, yesterday, your postcard from Stockholm, which I say to prove that all my friends have gone away, and that only the sick remain behind.

I am reading Morgan's novel with considerable pleasure, and in the same way in which I used to read in my youth, when I wanted to be the heroine and to utter noble words. The book is more than 500 pages long. I have become so involved in it that everything else seems very uninteresting. At just such a moment yesterday, Rosette [de Matharel] came to take me to lunch. Suddenly she seemed such a little fool, but pathetic—penniless, with four children and a husband who earns nothing and does not even know how to work. She wants to find a job for Guy with the 1937 International Exhibition, where Roger Martin du Gard got an important post. How nice if, through him, Fedya could also find some work of a decorative nature.

We will see each other soon, Bubushkin, my dear. During your absence I lost five kilos. I have been starving myself most of the time, and my gymnastics have helped me. I kiss you warmly and embrace you in my imagination most tenderly, my dear Matushkin. Your V.

I still do not know whether or not you received the *Excelsior* clipping and my letter to Göteborg (Palace Hotel).

1936

[In Paris, in October 1935, Catherine Stravinsky's lungs were x-rayed and she was obliged to return to the sanatorium at Sancellemoz (January 12, 1936), where she had spent most of 1935. A letter from her husband, received January 16, informed her of his forthcoming South American tour. (Did he deliberately keep this from her in Paris?) On the 18th, another letter came from him explaining the scandal brewing over his candidacy for the Institut de France. She wrote to him on the 20th, mentioning a package from ''Vierochka'' (and indicating that the Stravinskys were supporters of Pierre Laval [!]). Stravinsky visited his wife for two days, January 26 and 27, then returned to Paris. On February 19, he and his son played the *Concerto per due pianoforte soli* in Milan, and were in Paris the next day. At the end of February, Stravinsky went to Rome for a concert, and was in Paris on March 4. He and Vera went to Barcelona for concerts on the 12th and 15th, and Vera wrote to Katya from there on the 14th. Igor and Vera were in Paris on the 17th, and Katya wrote to Igor the next day: ''Vera writes that it's very difficult to find an apartment and that she's sorry to part with her little house, but it seems to me

[1] The 1936–37 correspondence is entirely in Russian.

[2] Countess Anna Laetitia (Mimi) Pecci-Blunt, née Levy, niece of Pope Pius XI. Her Roman salon was renowned for fine concerts and conversation.

that this is absolutely necessary for her health. During the summer it's all right, but she will certainly have to move by the fall.'' On March 24 Stravinsky and his younger son left for a concert in Brighton. On returning home, March 30, they were met by Katya, who had left Sancellemoz for two weeks. Even then, however, Stravinsky did not remain at home but gave a concert with his son in Baden-Baden.]

Vera to Igor

[Rome]   March [?], 1936

My beloved Rimsky [i.e., Roman] (but not Korsakov) Bubushkin,[1] Returning from the railroad station, I bought Vichy water and newspapers, went to a café to get warm, then, after a hot bath, went to bed with hot water bottles. I slept well but woke with a headache, which disappeared after a cold-water rub. I will go to an oculist today and have promised to take Lyudmila Gavrilovna with me, since she is having trouble with her eyes. I am lunching with Ira today and going to dinner with Wolf. Meanwhile, I work on my flowers.

I look forward to our trip to Spain in a week. How happy I will be to leave everything behind! On Monday I must get my visa.

I wish you and Svetik much success and a good time (only not with Pecci[2]). I kiss you, my dearest, with all my heart. Write to me giving me the time that your train arrives on Thursday. Your Vera.

Vera to Igor

[Rome]   March [?], 1936

My dearest little one, I am not sure that you will receive this note, but perhaps it will come just before your departure. I spent half a day with Kirsta and made peace with her. On Saturday I went to the oculist who told me that I need glasses. He also advised dieting and gymnastics, which I already know and have not kept up because of the lack of time. It is quite cold here, whereas in Rome you are probably feeling the first breath of spring. I kiss you tenderly. Your Vera.

Vera to Igor

Monsieur Igor Stravinsky
Teatro Colón
Buenos Aires
Argentina   April 14, 1936

My dearest Igor, Felicitations for a happy Easter and many thanks for your cable. It came Sunday night, but since I knew that your family and the Beliankins had already received a cable from you in the morning, I was a little disappointed. I stayed home all day in expectation, and was rewarded at last. I am very happy to have it and I regret not to have money to send one to you. Easter seems so sad this year, and I was depressed after your departure. Your good-bye was hasty, not very tender, and at the last moment you did not call me ''Sobachkina.''

I hope the weather is good, the sea calm, and that after some rest and quiet your colitis will disappear. The last few days before Easter I did not have much time for work: I had to clean the house, I went to church, I fasted, and I gave up smoking. On Saturday, I took communion, and Fred[3] and Wolf came in the evening. Wolf annoyed me by keeping the radio on; I locked myself in the bathroom to escape the noise, and I wept a little. I often feel sad on Easter Eve. After church, both of them came to

[3] A letter from Catherine to Igor, April 14, mentions a visit to her house by Fred Osten-Saken. She says in the same letter that Ansermet called, that she invited him, but that he never came.

my house for supper. When they left I went to Ira's, where the family atmosphere was festive. The next day I felt tired and, since no one came to see me, I went to visit sick friends, first to the Russian Clinic to see my niece who had had an operation for appendicitis, then to Tulia who had had an ear operation; yesterday I visited Olga Sallard.

Ansermet, here for two days en route to Barcelona, telephoned me twice. He wanted to come to see me, but instead invited me to his apartment for tea. After replacing the receiver, I realized that he was calling from Hurtado's. I called back, got her on the phone, and we had a long conversation. She finally understood, I hope, that she had behaved very badly to me.

Yesterday, Arthur Lourié was to have lunched with me but he called a half-hour before the appointment saying he had been delayed in the country. I told him not to come, and that we would see each other at a later time. So: I saw neither Ansermet nor Arthur.

I went to the dentist today and will now go to Mme Auber's to mail this letter. Then I will start to work, for I want to exhibit my flowers at Ira's on the 20th. I have arranged to stop my electric heating but the weather has turned so cold again that I will have to buy wood. I saw Katya on Friday and we walked together on the avenue Gabriel. She sent me pink roses for the holidays, which touched me very much. She looks very well.

I hope that you have a comfortable cabin and that the food is good. I want very much to have your impressions of South America. Is Svetik pleased or is he bored? I embrace and kiss you with much tenderness, my dearest Matushkin. Your Vera.

Vera to Igor

Monsieur Igor Stravinsky
c/o S.S. *Cap Arcona*
Rio de Janeiro
Brazil   April 15, 1936

Igor dear, I just received your letter from Vigo, and I have no words to tell you how happy I am. I telephoned Katya this morning to tell her about your letter. I mailed a letter to you in Buenos Aires and am in haste now to send at least a few words to you in Rio. (I did not think in time of sending my letter there.) I enclose a photograph that Fred took at the railroad station. All is well with me; but I have already written everything in detail to Buenos Aires. Here it is raining, so we hope it will become warmer; the last days have been very cold, with frost at night. I am working at the moment, but for five days I did not work or smoke. I embrace Svetik. I am glad to hear that the sea was calm. Yours with all my soul, V.

Vera to Igor

Monsieur Igor Stravinsky
Teatro Colón
Buenos Aires
Argentina   April 22, 1936

Igor, my beloved, I look at the map and think: Oh God!, how far Igor has gone away! By now you have crossed the equator and are nearing Buenos Aires. Did my note with the photographs reach you in Rio? The heat must be tropical where you are and probably you are sporting your white suit. The weather here is terribly cold, and many flowers and trees have suffered. It is only 12 degrees in my little house, the electric heating having been turned off; I have only my wood-burning fireplace. The humidity and the cold bring on headaches that go away only when I spend a few hours in a warm place. The other day I had a permanent wave, and whereas I usually suffer under the dryer, this time the heat was agreeable.

A few days ago I had a very enjoyable visit from Baroness Stackelberg[1] from Cologne. She was very close to my family and still calls me "*la petite*." We were happy to see each other and I felt almost as if my mother had been to see me. She is staying with her sister here, and I am with both of them almost daily, driving them around Paris and shopping together.

I am preparing a flower basket for Ira's Tyrolean exhibition, which is to be arranged by an Austrian duchess. An article describing some dresses and hats with my flowers on them appeared in *Paris Soir*. I wanted to send you this clipping to show to Victoria but thought it would make the letter heavy and double the cost.

The other day Dushkin gave us very good seats for an interesting BBC concert. I went with both of the Dushkins and Fred. The orchestra, conducted by Adrian Boult, was very good, but he has not quite mastered the *Sacre*; at any rate, the first part went neatly but the second sounded dry, tentative, and dull. The piece was a great success, nevertheless, and the whole evening, with the people from the British Embassy, had the atmosphere of a gala. Fred liked Dushkin and found Louise charming. He asked if he could pay them a visit. I would have liked to invite them all to my house but it is impossibly cold there at the moment.

I had tea at Mika's last week, and I said good-bye to Katya on the phone before she left. I am going to the dentist daily, which is boring and will probably result in a huge bill. I will finish the letter now, by sending you, my Bubushkin, many tender kisses, and all my love—hoping to get as much in return. Do not forget your Sobachkina. Kiss Svetik.

Vera to Igor

Monsieur Igor Stravinsky
Teatro Colón
Buenos Aires
Argentina   April 29, 1936

My dearest, my beloved, Your letter was a joy. It arrived by zeppelin[2]—all of the stamps were very impressive. The same evening I had a phone call from Fedya telling me about your telegram from Buenos Aires. Everything that you say about Argentina is very interesting. The picture postcards with animals were interesting, too.

Here, the cold continues, and though the sun appears, the weather is no warmer. Taking advantage of a break of good weather, I went to Ira's—on foot, to give my car a rest. I talked to the garage owner. He does not advise me to buy a Simca, believing the Peugeot superior. Also, I am certain to receive a higher allowance on a Peugeot when I trade in my old one. He will be on the lookout to find a new one for me. I trust him and his honest blue eyes.

Instead of going to the dentist every other day, I decided to have only part of the work done now and to postpone the remainder until the autumn. The bill will use up all of my savings. Now that I walk to the dentist, I spend my time en route looking at apartments for rent. I found one on the corner of Avenue Mozart, very nice and sunny, but a little too expensive. The rooms are enormous, the bathroom alone being half the size of my whole house, Moreover, it has its own, separate, heating system, like the one at the Beliankins'.

I continue to make flowers because of the current fashion for them. I sold 200 francs' worth at the Tyrolean exhibition of Ira and the Austrian duchess. That show was a great success, incidentally, and one result is that Ira has many new clients. I was amused, also, to hear people say, while curtsying, "Will Your Imperial Highness make a special price?"

---

[1] A Russian aristocrat, refugee from the Revolution.

[2] The *Cap Arcona* and a zeppelin passed very close to each other during Stravinsky's return voyage from Rio de Janeiro to France, and he took several photographs of the aircraft.

I spent last evening at Fatima Hanum's, who thanks you for the cable. She still feels weak and looks awful, and when I stayed with her for dinner, she told me that she now divides people into those who have lost a close relative and those who have not. Imagine, she still writes letters to her dead husband! for whom she made a wonderful, flower-filled grave—which, she says, is "like Giselle's." Coming home, I felt very lonely.

Georgette and Pearce Bailey arrived from London for a few days. Their marriage is set for June. We dined together, went to a nightclub—the likes of which I never hope to see again—and I came home at 4 a.m.

The big news in Paris is that Markevich married Kyra Nijinska.[1] To get over this loss, Marie-Laure [de Noailles] ordered several dresses from Ira.

I am thinking of you with much love, dear Bubushkin, and I hope that you are in good health and enjoying your trip. Have great success, and do not think about rotten old Europe. Remember only me! I kiss you very, very hard. Your Vera.

Vera to Igor

Monsieur Igor Stravinsky
Teatro Colón
Buenos Aires
Argentina   May 6, 1936

My dearest little one, I have had no letter except the one from Rio, and this makes me sad. I would be sadder still if I were idle, but though I work all the time, running to Ira, to Nicolo, then back here, I make very little money. By evening, dead tired, I go to bed early, but my little house is as cold and damp as a cellar; I still buy wood and sit by the fireplace. The political events do not help to lift one's spirits, though the May 1 elections passed peacefully. Olga Sudeikina is still working with me. Tomorrow I am giving a big dinner for Mme de Frey, Tila de Flugge, the Osten-Saken brothers, and Valechka. I have not had these people in my house for quite a while and I must repay their invitations.

I saw Fedya twice, and he brought me the money, for which I am grateful. We walked together in the Bois, where he unburdened his worries about Denise, who has been ill but is better now and is soon coming to Paris. The two of them seem sound and solid, and I think the marriage will be a good one. I received a letter from Katya asking about the last date that she could still write to you in Buenos Aires, but not knowing myself (nor does Fedya know), I could not say. I think we can write only once more. A pity that the stamps are so expensive for letters of more than one page, and for enclosures of photographs.

I met Arthur Lourié the other day in the street. He looked bloated and pale and his greenish overcoat did not enhance his appearance. Things are very hard for him now, apparently. He wants to come and see me, but it would be about the same subject, and he feels deeply hurt.[2] Never mind. Our problems in Paris cannot be of much interest to anyone seeing the many interesting things that you see at the moment. I only hope that you will not be exhausted by all the rehearsals and aggravated by the bad players. I hope you have time to travel a bit, to see the country and the tropical forests with hissing snakes and lovely orchids—or perhaps it is not at all like that and looks like the outskirts of Pargolovo.

This dull letter reflects the kind of life we lead here, hurried and lazy at the same time. Good-bye, my dearest. I wait impatiently for your news. May God give you strength and health. I kiss you most tenderly. Yours with all my heart, Sobachkina.

[1] Daughter of Romola and Vaslav Nijinsky.

[2] Stravinsky had become estranged from Lourié after he published his book on Koussevitzky.

[3] Catherine wrote to Igor, May 11: "I haven't received an answer from Vera to two letters which I wrote her from here. I suppose that she is very busy now, and I'm

Vera to Igor

Monsieur Igor Stravinsky
Teatro Colón
Buenos Aires
Argentina   May 15, 1936

My nearest, my dearest, You were probably surprised not to have had a letter from me with the last mail. Meanwhile I received two letters from you and was tremendously happy.

For the past week I have had conjunctivitis, and my eyes have hurt me very much. I have had to stop working on flower orders, since the aniline paints that I thin out in denatured alcohol are one cause, and my diet of too much fish another—according to the doctor. Now I wear dark glasses, follow a strict diet, and my eyes are much improved. I am very nervous, however, since I have had no visual recreation. I could not send Katya your latest news, but at last I wrote her a sloppy-looking note with gigantic letters.[3]

On Monday I had dinner with Elena Hurtado and Ansermet, who returned from Spain. He wanted your Buenos Aires news, of course, and I think he is very jealous. When told that you were staying in Victoria's townhouse, Elena said, "Did you know that Victoria has become a communist?," by which she meant to insinuate that "Stravinsky is accepting the hospitality of a communist." Elena is a shrew and Ansermet is naive and a fool.

What do you think of Léon Blum becoming so important? People get the governments they deserve. It is said that the conservatives are waiting for their turn, but they will wait until it is too late. I am afraid to move under such political circumstances, since the expenses will increase wherever I go, and I doubt that my income is likely to increase.

I have quite a few orders at the moment, and Olga Sudeikina is coming to help me out, but my earnings are really small. I am glad to have been able to pay my debt to Ira. Fedya came to tell me about *Noces*,[4] but since he has written to you, I will not repeat his story. I would like to take Denise and Milene for a drive outside Paris. The weather is warmer now and we would like to gather some lilies of the valley. It is difficult to imagine that winter must be arriving in the part of the world where you are now. I look at your photo as I write, wondering how you will be when you return. Does crossing the equator change a person as much as wine does?

In view of Léon Blum and the victories of the Italians [in Ethiopia], we are not making many plans. Well, Bubushkin, my dearest, I will finish the letter and send you the tenderest kisses. *P.S.* I forwarded your letter to Fedya and telephoned Païchadze. Embrace Svetik for me. Your Vera.

Vera to Igor

Monsieur Igor Stravinsky
Teatro Colón
Buenos Aires
Argentina   May 23, 1936

Igor my dearest, Thank you for your letter of May 14/15, which made me so happy to receive. I took your letter to Dushkin to him immediately, telephoned Fedya and Païchadze, and wrote to Katya about everything. Fortunately my eyes are well again and I can read, write, and work. Yesterday, I met Bronia Nijinska's husband, who gave me news about the production.[5] I am very happy to hear about your success and I can imagine that the

not at all offended, though I would be happy if I were to receive a note from her. Perhaps it will still come."

[4] Theodore Stravinsky had designed a production of *Les Noces* in Brussels.

[5] Nijinska choreographed *Le Baiser de la fée* in the Teatro Colón in Buenos Aires. See illustration no. 77.

77 May 1, 1936. Buenos Aires. With Bronislava Nijinska, who had staged *Le Baiser de la fée* at the Teatro Colón.

78 May 1936. Buenos Aires. Stravinsky often swathed his neck in towels or scarves, or wore turtleneck sweaters, because of his fear of pulmonary infection. Ten months after this photograph was taken, a New York doctor discovered that the composer was suffering from active tuberculosis.

public there is very pleasant. But why all the fatiguing work? Are the musicians slow? Lazy? Used to dragging the tempo?

I had a letter from Victoria. She boasts about the great reception she gave you: "I hope we made them feel how glad we are to have them and how all of us are trying to please them."

The weather turned cold again. On Monday, a lovely warm morning, I went to Meudon with Fedya, Denise, and Milene. We walked for an hour and drank milk at a farm, but a few days later we had to unpack our winter coats again.

Ira is in a bad mood. Her father lost his job at the Café de la Paix. I am sorry for the old man.

[Since the signing of the Franco-Soviet Pact] the French feel panicky, expecting developments here similar to those in Russia. Many parties and celebrations, entertainments that would have brought money to Ira, have been called off. [Etienne de] Beaumont did not entertain this year and Sonya tells me that her English lady did not send any invitations or have any guests. Only the cinemas and cafés are full. On Tuesday, Dushkin and his wife will come here for dinner; he is making recordings and could not come until now. I will be obliged to spend some money for good cocktails. I hope that Louise buys some of my flowers. I am so interested to hear about your trip. May I come to meet you in Boulogne? Yes, Bubushkin, it will be very interesting. As you see, nothing happens here and life goes on uneventfully. I go to a café now and then, and, as always, to Nicolo's. Once I went to Longchamp with Fred, but no theater, no cinema. I am waiting for you. I embrace you tenderly and await your arrival. Your Sobachkina.

Vera to Igor

Monsieur Igor Stravinsky
Teatro Municipale
Rio de Janeiro
Brazil

May 30, 1936

My dearest Matushkin, Thank God for the beginning of June. Now it is less than a month before you return.[1] I hope that the last few days of your tour are smooth and successful and that we do not experience any catastrophes in our old and rotting Europe— though people sometimes seem to attract them with their fears. The political situation is really bad and I fear that Blum, the idealist, will play the role of Kerensky. (When *I* talk about politics, you will understand that nothing else is ever mentioned here.) Life is really difficult at the moment, and I am so overtired that I often think I will go to pieces. Since my eyes, hands, head, and stomach hurt, I have decided to take three days' holiday, and starting today, Saturday, I will stay in bed. Tomorrow I will walk and Monday go to Meudon forest.

The other day I had the Dushkins for tea. I also invited Argutinsky (an American acquaintance could be useful for him), Ira (Louise Dushkin could be a future client), and, to provide atmosphere, the Osten-Saken brothers. The next day I asked Denise, Fedya, and Tulia, who is a painter and was interested to meet Fedya. Yesterday I bought a first communion present for my godson, René de Matharel, a writing-table set in green leather. I saw Mika, who looked very fresh and extremely well, but Milene seems depressed, as if something sad were happening in her life. She looks frail, unhappy, ingrown. Only marriage could save her.

Perhaps we should move, except that this seems unsafe under the present political circumstances. The Russian revolution taught

me a lesson, yet I do not know what to do now. Should we liquidate everything, pack up and emigrate to another country? Fred was arranging an exhibition for Munich—with the support of the Louvre, which had given him permission to borrow some Degas paintings. He also wanted to add a contemporary section, but when Munich told him that modern painters with communist influences were not wanted, and asked him to be cautious in his choice, he promptly cancelled.

French Jews are very fearful of a wave of anti-Semitism if Blum is not careful, a situation that reminds me of Russia. Forgive this gloomy letter, but it would be a great pity if the "old lady" France were to perish in a general chaos. Meanwhile, I expect your letter and, soon, yourself. I kiss you tenderly, my dearest. May God help you to return safely. Yours with all my heart and soul, V.

Vera to Igor

Monsieur Igor Stravinsky
Teatro Municipale
Rio de Janeiro
Brazil

June 6, 1936

My dearest Igor, I want to send you one more letter from here but I fear that it will not reach you in time and not be forwarded. You must be anxious about the situation in Paris, but though it *is* serious, calm prevails and the strikes do not pose any danger. Three days ago, the Parisians were in a panic when bread, candles, macaroni, etc., suddenly disappeared from stores. It was a false alarm, however, and these and other commodities quickly reappeared in the shops and the restaurants. The strikes that threatened our gas, electricity, and water supply did not materialize, but gasoline is still unobtainable, which is very inconvenient for me, since I cannot use my car. On Thursday I found four gallons outside of Paris but I am saving them in case of emergency. I go about on foot in the cold rain (we have November weather) and from time to time I make a fire. The temperature and humidity in my little house remind me of a cellar.

Our businesses, Ira's as well as mine, have almost come to a standstill. Some ladies want to look beautiful, of course, no matter what the circumstances, but such people seem to be fewer all the time. Nothing has happened so far, but Paris is apprehensive. Yesterday the only newspapers that appeared were *Humanité* and *Action Française*, the latter actually calling for a pogrom. Most Jews are terrified and are staying home. Some say that in a few days all of this will be over, but we Russians, remembering the revolution, think otherwise.

Now that I do less work, I take better care of my health, walk every day, and have massages. I talked to Fedya on the telephone. All is well in your house; a few days ago I had a letter from Katya. Bubushkin dearest, forgive me for such an incoherent letter but I have neuralgia which affects my eyes, and writing is difficult for me. I embrace you tenderly and rejoice at the thought of your arrival. Your Vera.

Vera to Igor

[On the envelope]: Monsieur Igor Stravinsky, 31, rue de l'Assomption[2]
the S.S. *Normandie*, sailing December 18, Paris 16
Le Havre. December 17, 1936

My dearest, I salute you on the *Normandie*[3] and hope you will

---

[1] Stravinsky was in Paris on June 25. Catherine had returned from Sancellemoz on the 17th.

[2] While Igor was in South America, Vera had moved to a new apartment; this is the address of all her letters to him from Europe until 1939. On his return to Paris, Igor was disturbed to learn that his elder son was planning to marry (letter to

Victoria Ocampo, July 10, 1936). Another undocumented but shorter separation occurred in August 1936 when Vera was obliged to undergo treatment for high blood pressure in a Kurhaus in Wiessee, Bavaria.

[3] Vera did not go to Le Havre because Igor was accompanied by the Dushkins.

have a very good crossing on a calm sea, with a blue sky and peace in your soul, and that the crossing will not be boring but of the kind about which young girls dream. And with all of those wishes, dearest, I kiss you very tenderly.

Thank you for playing your music [*Jeu de cartes*] for me.[1] I was so sad because you were leaving that for the first time in fifteen years I found it difficult to listen. Now I am happy that I heard it, if only because I will be able to imagine it in New York, and because, when the reviews appear, I will understand references to details.

I am glad that the Dushkins are sailing with you. This, together with your own new knowledge of the English language, will make the voyage more pleasant, as well as easier for you. Do not forget to let me know the results of your Berlitz lessons.

Georgette's address is: Bailey, 17 East 96th Street, New York City.

Do not worry about us here. With God's help all will be well and no revolutions will occur. Return to us healthy, wise, and rich. Once more I embrace you lovingly. Do not forget your little Sobachkina. May God bless you. Your Vera.

P.S. Thank you once more for the money, with which I can now pay the rent.

Vera to Igor

Letter No. 1
Monsieur Igor Stravinsky
c/o Richard Copley
113 West 57th Street
New York, New York[2]   Monday, December 21, 1936

My own beloved Igor, Happy New Year 1937! I am thinking of you all the time and imagining you among the gay and elegant society on the *Normandie*. I read in the newspapers that your friend Edward G. Robinson is on board with you. If the ocean was calm, the trip must have been very agreeable and very good for you, a necessary change after so much hard work. Please write me about it, and tell me who was amusing and who was stupid.

I am cleaning and cooking a lot these days. I had Ira and Fred for lunch on Saturday, and again today, together with the Beliankins and a chemist called Prohorov. Later Wolf and Argutinsky came, the latter wanting money. The chemist, not a "man of the world," got terribly drunk, and we could not get rid of him until 5, when he said he had to see a doctor. I phoned Dr. Karasik and made an immediate appointment for him so that he had to leave. Today I must see what I can do for Argutinsky. Fred can give him 300 francs, but he needs more.

Feeling very tired the last few days, I have been going to bed early. Apparently I must be in a hurry all my life. I wonder if the time will ever come when I will no longer have to. I have constant visitors here. I do not mind, but must look for a more efficient maid. The one who has been working for me is very slow.

Katya told me on the telephone yesterday that she had received your first letter. I decided to phone American Express for the dates of steamer departures. Please send me some magazines, *The New Yorker*, for instance,[3] in which I might find a description of your arrival in New York.

I received my first bill for electricity today: 90 francs, which is not so terrible, considering that the lights burn all of the time in my house because of my many guests.

Tomorrow a possible buyer for my Peugeot is coming to see me, sent by my cleaners. Now that I expect to sell the car, I will have to give it a good washing.

I kiss you innumerable times, my little one. You did not tell me whether you received my letter sent to the *Normandie*. Your letter arrived yesterday morning. I wish you American blessings and much peace of mind, and I embrace you with all my love. Your Vera.

Vera to Igor

Letter No. 2   December 27, 1936

My dear faraway Bubushkin, I am sitting in my cozy, elegant apartment, enjoying it and resting. I received your cable and am very grateful for it. Meanwhile a great event has taken place in my life: my Peugeot is sold. It is gone, and I have received seven thousand francs. Everyone congratulates me, saying how lucky I am, not knowing how sad I was to part with it. I did not tell the truth and pretended to be happy about it, this being my character.

I am resting because of the holidays and because I have stopped making artificial flowers, a business that took a lot of time and did not earn enough money. My eyes used to swell from the tension, the dyes, and the odor of alcohol, and I was nervous and irritable. Also, I can't make deliveries now without a car.

As I wrote before, the man who bought it was sent by my cleaners, for which I will have to give them something. He came and sat for two hours telling me about his wife and his dog, while I kept hoping that he would buy the car, pay the money, and leave. Suddenly remembering that that was what he came for, he said, "The deal is done, here are seven thousand francs, and please give me a receipt." I gave the owner's license then and there, and he drove off in my car.

It has been bitterly cold. I am expecting Svetik, who promised to visit me. For Christmas dinner I had Ira, Fred, and Valechka, who drank a lot. He is very happy, feeling rejuvenated because a young man declared his love for him—a technique that should be used in beauty parlors and be introduced in my courses in cosmetics. The courses have also stopped now because of the holidays. Our whole class purchased a quantity of beauty products and divided them among ourselves. Unfortunately, I did not buy enough and now the price has gone up sixty percent; I'll have to look for special sales.

Bubushkin, my precious, where are you now? I am trying not to think about sentimental subjects, but at times my heart is very heavy. Please write, even if only short notes. I embrace you with all my strength and kiss you with great tenderness. Yours with all my soul, Vera.

1937

Vera to Igor

Letter No. 3
S.S. *Aquitania*, via Cherbourg
Hotel Sulgrave
67th Street and Park Avenue
New York City   January 1, 1937

My dearest Igor, I address my first letter in 1937 to you. I sent my last one in 1936 to my father,[4] from whom, the other day, I received a long letter. I am so happy to be corresponding with him again and to know that I can bring him some joy in his old age.

---

[1] From 1921 until his death, Stravinsky played his music to Vera as he composed it.

[2] All of Vera's letters to Igor in America, except for the one dated January 1, 1937, were sent to the same address.

[3] *The New Yorker* had published Janet Flanner's profile of Stravinsky at the time of his arrival in New York in January 1935.

[4] Artur de Bosset was living in Santiago, Chile.

This morning I received your letter sent from the *Normandie*. I was very glad to have it, partly because *Paris-Soir* published an article and a cartoon depicting life on board. The cartoon, which I enclose, is enough to provoke a jealous scene. What with Mary Glory sitting on your knees, your sufferings from the stormy sea seem to be an invention. Yes, Bubushkin, say what you wish, but here in *Paris-Soir* is an account in black and white of the way you spent your time. Judge yourself, by the cartoon, except that without the caption you could be mistaken for someone else.[1]

I did not do much New Year's Eve celebrating, was home at eleven-thirty, and at midnight sound asleep. I dined at the Kiev restaurant with Fred and Wolf, after which we went to Wolf's new bachelor apartment. What a fool! He sold his own nice clean furniture and moved into a furnished apartment with dirty curtains and worn rugs, all quite expensive. Though I had not written to Georgette, she asked me why I am angry with him. How did you find her? Did she meet your boat?

I had visitors today. Lyudmila Gavrilovna brought me cake and WC equipment. Ira came with her and gave us a very funny account of a big ball that she attended last night, where she made friends with Cécile Sorel. Arthur Lourié brought me a mimosa branch.

I had a very strange New Year's Eve dream. In it, you told me that I had to play your new concerto in your next concert, and that you would conduct. No matter how I tried to convince you that I did not know how to play, you insisted, and when the day of the concert came, I was horrified and worried sick. I woke up in a panic and shouting. So this is the kind of thing you make me do!

Since selling the automobile, I walk a lot. The other day I was in the Hôtel Drouot (the auction house) trying, without success, to find chairs for the apartment. Then I walked toward Dreyfus (near Sacré Coeur) to the old Pleyel—here I was besieged by memories: do you remember the Hôtel des Arts?—to the Opéra, and finally to the Métro station of St. Philippe-du-Roule, where I took the train. I stopped at corners and stared at shops like a woman from the provinces. So far the novelty of walking amuses me, but when spring comes I will miss the car, and on warm, sunny days I will feel like driving into the Bois or going to Versailles.

Now I only miss *you*, my Matushkin, and I am impatient to receive your letters. I embrace you from the heart and kiss you very, very lovingly. Your Vera.

When Svetik visited me yesterday, he brought me an azalea plant and 3000 francs. Thank you so much, dearest.

Vera to Igor

Letter No. 4   January 10, 1937

My dear beloved Igor, Still no news from you, except for the cable, which Svetik telephoned to me. Probably no ships left New York for a few days, otherwise I would surely have a letter from Georgette describing your arrival. Katya and I often telephone each other, always with the same question: "Is there news from Igor?" I always ask about Mika's health, but, so far, neither question has an answer.

As is now customary, I spent Christmas Eve at Ira's. Valechka and Madeleine were there, and the whole evening was spent gossiping. Valechka lives only for gossip now, which I do not consider appropriate conversation for Christmas. We also celebrated my birthday. I received an elegant coffee pot as a present, and Katya sent candy via Svetik and Milene, both of whom came to the Beliankin apartment after dinner. Ira had also invited Fred, but he is fighting the flu and stayed home. Everyone

has flu; it almost caught me, but I have ways to combat it: first go for a walk, then take a hot bath, then go to bed. The next day it will be gone.

The other day I went to Dr. Karasik, paid him part of the debt, and complained that I am beginning to gain weight again. He checked my blood pressure and it was even less than after Wiessee, and therefore very good, though I do not know which helped most, Wiessee or Karasik.

On Sunday, in spite of very cold weather, I went to the flea market and found a good, stuffed chair and a hassock to put in front of the dressing table. Both pieces cost only 80 francs, but the taxi was 25 francs. Here I missed my car. Naturally the furniture will have to be aired and re-upholstered.

I am very much annoyed with Akis-Bey. After completely disappearing, suddenly he sent that idiotic Bielosselsky with a screen for my fireplace, and this though I told him I did not want it and do not intend to pay 150 francs for it. And not only did he send it, but he also made me pay the taxi in which it was transported. This fire-screen is very rough-looking, more appropriate for a chicken coop. I did not pay for it, but, also, I do not know how to get rid of it. Though I wrote Akis-Bey asking him to take it away, I have not had a word from him, nor has he repaired my cupboard shelves.

I have begun to work on creams and lotions and have bought several kinds of chemical containers, as well as small scales. Our shop will be closed soon, which I already regret, since the work was becoming more and more interesting. When I pass the examinations, then what? I start to wonder if I can sell my products, though the business seems to be a profitable one.

I went twice to Olga Sallard's by railroad, a restful way to travel, since nobody bothers you, and you do not have to rush.

I have not wished you happy holidays yet, but I do so now and embrace you with all my heart. May God bless you. Your Vera.

The 12th: Katya just called to tell me that she finally received a letter from you, dated the 28th. That is very nice. Now I will be expecting one too.

Vera to Igor

Letter No. 5

S.S. *Paris*, via Le Havre   January 18, 1937

Igor my dearest, Before all else, I congratulate you on becoming a grandfather. I just learned that Mika gave birth to a girl. We expected it to happen last evening, for which reason Ira and Valechka were with me. The labor started at eight in the morning, and Mika, good sport, went to the hospital on foot. Nothing happened until eleven that night, and the only question was if the child would appear head first. This worried me, since the baby is Mika's first. Katya and Lyudmila Gavrilovna spent the whole day in the hospital and returned home only at two in the morning after everything was over. Katya and even the doctors said that they have never seen a happier mother. I will go to her in a few days. (I would probably not be admitted before.) You must have received a cable. I wonder where and when you found out that you were a grandfather. Except to be coquettish, I am not going to use that word again, which does not really suit you.

Not knowing your itinerary, I do not know where to imagine you at this moment. Your letter with the description of Christmas Eve and of Sert's rooms amused me very much.[2]

To maintain a reputation of erstwhile beauty, I began exercising again and having massages. Without the car, and living in warmth and comfort, I began to gain too much weight. But Karasik took my blood pressure and found it perfectly normal.

---

[1] The cartoon space is filled helter-skelter with people. Stravinsky is unrecognizable and no one is sitting on his knees.

[2] Aboard the S.S. *Normandie*; José-Maria Sert went to New York to paint frescoes in the Waldorf-Astoria Hotel.

79

79 1937. Paris, at home (25, rue du Faubourg Saint-Honoré), playing from the manuscript of *Jeu de cartes*.

80 1937. Paris.

80

I am busy with my cosmetology and am pleased with the results: now I know how to make all kinds of creams and lotions.

Akis-Bey appeared the other day and worked on the cupboard; he has not finished but it looks much better. He also upholstered a chair that I purchased in the flea market. I found wonderful material, beige with shiny dots, for the upholstering, of which I am very proud, since it is beautiful and will never wear out. (It is used for corsets.) Now that the bedroom is finished, I must do the entrance hall, but this is difficult because I cannot find the right carpet.

The other day I bought Céline's new book about Soviet Russia, *Mea Culpa*. He attacks the communists with great passion, in words that are clever, pertinent, and often indecent. He and André Gide have really compromised the Bolsheviks, but Céline's work, being that of a convinced communist, is the more valuable.

How is the influenza epidemic in America? It is very bad in Europe, less so, generally, in France. Tula just returned from winter sports, which amounted to ten days in bed with flu. The day after we were together, she phoned to say that her temperature was very high. She asked for a doctor, and I sent Karasik, who diagnosed pneumonia. Now she has a nurse and all of us are taking care of her. The poor woman is suffering, but Karasik says that she will soon be well again thanks to her iron constitution; still, she must stay in bed for two weeks. Olga Sallard is also in bed. I'll go to see her tomorrow.

Friends took me to the circus to see Grock, a very funny and touching old man. He has reappeared after four years' absence and is really wonderful.

What is most important, Bubushkin, is that *you* are well. I wish that for you, and much success (but not with women). I kiss you, my dearest. Your Vera.

Vera to Igor

Letter No. 6   January 24, 1937

Dear little one, I was at Mika's and saw that tiny creature next to her,[1] a touching sight that also made me reflect on the wonder of the birth of a new being. Mika, who looks marvelous, gave me a minute-by-minute description that was completely unlike the way other women have talked about it. Mika is ready to do it all over again.

Katya came to see me.[2] She has been very tired in the last few days and is resting now. She had not seen my apartment in such an advanced stage of decoration and found it cozy. Everyone, myself included, thinks it very attractive.

The weather is so warm that I keep my windows open most of the time. After my February examination in chemistry, I would like to go to Nice. I could stay there with my relatives in Tourrette-sur-Loup, or else at Georgette's mother's. If I could find a reasonable way of getting there—a special train, perhaps—I would certainly go. I want some sun and sea air. The exams should take place in about ten days. I'm really sorry that these studies are coming to an end; I would love to pursue them in a university. Do you think that if I could prove that I went to the University of Berlin,[3] I might be accepted here? Some people enjoy golf, or tennis, but I love to study. I am not yet making any money, it is true, but I have already learned a great deal. I am one of the first in the course, in laboratory work as well as in classroom chemistry.

[1] Catherine Yurievich Mandelstamm.

[2] Katya had described the birth to her husband in a letter, January 18, 1937, that should be read in juxtaposition to Vera's letter as, respectively, examples of extreme White Russian conservatism and New Russian liberalism. Catherine is grateful to "God and the Holy Mother" for the successful birth, rather than to the obstetrician, a "Russian Jew." (The letter goes on: "Not much Jewishness is noticeable in the child. The important question is what the nose will look like later. It will probably be here that her race will become apparent.")

Ira's collection of clothes will be shown soon. The pressure accompanying this is again noticeable. I am sorry for her, especially in the moments when she is not trying to be a snob or trying to pose.

I finally decided to have my bathroom chair repaired—by a woman who used to wake me with her bell at 9 a.m. She vanished when I moved, so I was glad to hear the "cry of Paris" again, and the sound of her bell under my windows.

I just received your letter and immediately telephoned Païchadze about the scores and parts.[4] He said that there was still plenty of time, and that he would send the music to you before then, even if he has to retrieve it from some place in South America.

You probably know that Svetik had pains in the area of the appendix. He is better now, but after his concert an operation will probably be necessary.[5]

I must take this letter to the post office. As is usual when I want to do that, it is pouring. A friend from my chemistry course is coming to prepare for the examination with me. I am enjoying all of this like a schoolgirl, and it makes me feel young.

I embrace you a thousand times, my dearest, and thank you for the letter and the congratulations for my success. Your Vera.

Vera to Igor

Letter No. 7
[Forwarded to:
Hotel Sulgrave
60 East 67th Street]   February 4, 1937

My dearest Igor, I do not know where or how to begin this letter which brings you sad news. We have all gone through, are still going through, terrible days and nights. On Tuesday, February 2, at 8:00 in the evening, Lyudmila Gavrilovna suffered a stroke when she was alone in the kitchen, making dinner. Grigory Pavlovich was sitting in the entrance-way, tinkering with something or other, and Ira had gone to a bar with Madeleine, but was expected back, since it was Grigory Pavlovich's birthday, supposedly a festive occasion. Suddenly he heard a cry from the kitchen, "Oh! I feel bad." He ran there and found Lyudmila Gavrilovna on the floor, tongue curled back, foaming at the mouth, eyes rolling. At this point the dogs started jumping and barking. No one else was in the apartment except Ganya, who was ill at the time and unable to help. Grigory Pavlovich ran to the concierge, who fetched a doctor, a surgeon who lives in the building. He had just sat down to dinner but came immediately and—with Grigory Pavlovich's help—carried her from the kitchen to the sofa, where he gave her a camphor injection. Then Ira arrived and, seeing her mother in this condition, ran to call Katya, shouting into the telephone, "Mama is dying."

Ira called me and asked me to find Dr. Karasik, which I was able to do, and to bring him there by 9:30. We had another doctor at 11:00, and a French professor in the morning, with whom there was a consultation. I did not go to bed until the next night; poor Ira has been up for forty-eight hours and is now on her knees trying to talk to her mother—who seems to recognize only her, once, yesterday, even smiling at her. Last night was the worst: the temperature reached 41 and the pulse 150, and I thought the end had come. From time to time, Ira would go into the kitchen to cry.

Today Lyudmila Gavrilovna is better. Her temperature is lower, and she seems to know what is going on around her, whereas on the first day she was not aware of anything, but only felt very ill and vomited a great deal. Now she asks about Ganya and others

[3] Before World War I.

[4] For *Apollo* and *Le Baiser de la fée*, which Stravinsky conducted on the program with the premiere of *Jeu de cartes* in the Metropolitan Opera House, April 27.

[5] The operation took place at the end of February 1937. See Theodore Stravinsky's letter to his father from Les Diablerets, March 1, 1937.

and is trying to understand what happened to her. It will be terrible if she succeeds, since the diagnosis is cerebral hemorrhage, as well as something that the doctors could not explain, but which is either brain concussion (from falling on the stone floor?) or meningitis.

Her legs are paralyzed but her upper body is not. Ira says she would rather see her mother dead than in such a state, or even in a wheelchair, pushed along by a nurse. There are two nurses, day and night, and the doctor comes twice a day, as well as a third doctor who relieves her bladder with a catheter. The tests show that she had high blood pressure and malnutrition, and that her kidneys were in poor condition; in fact she has all the symptoms of uremia.

At this moment she is talking, but most of the time without making sense. She also seems to feel that her legs are stirring. The poor, poor woman. I am so very sorry for her and for the whole family. What will they do without her? And even with the most favorable outcome her life is finished. That she could be up and around the house within a year is out of the question. She complains of pain in her side, and the doctors suspect that a rib was broken when she fell, but to find the break is impossible because she cannot be moved from the sofa and the position in which they first placed her. (Her dress was cut from around the body.) Any movement might start the hemorrhaging again.

We still had hope on the day following the fall, but not after the report on the kidneys. It must be horrible for Ira and Grigory Pavlovich to see her suffer like this.

On the first day, Katya could not walk—because of a stretched tendon—but she comes now and does not limp.

Ira has just come to talk to me; she asked me to send you a kiss. Karasik has examined Lyudmila Gavrilovna's reflexes: one leg might possibly be saved, but the other will be paralyzed.

This letter may seem incoherent: I am interrupted all the time. Ira had already started to show her collection, and the work room has to function, since buyers come every day. In the midst of that stampede of dress-making is a dying woman. But there is still hope.

I kiss you, my dearest. May God bless you. Your V.

Vera to Igor

Letter No.8
S.S. *Aquitania*, via Cherbourg
[Forwarded to:
Hotel Sulgrave
60 East 67th Street]   Tuesday, February 9, 1937

My dear, God, what sad days these are! I wrote you on Thursday. On the Tuesday, this misfortune with Lyudmila Gavrilovna befell us. Today is Tuesday, a week, in other words, since it all began, and poor Lyudmila Gavrilovna is still lying unconscious and delirious, with a temperature that reaches 40°. Suddenly she seems to be reviving, and exclaims that the milk is good—she is fed only milk and bouillon—or asks why Ira looks so sad. Then, seconds later, she does not recognize her husband and starts to recall events of forty years ago. This is terrible. To see Ira in such a state tears my heart. Grigory Pavlovich is also having a very painful time, though he keeps a tight hold on himself.

Yesterday Dr. De Gennes[1] consulted with Achabadzhan, an old

Russian professor and brain specialist. Both men were very pessimistic. Lyudmila Gavrilovna has a strong constitution, and her heart and pulse are still good, but no one can withstand such continuing high temperature. Every two hours she receives injections and has auto-vaccines of the blood (blood-letting from the veins). Saturday was the worst. Ira asked me to call a priest, and Father Nikolai came from the rue Daru.[2] We said prayers and Father Nikolai gave Lyudmila Gavrilovna the blessing. When Ira said, ''Mama, kiss the cross,'' Lyudmila Gavrilovna pursed her lips and kissed it. She seemed much better after that and her temperature began to fall. On Sunday her condition was stationary, and yesterday, Monday, she seemed better, or at least we thought so, since she was conscious more often, the breathing had improved, and her appetite was good. But after the doctors had a consultation, we all lost spirit. Until then Ira had managed to be almost cheery, making plans, even laughing a little.

Katya is here from early morning until lunch, then from four until dinner. I am here from early morning until late at night, doing housework, running to the pharmacy (this is where we miss the car), and answering the constant telephone calls of friends.[3] I sleep at home because not even Ira has a place for herself. Volodya,[4] who does the housework and continues to make yogurt,[5] sleeps on the living-room sofa, and Ganya is confined to bed with an injured knee. Ira takes turns with her father sleeping in his bed, if a few minutes now and then can be called sleeping.

Karasik comes twice a day and stays for an hour each time. He has just left and was not very encouraging, telling us that Lyudmila Gavrilovna's blood pressure has begun to drop too rapidly, and that her pulse is irregular. We closed Ira's studio today and dismissed the employees, not because shoppers had stopped coming, but because it would be awkward if someone had noticed that everyone was speaking in a whisper.

We hope for a miracle and interpreted as one the improvement after we had said prayers on Saturday. But I do not think she will recover, and it would be better for her and for the family if she dies. She has suffered in life and is suffering in dying, but to die would be better than to live for a few more years as an invalid and always with the fear of a second stroke. . . . I am terribly sorry for the whole family. Poor Ganya! Who is going to take care of him? The old man is becoming more and more dependent. Ira, unhappy girl, adored her mother.

My greatest concern is for you and how upset you are going to be when you receive our first letters. I advised Katya to send you a cable, ''Condition stationary,'' but in order to calm you, she prefers to send one only when some improvement has taken place.

Today I received your letter with the enlargement of the Alsace photograph. Thank you very much. God keep you. I embrace you with all my soul. Your V.

Vera to Igor

Letter No. 9
S.S. *Queen Mary*, via Cherbourg   Monday, February 15, 1937

Igor, my dear, I think of you all the time and wonder whether you were alone or whether anyone was near you, to make it easier, when you received the sad news about Lyudmila Gavrilovna.

[1] Dr. Lucien de Gennes. Stravinsky, on his return to Europe, wrote a letter to another doctor (Karasik?) dismissing him in favor of De Gennes: ''We just had a visit from Dr. De Gennes, called at the suggestion of Ekaterina Gavrilovna. He gave her medications to alleviate her breathing and to strengthen her heart. She reacted very well to Dr. De Gennes and has decided to follow his instructions very strictly. I am in accord. We will see if this improves her condition. Under the circumstances, I do not want to bother you any further. If you permit, I will let you know the progress of her condition.''

[2] From the Church of Alexander Nevsky on the rue Daru. The Stravinsky family and Vera had not been connected with this Church ever since it had recognized

the primacy of the Metropolitan of Moscow. Mika and Theodore were married in the Cathedral of the Metropolitan Anastasy, on the rue d'Odessa. In 1937, the Stravinskys and Vera became members of the diocese of the Church of the Sign of the Holy Mother, 32, rue Boileau.

[3] Theodore Stravinsky wrote to his father, February 9, 1937: ''Vera is helping out in whatever way she can.''

[4] An ex-Russian army officer, employed by the Beliankins.

[5] G.P. Beliankin was in the yogurt business at the time.

I cannot find words to describe our feelings, and especially Ira's, as well as all that we have lived through in these nerve-racking ten days. I cannot comprehend where Ira found the strength to continue. During the final 24 hours, she held her mother's hand and lay down next to her, looking into her eyes, and trying to smile, in case her mother became conscious and would then see her daughter's smile. It was impossible to watch without crying.

I am sorry for those who are left behind. Though their grief is very deep, they try to bear up and not behave hysterically. Ira says that now that the worst has happened, she is immune. Everything humanly possible was done: the best doctors were here, and a priest was present in the last moments to read the last prayer. She was buried on a sunny day, with birds singing. The cemetery[1] is in the country 40 miles from Paris, surrounded by the quiet of the fields and forests. Ten minutes after the coffin was lowered into the ground and covered with earth, bees were hovering over the flowers. It was all so peaceful that the sadness we felt in our souls was somehow wonderful. This is the first time that I have witnessed the death of someone close to me, and I cannot get over it.

Now the Beliankin house seems very empty, especially in the evenings when Ira's customers are not around. I will go there as often as I can to cook or simply to sit, until the initial grief passes and they can begin to put themselves back together. Ira is now holding on to her father, and Ganya, who suddenly seems grown up, is talking about everything in a completely different tone and acting like an older brother to Ira, stroking her hair and speaking tenderly to her. All of Ira's friends were at the funeral. They helped greatly, even with money. (The wife of Admiral Thouars brought 5000 francs to the funeral.)

Poor Katya comes to help and to clean up. She was devastated but bears up wonderfully. Maggi (Ira's friend) has put her country house at the Beliankins', Ira's, and my disposal for the month of March, and we intend to spend the coming weekend there.

Meanwhile, I received your letters and photographs and was very happy to have them. I am impatiently waiting to hear from you again.

I embrace you with all my heart, my dearest. May God bless you! Your Vera.

P.S. It is unfortunate that, because of the airmail to South America, our letters there took much less time than do those to New York.

Vera to Igor

Letter No. 10   March 1, 1937

My dearest little one, Where are you and what are you doing? I know nothing about you and cannot follow you on the map, knowing only approximately where you are.

We are having a very confusing season here; I do not know whether to call it winter or spring. At times it rains hard and is very windy, the sun coming out only sporadically. Everyone's nerves are on edge.

No sooner have I settled down to a quiet evening at home than I receive an urgent call from Ira. Obviously, I must help them until their affairs return to normal, which will not be very soon. I visit Ira daily, help her to write letters, checks, and everything else that requires accurate spelling.[2] Lately I have even been helping them to package the yogurt. I cannot go on doing it, of course,

which they will have to understand. Also, they are unbelievably obstinate and difficult. Fortunately they decided to take on an ex-officer, a Russian, who will live in and be a great help. You cannot imagine how terrible Ira looks. I have to admire her courage, getting up at 7 every morning and trying to do all of her mother's work, but she does not have the strength to go on for very long—no one has. Besides, she worries about her father and Ganya all the time and takes such good care of them and so cheers them up that we are amazed at her patience, especially since the old man is becoming irascible. I am sorry for him, but he can be extremely trying, even to Ira. Yesterday they were all here for tea.

We went to see Svetik in the hospital. He looks very well; his appendectomy went normally. The hospital is very up-to-date, big and white, not at all like our own hospital on the Avenue Janot. The patients are taken care of by nurses all dressed in white. I found the old man Mandelstamm[3] in Svetik's room when I arrived. He seems to be very nice and kind. Svetik will be going home on Thursday the 4th.

Oh yes, I almost forgot to tell you that I passed my chemistry examination. My professor was so pleased with me that he wanted to mark it "excellent," but could not do so because no such mark exists. "Very good," the mark I received, is the highest that can be put on a diploma. Now I am a "cosmetician," a worker, and a researcher in cosmetic chemistry.

I met and made friends at the school with a very nice Russian woman, Mme Maximovich. For many years—though she is still young—she was the director of the American Beauty Institute. She now plans to open one here in Paris. In the meantime, she and I are practicing the application of creams, lotions, etc.

Olga Ilinishna stayed here with me for three days and will soon be coming for two more. I was very glad to have her; with all the problems of late, I could not sleep and felt lonely and anxious. I am going to a new doctor now, not to that fool Karasik, who only increased my blood pressure and aggravated my nervous condition. The new doctor finds nothing organically wrong, just nerves. He calmed me, so I am continuing with him.

I have started to give lessons in making artificial flowers, which is fun and brings in a little money, a necessity, since, without a car, I must spend a lot on taxis. Also, I have a daily maid, who keeps everything clean and cozy: to come back home from the disorder in Ira's apartment is a great pleasure.

As I close this letter, I want to try not to tell you how much I miss you. With all my deep love, Your Vera.

Vera to Igor

Letter No. 11
Via S.S. *Queen Mary*   Monday, March 15, 1937, first week of Lent

Dearest darling Bubushkin, I see from the newspapers that all steamers from New York in May, June, and July are full, and all tickets sold out. Have you confirmed your reservations for the return trip? When do you plan to come? Though this is still two months away, I think about it all the time. Shall I come to meet the boat? I await your instructions.

Everyone seems so nervous here this spring, with all the deaths and misfortunes. I dread looking at a Russian newspaper, since it always announces the loss of another friend. Now, Maria Lange is dying. Though I was not very close to her, we did go to school together and shared many childhood memories. She has had heart trouble for a long time, so to some extent her family is prepared for her death.

I visit the Beliankins almost every day. Their financial problems are considerable, and while they always hope for good customers, the people who actually buy are personal friends, who must be given reduced prices. Ira again owes me money, and again she wants to pay me back with dresses. She rearranged her room, and now her father and Ganya are redecorating theirs,

---

[1] Ste. Catherine des Bois, on the road to Orleans. Mika was buried there in December 1938, Katya in March 1939, and Anna (Stravinsky's mother) in June 1939.

[2] Ira was scarcely able to write.

[3] Father-in-law of Lyudmila (Mika) Stravinsky.

trying to make them a little more comfortable. The old man commented: ''How strange that when Lyudmila was alive we lived like pigs, while now we are trying to be cozy.'' Ira answered: ''When dear mother was alive we did not need anything else,'' and in truth their whole life revolved around her. Ira has changed terribly. She looks so bad without make-up that her clients are appalled at her appearance. Trying to act and to look like her mother, she works straight through the nights. Let us hope that her youth will sustain her. Ganya, by contrast, is adjusting.

Exactly a year ago you and I went to Spain together. Now we rarely take any trips, which makes me sad. I am afraid that those lovely trips to Germany, sometimes for a month or two, can never be repeated. I think of them as I think of the remotest days of youth.

Sonia got tickets for me to go to the Opéra tomorrow to Sir Thomas Beecham's concert, a great gala under the patronage of the British Embassy. I will be glad to hear some music. The event will be a financial strain on me, since I must borrow a dress from Ira, take it in a taxi to my house, go to the concert in a taxi, and return the dress in one.

I am leaving for church in a few minutes. It has been moved to Auteuil, close to my house. Katya must have described all of this to you.

I am sorry for this depressing letter, but I am feeling sad and heavy in my heart. I would so love to be with you for even a minute. I embrace you, my dear and faraway one. Your Vera.

Vera to Igor

Letter No. 12
S.S. *Ile de France*, via Le Havre   April 2, 1937

My dearest Matushkin, What a pity that I do not have enough money to send you a cable of congratulations for the premiere [of *Jeu de cartes*] and tell you at the same time how happy I am at the thought of your impending return. In truth, I have no desire to write, for the reason that I am already anticipating how I will sit next to you in the railroad car, tell you about everything, and hear all of your news. Nothing remarkable is new here, where we simply go on fighting against the rising cost of living and looking forward to the Exposition—which, by the way, will not be ready until July.

The death of Misia's father, Cipa Godebski, has deeply touched me. He had been left alone in a clinic in Fontainebleau (while his daughter went to Paris to have a good time). Never again will we see the old man at concerts. Misia was not attached to him, but she will be affected by his death. You were inquiring about her some time ago. She was very considerate to Ira at the time of her bereavement and continues to be attentive to her.

All of the Russian churchgoers are very worried about the forthcoming taxi strike—and of subways and buses—wondering how they will get to church on Russian Easter. Luckily I live near the church and can walk. The new church is lovely, with good architecture and plenty of room, holding about five hundred people. Its finances are being managed better. But I will not give any details here, since I hope to tell you about everything as we ride together in the boat train. I cannot tell you how happy I am just thinking about your arrival and, with it, leaving behind old, dreary, sad winter: spring will be here. And so, my dearest, come soon and bring with you, as a present, joy and warm weather. I kiss you, my Bubushkin, and open my arms wide to embrace you. Your Vera.

[1] Stravinsky had sent a redwood sapling from San Francisco.

Vera to Igor

Monsieur Igor Stravinsky
Hotel Sulgrave
67th Street and Park Avenue
New York City
sur *Ile de France*
[Postmark: letter received April 20]   April 12, 1937

My little, my beloved Igor, The days run along, one after the other, and I am glad to be very busy filling the time before your return. The little green tree has not come, but I look forward to receiving it.[1]

Maria Lange's funeral was last week. She suffered terribly and no one was allowed to visit her: I did not see her until she was already dead. The spring was saddened by deaths of other friends as well, and I had to go to funerals, send flowers, and look at tear-stained faces. Olga Mumm's husband died, and I must write a letter of condolence—not an easy task, since no one liked him. You have probably read about the death of Karol Szymanowski.

Now, after this depressing introduction, let me tell you a few pleasant things. First, I am feeling much better lately and am pleased with my new doctor. I drink carrot juice and hot water with honey, and I have alternating cold- and hot-water rubs. I work at my cosmetics and read all sorts of scientific books on the subject at the Sorbonne library. I go on making flowers and giving lessons, and I try to put the finishing touches to my apartment, by re-covering my old furniture.

I will ask you to bring me six pairs of stockings. American stockings cost 35 francs here, but only a dollar a pair in New York, and they are wonderful stockings. My size must be 10, but you can ask one of the ladies, perhaps Georgette, to do it for you. She wrote to me that her second husband, Pearce, will have the same sinus operation that Wolf had had. This seems like her fate.

I have not seen much of Ira lately, since the buses and subways tire me. She cooks, mends clothes, and reads out loud to her male admirers, exactly as her mother used to do. Grigory Pavlovich is hurt that you did not answer him about the cemetery; he wants to reserve plots near yours. I told him that you can take care of this on your return but he fears that in the meantime someone else might buy the adjoining ground.

Except for tourists to the Exposition (which is opening piecemeal), Paris seems empty. I will be glad to come to meet you—in Cherbourg, I hope, since we would be alone for a longer time.

Katya is coming soon to have tea with me. I owe Svetik a good dinner after his appendix operation. I embrace you, my dearest, with all my heart and kiss you tenderly. It won't be long now! Your Vera.

Vera to Igor

Letter No. 13
Via S.S. *Queen Mary*   April 26, 1937, French Easter

Dearest Igor, I have not written to you for ten days because I felt so terrible and did not want to write in my state of depression. I do not know the reason for it. Perhaps it is the spring, or all the sad things that have happened lately, or your absence, or simply that I am growing older. In any event, I am very nervous, my heart is uncomfortable, and I am short of breath. Fred brought me medicine from Germany, but he insisted that I go to a specialist, who told me that the medicine was too strong and threw it out. He uses a more natural method of treatment: rest, diet, and hot compresses. I am still bothered by insomnia, for which I am taking medication. This type of ''cure'' takes time, unlike an appendix, which, once it is cut out, is followed by quick relief. The doctor thinks my problems are with my nerves. He advises me to keep busy, but I am already active all the time, working on my flowers, attending my chemistry lessons, looking after my

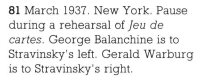

81 March 1937. New York. Pause during a rehearsal of *Jeu de cartes*. George Balanchine is to Stravinsky's left. Gerald Warburg is to Stravinsky's right.

82 1937. New York. Photo by Fritz Reiner.

83

83 May 1937. On the S.S. *Normandie* New York to Le Havre. With Natalia and Serge Koussevitzky, Samuel and Louise Dushkin, and an unidentified woman.

84 1937. Paris. At home, 31, rue de l'Assomption.

85 September 1937. Venice. Palazzo Ducale. Photo by Igor.

84

85

apartment. At the moment I am posing for Millioti for a portrait, which I think will turn out successfully.

Fred came from Germany last week and, as usual, brought me a variety of nice presents, including a copybook in which to record my chemistry prescriptions, an electric pan, kitchen knives, and other gadgets. Now he plans to go to England.

Today I went with Ira and Ganya to the cemetery. Ira has resolved to take good care of her mother's grave, and, indeed, it was covered with flowers. Ira has changed so much—she has even stopped using make-up—that her friends scarcely recognize her, though they are trying to keep her spirits up.

I read the other day in the newspapers that your name is being mentioned again for election to the Académie Française, for the place of Widor, who died. Florent Schmitt, it seems, is going to a lot of trouble to arrange this.[1]

The streets between Ira's place and mine are full of traffic because of the Exposition. I hate to use the Métro. We have all decided not to rush out to the Exposition but to go only in a month or so.

I am disgusted with Wolf and I criticized him sharply for not going to see Ira after her mother's death. You did not tell me whether or not you saw Georgette. I have not heard from her for quite a while, but I do know that her mother intends to visit her this summer.

I sent my father several of my photographs. He replied that he was disappointed in them and did not even recognize me. He said that I should send a passport photo, without any embellishments, and then he would recognize me.

If, my dearest, I wrote to you how I miss you, the letter would be long and tearful.[2] Therefore I had better hide my feelings. I saw Boris Kochno, who said he saw you in New York. He promised to come and tell me more, also about Sudeikin whom he saw frequently. I embrace you with all my heart and kiss you as much as I love you. Your Vera.

Vera to Igor

Monsieur Igor Stravinsky
Hotel de Rome
Riga
Latvia   December 12, 1937

My dearest Igor, I still have not heard from you in the far North.[3] Did you feel the nearness of Russia?

Here in Paris it suddenly feels like Russia, having become so much colder, and, also, Russians having found it so much harder to live. With the cold weather, prices have gone up, including those of bread and milk. I hear so many complaints. For myself, I am working so hard that the time seems to pass swiftly. I did not leave the house yesterday, ate some leftovers, and the day was over before I knew it.

Cosmetics are proving to be a wonderful field for my imagination and inventiveness. I showed my bath oil to Dr. Salmanov, who was very interested and, I think, will recommend it; he approved it, in any case, and also told me many interesting things. He wants to put his laxative on the market: purée of figs, raisins, and some herbs. I made this mixture into small sausages, wrapped them in purple cellophane, tied them with gold cord—in order to make them look like party favors—and am selling them for 3, 5, and 10 francs. No doubt Salmanov and I will go to jail. (I see you worrying already.) I went to him about my headaches and

was told that they come from the sinuses. Following his advice, I put my elbows in hot water and as a result I have had no pains for five days.

I feel very badly not to have congratulated Katya, or to have given her a present on her saint's day, but I did not go downtown for a week and, luckily, she phoned me herself to tell me about your telegram, thereby giving me the chance to explain everything to her. I then planned to send her a present through Milene, who was coming to see me but had to cancel because she was coming down with flu.

Ira telephoned complaining that she does not see me any more. When I told her that I was free the next day for dinner, she promptly invited me. I went, but the confusion and disorder there were such that we did not dine until 10 p.m. I talked to her for a few minutes during dinner and for about 5 more minutes on leaving, since she was busy working all the time. She signed a contract with Jacques Rouché[4] to do something for the Opéra. I do not know how she will manage it, in addition to going to Morocco. She asked me to help with fittings while she is away—which I will do, since she must have a rest. She really looks terrible.

I just phoned Ira to ask her to call your house and find out how Katya is feeling so that I could write to you about it; but none of the Beliankins had time to talk to me, which annoyed me, and I hung up. I could not call your house directly because both Katya and Milene are sick in bed. I embrace you darling and wish you and Svetik great success. I kiss you tenderly. Your Vera.

P.S. I just had a call from Katya Kessel,[5] who is back from Buenos Aires. She met Victoria Ocampo and was charmed by her but not by Argentina. Katya did not go to Santiago and therefore returned the money that I had sent to my father.

1938

January

1 For a pheasant dinner: Igor,[6] Valechka, and Fred.   **2** Go with Igor to see an interesting color film, *Vogue 38*.   **3** Terribly cold. Walk in the Bois. Ira returns from Africa. I go to see her at 9 p.m. to clear up questions about costumes but, instead, listen to her raptures about the desert.   **4** In the evening Igor and I listen to the radio concert in memory of Ravel.   **6** Igor leaves for Rome, and I go with him to the Gare de Lyon. He gives me azaleas. Cocktails with Svetik at Fouquet's.   **8** Arthur Lourié from 5 to 7.   **10** A postcard from Mother. I visit Mika. With Kugulskaya to the movies, *Desire* by Sacha Guitry.   **12** Meet Igor's train, the Rome Express, at 8:10 a.m.   **15** We go to a Pasdeloup Orchestra Concert with Prokofiev.   **16** Igor spends the whole day with me. Mika is very sick, and he is worried and sad. Fred joins us for dinner, and the three of us sit quietly in a kind of foreboding.   **20** A letter from Mother with photographs. Dinner with Igor at Prunier, then to the theater: *Alibi*.   **23** Igor spends the whole day with me.   **26** Dinner and cinema with Igor and Fred.   **30** Fred leaves for Mexico. Igor for lunch and the remainder of the day. Dinner with him at Prunier, then to a film.

February

3 Lunch with Igor. At 4, Borovskaya and Yvonne Casafuerte.[7] Valechka for dinner.   **4** Dinner at Tulia's with the Tolstoys.   **5** Lunch with Prince Argutinsky.   **6** Prokofiev comes from 10 to 1 and Igor at 3. We dine at Doucet, then see a movie.   **9** To Dr. Mascré 1:30–4. Igor, Arthur Lourié,

[1] See *Stravinsky: Selected Correspondence*, Vol. II, op. cit.

[2] This was Stravinsky's longest transatlantic tour, four and a half months as compared to three months in 1925 and 1935, two months in 1936.

[3] Stravinsky had concerts in Tallinn, December 13, and Riga, December 17.

[4] Director of the Paris Opéra.

[5] A long-time friend of Vera's, Katya Kessel survived the German occupation of

France and in 1948 emigrated to Israel.

[6] At this date—and from 1934—Stravinsky was permanently domiciled in Paris, and to spend an evening with Vera, therefore, was to choose *not* to spend it at his own home.

[7] The Marquise Yvonne de Casafuerte, one of the founders of the Serenade, a Paris chamber music society, was herself a violinist who later played more than a thousand performances in the orchestra of *South Pacific* in New York.

and Charles-Albert Cingria[1] for dinner here.   **10** At 9 a.m. a *panikhida*[2] service for Lyudmila Gavrilovna, after which I go with the Beliankins to the cemetery. Igor and I go to the Opéra Comique in the evening.   **11** I have not smoked for 10 days.[3]   **12** The Countess Tolstoy comes for tea.   **13** At the Serenade concert, I am with Igor, Ira, and Massine in the box of Marie-Laure de Noailles, who drives us home. Long telephone conversation with Igor.   **14** In the evening to the Comédie Française with Marcelle Meyer, Casafuerte, Vittorio Rieti.[4]   **17** Mme Levy from 11 to 12. Dinner with Igor at the Marignan, then to a film.   **18** At 6 Ira shows her collection. Igor leaves for Berlin to make recordings.[5] I go to Fatima Hanum's at 9.   **24** Munch[6] conducts Rieti's Piano Concerto with Marcelle Meyer as the soloist.   **25** Dine with Igor on the Boulevard and hear *La Création du monde* and *Jeanne d'Arc* on the radio.[7]

March

1 Dine with Igor at 8:30, then go to the rehearsal with him.   **2** With Igor to the rehearsal in the Salle Gaveau.   **4** To Igor's concert.   **6** Igor and Arthur Lourié for lunch. To the movie *Carnet de bal*.   **8** Prokofiev and Voronshenko come in the evening. White wine and sandwiches.   **11** Misia Sert, Igor, and Ira for dinner.   **12** Lunch with Ira. Visit Fedya and Denise at 9 p.m.   **13** Igor here all day.   **14** With Igor to a concert at the Ecole Normale.   **17** In the evening with Igor to a concert of the Serenade.   **19** Arthur Lourié comes in the evening.   **20** Igor here the whole day. To the cinema together.   **21** Igor goes to Sancellemoz to bring Mika home.   **23** Make arrangements for Arthur Lourié's concert.   **24** With Igor to see the *Corsaire* at the Théâtre Athénée. A reception afterward at Misia's for "tout Paris."   **26** Arthur Lourié for lunch. Dinner with Igor at Marignan, then to a stupid Sacha Guitry film.   **27** Igor for lunch and to a film in the evening: *Queen Victoria*.   **28** Dinner at the Ritz with Chanel.

April

1 Lunch with Igor near Gare St. Lazare.   **7** Annunciation Day in the Russian Church. Go to church with Igor, who is very depressed because of Mika's illness.   **8** Ira for lunch. Sumptuous dinner in Montparnasse with Ilya Zdanevich.   **10** The whole day with Igor, joined by Fred and Arthur Lourié for dinner.   **14** Lunch with Igor at Bernard's.   **16** A lovely day. Walk on the Champs-Elysées. Igor and Fred for dinner.   **17** Palm Sunday. To church and lunch with Igor. Dinner at Doucet. Cinema.   **23** Lunch at the Ritz with Igor and Lord Berners. Dine at Ira's with Igor, then go with him to the cinema.

---

[1] 1883–1954, one of the major Swiss writers of the twentieth century and a close friend of Stravinsky's from 1915. Cingria's *Pétrarque* (1932) was a book of great importance in Stravinsky's life, both because he set a text by Petrarch published in it, and because of Cingria's aesthetic arguments. Stravinsky wrote to him: "What a beautiful book your *Petrarch*. I am reading it with infinite joy, not stopping for a moment—I like that. Thank you, dear friend, for having sent it and with such a flattering dedication."

[2] Vera's presence at this intimate service, which Stravinsky and his mother also attended, seems strange.

[3] Vera still smoked until her death (in her ninety-fourth year), and though Stravinsky did not smoke after December 1956, he repeatedly said that he continued to crave cigarettes.

[4] Vittorio Rieti, composer (b. 1898), husband of Elsie Rieti.

[5] Of *Jeu de cartes* with the Berlin Philharmonic (Telefunken).

[6] Charles Munch (1891–1968). See the correspondence for November 1939. In 1942 Munch conducted *Le Sacre du printemps* at the Paris Conservatory. When he became conductor of the Boston Symphony Orchestra, succeeding Koussevitzky, Henrietta Hirshman wrote to Stravinsky: "Dear, Beloved Igor Fyodorovich: For three days now I've been living the *Canticum Sacrum*, but only today did I learn that you are in New York conducting. I feel like flying to you, embracing you, and thanking you for such a wonderful creation. . . . Munch was so inspired by the *Canticum* that I am sure he will work on and conduct *Agon* with the same reverence and grace. I want very much for you to meet him, really meet him, not in a crowd. Tomorrow he will be going on tour with the Orchestra, and on Wednesday he will be conducting in New York. Perhaps you will still be there. He will be performing the *Canticum*. Would it be possible for him to call you? . . . He is staying in the Ambassador Hotel, next to you. . . . You should recognize *this*!" (November 10, 1957). The reference is to a picture of the Hotel Hemenway, Boston, in which the Stravinskys lived after their marriage in March 1940.

[7] By Darius Milhaud and Arthur Honegger, respectively.

[8] Daughter of the pianist Leopold Godowsky. The one-time screen partner of Rudolph Valentino, Dagmar pursued Stravinsky with serious intentions from the

May

1 Igor is ill. A visit from Arthur Lourié.   **3** To Igor.   **8** Lunch with Igor at the Café Weber.   **10** See *Perce neige* with Igor at 9, a disappointment. Dinner with him at the Marignan.   **12** Igor and I dine at Doucet.   **14** To the funeral of Alexander Yakovlev.   **15** Igor lunches with me and stays until 6 p.m. Tomorrow morning he goes to Brussels.   **18** Up at 6:30 to fetch Katya at Dr. Dreyfus'.   **21** Take kefir [buttermilk] to Dagmar Godowsky.[8]   **23** Go to Godowsky regarding money matters.   **25** See Katya in the morning.   **26** Igor tells me about the dinner invitation at Ida Rubinstein's, which I do not like at all.[9]   **29** Igor for lunch. Igor, Fred, and Ira here for dinner. Cinema with Igor.   **30** Igor and I go to the 25th anniversary concert of *Le Sacre du printemps*. The performance is very well conducted by Manuel Rosenthal.

June

6 With Igor at 9:30 p.m. to the Serenade rehearsal.[10]   **8** To the "Festival Stravinsky" concert at the Serenade.   **9** Visit from Struve.   **11** To the races at Auteuil. Tea at Mme Errazuriz's.   **12** Igor arrives at 7 and we dine at Fred's on the Avenue Mozart.   **16** Dinner at Misia's with Igor, Dali, Chanel.   **18** With Misia. Cercle Interallée (Club) with Igor, Dushkin, Fred, Willy Strecker.   **20** Igor comes, depressed, and we sit and read.   **21** Dinner with Igor and Casafuerte at the Bouteille d'Or.   **25** Go to a café with Igor.   **26** Igor is very depressed all day.

July

1 Dine with Igor at Doucet, then to a film.   **3** All day with Igor and dine with him at Doucet.   **6** Dinner with Igor and Suvchinsky.   **8** To Fouquet's with Fred and Marussia.   **9** With Georgette and Pearce Bailey to Viledo, where we meet Igor, Suvchinsky and Roland-Manuel.[11] We all go together to Montparnasse.   **10** Igor comes for lunch. Then we go to a movie and dine at Doucet.   **13** To the cinema with Igor.   **14** Igor calls Dr. Salmanov for me at 10:30 p.m.   **15** Igor comes but frightens me with the thought that I might have diphtheria.   **17** With Igor to a church service marking the 20th anniversary of the assassination of Tsar Nicholas II. Lunch with Igor at Doucet. Dinner at home with Igor and Fred.   **19** Dinner at the Lebolo restaurant with Igor, Fred, Casafuerte, and her daughter.   **24** All day with Igor. We lunch at La Coupole, see the movie *Les deux de Stade*, dine at Marignan, and walk along the quay.   **26** Listen with Igor to Verdi's *Falstaff* on the radio. Afterward with Igor, Valechka, Suvchinsky, and Guy.   **31** Go to Fontainebleau with Igor and Dushkin. Dinner at Montigny-sur-Loire.

---

time that she first met him in New York in 1935. She first wrote to Stravinsky on September 10, 1936, asking him to bring her a certain French perfume on his next trip to the United States. In April 1938 she was visiting some friends on board the S.S. *Britannia* leaving New York for Le Havre, failed to debark in time, and arrived in France with only her pocketbook for baggage. Whatever transpired in Paris when she called Stravinsky, he never revealed, but the letter (see below) from her, sent to him at the Palais des Beaux-Arts in Brussels, was mysteriously preserved in his 1938 scrapbook. Even more puzzling is his request to Vera to take money to Dagmar (Diary, May 23), even though Vera was not yet aware of his "incident" with the ex-movie star. In May 1939, when Dagmar was arranging concerts in America for Stravinsky and it was necessary for him to telephone her from Sancellemoz, he asked Vera to translate his several-page message into German for him, since Dagmar spoke no French. Here is Dagmar's letter to Igor, May 16, 1938, sent from the Hôtel Edouard VII, Paris, published with apologies, but no longer suppressible, since Stravinsky's children placed no restriction on the family archives in the Sacher Foundation (Basel): "But once in my life—my beloved one— have I felt such utter misery as today. To have you send me away, when all I care about is you. All my dreams, all my life means you. [This] is hard to bear. I understand your motive and will respect it, but . . . I don't see how I will carry the burden. It is sad to love someone to whom one is merely an incident. And it is really you to blame who made me feel as I do. Now it is too late. No matter what you do to me, it cannot alter the fact that it is you around whom my whole life revolves. And you send me away coldly, unfeelingly, with only one thought: not to complicate your life. I am not reproaching you, but only myself that I wasn't capable of making you care. . . . Nothing seems to be able to stop the terrible pain in my heart. D." (Original in English) Miss Godowsky's memoirs, *First Person Plural* (1959) infuriated Stravinsky when they appeared, but he never denied the truth of her anecdotes about himself, including the description of a scarcely believable dinner with Josef Hofmann in Rio de Janeiro in June 1936.

[9] Mme Rubinstein had invited Stravinsky to collaborate with Paul Claudel on a work that would have a part for her as a *récitante*.

[10] Stravinsky's rehearsal for the European premiere of his *Dumbarton Oaks* Concerto.

[11] Nom de plume of Alexis Manuel-Lévy, close friend of Stravinsky and ghost writer of the composer's *Poetics of Music*.

August

2 For dinner here: Igor, Valechka, and Ira, who tells us about London. **4** Dinner with Igor at the Café Marignan. **7** At 8 p.m. meet Igor and Beliankin, then drive to the Grande Taverne, and later, at Fouquet's. **9** Visit from Marina Heiden.[1] **10** Lunch with Igor in two restaurants on the Boulevard Saint-Germain. **12** To Fontainebleau with Igor and Dushkin. **18** For dinner here: Igor, Ira, and Fred. **20** Igor and Suvchinsky for tea. **23** Cinema with Igor and Beliankins. **24** For dinner here: Igor, Marcelle Meyer, Carlo de Vieto, Ira. **26** Dinner at Nadia Boulanger's with Angelica Ocampo. **28** Igor at 3 p.m. and dinner with him and the Dushkins. **29** We spend the day at Antwerp and the night at the Queen's Hotel. **31** Dinner with Igor, then to the Cinema Rex.

September

1 Igor and Fred at 5 p.m. We go to a Leni Riefenstahl film. Dine with Igor at Doucet. **11** All day with Igor, dinner with him, then to the cinema. **14** Dinner at Ira's with Igor and Tchelichev. **16** Igor and Valechka for dinner at my house. **22** Dinner at Ira's with Eugene Berman.[2] **24** Prokofiev here for lunch; we work together. **26** Hitler's speech. **27** We listen apprehensively to Chamberlain's speech. **28** Many people leave Paris in a panic. Fred comes tomorrow from Germany, which is a bad sign. **29** Fred arrives by plane in the evening.

October

2 Igor comes at 6. Nothing is going well at his house. Dinner with him and Fred. **9** For tea here: Igor, Ira, Fred, Dushkins. At Fouquet's, then with Igor to the film *Amanda* (Ginger Rogers, Fred Astaire). **14** Dinner at the Plaza-Athénée with Igor and Victoria Ocampo. **15** For dinner here: Igor, Yvonne Casafuerte, Rieti, Valechka, and Ira. **16** All day with Igor, then with him to the cinema. **19** Go to Mme Schreiber to be paid.[3] Arthur Lourié for lunch. Igor puts Dr. Salmanov in charge of Mika's tuberculosis. To a café with Igor, Ira, and Olga. **23** Lovely day. Walk in the Bois and lunch with Igor. He stays all day and in the evening we go to the cinema and dine at Café Weber. **24** Early dinner at Café Weber with Igor. **30** Go with Igor to *Paris-Soir*, then dinner at Marignan. **31** We go to see the Spanish church, Ste. Thérèse.

November

3 Dinner with Igor. **6** Lunch with Igor at Doucet, then with him to the cinema and dinner at Café Weber. **8** For dinner here: Igor, Victoria Ocampo, Roland-Manuel, Cingria. **10** With Igor at Cercle Interalliée, where we see Alexandra [Duchess of] Leuchtenberg. **12** Dinner with Igor, then to visit Fedya. **13** With Igor from 3 p.m. until evening. We dine at Marly, which he likes very much. **18** Walk in the Bois. Igor dines with me. **20** Tea, dinner, and cinema with Igor. **21** I meet Igor at Weber's. He is very upset. **22** Prepare brilliantine for Igor: he leaves

---

for Rome at 7 p.m. **28** Igor in the Excelsior Hotel in Rome. **29** Igor's Rome concert, then Turin. **30** Mika dies at 5 a.m.; I go to get the priest. I meet Igor's train at 10:25 p.m., and spend the rest of the evening at Païchadze's.[4]

December

2 Mika's funeral. I go to the cemetery with Masha and Olga, and, on the return, to Ira's. Svetik comes there. **3** All day sad, alone. **4** Igor comes at 3 p.m. and I try to distract him as much as I can. We go to Ira's, and stay for dinner. Igor phones at 11 p.m. to say that Katya has a high fever. Ira goes to her. **11** The doctors advise Katya to go to Pau. **15** For dinner here: Igor, Angelica, Ira, Fred. **17** Dinner at Prunier with Igor, Valechka, Ira. **18** Igor does not come because he has difficulties with Yuri Mandelstamm. **24** Christmas tree in my house. Igor brings wine. **25** Igor gives me money for food. **26** Take Igor to the train for Turin. **29** I listen to Igor's Turin concert on the radio at Casafuerte's. **30** Igor returns from Turin on the 7:15 train. We go to the Café Louvre. Meet Suvchinsky. Svetik plays on the radio with Marcelle Meyer. We listen at Suvchinsky's. **31** Igor, Ira, and Fred for dinner.

Vera to Igor

Monsieur Igor Stravinsky
c/o Richard Copley
113 West 57th Street
New York City
[Forwarded to:
Sulgrave Hotel
60 East 67th Street]   September 26, 1939

Igor, my dearest, my beloved Bubushkin, This is my first letter to you.[5] On the day after you left,[6] I could not write, feeling even sadder than on the day of your departure, and with thoughts as dark as that railroad station. I slept very badly in the empty, forsaken bed. When I got up I decided to keep very busy, putting things in order, scrubbing, and laundering. I telephoned the steamship company and asked the location of the *Manhattan*. They laughed at me, saying, "The ship has other things to do than to broadcast its course to the whole world." Until you reach America, therefore, I will not know anything. I am sorry that I did not give you some little memento. In the evening I read Andersen's fairy tales and became totally depressed.

The next day, Saturday the 23rd, Svetik and Madubo[7] came to lunch with me. It was Svetik's birthday and I bought a bottle of cognac that he and I almost finished, sitting at the table until five

---

[1] Vera continued to see the Countess Heiden after World War II. She lived at 7, rue Christophe-Colomb, Paris.

[2] Eugene Berman (1899–1973) was to become a member of the Russian branch of the Stravinsky inner sanctum, along with Balanchine and Nabokov, though perhaps "Russian" is redundant, since only Russians could have comprehended much of Stravinsky's mind and character. On December 7, 1942, Stravinsky sent a design by Berman to Associated Music Publishers saying, "I want it to be used as a trademark on the cover of all my works published by you. . . . Mr. Berman has generously dedicated and presented the design to me."

[3] See Vera's letter to her in the diary, August 19, 1940.

[4] In a note to Stravinsky, November 30, 1958, Nadia Boulanger recalls the scene a day or so before the death: "Mika motionless, Catherine on her knees, Kitty calling 'mama'—they are there until now, as always, but even closer."

[5] The correspondence is in Russian except where otherwise specified. All of Vera's letters were sent from the 31, rue de l'Assomption address.

[6] From the second week in June 1939 to the declaration of war ten weeks later, Vera and Igor lived in Sancellemoz, where he completed the second movement of his Symphony in C. The couple returned to Paris at the beginning of September, and on the 5th, Stravinsky cancelled the lease on his Faubourg Saint-Honoré apartment (due to expire October 1, 1940) with the payment of 24,200 francs. He immediately moved to 7, rue Antoine-Chantin, but because of the almost nightly air-raid alerts requiring Parisians to go to cellars and shelters, Vera convinced him to spend the two weeks before his departure for America in Nadia Boulanger's country house in Gargenville. He had wanted to cancel his American engagements and remain in France, but Vera helped him to change his mind, and

on September 21, he left Paris for Bordeaux, accompanied on the train by Katherine Wolff, the sister of Blair Fairchild and Nadia Boulanger's assistant, who was returning to Philadelphia. Because of the great demand for space on the neutral American steamer, the S.S. *Manhattan*, embarkation was slow and the ship did not sail until the 25th. Stravinsky had to share a cabin with four other men. (One of them, a Mr. Brooks, Stravinsky saw again, in Cleveland, in January 1947.) Toscanini preferred to pace the decks and to sleep in the ship's lounge. (See Vera's letter of October 4.) The boat docked in New York on September 30.

[7] Mina Svitalski (1892–1956), governess to Stravinsky's children. In *Catherine and Igor Stravinsky: A Family Album* op. cit., Theodore Stravinsky writes that after the death of the governess Bertha Essert, in April 1917, the Stravinsky home was "a sad place, until Mina Svitalski came to us as governess." Actually, Mlle Svitalski had been employed by the Stravinskys since March 29, 1916. (Catherine wrote to Igor, March 18, 1936: " I would like to do something at the end of the month for the twentieth anniversary of Madubo's service with our family—I believe the date is the 29th.") Theodore goes on to claim that Mlle Svitalski "was to stay the rest of her life with one or the other of us," though for five of her seven years in America, she did not live with any member of the Stravinsky family. (Stravinsky wrote to Edouard Svitalski, October 27, 1953: "When my daughter and her husband came to live in Los Angeles in 1947, I asked your sister if she would also like to transplant herself. . . . Her experience here proved to be negative. For one thing, her life, first in my daughter's house and then in my son's, was contraindicated by everyone involved. . . . She continued to see as 'the children' people who had grown up and were married. From 1949, therefore, she lived alone and earned her living as a dressmaker, quickly attracting a devoted clientele.") Mlle Svitalski also did not stay with "one or the other" of the Stravinskys after returning to Switzerland (March 1954) but lived with her brother. (In the early 1950s, R.C. spent many illuminating hours listening to her invaluable recollections and insights about Stravinsky.)

in the afternoon. I had a hangover, but not an unpleasant one, and the rest of the day slipped by unnoticed.

I bought a radio "on approval" but sent it back because of the irritating way that it made voices sound—as if they were coming from a barrel. Nevertheless, it was very strange in the evening to hear German reports: *Der Polnische Krieg ist beendet* [the Polish war is over]—unbelievable! I felt like asking the speaker, "Is that all?" I must find a second-hand radio on sale because these reports are now very interesting.

Sunday was depressing. I felt very tired and spent almost all day in bed reading the newspapers and rereading old letters. A letter came from Victoria Ocampo—only seven days from Buenos Aires—asking for our news: "Tell me your plans and whether or not I can help you. Make use of me. I embrace you both." I will write to her immediately. Did you take her address: Elisalde 28–47?

Yesterday, Monday, was a good day. To begin with, I woke up feeling energetic, and then came your card from Bordeaux, cheering me tremendously. I immediately telephoned Svetik about it and wrote to Milene[1] and to Fedya. By the way, Milene writes me almost every day. She is doing well, and her temperature is normal.

A letter came from Kall.[2] To judge by it, he seems to be sympathetic and kind, so I'm glad that you are with him. The letter was typewritten; he says, touchingly, that he is practicing his typing to be worthy of being a secretary to Stravinsky.

I think constantly about your voyage. How did you manage with five people in the cabin? How was the sea? I wanted to warn you that you would probably be forced to do the emergency drills. And how did you make out with the gadget for the pear? I so hope that the sea weather was good. We had wonderful sunshine here, just like last year at this time when I wrote in my diary: "Peace, sunshine—what happiness!" When will I continue this letter . . .?

Yesterday, Monday, was a good day. Unexpectedly, the morning was spent in the *Mairie* of the XVth *arrondissement*. The night before, Katya Kessel phoned that she urgently needed three witnesses for her birth certificate. She is marrying Kessel, who in a few days leaves for the front as a correspondent. The witnesses had to be Russian, and as I am a Georgian citizen, I could not be one. I proved to be a good manager, however, and within an hour arrived at the *Mairie* with Suvchinsky, Fred, and Marussia Kugulskaya. For that, we will be treated in a few days to a good lunch.

Having been busy in the morning with someone else's birth certificate, I decided to occupy myself in the afternoon with my own. I went to the Ministry for my papers, paid seventy-five francs, and was promised them in three days. Incidentally, Katya Kessel will give me the name of a good lawyer, a specialist in divorce. I saw Misia in the street in front of the Ministry, very smart in a white coat, but with gray eyebrows. I walked from the Ministry to Argutinsky's to find out Valechka's address. (Several people were there, Alexandre Benois, Hirshman,[3] and others.) To my great surprise, Argutinsky said that Valechka lives at 51, Avenue Marceau. "In Saint-Honoré-les-Bains?" I asked, and he answered, "No, in Paris." Think only! Valechka has been sitting in Paris all this time and nobody knew it! I immediately jumped into a taxi and went to 51, Avenue Marceau. His apartment is small but beautifully furnished. He was sitting in a dressing gown, with Trubnikov and someone else. My voice was choking with indignation when I asked why he had not given us a sign of life

and did not even bid you good-bye before your departure. At first he looked peeved and then called us all idiots. What do you say to that? I was beside myself. As for the air-raid alerts, he said that he has not heard any. I did not reply that this means he must have become totally deaf.

I am going to the post office now to find out when the Atlantic Clipper leaves. I do not even know how to embrace you, my dearest, so that you would feel how I am thinking of you. I send you all my love and thoughts. May God bless you. Vera.

Vera to Igor
(Original in French)

Monsieur Igor Stravinsky   Wednesday, September 27, 1939
c/o Richard Copley   [Postcard]
113 West 57th Street
New York City

My dear Igor, Yesterday I sent you an airmail letter, but it will not leave Lisbon until October 3. I am writing this card (the first one) with no idea of boat schedules or on which liner it will go. Yesterday I had dinner at Nini's and spent a very charming evening with him. He had just received a letter from Theodore and Denise, who are well and who asked him to send them several things. He spends a great deal of time with Françaix[4] at his home in the country. Milene writes to me almost every day, and she is well. I saw her paintings at Nini's and was delighted by a very beautiful portrait. I had to take a taxi to return from Nini's, this being the only transportation available in the blackout.

I learned that the *Manhattan* finally left and is now riding the waves. I think constantly about your trip. Elsie Rieti returned from Bordeaux, where she had accompanied some friends to another boat. Having been refused permission to join her husband and son at Cannes, she will remain in Paris for the moment.

Nini does not have to present himself [for mobilization] until the 15th of October, unless he receives a written order for another date. Meanwhile he is taking piano lessons and working intensively with Isidor Philipp. The cold weather is beginning; we fear that the winter will be unbearable, which is all that we needed. I await news of your arrival with scarcely controllable impatience, and I send you all my thoughts and embrace you. Vera.

Vera to Igor
(Original in French)

Monsieur Igor Stravinsky   September 29, 1939
c/o Richard Copley   [Postcard]
113 West 57th Street
New York City

My dear Igor, The wind is blowing fiercely here, and since it is from the north, I fear that your crossing was not restful. I am counting the days until I receive your cable. I have not yet started to put my house in order, which is my only occupation at present. Ira goes to dinner from time to time at Jouvet's[5] and will soon have work in films. The stores are open and the women are beginning to make their hats and dresses. We have had two or three alerts, when everyone takes cover. Today at 11:30 a brief—40-minute—alert sounded just as I was dressing for a lunch with Antonini.[6] At her house I was shown a photograph of Kall taken in America by Mme Borovsky. Now I know what I am reminded of

---

[1] Milene was in the same tuberculosis sanatorium in Sancellemoz where her father had been and, before him, her mother and sister.

[2] Dr. Alexis Kall, classmate of Stravinsky's in the University of St. Petersburg Law School. Kall was living in Los Angeles in 1935 when Stravinsky first visited the city. The composer employed him as a secretary and translator during the winter of 1939–40, while lecturing and teaching at Harvard.

[3] Possibly the husband of Henrietta Hirshman. (See Vera's diary, January 8, 1922.)

[4] Jean Françaix (b. 1912), French composer.

[5] Louis Jouvet, the actor, was an intimate friend of Ira's.

[6] Mussia Antonini was a Russian friend of Vera's who had married an Italian count.

by this big "Woof."[1] Tomorrow, for my name day, I am having the Suvchinskys, Nini, and Madubo to dinner. Milene is well; Dr. Tobé is pleased and the treatment has been successful. She now has her radio. Do not forget to write to me the dates on which you receive my two cards and my letter. (This is my second card.) I embrace you with all my heart. Vera.

Vera to Igor

Letter No. 2
Monsieur Igor Stravinsky
c/o Richard Copley
113 West 57th Street
New York City
[forwarded to:
Sulgrave Hotel
60 East 67th Street]   October 1, 1939

My beloved little one, my dearest, I think and think about you but still cannot picture you on your trip. What is your mood? Thank God if it is not a bad one. You did well to leave, but I do not want to imply by this that conditions here are very hard. On the contrary, it is so quiet and peaceful that I ask myself: "Where is the war?" If it should flare up, however, you would not know what to do and would not wish to remain in Paris. And life in the provinces, so I hear, is difficult. Provincial people are prone to panic, and in the absence of newspapers, God only knows what is being invented and imagined in the country. Everyone able to return to Paris is doing so for the sake of its calm atmosphere, as well as to rest. The government is not pleased about this, it seems, so these people are being asked to leave.

Yesterday, my name day, I had the Suvchinskys, Svetik, Madubo, and Fred. During the day several friends came with candies and cakes, but not Ira who, of course, forgot. I had invited her for dinner without telling her the occasion, but she had a previous engagement. The weather was sunny, beautiful, and warm, and I thought about the year before. The best present for me would be a cable from you announcing your arrival in the USA, but the voyage will probably take eight to ten days.

I received another present, this one from the Ministry of Foreign Affairs: my birth certificate with all required seals and signatures. I will make an appointment tomorrow with a divorce lawyer. Katya Kessel, whose divorce was exceptionally complicated, said that everyone warned her it would take at least five years. Actually it was arranged in eight months.

Olga Sallard is returning to Paris and will stay with me. Her husband was called up, and since her government allowance could not be paid in Tours, she is coming here. We will sew and occupy ourselves with household tasks. What would I do if I had been stuck in some province? Here, if I feel depressed in the evening, I start to empty my cupboards, burrowing in them like a mouse, and thus pass the time.

I do not know why, but Fred always leaves immediately after dinner, sometimes even before nine o'clock. If I have no other guests, I am left alone, which can be dispiriting, since I don't like to go to bed before eleven or twelve o'clock. Fred's mood is low because he has not heard from [Marcel] Boussac.

I just heard a knock on the door—the concierge bringing me your cable, which has made me so happy. I'll tell all of our friends about it, and I am going to run to the post office immediately to send you a few lines. Please advise Copley that the cable will not have your name on it. Using a cable address costs only 38 francs, and therefore I will be able to send you one every week. I embrace you, dearest, and miss you very, very intensely. Your wire brought joy to my heart. Your Vera.

[1] "Stravinsky referred to Kall as 'Woof,' as we all did then, because of his comical way of saying 'woof' when he wanted something or just wanted to exclaim—as when he caught his breath after climbing the two flights to reach the top floor at Gerry's Landing where he and Stravinsky had their rooms." (Letter to R.C. from Elliot Forbes, November 15, 1981.)

[2] Ira lived in Vera's apartment for a time after she went to America.

Vera to Igor

Richard Copley   October 1, 1939
113 West 57th Street, Suite 1222   [cable]
New York City

All is well   Vera.

Vera to Igor

Letter No. 3
Monsieur Igor Stravinsky
c/o Richard Copley
113 West 57th Street
New York City   October 4, 1939

My dearest, dearest, Receiving your cable gave me such tremendous happiness that I am still living on it. I wonder when I will have your first letter? How complicated! What will we do if the Clipper stops flying in the winter? I am reconstructing the details of your trip from your postcard and from newspaper reports. The voyage of the Manhattan was reported in Le Jour, but most of the space was devoted to a description of how Toscanini ran about on the decks during the night in a fury. I am impatient to hear more.

I continue to work, putting the apartment in order. Madubo went through all of the boxes. Only a few torn towels and two sheets, which we will never see again, will remain for Ira.[2] Madubo guards everything like a Cerberus. Last night we all had dinner in Suvchinsky's kitchen: a cozy evening, eating, drinking, and enjoying animated discussions. But to return through the dark streets is spooky; the Métro and the buses stop running early, and at a late hour practically no taxis are available.

Sergei Nabokov,[3] whom I knew in the Crimea, was at Suvchinsky's. He is the son of the Nabokov who was assassinated.[4] He studied at Cambridge and is giving English lessons here. I made an agreement with him, and he promised me that I will be able to converse in English by spring. Today I had the first lesson, which was very tiring because he made me talk a lot. I like the work, since it makes me feel closer to the day of my departure.

I also went to see the lawyer. Everyone says he is very good, but I fear that he will charge a lot. Just how much, he will tell me the next time I see him, but, in any case, he promises to obtain my divorce in two months. According to French law, the announcement of intent must be published in an official paper ten months before marriage, in order to give time to anyone who wishes to oppose it. He does not know if a similar law exists in America and asked me to find out. When you have a chance, please ask about this. Also, should I come with a divorce paper dated about Christmastime, and do I have to wait before marrying again, or does America have such laws?

I have been very depressed these last two days and have been picking on Olga—who is staying with me—and especially on Fred; everything irritates me, but, above all, being obliged to cook. I do not know what put me in this mood. Perhaps it is because I was told that I would not be permitted to leave France, thanks to a new law. But no law exists that cannot be circumvented. I should begin working toward my goal quite soon—after Christmas, let us say. Some pessimists are surprised that I make precise plans for the future, as if the war had not happened and there were no dangers, but this is the only way that I can live and also keep my sanity. When I look at the people from the provinces and see how anxious and miserable they are, I feel happy merely to be in Paris.

[3] See Vera's diary, May 20, 1931. Sergei, brother of the yet-uncelebrated Vladimir Nabokov, committed suicide shortly after Vera went to America. She is identifying him for Stravinsky because the only Nabokov he knew at this time was Nicolas, Sergei's cousin.

[4] Sergei and Vladimir Nabokov's father was shot in the street in Berlin in 1922.

A postcard just came from Marcelle Meyer, in Rennes, where she has settled. The Paris radio station has been evacuated there and she will play three times a week on it. She is terribly unhappy about this move and begs me to come to visit her, but unless we have trouble here, I don't think I'll go. Fedya wrote to Madubo asking her to visit them, and also to invite me or Svetik. They must be bored. Milene, who feels very well, is annoyed that the sanatorium has reduced the living space and is relocating all of the patients on the first floor. This means that she won't have a balcony with flowers. Since most of the patients are gone, she is lonely and bored. I would like to visit her, but, Sancellemoz being in the war zone, I am afraid I will not be able to get a permit.

This letter will go by Clipper, but not until six days from now. Even so, I must mail it immediately. It will be delayed two more days by the censor and will take another three to reach Lisbon, before crossing the Atlantic.

My little one, my beloved, may God protect you. I am dreaming of coming to you and only hope that all goes well. Today's newspapers sounded optimistic, and immediately I started to hope for the end of the war. Oh! If only this would come true! I embrace and kiss you with deepest love and tenderly, tenderly. Your Vera.

Vera to Igor

Letter No. 4
Monsieur Igor Stravinsky
c/o Richard Copley
113 West 57th Street
New York City

October 10, 1939
(This letter was sent by boat. The last, No. 3, was sent by Clipper.)

My dearest Igor, my beloved, I am writing to you in a void, so to speak, since I never know when and with which boat the letter will go: everything is kept secret. I know only that the Clipper leaves from Lisbon on Tuesdays, that Paris to Lisbon takes three days, and that censoring takes two more. From day to day, I expect a letter from you.

Here we are, only at the beginning of October, and yet I look at the calendar thinking that time is not moving. I am usually occupied all day and time flies. I keep myself busy making order—this work calms me—yet I seem unable to accomplish anything. The big cluster of bottles near the cupboard is still there, but I finally moved the mirror, placing it on a small dressing table next to the fireplace. I try to make things cozy and to forget the war, but the thought of it is always there, spoiling everything. I also try to become accustomed to the sirens of the air-raid alerts. While I wash my hair I think, ''What if it starts now? Will I go to the cellar with wet hair?''

Everyone hurries in the Métro, hoping not to get stuck for hours between stations. That happened a few days ago, and a panic occurred, in spite of an announcement that the electric power was cut off, and that we could walk out through the tunnel to the next shelter. No one dared to do it, fearing electrocution. Now the papers have given notice that the trains will continue to the next station. The words ''alert'' and ''shelter'' have been incorporated into Russian émigré language.

The cold weather has started, but the house is without heat, and we do not know when and if the owner will provide it. We were waiting for a government regulation, but now it seems that the matter is to be decided by agreement between owners and tenants. In some houses, where conscription has left many apartments unoccupied, the owners simply do not want to heat half-empty buildings.

I think of you and wonder whether you could endure the hardships here. Most people are freezing and catching colds. I have found a stove and, for fuel, am making little rolls of newspapers, which I soak for several hours, then roll them up and let them dry well. They seem to be very effective, also in my fireplace. I am describing a wartime existence for you.

I saw Mme Rieti yesterday. She told me about a ship that sailed from Bordeaux for New York, on which, at the last minute, all non-

American passengers were ordered ashore, even though they had paid for their tickets. After waiting in Bordeaux for ten days, these people were permitted to sail on the S.S. *Washington.* I think Mme Rieti will go to America after Christmas.

My lawyer wants to try a different approach from the one he first proposed, which would have been costly and taken a long time. I may need a copy of Sudeikin's divorce from Olga, which was only a church divorce. Kramer has a copy of it, but that s.o.b. is hiding behind the skirts of Tulina and cannot be reached.

I have more guests now than before the war, most of whom come for lunch or dinner. Today, Olga Sallard and Olga Sudeikina will be here for lunch, tomorrow, Svetik, Suvchinsky, and Madubo for dinner. Ira asked me to invite her father and Ganya for dinner and even offered to pay me for it. They are rarely asked out, but Ira herself often goes to Maxim's and other expensive places.

I would so like to know the details of your trip. How are you feeling? I think so often about your health. I hope you did not catch cold on the boat. The news from Milene is very good: she has started going for walks. Also good news from Fedya, but I think he is bored, for what reason I don't know. I am not bored, since I am always busy, but I feel depressed in the evenings and am sleeping less well than usual. I often wake up in the middle of the night, and any night thoughts are likely to be gloomy ones. My little one, we will have to wait through so many days and nights. Courage, courage! We will achieve our goal. I kiss you tenderly. May God bless you. All my love, your Vera.

Vera to Igor

Richard Copley
113 West 57th Street
New York City

October 13, 1939
[cable]

Letter received   All is well   Vera.

Vera to Igor

Letter No. 5
Monsieur Igor Stravinsky
c/o Mr. Edw. Forbes
Gerry's Landing
Cambridge, Mass.

Sunday, October 15, 1939

My precious, Suddenly I feel so sad. And a long winter looms ahead, like a huge mountain that must be crossed. I should not complain, though, since I am busy all the time, which saves me. But this also means that I have a lot of people milling around for lunch, dinner, and tea, which costs me money. Today I expect the Beliankins (without Ira) for lunch, along with Madubo, who will probably be very sad: Svetik has been drafted; he left this very morning for Nevers. I did not write to you about it before, since it happened so quickly. On Sunday he received orders to present himself at the barracks in Nevers, where he will probably have to spend several months (seven or eight, I think) in basic military training. Fedya wanted to come here for one day to see him, but telephoned that he could not get permission.

Fedya and Denise want to come to Paris next week to spend a few days. They are bored, I suspect, and want to move. They also want to take Madubo back with them, but she does not want to go, and I think she is right. Someone should stay in the Paris apartment, where all letters, requests, and other business affairs are directed. Things are continually arriving there to be sent on to Milene or Svetik. Moreover, Svetik ought to have a place to go to when he has leaves of absence. If Madubo is away in the provinces, he would have a very difficult time getting to her and back. Above all, though, I think Madubo feels that she is not wanted for moral support but rather to cook and to keep house for Denise, who would like to turn her own attention to business affairs. Only yesterday Svetik said he thought it would be better for all of us if Madubo were to stay in Paris, at least for the

present. Besides, she is in a nervous state and should stay at home resting, mending the linen, knitting, and whiling away the time until Svetik's first leave.

I had Tara all day yesterday. He vacuumed, polished the floors, and seemed to be pleased with the work. I made *cassoulet toulousain* for lunch—for which, beside Tara, I had Olga Sallard, Fred, and Carlo di Vieto (the husband of Marcelle Meyer). Many clients came during the day and, unexpectedly, I took in 150 francs. Now I must either prepare new products or close the shop.

I am concentrating on my English studies and no doubt am making progress. My teacher promises me that by spring I will be speaking fluently. My lawyer wants to prove that my marriage was unconsummated, which is correct, and he will obtain an identity card for me in my maiden name, which would be ideal. I have not discussed the cost of this with him yet, since he only comes to Paris three times a week and I see him rarely. But I know him to be a serious man and not like the incompetent Kramer.

Since I want to send this letter by the Clipper, I must stop now. My Bubushkinsky, I kiss you with greatest tenderness. Having received your first letter, I look forward to more joys. The diary you kept on the *Manhattan* has not yet come. I send you all my loving thoughts and embrace you. God be with you. Your Vera.

I forgot to tell you that Svetik seems very vigorous and happy.

Vera to Igor
(Original in French)

Letter No. 6
Monsieur Igor Stravinsky
c/o Richard Copley
113 West 57th Street
New York City   October 19, 1939

My very dear Igor, Perhaps I am guilty of a stupidity. I was told that I could write my letters in Russian and did so, but perhaps for this reason they have been held up. I have already sent five letters with the Clipper—this is the sixth—two cables, and several postcards in French. I received your second letter, dated October 6, which took ten days.

Kall's illness is unfortunate, but I hope that by this time everything has been taken care of and that you are already in Cambridge. What is the date of your first lecture? [October 18] I so much want to have news about it immediately.

Nini, who left on Sunday, has already written that he sleeps under a tent and that everyone is very nice to him. He will not stay at Nevers but will be transferred to another barracks, perhaps at Bourges; I do not know as yet. Madubo often visits me and during the entire day knits all sorts of things for Nini—as I do, having begun with socks. Olga Sallard also stays with me for two or three days at a time and helps me with the housekeeping, since I continue to have many people for lunches and dinners. This is agreeable, both because it hides my loneliness a bit, and because to be surrounded by friends during this anxious time is good; but from the financial side the cost of food begins to count, even though I invent very economical dishes (often just *kasha* and fruit).

I am pursuing the question of my papers very energetically. You cannot imagine how much time is consumed filling out all of the separate forms. But the goal, my departure to come to you, is all that counts. I think of nothing else, and it is the meaning of my life. The rest is so sad.

Milene writes to me almost every day, and I write frequently, too. Today I have warm linen shirts to send her; Madubo bought them, and if Milene begins to paint, they will be very useful to her. Theodore and Denise wanted to come to Paris to see Nini but did not receive their "safe conduct." They will come one of these days to see Madubo and to try to take her with them to Le Mans. But she refuses to go, and it would be truly idiotic if she went there. Someone must establish a home base here in Paris. Milene

writes asking her to send this or that, and Nini, too. Yesterday, for instance, Madubo had letters from Bedel that have to be answered. Once at Le Mans, it would be very difficult to return to Paris, special permission being required for each occasion. And when Nini is able to rest a few days in Paris, where would he go?

The orchestra parts for *Jeu de cartes* and the two Tchaikovsky symphonies should be here with me. If not, Nini will write and tell me where to find them. For the moment, I do not know of anyone who could bring them; besides, the package would be very heavy. Perhaps Nadia might have someone, but I do not know where she is. No one answers the telephone at Gargenville or at the rue Ballu.

I am notifying you in advance that my next cable will not be signed "Vera" but "Sudeikina" as this is now the law: all cables must be signed with the family name. This will seem less intimate, but what can I do?

I am on my way to the Office of Georgian Refugees for my papers—am expected there in twenty minutes—and after that to the Ministry, the Prefecture, and my lawyer: you see the work.

I embrace you with all my heart and wish you the greatest success at Cambridge. Make a great stride for us. We are managing very well in spite of everything. I embrace you again and again. Your Vera.

Marcelle Meyer played *Petrushka* on the radio yesterday. She writes to me regularly and always sends her best wishes to you. Her husband is in Paris and often comes to see me.

Vera to Igor
(Original in French)

Letter No. 7
Monsieur Igor Stravinsky
c/o Richard Copley
113 West 57th Street
New York City   Saturday, October 21, 1939

My dear Igor, What joy to have your news again! Yesterday I received your third letter, together with your *Manhattan* diary. I was so happy. I think and think of you and try to imagine myself with you and Kall in Cambridge. How was the first lecture? That interests me enormously. And your health and mood? I imagine that Kall makes good coffee for you—I do not know why: is this his speciality, perhaps? Thursday will be exactly a month since you left, and I keep recalling all of the details, the gloomy railroad station and returning to my apartment alone. A month has already passed—six more to go, if only I can leave at the end of April. I dread to think of all the difficulties.

A new law for foreigners forbids them—and all women, as well—to leave France. But I hope that in three months this will change, and that after appealing on all sides, we will finally obtain permission. There are always exceptions, especially if the reason is a good one.

In this letter I want to ask you to begin taking certain steps. In order to be absolutely certain that my papers are all that is required, please talk to a lawyer. After receiving Kall's advice in your letter yesterday, I immediately stopped my lawyer here from continuing what he had begun—which angered him, since he will not receive some 3000 additional francs. Precisely to avoid this expense, I want to know as soon as possible if my papers are sufficient for America. I have my birth certificate from the Georgian government, legalized at the Ministry. Before going to America, I think I must have this translated and notarized at the American Consulate.

Like all foreigners, I must change my identity card, even if it has not expired, but those under the letter "S" will have their turn only after Christmas, and perhaps not until February. Will I be able to get a passport without the new card? There are instructions with the card. My lawyer wants me to use my maiden name, but this strikes me as too complicated in view of the amount of time that remains. How can I be assured that the passport will take two or three months and not, as I fear, an entire year? An affirmative answer from you (after you have been advised by someone who knows the law) will give me a little peace of mind. After Christmas, toward February, you should ask Mrs. [Robert Woods] Bliss to write from there for my visa, and if not her, someone else very important. Should Nadia write to her first? How do you see the matter? I am talking about it already because I see how everything drags and how each letter and each step takes so much time.

Madubo was here for lunch yesterday. She spent the whole afternoon knitting socks for Nini. Also, she brought me two letters for you, which I opened. One, from Forbes, dated September 26, was sent to 25, rue du Faubourg Saint-Honoré. What idiocy.[1] The other, from Mrs. Bliss, contained the special program for you of May 8, 1938,[2] which they had neglected to send. The letter was typed—by a secretary, I suppose—and Mrs. Bliss wrote, in ink, at the end: "We will re-open Dumbarton Oaks October 10 and are absolutely counting on your visit."[3] To forward these two letters would not be worthwhile, so I'll keep them.

I am beginning to feel the cold. Since the house is not heated, I have talked to the landlord about deducting the cost of the heat. He sent me his terms, and do you know that for three months without heat he allowed me a ridiculous 125 francs?

Today I am also writing to Victoria Ocampo; and to Nini, to ask him where I can find *Jeu de cartes* and the Tchaikovsky symphonies. I'll tell him what you said. He is to have his lungs x-rayed and to be inoculated against typhoid, tetanus, etc., before having a general medical examination. Milene is perfectly well, walking outside, and painting.

Tomorrow I have the Rietis for lunch. Olga Sallard comes for two or three days, as she does every week. Ira, still without a job, is becoming sullen, but as the cinemas and theaters are reopening, I am certain that she will succeed. Simply to keep busy, she asked to work in a canteen, but was told that no Russians are employed. Such things are very painful for us. Russians are refused everywhere.[4]

I wait impatiently for your answer to the question that interests me above all. I embrace you with all my heart and with the greatest tenderness. Your Vera.

Best thoughts to Kall, and, if you see Sam [Dushkin], give him my regards and thank him for his *pripiska*.

Here is the information on my birth certificate:
Office of Georgian Refugees
Certificate
This office for Georgian Refugees certifies that Mme Vera Sudeikina, born Bosset, of Georgian origins,[5] residing in Paris, 31, rue de l'Assomption, was born 25/XII/1892 in Petrograd. Her parents are Arthur Bosset and Henriette Bosset, born Malmgren. The present certificate was delivered to Mme Vera Sudeikina, born Bosset, replacing the document that she is unable to procure, given the present situation in the country of her birth.
The Director of the Office
Assathiany[6]

Vera to Igor
(Original in French)

Opened by the censor.
Letter No. 8
Monsieur Igor Stravinsky
c/o Edw. Forbes
Gerry's Landing
Cambridge, Mass.   Thursday, October 26, 1939

Igor, my dear, what joy to have your letters! I have just received the one of October 17, sent the day before your first lecture. That the letters take so long to come—mine, I mean—is heartbreaking. I see from yours of the 13th that you do not yet have any of my postcards or my third letter, sent by Clipper on October 5. I won't send any more cards; they go too slowly by boat.

Last Sunday, the 22nd, I had Theodore and Denise all day. They came to Paris for several days and for various reasons: to see what is happening in the apartment, Madubo, the bank, etc. Madubo successfully explained why she does not want to leave Paris. Theodore has a re-examination for the army next week. He looks well, if a little thinner. He and Denise are bored in Le Mans; at least this is my impression, but I never understood their reasons for choosing that city, and why they do not stay in Paris. Since the Le Mans area has no caves, people must go into the fields during the air-raid alerts. The prices of things are a bit less there than here, but nothing is cheap anywhere now, and little by little everything goes up.

I spent the whole of yesterday looking for a good down-filled sleeping bag for Nini, found one for 360 francs at the Hôtel de Ville, and have already sent it. He wrote that he is suffering from the cold. Madubo sends him underwear, socks, and all sorts of warm things. If she were not here, who would have done this? I am less aware of his measurements and of what he needs. Milene will send him some warm shirts. She is well, painting, and taking outdoor walks. Dr. Tobé is pleased with her progress.

The Suvchinskys invited Fred and me for dinner yesterday. Saturday they will come here to dine. Tomorrow I will have Madubo and Olga Sallard: I continue to feed people practically every day. One of these evenings, Valechka will come for dinner, on condition that I find a taxi for him. He has become very old and deaf. I went to his apartment for tea. It is in a hotel of small, but luxurious, furnished apartments, and he is very well situated there. The Ritz is completely full. Everyone has moved into hotels, to save money and to avoid the difficulty of heating homes. The cellar of the Ritz is splendid, lined with silk, and with a bar, bridge tables, etc.

Ira finally has a job making costumes for a film, not very well paid, but enough to restore her smile and good mood. Already she is working all night to make the designs: what organization!

I await an answer from Nini concerning the whereabouts of the parts for *Jeu de cartes* and the Tchaikovsky symphonies, after which I will try to find an opportunity to send them. Nadia is in Holland (living at the embassy); she was very ill with kidney trouble, the first time she has ever cancelled a concert. Everything is settled with Kitty: London will pay for her directly.[7]

In my cable, "letter received" refers to your first letter by Clipper.

---

[1] As the person responsible for Stravinsky's appearance as Charles Eliot Norton lecturer, Forbes must have known the date of the composer's departure for New York, and also known that he no longer lived at this address.

[2] The date of the premiere of Stravinsky's Concerto in E flat (*Dumbarton Oaks*) at Dumbarton Oaks, Washington, DC, the Bliss home, now the Harvard University Center for Byzantine Studies.

[3] Stravinsky stayed at Dumbarton Oaks during the New Year holidays, 1939–40, en route from Los Angeles to New York.

[4] This was in reaction to the German-Russian non-aggression pact; the French did not distinguish between "White" and "Red" Russians.

[5] Vera had no Georgian, and even no Russian origins, her father being of French descent, her mother of Swedish.

[6] Of the Office des Refugiés d'Origine Georgienne, 58, rue Boileau.

[7] Catherine Mandelstamm, then aged two and a half, was in a tuberculosis sanatorium in Leysin, Switzerland, supported by money sent in regular installments from Stravinsky's bank in London.

I wrote to Victoria telling her about our plans.

In spite of a torrential rain (I'll wear your old raincoat), I am going to the post office; otherwise this letter would not go out. I forgot to mention that Denise Mayer was here for three hours complaining about Ira's tiresome jealous scenes.

Misia is very ill, a heart attack or stroke, the second one. After a third one she would not be able to get around at all.

I embrace you, my dear, dear Bubushkin. May God keep you, and may time pass quickly. Your Vera.

Vera to Igor

Letter No. 9
Monsieur Igor Stravinsky
c/o Edw. Forbes
Gerry's Landing
Cambridge, Mass.   Saturday, October 28, 1939

Dearest, I want so much to write to you in Russian, French being somehow less intimate. If my first letters reached you, I do not see why this one should not also.

The wet, slushy autumn arrived with constant rain and frightful cold. We crowd near the fireplace, change wet boots, and dream about warm countries, warm coats, and hot sun, all of which seem very far away. This week in particular has dragged very slowly. At least ten times a day I count on my fingers: November, December, January, February, March, April. Let us say that we will not count April. Then five months of 30 days remain, which makes 150 days. And then what? Suppose I am not granted a visa, or not let out, or that I get sick, three possibilities more frightening than anything in the pessimistic present. But at other times I think that perhaps the winter will pass quickly, that I will hardly have time to learn English, sew and knit everything that I have planned, and even put all of my papers in order. Oh, if only it were so!

I am obliged to tell you about a very disagreeable surprise. Fedya and Denise came here yesterday from Le Mans. They have drawn out all of the money from the Paris bank and transferred it to Le Mans. The purpose of Fedya's visit was to tell me that my and Madubo's access to the account has been cancelled, and that from now on if I need money, I will have to request it from him—or, if he is conscripted, from Denise (!!!). The same is true for Svetik, who must be outraged, since the matter was not even discussed with him. Fedya manipulated all of this because he had heard a rumor that our bank might fail, but I do not see why trustworthy banks should exist only in Le Mans. He could have left the whole arrangement just as it was and, if he were really worried about our Paris bank, transferred the money to the Banque de France. Fedya said that, as the oldest, he has the right to decide such things, and that "Papa would have approved of my action."

Not being a member of the family, I kept quiet. Also, I did not want to say that the whole thing was engineered by Denise so that she could control the money and everyone would be beholden to her. I hope that they will not do anything foolish, and that the money, under their "management," will not be lost. Nothing can be done now, the money having been deposited in their names in Le Mans, nor can any of us go there to find out if their bank is reliable. Money questions are always delicate, more so among friends; and now this very unpleasant thing has happened, the worst part of which would be to have to receive money from Denise, especially after all that she has done to me. Her animated and self-satisfied behavior yesterday confirmed that this maneuver was a great success for her.

They returned to Le Mans without waiting to see Svetik on his twenty-four-hour leave. He and Madubo will come directly to my house. He will take a bath here (they have no water at home), and have dinner here with the Suvchinskys. The menu: *cassoulet toulousain.*

Forgive me, dearest, for having written this unpleasant letter, and believe me that I am not spiteful and have already forgiven Denise for her actions, though I cannot help being aware of her desire to dominate and to play a role. Fedya has nothing to do with all of this; if he had acted alone, he would have done so more tactfully, so that no one would have suspected him of manipulating. I wanted to say to him: "First ask your father's permission"—after all, the money is yours, and you alone can dispose of it—but I decided to say nothing. I do not understand why they did not say to me: "Take out your share, the money that is coming to you in May, and put it wherever you choose; we will take our share to Le Mans." But enough.

I embrace you fervently and once more ask you to forgive me for this disturbing letter. I was so upset all day. But maybe all will end well. I love you tenderly and embrace you tenderly. Your Vera.

Vera to Igor
(Original in French)

Letter No. 10
Monsieur Igor Stravinsky
c/o Mr. Edw. Forbes
Gerry's Landing
Cambridge, Mass.   November 1, 1939

My dear, my very dear Igor, I am in a very bad, not to say sad, distressed, furious mood these days. People and events are forever putting obstacles in our path. As before, I am beginning to think that it is necessary to experience a difficult life, full of deceptions, and necessary to develop an insane energy. But the struggle is in vain. I see no progress in anything. Three days ago a new law was passed whereby a Frenchman cannot marry a foreign woman outside of France. If he happens to be in America, he must go to Japan, for example, and be married there by the French Consul. Unless I have misunderstood the law, this means that we cannot be married in the United States. You must ask a French Consul or *homme d'affaires* there.

I am impatient for the answer to my letter of October 2 (No. 7), though I realize that your reply will do me no good, since I am certain you did not state that you are a French citizen. Conclusion: according to French law, in order to marry I must bring my divorce papers, which would take years; only then will it be possible for me to come to New York. What I need is a lawyer (not you) to tell Sudeikin that I will soon be in New York, and that I need my divorce papers. He will be obliged to hand them over. I can keep on writing to him from here, but he will not answer. In my letter of October 21 I spoke to you about using the name Bosset; but I prefer not to do that as it would be too complicated and could take an eternity, and I want to leave in April or May. I must take action after Christmas, but without my papers I do not know how to begin! A vicious circle. Americans here say that, once I am in New York, these difficulties are easily resolved. What do you want me to do here? I am nervous and struggling against the cold. Everyone is anxious and talks about nothing except politics; no one wants to do anything properly.

Something else. It seems that the Clipper will be discontinued, and that henceforth we will be obliged to wait a month for each letter. What a prospect! I am very upset, naturally, even though other people are in much worse predicaments. I wrote that six months remain to be gone through. And then what? Perhaps longer. I had begun to accept your absence with considerable courage and was preparing for my departure: it was my only reason to go on living. But these new laws have shattered my equilibrium. I don't know where to begin. I hope that you will speak to an *homme d'affaires* who knows French law, and that you will send me a reassuring letter. Above all—though only if necessary, of course—I hope that you will find Sudeikin, who cannot say "no" if I turn up. *He is not aware that my papers contain my divorce*. If he says "no," I can do him a lot of harm.[1] But enough of this. Let's talk about other things. On Saturday evening, when Suvchinsky was here, I received the letter that you wrote after your first lecture.

Nini could not get leave, but he will be here next Saturday. He wants a promotion and has asked me to buy some military books for him. His health is good, and we correspond frequently. Milene writes to me every day. She walks in the snow, works at her painting, and is not bored at all. Madubo, who will come for dinner tomorrow, telephoned me that Theodore has been excused from military service because of his hernia, his myopia, and his general health. I wrote to Nadia, who is recuperating in Holland, and hope to see her soon. Roland-Manuel is still at Nemours and in very low spirits. Ira, waiting for work in connection with a film, often comes to knit with me and to keep warm. The Païchadzes have moved in with the sister because their apartment was not heated; Mme Païchadze cannot endure the cold, and that is uppermost in everyone's minds. No doubt the cold is the cause of so much bad humor.

If you knew in what state of nerves I am and how often, you would excuse me for this boring letter, my dear. A ray of sunshine—the hope that you will be able to arrange everything—and all of that will disappear.

I miss my work. I have a few customers, but nothing in comparison to last year. I knit, keep house, cook. The afternoons and evenings are dreary. I have no desire to go out in the darkness and cold. Often I invite people simply not to be alone, but this is costly, everything having become much more expensive since September. Don't be annoyed with me because of my complaints: I must bare my soul. The prospect of being without letters from you—or when the Clipper has been discontinued, nearly without them—is not comforting. If only it were possible to have an entr'acte in the midst of all this and to see each other for even ten minutes! That would give me new courage!

Voilà. I am calmer for having written this letter. I will go to bed with a hot-water bottle and will pray for you, for us, and for God to protect us. I send you all my love and embrace you endlessly. Vera.

The five baskets are still here. Some day they must be transported to Madubo.

Tomorrow Olga Sallard comes for two days, so I will not be alone; for lunch I will have Madubo, Fred, and Rieti. Elsie Rieti left to be with her son in the South. She wants to go to America in the spring. I have already talked to her about the possibility of our going together. I am looking for an opportunity to send the Tchaikovsky symphonies and *Jeu de cartes*, but this has not yet presented itself.

Finally November. Yesterday I had a crisis because I thought it was already November. How slowly the time passes.

                                                                November 2

On rereading this letter, I am afraid that you will be irritated. Forgive me, but it must go with the Clipper, perhaps the last one I send this way. I am in a better mood today and once again ready to face any obstacles, providing[2] I see you in May. I embrace you with all my heart. Vera.

Vera to Igor
(Original in French)

Letter No. 11
Monsieur Igor Stravinsky
c/o Mr. Edw. Forbes
Gerry's Landing
Cambridge, Mass.   November 4, 1939

My dear Igor, What joy your letters bring me! I have just received the one with the article by A. Williams. I am so happy about your success. A letter from Nini came at the same time, with a photograph of himself in uniform. I would like to send it to you

but I am taking advantage of the last Clipper, and the photo is heavy. Where should I write to you after you leave Cambridge? The thought of no Clipper in the winter saddens me very much.

I spent the whole morning looking for military books for Nini, finally found them, and they are already on the way. He wrote a detailed description of his life, saying that he is getting along very well, and that his colonel congratulated him. He even sent me a drawing of a target with the positions of his bullets. I am so pleased that he is taking this positively. He is glad, too, that Theodore has been demobilized, since the life would be too hard for him.

Nini regards the money story as utterly stupid: "Why did you let it happen? In Father's absence, these decisions can only be matters of common agreement." He feels that Theodore and Denise have acted most inconsiderately toward all of us. You ask me how much money remains in the bank? I have no idea. Now only Theodore knows. Païchadze says that the bank had no right to ignore the proxies, but I think that precisely for this reason Theodore and Denise left 1000 francs in the account. Until now, all dealings with this bank have been impeccable.

Do not worry about Madubo. I have the impression that she is completely happy with her new, quiet life. She is like a mother looking after her son. Naturally she thinks of nothing except sending letters and packages to Nini and Milene, but after so many years of work, she finally has peace and is dependent on no one but herself. Moreover, all of our friends are very nice to her. She comes to pass a whole day with me, or with the Suvchinskys, where she spends the night. Yesterday she was invited to Ira's. I think of Madubo as of *somebody*, somebody who expresses great pride when she talks about Nini's courage and how he endures the cold. I know you understand what I am trying to say. She wants another kind of life. After having been a governess all of her adult years, she is practically a mother now. If she moves in with Theodore, misunderstandings with Denise will immediately develop. In the first place, she and Denise are not compatible. In the second, Denise, who likes to give orders, will tell Madubo to "do this" and "do that," and in a week Madubo will have become Denise's cook, housekeeper, and laundress, which is not very enviable. Madubo says that she will gladly go to their place for a week, but why undertake this expense when they have already been here twice? And now that Theodore is out of the army they will surely come here more often. Meanwhile, if Nini comes to Paris (he has a furlough on November 8), he can write to her there for anything he wants. The mail moves rather well between Paris and the provinces, but, like the trains, not between one provincial city and another.

I'll wait for Nini before sending your music.[3] He'll tell me what Dagmar wrote and the name of the person for whom I should ask at the Embassy.

Here are the addresses you requested: Kitty: "Les Oiselets," Leysin (Vaud); Nossenko: "Les Acacias," Leysin (Vaud); Schwarz: 10 Mont-Riant, Lausanne.

The situation with Yura Mandelstamm is as follows. When Nini was still in Paris, he telephoned several times to the newspaper, but Yura was never there. After insisting, Nini was finally told that Yura could be found playing cards in a certain café. I also know that Yura came to 7, rue Antoine-Chantin and was surprised to find no one there except Madubo. She said that he was in a good mood, very pleasant, a bit embarrassed to have to admit that he

---

[1] This seems to say that Sudeikin took Vera's papers with him when he moved to the United States, in the summer of 1922, but, if so, how could he fail to discover what the papers contained? Or is Vera referring to a divorce from a previous, pre-Sudeikin, marriage?

[2] "Providing" is one of the words that characterized Vera Stravinsky's English.

[3] Stravinsky had programmed *Jeu de cartes* in his Boston Symphony concerts in December, and *Jeu de cartes* and Tchaikovsky's Second Symphony in his San Francisco concerts immediately afterward.

earned very little money. Perhaps he will go into the army. This is all that we know about him. Madubo thinks he is content to be back in his own milieu. Perhaps he has someone (a woman), but this is only Madubo's supposition.[1]

Milene wrote me that she had a lung-tapping, and that it went very well, with scarcely any fever. One liter of fluid was drawn, but she has put on considerable weight since the tapping, when she lost a kilo. She has already recovered, is painting again, receives visitors, and amuses herself with her friends. My impression is that, in spite of the experience, she really is much better.

Ira is often very impatient and nervous while waiting for her film job. I must invite her father again, but I am beginning to consider how much time I can spend every day in both money and work. I have people here literally every day, the numbers increasing rather than diminishing as more and more people are unemployed; they come to save money, and because they have so much free time. Poor Fred is defeated by the Baltic story. What brutality, to tear the poor people from their land, place them on abandoned Polish farms, and make "Germans of the second zone" out of them. He is taciturn and does not want to do a thing, and the people who come here and take it out on him make me nervous and upset.

I like my English lessons much more, now that I am beginning to see results, but when I fear that the lessons are useless, I feel very sad; at such times nothing comes into my head.

I am eager to know what you will say about my papers, visas, the necessary steps, lawyers. Perhaps the simplest course would be to become Bosset, but I don't know whom to ask. Kramer is a dolt, and the others must be paid.

Olga Sallard has been here for three days and has helped me very much, but I think she has had enough. The work is too tiring for her. She will not come for ten days.

It is useless to tell you that I live from day to day and that this depends upon my good humor. I embrace you very tenderly and send you all my loving thoughts. How I would like to see you! Your Vera.

Igor to Vera

Vera Sudeikina
31, rue de l'Assomption
Paris 16

c/o Mr. Edw. W. Forbes
Gerry's Landing
Cambridge, Mass.
November 5, 1939
[Cable]

Demand immediate transfer for your needs three-quarters my money Paris Morgan your name one-quarter remains Le Mans Theodore's needs.

Vera to Igor
(Original in French)

Letter No. 12
Monsieur Igor Stravinsky
c/o Edw. Forbes
Gerry's Landing
Cambridge, Mass.   November 9, 1939

My dear, very dear Igor, I have just received your letter of October 31 and am so happy to have it. Your cable about the money came on Tuesday, and I sent a copy to Theodore so that he could return the seventy-five percent to the Morgan Bank. Before I go to Morgan to ask if I can share this sum with Madubo—I do not

want to have the account in my name only—I will have lunch tomorrow with Païchadze and ask for his advice how to go about it.

Your cable was a great relief. In the meantime I had received a letter from Milene saying she was "green with anger." Theodore wrote to her that his trip to Paris was on "business," but he did not say more about it. "Papa will settle everything and put things in their proper place," she writes. Nini was furious, too. Then I received a letter from Theodore containing very vague explanations and making nothing clear. When Nini challenged him, he answered: "Believe me that I certainly did not do it for my own sake but only out of prudence and for our common interests."

Nini has a 24-hour pass the day after tomorrow (Saturday). If he can come Saturday evening, we will have dinner together, and I will put all of your questions to him. I am in a hurry now to send this letter with the next Clipper. Since the "lost" letter was sent by boat, you might still receive it.

I wrote to Nadia and am still awaiting a reply. I just telephoned Madubo. The box that you want must be there with her. She is certain that she has seen it; when Nini comes, she will ask him where to find it. Madubo has the checkbook from the Morgan bank in London. Nini brought your little valise and took the contents of the small safe to the bank. Then Theodore took the empty safe to Le Mans. As for sending the London money, I will inquire about it tomorrow, but I think that a maximum of 5000 francs a month is allowed; someone told me this yesterday, but I will verify it myself at the bank. The arrangments for Kitty are confirmed. Nini saw to this before he left.

This week has passed more quickly than last. I was so upset then, which explains the desperate letters that I sent to you. Now the sun has come out, and everything is already better. Starting today, too, the heat has been turned on, a result of no one paying his rent. Now everyone has paid, and we are warm. You cannot imagine what it is like to live in a cold apartment, and the work involved with charcoal and wood. I have two fireplaces to fill, which is expensive.

This week life is more civilized. Moreover, I have begun to go out, which changes one's ideas and makes one feel better. Yesterday I lunched at the Ritz with the Heylegers, who came for a fortnight from Cannes, a trip that requires a safe-conduct visa, as if one were traveling to some remote place. Today I'll lunch with Rieti, tomorrow with Païchadze, and Saturday with Nini. I'm bringing vodka, salted cucumbers, and herring. I am very happy to be seeing Nini, and Madubo, whose voice sounds different, is ecstatic.

Tuesday I had a surprise party here with Ira, Guitton Buffet (cousin of Gabrielle Picabia), and Roger Lefebure, who is now someone important at *Paris-Midi*. I have decided to see lots of people, which is good for all kinds of relations. For the moment, identity cards are obtainable immediately on request. At least this was Ira's experience, and she already has hers. A visa to leave France can be had, but not—and this is the twist—a return visa. The Americans, on the other hand, afraid that people will stay there permanently, do not give visas unless you already have the return one. But perhaps this problem can be worked out. So long as no obstacles like this arise concerning our marriage, I will continue being more hopeful.

Hurrying to the post office, I embrace you, my Bubushkin, with all my tenderness. I am happy for you that your lectures have been so successful, and I am sure that this will be good for you. What address shall I use after the first of December? I embrace you again and again. May God protect you. With all my love, your Vera.

---

[1] Since Yuri Mandelstamm's sister was alive in Paris in the 1960s, and received visits from Stravinsky's granddaughter, one wonders why Soulima or Theodore

Stravinsky seem not to have seen the woman and inquired about the fate of Yuri, who was vaguely known to have been murdered by the Nazis during World War II.

Enclosure November 12, 1939

My precious Bubushkin, I am adding a few words to Svetik's letter. He just left, having spent his first leave with us. He is magnificent. You cannot imagine how he has changed, how he bears all of the hardships, how he is trying, with good humor and positiveness, to work and to encourage the others. He looks well—tanned, slightly thinner, and somehow more endearing. If this continues, he will be an officer and maybe even a general. Today we had lunch at my place. He left at six, and I was sad. I will write to you in detail tomorrow; otherwise this letter will weigh too much. I embrace you, dearest, and kiss you endlessly and tenderly. Your Vera.

Vera to Igor

Letter No. 13[1]
Monsieur Igor Stravinsky
c/o Mr. Edward Forbes
Gerry's Landing
Cambridge, Mass. November 13, 1939

My precious, my beloved, I am writing to you under the influence of Svetik's twenty-four hours here. They were a great joy for us and for his friends, and Madubo was so radiant that simply to look at her was a pleasure. She prepared a sumptuous meal, and we dined with Svetik on Saturday when he arrived. We talked until midnight, and he told us so much that I feel as if I know all about his friends and his daily routine. Above all, I know that he has decided to do everything willingly and with enthusiasm. If he behaved begrudgingly at first, he has now adjusted to the lack of freedom, as well as overcome his former luxurious habits. He is actually finding pleasure in dismantling and reassembling his rifle, and in studying the instruction books that might help him to become a commissioned officer. The level of his associates is deplorable, though some nice people are among them. Evidently the conversation revolves around food, sleeping, defecating, and so on. That "so on" is out of the question, however, since bromides are added to the morning coffee. Only the Algerians seem not to be affected by this, and to go into their rooms at night is not recommended. Svetik described everything so well that I encouraged him to write it all down, eventually for a book, something like Céline.

Later I went out with Suvchinsky and Fred, but by midnight I was yawning: there had been an alert the night before, and I had been up since 5 a.m. The alert lasted until 6, and at 5:15 Fred arrived with delicious coffee and warm croissants. Another alert began tonight at 4:30, but Fred did not come; we had agreed that he will come only if the alerts are later in the morning. I got dressed but did not go to the cellar.

Yesterday (Sunday), after the church service, Svetik and Madubo came here for lunch with the Beliankins—not including the old man, who has a cold. (I had bought pastries especially for him, and Ira took them home with her.) Svetik talked again. He really is touching, with something of the little boy about him, though at the same time he seems to have grown up a lot. The one pleasant side to his new life is that he does not have to think about anything: he is taken care of by his superiors, and he seems satisfied with this. He says that his captain is "a wonderful type and I adore him." How fortunate that Svetik takes it this way! At 6 he left for home and from there he will go to the railroad station. I felt very sad. He asked me to write to him every day and to send him chocolate and preserves twice a week. Army food is good but does not include sweets. His company is moving from the village to a barracks in town, and he will be completely free on Sundays. I think that Madubo and I will be able to go there and have lunch with him in a restaurant, but not this Sunday, because he has to have a second injection; the first one did not take.

[1] Stravinsky wrote "received Nov. 23." on the envelope.

[2] Stravinsky wrote "received November 24" on the envelope.

Svetik and I looked for the Tchaikovsky orchestra parts but could not find them. Probably they are in a cellar at Païchadze's. I will ask him again. We did find the parts for *Jeu de cartes* but not the score. Svetik was surprised that you had not taken the Tchaikovsky with you. The question is how to send the music. Nobody wants to carry it because of the weight, the responsibility, and the trouble at customs with censors. Perhaps it could be sent in several registered packages, but only two kilos are accepted, and the censor might take two months to examine the contents.

I lunched with the Païchadzes the other day; since it was very cozy, I stayed until 5 o'clock. I gave them your news and told them how nice Koussevitzky had been to you, which greatly pleased them. We talk about the difficulties of getting permission to leave France. Yet Koussevitzky's niece, Tanya, left for America a few days ago, which means that it is possible. I am optimistic these days.

I haven't been feeling very well and thought that my blood pressure might be up. Païchadze recommended a very good and inexpensive Russian physician, Dr. Ochan, who lives near me, and I went to him on Saturday. He found me in good condition and the pressure not too high. In fact, he said I was in tip-top shape except that my nervous system is bad. He gave me several medicines, one of them a sedative, and I feel better already. He also told me to change from cold baths to warm ones, and told me to give up alcohol and coffee—except for one cup, with milk, in the morning. I look well, and yesterday Madubo complimented me.

Svetik and I decided to transfer the money not to Morgan but to Crédit Commercial, where it was before. He said that "since Father decided this in the beginning, it should stay that way." I'll make more inquiries, but when I ask people if the bank is reliable, they laugh. The Morgan bank requires references, which is quite complicated. As I said, I do not want to have the account in my name only.

I sent Fedya a letter enclosing the copy of your cable. When everything is resolved, I'll probably send you a cable saying *tout fait* [all done], which will refer to the bank affair.

My dearly beloved, I embrace you from my heart. Oh! If only a recess could be arranged and I could see you even for a moment. I kiss you very tenderly, my dearest. God be with you. Your Vera.

Vera to Igor

Letter No. 14[2]
Monsieur Igor Stravinsky
c/o Edw. Forbes
Gerry's Landing
Cambridge, Mass. November 16, 1939

My dearest Igor, It is warm today, almost like spring, and now that the apartment is heated, my mood is much improved.

I constantly hear about people coming from and going abroad; therefore travel is possible, a consoling thought. About our getting married, I am assured that "Once over there, you can arrange it easily." I only hope that there will not be any new laws! One phrase in your letter made me as happy as if I had seen the first swallow of spring: "Bring me the hand-painted wooden box when you come, since I forgot to take it with me." When you say such things, I am full of hope and happiness.

My English teacher praised me very highly yesterday. I can write compositions on various themes now and am translating Andersen's Fairy Tales for him. I write reasonably well, but I still cannot speak. I'll write to you in English, if you like, but I will not send the letter by Clipper, since it would be a shame to waste money.

Olga Sallard came yesterday to stay with me for two or three days. Tomorrow Madubo is coming for lunch, after which we will sit together and knit. I'm knitting a pair of socks for Svetik. I already sent him some sardines and two rolls of toilet paper and in a few days will send him some sausages. Madubo sends chocolate and other sweets. I wish we had a chef from Prunier, but with his present appetite, he needs only a few things. Dear Svetik left us with such a good and touching impression.

I received a postcard from Milene: "I feel better all the time, am getting fatter and fatter, walk every day and am much less short of breath. It is lovely and warm here." For her name day I sent an ornament for her lapel: a little drum, which is very stylish.

A few days ago we were subjected for several hours to the sound of bombardment, a DCA beating off German airplanes. We no longer have daytime alerts, which interrupted work, but we are warned to avoid being in the streets because of shrapnel. That happens more often in the suburbs, and in Saint-Denis and Clamart three people were injured. At such times I stay at home or sit in a café, but most people run about as if nothing had happened. Altogether Paris seems more and more animated; automobiles and pedestrians are numerous both in the center of the city and on the boulevards. Little by little the theaters are reopening, and tomorrow I am going to one, to see a Franco-British gala. The Opéra is also reopening, with Lifar dancing, but as yet there are practically no concerts, and the radio programs are *merde*. There are no races.

I don't know what to do with Fred. He seems to be fading away, and everyone remarks on how bad he looks. He is worried because he has only enough money for a year, and then what? He used to cheer everyone up, but now we have to do it for *him*. I feel sorry for him, but he irritates me. Since people visit me continuously, he could help me wash the dishes and clean up the rooms. When I go out for the day, he says: "I tried to look in on you yesterday" or "You are never home."

Tonight I'm dining with Suvchinsky. He saw Svetik off at the railroad station and met some of his friends. Since I now know these people by name, Svetik having sent most of them to meet me, I would like to have more details. Suvchinsky told me on the phone that Svetik seems to be popular with all of them.

I am very pleased with my new doctor and feel ever so much better. The spasms have gone, and I even feel sleepy in the evening. I was under such tension before that I was almost afraid of the night and the quiet and could sleep no more than 3 or 4 hours. Olga used to say, "You have so much energy, you could have been a tank." Now I feel so relaxed that I go to bed earlier.

I went to see Valechka the other day and found him sitting in his warm room playing patience. I showed him a new kind and had scarcely reached home before he was on the phone asking, "Do you use six or eight cards in your version?" He has aged greatly; he does not want to come to dine at my house because "I cannot move around in the darkness." Every time we talk, he sends you a kiss.

Little one, I embrace you very tenderly. I am waiting for your letters. It is nine days since the last one. Yesterday I had a letter from Fedya, who writes: "I am very pleased to have father's cable because it absolves me of all responsibility in that business." Supposedly he is sending the money to me. In answer to his reproach, "Why didn't you tell me immediately that you did not agree?," I answered that it was not my money, and that for this reason I wrote to you, whose instructions had been disobeyed. You are the principal person in this case. I should have told him that I do not understand anything in banking myself and needed time to inquire. Besides, everything was done in such a rush that I did not have time to open my mouth. Thank God all is settled now.

My dearest, I kiss you many, many times and love you with all my soul. Vera.

Vera to Igor

Letter No. 15[1]
Atlantic Clipper
[Opened by] Contrôle Postal Militaire
Monsieur Igor Stravinsky
c/o Edw. W. Forbes
Gerry's Landing
Cambridge, Mass.   November 19, 1939

My dearest, I received your two letters, one of them dated November 9, the other containing your letter to Fedya. He will answer you: "I *did* let Vera and Madubo know," and, "*Svetik did not come that day* because he did not get permission." The truth is that Fedya informed us only a half-hour in advance and gave us no opportunity to think about the matter. But never mind, since everything is now settled. I am waiting for a check which I will deposit in our old bank according to your former instructions. Hasn't Fedya written to you? I sent him a letter asking him to write first of all to you, since the money is yours.

You now know that our apartment is finally being heated, and that it is quite warm. My doctors told me that the cold was partly to blame for the bad state of my nerves. The "knots" have dissolved now, and I am feeling much better.

I regret that you have not written to me about a lawyer and that you have no new information. Did you receive my letter about the new law that a French citizen cannot marry a foreigner except in places with French consuls?

Everyone says that I should leave now, that by spring the crossing will be dangerous because of mines, and that new emigration laws may be enacted. Going now would be simple, except that the French do not issue the return visa without which one cannot obtain the one for America. I realize that I keep repeating these things and that I myself have not started to do anything, which I will regret later; but I am waiting to hear from you. Please ask someone competent about this question of the visas.

Not having had an answer from Nadia Boulanger, I must write to her again. Since Madubo is coming for lunch today, I will go out and buy something and also mail this letter. Denise Mayer will be here for dinner. And so the days pass in cooking and washing dishes. Prices have gone up tremendously. Cigarettes are six francs now instead of four, etc. Ira finally has the film job and is delighted.

I am so happy when I receive one of your letters. Yesterday Suvchinsky called on me and asked me what I was doing. I said: "Looking under the door in the hope of a letter from America." Incidentally, he advises me to send the music in small packages, but I fear that this would take months. My letter No. 4, as you remember, took a very long time.

Don't worry about the money from London: everything will work out. When I last heard, the bank there had eleven thousand. Milene writes that she feels good and has gained 1 kilo, 300 grams in the last week. I would love to visit her, but this has become very complicated, involving a month's work, in addition to at least three month's work for America. I kiss you, my dearest, a thousand times, with great love. Your Vera.

Igor to Vera

31, rue de l'Assomption   Gerry's Landing
Paris 16   Cambridge, Mass.
                                             November 21, 1939

Vera Dearest, Yesterday I had dinner with Sergei Alexandrovich and Natalia Konstantinovna [Koussevitzky]. I've already told you of their truly touching sympathy toward our forthcoming union. At

---

[1] Stravinsky wrote on the envelope: "No. 15, sent Nov. 19."

their home I met Tanya, the younger sister (twice as young) of Natalia Konstantinovna by their father's second marriage. Tanya is married to Dr. Joseph Iorgy, and the couple have just flown from Paris. He has been appointed General of the Union Féminine Française. When I told him of your plan to come to America, he was very enthusiastic and quickly thought of the possibilities of our connections and of how they could be used for the welfare of our dear France and the great work that he represents. Think only of our friends, Ambassador Bliss and his wife, the Koussevitzkys, the Monteuxs, the [John Alden] Carpenters. And think of my friends in Hollywood, Charlie Chaplin, the [Edward G.] Robinsons, Douglas Fairbanks, Marlene Dietrich, and of all the powerful Americans with whom you have connections. How much money can you collect to help me with the work for France?

I enclose letters from Dr. Iorgy, one of them addressed to you, the other to Colonel Capdeville, Commandant of the BCR (Bureau de Commandement de la Région).[1] You must take them to Colonel Capdeville, Avenue de Tourville (near the Invalides), approach a guard and demand to see the Colonel (in order to be received ahead of the others). Give the guard a calling card indicating that you are a bearer of a personal letter to the Colonel from Dr. Joseph Iorgy, Delegate General of the Union Féminine Française in the United States. The Colonel will give you a military visa, a paper with a seal, to leave France. Colonel Capdeville is a very eminent man who does a great deal of good in helping ordinary soldiers. I want to contribute 1000 francs for this cause and I ask you to do it for me, at the time of your talk with him. This will be a charity placed in proper hands.

I continue: with this visa you must go to the Prefecture and obtain a stamped paper, an application for a United States passport. At the same time, ask for a visa, on a special card that must be attached to the military visa you receive from the Colonel, for permission to leave France. Understand that the request for this visa cannot be submitted until three days before you leave France: the visa is valid only during those three days. As soon as you have your passport, cable me and, through Sam [Dushkin]* in Washington, I will arrange to have the American Consul in Paris send the necessary permission to give you a visa for this new passport. I will be in New York from about the 5th to the 25th of January, following my stay with Kall in Los Angeles (as you already know). It will be too difficult for me to concern myself with these questions from California.

Only, Vera, I want you to do all these things as quickly as possible and not wait to come to the United States until spring. How we will live until my courses at Harvard are over is another question, one that I will not discuss today, or anything else except your move to America. Do not forget that Iorgy's politeness requires an immediate and affirmative acknowledgment. His name is pronounced with a hard ''G'' (as though it were written with an ''H'': IORGHY). It would also be a good idea to write to Georgette Bailey, since I am certain that she will not allow you to go to California (as I intend to do after my Harvard lectures) without visiting her. This could be a solution to the problem of your stay in America before the end of my courses.

I have received nothing from you since my cable of November 6 concerning the transfer of three-quarters of my money to your name from Le Mans to Paris, and no letter from Theodore. On the other hand, a very nice letter came from Madubo. Tell her that I will write to her as soon as possible, and that I thank her with all my heart. A letter came from Milene, dated October 28 (before the tapping of the fluid).

I enclose a letter to Nadia Boulanger that you may read but must forward to her immediately. I am very, very happy that you have thought about Theodore's precarious health. I hope that he has

begun to regain some weight. I await your letters with great impatience, as I place a final period on this one.

*It will be more practical and time-saving if you cable him directly. His address is 1075 Park Avenue, New York City. I have already advised him.

Vera to Igor

Letter No. 16
Monsieur Igor Stravinsky
c/o Mr. Edw. Forbes
Gerry's Landing
Cambridge, Mass.   November 23, 1939

Dearest Igor, I have replied to your two letters concerning the money story and told you that I will forward your letter to Fedya. But I have not sent it, for this reason: people who are close to each other and who suddenly find themselves separated and living in nerve-racking circumstances—you because of your concerts and your work, we because of the war and constant fear—should not write such letters. What you wrote to Theodore is so harsh that I take pity on him. One result of the letter would be the beginning of endless explanations, or, at the very least—because of the discontinuation of the Clipper—of explanations lasting a year or more. Besides, he wrote to me twice, intending to make apologies, and he clearly understood from your cable how you felt about the whole affair. Moreover, Svetik expressed *his* opinion to Theodore. And, finally, I have received the money now and the matter is settled. (I enclose a separate page with a complete accounting.) Thanks to your cable, everything has returned to normal.

I do not want Fedya to be upset all over again by your letter. Consider only that he cannot go to you to explain—this is a terrible problem—and that for a whole month you would have a sad correspondence. If something were to happen to any of us, a bitter feeling would be left for life. Nowadays Ira, on leaving her house, makes peace with her father and brother (if she happened to have quarreled with them beforehand) so that if she is killed by shrapnel, they would not have bad memories of her. Forgive me for writing such depressing things, but a war is going on here and people are perishing every day, not only at the front but behind the lines, too. Nervous tensions prevail, and though we try to hide them, they are always there and we do not become accustomed to them. To insist on things that, thanks to you, have been straightened out, seems to me pointless. If you would write to Theodore that you could not understand his actions, that you disagreed absolutely, but that all is now resolved—well, that should be sufficient. We had trouble enough with the story in Sancellemoz[2] without another one, especially in our state of nerves. It would be impossible to explain things at this distance. I hope that you will agree with my decision and that you will write me about it.

In a few days (December 5–8) I must change my identity card. Perhaps, as the lawyer advised, this would be a good moment to change my name to Mlle B., my maiden name. But I am afraid to do it because of the expense and trouble, and because months might pass before all of the information can be obtained. For these reasons I am eager to have your reply. Perhaps we can avoid all of the bother, but if, after I have *not* changed the card, you were to write, ''It is better to make the change,'' I do not want to have missed the opportunity. How complicated to write about such things.

At this very moment a letter arrived from Svetik. He might be given some leave on Sunday the 26th, and he asked me to arrange a lunch with the Beliankins. He so looks forward to this

---

[1] The letters are dated November 20, 1939. Stravinsky kept carbon copies of both of them, writing out in his own hand the last three lines of the one to the Colonel, which did not come out in the copy.

[2] In a letter to ''Vera Arturovna,'' August 16, 1939, Suvchinsky writes: ''I am glad

that the conflict with Fedya and Denise has been resolved satisfactorily.'' Whatever the cause of this ''conflict,'' Stravinsky ordered Theodore and Denise to leave Sancellemoz. Then Vera persuaded Stravinsky to forgive them, and they returned until the end of August.

and hopes that it will take place. I am sending him packages with all sorts of "goodies" so that he will have some consolation if he is not permitted to come. And if he does come, the package will be waiting for him on his return on Monday.

Madubo just telephoned to say that a telegram came for you from Amsterdam. They want you to take Artur Schnabel's place at the piano—a "Klavierabend"—on December 12. I will see her tomorrow and answer them that you are in America, since the fools do not know it. All of these telephone calls, visits, letters, and all of this cooking, cleaning, visiting (Mussia Antonini came in) filled my time so that I cannot get downtown until tomorrow. I also must write to Fedya that I received the check, and write to Milene, who complains that I have written less often lately.

You left two months ago tomorrow, but it seems to me that all of these days, weeks, and months of separation will never end. I had a bad moment today and became very anxious. Everything gets on my nerves and I blame everybody, especially Fred, who arrived for dinner nonchalantly, since everything had been prepared for him. The pessimism that he emanates drives me to distraction.

My dearest one, I embrace you in my thoughts and would so much like to do it in reality. Write me a few real Bubushkin words; I need them so much. But if the Clipper stops flying, how will I receive them? I embrace you very tenderly, my beloved. Your Vera.

P.S. Yesterday, a beautiful, fluffy, and affectionate pussycat came into my house and slept with me all night. He left in the morning and did not come back. What a pity. He purred so cozily as he washed himself.

It seems that Misia is very ill. She has been in bed for three weeks, and Sert does not leave her for a moment, which is a consolation for the last days of her life.[1]

I will either send your letter to Theodore or burn it. I prefer the latter. If I ever received a hundredth part of the reproaches you sent him, I would lose my sanity. Fedya is very sensitive and would suffer. He is not stubborn and does not insist; otherwise he would not try to explain to me and write me letters. Please, my darling, leave him in peace now.

Separate Enclosure   November 23

Tonight we had another alert, and I am tired and nervous for the additional reason that I had to rush around again so much. For the first time today, the window panes rattled from the bombing. Olga Sallard spent the night with me. We did not go down to the cellar—where one can die from the cold—but stayed here and studied English together. It has been freezing lately, and it just would happen that we have not had heat and hot water for the last two days. An attempt is being made to repair the heating system, but in the absence of workmen, this will take some time. I am running now, and in a hurry. I kiss you. When will there be an end to all this?

Here is the state of our finances: tomorrow I will deposit 79,500 francs into our old bank. When Fedya came to transfer the money, the balance was 132,329. Fedya took 19,034 for me, Madubo, Svetik, and to pay Bedel's bill before January 1, 1940. I took 8,000 from the 19,034. After subtracting the 19,034, 113,295 remained. Fedya left 1,295 in Paris and transferred the rest to Le Mans; therefore 112,000 was deposited in Le Mans. From this sum he took 3,000 on November 1 and 3,000 on December 1, in order to have enough money until January 1, 1940. This leaves 106,000 which, divided four ways, comes to 26,500 each. Multiplied by 3 this equals 79,500. Add the 1,295 and the total is 80,795 to remain in the bank beginning tomorrow. Apart from all this, G. Clément, your ex-real-estate manager,[2] wants me to pay 800 francs interest. I was supposed to see to all of these things in the morning, but, because of cooking and conversations, I did not have time.

[1] Misia Sert, born in 1872, did not die until 1950.

[2] He had disposed of Stravinsky's apartment at 25, rue du Faubourg Saint-Honoré.

Olga sleeps here these days. Katya Kessel is upset. She was to have been married in the town hall, but irregularities were found in her divorce papers and she has to start all over again—a process that will last at least two years. She must present her birth certificate from Russia, but this is impossible to obtain. I do not understand anything and am impatiently waiting for your news. Did you consult a lawyer about the divorce and the papers? I try to keep calm but am most upset.

Milene still had 11,000 francs recently, or so she wrote to me two or three weeks ago.

Vera to Igor

Letter No. 17
Monsieur Igor Stravinsky
c/o Mr. Edw. Forbes
Gerry's Landing
Cambridge, Mass.   November 25, 1939

My dear Bubushkin, You cannot imagine how much your letter encouraged me. Having been very nervous lately, I decided to spend yesterday in bed to rest. I told everybody that I felt sick, which was not true; I am just too tired from constant hurrying, cooking, washing dishes, cleaning, and I wanted to show that I had had enough. Olga went away, Fred went to a restaurant, and I enjoyed my warm bed and had a good rest.

Even so, I had to get up at 5 o'clock because several people arrived—Nabokov (my teacher), Suvchinsky, Ira, Fred, Kugulskaya—and once again I was left with a lot of dirty dishes and cups. Ira went away to prepare dinner for Jouvet, whose cook left him in the lurch, but she likes doing this, since the Jouvet house is well-to-do, and she can spend as much as she wishes on butter as well as order anything she fancies. What is tiresome about cooking now is that one has to think not only of what is inexpensive but also of where it can be found. We shouldn't complain, but from time to time some products disappear from the market. Lemons were unobtainable a while ago, then bananas, and now the only available coffee is very dear, the cheaper quality having been sent to the army.

Tomorrow, Svetik's leave, I am giving a big family lunch for the Beliankins.

I sent your letter to the Morgan bank, wrote to Milene, and asked Roland-Manuel to come to Paris. (He did not know that your first lectures were successful.) I discussed your question about leaving the Société des Auteurs only with Suvchinsky, who does not think it a good idea, for the reason that you became a Frenchman (French citizen) only recently. As always in wartime, chauvinism becomes very strong. Marcelle Meyer told me that she has had difficulty in programming *Petrushka* because it is too Russian. Most French people do not make any distinction between Soviet Russians and Russian refugees. Many Russians here have lost their jobs and are starving, though of course this is often their fault.

Today I will try to locate Nadia myself, since no one seems to know her whereabouts. The Tchaikovsky symphony was found, at last, at Païchadze's. (He is in his office only twice a week.) Two days ago I deposited the money that Fedya sent in our old bank— and discovered that the old man with the small beard who alarmed Fedya by giving him false information is no longer there. All of us are relieved that the money episode is over, and I wrote to Milene that her proxy to draw on the account is again in effect. She was worried about it and angry with Fedya, but we have all promised each other not to talk about it anymore, especially since Fedya, in his last letter, sounded so upset, which means that he realizes his gaffe.

A letter came from Lanvin asking you to pay your bill of 2,267 francs.[3] What shall I do about it? Pay something on account? The

[3] In view of the money worries discussed in these letters, this seems like a remarkably large sum.

Minister of Trade has asked all of the big *Maisons de Couture* to keep their workrooms open and to continue production. It was also announced that a special effort will be made to collect bills. I will pass by there and tell them that I forwarded their letter and am awaiting your response.

If I do not find Nadia, Suvchinsky will try to make an appointment with Munch.[1] I often hear about people traveling and I hope that someone will bring the music, especially after your nice letter.

This very minute I received a charming letter from Svetik, lovingly thanking me for my letter and the sausages I sent him. He is so warm that he makes me happy. Milene also wrote me a very warm letter. Svetik obtained some Russian songs through Païchadze and is teaching them to the soldiers in the evenings.[2]

A half hour ago your *Fireworks* was played on the radio, but before the end of the program the announcer interrupted, saying, "In a few minutes you will hear the news." Imagine the voice over your music! Pretty cold attitude to music! I embrace you from my heart, which misses you. God bless you, my beloved. Your Vera.

P.S. Remember me to Kall and thank Dushkin for his trouble on my account. Should Nadia write to Mrs. Bliss about me or not? And if so, when? Will Dushkin's efforts on behalf of my visa be sufficient? I think that America is primarily worried about people who might become public charges.

Vera to Igor

Letter No. 18
Monsieur Igor Stravinsky
c/o Monsieur P. Monteux
Empire Hotel
San Francisco, California
(Opened and examined by
Contrôle Postal Militaire)   November 30, 1939

My dear little one, I am writing to San Francisco, since a letter to Cambridge would not arrive in time. I said in my last letter that we were expecting Svetik. Well, we gathered at his place on Saturday, but a telegram came from him saying that his leave was not granted. Poor Madubo basted the roast with sauce and with her tears. According to a subsequent letter from him, the leave papers were stacked against him by someone in his regiment, and this even though he was very good at target practice (five bull's-eyes and the praise of his superiors).

Sunday, the Beliankins gathered at my house, and we spent the day in a family atmosphere. Grigory Pavlovich slept in a chair for a couple of hours and he did not criticize anything. Now we expect Svetik on Sunday the 10th. By that time I hope to have a letter for him from you. He is looking forward to it so much.

I finally found Nadia—in Gargenville, resting after her illness—and yesterday I talked to her on the telephone. Yesterday, too, I found Munch's phone number and talked with his wife. He leaves around the 20th of December and will be glad to take your music. I think he was horrified at the quantity of it; he has a lot of his own to carry. Perhaps I will give him only one package, the Tchaikovsky symphony, and try to find out from Eschig[3] how he sends music to America. It seems—so I heard from Rieti—that Eschig sends it regularly and has a permit to do so.

December begins tomorrow and I am counting the hours. Today is the anniversary of poor Mikusha's death; I have been re-living all the terrible details of last year. A few days ago I went to Father Vasily to order a *panikhida* service, but Yura had already

ordered one, which will take place tonight at 8. (Father Vasily is busy all day.) After the service, the Beliankins and Madubo will probably come to my house.

I have no news from Roland-Manuel, though I asked him to let me know immediately when he can come to Paris. Finding anyone seems to take so long now, and obtaining an answer even longer. Many people seem to think that it would be best for you to become a member of ASCAP. Hard times are predicted when the war is over, with very little work in Europe. Charles Boyer[4] took a Clipper to America, and it seems that he applied for American citizenship.

I am studying English intensively and I now read English novels easily, but I am annoyed that I still cannot talk freely and am tongue-tied. I imagine how dull it would be for an American to hear me mumbling. Still, with some assistance I can discuss almost anything.

Starting tomorrow, I will try to procure my identity card. It now seems that the old cards are being retained with new photographs in profile pasted on them. Since the ear must not be covered, I have to have a new picture taken.

I long to know the details of your work with the students and of how you spent the weeks in Boston. I heard your *Jeu de cartes* recording on the radio yesterday, and Ira heard *Apollo* and *Jeu de cartes* from Germany.[5]

That is all for today, my dearest. I am hurrying to the post office to send packages to Svetik and to send you a million letters to be forwarded. I must also pay the telephone bills for our September conversations between Paris and Gargenville. I embrace you, my dearest Igor, with a great feeling of love and tenderness. Your Vera.

Vera to Igor

Letter No. 19
Monsieur Igor Stravinsky
c/o Monsieur P. Monteux
Empire Hotel
San Francisco, California   December 3, 1939

My dearest, You cannot imagine how happy it made me to receive your letter asking me to come sooner. I could not sleep, planning how to organize it successfully. I am not quite certain when you want me to come, since I know that you would say, "When everything is ready," and I do not expect this to be the case before the end of January. But would that be too soon? Please answer immediately. What worries me is that my passport is valid for only six months, and that if I spend a month here, only five will be left. I have heard that the Americans do not give visas for passports of such short duration, but I will find out about this here and not disturb you with the matter.

A woman told me yesterday that a French friend of hers was obliged to undergo a medical examination before leaving for America and to submit to some analysis, which took a month. If you intend to purchase the ticket in New York, you will probably have to send me some kind of certificate. I was told not to believe any official who says that the return visa to France will be arranged by a French Consul in America, since this is not within a Consul's jurisdiction. I repeat this rumor to you only as a precaution. I'll start working on the whole thing immediately, and by the end of the week, answer Iorgy's kind letter and go to see the General about my identity card.

Dearest, you cannot imagine the happy inner flutter from the thought that I don't have to wait until April or May. I've already written to Georgette Bailey.

---

[1] Charles Munch, the conductor, was about to leave for America. He brought the music that Stravinsky wanted.

[2] This seems unlikely in view of the hostility to Russians described in the previous letter.

[3] Editions Max Eschig, Paris music publisher, was the representative in France of

[4] B. Schotts Söhne, publishers of *Jeu de cartes*.

[4] Boyer was a friend of the Stravinskys both in Paris in the late 1930s and throughout the Hollywood years.

[5] Stravinsky's European royalty statements during World War II indicate that his music was performed in the occupied countries but not in Germany.

After Thursday night's memorial service for Mikusha, Ira and Valechka came to my place; Madubo went home, since she would have no transportation later at night. Yura Mandelstamm apologized profusely for neglecting to send me an announcement. I invited him for dinner and, of course, he came with his whole family. The same day we heard the news about Finland and were all very depressed. So many dramas!

I'll go to the post office now, and, if not too expensive, will send you a cable to tell you how happy I am. I expect Madubo for lunch, and I intend to write to Svetik. I spend half of the day in the kitchen, the other half in the post office or in government offices trying to get permits. My beloved Igor, I embrace you with all my being. I crave more news, and I wish I could find something interesting to tell *you*. Your Vera.

I forwarded your letter to Nadia. Since Roland-Manuel does not answer letters, I will try to telephone him. Which music is the most important to be sent over to you with Munch?

Vera to Igor
(Original in French)

Richcop
New York

Paris
December 3
[cable]

Happy to come earlier all is well Vera.

Igor to Vera

Vera Sudeikina
31, rue de l'Assomption
Paris 16

c/o Richard Copley
113 W. 57th Street
New York
December 6, 1939

Vera mine, Today, Wednesday, St. Ekaterina's day, I am in New York, where I arrived yesterday. We leave today, myself and Kall, for San Francisco, where I will be on Sunday at 8 a.m. At 10 I have a rehearsal. Yesterday Drake of the Copley Agency gave me your cable, which I am tremendously happy to have. I learned from it that you finally received my letter of November 21, since there was no answer by Clipper (as there could not have been).

Whether you would be able to come before May is not yet clear, but to expect you before January would seem to be impossibly soon. I am leaving everything concerning your arrival in Dushkin's hands. Yesterday at the railroad station I gave him my instructions. He has just returned from the funeral of Louise's father in Cleveland. Today, in the event that somehow you might arrive this month—while I am away—I plan to discuss everything with Sam. If necessary, I will ask him to pay $500 for the ticket on the Italian liner. The swine demand that we pay for the return ticket at the same time, though on the understanding that the money will be reimbursed later.

Forgive the incoherence of this letter, which I am writing in a great hurry, and which I will finish and send from Chicago, where I have a two-hour stop before leaving for San Francisco. At the railroad station just a moment ago, I received a wire from Drake (Copley) saying that I will be conducting the New York Philharmonic from January 4 to 8, which means that I will not be in Los Angeles for Christmas. I plan to spend one day on the way east at the Grand Canyon.

Tell Fedya that his vernissage [in New York] will take place immediately after my Philharmonic concerts. I'm organizing a cocktail party and reception for the public. Obviously Dagmar is involved; she will invite many people. I embrace you, my Vera, with all my love, also the children and Madubo.

---

[1] US Ambassador to France, Robert D. Murphy. Stravinsky wrote to him asking for his aid in securing a visa for "my best friend, a friend for a very long time, Mme Vera Sudeikina." Stravinsky guaranteed to post the $500 bond required before Mme Sudeikina is permitted to enter the United States, and he adds that she has a Nansen passport.

Vera to Igor

Letter No. 20
Monsieur Igor Stravinsky
c/o Dr. A. Kall
143 South Gramercy
Los Angeles, California, USA
[Atlantic Clipper]

December 8, 1939

My precious one, I received your letter today, the one containing the copy of the letter to Murphy.[1] I have just returned home after a long day wandering through ministries and police courts. Colonel Capdeville is not here any more, and everything has changed in the Passport Bureau. Even the nice secretary who helped me when I tried to arrange your papers is no longer working at the Ministry. A change takes place every two weeks. You must not forget that this is wartime.

I have a new plan of action, which is to press all of the buttons and to exert all of my strength. I still hear that it is possible to obtain a passport in ten days, but only with a return visa: the French Consul in the United States is powerless without a request from Paris. I do not believe any of it. If only they will let me out of France and permit me to enter America!

I have several important dates for Monday, and Païchadze promised to find out the new address of Colonel Capdeville, who was moved to another department. I think and live only for this.

We expected Svetik tonight, but he cannot come until tomorrow evening, when we will have the usual dinner at his house. Sunday I will have it in my house; I am preparing for ten people and doing everything myself. Besides the familiar crowd and the Beliankins, I will have Valechka, Olga Sallard, and Rieti, who will come to see Svetik.

When I visited Ira yesterday, I found everyone very downcast. Ganya was ill and Ira's knees are swollen. She has stubbornly refused to go to a doctor, though yesterday I think that I convinced her to do so. Grigory Pavlovich came to me and said: "Don't go away. We will be like orphans if you leave us." That is true. Madubo is the only one left here.

I went to the Italian Steamship Line and found out their schedule: *Rex*, January 2; *Conte di Savoia*, January 16; *Rex*, January 27; *Conte di Savoia*, February 10; *Rex*, February 25. The *Vulcania* and *Saturnia* leave from Trieste, not from Genoa. It is difficult to say how long the reservations will take, and what shall I do about the ticket? The steamship line in New York will cable to the steamship line in Paris that the ticket was paid for, but what if the visa is delayed? In the eventuality that I did not take the boat in time, would it be possible for me to use the ticket for another boat? I hear that the Italian visa can be obtained quite quickly. On Monday I will go to the American Consulate and try to see Murphy through a Russian woman I know who has worked there for fifteen years.

Nadia does not answer letters, which is surprising; I have telephoned her and forwarded your letter. I talked to Roland-Manuel on the telephone. He promised to come to Paris this week but did not do so. Everything has slowed up here. I am told that Serge Lifar is all-powerful and can arrange round-trip visas. I prefer to find someone else.

My dearest, you can judge by this letter that I am trembling inwardly at the thought of my departure and am also afraid of the obstacles. I embrace you, my beloved, with all the strength of my soul. Your Vera.

Igor to Vera

31, rue de l'Assomption
Paris 16

San Francisco, California
December 11, 1939

Only yesterday I received the long-awaited letter from you. To my regret, I saw that letter 15 has been lost. What was its date? The last letter from you that I received in Cambridge was No. 14, dated November 16.

86 Summer 1938. In the French countryside.

87 December 1939. Los Angeles. The photograph was taken on the day that Igor cabled the ticket money to Vera for her passage from Genoa to New York. Photo by Edward G. Robinson.

86

87

Since you did not forward my letter to Fedya, I am momentarily inclined to agree with your advice concerning it. But I feel that he should answer my two questions: why did he draw out the money from the bank *secretly*, not telling you and Madubo, and why did he take it to Le Mans? Following your recommendations, I will not insist that my letter be sent to him: you can destroy it. But I will be satisfied only when I have an answer from him to those two torturing questions, together with his apology for his actions. Without that, I cannot write to him as if nothing has happened. Therefore, feeling tormented in my soul, and at the same time not wanting to hurt him, I will not write to him at all. Still, I want him to know the reason* for my silence.

At the same time as your letter, I received one from Denise (with a note from Fedya) for the anniversary of Mikushina's death. I read it with a heavy heart, for I do not believe her any more. I do not want to miss the mail pick-up and therefore am writing only this little page in answer to your dear letters. I am in a hurry to send it. I will try to write again in a few days. I embrace you, my Vera. Yours[1]

My recordings in January for Columbia do not seem to be materializing. I'll probably return to Cambridge after the New York Philharmonic concerts.

*I think that he does not know, but that Denise does.

Vera to Igor

Monsieur Igor Stravinsky   December 13, 1939
Empire Hotel   [cable]
San Francisco

Will obtain all visas by the end of December awaiting your instructions Vera.

Vera to Igor

Letter No. 21
Monsieur Igor Stravinsky
c/o Dr. A. Kall
143 South Gramercy
Los Angeles   December 16, 1939
[Forwarded to the New York Philharmonic, Carnegie Hall, New York; by the Philharmonic to the Great Northern Hotel, West 57th Street; and by the Great Northern to the Pittsburgh Symphony, Pittsburgh, Pa., where Igor and Vera received it on January 17, 1940]

My very dear one, These few words in a great hurry, since Monsieur Munch will take the music with him by airplane. Your telegram just arrived. If all goes well, I will leave January 4 on an American ship. I believe that these boats are very small. I still do not know if you intend to send the ticket or if I must buy it, but the latter is almost impossible because payment must be in dollars. I suppose that you will send it to me, or instructions for the American Lines.[2]

I'll have the exit visa on the 26th, or thereabouts (at any rate the Prefecture has promised this), and the military visa at about the same time. After that I will not pick them up until nearer the 31st, however, because I have only three days after that in which to leave France. The Americans will give me a visa only when I have the passport with the other two. If everything is prepared, if there is no hitch, and if God wills, I will be with you on the 12th of January (the 4th + 8 days). Since today is Saturday and everything is closed, I do not know when the boat will arrive. I telephoned American Express and asked if the crossing from New York is likely to take more than eight days. I am rushing

[1] The signature is missing from this carbon copy.

[2] Stravinsky cabled the travel money to her (in dollars) from Beverly Hills, December 23, 1939.

[3] Vera wrote to Dushkin on December 26: "My dear Sam, thank you for the nice

about in a way that you cannot imagine and scarcely sleep at night.

I saw Roland-Manuel. He says that he cannot offer any advice and he refers you to M. LeBail [Stravinsky's attorney], 1, rue Valleret de Joyeuse, for all questions concerning the Société des Auteurs. I gave Mr. Munch three packages of cigarettes for you. Since large boxes are no longer to be found, I was obliged to buy little ones and fill them with what I had. Tobacco has become very expensive, and soon there will be none. Already coffee is unobtainable.

Nini came today. I will eat with him this evening. Olga, who lives with me, has helped me very much in the preparations for leaving.

I will bring the remainder of the music to you myself. How happy I am at the idea of being in New York soon.

Is it true that if I have the American visa, I do not have to do anything else? If absolutely necessary, please be with Kall when the boat docks and help me in the event of any difficulties.

If only everything would take place here without delay. I embrace you strongly. My heart and I are very impatient. Vera.

Vera to Samuel Dushkin
(Original in French)

1075 Park Avenue   December 18, 1939
New York   [cable]

Tell Stravinsky that I prefer *Rex* tourist class American boats take fifteen days Sudeikina.

Vera to Igor

[No envelope]   December 25, 1939

My dearest, Even if I do arrive on the *Rex*, this letter might get there before me, and I want to explain in advance why I insisted on taking this boat. When I received your letter suggesting that I should come earlier, I made my plans based on a sentence in your letter. You wrote: " I hardly dare to imagine that you might be in New York in the beginning of January when I am there, and that you will be coming on an Italian ship." From this moment on, I started to think about going on the *Rex*, whose second class is only slightly more expensive than first class on the *Manhattan*.

Already in the beginning of December I indicated my intention of leaving on an Italian boat. I can change this, but I do not know how long it might take. To postpone my departure three or four days is one thing, but a postponement of three or four weeks is quite another. The laws are constantly being revised and surprises occur every day, for which reason everyone advises me to go as soon as I receive my papers. An Italian boat is also recommended for the reasons that the small boats leaving from Marseilles take 15 days, and that if the *Manhattan* and *Washington*, which leave from Genoa, should stop in Monte Carlo during rough seas, they would stay in port three or four days. In this eventuality, what would I do about my visa?

Everything is much more complicated than you imagine. For instance, in the three months since you left, many changes have been instituted in the filling out of papers, and any misleading answers to such questions as "Through which frontier do you expect to leave and with what ship?" are punishable offenses. I will not go into all of the problems now, however, but only when I see you. When I cabled you that I would have the visa at the end of December, I was assuming that I would have the ticket in a few days: I must show the ticket in order to get the visa.

I had a letter from Sam[3] saying that he is ready to help

letter and for all the care that you are offering me. Meanwhile, everything has been managed and if it takes place as planned, I will leave on the *Rex* from Genoa on January 2. I was sad to learn of the death of your father-in-law and I ask you to convey my sympathy to your wife. I know how attached she was to him, and I understand the loss she must be feeling. I am counting on seeing you at the debarkation; this will add to the joy of my arrival. With my love, Vera Sudeikina."

whenever I need him. Here, spending sleepless nights worrying about the whole thing, and then receiving such calm, unhurried messages, I realize that an altogether different mentality prevails in the neutral countries. The next day I received a wire from Cook's mixing up everything, including my telephone number.

Tomorrow I expect to know the name of the ship that I will take. How sad if it isn't the *Rex*, especially since you are free until Pittsburgh. I had a letter from Georgette. She is delighted and says that I may stay with her as long as I wish, and you too; she has a very nice guest room. I can economize there more than in Paris.

I'm in the middle of everything now and have guests all of the time; the Beliankins, Olga, Madubo, Suvchinsky, Nouvel. Svetik came during his three Sundays off-duty. Many others have been useful in procuring reference letters for me, without which it is impossible to move nowadays. I am looking forward to a good rest on the sea, if it is not too rough—still another reason for taking a large ship that makes the crossing in eight days.

It is very cold here, the radiators are barely warm, and I must buy wood. I hope not to have any unpleasant last-minute surprises. To take the *Rex* second class to New York and third for the return will cost only 50 dollars more than the *Manhattan*. Finally, all that matters is to get away. I will not send New Year's and Christmas greetings, so I send my best wishes now.

In your last letters you sound somehow sad. I want you to feel joyful thinking of our impending reunion. Bubushkin, dearest, I embrace you with all my heart.

P.S. Maybe by Christmas I will be on my way. I can hardly believe it. I can picture you meeting me at the dock. I pray to God that all is well and successful. Your Vera.

Vera to Igor

Monsieur Igor Stravinsky   rue de l'Assomption
Paris
December 27 [?], 1939
[Cable]

Dearest I am leaving on the *Rex* tourist class terrible problems have to prolong my visa by one day no end to my joy at the thought of seeing you Vera.

1940

January

1 After a nice dinner with Ira at the railroad station, and the sadness of parting,[1] a feeling of relief from the problems of the last days in Paris. I have a couchette to Chambéry. Frost-covered window. At midnight I want to say "Happy New Year" to three officers but am tired and sleep instead. At 5:25 a.m. I jump up in terror thinking I have missed Chambéry, but the train is late. At 6 a conductor comes to transfer my baggage to another car. At the frontier is a crowd waiting to go through the formalities with the checking of all papers. At last we are in Genoa, at the Hotel Colombo, where I drink tea, eat sandwiches, take a bath, write postcards to Fred and Ira, go to bed and sleep well. **2** At 11 a.m. I go aboard the S.S. *Rex*, cabin 565, tourist class. On the advice of someone who has made the trip before, I give twenty dollars to a steward to get me a better cabin. At lunch, Eve Charpentier, a pretty woman I met in the train, proposes to share a table with me, and a fat Spanish woman, Señora Honda, joins us, saying she'd like some French conversation. She is

vivacious and nice. **3** Naples. We depart at noon, to the sound of band music. The view is fairy-like, blue with pink and white palaces. I throw Madeleine's carnations into the sea, then go to the cinema. Letters to Madubo, Olga, Fred, Milene. First-day acquaintanceships on the *Rex* deepen. **4** Gibraltar. A long stop, from 6 a.m. to 2 p.m. A tremendous aggregation of ships around the big rock; to navigate through them must be difficult. The refugees and immigrants with children crowding our decks are a strange contrast with a party of young people carrying skis. I make friends with Tila, an attractive young woman, and we exchange impressions and apprehensions. She says: "If you like Paris, you will never become accustomed to America." At 2 we finally start for Lisbon, sailing by white mountains against a blue sky. Can natural beauty make life happier? Yes, by inspiring the human senses. **6** Lisbon. I send a cable to Igor, "*Bon Noël*," and the operator says, "You are too late." I explain that tomorrow is *Russian* Christmas. Post letters to Ira and Fred. **8** The Azores are in view in the morning, through fog. The boat rocks more and more. In spite of taking Varsano, I have a fierce migraine, go to bed, and sleep all day. Terrible rocking. Mme Honda says that the dining room is empty. **9** At 11 a.m. I receive a cable from Igor. What joy! At lunch I order Asti Spumante for everyone. But the rocking is stronger, and I spend the day watching the clock. I have no stomach for the movies and go down to my cabin. **10** I stay in bed until 4, then play cards, read, and look at the waves. How the time drags! Trips like this are for old people. A gala dinner and dancing. Some Russian Bolsheviks occupy one table; they do not eat much but try to look like intellectuals. Red ropes are everywhere which the passengers hold onto, yet there is dancing in the bar. From time to time, people with drinks in their hands fall over each other and over tables. **11** The sea is calm but the Gulf Stream air is stifling, and we are not allowed to open our portholes. And, horrors, I have completely lost my voice! How will I tell Igor tomorrow about Paris? After seeing a documentary at the cinema, I go to bed at 10 very tired. **12** Slept well until 6. Put the clock back the final 45 minutes. My voice has not returned. I look at my watch every few minutes and pass the time repeating English phrases. At 5 p.m. New York appears in a pale blue fog. Millions of lights in a blue mist. Floating ice in the harbor, which we enter very slowly, docking at 7. Some of the passengers are shut off in a salon with a sign on the door, "Ellis Island." How humiliating! Suddenly I see Igor on the pier, with Kall, Dushkin, Bolm, and Kyra.[2] Now they will take care of me. My voice comes back a little, and I ask a woman next to me to shout down to them: "She is all right but has lost her voice." Bolm suggests that we go to the hotel first and have drinks in the bar, "Then we will show her something she has never seen before, a cafeteria." We go to the Great Northern Hotel. I am half drunk from all the excitement. **13** I still feel the pitching of the ship. Everything is so strange here! Igor cannot come and chat with me in my room because I am not his wife. We go to the Park Lane Cafeteria and at 3 p.m. Koussevitzky's concert in Carnegie Hall. I am in a loge with Countess Alexandra Lvovna Tolstoy and during intermission I see Elena Mumm. **14** Go to Fedya's exhibition in wind and pouring rain. Dinner at Sam Dushkin's. **15** Pittsburgh. Ferguson Webster, brother of Beveridge, meets us at the station.[3] In the Hotel Webster Hall, Igor makes a great mistake, registering us as husband and wife. The rectification of this is embarrassing. **17** A cold and dirty city. I stay in all day, helping Igor to write letters. In the evening, Igor reads Chekhov to us aloud. I write to Soulima: "This hotel does not belong to Beveridge Webster. Websters are as numerous here as Ivanovs in Russia and Duponts in France. It is five days since my arrival in America, and I still do not realize where I am. The approach to New York made the greatest impression so far. . . . I was glued to my porthole, searching among the shouting, waving figures on the dock. I saw Dushkin first. Seeing me, he ran and returned with Papa, Louise, and Dr. Kall.[4] They all shouted and waved at me with handkerchiefs and flowers, but I had lost my voice during the last two days at sea. A long time elapsed before we could leave the boat. Finally, a government official provided an escort. . . . The voyage was very tiring. Two of the eleven days were very stormy and another four were quite bad. The boat was very hot inside while the decks were bitterly cold. It is the same in the hotels here: outside it is cold and snowing but

---

[1] According to a letter to Vera, December 15, 1961, Ira left Paris "on foot, as a refugee" in 1940. The two women did not see each other again until April 19, 1971, in Marrakesh.

[2] Adolph Bolm, the dancer (*Firebird*, 1910), and his daughter Kyra Hubbel. Bolm and his wife Beata are the most frequently mentioned friends in the early California years of Vera's diary.

[3] On September 24, 1973, Mrs. Stravinsky, on board the S.S. *France* from New York to Le Havre, received a letter from Ferguson Webster's cousin, a fellow passenger who had seen the Stravinsky name on the passenger list, and who reminded Mrs. Stravinsky that they had gone to stores together in Pittsburgh in 1940.

[4] The reason that Vera does not mention Bolm and Kyra Hubbel may be that Soulima did not know them.

the rooms are so hot that I am bathed in perspiration and want to wear summer dresses. Probably for this reason everybody here drinks ice-water.

"On my first evening we sat up until 2 talking—after eating with the Dushkins in a cafeteria, an amazing kind of restaurant in which you take a tray and serve yourself. The next day, Saturday, we went to Koussevitzky's Boston Symphony matinée in which Jesús Maria Sanromá played Papa's *Capriccio*. The performance was a great success and Papa came out to take a bow. I am so sorry that I arrived too late for Papa's New York Philharmonic concerts, which were sold out and, I hear, a great success.

"In the evening Papa took me out to admire the city. It is phenomenal, but so far all those lights, all the hugeness, and the crowd on Broadway, depress me. Too many strings hold me to Europe, and I think of the coziness, the dark, and the sadness of Paris. There I loved so much to go out into the street to buy a newspaper and exchange a few words with the shopkeeper. But here, from the twentieth floor, I have not gotten around to buying myself a pair of stockings, some thread, or any of those small things. If you go into the street at all it is for business, to dine, or to visit somebody.

"After only two days in New York we went to Pittsburgh where Papa has a concert on the 24th. We came ahead of time so that he could enjoy some freedom, but acquaintances have already begun to appear. Beveridge's brother invited us to dinner with his mother and Bakaleinikov, a conductor who alternates with Fritz Reiner. Bakaleinikov was so happy to meet us Russians that his delight is difficult to describe. . . . Pittsburgh is a sad provincial city full of factories; or, more exactly, it is a colossal city consisting mainly of factories. Everything is black and covered with soot, and though it snows as hard here as in Siberia, it quickly turns gray.

"On March 15 Mrs. Bliss is arranging a concert of Papa's music in [Town Hall] New York, for *charity*—French war benefit. Part of the proceeds will go to French artists." **18** Receive letters from Europe and almost cry. **19** Go to a concert conducted by Bakaleinikov in which Josef Hofmann plays the Schumann concerto beautifully. **21** We see Garbo in *Ninotchka* (she laughs). In the evening Igor and I cut and paste newspaper notices. **22** Two letters from Fred. Today is the first time I shop alone. Igor's first rehearsal from 10 to 12:30, second rehearsal from 3 to 5:30. **23** I go to the rehearsal of *Apollo* and *Jeu de cartes*, after which Igor and I read Chekov to each other. **25** At the rehearsal Igor polishes the orchestra "with a toothbrush," as he says. **28** Concert 3–5 p.m. Very nice evening at Bakaleinikov's. **31** Dinner at Fritz Reiner's. Write letters to: Madubo, Svetik, Ira, Fred, Milene, Theodore, Olga, Valechka, Victoria Ocampo.

February

1 We leave Pittsburgh at 10 a.m. and arrive at the Great Northern Hotel, New York, at 7 in the evening. We meet Feodor Chaliapin. A telephone call at 11 p.m. Igor answers but, recognizing the voice of a woman from the press, he pretends to be someone else. "May I speak to Mme Stravinsky?" "There isn't a Mme Stravinsky." "Then with whom did you travel to Pittsburgh?" **3** Dushkin helps us move to another hotel. At lunch Igor is angry with Kall. After dinner at the Dushkins' I go to the railroad station. As soon as the train pulls out, an American says to me, "Your heart seems to be broken; you must have a drink." Then he and I and a woman who has just been seen off by three daughters go to the club car. **4** Georgette and Pearce Bailey meet me at the North Charleston station at 3:30 p.m. This does not look like an American city. In the evening, in a café,[1] a waiter brings us champagne, sent by a man sitting nearby, with a note: "This is for the nice French girls." **5** The clock on Georgette's night table shows Paris time. In town: palm trees, little white houses, negroes. Two pairs of stockings, $1.30; kleenex, witch hazel, 39 cents; Chesterfields, $1.00; taxi, 35 cents.[2] **6** At Mrs. Wigglesworth's cocktail party, I am obliged to reveal that next month I will marry Stravinsky, and am an immediate social success. Write letters to Igor and Fred, and spend the evening with Georgette and Pearce, who

takes my blood pressure; it is high. Rain. **9** An English lesson, after which we go to the seaside. **13** An English lesson in the morning, then walk with Georgette to the Hotel Sumter. **14** Third English lesson. A terrible wind at night, lamps falling from tables, papers flying around. A letter from Igor who has had good news from Europe. **15** We photograph Charleston architecture. To the cinema to see *Gone with the Wind*. Read Zola's *Nana* in French and in English. **16** Write to Ira: "How happy I was to receive your letter. Letters from Europe mention how cold it is, and here I am writing about the heat. Charleston is charming. One would not think that one is in America. It is more like Toulon or some other Mediterranean city. The houses are pink, yellow, and other light colors and have beautiful iron-grille balconies. The sun, the palms, the negroes (it seems they are sixty percent of the population) look so southern. Georgette has a very nice three-story house with a garden, black waiters and a cook.

"Although the city is cozy it does not have theaters or concerts, only movies. No bar or restaurant exists to which one could go on a spree. Drinks are forbidden except for beer (here every state has its own laws concerning alcoholic beverages). Nevertheless, cocktail parties take place every day and people frequently get drunk at them. Many people speak French, and so long as I am with Georgette and Pearce, I will never learn to speak English. I have made some progress, however, and can go shopping by myself and make complicated purchases.

"In the evenings Georgette and I knit and try to get France on the radio, not always successfully." At 8 to a performance by Martha Graham of a skeleton dancing with great technical proficiency. Afterwards, at La Boîte, a man at the next table sends a message through the waiter that he wants to pay for us. **17** A telegram from Igor. **18** All-night storm and rain. Finish *Nana*. **19** I have an English lesson. **20** A telegram from Igor in Chicago.[3] English lesson. **21** Reading Mauriac. **22** To Henri's bar. A very hot night. **23** English lesson. To the movies with Georgette. **25** Study English. **26** English lesson. Write to Svetik: "From Ira's letter of February 6, I believe that you still have not received my first letter. There was a great delay in the mail at the end of January because of storms, and because the English began to censor all mail on Bermuda. We hear that the Clipper will now take a different route, avoiding British territory. . . ." **27** English lesson. **29** The Baileys' guests arrive, and I am moved into a smaller room. The guests drink a lot before, during, and after dinner. While finishing the best cognac, Georgette is on the verge of saying many disagreeable things about America.

March

1 At midnight Pearce and Georgette take me to the station, a distance of 20 kilometers. The train should have left Charleston at 12:28 a.m. but is two and half hours late; we watch fifteen trains go by, including the "Florida Special," which seems to make the ground tremble and which frightens me. **2** The train arrives in Boston at midnight instead of 8:45. Igor and Kall are at the station and have been there since 8. We go to the Forbes's, a lovely house, filled with flowers; my windows look out on a greenhouse. After conversation by a fireplace, I go to bed very tired. In Charleston I felt sleepy all the time and could not make myself do anything except talk about Paris where the principal occupations, so we agreed, are food and criticism. We drove out of Charleston four times, and the surroundings are beautiful. I wonder whether people should marry foreigners[4] and what is the wife's role in a childless marriage?[5] How should one serve at table, according to the customs of the country or not? Once in a discussion with Georgette I said that if I felt as rebellious as she does, I would take the Clipper and return to France. Imagine, keeping her clock on Paris time! Her husband has a right to be irritated. After all, she speaks with an awful accent, mixes up all the words, and does nothing but criticize his country. **3** Igor wakes me up in the morning on his way to a rehearsal. The ground here is covered with snow except for dry patches of moss. Forbes's daughter, Zazy, an actress, fetches me and we have a glass of sherry, awaiting the return of Igor with Kall and Teracuzio.[6] After lunch we drive to Bedford to get a marriage license. Teracuzio has a small house here, surrounded by pine

---

[1] Actually the restaurant Henri's; in February 1950 Mme Stravinsky and her husband dined at what, so far as she remembered, was the same table.

[2] Stravinsky seems to have requested that all expenses be listed. Accordingly, every penny is accounted for in nearly every entry in Vera's diary.

[3] Stravinsky (with Kall) was in Chicago to conduct a pair of concerts with the

Chicago Symphony.

[4] Dr. Pearce Bailey was American.

[5] Mrs. Stravinsky's own case.

[6] Timothy Teracuzio, of the Slavic Languages Department at Harvard University.

woods. After tea, Igor returns to Cambridge, and I am alone. In the evening the Teracuzios go to a rehearsal for an amateur performance and I go to bed and read Dostoevsky. **4** Try to talk English with Evelyn, Teracuzio's attractive, blonde wife. Read more Dostoevsky. A squirrel outside my window, and a dog called Chappy. **5** My divorce is effectuated from 9:30 to 12:30.[1] Lawyer John Divine. Also a judge. Lunch at the Forbes house. I rest in Igor's room until he goes to a rehearsal at 5, after which I return to Bedford with Teracuzio. I am so very tired that Igor thinks I am not well, but I am simply preparing myself to be Mrs. Igor Stravinsky. **6** Igor's concert. **8** Igor gives a lesson to Robert Stevenson. In the evening, Igor's concert. Meet Mrs. Bliss and Mrs. Walter Gropius. **9** At 12:30 the Bedford Town Clerk performs our marriage ceremony. We go to the Hotel Hemenway in Boston. **10** Koussevitzky gives a lunch for us, actually a wedding feast with a table full of white flowers, very hospitable, elegant, and cozy. Gregor Piatigorsky and Teracuzio are there. **11** To the French Consul, a cold, malicious bureaucrat who leaves me with a painful impression all day. Boaz Piller[2] takes us to an immigration lawyer and to a dentist, Dr. Fink.[3] The lawyer[4] calmed me, promising to straighten my papers. **12** Igor at the dentist. Later he reads his lecture to me. **13** Cable of felicitations on our marriage from Madubo. Dinner at the Forbes house. Olga Naumovna Koussevitzky drives us to the lecture. Not many people are there[5] and Igor was not pleased. He reads very well and afterward takes the night train to New York. **14** Igor's matinee concert in Town Hall, New York for the benefit of French musicians. He conducts the *Dumbarton Oaks* Concerto, *Histoire du soldat*, the Octet, and, with Adele Marcus, plays his *Concerto per due pianoforti soli*. **15** Boston. Lunch in the Amalfi restaurant,[6] and dinner at home. Write to Ira: "My dear Irusha, I am your aunt now. It happened on March 9, in a village near Boston. We were so busy with obligations on the wedding day and the day after, that only two days later could we send a wire to Madubo telling her to inform the children and you about the event. Igor—my husband (I must become accustomed to the word)—left for New York, where he is giving a concert for the benefit of French musicians, under the patronage of the French Ambassador. I decided that to go for a day and two nights would be too tiring, so I took this opportunity to attend to some chores. Igor will be in New York again from the first to the eighth of April; I will go with him then. On April 8, we go to Washington to visit Mrs. Bliss and attend a reception at the Embassy. This is very important, since the French Consul is a pig: he refused to do anything about my passport or transferral of my French citizenship, whereas, since I am still a French subject, he should have taken care of me. I speak English well enough now and know many people who could help.

"I wrote to you from Charleston where I had a very enjoyable time with Georgette. I left on a very hot day, after seeing some marvelous plantations and gardens of azaleas and camellias. I took the Florida night train to Boston, which was full of snow. The day after my arrival I was taken to the country to a Russian friend married to an American (who did not know a word of Russian). I stayed there for a week, surrounded by mountains of snow near a pine forest, in a country house guarded by big dogs. Meanwhile, my divorce papers and other documents were put in order.

"During that week I went twice to Igor's concerts and receptions in Boston. On Saturday we were married in a little country house. A clerk told us to keep our hands raised and to swear that we would be with each other in health and sickness. We said 'yes,' drank champagne, and left immediately for Boston." **16** At 5:30 Igor's lesson with Stevenson. **17** Lunch at the Forbes' house. A tall, gray-haired beautiful woman there reminds me of Lyudmila Gavrilovna. Betsy Forbes, a good-looking girl with a big behind, blows in like a dog released from a leash, and kisses Igor and me. The food is very good. The hostess carves the meat, which is served by two white maids, less ceremoniously than in Charleston, where the servants were black. After lunch we go to Back Bay railroad

station to meet Adele Marcus. Arrive at the Exeter Inn at 6:45. Igor's lecture and the performance of the *Concerto per due pianoforti soli*. Woof talks on the phone with Dagmar Godowsky in New York, then makes a scene with Igor. **19** I shop by myself today, and when I refuse a bad chicken, saying, "I am from Paris and am accustomed to having chickens with full breasts," the butcher says, "You mean a *poule de luxe*!" **20** In Koussevitzky's car to Igor's lecture on Russian music. He had two topographical maps, of Europe and of France. He looked so slim and young and spoke so well. Mme Koussevitzky looked like an eagle. Her niece[7] is very polite, with a meek voice. Mme Gropius looks as if she is resolved to live well in America, her face saying, "Everything is wonderful here, and it will get better and better." I saw a young Frenchman, Pierre, whom I had met in Rome. The Russians who were present thought Igor's lecture was too dogmatic. **21** Piller comes with Moses Smith,[8] a representative from Columbia Records. **22** 4–6, Igor meets with the students. Teracuzio for dinner. **23** To Winchester to see Dobouzhinsky's exhibition. **24** Igor gives an interview, with photographers, for the newspapers. The *Post* interviews me, and I have to manage by myself, since Woof arrives only at the end. **25** Igor's orchestra rehearsal at 10 a.m. In the evening to Koussevitzky's charity concert at Symphony Hall with Lily Pons. To the French Consulate for Igor's passport. **26** Rehearsals at 10 and 4:45. Much ado about the contralto for *Oedipus Rex*: she lost her voice. Send to New York for another singer. Dinner at Amalfi. **27** Tenor Jobin at 11 a.m. Igor rehearses with the new singer, Peable. 6:45 dress rehearsal. **28** *Apollo* rehearsal at 10. At 8, Igor's concert at Cambridge: a sell-out and a great success. **29** Igor rehearses with the new singer from 10 to 11. Concert in Boston at 3, absolutely packed. In the evening to a cinema with Igor. **30** Igor angry at Woof, who did not take care of money matters and letters. Igor's concert in Boston at 8. **31** Our honeymoon trip! We leave for New York at noon, but Woof forgot the tickets at the hotel and we have to return. Igor is furious. Then Woof loses two suitcases and a pocketbook on our arrival in New York. Igor outraged. Spent the evening with the Dushkins. Fantastic night-view of Central Park from the Barbizon Plaza Hotel.

April

1 Igor's rehearsal with the New York Philharmonic at 10 and 2. The old story with *Le Sacre du printemps*: the score is from the revised version but the parts are from the old one. **2** Igor's rehearsals in Carnegie Hall at 10 and 2. Journalists at 5. **3** Igor's rehearsal at 10. He rests afterwards, then works on the score. I walk for an hour in Central Park. Concert at 8:45. After it, sandwiches and beer in our hotel rooms until 1 a.m. **4** Igor records *Le Sacre du printemps*. I go to see Dr. Joseph Iorgy. Later, waiting for Igor, I have tea with the Dushkins at Rumpelmeyer's. Igor returns at 6 exhausted. We dine in a small restaurant. Write to Fred Osten-Saken: "Kall constantly forgets things, wrongly addresses important letters, gets drunk, and has difficulty waking up in the morning. In spite of his good side—he is an educated and highly sensitive man—he irritates Igor beyond endurance. Igor would not have employed Kall as a secretary if his deterioration to such an extent had been suspected. I have taken on some of Kall's duties, since my memory is superior to his, but Igor is still extremely annoyed by him. This charming companion with interesting memories of another life in St. Petersburg should not be allowed to come near any business matter. At the moment, Igor has a hellish job making recordings. I look after him, prepare food for him, change his underwear when it is drenched in perspiration, and, in general, organize our life. I have to keep journalists away, and I am afraid of Sudeikin. Tales have appeared in newspapers about 'the greatest love story,' and 'the beautiful Vera working with Sudeikin for Diaghilev'—trash of that sort. I am looking at New York from the 29th floor." **5** Igor's concert in Carnegie Hall at 2:30. Dinner at Mrs.

[1] For a documented account of this see *A Stravinsky Scrapbook*, Thames and Hudson, London and New York, 1983.

[2] Russian-speaking contrabassoonist of the Boston Symphony Orchestra. He had been introduced to Stravinsky by Pierre Monteux, June 10, 1922, in the composer's quarters in the Rue Rochechouart, Paris ("you made your appearance à la Liszt in a robe de chambre"). When Stravinsky returned from his Chicago concerts in February 1940 he took Piller in his confidence, "and I learned about your intended marriage. I got you the apartment near Symphony Hall (as you requested) and you invited me to come every day for 5 o'clock tea. I recall the wedding luncheon I offered at the America restaurant, Durgin and Park, and your indignation when you found out that they did not serve wine. But Piller knew how to get it and . . . got it." (Letter to Stravinsky, June 17, 1957.)

[3] 100 Boylston Street.

[4] David Greenberg, 80 Federal Street.

[5] Stravinsky lectured in French.

[6] After dining here in February 1949, the composer became ill with food poisoning.

[7] She became the next Mrs. Koussevitzky, after the death of her aunt (1943).

[8] Director of Masterworks at Columbia Records, best remembered for his biography of Koussevitzky which the subject tried to suppress.

88

88 March 9, 1940. Bedford, Massachusetts. Before the wedding. With Evelyn Teracuzio.

89 March 9, 1940. Boston. Leaving for the wedding.

90 June 1940. Hollywood. Farmers' Market, with Dorothy and Edwin McQuoid.

91 November 1940. Cincinnati.

90

89

91

Mitchell's,[1] with Fritz Kreisler and his wife, the Dushkins, and Olga Samaroff, the first wife of Stokowski. A wonderful house, flowers in profusion (worth at least $100), and a French chef and waiters. **6** Golubev[2] comes with flowers, and we lunch at the Central Park Zoo. Lovely weather. Igor's concert at 8:45 in Carnegie Hall.   **7** Igor's final Philharmonic concert at 3 p.m.[3] In our box: Katherine Wolff, Olga Baklanova[4] with her husband (a writer), and a Mr. Hearst. Zosia Kochanska, Katya Sergava[5] with Eugene Berman, and [Mrs. Charles B.] Goodspeed come to see us. For dinner: Dushkin, Golubev, Kall. We leave for Washington at 10 p.m.   **8** Washington. Lunch with Ginny Hill.[6] Dinner at Mrs. Bliss's.   **9** Lunch at the French Embassy. Igor sits next to Mrs. Winslow, a lookalike friend of Nadia Boulanger, while I am between the Ambassador and Mr. de Rosen. Terrible news: Denmark and Norway are occupied by the Germans. Mr. Bliss, Igor, and I have dinner together. Leave for Boston at 9 p.m.   **10** In Boston, 7:35 a.m., Igor goes to bed. Igor's lecture in the afternoon, then a reception at the Forbes house. **11** Igor begins composing the last movement of the Symphony. At 6 we go to the cinema, which is very dull.   **12** We make up a small dictionary of political and military terms, such as "to shell" and "to wreck." **13** Igor's lesson to Stevenson.   **14** Igor and I shop in the morning, and at 3 we go to kosher shops to buy things for a dinner that we are preparing. Igor is nervous because we must get references from the French police for our US quotas. I read a novel to him.   **15** We are at police headquarters from 2:30 to 4, and, in the evening, at the Chamber Music Club.   **16** Teracuzio for lunch. Golubev cooks. In the evening, a good film with Charles Laughton and Vivien Leigh.   **18** Roses from Dagmar Godowsky. Igor meets with students. I send three regrets for invitations, and write to Victoria Ocampo: "Igor and I were married on March 9 here in Boston, where we will stay until the end of his course at Harvard, May 5. Leaving Boston, we will be in New York (Barbizon Plaza) May 5–10, then go by boat to New Orleans and Galveston, and from there by train to Los Angeles. Igor needs tranquillity in which to complete his symphony, his entire concert tour next season being based on the performance of the work. Our address in Los Angeles for the moment is c/o Dr. A. Kall, 143 South Gramercy. Igor has some concerts in Mexico City and we will go there about the 15th of July, the only absence during the entire summer and until the end of October. If you think that it is possible for us to come to Buenos Aires in 1941, the joy of seeing you again would be very great. Should something be done about this now? We receive very few letters from Paris and these tell us only about a very sad life. The most recent political news simply bewilders us." **20** Read to Igor. He gives a lesson to Stevenson, who stays for dinner. We go to a Koussevitzky concert: Hindemith and Scriabin. Piller invites us afterward to the Café Rouge.   **23** Receive a postcard from Picasso. Call off a dinner engagement at Pitirim Sorokin's and go to the cinema. **24** Piller for lunch. Igor works with Burgin,[7] who stays for dinner. Igor spends the whole evening working with students.   **25** Igor's lecture, from 4 to 5, is followed by a concert. The students include boys with pink socks and girls with pink hair ribbons. In the evening Igor reads to me

the 12 Gospels used in the Russian Church Service.   **26** To the Russian Church at 9. The priest has a strange, high, penetrating voice.   **27** Igor's lesson with Stevenson.   **28** Russian Easter. Send flowers to the Koussevitzkys. Lunch at Oyster House. To the zoo.   **29** Professor Tilman Merritt[8] takes us to Mrs. Edward Ballantine's for dinner.   **30** Burgin at 6. Dinner at Louis Speyer's.[9]

May

1 At 5 a singer, Olga Averino. At 9 we go to the Russian Bear restaurant.   **2** To Mme Gropius at 3:15. Dinner with Walter Gropius and Edward Forbes.   **3** Otto Klemperer[10] comes: a very moving encounter. He looks ill but elegant, and he brings a rose. To Dobouzhinsky's exhibition. Dinner at Mrs. Sach's.[11]   **4** A young man comes to show his compositions. Igor gives Forbes the manuscript of the lectures for publication.   **6** To the dentist, Dr. Fink, who takes movies of us. A farewell reception at 5, then with Balanchine to "Southland," to hear a wonderful Negro orchestra.   **7** We go aboard our boat at 5:50 p.m. **8** Up at 6 to admire the view of New York. Dushkin meets us.   **10** Shaken by events in Europe.   **11** Buy a blue straw hat at Macy's for $4.85. **12** Lunch with Carl Engel.[12] Evening at the Dushkins' with Vladimir Golschmann.   **13** Dinner with Dr. Garbat.[13]   **14** Sedan is captured by the Germans.   **15** Our boat, the *Seminole*, sails at noon. Igor and I play bingo, though we are upset on hearing the bad news on the radio.   **16** A rough sea. Study English with Golubev, then play poker.   **17** We listen to the news.[14]   **18** At 6 a.m. we watch our boat nearing Miami. On shore we see crocodiles being beaten on the head to make them move. **19** Beautiful blue sea. I would like to be a water nymph in the Gulf of Mexico.   **20** Cocktails with Veronica Hart. Big gala on board. Woof recites poetry (Turgenev).   **21** Galveston. Met by Rodolfo Gonzales, representative of Teatro Rex, Monterrey, Mexico. We are stunned by the news from France. Mrs. Gilman spends the day with us, until we leave for Houston by train.   **23** We arrive in Los Angeles like refugees, and spend a very uncomfortable night in Kall's very poor house. We decide to move into an apartment tomorrow, and not to look for a house until after Mexico. We have been very nervous and even mean in the last few days, because of the terrible news we heard in Galveston.   **24** Final quarrel with Kall. His house has no electricity, no gas, and no telephone, since none of these utilities has been paid for. But of dirt there is a great deal. **25** At 4 p.m., Klemperer.   **26** At 2 p.m., Dorothy[15] takes us to her house. **28** The Belgian Army surrenders!   **29** All Saints' Day. A morning drive with the Bolms. Igor stays home and sleeps. Dinner at Rodakevitch's.[16] **31** Drive around all day looking for a house. I write to Moses Smith: "As promised, I am sending you an account of our trip from New York to Galveston. . . . At Miami we took a taxi to visit the city, the beach, the Indian village—an agreeable and cool promenade. In the evenings we had lotto, races, and dances to watch. And there was a swimming pool. The sea in the Gulf of Mexico is an unforgettable blue and the night breeze is so soft and perfumed that the memory of it will last all my life.

---

[1] On October 3, 1941, Mrs. Charles E. Mitchell sent Stravinsky a copy of her book, *Music with a Feather Duster*, together with a letter offering "warmest remembrances" to him "and your charming wife." The book describes a meeting with Stravinsky "seventeen years ago," and the authoress says that she ate *blini* with him more than once at the Café La Rue in Paris with a "mutual Russian friend." After correcting an error in the margin, Stravinsky answered: "Very dear Madame, How can I thank you for your kind words and for the book that I just received? The few fragments that I have had time to look over make me want to read the book in its entirety, and as quickly as possible, because I recognize the good humor and the spirit so characteristic of its author. A thousand thanks. All the best to you. I. Str." [Original in English]

[2] Gregory Golubev was one of Stravinsky's numerous agents.

[3] This was the first Stravinsky concert that R.C. heard live.

[4] Star of the 1916 Russian film *He Who Gets Slapped*, and a friend of Vera's since 1915, in Moscow.

[5] The Russian actress, Catherine Sergava, then living at 66 West 55th Street.

[6] Ginny Carpenter Hill (Mrs. Patrick Hill) was the daughter of John Alden and Rue Carpenter.

[7] Richard Burgin, concertmaster and assistant conductor of the Boston Symphony Orchestra.

[8] Professor of music at Harvard University.

[9] The English-hornist of the Boston Symphony Orchestra.

[10] Klemperer was conductor of the Los Angeles Philharmonic.

[11] Mrs. Paul Sachs, sister-in-law of Arthur Sachs. Paul Sachs was the director of the Fogg Museum.

[12] Editor of *The Musical Quarterly*.

[13] Stravinsky's physician in New York since 1925.

[14] On May 17, aboard the S.S. *Seminole* (Clyde-Mallory Lines), Vera wrote to Mrs. Edward Forbes, thanking her for the red roses that she had sent to the boat and for the farewell party at Gerry's Landing: "Our stay in New York and the voyage would have been very agreeable if the news from Europe hadn't been so terrible. We listen constantly to the radio from which, between a rhumba and a foxtrot, comes a description of a battle more fierce than has ever been seen before. It is terrifying. . . . The boat is small but quite steady in a sea that was rougher the second day than the first. The food is not bad and there is a cinema in the evenings. We already feel the tropics, and I am thinking of the heat that we may expect tomorrow in Miami. The blue of the water is dazzling and there are flying fish. . . ." Stravinsky signed the letter, "votre Igor."

[15] Dorothy McQuoid. Her husband, Edwin, was a professional photographer.

[16] Second husband of Margaret Adams Plummer, who had married Curtis Bok of Philadelphia in 1924, and in 1933, two years after the birth of their son Derek (now—1985—president of Harvard University), obtained a divorce on grounds of cruelty. In the mid-1940s she divorced Rodakevitch, a film director, and married the surgeon William Kiskadden. Peggy Kiskadden was a close friend of the Stravinskys and Huxleys.

Galveston was terribly hot and the bad news from Europe so shocked us that we gave up our idea of going to the Grand Canyon and came directly to Los Angeles. My husband received your letter and at the same time the packages with the records. . . ."[1] [Original in French]

June

1 The Bolms drive us to Palos Verdes to dine with the Remisovs.[2] This is a lovely country! What a view! **2** At 5 the Bolms drive us to Hageman's.[3] **3** Paris is bombarded and 45 people are killed, 200 wounded. A gray day: Where is the blue sky of California? Letters from Ira and Madubo that make me cry. Bad news about our quota. At 7, Igor and I look at a house, 124 South Swall Drive, and like it so much that we sign the contract immediately. **4** To the cinema, where I cry at the sight of refugees in the newsreels. **6** We move in three automobiles into the new house. **7** A service for Igor's mother in the Russian church.[4] The piano arrives. Dinner at the Ambassador Hotel with Mr. Wulsin.[5] **9** We eat in Dorothy's garden. Russian food (shashlik). At home by 6 p.m. Igor writes to Carlos Chavez. **11** Golubev drives Igor to the dentist. Very low spirits because of Paris. **13** Possibility of surrender of Paris. At 2 p.m., lawyers. **14** Paris is occupied by the Germans! **15** At 4:30 we go to Bel Air with Klemperer. For dinner in our house: Varvara Christophorovna and Bertensson.[6] **17** France asks for peace. **19** We go to a garden party at Edward G. Robinson's, with Marlene Dietrich, Josef von Sternberg, Erich Remarque, Amfiteatrov.[7] **20** I pass the examination for my driving license, and we look at cars. **21** We buy a car—insurance $70—and I join the Automobile Club. **22** Armistice! **25** A day of mourning for France. At 5, Arthur Bliss, an English composer. **28** At 4:30, Baron de Meyer.[8] **30** A garden party in honor of Bruno Walter at Mr. Harvey Mudd's. A woman there whom we knew in Frankfurt, Dorothy Huttenbach.

July

1 Igor gives me $10. Mussia Antonini is here. **2** I now read newspapers at length in English. **4** Independence Day. Golubev, with his lady friends, calls on Igor, which greatly annoys him. **5** Dinner at Erich Korngold's with Max Reinhardt, Jarmila Novotna, and Baron Georges Dauber. **8** Georgette arrives at 8 a.m. Lawyer from 3 to 5. **9** Dinner in a drive-in. **10** Dinner at Edward G. Robinson's with Marlene Dietrich, Remarque, Max Steiner, Hedda Hopper, Baron de Meyer, Bernardine Fritz, Anatole Litvak.[9] **12** Lawyer from 11 to 4. Terrible heat. John Barbirolli comes. We go to his Hollywood Bowl concert. **13** Igor works a lot and is very tired. The two of us dine alone together at Swiss Chalet, where we see Nina Conan Doyle with Prince Mdivani, her brother. **14** Write to Ira: "Dear Irusha, I am writing this in the office of a lawyer. We have spent an entire month sitting in this office, every visit—several times each week—lasting for half a day. We are trying to get permits to remain in this country and to get visas to go to Mexico. Regulations are very strict now, and all sorts of permits are necessary for exits and re-entries. We are frightened of being stuck in Mexico. We will not go by airplane (15 hours) but by train, which I do not mind, since it will give me an opportunity to rest from all the parties, the visits, the chauffeuring, the telephone calls. The distances are enormous here, and I drive as much as 150 kilometers a day.

"Igor is very nervous, always waiting for news from France and reading the papers. I get up every morning at 7 and almost always go to bed after midnight. The whole day is spent in work and in hurrying, worse than it used to be in Paris.

"Yesterday a letter came from Fred dated May 29. His whole letter is

about horses. So many world events are taking place, yet he still writes only about horses." **15** A wedding party at Simeon Aller's. Igor got drunk. **16** Phone call from Mexico. We are nervous about the quota problems and the expected answer from Washington does not come. Instead, we received some gossip about the behavior of the New York Philharmonic Orchestra when Igor conducted them. **17** Lawyer at 11. Cocktails at Kall's with Mischa Auer. **18** Leave for Mexico at 8. **21** Third day traveling. The stations are not quite so forlorn as yesterday, though there is enough dirt and wretchedness. Guadalajara, a charming town surrounded by eucalyptus. Bluish mountains in the background. **22** Mexico City at 9 a.m.: music at the railroad station. **23** Lunch at the Paseo, bad and expensive. The Bal y Gays. We met them in Madrid in 1933; she is the pianist Rosita Bal. We go to the Palace of Maximilian and to the park. Trees! **24** Lunch at the Prendes restaurant with Bal and Salazar.[10] Siesta from 3 to 5, then tea at One-Two-Three, then journalists from papers and magazines. **26** Igor's first concert in Mexico. **27** We go with Elena Ponce to see the pyramids of Teotihuacan. **28** Igor's second concert. Afterward to Lady Baltimore's[11] with the Bals. **29** Marcus arrives.[12] Lunch at Chavezs'; he is Mexican, she is Viennese.

August

2 Igor's third concert. **4** Igor's fourth concert. Go to Cuernavaca with Pierre de L. Boal, Counselor of the United States Embassy in Mexico. To Guadalupe. **5** Leave Mexico. **8** Reaching Nogales at 12:50 p.m., we spend three hours on the frontier filling out papers and being examined by doctors. At last all is in order and the US Consul drives us to our railroad car. **9** Arrive at 7:30 a.m. in Los Angeles, which feels like home. Met by Bolm and photographers. Igor writes to Zimmermann concerning his article about the bad behavior of the New York Philharmonic. I write to Ira: "No one told us that reading was impossible on that terrible train to Mexico because of constant and violent shaking, and that the food in the restaurant car would be inedible. After the frontier, the train, already hot and airless, filled up with families of shrieking Mexican children. It was not possible to lie down, and scarcely possible even to sit on the bench-like seats. But the sights were unforgettable: the Indians on mules riding in a dry river-bed; the terrible poverty of the villages; the big buzzards with white necks sitting on crooked telephone poles; the old cars filled with women and naked children: there are so many children in the country! At the stations, instead of the expected small villages, we saw only one or two huts in open fields with cactus. The names of most stations were barely legible on rough boards covered with white paint. We rode through deserts all day and only toward evening did the first few small stations appear. In spite of the terrible heat, we left the train at many of the stations. We saw people sitting at tables in darkness, except for candles, eating bread and drinking tequila. At some stations merchandise was piled up and at all of them dirty children in tatters were selling fruit, drinks, chickens. We bought mangoes, which I ate for the first time, and Igor was enticed by the bananas, which really tasted much better than any that we ever had in Europe. If we hadn't heard that we shouldn't drink tap water here, or eat raw fruit, I would have bought everything that I saw at those stations. At bigger stations, ice was loaded on the train, and the children tried to steal pieces of it.

"During the daytime stops, horsemen came near the train. They wore pink shirts, green or brown trousers, big sombreros, spurs on their boots, and some of them had lassoes in their hands. What we saw was real life and not something prepared for export.

"On the third day we arrived in Guadalajara. Since the train stops there for one and a half hours, we took a taxi to see the city and the

---

[1] The test pressing of *Le Sacre du printemps*.

[2] Mr. and Mrs. Nikolai Vladimirovich Remisov. He was a Russian painter who had exhibited in Paris with Bakst and Sudeikin in 1921.

[3] Richard Hageman (1882–1966), Dutch-born conductor and film composer.

[4] The Stravinskys attended the Russian Orthodox Church on Micheltorena Street when they first moved to California, and in later years there, the Russian Orthodox Church (bulldozed in the 1970s) at 5433 Fountain Avenue, Hollywood, because this was the church of Vladimir and Lisa Sokolov. But "attended" begs a question. They went only on their birthdays, Christmas, and Easter, and on anniversaries of the deaths of Stravinsky's mother, first wife, and daughter, though even this practice was soon discontinued. Stravinsky never entered a Russian Church after the mid-1950s.

[5] Lucien Wulsin, director of Baldwin Pianos, first met Stravinsky in Nadia Boulanger's Paris apartment in 1935. He died in Cincinnati, January 13, 1964.

[6] Dr. Sergei Bertensson, Mussorgsky's biographer.

[7] Film composer. Stravinsky had known him in Turin in 1933.

[8] Adolphe de Meyer (1868–January 6, 1949), best known for his photo portraits of Nijinsky. The title of baron was conferred by the King of Saxony at the request of his cousin, King Edward VII. See *De Meyer* by Philippe Jullian, New York, Alfred A. Knopf, 1976.

[9] Miss Fritz was the niece of Henrietta Szold, founder of Hadassah. Litvak was the Russian-born (1902) film director, best known for *Mayerling* (1936).

[10] Adolfo Salazar, musicologist. Stravinsky met him in Madrid in 1916.

[11] A chocolate and tea shop in Mexico City.

[12] The immigration lawyer from Los Angeles. He accompanied the Stravinskys on their re-entry to the United States at Nogales.

cathedral. The air was wonderfully fragrant, in spite of the dirt and dust.

"At Mexico City we were met by Chavez and his wife, a German woman with a reddish face, by Ricardo Ortega, the orchestra manager, and by a crowd of photographers. At the Hotel Reforma, photographers and interviewers invaded us all morning. After lunch and a rehearsal, friends came: Alfonso Reyes,[1] Salazar, Bal. The city itself does not make a great impression, but the view around it, the mountains, the air, and the sun are extraordinary. We were warned so much about food, water, and the altitude, but we were not affected by them. The next day I went to see the cathedral and the museum, where we were surprised by the characteristic expression of the Aztec sculpture. In the nineteenth-century section a guard asked me to sit on a stool and put my fingers on a harpsichord.

"We ate at Paolo's with Bal and Azev, then went to Chapultepec Park with its old trees: how much history they have witnessed! We also visited Maximilian's Castle, but toward evening felt tired. Reyes arrived, however, and took us to his house for a 'café au lait' and an omelette. (Mexicans do not eat a heavy meal in the evening.) He is very proud of his house and his library, which is large enough to be a public one. It is said that Reyes abducted his wife on a horse, supposedly a custom here." 10 [Hollywood] Awful heat. First day of our new cook, Bessie Nebraska. At the lawyer's all morning: we receive our first papers! At Baron de Meyer's from 4 to 7 p.m. 12 Igor and I dine at Bit of Sweden.[2] 13 Kall at 6 p.m. Igor does not feel well. We do not go to the Hollywood Bowl. After the Hageman concert, a party at Harry's Cohn's. 15 A party at Montemezzi's,[3] but Igor is too tired, and I go with Antonini and Baron de Meyer. 17 Rehearsal of Firebird. Igor very nervous. I am given flowers and photographed. Dinner with Cecil B. de Mille. Very pleasant company. 19 Zoya Karabanova for tea.[4] I write to Eleanor Schreiber, 141 Alte Landstrasse, Zurich: "Dear Mrs. Schreiber,[5] My husband and I thank you with all our hearts for your kindness. Your telegram and letter, our most recent news from Europe, gave us great joy. Until now we have received letters from Theodore, my husband's elder son, who is with his wife in Haute Garonne, from Ira Belline, who is in Auvergne, and from Milene in Sancellemoz. That is all. We know that Mlle Svitalski remained in Paris and that Nini is somewhere in Nevers, and we impatiently await letters from them as well as from Olga Sallard, whose last letter is dated June 7!

"Milene wrote to us that she is without money and is unable to receive any from Paris. We wanted to send her some, but even the Red Cross refuses to do it. Switzerland is the only country from which money can be sent. Do you think it would be possible to forward to her the $50 that we sent you through the Bankers Trust Company in New York? Please forgive the inconvenience. Surely you have enough to attend to without this, but I am counting on your goodness. Milene wrote that the best way would be to send the money to the Société Generale's branch in Chamonix—unless you know of a better method. Milene Stravinsky's address is: Sancellemoz (Sanatorium), Haute-Savoie.

"Could you write to Olga and tell her how much I think of her and how happy I would be to correspond with her again? We will stay in California until November 1, after which we go on a concert tour of North America. Toward February or March we expect to return to California, which pleases both of us very much—the sun, the climate, the beautiful countryside, the charming homes. Everything is marvelous here, and life is less expensive than elsewhere.

---

[1] Stravinsky had met the Mexican poet in Buenos Aires in 1936.

[2] A restaurant at the corner of Sunset Boulevard and Doheny Drive.

[3] Italo Montemezzi, composer of the opera L'Amore di tre re.

[4] Former Russian film actress, best known for her performance in Yakov Protozanov's Woman with a Dagger (1916). She and Vera had been friends in Moscow in 1915.

[5] Vera seems to have known Mme Schreiber from the mid-1930s, possibly at Davos and through Olga Sallard, a mutual friend.

[6] Victor Babin and Vitya Vronsky, the duo-pianists, later became very good friends of the Stravinskys, and Mme Stravinsky and Mme Babin continued to see each other after the deaths of their husbands in, respectively, 1971 and 1972.

[7] See the chapter on Firebird in Stravinsky: Selected Correspondence, Vol. II, op. cit. When Fokine died, a few months later, Stravinsky telegraphed his widow, care of Hurok Attractions, 711 Fifth Avenue: "Accept my heartfelt condolences in your great grief. Am deeply shocked and mourning my collaborator who gave the world unforgettable visions." [Original in English]

"I thank you again, my dear, for all the news you so kindly sent us. I also thank you in advance for all your efforts. I hope to hear a little something from you, which I would read with great joy. My husband sends you his respects, and I embrace you with all my heart. Affectionately, Vera." [Original in French] 23 In the evening to a concert by Vronsky and Babin at Hollywood Bowl.[6] 24 Igor's rehearsal at 9 a.m. Lunch with Deems Taylor. To the Bowl again in the evening to see Remisov's costumes. 25 To Santa Barbara for lunch. Igor and Bolm send a telegram to Fokine.[7] 26 Igor's rehearsal in the Bowl at 7:30 p.m. Write to Ira: "In a few minutes I am going to the rehearsal of Firebird in Hollywood Bowl. (Remisov made the sets; he lives in a lovely place with a beautiful view of Catalina Island which is illuminated in the background across the lovely velvety sea.) Even an ordinary outing such as going to a concert in the Bowl entails many difficulties. For instance, parking the car: try to imagine twenty thousand people getting there, all with their own automobiles. To park takes at least half an hour, and the parking lot is half a kilometer uphill from the Bowl. When you finally arrive, you still must walk a considerable distance and then find your seat. Even thinking of it makes me lose all desire to go. Most women sit at night concerts there in fur coats, for no matter how hot in the daytime, the Bowl is always very cool at night. . . . I like California for its beautiful landscapes, the sea, the mountains, the orange groves, the real cactus desert. . . . But the taste of food is questionable here. Fifty years ago this was desert and it hardly ever rains. Therefore everything that grows is artificial (irrigated). By now, however, I am accustomed to the relative tastelessness of California vegetables and fruit. Americans serve their food decorated, even cutting up fruit into little squares and balls. . . . I spend much of my time fighting off invitations; we have several for each day. . . ." 30 To Marcus for fingerprinting. Babin and Vronsky come for high tea. After the concert at the Bowl, and the reception, we drive Basil Rathbone's niece to Bel Air.

September

2 Go at 4 to Edward G. Robinson's ranch: Rouben Mamoulian, Lillian May, Bloomingdale, Lovet Lorsky (the sculptor), Harry Lachman, a Chinese woman. 6 Drive to Carmel for dinner (the Blue Bird Inn), and spend the night in Monterrey at Mrs. Stein's. 7 Cypress Groves and Point Lobos. At Cora Felton's,[8] Louise Varèse.[9] 8 To Los Gatos, then dinner with Mrs. Marcus S. Koshland.[10] 9 San Francisco. In Mrs. Koshland's car for lunch at Cliff House. To an exhibition, then tea at Hospitality House, where Igor's music is played on the radio. Dinner at a club. Then the film Cavalcade. Spend the night at Cora Felton's. 10 Lunch at Olympic Country Club with John Rothschild. Dinner with the Darius Milhauds. 11 Exposition.[11] Lunch with George Creel (president). Aquacade. 12 Drive to Yosemite and spend the night at 7500 feet. 13 We leave at 5 a.m. and reach Hollywood at 5 p.m. 15 In The New York Times: De Basil's ballet is giving Pulcinella and Petrushka, Massine's ballet Jeu de cartes and Petrushka. 19 Dinner at Mussia Antonini's (I lend her $100 by check), with Nina Koshetz [the soprano] and Zoya Karabanova. 22 Drive with Igor to San Pedro, the port of Los Angeles. My first English lesson. Birthday dinner at Bolms with Bronislava Nijinska. 28 To the English Consul's, then lunch at Vicki Baum's.[12] 29 We celebrate my name day with a lot of people at the Remisovs': the Sokolovs,[13] the Tamirovs,[14] the Sergei Bertenssons, Varvara Christophorovna.

---

[8] After returning to Hollywood, Mrs. Stravinsky wrote her first letter in English to Cora Felton: "We have enjoyed so much staying in your lovely country home and also in San Francisco. . . . Your hospitality and the charming evenings will always be a beautiful remembrance. . . ."

[9] Translator from the French and wife of Edgard Varèse.

[10] Later, from Hollywood, Mrs. Stravinsky wrote to Mrs. Koshland: "We thoroughly enjoyed your lovely house as well as your charming self. We left your beautiful city regretfully and we look forward with much pleasure to another visit. . . ." Learning of the Stravinskys' next visit to San Francisco, Mrs. Koshland invited them to stay in her 3800 Washington Street home, but Vera wrote that her husband "feels that we should stay this time at a hotel, since it will be more convenient for rehearsals. . . ."

[11] The San Francisco World's Fair.

[12] The best-selling novelist was married to conductor Richard Lert.

[13] Vladimir Sokolov, the actor, and his wife Lisa were to become the closest friends of the Stravinskys in Hollywood in the period 1944–48. Lisa and Vera opened the art gallery La Boutique together in 1945.

[14] Akim Tamirov, the actor, and his wife.

October

4 My fourth English lesson. [Gregory] Stone [agent] works with Igor all morning. Igor is in a state of nerves. **5** Vladimir and Odette Golschmann for dinner. **6** I study English diligently. Dinner at Chasen's with Carl Engel, then to Bolms' with Lichine [dancer] and Riabushinska [dancer]. **7** Fifth English lesson. Lunch at, and tour through, Paramount Studio. **9** Igor aggravated by telegrams and phone calls. **10** Letter from Milene. Igor sends $100 to her and Ira. A buffet supper with the Dmitri Tiomkins. **11** I walk with Igor on the Santa Monica pier. He postpones Walt Disney until the 12th. **12** We go to Walt Disney's studio, which is a whole city. Igor is horrified by the bad taste. We see *Fantasia*, in which Deems Taylor talks nonsense and Stokowski goes up and down a staircase bathed in red light. **13** Igor conducts an orchestra of wonderful young people who sightread his Violin Concerto played by Sol Babitz. Afterward we eat lobster at Redondo Beach. **14** Our church wedding.[1] Lunch at the priest's. In the evening Walt Disney's director, Rose, is here. **15** Seventh English lesson. Lunch with Antal Dorati, his wife, and their baby daughter. Golubev and Stone work with Igor on the Tango until 1 a.m.[2] **16** We go to the ballet—*Scuola de Ballo*, *Berlioz Symphony*, *Graduation Ball*—and see Nemchinova, Tchernicheva, Romanov. Tea with Dorati. Lecture about Igor by Kall and Golubev. **17** Eighth English lesson. Again to the ballet, with Walt Disney and Eugene Berman. A great disappointment this time, very dull. Fokine Ballets Russes made worse by Rachmaninov's music. *Coq d'Or*. Paganini with Sudeikin's decors. **19** To Palm Springs, and "Los Arbeles," where we meet Hageman. We are angry because of the heat and because of all the parties that pursue us. **22** Ninth English lesson. At 8, a dinner party here: the Montemezzis, the Edward G. Robinsons, [Lou?] Levy, the Baron. **23** Discuss *Renard* with two Disney directors. **25** Tenth English lesson. Denise wrote that they received the money. **26** While I am downtown, Igor, alone, is distracted by people, and telephones.

food	1.65
gas	.95
blue and green material for a housecoat	10.01
blue veil	1.00
three pairs of stockings	2.37
air mail	.10
furrier (check)	35.00
belt repair	.25
newspapers	.10

27 Igor works with Sol Babitz on the Violin Concerto and is furious because of mistakes in the score. **28** Igor is very nervous because of indecisions about Walt Disney and ASCAP. Golubev brings the Disney contract. **29** Bertensson for dinner, during which I discover that he knew my father's cousin, Admiral Theodore de Bosset. **30** We go to a drive-in cinema. **31** Halloween, children in masks demanding candies.

November

2 Leave on the "Chief" at 11:30 a.m. Gleb Deruzhinsky, the sculptor, is on the train and annoys Igor at first by chatting too much; then we get used to him. **4** Chicago at 1:25. Carpenter[3] meets us at the station and takes us to his old and cozy house, where we live as if we were in a hotel, and do not see our hosts. Toward evening Ellen[4] appears in evening dress, since she is going to the opera. We dine with Mr Carpenter. Igor speaks English very freely, but I feel less at ease with it. **5** Igor's first rehearsal with the Chicago Symphony. Igor finds a quantity of mistakes in the score.[5] An old German, Handke, sits up with him until midnight correcting the parts. We dine downstairs with some people who are going to the opera. I read a book about Isadora Duncan and begin to change my opinions.[6] Roosevelt is elected. **6** I walk to Symphony Hall, where Igor has been rehearsing since 10 a.m. After

lunch I go to the Chicago Art Museum, look at French paintings, then return to the Hall and the afternoon rehearsal. Igor does not have time to eat. **7** Igor at Symphony Hall. We lunch with Stock[7] in a good restaurant where we run into Alice Roulier. Igor goes to sleep early. While I dine with the Carpenters at Claire Dux's, Igor has dinner in his room on a tray. Concert: the premiere of the Symphony in C. **8** Igor's matinée concert. Afterwards tea at the Club (Goodspeed). Paul Stoes[8] comes to discuss business with Igor, and a young girl interviewer from *Time*. Dinner at Carpenter's. Ellen promises to make arrangements with the Red Cross about packages to France. **9** Igor's rehearsal at 10. I walk there. Dinner at Mrs. Kirk's (her husband is director of the opera): a wonderful apartment, and they have a great cook. They take us to *Manon*, but we cannot bear more than two acts. **10** A big lunch at Carpenter's: the Stocks, Goodspeed, Leyssac, and some university people. To a matinée at Ballet Theatre, where we see Dolin and Tudor. Program: *Les Sylphides*, *Peter and the Wolf* (ill-fitting music by Prokofiev, a ballet for backward children), and *Jardin aux lilas*, a charming surrealist dream—story by Maupassant—with Chausson's music. **11** Igor rehearses in the morning. Leaving the house later, I am caught in a "windy city" storm, people all around are grasping trees or whatever they can find. Suddenly it starts to snow, which makes me feel more at home. Dinner at Mrs. Langhorne's, during which I had to speak English exclusively. Then to Chaplin's *The Great Dictator*, which we find long and uninteresting. **12** Lunch in a club with Chauncey McCormack. Igor's concert at 2:15. Meet Sister Edward and Sister Louise, whom the Goodspeeds could not invite to their box because of the unsuitable company there—Elsa Maxwell and Grace Moore. Sister Edward gives us news of Nadia Boulanger. To *Carmen*, where we greet Anton Dolin. **14** We go to Stock's concert. **15** To a ballet rehearsal especially for us, where we see *Jardin aux lilas* once more and a dull *Swan Lake*. Tea at Chauncey McCormack's (his wife is born Deering). A fine collection of paintings. Dinner at Edward Ryerson's, president of the Orchestra Association. **16** Igor goes to a rehearsal of Carpenter's symphony. Tea at home with Mrs. Rudolph Ganz and Carleton Sprague Smith. **17** Leave for Cincinnati and arrive at 6:05. Stay at Lucien Wulsin's: cozy surroundings. **19** Igor has two rehearsals. The numerous Wulsin family is very friendly. The 80-year-old mother gives me books in French (Maurois and René de Chambrun). **20** Igor has two rehearsals. To the Taft Museum with Mrs. Wulsin, then lunch at the Netherland Plaza Hotel. I go to Igor's afternoon rehearsal. **21** Thanksgiving. Obligatory turkey. I go to Igor's rehearsal with him. Tea at Goossens'.[9] Press conference at 6. **22** Igor is wilting from the very hot day. After his matinée concert, fifty people come for tea, including Hoity Wyborg, who brings the latest gossip about Paris: Lifar is having an enormous success, Chanel is thinner, etc. After dinner we go to the cinema. **23** A drive to see the country, the horses, the hunts. Igor's concert at 8:30 is a tremendous success, the public refusing to leave. A party afterward at Mrs. Walter Freiberg's, a gruff old lady, but very nice. **24** We go to the zoo and eat hot dogs. I find a dying little bird, a dead snake, and a dead rat. In the evening, to the film, *The Letter*, with Bette Davis. **25** At 5:39 p.m. we leave for New York. **26** In New York at 8:30 a.m. Pretentious and dull dinner at Dushkins', because of the presences of mother and brother. Snow storm. **27** Lunch with Vittorio Rieti in a French restaurant. We dine at Tony's, then go to Balanchine's and Vera Zorina's[10] apartment. **29** Igor is in a bad mood. We have an expensive, good lunch at Longchamps, then go to Cartier's where we run into Dukelsky,[11] who makes a bad impression on us. Encounter Hoity Wyborg in the street. At 5, Nikitina for tea. Igor sleeps, then plays Bach. **30** The second anniversary of Mika's death: we go to the Russian Cathedral.

December

1 Late lunch at the zoo, then go to the 69th floor of Rockefeller Center, to

---

[1] This took place in the Russian church on Micheltorena Street.

[2] Golubev and Stone were attempting to compose "lyrics" for the piece.

[3] John Alden Carpenter, the composer.

[4] Ellen Borden, sister of Adlai Stevenson.

[5] Of the Symphony in C. This was the first time Stravinsky had heard the music. His November 5 errata sheet is in the Sacher Foundation.

[6] Vera lived in the same building as Isadora Duncan in Paris and knew her well.

[7] Frederick Stock, music director of the Chicago Symphony.

[8] Stravinsky's New York concert agent.

[9] Eugene Goossens, conductor of the Cincinnati Symphony and a friend of Stravinsky's since 1921.

[10] Mrs. George Balanchine, later Mrs. Goddard Lieberson.

[11] Vladimir Dukelsky (Vernon Duke), composer, author of books and criticism hostile to Stravinsky, who hit back in 1965 with an article titled "A Cure for VD."

admire the view of New York. **2** To the Ballets Russes de Monte Carlo. After the performance we go for supper with Colonel de Basil.[1] **5** Heavy snow. To the dentist at noon. Igor and I go to the movies in the evening and eat in a small joint. **7** At Zosia Kochanska's in the afternoon, with Tchelichev and Mme Chaliapin. **8** Tchelichev at 4. **9** Dushkin comes with Stock to see Igor. Balanchine dines with us in a Russian restaurant and takes us to see *Cabin in the Sky* with Ethel Waters. **11** Lunch with Tchelichev and Balanchine in Reuben's, a noisy restaurant. **13** Lunch with Denham and Balanchine. **14** Leave for Chicago and Minneapolis. **15** Hotel Radisson, Minneapolis, at 5:45 p.m. **16** Igor has two rehearsals each day. It is so snowy and slushy that I go out only to buy galoshes. **18** I give an interview for a newspaper (*Star*) and am photographed.[2] **20** The last rehearsal, and, at night, the concert. **21** Train at 8 to Chicago and New York. **22** New York at 9:30. **23** Igor has a cold. Dinner at Dick Hammond's with Nadia Boulanger and Mrs. Porter, the sister of Marcelle de Manziarly.[3] **24** We go to Balanchine's to see his Christmas tree. **25** Igor has a bad cold. **28** Sudeikin telephones: he wants to see me. Igor rehearses the Violin Concerto with Dushkin. **29** Nadia comes at 4, stays for dinner, and from 5 to 6 I go downstairs and talk to Sudeikin. **31** Lunch at Dushkins' with Walter Damrosch's daughter and Mrs. Mitchell, who tells us she will not speak French since she does not know the use of the subjunctive. Balanchine comes, Nicolas Nabokov with his wife, and the young Limantour (whom we met in Mexico and who wants to conduct *Sacre*). At 7 Nadia comes with the Arthur Sachses, who talk us into greeting the New Year with them at a restaurant, the Mirleton. It is very pleasant and almost empty. Outside, and in other restaurants, are orgies of noise and whistles of New Year's Eve revelers. Later in the night we hear the noises of the disturbed denizens of Central Park Zoo.

1941

January

1 A sunny, invigorating day. Igor's first outing after his influenza; we go for a walk in Central Park, eat lunch at the zoo, watch a family of seals, and feed nuts to pheasants and squirrels. Nadia Boulanger comes in the afternoon. I visit Georgette, who came home from a party at seven a.m. I promise to return with Igor before dinner, but she and her husband think that Igor can only find them boring, and could not really want to see them. In the end, all of us go to dinner together at the St. Regis Hotel, where there is an ice show. At the table next to us: Charlie Chaplin with a girl. **2** Snow turning to rain. Igor and Balanchine rehearse *Balustrade*. **3** We pack all morning, Igor, as always, becoming very nervous. Our train for Washington leaves at 4. The Hay-Adams House is very distinguished but not very generous. Igor was not met at the station and he does not even know the time of his rehearsal tomorrow. Nadia phones at 11 p.m., after her lecture, and Igor delegates her to find out the rehearsal time. **4** Igor's rehearsal of the National Symphony Orchestra at 9:30. This city, though very important, is also very dull. Dinner at Mrs. Winslow's with Mr. and Mrs. John Lodge (he is a well-known sinologue). **5** We go with Nadia to a Rouault exhibition, but in such quantity the paintings are not very pleasing, and the colossal black and red heads of clowns nauseate me. He reminds me of Kokoschka. **6** Igor has two rehearsals and I go to the one after lunch. I talk to Kindler,[4] who makes a poor impression. Interview with journalists. Our photographs are taken.[5] **7** Russian Christmas. Igor's concert in Baltimore. The trip to Baltimore and back is uncomfortable and tiring. The hall is huge and absolutely full, but I do not like the too-velvety acoustics. **8** In the

morning Samuel Feldman, the orchestra manager, takes us for a ride along the Potomac and shows us Washington. (Igor calls him Friedman all the time, but he doesn't mind.) Igor rests, and later in the day we pack. The concert in Constitution Hall is a great success. Mrs. Roosevelt is in the audience, and I am in the loge with Mrs. Chanler, Miss Winslow, and the wife of the minister from Czechoslovakia. A very full hall and a good audience. **9** New York. At seven a.m. we go to the drugstore for coffee. Pigeons come to the window of our rooms to receive their daily ration of bread. **10** Teddy Chanler[6] comes with his wife. I receive them downstairs while Igor talks to journalists upstairs. I telephone Igor every quarter-of-an-hour to ask when we can come up, but only succeed in annoying him. Unexpectedly enjoyable evening at the Rietis'. The Hindemiths and Berman come, and we leave at three o'clock in the morning. **11** We pack all morning, and at two o'clock leave for Boston. Mr. and Mrs. Forbes meet us with embraces and kisses, as if we were members of their family, but the only guests at dinner are Nadia and two young people: all of the Forbes children have flu. Later in the evening, a photographer takes pictures for the newspapers. **13** Sun and snow. Igor's first rehearsal. Nadia goes with him and I come later. Lunch at Amalfi restaurant. Igor is in despair because of mistakes in the parts of the Symphony in C and because the orchestra is so bad. **14** To the Gardner Museum. The cold is so penetrating that my feet feel as if they might fall off while I wait for a tram. **15** Nadia gives a party for us at the Forbes house. I snub the French Consul. **16** Igor's concert with the Boston Symphony Orchestra at Cambridge. **17** Igor's concert in Boston in the afternoon. Dinner at Professor Edward Ballantine's. **18** Igor's evening concert in Boston, a colossal success. **19** Our train leaves from Back Bay. Edward Forbes left a very pleasant impression. Even though he often seems to be on the brink of insanity, he is very kind. When we arrive in New York, at 7:47 a.m., Igor says: "It is like our own town." **20** Rehearsal of *Balustrade* at 10:30. **21** Ballet rehearsal at 10:30. **22** First performance of *Balustrade*. Almost a historical audience, a theater full of French refugees, including Jean-Michel Frank, Vogel, Mainbocher, and old acquaintances from Baliev's[7] Chauve-Souris, like old times in Paris. I sit with Mrs. Hamilton Russell. *Balustrade* turns out marvelously and is a great success.[8] The applause is so great that the curtain does not go down for ten minutes. People came from Boston, Forbes and [Tilman] Merritt. I saw Sorin and Sudeikin from a distance. **23** Igor is carried away by his work orchestrating "The Blue Bird" (Pas de deux) from the *Sleeping Beauty* for Pleasant.[9] Many telephone calls congratulating Igor on yesterday's success. **24** Cold and snowing: Central Park is white.[10] The lions in the zoo roared all night. Second performance of *Balustrade*. Party at Richard Hammond's,[11] with Mrs. Forbes, Betsy, Mr. Porter, Theodore Chanler, Nadia, and Dubinsky.[12] I said to De Basil: "I can imagine how this ballet horrifies you." **25** Igor feels that he has influenza. **26** Igor is sick; Dr. Garbat comes. After the third performance of *Balustrade*, which went smoothly and was a great success, phone calls from Rieti and Dushkin. How provincial the theater,[13] the backstage, and the audience. **28** Igor's temperature is normal. Sam visited him but did not stay long. **29** At 6 a.m. I watch the change of light in Central Park, but the most beautiful time is around 7 when the lanterns look like black diamonds. **31** We lunch at the St. Moritz, then go to the bank, the doctor, and the dentist. We take a photograph to Babin and Vronsky and ask them to come to see us. When they come, Igor plays his Tango for them. He gives it to them to arrange for two pianos. We dine with Salazar, who tells amusing stories, especially one about his concierge in Paris who said that when the Germans first arrived, they behaved like gentlemen and, unlike the French police, "did not hit me on the head."

---

[1] Of the Ballets Russes de Monte Carlo.

[2] The interview and photograph are reproduced in *A Stravinsky Scrapbook*, op. cit.

[3] Mimi Porter lived in Ojai, California. Her brother, Sasha de Manziarly, was French Consul in Los Angeles at the time, and until succeeded by Roman Gary. Marcelle de Manziarly, assistant to Nadia Boulanger, was a skillful sightreader at the piano, for which reason Stravinsky chose her to play *The Rake's Progress* with him for a gathering one evening in New York that included Billy Rose.

[4] Hans Kindler, conductor of the Washington Symphony at the time, played the cello part in the first performance of *Pierrot Lunaire* and conducted the first performance of *Apollon Musagète* (at the Library of Congress, April 27, 1928).

[5] The photos in the *Times-Herald* are reproduced in *Igor and Vera Stravinsky: A Photograph Album*, op. cit.

[6] Composer, pupil of Nadia Boulanger, son of Mrs. Chanler.

[7] Nikita Baliev (d. 1936) founded the Chauve-Souris. Meyerhold staged Tchaikovsky's *Queen of Spades* for Baliev's theater. See the writings of Hugh Walpole on Russia, particularly his novel *The Secret City*, with its many references to the cinema. (Walpole lived in Petrograd and worked as an agent of the British Foreign Office.)

[8] Compare this report with the notices by music and dance reviewers.

[9] Director of Ballet Theater.

[10] The Stravinskys' suite in the Barbizon Plaza was on the twenty-ninth floor.

[11] Pupil of Nadia Boulanger. Stravinsky had met him in 1921. See *Stravinsky: Selected Correspondence*. Vol. I, op. cit.

[12] Possibly Arkady Dubinsky, composer and violinist in the New York Philharmonic.

[13] The Fifty-First Street Theater, which had been only partly heated during the rehearsals.

February

2 Walking with Igor, we meet Dubrovska and Vladimirov [dancers].
3 Adele Marcus plays for Igor.[1] To Radio City to see Katharine Hepburn in *The Philadelphia Story.* Dinner afterward. **4** In the Russian Tea Room we meet Gladys [Mrs. Edward G.] Robinson, Hurok, and Borovsky.[2]
6 Igor has colitis and is in a rage. Balanchine comes to say good-bye; he has had a nose operation. He stays for lunch and sees us off at the railroad station. **7** Chicago, 8:40 a.m. We go to another station to change trains. Gladys Robinson is on the same train. **9** We are up early to see the beginning of the warm country and of spring. After San Bernardino: mimosa, orange groves, lemon trees, all in bloom, and small houses drowning in roses. We are met by a photographer and by the Bolms. At the Château Marmont, 8221 Sunset Boulevard, Hollywood, we have nice rooms, cozy, in good taste, and we are very pleased. **10** Poor Igor slept badly, and he has to conduct two rehearsals. I look at houses with Mrs. Abeman, most of them execrable, and only one roomy enough and with a garden. At 3 we go to look at automobiles. A problem with tomorrow's reception: the invitations "In honor of Mr. and Mrs. Stravinsky" are already printed, but we must refuse. Mrs. Irish[3] even telephoned the doctor to see if we are faking. **11** I go for the car, sign the papers, and bring it home. It is a dark green beauty.[4] **12** Igor returns at 6 p.m., exhausted, after rehearsing from 9 this morning. **13** I look at houses with Mrs. Abeman but see nothing suitable. Igor is tired and nervous (colitis and nose). At his Los Angeles concert, encounter with the Baron. Great success for *Firebird* and *Capriccio*, less for *Jeu de cartes*, and very little for the Symphony in C. The public prefers "oldies." **14** We go directly from the doctor's to the concert hall for the 2:30 matinée. A tropical downpour, in spite of which almost all of the seats are full. Run into Tatiana Chamié; we met in London on November 2, twenty years ago.[5] After the concert, the Wulsins come for tea. **18** To San Diego. A beautiful day. Thank God this San Diego concert is the last one. A very provincial audience. Only *Firebird* and *Jeu de cartes* are successful. Luckily we avoid all parties. **19** San Diego. Sun, lovely air, and the end of our concert season. We slept well and feel pleased and happy. Tour the city, the museum, and the zoo, lunch at a club, and leave for Hollywood at 3:30, gathering lemons, oranges, and avocados from trees along the way. **20** At home, the rain continues boringly. We look at houses. **21** We go to Ernest Anderson's, a future pupil of Igor's. He offers us his house as a temporary residence. **22** We take an apartment in the Château Marmont, and Igor orders a piano there, where we will settle for at least a month. **25** Igor went out with Levy and found a house with an enormous garden. I find a tiny, cozy house on a hill. **27** [I.S.: First lesson with Anderson.[6]]

March

1 We talk about the white house on Wetherly Drive and go to look at it. A pretty maid there plays for us on an electric guitar and asks Igor to autograph a book for her. Strange behavior! Igor likes the house and discusses the possibility of building a studio. **2** A *panikhida* service for Katya. We are in church from early morning, going to confession and taking communion. The beginning of the first week of Lent. **3** I am in a bad mood and Igor is in a worse one because of the pestering by real-estate agents. A letter from Darius Milhaud, whose mother sends money to Fedya.[7] [I.S.: Anderson's second lesson at 5 p.m.] **6** Igor stays home with a pain in the knee. I drive the Baron to the Wetherly Drive house, take him to dinner with us, and drive him home. I am reading Saroyan's *My Name is Aram.* [I.S.: Anderson's third lesson at 11 a.m.] **8** From Anderson's $25: silver, 6.00; lamps, 5.00; bird cage, 5.00; food, 2.00; gas, 1.00; food, .70. [I.S.: Anderson's fourth lesson at 4 p.m.] **12** I take Igor to

the doctor for treatment. Igor very worried by my absence in downtown Los Angeles, but the Baron stayed with him. The doctor comes to see Igor again to calm him. **14** [I.S.: Anderson's fifth lesson at 11 a.m.] **17** [I.S.: Anderson's sixth lesson, 4 to 5 p.m.] **20** Upsetting news at the bank about restrictions on withdrawing money. **21** We inspect the house, and dream of moving in as soon as possible. Dinner at the Pig'n Whistle.[8] Igor very depressed by the political news. [I.S.: Seventh lesson with Anderson, 11:30 a.m. to 1 p.m.] **23** [I.S.: Eighth lesson—Anderson 11 to 12:30 p.m.] **24** Downtown to sign interminable papers about a loan. We understand nothing and could be signing almost anything, which makes us nervous. At the Campbell glass shop we see an artisan, the first one in America! Still nervous when the Bolms come for dinner, I take Valerian drops. **26** [I.S.: Anderson—ninth lesson.] **27** [I.S.: 12 to 1:30 p.m., tenth lesson.] **30** [I.S.: Eleventh lesson with Anderson—almost forgot to give me the check.] **31** [I.S.: A tooth extracted.]

April

1 Dine at Villa Nova on terrible and very expensive food, but we delight a waiter because we know his native Florence. Today we have a telephone number: Crestview 1-4858. [I.S.: Anderson 12th lesson in the morning.] **2** I bring suitcases to the new house, buy food, and feed Igor. [I.S.: 3 teeth extracted.] **4** We transport suitcases in pouring rain. Igor to the dentist. **5** Sunshine! We eat lunch and dinner, served by Wanda, in the new house. [I.S.: Anderson 4 p.m., 13th lesson, in the new house.] **6** A most wonderful day. [I.S.: We moved into the house—1260 North Wetherly Drive.] **7** Slept very well the first night, but troubles begin in the morning: 1) no hot water; 2) problems with gas appliances. [I.S.: Four teeth extracted from the upper jaw.] **8** [I.S.: 14th lesson with Anderson 11:30 a.m.] **9** A cable from Fedya, in Switzerland, asking us to send dollars. **10** [I.S.: Write to Victoria Ocampo: "These few lines to inform you that we have settled here in Hollywood in a ravishing little house, which we purchased because nothing habitable can be found for rent. . . . Everyone comes to Los Angeles. We have been here since mid-February when I was conducting concerts with the Los Angeles Philharmonic here and in San Diego. Now we shall stay here for a while, after four months of hard work in the East, interrupted by interminable illnesses. The winter was bad. My next engagements are in Mexico, where I conduct my new Symphony in the second half of July. . . . I completed it last August and have performed it everywhere this season. . . . I did not see Maritain, but Darius Milhaud told me that he is in New York. Of all the French refugees, I have seen only Milhaud. . . .

"From time to time we have news from Theodore and Milene, who are still in the same place. Nini is in Paris; I have learned indirectly that he gave a successful concert in the Salle Gaveau in December. The problems of food and clothing are becoming tragic there.

"Aldous Huxley is here in Hollywood. I read that Virginia Woolf drowned herself. Why not Hitler? That question is as futile as it is stupid. . . . Send quickly the good news of your arrival here."] **11** [I.S.: Anderson 15th lesson 11:30.] **13** [I.S.: Anderson 16th lesson at 11:30.] **16** A visit from Ushakov, a former Russian Consul in Stockholm now selling *Encyclopedia America.* We go to Pasadena and on the return buy a rubber tree. [I.S.: Anderson 17th lesson.] **18** [I.S.: 18th lesson with Anderson 10:30.] **22** [I.S.: 19th lesson with Anderson in the morning. Lunch at Bit of Sweden restaurant with him, then audition James Sample[9] for his music.] **23** We go to Marcus about our permit for re-entry from Mexico. [I.S.: Bought music $41.] **24** At 4, Igor and I go to Gregory Stone's, who reads to us from his diaries about Yvette Guilbert and Lady Mendl.[10] I begin to knit a carpet. [I.S.: Anderson's 20th lesson. New denture (2nd one).] **27** [I.S.: Anderson's 21st lesson.] **29** [I.S.: 22nd lesson Anderson.]

---

[1] Stravinsky was coaching Miss Marcus in his *Capriccio*, which she was to play with him in his concerts in March with the Los Angeles Philharmonic.

[2] Probably the pianist, Alexander Borovsky.

[3] Mrs. Leland Atherton Irish, president of the Los Angeles Philharmonic Society.

[4] The Stravinskys had this second-hand Dodge until January 1950.

[5] Mme Chamié was a dancer. The date was that of the premiere of *The Sleeping Princess*, in which Mrs. Stravinsky played the role of the Queen.

[6] The entries thus demarcated are in Stravinsky's hand, in red ink and in a small black book.

[7] Between March 1941 and December 1943, Stravinsky transmitted money to his

elder son and daughter by means of a cabled message ("Stravinsky's health improved") that Darius Milhaud sent at intervals to his mother in Aix-en-Provence. On receipt of the wire, Mme Milhaud would forward 30,000 francs to Milene, for which Stravinsky would reimburse Milhaud in dollars in California. See *Stravinsky in Pictures and Documents*, op. cit.

[8] The Stravinskys could not pronounce "whistle," which came out "whithle" (like Pithom becoming Phithom in the Douai Bible).

[9] Anderson's son-in-law, a conductor, led the first performance of Stravinsky's *Star-Spangled Banner.*

[10] Sir Charles and Lady Mendl lived near the Stravinskys in Beverly Hills, 1018 Benedict Canyon. As British press attaché in Paris, Mendl married Elsie de Wolfe (d. 1950) in 1927.

92 1941. Los Angeles.

93 1941. 1260 North Wetherly Drive. With Eugene Berman and Baron de Meyer.

94 1941. Santa Barbara. At the home of Arthur Sachs.

95 October 1941. Santa Barbara. Vera, Mme Georges Sachs, Igor, Nadia Boulanger.

May

1 Mercedes de Acosta[1] and Genia Berman come at 3:30 with a photographer, Muneaz, who arranges a very ordinary and disappointing group picture in front of the house. Mercedes makes a good impression, a very ladylike lesbian. [I.S.: 23rd lesson with Anderson.] **2** Igor works late at the piano. **4** [I.S.: Anderson 24th lesson.] **6** Igor has two extractions, and my stitches are removed. Igor is upset because the wind broke some flowers in our garden. [I.S.: Anderson 25th lesson.] **7** A windy day again and very hot, which makes Igor nervous. The Baron is here since this morning. **9** We both go to the dentist. Later, in the evening, with Genia Berman and the Baron to a vegetarian meal at Mercedes de Acosta's. [I.S.: Anderson's 26th lesson.] **11** [I.S.: Anderson's 27th lesson.] **12** In the morning Masha, a Russian servant, who will be with us until Elisaveta Alexandrovna is free. **13** Read in the newspapers about Rudolf Hess. [I.S.: Anderson 28th lesson.] **14** Lunch at the Baroness d'Erlanger's. A very large house,[2] which she arranged with much imagination but in eccentric taste, and an enormous garden. **15** [I.S.: Anderson 29th lesson.] **18** Princess Christov phones: she received a letter from Mussia Antonini saying she had been detained in Bermuda for two weeks. Elisaveta Alexandrovna begins working for us. [I.S.: Anderson's 30th lesson.] **20** [I.S.: Anderson 31st lesson.] **22** Sound-proofing Igor's studio. In the evening, with Igor to a movie. [I.S.: Anderson 32nd lesson.] **24** [I.S.: Anderson 33rd lesson.] **25** Picnic at San Juan Capistrano, walk on the sand at Long Beach, and return to Los Angeles in the evening. **26** Take Igor to the dentist, who extracts a tooth—unexpectedly. I read to Igor in the evening. **27** [I.S.: Anderson's 34th lesson. Write to Victoria Ocampo: "I am typing these few lines in the hope that you receive them before your departure for the United States (assuming that you have not cancelled the trip). Would it be indiscreet to burden you with an errand? . . . I would so much like to give Vera a gift of a cowskin rug (black and white) for our new house, as well as a map of the Americas to place above our living room fireplace. Is it possible to find a rug before you leave? Possible or not, come to see us, dear Victoria. We leave for Mexico at the beginning of July. . . ."] **29** [I.S.: Anderson's 35th lesson.] **31** [I.S.: Anderson's 36th lesson.]

June

1 Igor is in a bad humor because of his teeth. We decide not to go to Santa Barbara. With the Bolms to lunch at Dr. Bernstein's, then a drive by the ocean. To the movie *Major Barbara*. Dinner at a drugstore. **2** [I.S.: Anderson 37th lesson.] **3** With Marcus to City Hall for our re-entry permits, then to the Mexican Consulate.[3] Problems again with my passport. **4** To the French Consulate at 10:30, then for passport photos. At 3 p.m., back at the French Consulate, where everything is finally in order. [I.S.: Anderson's 38th lesson.] **5** [I.S.: A trip to Santa Barbara with De Acosta, Bolms, G. Berman.] **6** Spend the day very plesantly, starting at the botanical gardens, then visiting a painter, under Picasso's influence, called Lebrun.[4] After lunch to Wright Luddington's[5] house, which has a room with Berman's murals. The garden is like Versailles. Tea with Mildred Bliss. **7** [I.S.: Anderson's 39th lesson.] **8** Hollywood. Russian Whitsun Day. At 11:30, to church with Elena Alexandrovna. Later to Ermoliev's housewarming celebration and blessing-of-the-house service. A Russian woman is there, Vera Johnson, whom I had met at the Ritz Hotel in Barcelona. We leave at 1 a.m. **9** [I.S.: Anderson's 40th lesson.] **10** [I.S.: Two teeth extracted from the left lower jaw.] **11** [I.S.: Anderson's 41st lesson.] **13** With Igor, after lunch, to buy flowers at a Swiss nursery. Igor picks avocados from the tops of the trees. In the evening, I paste flowers and leaves on for a collage while Igor polishes a frame. [I.S.: Anderson's 42nd lesson.] **15** With the Bolms to Mount

Wilson Observatory. We walk in this wonderland of crystal clear air and heavenly quiet, returning home, after a dinner in Pasadena, only at 10 p.m. [I.S.: Anderson's 43rd lesson.] **17** The newspapers mention Igor's birthday [tomorrow], though he has tried to hide it. Fetch the pajamas for Igor, the plant at the Swiss nursery, and a cake from Delhaven. [I.S.: Anderson 44th.] **19** [I.S.: Anderson 45th.] **20** [I.S.: Anderson 46th.] **22** Prince Galitzin[6] comes at 4 p.m. and prescribes salicylate (something like Urodonal) and heating pads for my leg pain. [I.S.: Anderson's 47th.] **23** [I.S.: A gardener called Tihominov began working.] **24** A cable from Fedya asking for money. We telegraph Milhaud and wait for an answer. Also send telegram to Mexico. [I.S.: Anderson 48th.] **25** [I.S.: Anderson 49th.] **26** [I.S.: I begin a naturopathic diet called Friend.] **27** [I.S.: Anderson 50th.] **29** [I.S.: Anderson 51st.]

July

1 [I.S.: Anderson 52nd.] **2** Take Igor to the dentist, With Marcus to the Mexican Consulate, where we write that I am "a French wife"!! [I.S.: Anderson 53rd.] **3** We go to a terrible Soviet film, *Volga-Volga*.[7] [I.S.: Anderson 54.] **5** [I.S.: Anderson 55th.] **6** Tea at the Baroness d'Erlanger's with René Clair, Marc Chadourne, the Montemezzis, and Baroness Kuffner. Dinner at Dr. Bernstein's with the Bolms and a drama critic, Stevens. [I.S.: Anderson 56th.] **7** Drive Igor to the dentist. At the library, take out two books by Goncharov, one book from the USSR, and one book by Chadourne. Igor lunched at home with Woof; they have been writing letters. [I.S.: Anderson 57th lesson.] **8** [I.S.: Anderson's 58th.] **9** [I.S.: Anderson's 59th.] **10** The train for Mexico. We sleep and read all day—Akhmatova's poems, Alfred de Musset, Blok, *Eugene Onegin*. [I.S.: Departure for Mexico at 9:45 a.m. (via El Paso).] **13** Arrive in Mexico City on time (!) at 6 a.m., pale blue sky, lights on in the houses. At the station, twenty photographers and all of our Mexican friends. Prieto[8] has a car for us, and we lunch at his home. Carlos Chavez comes. We have tea at Corinto and are beginning to feel uncomfortable from the altitude. I read Bertita Harding's book about Maximilian. **14** Igor is pleased with the first rehearsal, having worried about the difficulties of the Symphony. We go to a tailor, Fausto Montero, from whom Igor orders a suit.[9] After lunch at Prieto's, to Guadalupe. Bal y Gay takes me to a picture gallery. Igor goes to Agea to hear a pianist, Ochoa, who will play the *Capriccio* in the concerts. Tea at Lady Baltimore's. **16** To the museum and to buy books. Then to Prieto. I look for old maps in the antique shops but in vain. Tea at Lady Baltimore's, then fetch Igor. Very formal dinner at Prieto, long and tiresome, with ministers, directors, *et al.* Quijano, the president of the orchestra, asks Igor if he went to the opera last night. Igor: "No, I do not like opera. *C'est une vieille tante qu'il faut respecter mais il ne faut pas y toucher*." Everybody is shocked by this and Señora Icaza hardly speaks to us. **18** I go with Igor to his morning rehearsal. Lunch at Prendes restaurant with Bal and Salazar. Igor's concert: Symphony in C, *Capriccio*, *Pulcinella*, Divertimento. Small party with Delia del Caril,[10] Ortega, Bal y Gay, Salazar, and some people from the orchestra. **19** We are up at 7, since Igor goes to record the Divertimento. I stay home and finish the book about Maximilian, shedding tears at the end. We lunch at Limantour's with Sir Thomas Beecham. I sit between Beecham and Chatto. **20** Igor's concert at 11 a.m., then lunch with Carlos and Adelita Obregon.[11] **21** Igor caught cold yesterday, but we go to Cuernavaca and Taxco, nevertheless, well stocked with brandy, argyrol, and pills. At Tres Marias restaurant we eat *resadillas*. **22** Igor has a temperature of 39°, and I call Dr. [Efren R.] Marin twice; but in spite of Igor's temperature, we lunch with Manuel and Clema Ponce. (They lived in Paris and are friends of the Cranes', she is a singer, very hospitable.) Afterward to the American Consulate and police

---

[1] Writer. The Stravinskys had known her in Europe before the war. See her memoir, *Here Lies the Heart*, New York, 1960, in which Muneaz's photograph is reproduced.

[2] The Stravinskys purchased this house in the spring of 1964, remodelled it, and moved there in the autumn. See Enid Bagnold's *Autobiography* for a description of the Baroness's London home (which had been Byron's). Her son was Sir Gerard d'Erlanger, her daughter the Princess Faucigny-Lucinge.

[3] Adolfo de la Herta was Mexican Consul in Los Angeles.

[4] Rico Lebrun (1900–1964) drew a portrait of Stravinsky and a stage design (curtain or backdrop) for *Pulcinella*. In the late 1950s, Mrs. Stravinsky attended his classes in drawing from live models.

[5] An art collector.

[6] One of the Stravinskys' physicians.

[7] Made by Mosfilm in 1938, directed by Grigori Alexandrov, music by Isaac Dunayevsky.

[8] Carlos Prieto was a banker and the "president of the committee of patronage of the Orquésta Sinfonica de Mexico."

[9] Stravinsky paid $621.50 for the suit, a high price in view of the value of the dollar at the time.

[10] The wife of Pablo Neruda and longtime friend of Vera Stravinsky's.

[11] Son of the former President of Mexico.

headquarters.   **24** A crowd comes to the railroad station to see us off, bringing flowers and presents, but we are happy to board the train: it was certainly not agreeable to be ill in that dreadful hotel and to have had to postpone the return to our lovely white house would have been such a pity.   **27** [I.S.: Arrived from Mexico this morning at 7:30.]   **28** [I.S.: Anderson's 60th lesson. He sent my *Star-Spangled Banner* arrangement to be copyrighted.]   **30** [I.S.: Anderson 61st.]

August

1 [I.S.: Anderson 62nd.]   **3** [I.S.: Anderson 63.]   **5** [I.S.: Anderson 64th.] **8** The work on Igor's room—installing a double door—continues. [I.S.: Anderson 65th.]   **9** Carpets are being put down in Igor's studio. In the evening, we go to a Balanchine preview. We see Gregory Ratoff, Remisov, and the Akim Tamirovs afterward and are obliged to compliment them on the play.   **10** [I.S.: Anderson 66th.]   **11** [I.S.: Anderson 67.]   **13** [I.S.: Anderson 68th.]   **15** [I.S.: Anderson 69th.]   **16** To Mercedes' for dinner. Man Ray is there, with his wife and Alla Nazimova.[1]   **17** [I.S.: Anderson 70th.]   **18** We go to Berman's. He has a visitor, Mr. Austin,[2] Director of the Hartford Museum. We dine together at Victor's, where Igor is twice asked for an autograph.   **19** [I.S.: Anderson 71st.]   **21** Varvara Christophorovna takes Igor to the dentist. Igor goes to the Baroness d'Erlanger's for cocktails and returns with Chadourne to show him our house. Later Artur Rubinstein with his wife and Zosia Kochanska come and we dine together at the Little Hungary restaurant. **22** [I.S.: Anderson 72nd.]   **24** Igor is very nervous. Bolms and the Baron for tea, but I do not feel sociable. When I lie down and cry, Igor bangs the doors. [I.S.: Anderson 73rd.]   **25** [I.S.: A carpenter took measurements of the Icon.]   **26** [I.S.: Anderson 74th. Received a letter from Fedya dated August 7.]   **27** Arthur Sachs sends a car to take us to Santa Barbara, a pleasant drive along the coast. Sachs has reserved rooms for us at the Biltmore Hotel. Their ''Hope Ranch'' is a lovely place with green grass all the way down to the sea. We have an enjoyable time eating, drinking, and talking with the Sachses and Nadia Boulanger. **29** [I.S.: Anderson 75th.]   **30** To the cinema, two good films at last: one by René Clair and Lubitsch's *That Uncertain Feeling*.   **31** [I.S.: Anderson 76th.]

September

3 A wire, invitation for cocktails, from Dagmar Godowsky, as if nothing had happened. Igor phones and asks her to come to see him. I leave the house and return only when I think that they have had time for their explanations, but she is still there, sitting on the sofa, and it seems that no special conversation took place. I give her a little vodka and we drive her home. [I.S.: Anderson 77th.]   **4** The masseuse, Liamina, for both Igor and me. We go to Darius Milhaud's concert at the Los Angeles Library and to a reception afterward at the Biltmore Hotel.   **5** [I.S.: Anderson 78.]   **7** [I.S.: Anderson 79.]   **9** With Mercedes to a cocktail party at Dagmar's. No stars, but several boyfriends: Gayelord Hauser,[3] Erich Maria Remarque, Franz Allers. Tables in the garden and a sumptuous buffet, vodka and whiskey (only!) at the bar. Dagmar takes me under her wing. By the table: three drunken bodies, those of the hostess, her maid, and another woman. A doctor is called. The men behaved better [I.S.: Anderson 80.]   **10** A reception at Richard Neutra's, the architect, in honor of Fernand Léger. Man Ray is there, and Trubetskoy and Orlova.[4] **11** Shopping with Igor. Dinner party at Bernardine Fritz's, which was a trap, since we were supposed to go to Léger's exhibition after an early dinner. She asked us for 7:30 and we arrived at 8, the others only at 9, at which time one of them, Mary Pickford, declaimed a monologue from *Othello*. Finally it was too late for Léger's exhibition, and we took Dagmar home.   **12** [I.S.: Anderson 81.]   **13** For dinner here: Fernand Léger and Mme Roux. After dinner: Varvara (a surprise for Léger), the Bolms, and Mercedes, whose car broke down; I had to drive her home, which means that I went to bed at 2:30.   **14** Lunch at the Montemezzis'

with John Barbirolli. [I.S.: Piano practice.]   **15** [I.S.: Anderson 82nd.] **16** [I.S.: Piano practice.]   **17** [I.S.: Piano practice. Doctor 10:30 a.m. Anderson 83.]   **18** To the chorus rehearsal of Igor's version of *The Star-Spangled Banner*. In the evening to Fernand Léger's personal presentation of ''modern and unique films.'' [I.S.: Piano.]   **19** [I.S.: Anderson 84.]   **20** To Santa Barbara, arriving at Hope Ranch in time for lunch. Art Sachs is away.   **21** At 11, Igor meets Mr. Siposs[5] and is delighted. He gives a lesson to me, too. In spite of a great cook and ten servants in the house, I work hard preparing borscht with *pirozhki*. **22** [I.S.: Anderson 85.]   **24** [I.S.: Piano. Anderson 86.]   **25** [I.S.: Piano.] **26** [I.S.: Anderson 87.]   **27** Leave for Santa Barbara at 10 but arrive too late for a lesson from Siposs—which is postponed until 6 p.m. We go directly to the swimming pool, then lunch with the Sachses.   **28** During the lesson at Siposs's, I see that he is only interested in Igor; he merely pours some water on me. Lunch at the pool with Rico Lebrun. Visitors: Uspensky, Ramón Novarro. Tea with Mrs. Bliss and Elliot Forbes. **30** [I.S.: Anderson 88. Piano.]

October

1 Mercedes at 7, stays for dinner, then unburdens her heart to me until midnight about her love for Greta Garbo. [I.S.: Anderson 89. Piano.] **2** Dinner in the garden at Dagmar's: Greta Garbo, Gayelord Hauser, the Artur Rubinsteins, Lupe Velez, Remarque. Since Hauser never left Garbo's side, I was unable to talk to her and give her Mercedes' message. [I.S.: Piano.]   **3** [I.S.: Anderson 90. Piano.]   **5** Santa Barbara. Igor's lesson with Siposs. Lunch by the Sachs' swimming pool.   **6** To a Russian film, *Suvarov*.[6] A marmalade cat comes to live with us. [I.S.: Anderson 91. Piano.]   **7** [I.S.: Piano.]   **8** [I.S.: Anderson 92. Piano.] **9** [I.S.: Sent *The Star-Spangled Banner* score to Feist.]   **10** [I.S.: Anderson 93rd.]   **11** To Santa Barbara. Lunch with Sachs at the country club. To Siposs's at 6.   **12** At Siposs's from 11:30 to 1. Lunch with Mildred Bliss, then home. Dinner at the Max Reinhardts'. They are not very talkative, which is a relief.   **13** We go to a 9 a.m. rehearsal of *The Star-Spangled Banner* by the WPA orchestra. [I.S.: Anderson 94.]   **14** To Saks to fetch Igor's blue suit, then the WPA concert and unending telephone calls about it afterwards. [I.S.: Premiere of *Star-Spangled Banner*.]   **15** [I.S.: Anderson 95.]   **16** Cocktails at the Artur Rubinsteins'. They have such a beautiful house, with lovely lawns, birches, and a swimming pool, that for the first time I feel envious. Ronald Coleman is there, Maureen Sullivan, Baron Kuffner, Sir Charles Mendl, the Basil Rathbones, Jascha Heifetz, Remarque, Jacques Duval. Dagmar got drunk. [I.S.: Piano.] **17** Telephone call from a news agency asking what dresses I wore at the Biltmore in Santa Barbara. I said that I wore one flower in my *gray* hair. Dagmar phones to say that she and Remarque were on a drunken binge, that Remarque told her that he loves me very much, whereupon I asked her whether she did, too. At 5 p.m. we meet Nadia Boulanger at the railroad station. [I.S.: Anderson 96. Piano.]   **18** Lunch at Montemezzi's. Quite dull but the food is good. Igor is in a hurry to return home to see the lawyer, Danielson, and to give a lesson to Anderson.[7] I go shopping and in the evening read to Igor. [I.S.: Composing a letter to Marx.[8]] **19** Mercedes comes with Mme Sides, who was once married to Raoul Nungesser, the French aviator. After dinner I read to Igor. [I.S.: Piano.] **20** Igor to the dentist. Dagmar and Mercedes for dinner, after which we see *The Little Foxes*, a well-made film. [I.S.: Anderson 97. Piano.] **21** [I.S.: Piano.]   **22** [I.S.: Anderson 98. Piano. 3 p.m. to the dentist. Two new jaws.]   **23** Rain! I take Igor to the doctor and buy a vase for Nella Rubinstein. Igor is angry all day because of his frozen royalities, and playing patience does not help. [I.S.: Piano.]   **24** [I.S.: Anderson 99. Piano. Write to Victoria Ocampo: ''No news from you in months. In July we were in Mexico where I saw Reyes, who had brief and vague news about you. Your silence worries me. . . .'']   **27** At Dagmar's, then to Remarque's to meet Elisabeth Bergner and her husband. A lot of drinking. We return home at 2:30 a.m. [I.S.: Anderson 100.]   **29** [I.S.: Anderson 101.]   **30** [I.S.: Anderson 102.]   **31** [I.S.: Anderson 103.]

---

[1] Alla Nazimova had moved to Hollywood in 1918 and purchased the Sunset Boulevard villa that was later (1927) to become the Garden of Allah Hotel. Leslie Howard, Ronald Coleman, Laurence Olivier, Charles Laughton, Somerset Maugham, and Scott Fitzgerald stayed there at various times. In 1951 the hotel was demolished and replaced by a bank.

[2] A. Everett Austin, Jr., of the Wadsworth Atheneum Museum in Hartford.

[3] Author of *Look Younger, Live Longer*, dedicated to Lady Mendl.

[4] Vera Orlova, actress, best known for her role in the 1915 Russian film *Nikolai*

Stavrogin.

[5] Hungarian gymnast and guru to Stravinsky. From this time until 1956, Stravinsky followed Siposs's routine of morning exercises which included headstands, push-ups, chinning on a bar, weight lifting, and stomach-muscle flexing.

[6] Mosfilm, 1941, directed by Pudovkin, music by Shaporin.

[7] Stravinsky's diary does not mention a lesson on the 18th.

[8] Actually Marks, a music publisher.

November

1 Our first American party. I am on my feet for twenty hours and there are five people in the kitchen. 2 Edward G. Robinsons, 2 Hagemans, 2 Bernsteins, 2 Marfiottis, 2 Hammonds [Richard Hammond and George Martin], 1 Richard Lert, 2 Max Reinhardts, 2 Rathbones, 2 Chadournes, 1 Bernardine Fritz, 1 Dr. Joseph, 1 Mercedes, 1 Anderson, 1 Baroness d'Erlanger, 1 Baron de Meyer, 2 Sachses, 2 Bolms, 2 Man Rays, 1 Sir Charles Mendl, 1 Elizabeth Arden, us. Only daiquiris for cocktails. For dinner, 8 bottles of champagne. Menu: light borscht with pirozhki, cold duck with cranberries and salads, ice in a pineapple, turkish coffee, cognac. [I.S.: Party.] **3** [I.S.: Anderson 104. Piano.] **4** [I.S.: Piano.] **5** The opening of an exhibition of Berman, Tchelichev, Leonid,[1] Christian Bérard. Later, we all go to the Café Gala, where the music is old-fashioned and in execrable taste. [I.S.: Anderson 105. Piano.] **6** Very hot day. Lunch at Romanoff's with Dick Hammond, Mercedes, Dagmar. I made myself a hat in five minutes. Igor works until late in the evening, while I read to him. **7** [I.S.: Anderson 106.] **9** Santa Barbara. We drive home and on reaching our house at 5:30, Igor immediately starts composing. **10** Read to Igor in the evening. [I.S.: Anderson 107. Piano.] **12** In the evening, Igor plays his new composition to me.[2] [I.S.: Anderson 108.] **13** Igor to the dentist. Igor receives news of the death of his brother Yuri in St. Petersburg.[3] **14** [I.S.: Anderson 109.] **16** Four men are now working in our garden. We attend a *panikhida* service for Igor's brother. The Baron comes for lunch and does not leave until 10:30 p.m. **17** [I.S.: Anderson 110.] **18** With Berman to Chadourne's lecture. He reads well and at the end is so moved about Paris that tears come to his eyes. We go with Mercedes to see Astaire's film, which everyone has criticized but which turns out to be very amusing. Dinner at Melody Lane.[4] [I.S.: Anderson 111.] **19** [I.S.: Anderson 112. Dentist.] **22** Take Igor to an NBC studio to record a talk. [I.S.: Anderson 113.] **23** [I.S.: I talk to Koussevitzky, who is in New York, about Tanglewood.] **24** Dagmar's birthday. Dinner at Mrs. Fritz's. [I.S.: Anderson 114. Dentist.] **25** [I.S.: Anderson 115.] **26** Letter from Ira, who is going to Paris. At last we see *Citizen Kane* and send a telegram to Orson Welles.[5] [I.S.: Anderson 116.] **27** We go at 6 to the Baroness d'Erlanger's. Victor Babin comes for dinner and stays to work with Igor. **28** Igor goes to the dentist and I buy blue pansies. **29** Buy flowers with Igor. We visit Mme Archansky, who has had an operation, then with Mercedes to see Katharine Cornell. [I.S.: Anderson 117.] **30** To a *panikhida* service for Mikusha. Lunch with Mercedes, who has a beautiful view of the sea and the mountains. Home by 6. Read to Igor.

December

1 [I.S.: Anderson 118. Dentist.] **2** We go to Brailovsky's concert. [I.S.: Anderson 119. He went to pay our real-estate taxes.] **3** [I.S.: Anderson 120.] **4** [I.S.: Anderson 121.] **5** [I.S.: Anderson 122. Dentist.] **6** A lovely warm day, and we eat on the balcony, water the flowers, and work in the garden. [I.S.: Anderson 123.] **7** At noon, Dmitri Stepanovich[6] phones to ask if we watered a certain flower and, incidentally, to tell us that Japan declared war.[7] [I.S.: Anderson 124.] **8** We listen on the radio to President Roosevelt declare war. Then we order tickets to St. Louis, though I have a difficult time convincing Igor that we should go. Later, we dine at the Brown Derby, where we see Charlie Chaplin. [I.S.: Anderson 125.] **9** Our radio does not work. I call a repairman and find out that no radios are working. The newspapers say that Japanese planes flew over San Francisco—a false alarm, it seems, but many rumors are flying around. Victor Babin comes to work with Igor. [I.S.: Anderson 126.] **10** The first blackout tonight. [I.S.: Anderson 127. At 4:30 a visit from the

representatives of the local musicians union.] **11** Take Igor to the dentist. The second blackout. **12** [I.S.: Departure in the evening to St. Louis.] **13** A wire is delivered to us in the morning. How did that s.o.b. Mandelstamm find out which train we took? He will send the books to the Coronado Hotel, in St. Louis. If he continues to annoy us, we will complain to the police. In two days: eight phone calls, a visit at 9 a.m., and now a wire to the train. We spend the day reading Berberova on Tchaikovsky, and playing gin rummy. **14** Crossing unending plains and seeing vast horizons: how huge and rich is America! **15** Arrive in St. Louis at 7:10 a.m. The train made up the four-and-a-half-hour delay in Kansas City. We are in a bad mood, not having slept enough. Our apartment in the hotel is tremendous, with a dining room and a kitchen. Igor's rehearsal at 2 p.m. **17** I fear that Igor may be catching the flu. I go with Odette Golschmann to look for antiques. **18** Igor is in bed all morning, but he goes to his afternoon rehearsal **19** Igor's St. Louis concert. **20** After the concert a very nice supper at the Golschmanns'. After the criticism for *The Star-Spangled Banner*, Golschmann will conduct it himself on Friday.[8] **21** We are happy to be leaving St. Louis. **24** Arrive at 6 a.m. I am so glad to be home and in California. At our house for dinner: 3 Bolms, Mercedes, Dagmar, Berman. After dinner, a Christmas tree and presents for all. **26** Read Dostoevsky's letters to Igor. [I.S.: Anderson 129.] **29** [I.S.: Anderson 130.] **30** [I.S.: Anderson 131.] **31** [I.S.: Anderson 132.]

Tango	500	Sale to publisher Feist
Washington	1,200	Concerts
Boston	1,250	
Bluebird	500	Ballet Theater commission
Balustrade	1,000	Conducting three performances
	4,450	
Stromberg Carlson	500	[fee paid for endorsing the radio]
1 Associated Music Publishers	1,103.75	April 23
2 AMP	64.88	December 8
3 AMP	1,216.25	July 3
4 *Bluebird* performance by Ballet Theater	100	
5 St. Louis Symphony	1,250	Conducting
6 Janssen, 2nd payment	500	Part payment, September 30, of the Werner Janssen commission for *Danses concertantes*
7 3 1/2% War Bonds	361.75	
8 Feist (*Tango* royalties)	7.39	
9 London	370.74	June 26
10 Pushkin article	75.00	
11 132 Anderson lessons @ $25	3,300.00	
	$11,163.01[9]	

1942

January

2 [I.S.: Anderson 133.] **3** Buy tickets to San Francisco. Igor nervous because of his frozen accounts. We call on the Baroness d'Erlanger and send telegrams to Monteux and Koshland. [I.S.: Anderson 134.] **4** [I.S.: Give donation to the church.] **5** A much-censored letter of December 1 from Fedya telling us about Milene's engagement and of the problem with her left lung—which worries Igor. Leave for San Francisco at 9 p.m. [I.S.: Anderson 135. Go to S. Francisco. Porter 75 cents.] **7** Igor has two rehearsals. Lunch after the first one with Monteux, and dinner at Monteux's. A birthday cake for me. [I.S.: Madeleine Milhaud. Went to the

---

[1] Eugene Berman's elder brother, husband of Sylvia Marlowe, the harpsichordist. She became a good friend of the Stravinskys in later years, above all in 1969–70, during the Essex House period.

[2] *Danses concertantes*.

[3] Yuri, an architectural engineer, had died of a stroke six months before. Stravinsky learned of it from a letter sent from Long Island (New York) by a descendant of the composer Borodin.

[4] In the early 1950s the Stravinskys frequently dined at this very modest restaurant.

[5] Later Welles urged Stravinsky to compose music for Robert Stevenson's film *Jane Eyre* (1944), in which Welles starred. Some of Stravinsky's sketches for the film score survive, in addition to the second movement of *Ode*, originally intended for the film.

[6] The chief gardener at the Stravinsky home until the mid-1950s.

[7] *Not* "attacked Pearl Harbor," a name the Stravinskys would not have recognized.

[8] At the rehearsal of Stravinsky's arrangement of the National Anthem, some orchestra members and others spoke against the version as "unpatriotic" (this was ten days after Pearl Harbor). Stravinsky objected to the way in which his arrangement was withdrawn and a conventional one substituted.

[9] The final pages of Stravinsky's diary contain his accounting of his income for 1941. It may be worth noting that he received far more from conducting ($4,700) and from teaching ($3,300) than he did from composing ($1,500 in commissions), or from royalties from all of his music ($2,863.01). His expenses for the year—the down-payment and mortgage payments from his house, the purchase of an automobile, the medical and food and clothing bills—were almost as much as his income.

bank.] **8** In the evening rehearse Igor's *Star-Spangled Banner*. **9** Igor's concert at 2:30. After the concert, John Rothschild drives us to Mills College, where Madeleine Milhaud gives a reception for us. [I.S.: Concert.] **10** [I.S.: Concert.] **11** [I.S.: Flowers $5.00. Leave San Francisco.] **14** Igor works on *Danses concertantes*; we take the score to be photographed. **15** Take Igor to the library to look up Delibes' music. [I.S.: Anderson 136. 10 cents to a beggar.] **16** Hear about the death of Carole Lombard. [I.S.: Anderson 137. *Danses concertantes* copyright.] **18** [I.S.: Anderson 138.] **19** Take Igor to Dr. Waitzfelder.[1] A nice dog seems to have adopted us. In the evening I paint a picture of the Black Sea. **20** [I.S.: Anderson 139.] **21** [I.S.: Anderson 140.] **23** [I.S.: Anderson 141. Plant lilies.] **26** [I.S.: Anderson 142. Plant more lilies.] **27** [I.S.: Anderson 143.] **29** Dinner at Edward G. Robinson's with Emil Ludwig and Melvin Douglas. **30** Presents from Emil Ludwig, a book for Igor, parrots for me. While Elena Alexandrovna unpacked the parrots, one of them flew away.

February

2 At 8:30, Igor's first rehearsal of *Danses concertantes*. I read Ludwig's book. **3** In the evening, go with Igor and Babitz to the rehearsal. Home at 11 p.m., I cook scrambled eggs for them. **5** I drive Igor to his rehearsal at 9:30 a.m. **6** At 10 a.m. I go to Igor's rehearsal. In the afternoon Igor plays his wonderful ''Elephant Polka.'' In the evening we see *The Man Who Came to Dinner*. **7** A rehearsal of *Danses concertantes* from 8 to 9 p.m., after which we go to Max Reinhardt's. Franz Werfel and Salka Viertel[2] are there. **10** Go with Igor to the doctor's, where we see Massine. Later with Igor to the cinema (Zorina). **11** Read Vladimir Nabokov's *Lugin's Defense* to Igor, then go to the ballet: *Serenade*, *Nutcracker*, *Gaîté Parisienne* (with Massine). **12** A letter from Fedya informs us of the death of Prince Argutinsky. Igor finishes the piano score of the ''Elephant Polka.'' **13** Lunch at Serge Denham's [ballet impresario]. Mary Pickford and Krassovskaya's husband come afterward. In the evening: Denham with Danilova and her husband Kokich, Rudenko, Tatiana Chamié, and Semenov. **14** At 5 we go to Massine's, where Igor discusses a proposal to compose a Donizetti ballet. Home at 11:30 p.m. **18** I mail ''Elephant Polka'' to Balanchine. We intend to go to James Sample's concert, but Igor decides not to when he discovers his *Berceuses du chat* is on the program. **22** Santa Barbara. Lunch at Sachses' with the Merillons, Chadournes, Mme Singer (niece [?] of the Princesse de Polignac). **25** Awakened in the middle of the night by air-raid alert sirens, we leave Santa Barbara after lunch.

March

2 Hollywood. We go to a church memorial service for Katya, after which Beata Bolm comes to help write letters. **6** Two men come to see Igor about writing music for a film. **7** Babitz for lunch. Later a musician [David Raksin] to talk to Igor about orchestrating the Polka for a military band. **15** With Berman to Santa Barbara. Puzzling behaviour by Rico Lebrun vis-à-vis Berman and Cagli.[3] **17** Hollywood. To a preview of Cecil de Mille's shockingly stupid and banal *Reap the Wild Wind*. **19** Tansman[4] for lunch. Igor irritable all day because of business letters and a cable from Milene asking for money. We send a telegram to Darius Milhaud. **24** [I.S.: Anderson 1st lesson.] **26** Igor reading and enjoying Mendelssohn's biography. **27** [I.S.: Anderson 2.] **28** To Santa Barbara. Dinner at Sachses' with Chadourne. A wild political argument until 2 a.m. **31** For lunch here: Berman, Charles Jones,[5] Elsie, Cagli. Igor upset at the thought of guests again tomorrow. [I.S.: Anderson 3 p.m.]

April

3 [I.S.: Anderson 4.] **7** [I.S.: Anderson 5.] **10** [I.S.: Anderson 6.] **12** Santa Barbara. Lunch with Mildred Bliss, dinner by ourselves. **14** [I.S.: Anderson 7.] **17** [I.S.: Anderson 8. Dentist.] **20** Stokowski conducts Igor's Tango, badly. **21** [I.S.: Anderson 9.] **22** Igor not feeling well. **23** Mercedes returns, and I meet her at the station and bring her to lunch. Igor is so nervous that I call Prince Galitzin. **24** We listen on the radio to *Le Sacre du printemps* and go to the cinema in the evening. [I.S.: Anderson 10. Dentist.] **25** Igor registers for defense work. **26** Santa Barbara. Lunch by the pool with Mrs. Singer, then to a charity golf match with Bob Hope and Bing Crosby. **28** [I.S.: Anderson 11.]

May

1 [I.S.: Anderson 12.] **2** Hear Donizetti on the radio at 6 p.m. I buy the score of *Lucia* for Igor. **4** For lunch here: Berman, Babin, and Vronsky. **5** [I.S.: Anderson 13.] **8** Dinner at the Baroness d'Erlanger's with the Chadournes, who put Igor into such a panic with their political conversation that he spends a sleepless night. [I.S.: Anderson 14.] **9** Buy newspapers for Igor so that he can see the good headlines about a victory in the Pacific. Leave at 5:30 p.m. for Santa Barbara. **12** [I.S.: Anderson 15.] **15** [I.S.: Anderson 16.] **19** [I.S.: Anderson 17.] **21** A telegram from Louis B. Mayer inviting us to a dinner for Russian War Relief. **22** [I.S.: Anderson 18.] **26** At the nursery, discover that one species of geranium, pale pink, is named for Igor Stravinsky. Send money to Fedya. [I.S.: Anderson 19.]

June

2 [I.S.: Anderson 20.] **5** [I.S.: Anderson 21.] **9** [I.S.: Anderson 22.] **10** Prince Galitzin comes to see Igor and stays for lunch. **12** [I.S.: Anderson 23.] **13** Cohen and Louis B. Mayer here from 2 to 6 p.m. The film business seems to be materializing. **15** [I.S.: Anderson 24.] **16** [I.S.: Anderson 25.] **18** Igor's birthday. He takes communion. After lunch at Bolms', we drive to Big Bear. [I.S.: Anderson 26. Make a deposit in the Bank of America.] **19** Night at Big Bear. Boat ride on Arrowhead Lake. Home by 6 p.m. The presents for Igor include a weighing machine. He is convinced that he has lost much weight since Europe. [I.S.: Sent a letter to Biram, County Tax Collector.] **20** [I.S.: Anderson 27.] **22** [I.S.: Anderson 28.] **23** [I.S.: Anderson 29.] **24** Igor receives a letter from the Tax Collector; we hurry to see Sapiro,[6] then go to the Court of Justice. Bad political news from Libya and Russia. **26** [I.S.: Anderson 30.] **29** [I.S.: Anderson 31.]

July

1 [I.S.: Anderson 32.] **2** [I.S.: Anderson 33.] **5** We eat on the dark terrace and watch the searchlights follow airplanes. **7** Igor goes with Tansman to the film studio, where a discussion takes place until late evening. The agent Meyer comes after that and says that he was never more certain that the business is now concluded. [I.S.: Anderson 34.] **8** The film business has fallen through, and everyone is disgusted except Igor and myself. [I.S.: Anderson 35.] **9** [I.S.: Anderson 36.] **10** [I.S.: Anderson 37.] **13** [I.S.: Anderson 38.] **14** [I.S.: Anderson 39.] **15** Waitzfelder gives me a tetanus injection because of a splinter. Tansman for lunch. A quiet, sad day. Igor and I worry about the future and send off more letters to the children with checks. **16** Igor composes all evening. [I.S.: Anderson 40.] **17** [I.S.: Anderson 41.] **19** We listen to Shostakovich's Seventh Symphony on the radio. Then to Berman's, to see his paintings. (He gives us one.) **20** Igor in a bad mood. Visit from Babitz. [I.S.: Anderson 42.] **21** Igor nervous. [I.S.: Anderson 43.] **22** Dinner at the Rachmaninovs'[7] with Nella and Artur Rubinstein. **23** [I.S.: Anderson 44.] **24** [I.S.: Anderson 45.] **26** At 8:30 p.m., a beautifully arranged party at Rubinsteins'. Nella dances and is very touching. **27** [I.S.: Anderson 46.] **28** [I.S.: Anderson 47.] **30** [I.S.: Anderson 48.] **31** Lunch at Artur Rubinstein's with Elsa Maxwell.

August

1 An invitation from Marlene Dietrich. Party in Basil Rathbone's garden. I am at the table with Milestone[8] and Lovet Lorsky. [I.S.: Anderson 49.]

---

[1] Frederic Waitzfelder, 6253 Hollywood Boulevard, was one of the Stravinskys' chief physicians for a period of twenty years.

[2] Widow of Berthold Viertel, the movie director in Isherwood's *Prater Violet*, mother of Peter Viertel, the screenwriter, and sister of Eduard Steuermann, Schoenberg's pupil.

[3] Corrado Cagli, the painter.

[4] Alexandre Tansman, film composer (*Flesh and Fantasy*) and author of a book on Stravinsky, who gave him an important manuscript of the *Four Norwegian Moods*.

[5] Composer, pupil of Milhaud; Jones' wife, Sally, had published a novel, *The Lights Burn Blue*.

[6] Aaron Sapiro, Stravinsky's Los Angeles attorney, 1942–59.

[7] They lived in Brentwood, at 12921 Mathon Street, which was not far from Schoenberg's.

[8] The film director Lewis Milestone was a native of the Ukraine. He is best known for *North Star*.

96 May 1942. Santa Barbara. At the home of Mr. and Mrs. Robert Woods Bliss.

3 [I.S.: Anderson 50.]   4 To Elsa Maxwell's lunch at Warner's. Visit from the Baroness d'Erlanger.   5 Dinner at The Players Club with Preston Sturges,[1] Mercedes, and Janet Flanner. Mercedes annoys Igor by nudging him and saying "Talk."   6 The Rachmaninovs here for dinner. 8 [I.S.: The work up the hill is finished.[2]]   11 Lunch at Dagmar's with Bliss, Seversky (aviator), Rubinstein, Admiral Johnson, Remarque, Louis Bromfield, John Gunther.   13 [I.S.: Began daily practicing on the piano.] 14 Lunch at Mercedes' with the charming and intelligent Janet Flanner. Cocktails with Denham and Berman.   16 Unexpectedly George Balanchine and Zorina arrive at our house from Buenos Aires.   17 [I.S.: Did not practice piano.]   23 Party at Hurok's.   25 [I.S.: Anderson 1.] 28 [I.S.: Anderson 2.]

September

1 [I.S.: Anderson 3.]   4 [I.S.: Anderson 4.]   5 Lunch at Elsa Maxwell's with Bette Davis, Bliss, Sir Charles and Lady Mendl. Then to a party in Kisling's new studio: a De Gaullist French society.   8 [I.S.: Anderson 5.] 9 Charles Mendl here for lunch. Read Leskov's *Journey with Nihilists* to Igor; we laugh a lot.   11 [I.S.: Anderson 6.]   12 For lunch on our terrace: Artur Rubinstein, Kisling, André David, Charles Montgomery, and Dagmar.   13 Seance at Corbett's.[3] Lunch at The Players.   15 Mercedes in the evening until 11. Igor working all the time. [I.S.: Anderson 7.]   16 Eye exercises at Corbett's.   18 Drive to Montecito for dinner at Sachses'. 24 Lunch here with Nadia Boulanger, who leaves by train.   25 At 4, a representative from Disney about the termination of his option. Dinner at Lourié's[4] with Jean Renoir.   26 Plant cactus under Igor's window. Lourié comes with a scenario. Marc Chadourne tries to convince Igor to give a lecture.   27 Bolm for dinner. Mercedes, Marcelle de Manziarly in the evening. [I.S.: Anderson 8.]   28 At 1:30 p.m. Igor rehearses with the studio orchestra. A letter from Milene and her fiancé.   30 My name day. Igor plays *Ruslan and Lyudmila* 4-hands with Marcelle de Manziarly.

October

6 [I.S.: Anderson 9.]   9 [I.S.: Anderson 10.]   10 Igor is reading Werfel's *Verdi*.   11 Alone with Igor in the evening.   12 [I.S.: Columbus day. 450 years.]   13 [I.S.: Anderson 11.]   14 Our church-wedding anniversary. Take communion.   15 [I.S.: Leo Wonder took the orchestration of *Polka* and *Norwegian Melodies* to proofread.]   16 [I.S.: Anderson 12.] 19 Santa Barbara. Igor plays his 4-hand sonata with Marcelle.   21 A party at Tansmans' with Fritz Zweig[5] and Ernst Toch.[6]   22 [I.S.: Anderson 13.] 23 Ingolf Dahl[7] for lunch   25 Igor, Marcelle, and I work in the garden. 26 Send Igor's *Norwegian Moods* to the publisher.   28 [I.S.: Anderson 14.]   29 [I.S.: Anderson 15.]

November

2 [I.S.: Anderson 16.]   4 Downtown with Igor to a music store.   5 [I.S.: Anderson 17.]   6 Werfel and Alma Mahler for dinner. Animated conversation about music.   10 [I.S.: Anderson 18.]   11 Hitler orders the occupation of all of France.   12 Mrs. Schindler[8] from 6:30 p.m. to 11 p.m. I am speaking English much of the time now. [I.S.: Anderson 19.] 15 Lunch with Werfel and Alma Mahler at the Beverly Wilshire Hotel. 16 Igor ill, calls Prince Galitzin, who recommends a diet.   17 Cable from Fedya asking for 3000 Swiss francs, required by the Swiss Government as a bond.   22 Santa Barbara. Mrs. Bliss for tea. Dinner at the Montecito Club, and cinema.   24 [I.S.: Anderson 20.]   25 Dinner at Sir Charles

Mendl's with Nella Rubinstein, Greer Garson, Reginald Gardiner, Nadia Petrova.[9] Valentina and husband, Claude de Biéville [Mme Chadourne]. 30 A church service for Mikusha. Mitchell Goertz [film agent] to see Igor in the evening.

December

3 Igor and I plant oleanders. Visit from Zoya Karabanova (Chauve-Souris) and Chamié. 21 years ago was the premiere of *Sleeping Beauty*. Zoya tells us that Spessivtzeva is now in an insane asylum. [I.S.: Anderson 21.] 4 [I.S.: Balanchine comes.]   5 We go to the ballet with Berman, Ona Munson,[10] and Gregory Ratoff. Backstage everyone compliments Agnes de Mille, but nobody compliments poor, fat, deaf and aged Bronia Nijinska whose "Snow Maiden" is dull and uninteresting.   13 After correcting *Circus Polka* all day, Igor is tired and angry with Leo Wonder.   15 [I.S.: Anderson 22.]   23 Igor receives a check for $60 from ASCAP. Was it worth the trouble to join?   24 Igor in a vile mood. 27 Heavenly weather. Igor sits on the balcony, naked.

January

1 Santa Barbara. To Emily Singer's lunch for eighteen people at Coral Casino.   5 Everyone comes to the station to see us off.[11] At home, we find that the hen coop is finished and that the parrots are well.   7 Hollywood. Though a year older today, I feel very happy. [Mitchell] Goertz takes Igor to see Sam Goldwyn, whom Igor likes very much. Igor spends the evening reading the film script.   8 Igor curses the script, saying it is a veritable *Schlafmittel* [sleeping pill].   11 Babin and Vronsky here for lunch, after which they play Igor's Polka and Tango for him, to his great delight.   16 Igor is in a bad mood. He dislikes the atmosphere in the film studios and the prospect of having to work for Goldwyn. Igor hopes that the contract is not signed.   17 Hurok here for lunch.   18 Neither Goldwyn nor Igor will compromise, and Igor is pleased that the film project will not be realized.   23 Sapiro here to discuss Deems Taylor's radio talk and magazine article which have upset Igor.   24 We leave for San Francisco on the 9 p.m. train.   25 We arrive in San Francisco four hours late. Pleasant dinner in Oakland at the Milhauds'.[12]   26 We go to the Ballet Theater opening and like *Pillar of Fire*[13] very much.   27 A three-hour rehearsal for Igor of *Petrushka*. Igor conducts *Petrushka*[14] and receives an ovation.   28 After lunch, visit from Monteux.   29 Hollywood. So pleasant to be home. A sign over the avocados in the market: "Honey, please don't squeeze me until I am yours."

February

2 Stokowski visits Igor to discuss the performance of the Symphony in C that Stokowski will conduct in a radio broadcast later this month.   7 At 5:30, the pianist Chavchavadze and Dmitri Markevich [cellist].   8 Igor's rehearsal. In the evening, he conducts *Petrushka* for Ballet Theater in the Shrine Auditorium.   9 Lunch at Lady Mendl's with Chavchavadze, Princess Galitzin,[15] Lester Donahue (pianist), Markevich, *et al*.   16 Igor upset because only six chickens have survived.   20 Igor and I listen to the broadcast of *Rigoletto*. A telegram from Hurok invites Igor to conduct *Petrushka* in New York.   21 Stokowski conducts Igor's Symphony on the radio, and we receive many phone calls about it and a telegram from Dushkin.   24 Our parrot dies. Igor very worried about Svetik, since the

---

[1] Sturges, the Paramount film director, owned this Sunset Boulevard café, with a small roof theater.

[2] The Stravinskys had terraced the hill behind their house, planted a vegetable garden on it, and built a staircase.

[3] The celebrated eye doctor, friend of Aldous Huxley.

[4] Eugene Lourié, a Russian-speaking friend of the Stravinskys in Paris since the early 1930s. He designed Jean Renoir's films *La Grande Illusion*, *La Bête humaine*, and *La Règle du jeu*.

[5] Pianist and coach of conductors (b. 1893). Stravinsky had known him since 1930 in Berlin. At this date Zweig lived at 8743 Holloway Drive. From January 1950 to March 1952 R.C. lived a few doors away, at 8624 Holloway Drive, in a house rented from Vladimir Sokolov.

[6] Ernst Toch (1887–1964), composer.

[7] Ingolf Dahl (1912–1970), Stravinsky's musical assistant, 1942–48.

[8] Wife of the architect.

[9] Later Mrs. Gardiner.

[10] Film actress (*Gone With the Wind*), later Mrs. Berman.

[11] Gas rationing had obliged the Stravinskys to make this one Santa Barbara trip by train.

[12] On arriving in Oakland, Stravinsky composed a little song "To our friends, the dear family Milhaud, Darius, Madeleine and Daniel, their little boy."

[13] Schoenberg's *Verklärte Nacht* choreographed by Anthony Tudor.

[14] The Ballet Theater production.

[15] Wife of Stravinsky's physician Prince Galitzin.

Germans are now taking people of his age for labor.   **25** We receive our ration books.

March

2 Igor and I take communion and give a memorial service for Katya.   **17** A visit from a homeopath.[1] The US War Department asks Igor to broadcast to Europe on the 25th anniversary of Debussy's death.   **21** To Igor's concert. It lasts until midnight.   **22** Igor works all day correcting *Apollo*. For dinner here: George Antheil and Aaron Copland, afterwards Sol Babitz.   **27** We leave for New York.   **29** At 2 p.m., arrive at the Blackstone Hotel, Chicago. We read in the newspapers about the death of Rachmaninov.   **31** Dushkin, Rieti, Mercedes, and Marcelle de Manziarly meet our train at Grand Central Station. Our apartment at the Ritz Towers is filled with flowers.

April

2 Igor conducts *Petrushka* at the ballet. Party afterward.   **4** Koussevitzky comes, and Forbes with his wife.   **9** Cocktails at Zosia Kochanska's for Artur Rubinstein. Nadia Boulanger comes at 7:30.   **10** Igor says a few words on the radio. To the ballet, then to a party at Hurok's.   **11** Tea at Balanchine's.[2]   **12** Igor conducts *Petrushka* with great success.   **14** At 2 p.m., Hurok, at 3, Bobby Jones.[3]   **15** Lunch with André Maurois.   **16** Dinner at Antal Dorati's. He speaks very unkindly about Fokine.   **17** Lunch with the Brailovskys and Nathan Milstein.   **18** To Matta's [the Chilean painter] with Berman.   **20** Igor helps Alexei Haieff[4] with his symphony. Teddy Chanler comes for tea. Marcelle and Vittorio play his charming valses.   **21** Igor annoyed because of too many appointments. He rehearses with Balanchine from 1 to 4. Dushkin comes from 5 to 6 p.m. Igor coaches Vladimir Golschmann in conducting *Danses concertantes*.   **22** Igor goes to the *Danses concertantes* rehearsal. Lunch with Golschmann. Then to Balanchine's rehearsal of *Apollo*. Tea with Balanchine and Zorina.   **23** Igor and I walk in Central Park.   **24** Golschmann at 9:30 a.m. At 11 Igor has two rehearsals of *Apollo*.   **25** Igor's *Apollo* rehearsals, first with orchestra, then with the dancers, all going very well; Hurok is so delighted that he kisses me. *Apollo* is a fantastic success. Party at the Casino with Balanchine, Hurok, and Karinska.[5]   **26** Igor conducts *Petrushka*.   **27** Rehearsal of *Danses concertantes*, then lunch with [Alexander] Ziloti, Casadesus,[6] and others. At 7, dinner with Pierre Claudel. At 9, to *Danses concertantes* in the Serenade concert at the Museum of Modern Art, and at 11:30 to a party at Chavchavadze's.   **28** At 5 p.m.: Pavlik Tchelichev and Zosia.   **29** Dinner with Germaine Tailleferre.[7]   **30** Dinner with Fernand Léger.[8]

May

2 Dinner with Sir Thomas and Lady Beecham at 8 p.m.   **3** Dinner with Hurok.   **4** Dinner at Charles Mitchell's with Count Rasponi and Chester Burden; lots of waiters.   **6** Salome Halpern[9] comes at 5. Dinner at the Acropolis where we see Renée de Veyrac.[10]   **8** Dinner with André Maurois.   **9** Tea with Yo and Phyllis Cuevas.[11] Igor conducts *Apollo*. Afterward to the Russian Tea Room.   **10** A visit from Koussevitzky. We leave for Chicago at 5:30 p.m.   **13** Hollywood. We have fifteen little

chickens and a hen.   **18** Igor rehearses *Dumbarton Oaks* with a pick-up ensemble.   **21** I drive Igor to the First Congregational Church for a second rehearsal of *Dumbarton Oaks*. Many musicians have come, including Klemperer, Antheil, Copland, Alexander Smallens. Poor Ingolf Dahl labors with the orchestra, some of whose players are new. Worse still, not everyone shows up. Igor leaves, disgusted, and he is in a bad mood all day.   **23** Our cocks crow in the early morning, disturbing not only us. We will probably have to get rid of them.

June

1 Igor plays the Epitaph for me, the last part of *Triads*,[12] which he finished composing today.   **5** We go to Santa Barbara with the chickens and Russian *Kulich* [Easter bread].   **9** Hollywood. Igor composes verses on the chicken coop theme. Dinner at Antheil's.   **12** Igor and I listen to a broadcast of *Così fan tutte*.   **18** Igor's birthday. He takes communion and we have a memorial service for his mother. 1943 is his father's centenary.   **22** To Hollywood Bowl for a "Russian Day." Stokowski conducts *Petrushka*.   **24** Anderson, Igor's pupil, dies very unexpectedly.   **26** Santa Barbara for dinner.   **29** To Dr. Waitzfelder and the film *Hôtel du Nord*, which fills us with nostalgia.   **30** To Anderson's funeral.

July

7 A rooster wakes us at 5 and does not stop crowing. Later in the morning I give him away. We go to Kurt Weill's *Lady in the Dark*.   **12** Igor to Dr. Schiell[13] about a broken tooth.   **13** To Hollywood Bowl: Igor's rehearsal of *Petrushka*.   **15** Lunch here: Kall and Kibalchich.[14]   **17** Igor conducts *Petrushka* in Hollywood Bowl. A party afterwards with Hurok, Lucia Chase, Dorati, *et al.*   **18** For lunch here: the Massines. For dinner here: Virgil Thomson, Berman, Mercedes.   **23** Very nice, cozy dinner at Franz Werfel's.

August

1 Buy begonias for Werfel. Igor unsuccessfully tries to find out whether or not the Werfels have invited Schoenberg.   **2** Dinner at Werfel's with Montemezzi.   **3** To Orson Welles's Mercury Show, the tickets given to us by Dr. Bernstein.   **5** Lunch at The Players with Nadia Boulanger.   **6** Dr. Waitzfelder. Mercedes for lunch.   **7** Work in the garden with Dmitri Stepanovich. Igor receives good news about money from London. He remains in a good mood and buys wine. We see *Grande Illusion*.   **8** For lunch: Berman and Bolms, who stay most of the day.   **10** Igor works with Babitz.   **14** Cocktails at Lady Mendl's.   **26** Igor lunches at Warner Brothers Studio to discuss a possible film about Gershwin.[15]   **28** Dinner at the Werfels' with Thomas Mann[16] and Jeritza [the soprano].   **30** For dinner here: Hurok and Artur Rubinstein.   **31** We leave for Santa Barbara.

September

4 With Nadia to buy presents for Igor.   **7** Home from Santa Barbara.   **11** Tagunov for dinner and until midnight, to help Igor with his income

[1] Dr. A. Dwight Smith, from Glendale.

[2] At this time, at 637 Madison Avenue.

[3] Robert Edmond Jones, who had staged *Oedipus Rex* with huge puppets at the Metropolitan Opera.

[4] (b. 1914). Composer, close friend of the Stravinskys'.

[5] Varvara Karinska (1886–1983), stage, film, and ballet costume maker and designer, since 1949 closely associated with George Balanchine. Born Varvara Zhmoudsky, in Kharkov, October 3, 1886. Vera Stravinsky had known her in Yalta in 1917–19.

[6] Robert Casadesus was living at Princeton at the time.

[7] Germaine Tailleferre (1892–1983), member of "Les Six," spent World War II at 60 Gramercy Park, New York City.

[8] On this occasion Léger gave the Stravinskys an ink drawing of a bird.

[9] At this time Salome Halpern (the Princess Andronikov) lived at 2 Sutton Place, New York.

[10] The Countess de Veyrac had known the Stravinskys in Paris, but when R.C. met her she was working as a waitress in Frascati's in Beverly Hills.

[11] Née Phyllis Nahl, dancer, better known by her stage name, Antonia Cobos. She choreographed the performance of *Histoire du soldat* that Stravinsky conducted in Royce Hall in June 1949.

[12] The first title for *Ode*.

[13] Dr. Lewis Shiell, 415 Camden Drive, Beverly Hills.

[14] Vasily Kibalchich, choral conductor. He had known Stravinsky since January 1915, in Château d'Oex, Switzerland.

[15] Stravinsky had been asked to play himself in the scene in which Gershwin visits Stravinsky in Paris in the hope of becoming his pupil: *Gershwin*: "How much do you charge?" *Stravinsky*: "How much do you make?" *Gershwin*: "About $100,000 a year." *Stravinsky*: "In that case I should study with you."

[16] About this period, Mann wrote: "We had, as I had hoped, come to see much more of Stravinsky and his wife—a thoroughgoing *belle Russe*, that is to say, an example of that specifically Russian beauty that radiates the most likeable of human qualities. Talking with him at an evening gathering at our house, I was struck by things he said—with Gide as a starting point, and speaking alternately in German, English, and French—concerning *confession* as the product of various cultural spheres: the Greek Orthodox, the Roman Catholic, and the Protestant. In his opinion, Tolstoy was essentially German and Protestant." (*The Story of a Novel*, 1961)

97 1943. Los Angeles. With the John Alden Carpenters and Bolms.

98 1943. 1260 North Wetherly Drive. With the Alexandre Tansmans; Berman; Kyza, Olav, and Beata Bolm; and Mercedes de Acosta.

tax returns.   **16** To Santa Barbara to surprise Nadia, after phoning her for her name day.   **23** Hollywood. Victoria Ocampo and Josephina Dorado for dinner.   **28** Igor is still in a bad mood because of yesterday's wire from Koussevitzky saying that he will conduct the premiere of *Ode*.
30 Here in the evening, many guests. Nobody likes Victoria.

October

2 Shop with Nadia at the Farmers' Market. Buffet dinner here for Darius Milhaud.   **9** Many telegrams concerning the Blue Network broadcast of *Ode*. Koussevitzky made a speech, with great aplomb but also with a very thick accent. Igor is sad because the *Ode* was badly played.
14 Our wedding anniversary. Communion. Lunch at Father Gregory's, then with the Sokolovs[1] to buy 27 bottles of wine. Dinner at Laure's[2] with Jean Renoir.   **16** A telegram from Koussevitzky about *Ode* seems to satisfy Igor. Nadia calls from Santa Barbara.   **17** A long walk in the hills with Igor.   **20** Dinner here with Ernst Toch.   **24** See a very impressive film about Stalingrad.   **29** Leave for Santa Barbara.[3]   **30** Marian Sachs'[4] birthday.   **31** Igor and I discuss the possibility of moving to Santa Barbara.

November

26 Read Bunin aloud to Igor.   **28** Nadia phones with the news of the death of the Princesse de Polignac in London. Babitz for lunch and to work with Igor.   **30** Memorial service for Mikusha.

December

1 Nadia works with Igor correcting *Sacre*.[5]   **4** Dr. Waitzfelder. We leave for Santa Barbara   **5** Igor works with Nadia.   **7** Read Bakunin to Igor in the evening.   **8** Igor finishes his Chicago lecture with Nadia's help.   **9** I telephone the end of the lecture to Maillette.   **12** Shura Cherkassky plays the *Three Movements from Petrushka* for Igor, who approves.
14 Balanchine for dinner here.   **15** Igor goes to a memorial service for Max Reinhardt.   **16** Finish the map of Naples.[6]   **17** Leyssac[7] takes his first lesson with Igor.   **18** Igor and Beata Bolm send Koussevitzky the fourth version of a telegram about program timing. Leyssac comes for his second lesson.   **19** Werfel very ill.   **30** Igor sick and in bed.

January

1 A telephone call from Western Union to say that our cable to Fedya was not sent because the text was thought to be helpful to the enemy. At Hammond's New Year party, Igor gets drunk on eggnog.   **7** Leave for Boston. Igor buys me a silver brooch and a little box from a vendor on the train.   **9** In Boston at 3:30. No sooner do we arrive than, as always, we begin to count the days until we return home   **10** Igor rehearses the Boston Symphony Orchestra from 10 to 1 and from 4 to 7.   **11** Igor rehearses from 10 to 1. Lunch with Henrietta Hirshman; many reminiscences of Russia and Paris.   **12** Igor rehearses from 10 to 1. We buy books at Schoenhof's in Harvard Square: *Don Quichotte*; the *Memoires de la Tour du pin*; *Journal d'une Femme de Cinquant Ans* (2 vols.); Thierry's *Histoire d'Attila*; Corpechot's *Souvenirs d'un Journaliste* (J.-E. Blanche, *et al.*); and the *Mémoires de la Marquise de Nadaillac*.
13 Igor's Cambridge concert. At this morning's rehearsal, Aaron

Copland, Arthur Fiedler, *et al.* Lunch with Henrietta at Amalfi restaurant.   **14** Igor's matinée concert in Boston. A good audience reception. The *Circus Polka* is played twice. Many people in the greenroom after the concert. At 5:30, dinner at the Viking restaurant.
15 Lunch at Amalfi with George Balanchine. We buy more books: Vercors' *Les Silences de la mer*, Gide's *Ecole des femmes*, Gustave Cohen's *La Grande clarté du moyen-age*. Igor's Boston concert tonight is broadcast.   **16** New York.   **19** Chicago. Hotel Shoreland. Igor rehearses *Histoire du soldat* in a room at the Baldwin Piano Company. At 4 he rehearses with the violinist Weicher. We are very late for dinner at John U. Nef's.   **20** Igor rehearses all day, and I go to the Museum. Remi Gassman and the pianist Willard MacGregor take me to lunch, after which I return to the Museum: Velazquez's *The Servant*. I pick up Igor at 5. His lecture at 8:30 is introduced by Robert Hutchins. Afterward to a restaurant with Artur Rubinstein and Jacques Maritain.   **21** Rehearsal from 10:30 to 12:30, then lunch at the hotel. Igor goes to the University of Chicago at 4:30 and stays there until his concert at 8:30. Reception at Nef's. To bed at 3 a.m.   **22** To Madison, Wisconsin, on the Milwaukee and St. Paul Railroad. Professor Brosa, violinist, meets us. When people talk about "Mademoiselle," they mean Nadia.   **23** At 11 a.m. the sisters from the Convent send a car for us and we spend almost the whole day with them.[8]   **24** From Madison to Chicago where we give a dinner for eight at the Shoreland Hotel: Maritain, the Nefs, Gassman, *et al.*
25 Arthur Sachs is on our train for Los Angeles. I step off the train at each station's stop to enjoy the snow.   **27** What joy to come home!

February

6 Work in the garden. Igor composes all day.   **7** To the film *North Star*.[9]
8 Cried throughout the film *Bernadette*.   **12** Leave for Santa Barbara at 4.   **13** Igor is in a bad mood, tired of visitors. Lunch on the terrace. Dinner at Merillons'. Igor plays his recording but regrets doing it, since nobody reacts.   **15** Klemperer[10] from 5 to 7 to listen to Igor's recordings.   **28** First week of Lent. To church with Igor.

March

1 A memorial service for Katya. Igor and I take communion.
4 Klemperers for tea. We are very sorry for the Klemperers. She tries to be brave, and both of them appreciate the visit with us.   **6** To an "Evenings on the Roof" concert: a very pleasant atmosphere.   **9** Our wedding anniversary. I buy forget-me-nots and pink primulas for Igor.
11 Dinner with James Hilton.[11]   **15** Igor writes an article about Rimsky-Korsakov for the Office of War Information (Mrs. Reed)   **23** Igor completes the forms for gas rationing: I am a music composer and conductor. I go to various motion picture studios and radio studios. I drive to and from work. I have irregular hours and in my type of work it is not possible to take other people. I have to carry my music and work very late hours. I average 460 miles monthly.[12]   **29** Good news from Fedya: Milene is getting married.   **31** Igor plays Landowska's recording of the *Goldberg Variations*.

April

2 In the evening to the film *Jane Eyre* (Orson Welles).   **5** Igor answers letters all day.   **8** A letter from Olga Sallard with the sad news of Guy de Matharel's death.   **18** Nathaniel Shilkret at 5 to ask Igor to compose *Babel*[13] for the *Genesis* suite.   **23** Quiet day. Reading Pushkin. Man Ray[14] brings the photo taken at Laure's at Easter. To a film (*Tarzan*).   **26** Igor

---

[1] Vladimir Sokolov, the actor, and Lisa, his wife, became members of the Stravinsky inner sanctum until Lisa's death in June 1948.

[2] Laure Ferren, ex-wife of the American painter John Ferren (1905–1970), had married Eugene Lourié. She had a sharp tongue, and when the Baroness d'Erlanger asked her, snobbishly, about her family background, Laure answered, "*Je suis métèque, madame.*"

[3] This was to be the Stravinskys' longest visit to Santa Barbara, and the most critical, since they considered moving there.

[4] Daughter of Arthur and Georges Sachs, now Mme François-Poncet, wife of the former French Ambassador to the United States.

[5] The revised version of the *Danse Sacrale*. Stravinsky gave her some of the manuscript.

[6] Stravinsky followed every development on the war fronts, inserting pins on maps according to the moves of the Allied armies.

[7] A Los Angeles musician, pupil of Stravinsky's for a short period.

[8] Nadia Boulanger's pupil, Sister Edward Blackwell of Edgewood College, Madison, continued to correspond with the Stravinskys until the ends of their lives.

[9] Script by Lillian Hellman, lyrics by Ira Gershwin, music by Aaron Copland (after Stravinsky withdrew).

[10] At this date Otto Klemperer was living at 1546 Clamart Court, West Los Angeles.

[11] The novelist, author of *Lost Horizon*.

[12] This first entry entirely in English was probably dictated by Beata Bolm.

[13] This entry reveals that the choice of text was not Stravinsky's.

[14] At this time, Man Ray was living at 1245 Vine Street. Part of this photograph, a close-up of the Stravinskys, appears on p.100, *Igor and Vera Stravinsky*, op. cit. and is wrongly captioned there as having been taken on June 18, 1942.

meets with De Bourg.[1] To the rationing board for permission to drive to Santa Barbara. **30** Dinner at Sokolovs' with John Houseman (producer for Paramount).

May

4 Leave for Santa Barbara at 4. **13** We lunch at the Sachs' pool with Mayette Meyneng[2] and Shiva Baring Gould. **16** Hollywood. Dinner with Balanchine. **20** Balanchine for dinner. **22** Dinner at Thomas Mann's[3] with the Rubinsteins, Mr. and Mrs. Singer, Karen and Ernst van Leyden,[4] Dr. Joseph. Quite dull, on the whole. **26** Dinner at The Players with Balanchine, Denham, Berman. **27** Igor has a hangover. Lunch with René Clair, Man Ray, the Sokolovs. **28** Igor works in the garden. Dinner here with the Louriés, then to the film *Tunisian Victory*.

June

1 For dinner here: Balanchine, Berman, Denham. **3** Beata writes letters for Igor. Dinner at Toch's[5] with Joseph Szigeti and Thomas Mann. Toch talks amusingly about his musical work with the studio. His inspiration for church music is a small model of a cathedral. **5** The invasion of Europe! **8** A wire from Billy Rose.[6] **9** Fog, rain, and cold, as in France. Igor receives a Viennese professor. We worry about the news from France and walk in the hills. Walking on Sunset Boulevard we meet Balanchine near our corner. **10** Telegram from Anton Dolin.[7] **12** Buy the Guide Michelin and old Baedekers in order to follow the invasion on maps. **13** Telephone call from Billy Rose, in New York, after which Igor telegraphs Winter[8] about it, and Dolin calls us for the results. **16** Dolin works with Igor from 12 to 2, Balanchine from 4 to 7. A telegram from Winter: "Billy still stubborn." **17** Igor takes communion. A big lunch here with Man Ray, Balanchine, *et al.* **18** To Santa Barbara. A celebration, with presents, for Igor's birthday. **19** With Nadia and the Sachses to see a film on the invasion. **23** Nadia for lunch and until 5. **27** Dinner at Werfels' with Mme Reinhardt and Alfred Hitchcock with his wife. Igor likes Hitchcock and is friendly to him: they talk until late. **30** We go to Balanchine's rehearsal. Very good choreography but bad dancers. Drive an exhausted Danilova home.

July

1 Examination for my driver's license: I am nervous, but I pass. Dinner at the Beachcomber restaurant with Balanchine and Denham. **5** We watch Dmitri Mitropoulos's rehearsal in Hollywood Bowl. Berman brings his *Danses concertantes* sketches; they are not at all what Igor had in mind, which is embarrassing, since Igor leaves the room to work and I am left to smooth everything out. **7** Take photographs of Igor and Mitropoulos in Hollywood Bowl. I go to Berman who revises the sketches of the sets as I watch. I take them to show to Igor, who likes them. **11** To Mitropoulos's Hollywood Bowl concert. Meet Yehudi Menuhin there. Spend the late evening at Dorati's. **14** A Bastille Day Celebration at Claude de Biéville's. To the newsreels with Man Ray, then dinner here. **16** Dahl for lunch. Laure helps with the translation [of *Poétique musicale*]. **17** The *Examiner* publishes a scandalous story about Igor. We translate Igor's Tchaikovsky article with Laure. **18** Go to Marion Anderson's concert and afterward to Hurok's party for her. **20** To Mitropoulos's rehearsal. He conducts and plays Prokofiev's Third Concerto. I walk with Igor in the evening. **21** Igor is angry with Bolm because he sides with the audience who disapproved of Mitropoulos's kissing Marion Anderson's hand. **22** Igor and I go to the newsreels, then to Miller's to buy a photostat of a Michelin map. Laure and Igor work on translations until 11:30.

23 Mitropoulos here, talks to Igor until 2 a.m. **24** Ingolf Dahl in the afternoon,[9] Balanchine in the evening. **25** Mercedes for tea. Igor locks himself in his room and works. **30** Dahl works with Igor.

August

4 Lunch at Artur Rubinstein's. André David is there and someone from "Information Please." **7** Balanchine comes with two bottles of wine. **9** Dolin for lunch, Balanchine for dinner. **11** The Americans are approaching Paris! To a rehearsal in Hollywood Bowl. Dolin and Markova for lunch and to hear Igor's *Scènes de ballet*. Balanchine and Archansky come. **12** Igor conducts *Petrushka* in Hollywood Bowl. **17** Listen to the news on the radio every fifteen minutes. The Americans are in Chartres! **18** The Germans have retreated to Versailles. **25** Paris has been captured by the Americans and French partisans! **26** With Igor to Leonard Bernstein's concert in Hollywood Bowl. Igor is disappointed in his conducting (Mendelssohn, Gershwin, *Firebird*). **30** Igor rehearses in Hollywood Bowl. **31** Igor conducts *Petrushka* in Hollywood Bowl. After the performance to the Café Gala with Catherine d'Erlanger.

September

8 Dinner at Ona Munson's, a very attractive house with the Berman touch. A pleasant time, though Igor, with so much work on his mind, was very reluctant to go. **9** Victory party at Elsa Maxwell's for 200 of the "most beautiful" and "most famous" people. Wonderful dresses and diamonds. I am at the table with José Iturbi, Lady Mendl, Katina Paxinou, Gene Tierney, and Pasternak. Igor is at a table with Bette Davis and Orson Welles. **10** I cry seeing Paris in the newsreels. **11** Telegrams from Balanchine and Berman on the success of *Danses concertantes*. Igor goes with Dahl to record the new ballet.[10] **12** We go to Dahl's recording, second session, of the piano version of *Scènes de ballet*. **13** Application to the rationing board. Work in the garden. Babitz for dinner: discussion of Karl Marx. **14** Dr. Waitzfelder. Dahl brings Igor's recordings.[11] **17** I am one of the hostesses at a garden party at Arutunov's (580 North Beverly Glen) for the Russian American Actors' Mutual Aid Society. Igor is at my table. **18** We buy the *Encyclopedia Britannica* at Pickwick, 25 volumes for 15 dollars. **21** Dr. Waitzfelder. Birthday of the Mother of Christ.[12] **22** Dinner with Lyudmila Pitoëff.[13] **25** Dinner at Hagemans' with Lion Feuchtwanger, Will Durant, and Montemezzi. I do not enjoy the company. **28** Zoya Karabanova for lunch. Cocktails at Hammond's with Ginger Rogers, Ona Munson, the Bernsteins, Princess Pignatelli. Igor sick afterward from the food. **30** Leave for Santa Barbara.

October

3 In the morning, group photographs are taken, to Igor's annoyance. We return to Hollywood. **5** Dr. Waitzfelder. André David, for lunch, talks with Igor until 5 p.m. **8** Dr. Waitzfelder. Sir Charles Mendl for lunch. Dinner at The Players with René Clair, then cognac at his house and a very long but interesting discussion. **14** Our wedding anniversary. We take communion, then lunch with Father Gregory. **15** I cook dinner here for the René Clairs. **22** Dr. Waitzfelder. Nadia and Igor work together the whole day. Babitz comes to discuss a proposal from a group of musicians who wish to take lessons from Nadia. To Werner Janssen's concert with *Dumbarton Oaks*. Supper afterward at the Brown Derby. **23** We leave from Glendale for San Francisco at 9:27 p.m. **24** Met by Madeleine and Darius Milhaud, who is on crutches. Their house is very "bohemian" and untidy, but also cozy. Madeleine and I prepare lunch. Germaine Schmitz comes, and, in the evening, 25 professors and their

---

[1] Of the Swiss Legation in Washington.

[2] This French-born senior student at Santa Barbara State College had recently published a novel, *The Broken Arc* (Harper), which the Stravinskys had read.

[3] At 1550 San Remo Drive.

[4] Painters, both of them, who later lived in Venice near the Zattere.

[5] At this date Toch was living at 811 Franklin Avenue, Santa Monica.

[6] This was the first step toward commissioning Stravinsky to compose a ballet (*Scènes de ballet*) for inclusion in Billy Rose's *Seven Lively Arts*.

[7] The Stravinskys had known Dolin (d. 1983) since he joined Diaghilev's Ballets Russes. He choreographed *Scènes de ballet*.

[8] Hugo Winter was Stravinsky's publisher in New York.

[9] Dahl was arranging *Scènes de ballet* for piano as Stravinsky composed the music.

[10] Stravinsky did not have a copy of this performance in his collection of privately made recordings.

[11] These were sent to Billy Rose in New York, for ballet rehearsals (*Seven Lively Arts*).

[12] This is an important Russian holiday.

[13] She had danced the part of the Princess in the first performance of *Histoire du soldat*, September 28, 1918.

wives, "the most interesting people" in Mills College—supposedly.
25 Igor's lecture at Mills and a sit-down supper at President White's.
26 The president's car takes us to the San Francisco Station.[1] **28** At noon, the "March of Time" films us on our terrace; many people in the film crew and managing the electric lights. Shop with Nadia. **29** Nadia gives a lesson to Babitz and others. **30** Drive Nadia to Santa Barbara for Marion Sachs' birthday.

November

2 Denham telephones Igor inviting him to conduct *Danses concertantes* in San Francisco. **7** We follow the elections on the radio. Thank God Roosevelt beats Dewey. **8** Igor wakes up deaf in one ear. I drive him to the doctor, who says it is only a cold. Igor is very animated at dinner—with Berman—in spite of the deafness. **11** To Glendale to meet Nadia, who helps Igor to write an article and some letters. **13** Igor has laryngitis and stays in bed. **16** Dr. Waitzfelder for Igor. To Schwab's drugstore[2] for Igor's medicines. **23** Thanksgiving Day. Turkey dinner with Jean Renoir. **25** *Life* magazine photographers take Igor's picture for Billy Rose. **26** At 3 we go to Villa-Lobos' concert. **28** For dinner here: Villa-Lobos. **30** Memorial service for Mikusha. Telegram from Dolin. Drinks at La Rue's with Balanchine and Danilova. See a propaganda film at the General Service Studio with Renoir.

December

1 To the ballet rehearsal of *Danses concertantes*. Igor is pleased. Lunch at the Biltmore with Denham. The ballet is a big success. Party afterward at Sokolovs' until 4 a.m. **3** Dr. Waitzfelder. Balanchine and Krassovska [the ballerina] for tea. I cook dinner and stay up until 2 a.m., while Nadia, Igor, and Balanchine work on music. **5** Lunch with Nadia, Princess Pignatelli, Balanchine, Danilova, *et al.* Supper at the Biltmore after the "Gala Ballet Balanchine" with Denham, Nadia, and ourselves. **6** Once more to the ballet to see *Danses concertantes*. Dine with Denham.
10 Read, with much interest, Elsa Triolet's[3] *Mille Regrets* and *Personne ne m'aime*. **11** Here for dinner: Balanchine, Berman, the Sokolovs.
13 Dinner at René Clair's **18** Shop with Nadia. Igor frames his portraits of Gogol and Griboyedov. **19** Cocktails at René Clair's. Banquet at Pierre Blanchar's, then again later with René Clair. **21** See two French films at the Esquire Theater with Blanchar. **27** Telephone call from Billy Rose. **28** To Szigeti's house at Palos Verdes from 5 to 12 p.m. Igor and Szigeti play the Duo concertant. **29** Billy Rose and Maurice Abravanel [conductor] telephone Igor. **31** Santa Barbara. Lovely walks. For dinner: Nadia's pupils, the Abbé Fortier and two Sisters. Elliot Forbes, Rico Lebrun with Helen. Sparkling conversation all evening.

1945

January

1 Heavenly weather. Dinner with Stark Young.[4] **6** Hollywood. I take communion. We bring wine to Kall. At 6, Nadia comes with Berman, Nadia, Igor, and I light the Christmas tree [Russian calendar] and go to church, dining at home with Nadia afterward. **7** The birthday of the little Vera and also of Jesus Christ. **9** Our two loudest roosters are taken away. **10** Sapiro for lunch. **11** Bolms in the afternoon, Sokolovs in the evening. **12** Carlos Chavez here for dinner. **17** Igor and I plant roses.
18 Igor has a tooth extracted. **20** A quiet dinner here with Nadia.
21 The Louriés for lunch, the Sokolovs, Bolms, and Berman later. To the newsreels at 8, then to a bistro with Nadia, the Sokolovs, Berman. **24** Up at 8 for the 10:15 train from Pasadena. Meet Frank Sinatra on the Chicago-

bound train. **26** Meet John Houseman with Joan Fontaine on the train.
27 New York. The Drake Hotel. A thousand phone calls. Lunch at Giovanni's restaurant. **28** Igor dines in the evening with Balanchine and Zorina. **30** Igor's first rehearsal with the New York Philharmonic, but he has a high temperature and we call Dr. Garbat who gives him sulfa drugs. At 9 p.m. we hear Rieti's two-piano concerto. **31** I go with Igor to two rehearsals. Arthur Sachs orders a car and chauffeur for us for the whole week.

February

1 Igor's morning rehearsal in Carnegie Hall. I have a temperature too, but in spite of it I go to Igor's concert. In our box: the Sachses, Baring Gould, Rieti, Kyriena Ziloti[5], Alexis Haieff. **2** To Tchelichev's exhibition and to Igor's afternoon concert. **3** Igor's concert at 8:45. A big gathering at Reuben's restaurant afterward and until 4 a.m. **4** Igor's Sunday broadcast concert at 3 p.m. In the evening: Balanchine and Nicolas Nabokov. **5** Igor has a long and tiring recording session (10 sides) with Columbia—*Scènes de ballet, Ode, Norwegian Moods, Circus Polka*. A late dinner with Goddard Lieberson [of Columbia Records] in a Greek restaurant. **7** Germain Prévost plays Igor's *Elégie* for him, after which we go to Professor Telberg's on Riverside Drive (bus no.5) for tea.
8 The pianist Vincent Persichetti comes from Philadelphia to work with Igor.[6] **9** In the evening we go to see *The Tempest* [with Vera Zorina].
11 Spend the whole day at Kyriena Ziloti's. After lunch, a gathering of her pupils and some young composers. At 5:30 to Szigeti's concert, and in the evening to a concert of the Pro Arte Quartet in which Prévost plays Igor's *Elégie*. I give him a rose. **12** At 8 p.m., dinner at Leone's, with old bankers and their wives. At mid-point Igor asks me in Russian: "Is it at least half over?" **13** Igor, reading his Philadelphia lecture, is in a bad mood. Dinner with Balanchine, *et al.* In New York, one is more conscious of the war and one feels more the proximity of Europe. Here the pace is frantic, and our nerves are so taut that we feel like crying without any reason. A great lack of things and at the same time tremendous waste. It is terribly cold: I feel it in the soles of my feet. So far I have not seen much, but have gone to rehearsals and Carnegie Hall. Igor's rehearsals are filled with countless friends. I haven't eaten anything but millet porridge for the last three days. One of Igor's fingers is swollen—we don't know whether it is from a bedbug bite or from the sulfa drug. All of these illnesses occur in an atmosphere of constant nervousness and terrible hurry. The telephone never stops and the most difficult thing is to find excuses not to accept the invitations: everyone is so insistent. But people are afraid of infection, and when I told Tchelichev that I had a high temperature he bounded out of my room, afraid that I had flu. Nabokov's face looks crooked. I do not know what it is but it looks like paralysis. He is going with us to Philadelphia just to be able to find time to talk to Igor on the train. **14** Igor rehearses *Apollo* from 8 p.m. to 11 at the Columbia Broadcasting System, then conducts the performance at 11:30. Afterward we go to the Russian Tea Room with Balanchine, Ziloti, Haieff, Marcelle de Manziarly, Rieti, and David Diamond. **15** Igor lunches with Bruno Zirato[7] and receives the commission to compose a "Victory Symphony."[8] **16** We go to a preview of *Oklahoma*, then visit Katya Sergava. **18** Marcel Hubert[9] with Igor. Lunch at Kyriena Ziloti's. Two young men, Arthur Gold and Robert Fizdale, come to play Igor's music. **19** Koussevitzky comes at 5. **20** Igor and Balanchine discuss music. Igor writes a speech to be recorded and broadcast in France and Belgium; he records it at 5 p.m. **21** Igor goes to Philadelphia, Barclay Hotel, and gives his lecture at 8:30. **22** Lunch at the Mirleton (11 East 58) with Lieberson. In the evening to the Monte Carlo Ballet to see *Danses concertantes*. **23** 10–12:30: the photographer Martini. Tea at Mercedes' with Stark Young and Zosia Kochanska. Newsreel (Stalin to Roosevelt: "I said Yalta, not Malta"). **24** Lunch at Virgil Thompson's with Maurice

---

[1] Mrs. Stravinsky wrote to Mrs. White from Hollywood: "I hope . . . that being without your car for the whole afternoon has not disturbed you too much. We shall certainly remember with great pleasure our visit to Mills College. . . ."

[2] At the corner of Sunset Boulevard and Laurel Canyon, closed permanently in 1983.

[3] French novelist, wife of Louis Aragon.

[4] Stark Young, novelist (*So Red the Rose*) and former drama critic for *The New York Times*, shared a New York home with William McKnight Bowman. Both were friends of the Sachses, and, through them, of the Stravinskys.

[5] Daughter of Alexander Ziloti. She had known Stravinsky since at least 1907. She

lived on West 73rd Street while the Stravinskys lived on East 73rd.

[6] Stravinsky was to give a lecture in Philadelphia and to play his Sonata for two pianos there with Persichetti.

[7] Of Columbia Concerts, 113 West 57th Street; also manager of the New York Philharmonic.

[8] The Symphony in Three Movements. The money, $5,000, was given to the Philharmonic by Arthur Sachs who also purchased the manuscript and donated it to the New York Public Library.

[9] The cellist. He played the Lalo Concerto, conducted by Stravinsky, in Montreal, March 5.

Grosser and John Cage. Arthur Berger at 4.   **25** At 6 p.m.: Tchelichev.
26 At 12:01, the train to Rochester. Haieff and others come to the station.
Rochester is very provincial.   **27** Igor's first rehearsal.   **28** A morning
rehearsal, then a reception by the president of the University (Eastman
House). The Gordon Quartet plays Igor's music. A second rehearsal at
8:30 p.m.

March

1 Rehearsal at 9:30 a.m. After Igor's concert (at 8:30 p.m.), we leave for
Montreal.   **2** At the Montreal station, photographers, reporters,
Kudriavtzev. Press conference 2 to 3 p.m., rehearsal 3 to 6. A second
rehearsal from 8:30 to 11:30 p.m.   **3** Rehearsal at 9 a.m. Buy books:
Péguy, Bernanos, Radiguet, Chesterton.   **4** Igor talks on the radio. We go
to a students' club where Igor answers their questions. A dinner for 20 at
the Ritz Carlton.   **5** Rehearsal from 9 to 12:30 p.m. Igor is catching a cold.
His concert is a tremendous success, and after it many young people
follow him to his car.   **6** Igor has a temperature. Leave for Chicago at
11 p.m.   **7** After a tiring day on the train, we spend the night at the
Blackstone Hotel, Chicago.   **8** We leave on the "Chief" at 12:01 p.m.,
cross the Mississippi at 5, and are in Kansas City at 9:45.   **9** Our fifth
wedding anniversary. Igor gives me an Indian bracelet.   **10** Home at
last—like in heaven.   **11** Nadia comes.   **12** Lunch with Igor at the
Farmers' Market.   **31** To Dr. Waitzfelder, then leave for Santa Barbara.

April

2 Lunch with Rico Lebrun and Baring Gould.   **8** Hollywood. At 2:15, to a
concert by Szigeti, who plays Duo concertant; at 5:30, a party at Atwater
Kent's.[1] For dinner here: Nadia, Berman, Sokolovs.   **12** Roosevelt dies.
Everyone is upset and Igor is ill.   **28** Wait all day by the radio expecting
news of the end of the war. Nadia arrives.

May

1 Hitler is dead, perhaps murdered.   **3** Berlin is occupied by the
Russians.   **5** An Easter eve supper at Akim Tamirov's.   **7** To the
newsreels: atrocities. We are deeply shaken.   **8** VE-Day. We hoist our
flag. I go out with Sokolovs very late for lunch and return to find Igor
standing in the garden waiting for us.   **14** Igor's rehearsal at 10 a.m. of
Firebird in the Shrine Auditorium.[2] Lunch here at 2 p.m. with Nadia and
Abbé Fortier. Igor answers letters from France.   **15** Igor's Shrine
rehearsal at 5 p.m. We also hear Prokofiev's very nationalistic *Alexander
Nevsky*.   **20** Afternoon visit by two French correspondents from San
Francisco.[3]   **23** My English lesson with Anita Loos.   **26** For dinner here:
Pierre Schaeffer,[4] Nadia, *et al*. Listen to recordings.   **28** To the French
Foundation to hear a *causerie* by Pierre Schaeffer.

June

2 Nadia gives a lecture but forbids us to come.   **6** My English lesson with
Anita Loos at 10 a.m. Later, while I am out, the Baroness d'Erlanger stays
with Igor to answer the telephone.   **8** Lisa baby-sits with Igor while I am
out.   **9** Lunch with Igor and Lisa at Grandma's on Ventura Boulevard.
14 My English lesson with Anita Loos. Szigeti.   **15** While I am out, Zoya
stays with Igor.   **16** My English lesson with Anita Loos. We see *Carmen
Jones*.   **28** Virgil Thomson to see Igor. Cocktails with John Houseman at
Joan Fontaine's (703 North Rodeo).   **29** My English lesson with Anita
Loos. Dinner at Lou Levy's,[5] where we meet Bing Crosby.

July

1 Anita Loos at noon.   **4** Virgil Thomson, George Antheil, Stein.   **5** Lisa
comes to discuss details about our shop.[6]   **6** Lesson with Anita Loos.

[1] Kent's mansion was at 801 Bel Air Road.

[2] For the Russia-America benefit concert jointly conducted by Stravinsky and
Klemperer.

[3] The correspondents had been attending the meetings for the foundation of the
United Nations Charter.

[4] The animator of *musique concrète*.

[5] Of Leeds Music Corporation.

7 We see two Russian films in the Esquire Theatre, Chekhov's *Wedding*
and Stalin's speech.   **8** My final English lesson with Anita Loos.   **13** To
the film *We Accuse*, in which the Russians charge the Germans with
barbaric behavior in Russia.   **20** At 4:30 Anita Loos.   **25** At 5:30 Berman
comes to the Boutique to help with decoration, and in the evening Igor
comes to see it.

August

1 George Antheil for lunch.   **14** Victory! Stores close and people run out
into the streets. Sirens sound. I hurry home, but Igor has already heard
the news.   **15** Two days of celebrations.   **16** We celebrate the victory at
René Lefebure's.   **25** Party at Hageman's with Elsa Maxwell.   **26** Franz
Werfel dies.   **27** Send our second naturalization papers to Sapiro, after
Igor worked all day on them. Note to remember: I married Sudeikin
February 11, 1918 in Yalta and divorced him February 20, 1920. To a
cocktail party at Sir Charles Mendl's.   **29** At 3 to Werfel's funeral.
30 The Boutique opens at 6: five to six hundred people. We try to get rid
of our guests by 11.

September

7 Elsie Rieti comes. Elsa Maxwell talks on the radio about "Vera, the
charming wife of Stravinsky, who opened La Boutique."   **8** At 10 a.m. an
interview and photographers from *Life* at the Boutique. To a French film
with Fernandel at the Esquire Theater.   **20** Shop open from 2 p.m. to
10 p.m. From 5 to 8 Lisa and I, and from 8 to 10 Lisa. It is gloomy there in
the evening if there are no customers.   **21** A mob in the shop, including
two Princesses Galitzin, van Leyden, Baring Gould.   **23** Photographers in
the Boutique in the morning take pictures of us and of Berman. Lunch at
The Players. I work on icons and frames. Igor drives a car for 10 minutes.
Sold an icon for 51 dollars.   **26** Working on a black icon. Photographers
from *Life*.   **28** First dinner at our new round table: Szigetis and Goddard
Lieberson.

October

6 Igor works with Szigeti.   **10** To the post office to send four packages, to
the Marions in Beaujeu and to Olga Sallard.   **11** Igor records Duo
concertant with Szigeti.   **14** The fifth anniversary of our church wedding.
We go to church and receive communion. Champagne lunch with
Sokolovs.   **18** We take our citizenship examinations with Edward G.
Robinson and Beata as our witnesses.   **22** Igor nervous because I am late
returning from the Boutique. In the evening to a wonderful Bach concert
conducted by Klemperer.   **26** Worried about the absence of news about
the *Firebird* performance in New York.

November

4 Gilbert Grau for lunch and work with Igor. The Sokolovs for dinner.
5 People from *Harper's Bazaar* at the Boutique.   **6** To Lily Pons' cocktail
party in the Beverly Hills Terrace Room.   **16** Rehearsal of *Babel*.   **17** At
3:30, go with Igor to Werner Janssen's rehearsal of *Babel*.   **18** At 2:30
with Igor to Janssen's rehearsal. At 8:30 to Janssen's concert.   **30** To
Ballets Russes de Monte Carlo opening night. Denham takes us to supper
at the Biltmore Hotel.

December

9 Opening of our Pavel Tchelichev exhibition of drawings and gouaches
at the Boutique.   **15** We hire Evgenia Petrovna, Mrs Gate, as our cook
and housekeeper at $100 a month.[7]   **24** We open the shop for Nathan
Milstein.   **28** We are American citizens! Lunch with Ralph Hawkes at the
Biltmore.   **29** Our celebration party: the Edward G. Robinsons, the
Baroness d'Erlanger, *et al*.   **30** Eggnog party at Bernstein's.

[6] "La Boutique," on La Cienega Boulevard.

[7] She had emigrated to the United States from Shanghai after the Russian
Revolution, married a Mr. Gate, and changed her name to Jennie Gate. In 1948,
Mrs. Stravinsky wrote to Olga Sallard apropos "my cook Evgenia Petrovna. One of
her predecessors loved having guests. This one hates them and even becomes
quarrelsome every time she hears that we expect anyone for dinner. I have tried
to explain that Igor Fyodorovich's position requires that he receive people on
business, to which her answer is that we should arrange big receptions a few
times a year and hire waiters. She does not understand that often people simply
pass through Hollywood and we can see them only then. Igor Fyodorovich, who is
working very hard now, likes to relax with friends at dinner. . . ."

99

99 August 1944. 1260 North Wetherly Drive.

100 1945. Ambassador Hotel, Los Angeles. Victory party with Sir Charles Mendl.

101 1945. Hollywood. Eugene Berman's poster for La Boutique.

100

LABouTiQUE

957 NO. LA CIENEGA

Will present

1946

January

9 To a concert by the Pro Arte Quartet in the evening—surprisingly small attendance. **11** Associated Press photographers in our house. **15** *Harper's Bazaar* photographs Loretta Young in the Boutique. **16** At 12:20 we leave for New York on the ''Chief.'' **19** New York. A terribly cold day. We have a nice apartment at the Sherry Netherland Hotel. **20** I have a high fever but am taken care of by Leonard Bernstein and Balanchine. **21** Igor is at Zirato's at 11 a.m. At noon, to Balanchine's rehearsal for a charity performance for Infantile Paralysis.[1] **22** Igor rehearses at 9:30 and again from 2 to 5:30 p.m. **23** Igor has not slept and is not feeling well, but he gives interviews to Howard Taubman from *The New York Times* and to Miss Scott from *Time*. Champagne and sleeping pills. **24** At Igor's rehearsal: many Nadia Boulanger pupils. Igor gives an interview to *The New Yorker*. Lunch at the hotel with Alyosha Haieff. The hall is completely full for Igor's concert and, unexpectedly, the Symphony has a great success. We drink wine and eat sandwiches at our hotel afterward. **25** At Igor's 2:30 concert: Gertrude Hindemith and Balanchine. Dinner with Balanchine. **26** Visit from Henrietta Hirshman. Igor goes to Balanchine's to practice the piano. Go to Igor's evening concert with the New York Philharmonic. **27** Igor's fourth and final concert at 2:30 p.m. (broadcast): Hirshman, Haieff, Stark Young. Many people come after the concert, then Igor and I go *alone* to a newsreel. **28** Telegrams of congratulations from Los Angeles. Igor records from 2:30 to 6 p.m. At Iolas's gallery to see Corrado Cagli's exhibition, I meet Varia de Gramont (Princess Ruspoli), Saul Steinberg and his wife Hedda Sterne. **30** At Iolas's again we meet Cagli, and Igor buys one of his drawings. Go to Balanchine's charity performance for the March of Dimes. Igor rehearses the *Symphony of Psalms* and wind-instrument Chorale, and conducts the CBS broadcast at 11:30 p.m. **31** Igor sees Hawkes in the morning and we lunch with Lieberson.

February

1 At 8:30 we go to *On the Town*.[2] **2** Igor works with Woody Herman. **4** We move to the Waldorf Astoria and Igor goes to Baltimore. **5** At Peggy Guggenheim's gallery I meet Jackson Pollock, at Kirk Askew's, Esteban Frances and Kurt Seligmann, and at the Matisse Gallery, Chagall. Igor's lecture in Baltimore. **6** Igor's concert in Baltimore. **7** Igor returns from Baltimore and rehearses with Szigeti and Claudio Arrau. **8** In the evening, the New York Philharmonic pension concert: Igor and Szigeti play Duo concertant in Carnegie Hall, and Claudio Arrau plays Igor's Serenade. **9** Chagall comes at 4 p.m. We go to Tchelichev's at 6, then to a dinner party with Archibald Macleish and Gerald Murphy.[3] **11** Igor rehearses the *Symphony of Psalms* at CBS Playhouse, Studio 4, 53rd Street west of Broadway. **12** The recording of the *Symphony of Psalms* is cancelled because of a strike. We go with Balanchine to Tatiana Chamié's studio for a rehearsal of Tallchief and Franklin, then to the Russian Tea Room. **13** With Igor to the Matisse gallery. Dinner at Dushkins' with Lin Yutang.[4] **14** Rehearsal 2 to 4, at Balanchine's school. **15** Rehearsal of *Le Baiser de la fée* at Balanchine's school, then to Sammy's restaurant with Balanchine, Dubrovska, Vladimirov, Danilova, Brianskaya [all were dancers]. **16** 10 to 12:30, *Le Baiser de la fée* dress rehearsal. Tchelichev brings a lovely drawing as a gift. **17** At noon: Claude Lévi-Strauss, cultural attaché of the French Embassy. A nice lunch with Chagall's son-in-law. The performance of *Le Baiser de la fée*: we send roses to Danilova and Tallchief, and four bottles of wine to Balanchine. **18** Boston.

Igor goes directly to his rehearsal. **20** Igor's third rehearsal and first concert, at Cambridge. Supper afterward at Gerry's Landing with the Forbes family. **21** Igor's morning rehearsal for the Boston program. Lunch with Henrietta Hirshman and Haieff. Igor meets with a group of young musicians. **22** Igor's first concert in Boston. Dinner at Koussevitzky's. **23** Lunch in a Greek restaurant with Haieff and Spies.[5] Concert in Boston. **24** We take the ''Silver Meteor'' for Miami. **25** Jacksonville in the morning. No rooms are available in Miami, but we finally find a very small room for the price of our suite at the Waldorf Astoria. **26** We fly to Havana: a beautiful view from the airplane. Hotel Nacional. Igor is worried because the score of *Firebird* has not yet been received. A visit from the president, Aixala, then from Gustavo Pittaluga. **27** Igor rehearses. In the evening we tour the city and dine with the Pittalugas at the Zaragozaña. **28** Igor's rehearsal. Dinner at the Pittalugas'.

March

3 Igor's first Havana concert is at 10:45 a.m. A tremendous success and a crowd of autograph seekers. Lunch at the Country Club with the Pittalugas and Josephina Tarafa.[6] **4** Igor's evening concert. **5** To ''Fifi'' Tarafa's sugar plantation, on her private train. **6** Tour the Tarafa sugar plantation and factory. **7** Spend the night at Tarafa's cozy country home. **8** Return to Havana. Dinner at the Pittalugas'. **9** Meet Georgette and Pearce Bailey in the lobby of the Hotel Nacional. Fly from Havana to Miami. **10** Train to Jacksonville, and change there for New Orleans. **11** Massimo Freccia and his wife Nina meet our train at the New Orleans station.[7] **12** Arriving in Dallas at 12:35 p.m., we are met by reporters and photographers, but not by our baggage, which is missing; I go to buy shirts for Igor. Dorati[8] comes. **13** While Igor rehearses I return to the station for our luggage, which has been found. I light a candle to St. Anthony. **14** Igor rehearses from 10 to 1. In the evening to a Russian film, *Summer Storm*. **15** Igor rehearses from 10 to 1. **16** Igor has two rehearsals. At 6 to Mrs. Stanley Marcus's. **17** Igor's concert at 3:15 in the Fair Park Auditorium. At 10 p.m. we leave by airplane for Los Angeles. **18** Approaching San Diego, we descend through a solid cover of white clouds, which makes Igor nervous. Change airplanes at the Los Angeles Airport for San Francisco. Fairmont Hotel. A beautiful view. **19** Igor rehearses from 10 to 1. Dinner with Monteux at the St. Francis Hotel. **21** Igor rehearses from 9 to 1. Lunch with John Rothschild, who takes us for a drive. Dinner at the Musicians' Club where Doris Monteux makes a good speech. **22** Igor's first concert: 2:30. Then an excellent dinner party. **23** Igor's concert at 8:30 p.m. **24** John Rothschild invites us and Milhaud for lunch. At 9 p.m. we leave for home. **25** 8:30 a.m.: the Sokolovs meet our train at Glendale. **27** At 9 p.m. Judith Anderson comes with Luther Green.[9] Send a telegram to Koussevitzky for Païchadze's arrival in Boston. **29** We listen to *Ebony Concerto* and send a telegram to Woody Herman.

April

4 Igor spends the whole morning with Balanchine and Nicolas Kopeikin,[10] and they come again at 8 p.m.[11] **5** Balanchine for dinner. **14** We go to church and also visit the Arensbergs.[12] In the evening here: Balanchine and Kopeikin. **17** Lady Mendl comes with a child and a madman. **20** Our Chagall exhibition opens in the Boutique. We go to a Russian Easter supper at Kall's, then to another one at Balanchine's. **21** A Russian Easter reception here: Balanchine, Kopeikin, *et al.* **22** We sell two paintings by Chagall. My interview in the Los Angeles *Examiner*. Dinner at Chick Austin's. **27** A musical evening listening to Igor's recordings

---

[1] Ten years later, Balanchine believed that by having given Tanaquil LeClercq the role of a paralyzed person, he foreshadowed her future. (Translator's note)

[2] The Bernstein-Robbins musical.

[3] See Vera's diary, July 1, 1923.

[4] Jeanyee Wong, who had illustrated Lin Yutang's Modern Library translation of *The Wisdom of Confucius*, gave the book to Mrs. Stravinsky in 1943.

[5] Claudio Spies (b. 1925), an authority on Stravinsky's music and a professor of music at Princeton.

[6] Josephina Tarafa's sugar plantation in Central Cuba, Pedro Betancourt, Matanzas, was one of the largest on the island.

[7] Freccia, a protégé of Toscanini, was the conductor of the New Orleans Symphony.

[8] Antal Dorati had become conductor of the Dallas Symphony.

[9] Miss Anderson's agent. She had wanted Stravinsky to compose incidental music for Robinson Jeffers' *Medea*.

[10] Balanchine's—and, before him, Diaghilev's—rehearsal pianist.

[11] On April 4 and 5 Balanchine and Stravinsky composed the scenario for *Orpheus*.

[12] Owners of the Walter Arensberg collection of modern art, now in Philadelphia.

102 1946. 1260 North Wetherly Drive.

103 1946. On the garden steps at 1260 North Wetherly Drive.

104 In the text, by George Balanchine, the first letters of each line in the original Russian form the acrostic IGOR:

Nameday and birthday!
Guests, noise, and animation!
Get drunk on Grand Marnier!
Don't forget a glass for me!

On seeing Balanchine's melody, Stravinsky told him to set it ''for five voices instead of four,'' whereupon Balanchine said that he was not a composer. Stravinsky, taking a piece of music paper, harmonized the tune himself.

102

103

104

with Eric Zeisl.[1] **28** The Sokolovs and Louriés for dinner (which I had to cook, as well as wash dishes). Millier wrote a nice article in the Los Angles newspaper. **29** I drive Igor to the dentist.

June

1 Dinner with Milhaud, Balanchine, Kopeikin, Berman. **10** Fedya writes that he has become a Catholic. **11** Igor to Dr. Epstein at 10:30 a.m., then Balanchine and Kopeikin. **18** Igor and I take communion, then lunch at the Farmers' Market. For supper here: Balanchine, Kopeikin, Igor Youskevitch,[2] et al. **21** A farewell party for Balanchine. **24** Georgette and Pearce Bailey at 6. Igor, Balanchine, and Berman discuss a project for a new production of Scènes de ballet. **29** Take Vaska [the Stravinsky's cat] to the veterinarian.

July

2 In the evening to Henry V, a wonderful film with real actors! **3** Dr. Epstein 10 to 1. Write to Rosette de Matherel: "To think that René has already had his eighteenth birthday! In my next packet I will include a little memento from his American godmother. . . . I am happy that you spend your vacations at Villiers, Pasredon, and Isthmia, in all of which I have known marvelous times. . . . Igor's daughter will come here. We sent affidavits for her, her husband (she married a Frenchman whom we do not know), and the governess who raised all of Igor's children. At this very moment I am preparing the house that we bought for them, which is complicated work because of so many scarcities and the limited choice of materials. I also have an art gallery in Hollywood that keeps me very busy. . . ." **6** The Milhauds arrive from Mexico.[3] **9** Igor and I have cardiograms. Dr. Waitzfelder thinks that Igor should stop smoking.[4] Igor and I go to see Carmen. **15** We leave with the Sokolovs for Mexico. **16** El Paso. **18** Mexico City. Bal y Gay and Salazar are at the station. Lunch at Prendes. Cocktails at Lady Baltimore's. **20** Feeling ill, we ask for a doctor, Raoul Fournier. **21** Spend the evening with the archeologists and historians, Alice and Wolfgang Palen. **22** Igor rehearses. **23** Guadalupe. Tea at San Angel, at the home of Eduardo Villaseñor. **26** Igor's first concert at 9 p.m. **27** Lunch with Dr. Fournier at San Jeronimo. **28** Igor's 11:15 a.m. concert. Lunch at Chavez's, then visit the Prietos. **29** Go with Salazar to Cholula and Puebla (365 churches).

August

1 We leave Mexico. **3** Up at 5 a.m. for the Mexican, then, at El Paso, the American, formalities. **4** Los Angeles. Alyosha Haieff in the station. Lisa has to be taken from the station in a wheelchair. We call Dr. Waitzfelder for her. **5** Lisa has jaundice. **15** Balanchine marries Maria Tallchief. **26** Igor conducts Firebird at Hollywood Bowl.

September

1 For cocktails here: Man Ray with Juliette, and Roland Penrose. **4** Visit from Max Ernst, on his way to Reno to get a divorce. **5** George Platt Lynes takes photographs of Igor for Vogue. **9** Cocktails at Ona Munson's: Ruth Ford,[5] Hatfield (Dorian Gray), Penrose, Man Ray. **10** Haieff now lives in Milene's house. **13** Take Igor to Dr. Epstein. Dinner with Igor at the Brown Derby. **14** Igor to Dr. Epstein. With the

Huxleys in the Farmers' Market. **16** Otto Klemperer and his wife here for dinner. **20** Darius Milhaud here for dinner. **21** A big champagne lunch here for the French Consul, Darius Milhaud, Lehman (director of the Paris Opéra) with his wife and two daughters. **29** A surprise name-day party with Father McLane and family,[6] Eleanor Clark,[7] Katherine Ann Porter, Haieff.

October

3 Vernissage of Suzanne Nicolas.[8] Supper at the Huxleys'. **8** Lunch at Romanoff's with Arthur Bliss [British composer], Artur Rubinstein, et al. **9** Here for dinner: Yves Baudrier [French composer]. **14** Our wedding anniversary. We go to church and take communion. **15** Lunch at the Farmers' Market with the Huxleys. Go to the lecture by Yves Baudrier, who comes to our house for dinner. **27** Igor: "L'abondance, ce n'est pas une quantité, c'est une qualité." **28** We go to La Forza del Destino, by the San Francisco Opera in the Shrine Auditorium. **31** Lunch at the Farmers' Market with the Huxleys.

November

3 We spend the whole day in Huxley's "desert de luxe."[9] Wessbergs.[10] Return with Nicolas.[11] **4** Clifford Odets comes to La Boutique. Daniel Milhaud [son of Darius and Madeleine] moves into Milene's house. The Milhauds here for dinner. **6** Igor and I read, and like, Camus' L'Etranger. **8** Lunch with Igor at the Town and Country Market. Igor to Dr. Epstein at 3. **9** We go to Santa Barbara, where Arthur Sachs' paintings are on exhibit. **17** The Milhauds come for lunch. Madeleine works with Igor on Perséphone.[12] Suzanne Nicolas with her two daughters. Claire interviews Igor.[13] **18** Sapiro for lunch. **28** Thanksgiving. Berman, the Baroness d'Erlanger, Milhaud, Sokolov, and the Bolms for dinner. **29** Igor to Dr. Waitzfelder.

December

3 We leave for New York from Pasadena. **5** Chicago. To the exhibit of Turner, Hogarth, and Constable at the Museum. Also Chagall. **6** 9 a.m. New York, Grand Central Station. We take the train for Montreal at 11:55 p.m. Rest in Mercedes' apartment and receive a visit from Julien Levy and Leonid. **7** 8:25 a.m. Montreal. Pierre Béique meets us at the station. **8** 9 a.m.: Igor's first rehearsal. **9** Igor has a difficult rehearsal, since the orchestra is not good. We visit the Mayor for photographs. **10** Igor's rehearsal at 9:30 a.m., his concert at 9 p.m. **11** The Mayor wants to send his car to show us the city, but Igor decides against it. Igor's second concert with Les Concerts Symphoniques de Montréal at 9 p.m. **12** 9:30 train to New York, arriving at 7:30 p.m. **13** For lunch, François Valéry, a very pleasant young man. At 3, James Fasset with Bernard Herrmann, whom Igor rates very highly.[14] We dine in the Sert Room at the Waldorf Astoria with Victoria Ocampo. The police are everywhere because Molotov is staying here and Frank Sinatra (bobby soxers). **14** Dinner at Balanchine's. **16** Igor goes with Balanchine to hear the singers for Renard. Meet Pierre Claudel at Cartier's. Mercedes tells us about Karsavina in Paris (she is old and sad). **17** Igor goes to a rehearsal of Renard at Balanchine's school. Alexeichik Haieff for lunch. Igor and I walk and go to a newsreel. Igor goes to the Symphony of Psalms chorus rehearsal with Felix Wolfes. **18**[15] To Balanchine's rehearsal of Haieff's Divertimento. George's choreography is the creation

---

[1] Composer. Mina Svitalski (Madubo) became the governess and French tutor to Zeisl's daughter Barbara, who later married one of the sons of Arnold Schoenberg.

[2] The dancer. He had performed the title role in Stravinsky's Apollo many times.

[3] Darius Milhaud opened one of his bags in Stravinsky's bathroom, and later Stravinsky found a scorpion in the sink. Stravinsky used to tell a story about how he eventually managed to destroy the arachnid by surrounding it with lighted matches.

[4] Stravinsky smoked heavily until the autumn of 1956. He purchased the tobacco and paper and rolled his cigarettes himself on his own machine.

[5] Actress, later Mrs. Zachary Scott, sister of Tchelichev's friend Charles-Henri Ford, and friend of William Faulkner.

[6] In the late 1940s and 1950s, the Reverend James McLane (d. 1960), his wife Mary, and their children Augusta and Louis, became close friends of the Stravinskys and of Alma Mahler. McLane had a superb collection of paintings by Chagall, Balthus, and Giacometti, as well as two of Picasso's owl sculptures.

[7] The writer, now Mrs. Robert Penn Warren. She and Katherine Ann Porter were friends of Haieff's; both women stayed in Milene's house.

[8] Sister of Maria Huxley.

[9] Aldous Huxley's description of Hollywood, but the reference here is to the Wessberg home at Wrightwood, California.

[10] Maria Huxley's youngest sister, Rose, was married to Wessberg.

[11] Joep Nicolas, husband of Suzanne, was a sculptor.

[12] Mme Milhaud was the récitante in a performance of the work conducted by Stravinsky in New York in January 1947.

[13] She published a description of this visit that provoked a considerable uproar. See Stravinsky in Pictures and Documents, op. cit.

[14] Herrmann, composer of the score for Citizen Kane, was the conductor of the CBS broadcast concerts.

[15] On December 18, Olga Sallard wrote to Vera from Illats (Gironde) describing a trip to Paris: "Valechka Nouvel is sick and old. He dreams of seeing you and Stravinsky."

of a genius. At 6:30 to the CBS Theater at 254 West 54th Street, where Igor rehearses the *Symphony of Psalms* and, at 11 p.m., conducts the broadcast concert. **19** Igor records the *Symphony of Psalms*. Victoria Ocampo gives us her tickets for *Harvey*, and we go with Kyriena Ziloti. **20** Dinner at Balanchine's with Tchelichev, who talks about illness, astronomy, and chemistry, and does not let anyone else speak. **21** William Hess, the tenor in *Renard*, calls for Igor. Dinner at Rieti's with the clavecinist Sylvia Marlowe. **22** At 5, François Valéry. We dine with the Milhauds and François Valéry. **24** Igor rehearses *Renard* at the Ballet School. Very pleasant dinner at the Milhauds'. **25** At 4, Miss Nell Tangeman comes, Jocasta in *Oedipus Rex*. At 6, with Corrado Cagli to Todd Bolender's, the fox in *Renard*, then to Rieti's, where Cartier-Bresson takes photographs. **26** At 10 a.m. Igor's rehearsal of *Renard*. Lunch with François Valéry and Mercedes. At Balanchine's, Hess and Madeleine Milhaud. Dinner at the Milhauds' with François Valéry. **27** Igor's *Renard* rehearsal at 10 a.m. Arnold Newman takes photos of us for *Harper's Bazaar*. **28** We leave for Cleveland. **29** (Sunday) Cleveland, met by C.L. Vosburgh, manager of the orchestra, who takes us to the Wade Park Manor Hotel. **30** Igor has two rehearsals. **31** Igor has two rehearsals. To the Museum. For the New Year, order oysters and champagne.

1947

January

1 With Igor to the Museum to see *The Temptation of St. Anthony*. **2** To Igor's rehearsal and concert (8:30 p.m.), in the loge of Mrs. George Szell. A very rich, very dull public. **3** Cocktails with James C. Brooks (18300 Shaker Boulevard), who shared a cabin with Igor on the *Manhattan*. **4** Igor's broadcast is at 6 p.m., his public concert at 8:30. He does not leave the greenroom between the two, and I prepare a light meal for him. **5** We leave Cleveland from the 55th Street station, but the redcap is late putting our luggage on the train, and it is sent to Pittsburgh with the next one. **6** Arrive in Philadelphia, the Warwick Hotel, at 7:30 a.m. Igor rehearses the Philadelphia Orchestra from 10:30 to 1. **7** To the movies, then birthday champagne. **9** Igor rehearses 10 to 12. **10** Igor's concert at 2:30, unexpectedly a tremendous success. **11** Igor's broadcast from 5 to 6:30 p.m., then the public concert, at 8:30—a colossal success. We have a police escort to the hotel. **12** Alyosha Haieff meets our train in New York and we lunch at our hotel (Ambassador). At 9 p.m. we go to a League of Composers reception for Koussevitzky. He talks at length about philosophy. **13** Igor's *Renard* rehearsal at 9:30 a.m. Many people in the hall [including R.C.]. Igor lunches with Ralph Hawkes and signs a contract with him. Igor's *Perséphone* rehearsal at 3:30. Igor goes to Balanchine. Arthur Berger comes. Then, after 10 minutes' rest, we go to *Renard*[1] with Victoria Ocampo. Supper at Lucia Davidova's. **14** At 10 a.m., Igor, still slightly drunk from last night, rehearses *Perséphone*. At night we go to the second performance of *Renard*. **15** From 7 to 12:30 p.m., Igor's rehearsal[2] and performance of *Perséphone*. **16** Dinner with Balanchine, Maria Tallchief, and Alyosha at Tony's. At 11:45 we leave for Buffalo. **17** Buffalo. Our train is very late and Igor does not get to his rehearsal on time. William Steinberg comes for lunch. **19** To Niagara Falls with Mrs. Farrar and her sister Miss Sibirsky, with whom we have a very good time. **20** Igor has two rehearsals. A very stiff dinner at Mr. and Mrs. Edgar F. Wendt. **21** Igor's rehearsal in the morning and concert at 8:30. The orchestra is not very good, and the public is not very interesting. We leave at 4 a.m. in a snowstorm. **22** Traversing enormous America. **23** San Antonio at 6:30 a.m. The city is charming, the hotel very good. **24** Spring weather: we walk without overcoats. Crowds of Mexicans. Blue arcades. Visits from Mr. Oppenheimer,[3] Max and Pauline Reiter.[4] From the newspaper: "Mrs. Stravinsky doubles as social and

business secretary to her famous husband and when he's rehearsing dashes out to do a bit of shopping." We go to a Hedy Lamarr film. **25** Reporters at 11. To Max Reiter's concert (with Robert Weede as soloist). Supper after the concert at Pauline Reiter's—charming. **26** A dull dinner at Oppenheimers' (rich, dull people). **27** Igor's rehearsal. We go to a lovely film, *My Darling Clementine*. **28** Igor has two rehearsals. Dinner again at Oppenheimers', *en famille*. **29** We go to the San Juan Mission and the zoo. **30** To Randolph Field, the "West Point of the Air."[5] Dinner with Fritz Reiner. **31** Igor's rehearsal. To Reiner's concert (very few people) and dine with him after it. Reiner snubs Reiter.

February

1 Igor's concert is a great success, and we leave at night after it, escorted to the station by Pauline and Max Reiter. **2** On the train to El Paso we meet Mischa Elman.[6] **3** Home. The Bolms, Sokolovs, and Berman are at the station. **4** Automobile license. I write to the French Consul in New York: "Cher monsieur, we want to ask one more favor of you. Can you obtain reservations for Stravinsky's daughter and her husband on the 'Chief,' a drawing room in a through car, possibly for two different dates, in the event that one of them is not possible? We want the children to be here as soon as can be realized since we ourselves are leaving for New York on April 20." **6** Igor to Dr. Waitzfelder. **7** At 4 to Dr. Epstein's: x-ray for Igor. Buy files for Igor, whose studio will soon look like an office. We listen to the *Genesis* Suite on the radio. **8** Catherine d'Erlanger for dinner. We listen to Igor's recordings and to the *Magic Flute*. **12** To Dr. Epstein at 11: Igor has three teeth extracted. **18** At 10:30, Igor to Dr. Epstein. **20** Igor to Dr. Epstein at 11. Party here for Lady Abdy, the Baroness d'Erlanger, *et al.* **26** Lunch at the Farmers' Market with the Huxleys. **27** To Dr. Waitzfelder. A party at Annabella's[7] with Simone de Beauvoir. Dinner at John Houseman's.

March

2 At Szigeti's (Palos Verdes) with Benny Goodman. **3** Dinner at the Bel Air Hotel with Charles Munch. Later we drink champagne in our house. **6** We go to Charles Munch's concert with the pianist Gilles Guilbert. **7** To Dr. Chambers. Sokolovs for dinner: Napoleon made by Marie Le Put. **12** To a very beautiful concert by Klemperer: Haydn's *Farewell* Symphony. **15** We see a terrible Russian film, *Stone Flower*. **20** Igor goes to Monteux's concert with the Bolms. **23** With Igor to see a wonderful film, Malraux's *Man's Hope*. **26** Lunch at the Town and Country Market with Sir Charles Mendl and Cary Grant. Work on our terrace with Dmitri Stepanovich. In the evening, a double feature: *13 Rue Madeleine* and *To Each His Own*. **27** Go with Igor to Dr. Epstein. Country Market. Go to bed early and read Julian Green[8] with great pleasure. **28** John Hammond, of Keynote Recordings, to see Igor.[9]

April

2 Dr. Chambers at 10:30. Lunch at the Town and Country Market with Igor and the Huxleys. **3** At the Town and Country Market: Lady Abdy, the Huxleys. To Dr. Epstein at 3. I enjoy reading Paul Valéry. **4** A telephone call from Milène and Andre in New York. **8** Milene and Andre arrive at 3:15 p.m. **13** From 2 to 11 we have a big reception for the children, thirty-two people in all. **18** At 5, photographers here, me with Benny Goodman.[10] **20** We leave for New York on the "Chief." **22** Chicago: to the Henry Moore exhibit between trains. **23** New York. Alyosha Haieff meets us at the station. Igor talks to the manager, but we have to wait in the lobby until 8 p.m. for our rooms. **24** Igor rehearses the *Dumbarton Oaks* Concerto all day. **25** Train to Washington. At 8:30: Igor's concert in Dumbarton Oaks. From 12 to 3 a.m., at Mischa

---

[1] Léon Barzin conducted this and the second performance.

[2] A photograph survives of Stravinsky at this rehearsal with Walter Hendl, Lukas Foss, Claudio Spies, and R.C.

[3] Dr. Frederic G. Oppenheimer. His son Frederic Joske Oppenheimer was the first husband of Laura Wells, later Mrs. Eduardo de Villaseñor. The Oppenheimer collection of old masters is now in the McNay Art Museum, San Antonio.

[4] Max Reiter, conductor of the San Antonio Orchestra, had known Stravinsky in Turin in 1933.

[5] Photographs of the Stravinskys on this visit show that he conducted the Air Force band, and that his performance was recorded. He also sat in the cockpit of one of

the airplanes.

[6] Stravinsky had known Elman since the first decade of the century, when the violinist played the solos in *Swan Lake* for Pavlova.

[7] French actress, wife of Tyrone Power.

[8] *Si J'étais vous* and the first three volumes of the *Journal*.

[9] At this meeting Stravinsky agreed to record the *Dumbarton Oaks* Concerto in New York on April 28, 1947.

[10] One of these pictures is reproduced in *Igor and Vera Stravinsky*, op. cit.

105 January 1947. Philadelphia.

Schneider's.[1] **26** Concert at 4 p.m. Reception at Mrs. Bliss's from 6 to 8 p.m. Then fly to New York with Haieff, Ralph Kirkpatrick,[2] and Nabokov with a young woman. Late at night, a light supper in our room with Alyosha Haieff. **28** Igor records from 9 to 12 p.m. **29** To Leonor Fini's exhibition at Iolas's. Tea at Tchelichev's. Dinner with Nicolas Nabokov at L'Auberge. **30** Igor and I go to the Lipton Librairie Française, to dinner with Denham at L'Auberge, and to see *Apollo* performed by Lucia Chase's company.

May

1 Lunch with Lincoln Kirstein and Nabokov, Lady Abdy and Mercedes. Leave New York at 6 p.m. **4** Arrive in Pasadena on the "Chief" at 9:30 a.m. Lunch with Sokolovs at South La Peer. **12** While Evgenia Petrovna was cleaning the cage, the bird flew away.[3] To the movies in the evening with the Sokolovs. **13** Lunch with Huxleys at the Town and Country Market. Babitz to see Igor at 4. Late in the evening, a pessimistic phone call from Milene: she thinks nothing will result from the conversations about Andre's job. **19** Lunch at the Market. Igor works all day. **23** A very animated dinner at Jean Renoir's with Charles Boyer. **25** In the evening, to a rehearsal of *Camille* at the Coronet Theater. **26** At the Market with Greta Garbo. **27** Cartier-Bresson takes photographs of us. To the Roth Quartet concert with Benny Goodman. **29** Documentary film at the Coronet Theater.[4]

June

2 Work in the garden from 8:30 a.m. To Dr. Epstein at 3:30 p.m. Walk with Igor in the hills. Read Théophile Gautier in the evening. **3** I take $150 from the bank for Milene. **4** Lunch with Huxley at the Farmers' Market. **8** Nice lunch (*bourride* [Provençal fish soup]) in the children's garden with the Sokolovs and the Baroness. **9** René Clair's *Chapeau de Peau* at 7:45. **10** I read *The Skin of Our Teeth* to Igor. **11** Igor and I go to the opening at the Coronet Theater of *The Skin of Our Teeth*. **17** With Huxley to Benjamin Britten's *The Rape of Lucrece*. **18** Igor's birthday. Communion. Lunch at Xenia Stepanovna's. **20** Milene phones me asking about the purchase of a second-hand car for them. Igor in a very bad mood but, toward evening, he consents. Tea at John Houseman's with Henry Schnitzler[5] to discuss the staging of *Histoire du soldat*. **21** With Berman and the Sokolovs to a terrible film, *Bel-Ami*, with music by Milhaud. **24** Dagmar here for lunch. To Jerry Westmore [hairdresser], where I see Tamara Geva[6] and Mischa Auer's wife. Andre does not get along with Canizaro. **25** Jeanne Gautier[7] with Annie Chorrard for dinner here. **26** Cocktails at Charles Boyer's. **27** For lunch: Jeanne Gautier with her girl friend. I take them to Malibu Beach. With Igor in the evening to a French film, goose pimples guaranteed. **28** At 9:20 p.m. we leave with the Sokolovs on a train from Glendale to San Francisco. **29** San Francisco, the St. Francis Hotel. Terrible food at a Chinese restaurant with the Milhauds. **30** Dinner at Milhaud's (*bourride*).

July

2 Take the "Daylight" to Glendale. On arrival, the children for dinner. **3** Dr. Epstein for Igor. Madubo walks to our house for dinner and spends the night.[8] **4** For dinner here: Jean and Dido Renoir, and the Baroness d'Erlanger. **8** We buy a car for the children, after going to the bank and the Automobile Club. **10** Massage by Dr. Waitzfelder. Take Igor to Dr.

Epstein. Dinner at John Houseman's with Jeanne and Annie, who tells very interesting stories about Australia. **23** Vladimir Golschmann for lunch. We take him to the Coronet to see a film of Picasso drawing. A champagne dinner at Father McLane's to celebrate his new (10th) Chagall. **26** A good-bye party for Alma Werfel, who is leaving for Vienna. **30** See Bertolt Brecht's *Galileo*, which we like very much.

August

3 Lunch at Malibu Beach with Karinska, Rhonda Fleming, and Ingrid Bergman. **5** Madubo now spends all her time in our house. Beata writes letters for Igor. **6** We go to *Galileo* a second time. **7** To the ballet at Hollywood Bowl: *Nutcracker* and *Rodeo*. **12** Beata writes letters for Igor. Indra Devi[9] and Bernardine Fritz. **14** To Dr. Epstein who extracts Igor's tooth. Milhauds here, preparing to sail to Europe. Party here: Renoir, the two Gautier girls, *et al.* **15** The Milhauds dine here. **16** We go to the Renoirs' for dinner with René Clair, just arrived from Paris. **17** To Long Beach to see the Milhauds[10] sail for France. **18** At 4 to Milene, who is working at Karinska's. **19** To the Biltmore to visit sick Georgette. Igor, home alone, summons Milene for a serious talk. **20** I read Sartre's *No Exit* to Igor, in English. **21** 7:30 a.m.: George Balanchine arrives from New York. We go to Howard Warshaw's vernissage at the Coronet and to the premiere of *No Exit*,[11] a bad, amateur performance. **22** To the Country Market with Balanchine. For dinner here: Balanchine. **24** With Balanchine to visit Berman. **25** Country Market. Rose Wessberg takes photos of George Balanchine and Igor. See *Poil de carotte*—a great disappointment.[12] **26** At 6:30 we see Balanchine off for New York. On the way back, pick up the children and go to the Town and Country Market for dinner. **28** Madubo moves into our house. **30** Indra Devi. We lunch at the Town and Country Market with Huxley.

September

1 The children come unexpectedly for dinner. Afterward to an interesting talk by Indra Devi. Late tea at home (1 a.m.). **5** At 11:30 Richard Gilbert takes Igor to his recording session (RCA Victor). **6** We are horrified by a letter from Georges Sachs about Arthur's interest in another woman. I write to her: "Ma chère Georges, Your letter stunned us. It was so completely unexpected that I read it again and again, and I wanted to cry. What you say is not possible. You know how much we regretted your departure and how terribly painful your prolonged absence was for us. The news that you give us now is very serious. I put your letter away, in order not to see it and in the hope that it would turn out to be a bad dream. But, unhappily, what you write is very clear.

"Give us details: it is terrible not to know exactly what happened. Whose fault is it? Isn't it just a little bit your fault in not having returned to Santa Barbara while knowing how much Arthur likes his country and California in particular? When we saw him the last time in our house, a year ago, he seemed very sad at being obliged to return to France. It was as though he were bewitched by the beauty of California and he adored his house. What we hear from Paris about both of you is always that Mme Sachs wants to stay in Europe and that he is nostalgic for America. I tell you this only because he gives the same impression to everyone.

"Who is the woman and how did she succeed in invading your life with Arthur? I do not want to ask you any questions. Do not think that we have forgotten that for us you are the well-loved Georges, the charming

[1] First violinist of the Budapest Quartet.

[2] Harpsichordist (1911–1984), soloist in Manuel de Falla's Concerto conducted by Stravinsky.

[3] Eugene Berman wrote to "Chère Big Vera" from Mexico City on May 21: "Welcome home. . . . I learned from Ona [Munson] that your talking mechanical nightingale flew away. . . . I count on seeing you soon. . . ."

[4] Probably *Night Mail*, with script partly by W.H. Auden.

[5] Stage director, son of the playwright Arthur Schnitzler.

[6] Dancer, the first wife of George Balanchine.

[7] Violinist, in Hollywood to work with Stravinsky on an arrangement for violin and piano of the "Ballad" from *Le Baiser de la fée*. He had met her in Paris in November 1916. In 1954, in Turin, she played Stravinsky's Violin Concerto with the composer conducting.

[8] This would suggest that Madubo's difficulties with the Marions had already

begun, since the all-uphill walk from the Marions' to the Stravinskys' is a strenuous two miles, but Olga Sallard's letters to Vera confirm the growing crisis. On January 26, 1947, Olga had written to Vera, warning her about Marion's "authoritative disposition." In a letter of May 28, 1947, Olga says that she is not surprised to hear that Andre does not want Madubo to live with them, since he was always afraid of her, even though she stood in queues in the cold, shopping for them in Paris during the bleak days at the end of the war. On January 19, 1948, Olga wrote that Madubo was "on to" Marion from the beginning, and blamed Milene's illness and shyness as obstacles in her choice of men. In a letter dated June 4, 1948, Olga remarks that Madubo had "intuitively felt that Andre suppressed Milene's gifts."

[9] The wife of Doctor Sigfrid Knauer, Indra Devi was a Russian woman who had lived in India for many years.

[10] See the photograph on p.106, *Igor and Vera Stravinsky*, op. cit.

[11] Warshaw had designed this production.

[12] The Stravinskys greatly admired Jules Renard's book, but did not like Renoir's film of it.

friend. Whatever happens you can count on our profound friendship." **7** See Indra Devi at the Baroness's. **8** Igor records for Victor at Republic Studios. **10** Lunch at the Farmers' Market with the Huxleys. **13** Renoir comes (the Matisse book). At 5 p.m. Charles Olson, the poet, a friend of Cagli. **15** Write to Olga Sallard and tell her about Igor's recordings, Balanchine's reports about Paris, Milene's stopping work for Karinska, Andre's complaints that his French lessons are poorly paid, the letters from my distant relatives—Mietens[1]—about Lisa's amoebic dysentery, about Georgette's visit, about Renoir's portrait. Write to Georges Sachs: "What will Santa Barbara be without you? I can't imagine it. And ourselves without you as a neighbor, we who have put our roots in California, which we love to such an extent that we do not dream of going anywhere and we expect our trip to Paris to prove this to us. Why did you write that you understand us for not coming this year? Is it that bad? Balanchine, returning from Paris, told us how difficult it was for him to struggle against all the intrigues at the Opéra and the cost of living. He returned without a penny and as thin as a wick, and came here for a week for the sole reason of telling us in detail about his life there and how much he suffered.

"Lisa was very ill after her trip to Mexico with us, and she is still not well. Finally, after many analyses, amoebic dysentery has been diagnosed, and she is being treated against this dreadful tropical disease. Sokolov himself, with a group of other actors, has opened a ravishing theater, the Coronet, in which marvelous new things are given and which we frequent a great deal. The premieres are always very brilliant.

"At present, two French friends are here, two charming women. Berman is in Hollywood involved in a complicated relationship with Ona Munson, who has a very bad influence on him. He went to Mexico for three months on a Guggenheim Fellowship and did some very beautiful drawings but, better still, some remarkable photographs. He was not ill, but he was robbed several times.

"Since the arrival of the children I have many more worries than before. We had to find work for them. He gives French lessons in a kind of Berlitz school and she does attractive embroideries that she would like to sell to dress designers.

"Do you remember the party in our house after Igor conducted his *Danses concertantes*, how very lively it was and how you said you were so happy to be there? Now, while Igor was recording *Danses concertantes* for Victor, I thought of that night. Why did you leave for such a long time? Do you remember the nights that you slept on our couch? And the dinner in our tiny dining room? (It has shrunk now and become even smaller, for which reason we intend, at great expense, to enlarge it; an architect has proposed several different ideas.) And the house across from us that at one time you wanted to buy for $17,000? Now it is $35,000.

"(Later) I wonder if Arthur is coming to Santa Barbara at all, since he has been in America for 15 days and we have heard nothing from him.

"Thinking of your daughter gives me the greatest hope that everything can still be worked out between you and Arthur. Do not leave us without your news." **16** Nadia Boulanger's 60th birthday.[2] Igor records. **20** Igor records. Arthur Sachs visits us. Babitz here for supper. **21** For lunch here: Mr. and Mrs. Ingolf Dahl and Volodya Sokolov. The children here for tea. Later we go to visit Lisa who is sick. I cook our dinner at 10 p.m. **22** Igor goes to hear his recordings with Richard Gilbert (RCA Victor). **27** We leave for Santa Barbara at 11 a.m. In San Fernando Valley the heat reaches 105°. I put ice packs on my head. Arrive in time for a 2 p.m. lunch in Santa Barbara, where it is very cool. Jeanne Voilier. Georges's absence is felt: only Ivory soap in the bathroom and no one smiles. **29** Voilier leaves at 4. We drive to Santa Barbara to look for books. **30** It is my name day, but without Georges, Arthur does not remember it.

October

1 I write to Georges: "We spent a weekend at Santa Barbara and met

Mme V. This came about as follows: on September 20, Arthur telephoned and came to spend a half-hour with us. He said that he was in Los Angeles to meet two Frenchwomen who were in America for business reasons and who were arriving by airplane from New York. He invited us to Santa Barbara for the weekend. Of course we accepted, but Igor had to make a recording and we could not go until Saturday, September 27. We arrived for lunch, and immediately after it, one of the women (Mme D.) left for New York. The other, Mme V., stayed for two more days, then also went to New York (the car with the chauffeur took her to the Los Angeles airport). We stayed for one day in tête-à-tête with Arthur.

"As a result of your letter we were especially attentive, but we did not notice anything unusual. We were very natural with him, asking him several times for news of you. True, he did not offer many details, but he never does. On that last day he proposed that we send a cable to tell you how much we missed you. Did you receive it?

"He seemed somewhat distracted, but was as friendly and nice to us as always. He did not mention Mme V. except to say that she is in the publishing business and he asked us to talk to her about writers, life in America, and Paris. Seeing the two of them together, one would never imagine that anything intimate could have occurred between them— never, never. Your absence weighed very heavily on us: the house was dead, and we sorely missed your smile, your kindness, and your friendship. We also missed your guesthouse, where we had stayed with Nadia.

"Arthur told us that he plans to come with you and Marion in May and to spend the whole summer in Santa Barbara, and that perhaps we would all return to Paris together: Igor has had the idea of going to Europe next August for two and a half months.

"It is very difficult to describe the whole visit, dear Georges, since we do not know what has happened. Your letter uses only very enigmatic and vague terms. I wrote a reply and I would like to know if you received my letter—not knowing exactly where you are and fearing that my letter might have been lost." **2** To Doctors Waitzfelder and Edel. Lunch at the Town and Country Market. The children here for dinner. Andre sorts out our magazines and takes *Life* and *The New Yorker*. **3** To the Coronet Theater to see *Dark of the Moon*. **4** Lion Feuchtwanger comes at 6. **10** Renoir comes at 6. **14** Our wedding anniversary. We take communion, and lunch at home. **16** Igor has plastic surgery to tighten the skin underneath his eyes; the operation is performed by Dr. Ginsburg. **18** Dr. Ginsburg removes the stitches underneath Igor's eyes. **20** Igor to Dr. Ginsburg. **21** Igor to Dr. Ginsburg. **22** Igor to Dr. Ginsburg. We go to *The Marriage of Figaro*, performed by the San Francisco Opera in the Shrine Auditorium. **23** Drive Igor to Dr. Ginsburg. **24** Igor's picture on the front page of the newspaper because of *Firebird*.[3] To Dr. Ginsburg at 2:30. From 4 to 6 p.m. photographers and reporters from *Life* and *Time*. Milene complains about Madubo. **25** To Ginsburg at 11. Everybody is working at the Baroness's, unpacking 40 cases from her palazzo in Venice.[4] For late supper here: Gilbert Grau with his wife and Dahl. To bed at 3:15 a.m. **26** The "Summer Moon" story continues. **27** To Dr. Ginsburg. At 9 p.m. to Zeisl's with William Steinberg [the conductor], [Adolph] Heller [conductor], Adler,[5] and others. **28** Drive Igor to Ginsburg. **29** Igor to Ginsburg. **31** At the Town and Country Market with Charles Mendl and Yvonne Riley.[6] Go with Mischa Schneider and his wife to *Othello* at the San Francisco Opera. For supper here: Charles Cushing [a musician from Berkeley].

November

1 To *Don Giovanni* at the San Francisco Opera. **2** To a concert by the Budapest Quartet. Dinner at Gala with Catherine. **5** Dinner at Renoir's with Robert Florey.[7] **6** To a very good Chaplin film: *Monsieur Verdoux*. **10** I think the children are bored. Tamara Toumanova, telling me about her disappointments in people, says she adores Balanchine. **11** At 10 o'clock Wystan Auden arrives from New York. **12** Auden and Igor work all day on the libretto. **13** Lunch at the Farmers' Market with

[1] V. Mietens, Olga Mietens Faure (d. April 5, 1972), and her son Arnaud Faure. V. Mietens lived in Rouen, the Faures at 163, rue de Sèvres, Paris.

[2] Stravinsky wrote a short 2-voice canon for the event on a text by Jean de Meung.

[3] Stravinsky had sued the Leeds Music Corporation for publishing "Summer Moon," a melody from *Firebird* with lyrics and harmonization by someone else. See the chapter on *Firebird* in *Stravinsky: Selected Correspondence*, Vol. II, op. cit.

[4] Catherine d'Erlanger had written to Vera from Venice on October 3 describing the depredations she had found in her Venetian Casa Rosa which she emptied and

sold. (One of the packing cases contained documents concerning Diaghilev's funeral in August 1929, proving that Catherine d'Erlanger had paid most of the expenses.) Her letter, with its references to the coming of Bolshevism in Italy, influenced the Stravinskys in their decision not to go to Europe in 1948.

[5] Kurt Herbert Adler, the director of the San Francisco Opera.

[6] Though Miss Riley was fifty years younger than Sir Charles Mendl, he married her and he survived her by several years.

[7] Film director, best known for *The Beast With Five Fingers*.

Auden. Go to a concert, then to the opening performance of García Lorca's *La casa de Bernarda Alba* at the Coronet. A party here afterward with John Houseman, Berman, Auden. **14** Igor and Auden work all day. **15** Igor and Auden. In the evening to the newsreels. **16** Lunch with Auden at The Players. With Auden to *Così fan tutte*. **17** Auden and Igor. **18** Auden has a pain in the ear; I drive him to Edel.[1] Auden finishes a wonderful libretto. Berman and Lisa for dinner. Auden should have gone to New York but his flight was cancelled. **20** To *Shoe Shine*, a wonderful Italian film. **23** To the Rembrandt exhibition at the Museum. **28** Lunch at Yolanda's [Farmers' Market] with the Huxleys. At 8:30 to the concert by Prévost's quartet, a program of Haydn, Mozart, and Igor's Concertino. Buffet supper here afterward.

December

3 The Sokolovs leave for New York, where he is to play in *Crime and Punishment*. For dinner here: the Huxleys and Berman. **4** Madubo and I go to Dr. Epstein. **5** Go to a small concert at William Wyler's [the film director], at 1121 Summit Drive (Benedict Canyon). **7** Igor walks with me on Santa Monica Beach. We go to a bazaar at the Baroness's. Milene and Andre come to discuss serious business and their future with us. **14** We walk on the beach and eat lobster. René Leibowitz, from Paris, visits Igor. We do not go to Hanns Eisler's concert (on the Roof), but the Babitzes, Edel, and Berman come to us after it. **15** Write to Olga about the complications between the children and Madubo. Dr. Epstein at 3. **16** Madubo comes for dinner, the children later. **17** Victor Babin for lunch. **21** George Balanchine comes with Nicolas Nabokov. Berman joins us for dinner. **23** Shop with Igor and Nabokov. Dinner with Balanchine, Nabokov, and Berman in the Naples restaurant. **24** Lunch with the Huxleys at the Country Market. **26** We are four hours at the airfield seeing Nabokov off. **29** Go to a Christmas show at the Coronet Theater with Adrian[2] and Joseph Cotton.

January

1[3] A lovely day. Igor and I walk in the hills. At 8:30 we go to *Mourning Becomes Electra*. Ona Munson has pleurisy and we drive Berman to a drugstore. To bed at 11:15 to read Isherwood. **2**[4] I write to Madeleine Milhaud: "We are grieved at the news that Darius has been ill ever since his arrival in France. We think of him constantly and hope that you have a good doctor. We hope that the cold and the difficulties in obtaining food are not tiring for you. . . . No doubt you would like to have news of *La casa de Bernarda Alba* at the Coronet Theater. Sokolov did a good job and did all that he could, but the results cannot be called a great success. Darius's beautiful music was very well played and it was the only attraction in this, so I think, not very interesting play, with its out-of-date realism and feeble construction. . . . Probably you already know that we plan to come to Europe in May and stay until the end of July or August. Igor must find some tranquility: he has to compose an opera on the subject of Hogarth's *Rake's Progress*, the libretto by the English poet, W.H. Auden, who was here with us." **3** Dinner with the children, then to see Maurice Chevalier at the Biltmore. I write to V.P. Preobrazhensky.[5] **7** Lunch with Sir Charles Mendl and several goodlooking girls. Write to Olga (doubts about our trip to Europe, Kugulskaya[6] and my flat in Paris, Balanchine, Madubo, Andre's bees[7]). **17** We listen to Ansermet's NBC Symphony broadcast, then go with Berman and Edel to a Cocteau film that annoys Igor, though Christian Berard's sets are good. **20** Dinner at Benny Goodman's[8] with Sascha Schneider.[9] Igor gets drunk on

champagne. **21** Sunbathe and drive Igor in the hills to air out his hangover. **23** A gay evening with Sascha Schneider and Berman—lobsters and 4 bottles of champagne—but Igor is in a very bad mood. **24** We listen to Ansermet's NBC Symphony broadcast. **29** Send *Orpheus* to Nadia and a manuscript page of *Le Sacre du printemps* to Brainerd Smith.[10] We decide to fly to Europe, since a cabin de luxe on the S.S. *America* costs $1600. I write to the Sachses: "We were so happy to be able to tell you the news from your New York agency that a cabin has been reserved for us on the *America* for May 12, but because of the price—$800 for each of us, one-way only—we must cancel the tickets and fly. We are very sorry not to be with you on the boat (I assume that you will not fly). . . . We leave for San Francisco on February 7, for Mexico City (by air) on the 20th, return to Los Angeles March 2, and on the 25th leave for Washington, New York, and Europe! The weather here is superb, and California is so beautiful that we leave it with great regret. The trip promises to be exhausting, exasperating, and expensive." **30** Igor and Babitz dine together, then Igor conducts an orchestra of film studio musicians. Later here: Grau, Babitz, Dahl, Aaron Copland. **31** We listen to Ansermet conduct the *Symphonies of Wind Instruments* on an NBC Symphony broadcast concert.

February

5 Very unpleasant phone call from Milene: Andre wants to get rid of Madubo and has actually consulted Sapiro about how to do it. **7** At 9:20 p.m. we leave from Glendale for San Francisco. **10** Igor rehearses the San Francisco Symphony for 4 hours. **11** The newspapermen pester Igor for comments about the musical scene in Russia. Rémy de Gourmont's *Art and People* strikingly anticipates today's situation with newspapermen. **12** Igor's first San Francisco concert. **14** Igor's second concert. **17** Lunch with Huxleys at Yolanda's. To a film with the Huxleys at 10 p.m. **20** We fly to Mexico at 10:45 p.m., a wonderful trip with enormous stars. **21** Land in Mexico City at 7 a.m. and are met by Rosita and Jesús Bal y Gay with flowers, and by photographers. We have a penthouse at the Ritz Hotel and drink coffee on the terrace. Fred[11] comes to see us and Prieto sends a car. We go to visit the Madonna of Guadalupe. Lunch, drink tequila at Prendes. **22** Fred, Igor, and I go to Topotzlan to visit a gold baroque church. **23** Igor's rehearsal from 9 to 12 a.m. **24** Igor's rehearsal from 9 to 12. See a Mexican film starring Maria Feliz. Dinner at Prendes. **26** Igor has two rehearsals. Lunch with Chavez. **27** Igor's concert, and a party at Bal's after it. **29** Go with Villaseñors to Topotzlan.

March

1 Go to Amecameca with the Fourniers[12] and lunch with them. **2** Leave Mexico at 9:45 a.m. Tiring trip, though good weather. Milene and Andre meet us at the Los Angeles airport at 4. Evgenia Petrovna says that we have a new cat sitting in the bushes near the kitchen. I bring him some food and milk, but he does not dare to come out because our Vaska is terribly jealous and won't let him. Since we are coming from Mexico, I name the cat, a beautiful fluffy one, Pancho. **5** To Dr. Mantchik. Write to Svetik and Françoise:[13] "People talk as if the Russians are about to swallow one country after another—Italy after Czechoslovakia. . . . In this disturbing atmosphere, Papa is unable to bring himself to sign contracts for European concerts. When we asked Washington for our passports, the answer was that we could have them only at our own risk, which is not encouraging. . . . If the European situation is really alarming, you should come here for some months. Perhaps we can find concerts for Nini while Françoise stays with us and avoids the bad times. We have just

---

[1] A large amount of cerumen was removed from Auden's ear.

[2] The costume designer and husband of Janet Gaynor.

[3] A letter to Vera from Olga Sallard dated January 1 mentions a broadcast performance on the Paris radio of Stravinsky's *Ode* and *Basler* Concerto.

[4] Olga Sallard wrote to Vera on January 2: "Andre Marion did not like Madubo and was irritated by her presence. Neither did she like him, and all of the Sancellemoz friends of the Stravinsky family detested Marion, even the curé, with whom you and Igor Fyodorovich once had lunch."

[5] Valentine Pavlovich Preobrazhensky, director of food and agricultural organizations for the United Nations, was living at 2000 Massachusetts Avenue in Washington. The Stravinskys had known him in Rome in the 1930s.

[6] Maris Kugulskaya continued to occupy Vera's apartment, 31, rue de

l'Assomption, until 1952.

[7] At various times in his first years in California, Andre Marion had considered becoming a restaurateur, a proprietor of a gasoline station, and a watch repairer.

[8] At this time the clarinetist was living at 945 Corsica Drive, Pacific Palisades.

[9] Second violinist in the Budapest Quartet.

[10] Friend of the McLanes, later a Los Angeles psychiatrist.

[11] Baron Osten-Saken was living in Mexico City at the time, on the Avenida Mazatlan.

[12] Dr. Raoul Fournier and his wife.

[13] Françoise Blondlat nad married Soulima Stravinsky in 1946.

learned that the Sachses will arrive in Santa Barbara on March 23. . . . Papa has a cold. He must conduct two concerts here in Los Angeles, on the 18th and the 19th, after which we leave for Washington and New York. . . . Is Papa's account in Paris sufficient to pay for your tickets from there to Los Angeles?'' **7** Every day now I have been trying to tell Vaska that he is stupid and that I love him more than the newcomer. But Vaska is heartbroken, miserable, and he has stopped eating. **8** To Dr. Mantchik. Rest and read Julian Green's *Journal*. Igor goes with Edel to Ingolf Dahl's Evenings on the Roof concert. **9** Our eighth wedding anniversary. Take Vaska to the veterinarian, who says ''If you love your cat, you must get rid of the other one.'' With Igor and Madubo to the cinema. **12** Svetik cables, guaranteeing that nothing dangerous will occur—as if *he* could guarantee that. We drive Pancho ten miles away, in Beverly Hills, and leave him in front of a home, with a little note, in the hope that children might find him; Pancho is so beautiful that they will love him and adopt him. On our return, Vaska receives us affectionately. **13** Evgenia Petrovna says that Pancho is back, sitting in the bushes, and very hungry. **16** Igor rehearses the Los Angeles Philharmonic Orchestra. Write to Nini and Françoise: ''This is the week of Papa's rehearsals and concerts here in Los Angeles, and since he has not fully recovered from the cold, the rehearsals tire him and he cannot write a letter. It is not necessary to tell you what a joy it was to have your cable announcing the decision to come here. . . . What most frightened us from coming to Europe was the impossibility of returning. All boats were sold out until October, and the airplanes, too, were nearly full. You can just see Papa seated in 'a city' waiting for the next departure!'' **17**[1] Igor's second rehearsal. **18** Igor's Los Angeles concert. **19** Igor's second Los Angeles concert. Friends here in the evening. **23** At 9:30 a.m. Igor broadcasts his message for the 30th anniversary of Debussy's death. Lunch with the Huxleys. **24** To the French Foundation cocktail party for Walter Lippmann. **28** At 11:28 we leave for Chicago on the ''Chief.'' **30** In Chicago, an exhibition of French tapestries. **31** On the train to Washington, Igor cannot sleep. From the window I watch the foggy view of the river approaching Pittsburgh. On arrival in Washington, go to the Hotel Raleigh. We spend all day with Auden and Craft.

April

1 Igor goes to his 10 a.m. rehearsal with Craft (Auden returned to New York last night). In the evening we go to a Mozart concert at Dumbarton Oaks and a reception by John Thacher. ''Power corrupts, absolute power corrupts absolutely.''[2] **2** Igor's rehearsal. Go to the second Mozart concert and to Thacher's party. **3** Igor has a morning rehearsal. We go to the National Gallery exhibition of German painting. Lunch at Mildred Bliss's with the Nicolas Nabokovs and Professor Vassiliev, Director of the National Gallery. Igor sees Ralph Hawkes at 5:30 p.m. The Nabokovs take us to dinner at the Salle de Bois. **4** Igor has a morning rehearsal. Igor's National Symphony Orchestra concert at 4 p.m. We take the night train to New York. **5** New York. Ambassador Hotel. Go to Bach's *St. John Passion* in Carnegie Hall. See Hindemith, who plays the viola sola, after the performance, then to a strange dinner at Auden's. **6** At Noguchi's[3] atelier we see his wonderful construction for the *Orpheus* set. Dinner with the Sachses at the Pavillon. At 11 to a party for Saul Steinberg. **7** Igor goes with Haieff to Craft's rehearsal at the Nola Studios, 1657 Broadway. Georges Sachs confides in me. *Orpheus* rehearsal and dinner at Balanchine's. **8** At 11 a.m., Igor at Zirato. Lunch with Haieff at Del Pezzo where we see Massimo Freccia. Buy flowers for Maria Tallchief and the Sokolovs. Igor plays *Orpheus* at Kyriena's. **9** From 10 to 1, Igor rehearses his *Symphonies of Wind Instruments*. Lunch with Craft and Lisa. *Orpheus* rehearsal at Balanchine's. **10** Abram Chasins interviews Igor, Balanchine, Kirstein, and Craft at 7:30 p.m. on WQXR. **11** Rehearsal

in Town Hall from 10 to 1. Tickets to: Balanchine (2), Nabokovs (2), Harold Shapero (2), Stark Young and Bill Bowman, Kyriena and friend (2), Pavlik Tchelichev (2). Concert at Town Hall at 5. **12** Betty Bean[4] and photographer Gene Fenn. Saul Steinberg. **14** Igor to Dr. Ruskin.[5] **15** Igor to Dr. Ruskin. Craft and Haieff for lunch. **16** Igor delighted with Dr. Ruskin. Dagmar[6] from 5 to 7 p.m. Supper at Lucia Davidova's **17** The weather is lovely, New York is beautiful. Telephone Virgil Thomson concerning Igor's letter about R. Craft. We go to Koussevitzky's matinée concert: an atmosphere of flattery; Igor says that the boxes are filled with old people who have taken trips with Koussevitzky down the Volga. Dinner at the *Crémaillère* with Balanchine, *et al.* **19** Igor to the doctor. Rehearsal at Balanchine's. **20** We go to Ballet Theater to see Balanchine conduct the orchestra in Tchaikovsky. Dinner afterward at Lucia Chase's with Varvara Karinska. Victoria Ocampo's picture is in the *Tribune*, in connection with a scandal about how much her visit to London cost the taxpayers (nearly $3,000); this is debated in the House of Commons. **21** At 11:30 a.m. a photography session with Gene Fenn, then an unsuccessful luncheon with R. Craft.[7] To Balanchine's rehearsal. **22** Lunch with Stark Young. To *Oedipus* at the Juilliard School. **23** *Orpheus* orchestra rehearsal. In the evening to the New School for Social Research: a symposium with Nabokov, Mary McCarthy, Edmund Wilson, and others. Dinner with Balanchine at the *Crémaillère*. **25** In today's *Tribune*: ''The Baroness Catherine d'Erlanger, portrait painter and active London society figure, reported today the loss of $31,900 in jewelry and $5,000 cash in a burglary of her rambling Hollywood house.'' **26** *Orpheus* rehearsal at the City Center with the dancers. Orpheus' mask horrifies us and we protest. *Apollo* rehearsal from 1 to 3. *Apollo*: in our box, Bob Craft, Sapiro with Lady Owen, Haieff. **28** The *Orpheus* dress rehearsal from 9 to 12. A lighting rehearsal from 2 to 4, then the premiere of *Orpheus*.[8] Party at Lucia Davidova's, then at Reuben's until 5 a.m. **30** At 12: interview with *The New Yorker*. At 1:30 Igor to Dr. Ruskin for sinuses.

May

2 Russian Easter. Lunch with Stark Young and Bill Bowman in their house at Waccabuc. **4** At lunch at Maria's restaurant, see Prince Troubetzkoy. Train to Los Angeles. **7** Arrive early in Pasadena. **12** At Yolanda's for lunch we learn that Huxley is ill. We visit him with flowers. **13** Cocktails at Charles Boyer's. **16** Santa Barbara. We ransack the Sachses' guesthouse for old furniture for Svetik. **20** Hollywood. Rehearsal of *Histoire du soldat* from 11 to 2 p.m. Koussevitzky telephones. **23** Write to Olga that Andre does not have a job and that Milene is completely under his influence. **27** Lunch with Huxley, who will soon be leaving for Italy.

June

5 Dinner at the Huxleys' with Peggy Kiskadden, Lesley Le Crou (a counseling psychologist), and Frederick Barienhock (architect). **6** To Joseph Szigeti's at Palos Verdes. **22** Lisa dies. **24** Lisa's funeral. **25** Svetik's arrival. **26** We go to the Rubinsteins' for cocktails—for the children, so that they can see real live movie stars.[9]

July

2 With Volodya Sokolov. Rest in bed and read *Brideshead Revisited*, which enchants me. **7** Ormandy's dinner for Alma Mahler, in the Crystal Room of the Beverly Hills Hotel, is terribly boring.[10] **13** Photographers from *Time* magazine. Very pleasant dinner and evening at the Szigetis'. **14** Igor, not well, blames the fog, but I am sure he feels ill from drinking.

---

[1] On March 17, Olga Sallard wrote to Vera: ''To judge from Milene's letters, Andre's father has a terrible disposition—a despotic character that Andre has partially inherited. Milene, of course, is extremely timid, and in the sanatorium she was always afraid that her bills would anger her father. I hope that Marion fears Stravinsky and you. I am particularly sorry for Madubo, who gave her life to Stravinsky's children. I am glad that you are taking her under your wing.''

[2] Lord Acton's line, which Mrs. Stravinsky had learned from R.C.

[3] Isamu Noguchi, the sculptor.

[4] Director of the New York branch of Boosey & Hawkes.

[5] Dr. Simon L. Ruskin, 32 East 67th Street.

[6] At this date Miss Godowsky was living at Delmonico's Hotel on Park Avenue.

[7] See the account of this in *Present Perspectives*, New York, 1984.

[8] A letter from Tchelichev to the Stravinskys, July 12, 1948, describes ''the dense crowd of admirers, flatterers, and the stupefied,'' who made it impossible ''for an ordinary mortal like myself to get through to you. . . . *Orpheus* sounded particularly wonderful when you conducted.'' The letter reveals that Stravinsky had agreed to sit for a portrait by Tchelichev—never realized.

[9] According to a clipping from the *Los Angeles Times*, Clark Gable, Nelson Eddy, and Cole Porter were among the guests, but Stravinsky's name heads the list.

[10] According to the *Los Angeles Times*, July 8, 1948, Schoenberg attended this dinner as well, and Thomas Mann, Montemezzi, Korngold, Antheil, Gruenberg, Toch, Bruno Walter, Szigeti. Ormandy conducted Mahler's Eighth Symphony in Hollywood Bowl, July 29.

I am now doing the shopping for all three houses, ours, Svetik's, and Milene's. At last Milene and Andre have a confidential talk with Igor. **18** At 7:30, leave on the train for Denver. **19** Denver, the Brown Palace Hotel, a terrible hotel. **20** Spend most of the day in Charles Bayly's wonderful house.[1] **21** Igor's first rehearsal. Denver needs an auditorium. **22** Two *Life* photographers from Hollywood taking our pictures all afternoon at Red Rocks, in terrible heat. In the evening we go to Central City, a ''ghost town,'' and attend a performance of *Così fan tutte*. **24** In the evening to Virgil Thomson's opera, *The Mother of Us All*. **26** Rieti and Renée de Veyrac at Lamy.[2] **27** At 7:13, arrive in Pasadena, and at 7:45, home! **28** Lunch with Catherine d'Erlanger in a restaurant called Wanda's which Andre would like to buy. Much discussion about Andre's problems. **29** At 7:30 go with Dick Hammond to hear Mahler's Symphony in Hollywood Bowl. **30** Bob Craft for dinner, directly from Mexico.

August

1 Discuss the Marion problem with them. Party here: Father McLane (3), Hammond (2), Berman (1), Bob Craft, Nini, ourselves. **2** Bob here for lunch. Sapiro makes an appointment with the restaurant owners for me, Andre, and Milene, but the negotiations fall through deliberately, on Sapiro's advice. **3** Lunch at the Farmers' Market with Bob. We go with him to Forest Lawn's Whispering Glades. Dinner at Françoise's with Edel and Craft. **4** For lunch here: Bob and Edel. To buy books at Pickwick with Bob Craft. **6** Lunch with Bob at the Farmers' Market. Drive Bob to Bel Air and UCLA. Here for dinner: the Dahls, Grau, the children, and Bob. **7** For lunch here: Bob and Max Edel. With Bob and Françoise to the book shop to buy, as he calls them, ''investments.'' Very gay lobster dinner at the ocean. **8** For lunch here: the children, Berman, and Bob. Then to Griffith's *The Birth of a Nation*. We dine at the Naples restaurant. **9** Drive Bob to Burbank airfield. Buy a car for Svetik from Charles Mendl. **10** To Artur Rubinstein's with Dick Hammond. **14** Lunch at the Rubinsteins'. **22** Write to Bob Craft: ''Merthi for your letter, your literary and kind letter. Thank you also for all the books coming from London. I became more and more a Waugh fan. E.W. is somebody from the family. I imagine how he would react on this: You certainly are not a cousin of mine. Nevertheless, he *is* one. Everybody is alright but I, who have a sore finger. Opening a wine bottle I hurt it. Popka is very irritated. He has sex troubles. Don't ask me, What do you mean by that. Apropos: I gave once a book to Mr. Sapiro, Maupassant's *Tales*, 'You can read it in bed.' He looked at me very suspiciously and said, 'What do you mean by that?'' **23** The Renoirs take us to see their house, then to dine together. **27** Milene and Andre come to discuss a new possibility for a business, a candy shop.

September

1 To Edel. Archansky for lunch. At 3, Sascha Schneider with a Cadillac [for sale]. **6–8:** Bill Copley and John Ployard. **3** Drive to Santa Barbara. In contrast to the heat inland, the sea is foggy and cold. To the Milhauds' in Carpenteria (the Keith School). Dinner at the Country Club with the Blisses. **4** Darius's birthday. Lunch at the Chanticleer. We see *Medea*. Igor and the children like it, Madeleine [Milhaud] and I do not. **9** We hear the news that Dr. Kall is dead. Lunch in the Brown Derby with Georgette Bailey. **10** Kall's funeral. **16** We take Svetik to Burbank for his flight to New York. **18** An unexpected spree with Igor. He listens to his records at Edel's. We eat lobsters on the beach, then go to the *Mermaid*. **22** Svetik arrives in the morning and comes to lunch here. **25** I take Igor to Dr. Loewenthal. **27** Soulima's concert—plays well, great success. We have a party after the concert for 27 people. **28** Take Igor to the doctor.

October

1[3] Dr. Loewenthal for Igor. **2** While waiting for Igor at Dr. Loewenthal's,

I read Osbert Sitwell's autobiography. **4** Igor to Dr. Loewenthal. A program of Stravinsky music at Evenings on the Roof, but Igor and I do not attend. **5** Igor and I go to a Paul Klee exhibition. **7** Igor and I take Sokolov to The Players for dinner—in order not to sit with him at home: he gets on Igor's nerves. **8** Take Igor to Dr. Loewenthal. **13** Milene comes for a check, and I give her an additional $50 of my own to help her forget her disappointments. **14** Our wedding anniversary. We take communion and learn of the death of Prince Galitzin. **16** Prince Galitzin's funeral. Dinner with Mme Charles Boyer, Mr. Verneuil, and Lili Palmer. **20** Igor and Dahl to the opera, *Elisir d'amore* which delights them. **24** At 2:30 Igor and I go to hear Carol Brice[4] in the Philharmonic Auditorium. **25** Igor to Dr. Loewenthal. **26** Dinner at Edward G. Robinson's with Charles Mendl, Bronislaw Kaper, Constance Collier [actress]. *Blini* and caviar, but the boors in the crowd would make good material for Waugh. **28** At 8, Igor and I to *Don Giovanni*. Afterward, at home, we play *Don Giovanni* again on records. **30** A wire from the Sitwells: ''Our homage and gratitude to the greatest creative artist of this time for his message of welcome by which we were profoundly touched. Edith and Osbert Sitwell.'' Milene, crying again, and Andre.

November

13 To Charles Munch's concert with the touring French orchestra. **14** Lunch at the Tricolor for the whole French orchestra: a very well organized party in the garden at the French Consulate. **15** We go to the Yves Tanguy exhibition at the Copley Galleries. Igor buys a Tanguy as a Christmas present for me. **22** With Françoise and Nini to Palm Springs. **23** Spend the night on Arrowhead Lake. **24** Return from Palm Springs. **26** For dinner here: Charles Bayly, Father McLane, John Ployard, the Soulimas, Berman. A conversation *à la* Waugh: Father McLane: ''You must come to our church. It was so beautiful on All Souls' Day, the flowers and black coffin, you would like it.'' **28** Cocktails at Vincent Price's. After dinner, André Maurois comes to see us. **30** [On this date Auden wrote to Kallman: ''Went to the Yiddish Y yesterday to hear a concert performance of *Mavra* which I thought a lovely work, all about a Huzzah (Hussar) in drag.'']

December

1 Go to Francis Poulenc's concert at the Wilshire Ebell. **2** Poulenc and Pierre Bernac here for lunch. **12** Igor and I go to Miramar to see Victoria Ocampo. **13** To the opening of Man Ray's exhibition at the Copley Gallery. **22** Write to Bob Craft. Dinner at Françoise's. **25** For dinner: the whole family, Edel, Berman, Bolms, John Ployard. **26** Igor writes letters with Andre. To Berman in the afternoon. Dine at Naples. **27** Fedya's book arrives. Igor and I buy a scrapbook for *Life*'s reproductions of Giotto. **28** Sapiro: ''We won the motion,'' in the lawsuit. Michael Mann comes.[5] Three years of our citizenship: we celebrate with champagne.

January

6 Aaron Copland for dinner. **7** Dr. Greene extracts three of Igor's teeth. Igor goes to the Philharmonic matinée concert to hear a piece by David Diamond. **9** Igor plays the first act of the *Rake* for Berman. It is wonderful. A reception for Max Ernst at the Copley Gallery. All the ladies get drunk and kiss each other. **13** Elegant dinner dance at Al Lewin's,[6] with Max Ernst and the Copley Gallery people. **16** Igor finishes Act One of the *Rake*. **18** Igor to the doctor. Unsuccessful trip to the Museum to see the German paintings. Crowds of people and police— only the barbed wire was missing. **23** Igor and I leave for Houston on the Sunset Limited. **25** The Rice Hotel, Houston. **30** Lunch at Efrem Kurtz's after Igor's rehearsal. **31** Igor's concert in the evening. Party at Clayton's in his charming house.

---

[1] A descendant of Henri Beyle (Stendhal), Bayly used to send shells to the Stravinskys for their collection; one shipment, in the summer of 1950, had been gathered at Zanzibar.

[2] The railroad station for Santa Fe, which would become very familiar to the Stravinskys a decade later.

[3] On this date W.H. Auden wrote to Chester Kallman: ''The first [scene] of [*The

Rake] is finished. . . . The Maestro only says, 'Eet vill be vary eesy to leesten to.'''

[4] Contralto (d. 1985), the first black musician to win the Naumburg award.

[5] Violist, son of the novelist. Stravinsky coached Mr. Mann in the *Elégie*.

[6] One of the most gifted scriptwriter directors in Hollywood. The Stravinskys knew him through the Baroness d'Erlanger.

February

1 We leave for New York. **3** Arrive at 6:55 a.m., Bob and Auden meeting us in the station. Lunch with Dushkin and Bob. 2 p.m.: Richard Mohr from RCA Victor. At 5:30 p.m.: Auden. **4** Dinner with Evelyn Waugh. **5** With Bob to Boston. **6** The Sheraton Hotel, Boston. **7** Igor's first rehearsal with the Boston Symphony. **8** Rehearsals. Igor's concert at Cambridge. Supper afterwards at Forbes'. **10** Dr. Rinkel[1] for Igor at 7 a.m. Both Igor and I have high temperatures. Igor's rehearsal at 10 a.m. **11** Igor's Boston concert. **14** Igor's rehearsal. **15** Igor's rehearsal. We return to New York. **16** Igor's New York concert with the Boston Symphony. **17** Igor's Newark concert with the Boston Symphony. **18** Igor's Brooklyn concert (Academy of Music) with the Boston Symphony. Lunch with Nabokov. **19** Igor's New York concert with the Boston Symphony. **20** 11:30 a.m. Igor at Dr. Dreyfus's. Igor's 2:30 rehearsal of the choir in St. Thomas Church. **21** Bob at 11:30 a.m. Auden's birthday dinner.[2] **22** Igor records *Orpheus* in Manhattan Center (34th Street) for 3 hours. **23** Igor records *Orpheus* from 9 a.m. to 1 p.m. Koussevitzky comes in the afternoon. 7 to 10 p.m.: rehearsal of Mass. **24** 1:15 p.m. Igor to Dr. Dreyfus. Igor records the Mass from 2 to 5. **25** 9:30 a.m. to 12 p.m. Igor records the Mass and the Three Sacred Choruses. **26** Concert at 5:30:[3] Mass. Big dinner at Maria's restaurant. Later at Abram's. **27** Lunch with Chanel at Maria's. Dinner at Maria's with Balanchine *et al*. **28** We leave for Urbana.

March

1 The University of Illinois sent a car to Chicago for us (120 miles to Urbana). Françoise continues to Los Angeles. The Lincoln Hotel, Urbana. Igor's evening rehearsal. **3** Igor's Urbana concert. **4** By train to Denver. **7** Denver. Igor's rehearsal. At 5:30 p.m. go to Bayly's with the President of the Central City Opera Company (Ricketson). **8** Igor's rehearsal and concert—a triumph. Party at Bayly's. **9** Leave Denver. **11** Los Angeles. **18** Much discussion about Igor's refusal to give his name to welcome Shostakovich to the United States. **26** We drive to the desert with the Marions. Lunch at Palmdale—Joshua trees—and spend the night there. **27** Wonderful desert flowers. Drive home via the National Monument, Indio, Palm Springs. Go to Harold Byrnes's Chamber Music Concert—an hour late. **28** To Nathan Milstein's concert. **31** Meeting here on the subject of the *Soldat*: Henry Schnitzler, Sapiro, Franz Waxman. We go to Milhaud's concert.

April

1 Benny Goodman comes at 3 p.m. **7** Igor goes with Dahl to see about recording the *Concerto per due pianoforti soli*. **8** Nini and Eula Beal give a concert in the Philharmonic auditorium. Unexpected party here for 18 people. **9** Lunch with the Huxleys at Yolanda's. **10** To the nursery with Igor. At 4, broadcast of Svetik and Dahl in the *Concerto per due pianoforti soli*. Stuckenschmidt[4] from 5 to 7 p.m. Explosion between Françoise-Nini and Madubo.[5] **12** At Daisy Fellowes[6] with Greta Garbo, Cole Porter, the Salvador Dalis. **13** For dinner here: the Huxleys.

---

[1] Dr. Max Rinkel, president of the Massachusetts Society for Research in Psychiatry, author, pioneer researcher in the effects of LSD, remained a close friend of the Stravinskys'.

[2] On this date Auden wrote to Kallman: ''I went off to the Ambassador Hotel to go through Act [I]. All your suggestions were conveyed and enthusiastically received; I wish you had been there to get the credit. I'm afraid you'll have to swallow my couplet for the Cabaletta:

Time cannot alter
My loving heart
My ever-loving heart.

I was faced with fitting it into the music and it was the only thing I could think up that would fit. The performance was from the piano score with the maestro at the piano, Bob Craft, Balanchine, self, etc., screaming parts.''

[3] In Town Hall. Stravinsky conducted the Mass (second performance anywhere), Soulima Stravinsky and Beveridge Webster played the *Concerto per due pianoforti soli*, and R.C. conducted the Octet.

[4] Hans Stuckenschmidt, the Berlin music critic, was in Los Angeles to see Arnold Schoenberg.

[5] After this, Madubo left Soulima's house and spent her remaining years in California working for Vera Stravinsky and Maria Huxley.

15 For dinner here: Benny Goodman. **16** Lunch at the Farmers' Market with Huxleys. Dinner with the Huxleys and Edwin Hubbles.[7] **19** Bob Craft conducts *Noces* in Town Hall, New York. **20** Igor and I take communion. **21** We were expecting a telephone call from Bob, but it does not come. **27** Igor and I go to *The Marriage of Figaro* at the Shrine Auditorium.

May

6 Igor and I to *Elisir d'Amore* at the Shrine Auditorium. **7** Dinner with the Renoirs. **14** *Negationism*: to derive pleasure from not doing things you never intended to do, but never got around to not doing. **18** Igor to Loewenthal. To a concert for the benefit of Israel in the garden. **22** For lunch in our garden: the Milhauds and Renoirs. **24** At a concert of Milhaud's music at UCLA, I have a run-in with George Antheil— *scandale*.[8]

June

1 Bob Craft here for breakfast and dinner.[9] For dinner: Nini and Françoise. **3** David Diamond here for lunch in the patio. **5** Svetik helps Bob to sort things out.[10] **8** Lunch at Country Market. For dinner here: Berman and Ona Munson. **9** At 8:30 we see *Figaro* at UCLA. **10** Antonia Cobos arrives. A visit from Roger Wagner, a chorus conductor. **11** Igor's rehearsal at 7:30 p.m.[11] **12** Igor's rehearsal at 7:30 p.m. **14** 7:30 p.m. rehearsal of *Histoire du soldat*. Dinner at 12:30 a.m. with Dahl. **16** Performance at Royce Hall, UCLA, of *Histoire du soldat*. **18** To church for Igor's birthday with Bob, Milene, Andre, and Nini. **23** Dinner at Renoir's: a charming house. **26** Stop at Catherine's to get a statue.[12] Visit from Balanchine. **27** Drive with Bob; buy bricks as a pedestal for the statue.

July

5 Igor to Dr. Loewenthal. **6** Igor has a sharp pain in his hands and does not sleep. Miss Churchill gives him a treatment and he is well by dinnertime. **8** Igor suffers all morning. Dr. Engelman for Igor, 1–2 p.m. I drive to Dr. Loewenthal's for the x-rays and to take them to Dr. Engelman. We install a hospital bed for Igor. Engelman 7–8 p.m. **9** A terrible night: Dr. Engelman. **10** Dr. Engelman at 12:30 p.m. **12** Igor has a good night. Dr. Engelman at 8:30 p.m. **13** Dr. Engelman 7–8 p.m. **14** Dr. Engelman 7–8 p.m. **15** Buy a Chrysler for Svetik. First day without Engelman. Marie comes to cook.[13] For dinner here: Efrem Kurtz, Bob; later Louriés. **16** Bob goes to Santa Barbara. **17** Balanchine and Nicolas Magellanes come and Bob and Svetik telephone from Santa Barbara. Go to the cinema with Igor. **19** Bob returns from Santa Barbara. Dr. Engelman at 8 p.m. **20** Bob and I drive to get *The New York Times*. **21** Dr. Engelman. To Hollywood Bowl with Bob to see Zorina in *Jeanne d'Arc au bûcher*. **27** Bob and I lunch at Yolanda's with the Huxleys. **28** Dr. Engelman. **29** For lunch, Albert Goldberg of the *Los Angeles Times*. Dr. Engelman. **30** From 10 a.m. to 10 p.m. Igor, Bob, and I drive to San Diego with the Marions.

---

[6] Mrs. Reginald Fellowes. The Stravinskys had known her in London before the war.

[7] The astronomer, director of the Mount Wilson Observatory.

[8] After reading Antheil's *Bad Boy of Music*, both Stravinskys vowed never to speak to him again. Passing him in the same row of seats at the UCLA concert, Mrs. Stravinsky snubbed him, but Stravinsky shook hands with him and was as cordial as ever. The *scandale* was between the Stravinskys.

[9] From this date R.C. lived in the Stravinsky home—in the den adjoining the composer's studio.

[10] Soulima Stravinsky was leaving his house to join the faculty of the Music Academy of the West near Santa Barbara, during which period R.C. stayed in the Hollywood house.

[11] Of a staged version of *Histoire du soldat*, directed by Henry Schnitzler (son of Arthur Schnitzler), danced (the Princess) by Cobos.

[12] A head-to-waist Greek marble that adorned the porch at 1260 North Wetherly Drive until 1964 and was stolen in 1965 from its pedestal at 1218 North Wetherly Drive.

[13] Marie Le Put and her husband were the chefs at the Deauville, the Baroness's nightclub restaurant. Later Marie Le Put worked for Aldous Huxley until his death.

August

2 Drive with Bob to Santa Barbara for Soulima's concert there. Dr. Engelman and Edel with Igor.   **4** The Balanchines for dinner.   **5** The three of us to the cinema (W.C. Fields).   **7** Balanchine comes. I read Faulkner [*Light in August*].   **10** Lunch with the Huxleys and Isherwood at Yolanda's.[1]   **12** Cocktails here: the Saul Steinbergs. Igor gets drunk.   **14** With Bob to the film *The Red Shoes*. With Igor to an ISCM concert (12-tone).[2]   **15** We go to the Huntington Library but it is closed. In the evening, the Steinbergs come to hear the Mass and Symphony in C.   **17** Lunch with the Huxleys. Drive Bob to Christopher Isherwood's.   **18** Lunch with Huxleys. To the beach.   **19** Lunch with Huxleys and two Israeli friends of Bob, invited by him.   **20** A dinner here with a lot of drinking: Isherwood and Bill Caskey, Berman and Ona.   **21** Bob working at Nini's. Visit from Phyllis Cuevas.   **24** With Edel to an unbelievably bad film.   **25** Go to the ocean with Bob. Tea at the Miramar, D.H. Lawrence's hotel. Edel for dinner here. All of us to the cinema: *Anna Lucasta*.   **28** Read Lawrence's *Virgin and the Gypsy*. Igor, Bob, and I drive on Mulholland.   **30** Koussevitzky comes from 5 to 6 p.m.   **31** I go alone from 5 to 7 to the birthday party for Alma Mahler at Mrs. Arlt's.

September

2 We go to San Diego after a dinner in Santa Monica (Ted's) with Isherwood. Stay at the Grant Hotel.   **4** To a *corrida* in Tijuana.   **5** Bob lost his bus ticket and came back.   **6** Bob leaves for San Francisco and New York.   **13** Farewell dinner at Lourié's (he is leaving for India[3]) with Renoirs and Toumanova.[4]

October

4 Paul Sacher comes with his wife, 5 to 7.   **5** Nini comes in the evening to tell us that he wants to move to New York. We approve but are upset by the decision.   **14** Our wedding anniversary. We go to church.   **15** RCA Victor broadcast at 3 p.m. At 5 we see Klemperer at the Roosevelt Hotel.   **22** Bob's concert in New York.   **23** We go to Harold Byrnes' concert here.   **28** Bob arrives.   **31** Terrible heat. To *Don Giovanni*[5] with Edel and Nini.

November

6 Bob flies to New York. I went to the airfield three times.   **8** Igor and I go to a beautiful concert of Medieval and Renaissance music.   **9** Read to Igor.   **11** Concert at Wilshire Ebell: Medieval music.   **20** Edel here for dinner. Igor plays the *Rake's Progress* for him. I send a wire to Bob.   **21** Bob conducts *Perséphone* in New York.   **22**[6] Worried—no news from Bob, no phone call, no wire. Igor dines at Nini's.   **24** Igor and Soulima go to Benjamin Britten's concert and Zizi[7] is left with me.   **25** A letter from Bob, at last. Igor goes to the Ballet Nègre with Edel.   **26** Walk on Mulholland. Igor to Byrnes' rehearsal. Zizi with me again.   **27** Byrnes' concert (Mass).   **30** Benjamin Britten visits us. Walk on Mulholland. Igor and I go to Britten's concert at UCLA.

---

[1] This was the first meeting between the Stravinskys and Isherwood.

[2] Ernst Krenek made a speech.

[3] Lourié was to be artistic director for Renoir's film on Rumer Godden's *The River*.

[4] Tamara Toumanova, the dancer.

[5] Performed by the San Francisco Opera in the Shrine Auditorium.

[6] On this date Auden wrote to Kallman: "Last night I had to put on tails and recite at Carnegie Hall in the midst of a Stravinsky program. *Pulcinella* (better than I thought though too long) and *Perséphone* which is very remarkable. Some of the Princeton choir who took part were very fetching. It conflicted with opening night at the Met, *Rosenkavalier* . . .''

[7] John Stravinsky, Soulima's son (b. 1945).

[8] In the Stravinsky home. An hour before this, as it proved, unhappy event, Miss Munson wept on Mrs. Stravinsky's shoulder, saying that she did not love Berman. He was well aware of this, but she inspired him as an artist; the only portraits that he ever attempted were of her. She had agreed to marry him, in a fit of depression after being passed over by Joshua Logan to play the female lead in

December

6 Igor in church for the rehearsal of the Mass.   **9** Igor goes with Grau to see Britten's *Albert Herring*. I stay home.   **10** Bob conducts *Mavra* in New York.   **13** We go to Sapiro's to sign our wills.   **15** Igor has an x-ray.   **16** Igor has a duodenal ulcer. Bad mood because of strict diet: only milk for two days.

January

3 Bob has pleurisy.   **24** To the Huxleys at 5.   **25** With Bob to Ojai.   **27** Berman marries Ona Munson.[8]

February

5 A good-bye party for us: Huxleys, Isherwood, Father McLane.   **6** We leave at four o'clock, eat Russian cutlets in the car, and sleep in the Barbara Worth Hotel in El Centro.   **7** Sandwiches in Tucson at 4:50. Visit the baroque church south of the city. Dinner in Lordsburg, New Mexico. Spend the night in Las Cruces.   **8** At 5:00 p.m. eat good turkey sandwiches in Marfa, Texas. Stay in the St. Charles Hotel, in Del Rio, Texas.[9]   **9** Lunch in San Antonio, dinner in Houston, sleep in Beaumont.   **10** Lunch in Baton Rouge. Stay in La Louisiane, New Orleans. Take the ferry to Gretna.   **11** Lunch in Biloxi, sleep in the Prince Murat Motel in Tallahassee.   **12** Ferry across the bay at St. Petersburg, and stay in the Sarasota Terraces Hotel.   **13** Miami.[10]   **14** Daytona Beach, the Riviera Hotel.   **15** Lunch at the Green Turtle, on US 1, before Jacksonville. Stay in Charleston, dinner at Henri's.[11]   **16** Stay at the Williamsburg Inn.[12]   **17** To Mount Vernon. Stay at the Drake Hotel in Philadelphia, dinner at Bookbinder's.   **18** Arrive at the Lombardy Hotel, New York, at 2:30 p.m.   **21** Igor conducts *Firebird* at the New York City Ballet. Willy Strecker arrives from London.   **22** *Orpheus*.   **23** Willy Strecker at 5. See the ballet, *The Prodigal Son*.   **24** Matinée at Carnegie Hall: Leonard Bernstein's *The Age of Anxiety*. Then to a Marlene Dietrich film at Radio City, and back to Carnegie Hall in the evening for Bach's *St. John Passion*.   **25** Matinée: Jean Giraudoux's *The Enchanted*.   **26** Lunch at the Auberge. Noel Coward's film, *The Astonished Heart*. A cocktail party at Sylvia Marlowe's for Berman. Dinner at Maria's with Nabokov and Bob. At the ballet: *The Age of Anxiety*.   **27** T.S. Eliot's *Cocktail Party* at the Henry Miller Theater, 124 West 43rd Street.   **28** Lunch with Lincoln Kirstein. In the evening to *Gigi* (Colette), with Audrey Hepburn.

March

1 Auden and Igor work together.   **2** Dinner at Lucia Davidova's with Cecil Beaton, Robert Sandbach, Berman, Natasha, Bob, then to the ballet.   **3** At 11 a.m. to the Metropolitan Museum, with Berman and Bob, to see the Viennese loan collection, then lunch with them at Maria's. Strecker and Igor together, 5–6. Ballet in the evening.   **4** We go to the Cloisters.[13]

Picnic. Berman asked the Reverend McLane to perform the ceremony, then decided to have a rabbi, and, finally, a judge—brought to the Stravinsky home by Aaron Sapiro. R.C. was Berman's best man.

[9] The hotel was a brothel, with peep holes in the doors, but the Stravinskys arrived at midnight and no other accomodation was available. In the absence of a porter, they and R.C. were obliged to carry their bags to their rooms.

[10] Discovering that personal checks were not accepted in hotels and restaurants, Stravinsky visited the John Alden Carpenters in Sarasota and borrowed money from them. Stravinsky also visited the Ringling Brothers Circus grounds: nine years earlier he had sent the manuscript of his *Circus Polka* here. The Stravinskys then drove to Key West, but were unable to find rooms there and had to return to Miami.

[11] Mrs. Stravinsky had been there exactly ten years before with Georgette Bailey.

[12] On this date Theodore Stravinsky wrote to his father announcing the sale of the manuscript score of the Octet to Werner Reinhart for 6000 Swiss francs. The composer gave the money to his son but was very annoyed with Reinhart for having refused to pay 7000 francs.

[13] On the day of her husband's death, Mrs. Stravinsky asked R.C. to take her there.

106 1948. 1260 North Wetherly Drive.

107 1949. 1260 North Wetherly Drive.

107

108 1949. 1260 North Wetherly Drive.

109 July 1950. Aspen, Colorado. In a circus tent. Stravinsky wore the same blue jeans and sandals for the first of his two Aspen concerts, a railroad strike having delayed the arrival of his concert and other clothes.

7[1] Lunch with Marino Marini. Later Stark Young (proposal to Igor for music).   **9** At the ballet: *Jones Beach*, good music by Andriessen.   **10** Kirstein comes, and Balanchine to say good-bye.[2]   **13** To Shaw's *Caesar and Cleopatra* at the National Theater.   **14** Lunch with Kirstein at Maria's. To the Frick Museum.   **17** Kirstein at 3, Auden at 4.   **18** Leave by train for Urbana (Chicago).   **21** Igor's concert at Urbana.   **22** St. Louis. Igor's concert.   **23** Leave for New York.   **25** Lunch at one with Walter Paepke (Aspen). Dinner with Poulenc.   **27** Lunch with Carlos Chavez. At night to the Morosco Theater: *As You Like It* with Katharine Hepburn.   **28** 5–7: a cocktail party at Claire Booth Luce's,[3] at 8:30 to Carnegie Hall to hear Virgil Thomson's Cello Concerto[4]—in a box with Poulenc.   **29** Huntington Hartford comes at 5.[5] At 8:30 we go to *The Beggar's Opera* at Juilliard (terrible).   **31** Igor records his Concerto with Nini, RCA Studio 2, 155 East 24th Street.

April

1 Igor records *Apollo* for RCA, 1 to 4.   **4** Party at Hurok's for the Artur Rubinsteins.   **5** Igor records at 7.   **13** Dinner at Stark Young's.   **17** Aaron Copland for lunch.   **19** Dinner party at Nabokov's.   **22** The Soulimas leave for France on the *Queen Mary*.   **23** Spend the evening at Arthur Berger's.   **24** Marino Marini works at his sculpture of Igor's head.   **25** Copland for lunch.   **27** We go to Matthew Huxley's wedding.[6] Dinner at Lucia Davidova's.   **28** Clare Luce.   **29** Visit from Claudio Spies.   **30** To a reception for the newlywed Huxleys.[7]

May

16 Stay in Monterey.[8]   **17** 6 p.m.: Arrival in Los Angeles.

June

18 Igor's birthday: 28 people come.   **24** Bob and Igor to lunch at Isherwood's.   **28** Françoise and Zizi for lunch.[9]

July

1 To the Biltmore Theater: Shaw's *Getting Married*.   **25** We leave for Aspen by car at 4:30 and stay in Salinas.   **26** Stay in a motel in Oregon at 5 in the morning [July 27].   **27** Portland, Olympia.   **28** Coeur d'Aline, Idaho.   **31** Aspen.

August

2 4 p.m. Igor's first Aspen concert. He conducts in blue jeans.[10]   **3** With Babin and Vronsky in two cars through Independence Pass to Taos, the Sage Brush Inn.[11]   **4** Visits to Frieda Lawrence and Mabel Dodge. To the San Domingo Pueblo, Santa Fe.[12]   **5** Visit to Witter Bynner's at 6. He gives us objects from his jade collection. Dinner in Los Alamos at the home of Cady Wells.   **6** Leave for Aspen after lunch, via Mesa Verde. Stay in Cortez, three of us in a small room. Bob collapses.   **7** Arrive in Aspen at 7 p.m.   **8** Igor's second Aspen concert.   **9** Leave for Los Angeles.   **10** Las Vegas.[13]   **20** (Sunday) To a benefit concert in Artur Rubinstein's garden.[14]

September

7 Automobile trip with Bob and the Marions. First night: Santa Rosa.   **8** Oregon coast. Second night: Gold Beach.   **9** Third night: Olympia.   **10** Fourth night: Columbia River.   **11** Crater Lake. Fifth night: Stockton.   **12** Home at 6:30. Learn of the death of Ralph Hawkes.   **13** Dinner with Milhaud at the Deauville.   **15** A party here for the Dahls and the Leon Kirchners.   **22** Last dinner with Mirandi and Bob Davidson at Deauville.   **24** Bob flew to New York.[15]   **27** Dinner at the Renoirs'.

October

3 Dinner at Alma Mahler's.   **9** Visit from the Babins.   **10** Igor and I see Menotti's *Medium* and *The Telephone*.

1951

February

4 Dinner at Alma Mahler-Werfel's.   **5** Evenings on the Roof. With Bob to Babitz's party.   **18** Visit from Carl Ebert.[16] To the Huxleys to see a film, on the Mayans, in their living room.   **20** Leave Hollywood in the car at 11 o'clock, lunch at the entrance to Twenty-Nine Palms, Indio at 2:45, Salome at 6:30, Wickenberg (Crestview Motel) at 7:30.   **21** Leave Wickenberg at 9:20. Demming (New Mexico). Stay at the Cortes Hotel (bad) in El Paso.   **22** Lunch near Carlsbad Caverns (Caverna Hotel—very good), and stay in the Rogers Motel (bad and dirty) in Breckenridge, Texas.   **23** Lunch at 1:15 in Dallas. Stay in Shreveport. Dinner there in the Mirror Steak House (very good).   **24** Lunch in Natchez. Mobile. Eat at Constantine's Old Spanish Fort.   **25** Pensacola at 10:45. Marianna, Lake City, Stark, St. Augustine (Travel Lodge—good but noisy). Dinner at the Neptune. No liquor on Sunday.   **26** Lunch at the Lafayette Grill in Daytona. Stay in Fort Lauderdale.   **27** Spend the whole day in Pompano Beach, Astor Motel on Highway 1. Lunch in Del Ray Patio.   **28** Fly to Havana.

March

6 Miami at noon.[17] Del Ray Patio at 2:45, Daytona at 8, stay in the Osceola Hotel.   **7** Daytona, Lake City, White Springs (bad lunch), Macon (stay in Magnolia Court).   **8** Chattanooga, Laurenceburg (dreadful dinner). Slept in a dreadful motel 14 miles from Bolivar.   **9** Memphis. Lunch in Little Rock. Stay in the Velda Rose Motel (de luxe) in Hot Springs.   **10** Lunch in Fort Smith. Webbes Falls. Bungalow Courts (nice).   **11** Elk City, Amarillo, Shamrock, Tucumcari, Santa Rosa, reaching Santa Fe (La Fonda) at 4. Miranda has a party.   **12** Gallup. Flagstaff.   **13** Williams, Kingman, Barstow, home.   **21** Nabokov arrives at 4 a.m., by plane.   **25** Drive Nabokov to Inglewood airport.   **30** With Edel to the Biltmore: *Don Juan in Hell* with Laughton, Boyer, Cedric Hardwicke, Agnes Moorehead.

April

16 Adia Bolm died in his sleep. Beata with us the whole week.   **24** Drive to San Diego with Huxleys.   **25** Stay at Escondido (Felicitas Motel) with Huxleys.

---

[1] On this date Auden wrote to Kallman: "Went through the libretto of Act III with Stravigor the other day. No changes wanted yet. The only thing I had to add was the exact figures for the bidding in the Auctioneer's song."

[2] He was leaving for Europe.

[3] She wanted Stravinsky to compose incidental music for a play of hers about St. Francis.

[4] The Philadelphia Orchestra, conducted by Ormandy.

[5] The A & P heir was momentarily interested in producing *The Rake's Progress* in New York.

[6] To the daughter of Brian Hovde, Director of The New School.

[7] The Stravinskys met Truman Capote and Audrey Hepburn at this party in Aldous Huxley's hotel rooms.

[8] The Stravinskys and R.C. drove from New York to Los Angeles by way of the Dakota Badlands, Yellowstone Park, and San Francisco.

[9] The Soulima Stravinskys, after a short vacation in France, again spent the summer at the Music Academy of the West. Olga Sallard wrote to Vera, November 26, 1950: "It seems that Françoise was peeved because Zizi did not become a

favorite of yours and your husband's."

[10] Stravinsky's concert clothes had been sent from Los Angeles but a railroad strike prevented them from arriving until his second Aspen concert (August 8).

[11] The Stravinskys met Mirandi Masacco (later Levy) in Taos; she became one of their closest friends.

[12] The corn dance was being celebrated in the Pueblo. The Stravinskys stayed with the Babins in Santa Fe, and dined with them and Dr. Eric and Suzette Hausner.

[13] In October 1983, when an interviewer for a University of Nevada newspaper asked R.C. a question about the Stravinskys and Nevada, he did not mention this visit, which had slipped his memory.

[14] For Harold Byrnes' Los Angeles Chamber Orchestra.

[15] R.C. conducted a concert (*Pierrot Lunaire* and Schoenberg's Septet Suite) in Town Hall, October 21.

[16] The stage director. Stravinsky had chosen him to stage *The Rake's Progress* in Venice.

[17] The Stravinskys were in Havana from February 28 to March 6. Stravinsky conducted two concerts there.

May[1]

5 Visit from Willy Strecker.

June

18 Igor's birthday. Picnic in Griffith Park. Dinner in Santa Ynez.
23 Dinner at Huxleys'. **25** Farmers' Market lunch with Bob and Huxleys. **27** [On this date Mrs. Stravinsky wrote to her stepmother, Irina Emilovna Mella, in Buenos Aires: "I am happy about the trip to Venice, although I would like to be a tourist, walk in the streets of my favourite Italian cities, go to museums, take sidetrips, see people. This will be a time of hard work for my husband: two rehearsals every day and all sorts of obligations. Friends and relatives will come to Venice, and I will have to be with them. . . . My husband does not want to go to Paris. So many of his friends, as well as three members of his family, died there. In November, we will return to New York, where I hope to stay at least a month. I love the exciting life of New York, so different from Hollywood, of which I am sick. All of our Hollywood friends are leaving, either for New York or Europe. Hollywood was very lively and interesting during the war, but not now. Also, our house became much too small for us, but my husband is very conservative; having lived in it for 10 years, he does not want to move. The distances here are great, so to go to the market or the hairdresser or a dressmaker I must drive for miles, whereas in New York everything is around the corner. At the moment, getting ready for the trip, I have a lot to do in order to leave the house in good shape, and I must also make myself a new wardrobe. Being accustomed to the California habit of walking around half dressed, I cannot stand hats, gloves, and long sleeves any more."]

July

1 Go to Father McLane's to see his new Balthus (*Georgette*). **11** For dinner at our house, the Italian Consul Ungaro, Huxley, Professor Passinetti, Catherine d'Erlanger. **13** Dinner with Renoirs. **16** Dinner at Huxleys' with Hubble, Christopher, Gerald Heard. **19** Dinner at Alma Mahler's.

August

7 Leave New York for Naples on the S.S. *Constitution*.[2]

October

15 Baden-Baden. Write to the Marions: "Yesterday's concert here was a great success. We will stay here two more days to rest. What a charming place, a real spa, marvelous air, surrounded by forests in autumn colors. The hotel is marvelously quiet, the restaurant first class. Naturally, Papa has had to go to the doctor every day, having lost his voice as a result of the cold he had in Cologne. No matter how prudent he is, avoiding

drafts, eating carefully, receiving vitamin shots, he is constantly catching something. At this very moment he is coughing and afraid that he has bronchitis. We will be in Munich until the 23rd, then Geneva. . . . Papa finally received a letter from Reinrich (Venice) saying that he knows nothing about the $13,500, that someone has used his name, and that he wants the number and date of the check. What a strange story."
31 Geneva. Hotel des Bergues. Write to the Marions: "*Mes chers*, I envy you. You are at home, you can rest, and you can see your friends and tell them about beautiful Venice. But we have twenty more days and perhaps a little longer. Nor will the airplane trip be restful. Papa is better, but his temperature is 37.2 or 37.3 nearly every day, which is not normal. He will go to see Dr. Gilbert,[3] who will probably tell him that he is still suffering from the after-effects of the flu that he had in Germany.

"We met the doctor at Theodore's, and yesterday this very nice man took us for a ride in his car to Gruyère and to Fribourg. . . . This week we will go to dinner at Ansermet's. He came to the hotel the day of our arrival to welcome us; our relations are now smooth.

"Papa cancelled the concert in Lausanne on the pretext of his health, but Desarzens[4] and the people there are furious. We are going to Lausanne for another reason, however: to see Aunt Vera[5] and Lyulya.[6] Papa is furious because it seems impossible to avoid this visit. We are leaving here the day after the concert, and will be in Rome (Hotel Hassler) on the 6th, where Papa has two rehearsals the same day and a concert the day after. Victoria Ocampo has just arrived in Rome, so we will see her there."

November

23 I write to the Marions: "*Mes chers*, We arrived in New York yesterday noon. The flight was marvelous—if only Papa had been less afraid, also Bob—and so much more convenient than those terrible ships and trains. We ate superbly (a dinner from Maxim's) and the women received Lanvin perfumes and orchid corsages. The landscape and views are extraordinarily beautiful, especially of London, completely unexpected with the green, orange, and blue lights, a veritable jewel.

"We stopped first in Paris, where Arthur Sachs came to see us and was as kind as always, bringing gifts. At Shannon, the second stop, we were delayed three hours because of a repair on one of the motors. (Papa was really frightened about that.) Then 14 hours over the Atlantic to Boston, where we lost another hour, and in 50 minutes we were in New York. Auden, Isherwood, Haieff, and Betty Bean met us at the airport, with her car. We went to lunch at the Lombardy, where everything has suddenly become expensive to the extent that within an hour we moved to the Gladstone Hotel, 114 E. 52nd Street, where we have a smaller and not at all modern suite. The Lombardy had been "modernized"—in a horrible style of thirty years ago, of course—and was not at all comfortable.

"The very same afternoon Papa went to a ballet rehearsal. He conducts *Le Baiser de la fée* at the ballet this Sunday. Poor Papa, he is still upside down from the airplane trip, and already he must work. I began to unpack, but now I am waiting for Alexis Haieff, who is coming to help me carry the many flowers that I have received."

---

[1] On May 27 Theodore Stravinsky wrote to his father trying to dissuade him from choosing Balthus to make the decors for the Venice *Rake's Progress*, mentioning the "Freudian elements" in the painter's work.

[2] At this point a gap of seven weeks occurs in Vera Stravinsky's diary. On August 21, Auden wrote to a friend from Naples: "Il Maestro arrived last week, thinking he had pneumonia. . . . Seats for the premiere are being sold on the black market at 180 dollars. September 3 we move on to Venice. On the 8th there is to be a Ball given by a Chilean millionaire to end all balls. We have not yet been invited, but it is rumored that we will. The Windsors are to be there and the Aga Khan, and food will be specially flown in from Paris." On August 23, the Baroness d'Erlanger wrote to Mrs. Stravinsky in Milan: "Yesterday evening Iris Tree [niece of Max Beerbohm] gave a reading of *King Lear* to her friends in my garden. They were seated around the swimming pool. Suddenly I was interrupted by a radio announcing that Igor was sick. I think all the time about you. No one had any information. Finally, this morning, I knew via Huxley . . . that you also had bronchitis. . . . I want to believe and hope that all is better with you both and I await your news with impatience. And Robert, I shall write to Venice." Stravinsky had pneumonia, three days out of New York on the voyage to Naples. Always hypersensitive to air-conditioning, he believed that the drafts in his stateroom on the *Constitution* were the cause of his illness. On arrival in Naples he was confined to bed. When his Milan rehearsals of *The Rake's Progress* were postponed, the press picked up the story. "Robert" was Robert Rounseville, operetta tenor, a protégé of Catherine d'Erlanger's. When no other singer had been found for the leading role in Stravinsky's opera, she suggested him. Stravinsky saw and heard him in a film of *The Tales of Hoffmann* and liked his

voice, but Rounseville did not have time to learn the long part and he was not a match vocally, or in any other way, for Elizabeth Schwarzkopf. On September 9, Auden wrote to a friend: "The music is quite terrific—one lovely tune after another. . . . One rehearsal Tourel missed her cue and [Stravinsky] went on for sixty bars without realizing that she wasn't singing. . . . If we get through the performance without disaster it will be a miracle. But it really *is* a masterpiece." On October 2, Maria Huxley wrote to the Stravinskys in the Hotel Excelsior in Cologne: "Bob's letter came this morning and we are relieved to know that your health is restored. . . . We are unhappy not to have been present at the Venetian ovation, but you were surrounded by so many old friends that perhaps we would have been a little jealous. . . . I recommend the Hotel Flora in Rome: the rooms are much larger than those in the Hassler. . . . I see Madubo frequently; she is completely lost without you . . ."

[3] Dr. Maurice Gilbert. Years later, Stravinsky gave him the manuscript score of Duo concertant in payment for medical service to Catherine Mandelstamm and Theodore and Denise Stravinsky.

[4] Victor Desarzens, conductor of the Lausanne Radio Orchestra.

[5] Dr. Vera Dmitrievna Nossenko had supervised the medical care of Stravinsky's granddaughter Catherine Mandelstamm in Leysin from 1939 to 1946.

[6] Olga ("Lyulya") Dmitrievna Nossenko Schwarz (1872–1953), a cousin of Stravinsky's; she is mentioned in his letters to his parents in the summer of 1900.

110 September 1951. La Scala, Milan.

111 September 1, 1951. La Scala, Milan. With W.H. Auden and Chester Kallman at a rehearsal of *The Rake's Progress*.

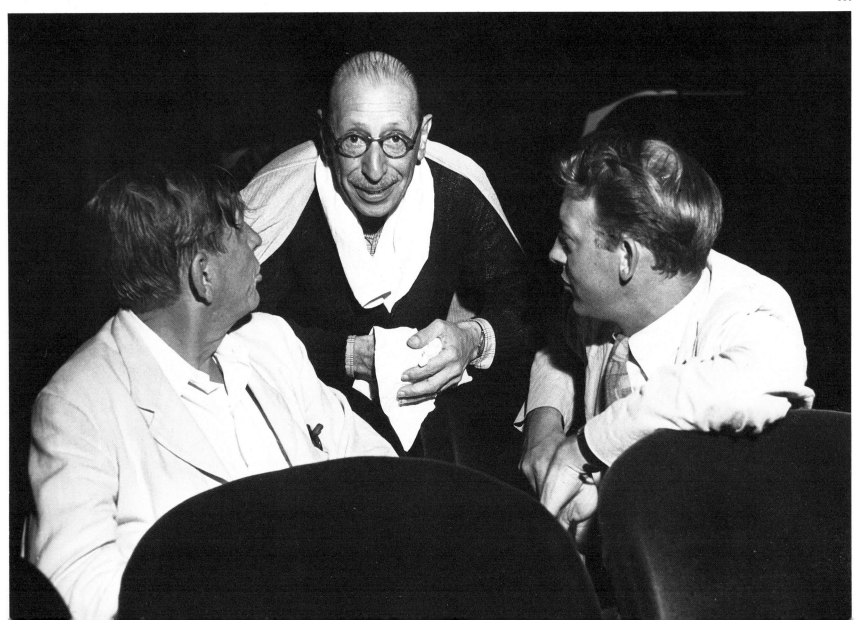

112 September 5, 1951. Arriving in Venice from Milan.

113 September 12, 1951. City Hall, Venice. The poet Eugenio Montale described this occasion as follows: "We crowd around the Mayor, who gives a well-received speech in which the names of Aeschylus, Hugo, and Arrigo Boito are intoned. Stravinsky, seated, received and thanked. He bows like a Russian in a sort of swan dive. I had the opportunity to exchange a few words with him and was not surprised to find him so simple and humanly solitary. Fame, Hollywood, and dollars have left untouched his essential nature of a little *barin* who is afraid of the Devil and would like all of life to be a beautiful opera closer to Tchaikovsky than to Wagner."

112

114 October 1951. Munich. Behind Stravinsky, in the leather coat, is Carl Orff.

December

8[1] I write to the Marions: "*Mes chers*, We are still here because of our baggage.[2] It is not lost, but God knows when we will have it, perhaps tomorrow, perhaps in a month. I went to the American Export Lines and took every possible step, but thus far without results. A moment ago I had a telephone call, from which I learned that the bags left Halifax November 28 and that we should have them by December 20, possibly a little sooner. . . . Our hectic life continues with dinners, lunches, theaters, and concerts everyday. To resist a Scotch and a cigarette at such times is very hard. Papa did not resist, and the doctor put him on a strict diet. Since then, life has become absolutely terrible.

"Bob is sometimes in New York, sometimes in Kingston. He is sad because his parents will sell the house in which he lived all his life. He cancelled his two New York concerts and will come to Hollywood with us.

"We lunched with Karinska in her beautiful apartment, which has large rooms, is very comfortable, and is full of works of art. The food was superb, and the apartment was so much to Papa's taste that he did not want to leave. She could arrange the rooms in her own way, however, only because she owns the entire building. This woman is really extraordinary. After years and years of misery (I have known her for 35 years), she has now attained this luxury entirely as a result of her own efforts.

"We have seen many ballets, including *Swan Lake*, Ravel's—and Balanchine's and Karinska's— *La Valse*, and *Tyl Eulenspiegel*. We often go to the Metropolitan Opera, always in Bing's[3] loge; this is much less amusing. We see friends and we have been to the country two Sundays in a row.[4] This Sunday we will be with the two pianists[5] who live not far from the Washington Bridge, in the house that they rented from Aaron Copland. The Sunday after that, we will go to the Connecticut home of Fritz Reiner, who, if everything works out, will conduct the *Rake* at the Met. We saw Christopher Isherwood's play.[6] The first act was very good, the last two much less so, but the success was enormous. From time to time we see Auden and other 'intellectuals.'"

January

1 Arrival at Pasadena. Our house is clean and smiling with welcome. We are all happy. How long will it last?   **7** I start work on my commission and trace the whole picture.[7]   **10** Fred for dinner, with Renée de Veyrac.   **11** Flowers for Bob's mother.[8]   **12** Igor's rehearsal at Royce Hall, 10 to 12:30. Maria Huxley had an operation this morning that was kept a secret from everyone. Aldous here for lunch, then we take him to the hospital. Igor's second rehearsal 7 to 9:30 p.m., then a late dinner in Melody Lane.   **13** (Sunday) Igor's rehearsal 10 to 12:30. Aldous for lunch.   **15** Terrible rainstorm. Igor's concert. With Aldous afterward to a party for Igor at Alma Mahler's.   **20** Aldous for tea.   **25** We go to a Los Angeles Philharmonic concert at 2:15 (Berlioz).[9]   **26** Goddard Lieberson for lunch.   **27** Dinner at Ludovic Kennedy's[10] with Moira Shearer, Frederick Ashton, Aldous, Frieda Lawrence, Angie Ravagli.

February

6 To Huxley's at 6:30 to see Frieda Lawrence and Angie.   **23** With the

---

[1] The Baroness d'Erlanger had written to Mrs. Stravinsky on December 3: "What joy to hear from you that you are 'nearly' home: our hill is so sad without you. . . . The Deauville, now all rose colored, is doing very well. . . . Be careful of the cold in New York. Here the orange trees are blossoming."

[2] When the Stravinskys decided to fly from Rome to New York, they sent their baggage by boat. Because of a longshoreman's strike in the United States, the bags were eventually unloaded in Nova Scotia and forwarded by train.

[3] Rudolph Bing, then general manager of the Metropolitan Opera, had signed a contract to present *The Rake's Progress* in the 1953 and 1954 seasons. His wife, Nina Schelemskaya-Schelesnaya Bing, a former ballet dancer, had been a friend of Vera's in Moscow before the Revolution.

[4] One of these excursions was to Stark Young's in Waccabuc. Young wrote to Stravinsky afterward: "When you spoke of [Horace] Armistead and the scenery [for the *Rake*] I could not bring any image to mind of a setting of his. Then I remembered it for Menotti's *The Consul*. There the play indicated a chance for a very effective setting. But Mr. Armistead missed it very badly. This of course does not mean that he would do it every time or often. Just the same, I wanted to tell you, so that you could keep a sharp eye on what he does. . . ."

Huxleys to the Huntington Museum in Pasadena to see the Turner show and the gardens. Tea at the Hubbles'.   **24** Bob's concert at USC.[11]   **28** Party at Frieda Lawrence's with Dudley Nichols [screenwriter] and Richard Tregaskis.[12]

March

5 Go to the Huxleys' good-bye party for Frieda.   **8** Lunch at Palmdale. Snow in the desert.   **10** To the Evenings on the Roof concert: Suzanne Bloch, lute.   **11** To Carlos Chavez's concert.   **12** Dinner here for the Vincents and Chavez.   **22** Take Igor and Marion to the Inglewood airport at 1:45. They are staying in the Hotel Del Prado, Mexico City.

Vera to Igor

Mr. Igor Stravinsky   1260 North Wetherly Dr.
Hotel Del Prado   Hollywood 46
Mexico City
Mexico   March 25, 1952

My dear Bubushkinsky, How do you manage at that height and without me? We saw you clearly between two windows of the airplane, as you were putting drops in your nose. All day yesterday we were expecting a telegram. Milene was very worried. Then she telephoned me at eleven in the evening at the McLanes', where Bob and I had dinner, to say that your flight was four·hours late, which often happens when one has to change planes. As for us, we had a very pleasant time, as always. Brainerd was not there, but in Denver, where his mother died.

A letter came today from Paris with sad news: Desormière[13] had a stroke, in Rome, and is paralyzed. He suffers terribly. He can use his hands and legs but is unable to talk. How terrible, the more so in that he has no money.

The Huxleys are back. I talked to Maria on the telephone but have not seen her yet. Today I drove Milene, Madubo, and Evgenia Petrovna to see the flower show, which is very large but not impressive, since it is in an enclosed space and has artificial lighting. I worked a lot in the last two days and will have some "*chef d'oeuvres*" to show you. It is always a great pleasure to show you the results of my efforts after days or weeks of work.

Don't be lazy; send me a postcard at least. I am interested to know how you found all of our old friends. I kiss you tenderly. My best to Andre. God bless you. Work well and keep well. Your Vera.

Igor to Vera

Vera Stravinsky   Hotel Del Prado
1260 North Wetherly Drive   Mexico City
Hollywood 46   March 27, 1952

Dearest Vera, I was very happy to have your few lines. Now it is 12:15, past midnight Wednesday, or, more precisely, Thursday.

---

[5] Arthur Gold and Robert Fizdale.

[6] *I Am a Camera* with Julie Harris.

[7] The Baroness d'Erlanger had asked Mrs. Stravinsky to copy an 18th-century Venetian carnival scene, featuring a pyramid of acrobats (standing on each other's shoulders on five levels). In circuses throughout the world, tiers of acrobats standing on each others' shoulders are known as the Zorros' act.

[8] She was in hospital for a serious operation.

[9] *Romeo and Juliet*, conducted by Alfred Wallenstein.

[10] The Kennedys had rented Marion Davies' Santa Monica beach house.

[11] Schoenberg's Septet-Suite Op. 29 and Webern's Quartet Op. 22.

[12] Author of *Guadalcanal Diary*.

[13] Roger Desormière, conductor of the Diaghilev Ballets Russes in the late 1920s, was in his early forties. He died soon after. See the Nabokov chapter in *Stravinsky: Selected Correspondence*, Vol. II, op. cit.

We have just returned from dinner at the Villaseñors'. His young wife, the ex-love of Chavez, sends you greetings—like everyone else—and is sorry that you did not come along. All of our friends are just the same, but the Bal y Gays have aged noticeably: she has become much whiter and her smile is older. Salazar, too, is so much older that he seems to have shrivelled.

Yesterday I went to Guadalupe with Andre. It was windy, hot, and dusty. As before, there were tremendous fair-like crowds in the churches and a long queue waiting to enter them. The shrine of the Virgin was lighted by millions of candles. I was very tired and had palpitations because of the altitude, to which I cannot become accustomed, so we returned to the hotel.

Today in a studio outside the city we saw two very good Buñuel films, one of them with music by Pittaluga. The first one reminded me of *Bicycle Thief*, the second (Pittaluga's) is very well directed, has some good dancing, and is gay and successful, but was less enthusiastically received in Europe than the other film.

I must stop now but will continue tomorrow. Andre received a letter from Milene.

Thursday, 7 p.m. I went to bed but did not sleep all night, and in the morning I had a tiring rehearsal with a very mediocre orchestra from which, as in Cuba, it is impossible to extract any sense. After that unpleasant experience, I went directly to the Prietos' for lunch with the Villaseñors, Raoul Fournier and his wife, the Minister of Culture and his wife, Bal y Gay without his wife, Salazar, and the very old mother of Mme Prieto and her sister.

I went with Andre to buy sweaters but found only one—for me.

In the evening we went to dinner with Pittaluga at La Rue's (recommended by English[1]). Here at the hotel the food is bad and the atmosphere dreary. Nice, crazy Edward James[2] came to the rehearsal. He brought me an XVIIIth-century Santo.

Now I'll lie down for half an hour, then dress for dinner. We'll go to bed early. The last rehearsal is tomorrow at 10:30 and the concert is at 9 p.m. I doubt that I'll have time to write tomorrow. Besides, my letter would not get there before we arrive on Sunday evening at 9. I embrace you. Your Igor.

The Mexican spring is hot, with no air stirring, and very tiring. Huge crowds are everywhere, but thanks to Prieto's car, we are able to manage. Even at 4 o'clock in the morning, when we arrived, the car was waiting for us.

On Monday I was exhausted from the lack of oxygen, but I am bearing up.

P.S. Poor Desormière. What horror!

[March diary continued]

30 Meet Igor's Pan American flight at Inglewood at 9:40 p.m.

April

6 Bob and Andre finish the translation.[3]   **8** Start to move furniture to the

Baroness's house.[4]   **14** Bob's concert. Guests at our house afterward.
23 We fly to New York from Inglewood at 9:30 a.m., American Airlines. California and Arizona from the air: beautiful Klees, Kandinskys, Mondrians, Dubuffets; nature imitates art. Stop at Dallas: storm afterward.   **28** TWA to Paris at 5 p.m. Stop in Gander and chat there with Charles Munch. Very tiring without sleepers.   **29** 2:25 p.m.: arrive at Orly. Nabokov meets us with photographers, reporters, etc.[5] Fly to Geneva, arriving at 5:30. We go to a rehearsal of *The Rake*, and to bed at 2 a.m.

May

1 Igor and Bob lunch with Dr. Maurice Gilbert.   **2** The performance of the *Rake*.[6]   **3** Fly to Paris on Swissair at 3:30. Dinner with the Nabokovs. *WOZZECK:* the biggest impression.   **4** Lunch with the Sachses in their marvelous house. Dinner at Marie-Laure de Noailles's with Poulenc, Sauguet, *et al.*   **6** Electric train to Versailles, back by taxi. Dinner at "La Mère Catherine" in Montmartre with Sachses, Phyllis,[7] Bob.   **7** Olga Sallard arrives. Lunch at the Trémouille. At 5 to a concert in the small Théâtre des Champs-Elysées. Messiaen and Boulez play something by Boulez, a girl hisses and a man jumps over three rows and slaps her, after which the police take him away.   **14** Igor's *Orpheus* by the New York City Ballet. Party at Sachses' afterward.   **19** *Oedipus Rex* at the Théâtre des Champs-Elysées. Party at Hervé Dugardin's.   **22** Igor's concert.

June

16 Taxi from Detroit to Flint at 9 a.m.: a line of people waiting for their cars.[8] Leave Flint at 3:35. Spend the night at the Holiday Motel (excellent) 126 miles north in Michigan.   **17** Leave at 8:30 a.m. Ferry across the straits (Mackinaw). Lunch (whitefish) at Fisher's Epoupette. Evening dinner (rather bad) at Mertens, Iron River.   **18** Leave at 8:45. Igor's birthday lunch (iced red Beaujolais!) in Duluth at The Flame. Bob invites. Spend the night (bad) in Bemidji.   **19** Night at Minot, the Clarence Parker Hotel (excellent).   **20** Lunch in Culbertson, Montana. Stay at the Hotel Havre (noisy). Café Dutch.   **21** Lunch at Browning. Kalispell in the rain. The Morris Motel. Hennessey Steak House (very good).   **22** Leave at 9. The Glacier National Park is most exciting: rain, fog, snow. Lunch in an Indian reservation. The Canadian border, spend the night in Calgary, Hotel Palisser.   **23** Leave at 10. Banff. Lunch at Lake Louise. The night at Radium Hot Springs, after bad roads.   **24** Leave at 7:50 and cross the border, Kingsgate, at noon. Night at the marvelous Caravan Desert Motel in Spokane.   **25** Leave at 8 via 395 to Portland. Dinner and the night at McMinnville (nice).   **26** Lunch at Coquille. Night at Orik.   **27** San Francisco, the Huntington Hotel. Dinner at the Fisherman's Wharf. **28** Lunch at Carmel. Dinner and the night (El Carlos Motel) in San Luis Obispo.   **29** Los Angeles at 1 p.m. Gasoline for the whole trip: $110.95.

July

25 Dinner at the Huxleys'.

August

7 Bob at a rehearsal. The Huxleys after dinner. Igor feels badly.
10 (Sunday) To Gerald Heard's lecture: extra-sensory perception,

---

[1] Harold English was a friend of the Stravinskys' in Hollywood. In 1959 the daughter of English's wife's sister, Arminie Montapert, became one of the Stravinskys' lawyers. See the essay "Cher Père, Chère Véra," in *Present Perspectives*, op. cit.

[2] Edward James (1907–1984), illegitimate son of King Edward VII and proprietor of the 6000-acre West Dean estate near Chichester, in Sussex. James had financed Balanchine's Ballet Trente-Trois, commissioned the *Seven Deadly Sins* from Brecht and Weill, and acquired the largest collection of Magritte and Dali in the world. James was a disciple of Gerald Heard in Los Angeles. He died in his home in San Remo, the location of John Huston's film *Beat the Devil*. Huston's *Treasure of the Sierra Madre* was filmed on James's finca in Mexico. The problem of his royal illegitimacy was solved by his being named godson. James's mother, a renowned beauty, was hostess of Marlborough House. See *Stravinsky: Selected Correspondence*, Vol. I, op. cit.

[3] Of Theodore Stravinsky's *Le Message d'Igor Stravinsky*.

[4] Actually to the Baroness's guest house, which became R.C.'s residence in Hollywood until September 1969.

[5] For the festival, the Arts of the Twentieth Century, of which Nabokov was the director, and to which Stravinsky would return on May 3, after hearing *The Rake's Progress* in Geneva.

[6] A collection was taken up in the audience to help pay the costs. The sets and costumes were by Theodore Stravinsky.

[7] Mrs. Phyllis Crawford, sister of R.C.

[8] The Stravinskys had traded in their Buick in Los Angeles for a new car to be picked up at the factory. Alexis Haieff flew from New York to Detroit and rode to Los Angeles with them. The blank pages for the end of May and the first half of June can be attributed to the increased activity during this period in Belgium and Holland.

115 May 1952. Paris.

116

116 June 1952. Amsterdam. With Lord and Lady Harewood (née Marion Stein, daughter of Schoenberg's pupil, Erwin Stein, Stravinsky's editor at Boosey & Hawkes) and Mr. and Mrs. Peter Diamond.

117 November 1952. 1260 North Wetherly Drive. Inscribed by Stravinsky the following year.

1953

parapsychology. *Paideia*[1] (Greek for "culture"). **12** To Hollywood Bowl with Aldous for Igor's concert.[2] Party here for 17. **17** Isherwood and Bill Caskey for dinner.

September

2 Dinner at Alma Mahler's. **3** Aldous for dinner; Maria is again in the hospital. **7** To Isherwood's. **8** Igor and I go to Bob's rehearsal of Schoenberg's Serenade.

December

6 [On this date, Stravinsky and Marion flew from Los Angeles to Cleveland and on December 15 from there to New York, where Mrs. Stravinsky, recuperating from a thyroid operation,[3] joined them, after traveling East by train. The following correspondence dates from this time.]

Vera to Igor
(Original in Russian)

Mr. Igor Stravinsky   December 7, 1952
Wade Park Manor Hotel
Cleveland 6, Ohio

Bubushkin dearest, Why didn't you add in your wire that you had freezing weather? After we saw you off and your plane started, Lourié appeared, running. Milene had told him that the plane was leaving at 9:15 and he understood 9:45. After having said good-bye to Christopher Isherwood and Lourié, Milene, Bob, and I drove to a Los Angeles suburb, a real slum area, to see the Towers. They have been, and still are, being constructed out of broken bottles, sea shells, etc., by a 72-year-old Italian.[4] We watched him continuing to work on them, after thirty years. Some of the towers, 100 feet high, remind me of Barcelona. A few photographs of them are in the December *Harper's Bazaar*. They should be seen in sunshine, but a dense smog covered them when we got there and the bright colors seemed gray.

In the evening we saw the Bali dancers from the first row, where it was interesting to observe the way they move their fingers and their eyes, and to look at the embroidery on their dresses. Milene, who sat far away and did not see the details, thought the performance dull, as did many other people.

It is rainy today. I stayed in bed until lunch, then cleaned up the studio and wrote letters. This evening Catherine invited us to dine at the Deauville—the restaurant's last evening, as it happens, Johnny Walsh[5] having sold it yesterday, quite unexpectedly, for a very good profit.

I had a letter from Denise expressing thanks for the money you sent them. She works a great deal, is very tired, and her letter was in pencil. She says that she went to bed on Saturday at 6 p.m. and woke up on Sunday at the same time. Fedya has many projects, much work, and several pupils.

Our monstrous mailbox[6] has been installed, and now I am waiting for the plumbers. Please do not overtire yourself. Rest a lot, lie down if only for ten minutes at a time, and do not drink too much. I am enclosing two bank statements. How is Andre withstanding the cold? Embrace him for me. I kiss you tenderly. With love, Vera.

Igor to Vera
(Original in Russian)

1260 North Wetherly Drive   Wade Park Manor
Hollywood 46, California   East 107th at Park Lane
                         Cleveland, Ohio
                         December 10, 1952

Verushkinsky dearest, I was happy to have your letter. How interesting that you saw those extraordinary towers by the Italian, Rodia, only you forgot that you yourself showed me the *Harper's Bazaar* article (with photographs) about them, and a similar tower by a Frenchman (not far from Gertrude Stein's home in France).

I spent two days with the Soulimas. All three of them look very *Ladies' Home Journal* in style. Zizi has grown but is still very noisy, running around the rooms and the hotel corridor hunting Indians with revolver in hand. I played cards with him. He learned that from his friends. He uses middle-Western slang, mixing it with many French words. (He thinks that with me, as with his parents, he must use a little French.) His French is full of mistakes, and, in particular he is not able to master the verbs; but he is very amusing. Yesterday they dined here (an hour and a half), then went to the railroad station, where they were allowed to occupy their rooms ahead of time and go to sleep. Both Svetik and Françoise will come to New York at the end of January for the *Rake*.[7]

The rehearsals proceed smoothly enough, but the orchestra, not too bad on the whole, has great difficulty in mastering the almost chamber-music quality of my Symphony [in C]. Evidently Szell does not require from them what I am demanding, but, of course, this is the same everywhere. The singers are mediocre [in *Pulcinella*], the woman not too bad but the two men just average, though they are agreeable and trying very hard. I hope that I will not have to blush over the recording.

In the last two days we have had storms, lightning, fires, firemen, and sirens. And it has been stifling. My nose trouble is subsiding, and so are my heart palpitations. I hope that all of this will right itself. Today was terrible, what with two rehearsals, 10:30 to 12:30 and 2 to 4:30. It is almost seven o'clock now, and we will eat in our suite. Then I will play solitaire and go to bed with a book. Andre heard from Milene that our kittens made a mess in the living room and that you had to clean it up. Not bad!

Sunday night at seven we fly to New York. I hope there might be another letter from you. I embrace you. Your Bubushkinsky.

Vera to Igor
(Original in Russian)

Mr. Igor Stravinsky   1260 North Wetherly Drive
Wade Park Manor   Hollywood 46, California
East 107th at Park Lane   December 10, 1952
Cleveland 6, Ohio

Igor dear, Thank you for the postcard. All is well at home. The pussycat will give birth any moment, I hope before my departure. Varzhinsky [the Stravinskys' gardener] has promised to make a small opening in the kitchen door, and Milene will bring some sawdust to lighten our housekeeper's task. At Renoir's, Bessy takes care of the newly born puppies without grumbling. The

---

[1] The Stravinskys were reading Werner Jaeger's classic.

[2] Stravinsky conducted Tchaikovsky's Second Symphony and Soulima Stravinsky played the *Capriccio*.

[3] On November 17, Stravinsky wrote to Theodore: "I can now give you good news about Vera. She is better and better each day. During the operation, which took four hours, it was difficult to introduce the tube for the anesthetic down the trachea, owing to the considerable hypertrophy of the thyroid. The pain is going away slowly, and in a few days she will be able to leave the hospital. She must rest for at least two weeks."

[4] The Simon Rodia Towers, in Culver City, California, resemble the work of Gaudí. When the City of Los Angeles threatened to demolish them for a building site, Mr. and Mrs. Sol Babitz organized a committee to preserve them, with help from the Stravinskys.

[5] Singer and friend of Catherine d'Erlanger.

[6] Because of the large number of letters that Stravinsky received each day, he installed a mailbox five or six times larger than the standard size.

[7] Since the premiere was broadcast, Stravinsky's son and daughter-in-law did not come.

weather is marvelous here, as in the rest of the country, I expect. Rosenthal[1] picked up the manuscripts. He will be in New York in four days. I am dining today with the Baroness and tomorrow at the McLanes'. I kiss you with all my heart. Best wishes to the rest of the family. Do not get overtired! Your Vera.

I wrote to Dick Hammond and Berman to suggest that we should all lunch together on the 20th, since Dick is leaving for Beverly Hills on the evening of the 20th.

Igor to Vera
(Original in Russian)

1260 North Wetherly Drive Hollywood 46, California	Wade Park Manor East 107th at Park Lane Cleveland 6, Ohio 6 p.m., December 12, 1952

Verusha dearest, My first concert is over. It was very successful, and at the end, after *Pulcinella*, there was an ovation. The orchestral ensemble is not too bad, but the solo woodwind players are far inferior to Bob's Hollywood ones.

Today it is snowing and raining. Two fat envelopes arrived from you, one of them containing your letter. Thank you. Perhaps there will be another one tomorrow. I forgot to pack something very important, my wonderful gloves, double-leather and wool, the ones that we bought in New York. Do you remember? They are in the lower cupboard near my chest of drawers. Evgenia Petrovna knows where, since she put them away, with the woolen shawls. Please bring them.

How are you feeling? Did you already pack most of the things in the black and gray trunk? Are you getting plenty of rest? So, Edward James has not returned, and his trunk will remain for years behind an upholstered chair in our living room?[2] I embrace you. I. Bubushkin.

Vera to Igor
(Original in Russian)

Monsieur Igor Stravinsky Wade Park Manor East 107th at Park Lane Cleveland 6, Ohio	1260 North Wetherly Drive Hollywood, California December 13, 1952

Bubushkin dear, It is terribly hot. Bob went swimming in the pool. Last night we went with Milene to the small theater (Players Ring) where you and I saw *Androcles and the Lion*. We really had a lovely time and laughed a lot— at a very amusing comedy, a satire on the Ballets Russes, *Look Ma! I'm Dancing*. Tonight I am dining with Bob at Huxley's. I have a lot to do before leaving. I cannot ignore Christmas and am sending fruit and flowers to friends—Beata Bolm, Lourié, Babitz, Zeisl. Am in a hurry to get dressed for dinner. I kiss you tenderly. We will see each other soon. Your Vera.

28 A letter from Catherine d'Erlanger: "I miss you so much. I look at the door but you don't come anymore. . . . A heavy packet came for Bob, but his door is closed. The Landsbergs[3] are staying with me, which is very tiring—and I have to go sightseeing! I like my quiet life. I miss Bob's reading."[4]

---

[1] Erwin Rosenthal, manuscript dealer in Berkeley, California.

[2] James was in the habit of leaving the manuscripts of his poems and other writings under chair and sofa cushions in the Stravinsky house, to be retrieved months later, and of hiding paintings and other possessions in closets and calling for them at unexpected times.

[3] Of the Villa Malcontenta, on the Brenta. The Baroness had given them this masterpiece by Palladio.

January

2 Igor, Bob, and I to the ballet. **3** We go to *The Importance of Being Earnest*. **5** Igor's rehearsal in the morning. Cocktail party at Dubrovsky's. Natasha Nabokov for dinner. To the ballet. **6** Igor's rehearsal. **7** Lunch with Auden, Chester, and Bob. To *La Bohème* at the Met in the evening. **11** Balanchine here from 5 to 7. I walk with Bob to the dinner at Lucia Davidova's. **12** Igor at Balanchine's. **13** Igor, Bob, and I at *Euryanthe*[5] at 8:15. **16** Igor and I go to a party at Virgil Thomson's: Nabokov, John Houseman. **19** Lunch with Berman and Sylvia Marlowe. In the evening to see *The Children's Hour*: unpleasant theme, very good cast. **21** We go to *Pal Joey* (marvelous!). **22** Dinner at Weissberger's with his Uncle Pepe[6] and Anita Loos. **23** Cocktails at Zosia Kochanska's (Chavchavadze, Palavicini). **25** To Hindemith's 5 o'clock Town Hall concert; Tourel sings. **26** Igor has the flu.

February

5 Exhibition at Betty Parson's of William Congdon (marvelous). **7** To an exhibition of Lovis Corinth. To *Love's Labor's Lost* in the evening. **10** To the theater: *Dial M for Murder*. **11** Rehearsal of the *Rake* at the Met from 10:30 to 3. **12** Dress rehearsal of the *Rake*. Afterward we go with Balanchine and Lucia to Radio City to see a film about Hurok. **13** I go for the third time to the Congdon exhibition. **14** The premiere of *The Rake's Progress*. **15** Igor goes to Baltimore on the 3:30 train, accompanied by Edward James. **18** Igor's Baltimore concert. **19** Igor returns from Baltimore. We go to the second performance of the *Rake*. **20** To the theater: *The Seven Year Itch*. **21** We go to *Rigoletto* and a dinner after it, at 11:30, with Bob and Berman. **24** Igor has two rehearsals for his Philharmonic concert. **25** To Inge's play, *Picnic*. **26** Igor's first concert with the New York Philharmonic. **27** Igor's second concert.

March

1 Igor's third concert. Igor records the *Rake*. **11** We fly at noon to Hollywood. **23** Igor has the flu again. **25** Bad night for Igor, two doctors, Knauer and Mantchik. **31** At 8 a.m. Bob drives Igor to the airport [for his flight, with his son-in-law, to Havana].

Vera to Igor
(Original in Russian)

Monsieur Igor Stravinsky Hotel Presidente Havana Cuba	1260 North Wetherly Drive Hollywood 46, California April 2, 1953

Christos Voskros! Dear Bubushkin, I am relieved that you arrived safely and that the weather is good. Thank you for the cable. On the day of your departure, after watching your airplane disappear in the fog, I went to buy some flowers, and I have worked in the garden planting them ever since. I called Varzhensky to come, and we have been cutting trees together. When Alfred Wallenstein[7] came to see us the last time, some of his hair was torn out by low branches. Now a lot of them have been cut and the passageway is clear.

I took Evgenia Petrovna to the Farmers' Market, which she had never seen, and she was wild about it. I try not to eat at home in order to give her a rest. Bob and I were invited for lunch yesterday by the Baroness, and today it will be by Edward James.

---

[4] R.C. read to her for two or three hours daily, as a means of earning his living.

[5] A concert performance of Weber's opera in Carnegie Hall.

[6] Pepe Weissberger, a friend of Aldous Huxley's, was an authority on Spanish art.

[7] Conductor of the Los Angeles Philharmonic.

118

119

120

121

163

The Milhauds came to see me yesterday between two lectures—hers in the morning and Darius's in the afternoon. I was very touched. They both look thinner and younger, after dieting for a month. They asked me, Bob, and Milene to lunch with them on Sunday: Madeleine will cook.

I kiss you tenderly. Your Vera.

Vera to Igor
(Original in Russian)

Monsieur Igor Stravinsky
Hotel Presidente
Havana
Cuba

1260 North Wetherly Drive
Hollywood 46, California
April 6, 1953

Igor dear, I received your cable this morning and thank you. I am happy that all is well, your health, the concert, the weather. Dr. Mantchik telephoned to ask about you. On Friday Bob and I went to Father McLane's church and I took some lilies there. On Saturday at midnight we went to the Russian Church, but so many people were there that we had to stand outside. It was cold, rainy, and the candles were blowing out. The crowd looked poor, gray, and sad, but touching. On Sunday we lunched at the Milhauds' in their lovely house with a view to the sea and the mountains, a very good lunch, and both Milhauds were nice and amusing. Tomorrow I will go to Darius's concert with Edward James, Bob, and Lawrence Morton, who will dine with me before. I did not go to any of the receptions in Milhaud's honor.

Catherine [d'Erlanger] is leaving tomorrow for New York and Italy. How amazing she is, not at all anxious about the trip. She brought a lady photographer to my studio to take pictures of me and of my paintings for *Vogue*. Her cats come to my studio now and even sit on my knees—difficult to work with those hairy lions in my lap—but they are offended that Catherine is leaving, and therefore more friendly to me.

I am taking care of the garden; it will look nicer for your arrival. Varzhensky is helping me. We had to obtain permission from the city to cut down the tree in front of the garage. Dmitri Stepanovich is still drunk from Easter. Evgenia Petrovna went to Balboa for Easter and came home very pleased.

I am working better now, and am following your trip with interest, wondering what you will think of Caracas. Andre must be enjoying the South. It is very cold here. I embrace you from my heart and kiss you tenderly. Your Vera.

Igor to Vera
(Original in Russian)

1260 North Wetherly Drive
Hollywood 46, California

Hotel Presidente
Havana
Monday, April 6, 1953, 4 p.m.

Verushkinsky dear, I am writing this sitting on the bed in my underwear, bathed in perspiration. The rehearsals were an inferno, and I have never perspired so much. Yesterday morning's concert was bearable only because the hall was air-conditioned, but I am still thinking about the torture of perspiring. I cannot understand why it was so bad, since a nice breeze blows from the sea.

The orchestra (almost all the same people[1]) is quite competent on the whole. The success was great, but the first few rows of the

---

[1] i.e., as in 1946 and 1951.

[2] Dr. Pittaluga, father of the composer, had been Stravinsky's physician in Havana in 1951.

[3] John Thacher, director of Dumbarton Oaks, had commissioned Stravinsky's Septet.

[4] R.C. had argued that the piece should not be shelved for more than a year simply because of scheduling problems at Dumbarton Oaks.

---

parterre were far from full. I was told that the hall was sold out but that subscribers did not come because of a 12-hour service on Easter morning. This is possible, of course, but we shall see how it is tonight.

I went with Andre to visit the old Pittaluga.[2] Everything is the same as before. Gustavo is in Brazil for three months, organizing an orchestra in São Paulo.

Yesterday I received the letters you forwarded. Thank you. The "Union Pacific," understandably, went into the waste basket, but the letter from Thacher[3] cannot be disposed of so easily. To a certain extent Bob is right, in his note, although he is dreaming of doing the premiere of the Septet himself, in Venice.[4] Perhaps the matter will be concluded this way. If Thacher insists that I donate the manuscript and insists on the word "commission," I will refuse both conditions. I am not dedicating the piece to them but only giving them the title *Septet 1953* and the premiere—at the end of January 1954—for one thousand five hundred dollars.

Andre is in the next room tapping letters on the typewriter; the heat bothers him less than it does me. Here I am, on the bed, feeling nauseous and running to the bathroom. I also swallow a lot of codeine.

Not a word has come from Caldwell in Boston.[5] Can it be that this whole project will fall through? If so, I should be notified so that I can change my tickets and fly home directly from Caracas. In this case it will be annoying to have to make a special trip from Los Angeles to Chicago.[6] I read Maigret with pleasure. I also found Simenon's *Act of Passion*, for which I paid 60 cents in a small kiosk, and I have already started it, though the print is very poor. Have you read it?[7]

I will be called for in three and a half hours: the concert is at half-past nine in the evening. Tomorrow we will pack, and Wednesday at eight fly to Caracas. A beautiful new highway connects Havana with the airfield, and the ride takes just 20 minutes.[8] I embrace you. Your I.

Vera to Igor
(Original in Russian)

Monsieur Igor Stravinsky
Hotel Potomac
Caracas
Venezuela
[Stravinsky has written on the envelope: "Sheraton Plaza Hotel, Copley Square Boston, arriving April 14"]

1260 North Wetherly Drive
Hollywood 46, California
April 10, 1953

Bubushkin dear, I am glad that you are having a good time—to judge by the letter that Milene received. Too bad that you did not take a direct plane and had to spend so much time flying. Tomorrow, Bob, Milene, and I are going to Palm Springs and Indio to look at the flowers. Huxley, with whom we spent yesterday evening, told us so much about the beauty of the desert flowers that we decided to see them. I only hope that it won't be too hot.

On Friday I will find out about the state of my liver. Edel made several complicated tests. I lunch today at Frascati's, where the Countess Renée de Veyrac works as a waitress. It is not an easy job and she has a lot of courage. I am dining at Laure's today. Evgenia Petrovna is delighted not to have to work. I wish you great success for your concert tomorrow and hope you will not be overtired. A big kiss. With love, your Vera.

---

[5] Sarah Caldwell had invited Stravinsky to conduct *The Rake's Progress* with her Boston University opera group.

[6] Stravinsky had agreed to conduct a concert in Chicago in June only because he expected to return from Boston to California via Illinois, but the Chicago concert was cancelled.

[7] Stravinsky read as many as a hundred novels by Georges Simenon, and he was especially fond of the Maigret detective series.

[8] When Mrs. Stravinsky was in Havana in 1951, this road was marked by craters.

122

122 March 1953. 1260 North Wetherly Drive. Some of Stravinsky's collection of mollusca can be seen on the shelf to his left, and, behind his right shoulder, part of his large library of Henry James.

123 March 1953. New York. Recording *The Rake's Progress.*

123

Monsieur Igor Stravinsky   1260 North Wetherly Drive
Hotel Potomac   Hollywood 46, California
Caracas   Monday, April 13, 1953
Venezuela

[This letter was forwarded to Stravinsky in New York and from there to Boston, as he reminded himself in a note on the envelope.]

How are you managing in Caracas, Bubushkin dear? How is the weather? How do you feel? At night it is only 42 degrees here. The heating has been on full blast, and the other day we almost had a fire. The house was full of smoke and Evgenia Petrovna telephoned me in the studio in a panic. It was a Saturday and we had to call a man who charges double on Saturdays. He said that the motor had burned out and we had to install a new one, since we couldn't have stayed there without heat.

On Sunday there was a concert by the New Music Quartet: Schoenberg, Webern and Berg. Bob asked Mrs. Schoenberg if she would like to come to my house and go to the concert together. She accepted with pleasure and arrived with her beautiful daughter. I gave them some Scotch. The first thing she said was: "This should have happened twenty years ago. It was not Schoenberg's or Stravinsky's fault, but that of people in between." She is very nice, very direct, but very nervous. She talks a great deal and drinks copiously. She gives the impression of someone who has been hurt all her life. We went to the Knickerbocker Hotel for dinner and then to the concert. We met Father McLane there and all of us went to his house afterward to look at his Chagalls and the Balthus. You are probably thinking, "Very chi-chi." But it was cozy, since McLane is quieter and does not talk so loudly anymore.

Tonight Bob and I are going to the Huxleys'. They go again to the desert for a few days.

I work—at times successfully and at times in despair. Zoya Karabanova is staying at the Baroness's to take care of the cats. "Who is that monster?" Bob asked about that one-time famous beauty! Now she drinks a lot, is very fat, and does look awful. She has a horrible life, suffers from asthma, and works as a cashier in a restaurant till 5 a.m. I am expecting your letter describing Caracas. Big and tender kisses. Keep well. God bless you. Your Vera.

Igor to Vera
(Original in Russian)

Mrs. Igor Stravinsky   Hotel Potomac
1260 North Wetherly Drive   Caracas, Venezuela
Los Angeles 46, California   Sunday, April 12, 1953
USA

I received your sweet letter, Verushkinsky beloved. I have many small impressions of Venezuela and Caracas that I will tell you about when I see you, since they are too complicated to convey in writing. The orchestra here is so-so, but better than I expected. Some individual elements are not bad (the solo players of different sections), and this facilitates my work. Rehearsals take place every day, and in them I am obliged to explain very obvious things, which is dull, unrewarding work. The only consolation is that I am paid very well.

We fly to New York on the morning of the 23rd, and should be in the city at 9 p.m. Except for rehearsals and inescapable lunches and dinners, not much is to be done here,[1] and I will be glad to be back in New York. The hotel is very good; the owner is a very thoughtful German[2] who speaks several languages. Good night; I will continue tomorrow.

[1] Stravinsky had been to a concert by Segovia the night before writing this.

[2] The Viennese, Schlesinger. See *Chronicles of a Friendship*, New York, 1972.

Tuesday, April 14th

Yesterday, Monday, I could not continue, since I had a very busy day. On Friday, Christian Dior and his models will fly in from Paris for a big benefit show ($50 entrance) all of them returning to Paris the next day, Saturday. Not bad! In spite of being in the tropics, the air is very good here, at the height of 1,000 meters, an altitude that I do not mind.

I had a cable from Boston to the effect that Caldwell is writing to me, and that everything is proceeding normally. The performances will take place on May 17 in the afternoon, and on the 18th in the evening. This means that you will have to send my morning coat with striped trousers and the Venetian full-dress tail-coat. For God's sake, do not forget. When do you expect to send them? Perhaps it would be better to wait until I give you the name of my hotel there, which should be in Caldwell's letter, which I expect each minute.

I just received your letter with two letters enclosed: 1) Royal Philharmonic, London; 2) José Ferrer with his proposition. Thank Bob for the commentaries and Mirandi for the elephant. I will send her a few lines when I have time. Good postcards do not exist here, but a friend gave me several postcards that I will bring along.

I expected Max Edel to put you on a strict diet, and I only hope that you will keep it. As consolation, I will tell you that Alexandre Benois's doctor put him on the strictest diet, and he now eats only once a day.

I must close but will continue very soon. As I expected, ASCAP has not moved. Love and kisses. Your Igor.

I heard from Caldwell at last. It seems that she sent me two letters that I never received. Send my clothes to the Sheraton Plaza, Copley Square, Boston. Write me if you receive the ASCAP payment and tell me how much it is, also how much from the Société Dramatique, Paris. You tell me that you deposited checks in the bank but not which checks, and this is important for me to know. How is your painting and your work progressing?

Vera to Igor
(Original in Russian)

Monsieur Igor Stravinsky   1260 North Wetherly Drive
Hotel Potomac   Hollywood 46, California
Caracas   April 14, 1953
Venezuela

Dear Bubushkin, Thank you for the cable and the letter from Caracas; I am sending you two letters written by Bob in such small letters that you will need a lamp to read them. His manuscripts are written in even smaller letters.

I went to see Dr. Mauer yesterday. He was very strict and said that if I do not reduce he will not keep me as a patient. He said that Father McLane, the pig, had gained 10 pounds *during Lent*.

I had dinner yesterday at Bel Air with Edward James and I ate only a steak and black coffee, which will be my menu from now on. Bob writes you that James bought a house on the beach for $23,000. Somehow the Baroness found out that Iris Tree received a commission for the sale, which greatly upset James, since he has always been so generous to her and even dedicated a book to her.

Mirandi sent us Easter presents: gold earrings for me and a little turquoise bear for you. I kept the bear for myself—for good luck. Please send her a postcard.

I spent an evening with Beata who told me that she sent her manuscript about Adia to Merle Armitage, who answers saying that she should not use so many superlatives on the very first page.

You received a check from ASCAP today for $1,279, which I will deposit.

It is very cold here and we are dreaming of hot weather. Love and kisses. Best to Andre. Send some nice postcards. Be well and happy! Your Vera.

124

124 May 1953. Boston. Talking with Arthur Fiedler at a party.

125 1953. 1218 North Wetherly Drive. Vera in the Baroness d'Erlanger's pool.

125

[*April diary continued*]

28 Reach New York in time for lunch. Bob goes directly to Boston to begin the rehearsals. **29** Igor has the flu. Dr. Pierre gives him penicillin. **30** Igor is better.

May

2 We fly to Boston, the Sheraton Plaza Hotel. **8** Igor rehearses the singers in the hotel. Rinkel. **17** *The Rake's Progress* performance at 3:30. Chester Kallman, David Protetch, and Lucia Davidova come from New York. **18** I am cyclothymic.[1] Second performance of the *Rake*. **20** Igor goes to Dr. Graves for an examination. Two nice people come from *Esquire* magazine.[2] **22** Dylan Thomas comes in the morning. **27** We leave Boston in the afternoon and dine in New York at the Gladstone. **28** Drive to Pittsburgh. **29** Stay in Richmond, Indiana. **30** Stay in a motel after St. Louis. **31** The Skirvin Hotel in Oklahoma City.

June

1 Stay at Amarillo. **2** Albuquerque. **3** To Socorro, Springerville, and Phoenix. **4** Reach home, via San Diego, at 8:15. **10** Dr. Waitzfelder for Igor. **12** Dr. Knauer. **14** Dr. Waitzfelder (second time). **15** Waitzfelder, third time. **16** Waitzfelder, fourth time. **21** Dinner at Huxleys'.

July

6 Benzedrine and bromides: modifiers of consciousness.[3] **22** Igor to the doctor's. The Fakir.[4] **23** Igor enters the Good Samaritan Hospital. **24** Igor's prostate operation. **26** Dinner at Huxleys'.

August

2 Lunch at Huxleys'. **3** Igor is released from the hospital. **6** Dinner at Huxleys' with Tara Bey. **13** We go to Hollywood Bowl for William Walton's concert. **14** Walton and wife come at 4, Isherwood and Bill Caskey at 6.

September

6 Dinner at Aldous's with Julian Huxley and Gerald Heard. **13** Construction begins on our dining room. **18** For dinner here: David Oppenheim and [his wife] Judy Holliday. **25** Dinner at the beach with the Huxleys. **29** Big dinner at La Rue by Edward James.[5]

October

19 Bob's Evenings on the Roof concert: Stravinsky jazz. **22** The Huxleys for tea. **24** Dinner at Huxleys'. With Aldous to see *Mme Butterfly*. **28** With Edward James to *The Masked Ball*, dinner afterward at the Statler. **30** To *Turandot* at the Shrine Auditorium.

November

1 (Sunday) To *Die Walküre*[6] with Lawrence Morton. **9** Dylan Thomas died. **10** Isherwood and Caskey for dinner. **17** Igor's Santa Barbara concert with the Los Angeles Philharmonic. **18** Igor's Pasadena concert with the Los Angeles Philharmonic. **19** Igor's first Los Angeles concert. Here afterward: Bob, 3 Huxleys (Peggy Kiskadden and Mrs. Nys[7]), the Baroness d'Erlanger, Gertrud and Nuria Schoenberg. **20** Igor's second Los Angeles concert. **21** With the Huxleys to the Musica Antiqua concert[8] in Hancock Auditorium, USC. **23** Jerome Robbins comes from New York.[9] **27** Photographs of Igor and me for Stromberg Carlson. We drive to Palm Springs and sleep there. **28** To La Jolla. **29** Home at 2.

---

[1] Mrs. Stravinsky was no such thing, of course, but she had been reading Huxley and Gerald Heard.

[2] In its December 1953 issue, *Esquire* published a long article by Martin Mayer on Stravinsky recording the *Rake*.

[3] Mrs. Stravinsky had noted this after Gerald Heard's lecture on July 5.

[4] Tara Bey. The Huxleys were helping to sponsor his American tour.

[5] Stravinsky was seated next to Gertrud Schoenberg.

December

6 A very nice lunch at the Italian Consul's. Igor receives a decoration. **9** To the Sadler's Wells Ballet to see Berners' *Wedding Bouquet*. **10** To the Sadler's Wells Ballet to see *Sleeping Beauty*. **15** To the Sadler's Wells Ballet to see *Sylvia*. **16** Aldous after dinner.

The following correspondence dates from the end of December 1953 and the beginning of January 1954, while Stravinsky was conducting the Philadelphia Orchestra:

Vera to Igor
(Original in Russian)

Mr. Igor Stravinsky   1260 North Wetherly Drive
Gladstone Hotel   Hollywood 46, California
East 52nd Street   (Morning) December 25, 1953
New York City, NY

My dear Bubushkinsky, Merry Christmas and thank you for the telegram. It seems that Christmas has to be with a tree, presents, squealing children, and that otherwise it is too sad. I have not written to you in the last few days because I had a lot of work to do. I shall not send any Christmas cards next year and am beginning to tell this to everybody now, but I didn't have the courage to do it this year. Having been deluged with cards, I started to respond, but do not have enough cards, stamps, or even all of the addresses. Then came the problems with gifts. I forgot several people and had to chase around at the last minute, when the stores were most crowded. Since a few small presents, the cards and the telegrams cost about fifty dollars, wouldn't it be better to find ten poor people and give five dollars to each of them?

Mr. Wright, the contractor, took a lot of my time and was also disagreeable. I had innumerable telephone conversations with him, yet he pretended to be surprised that you left without paying him. Finally he came and repaired everything, cleaned up, and I gave him a check marked "Paid in full," so as not to be bothered any more. The radio repairman came and changed the loud speakers. They are very good, and I have asked Bob to check them. Varzhensky finished his job, and now Evgenia Petrovna and I will plant flowers on the hill.

I tried to do some work but so far without success. The McLanes gave a very nice dinner party, but you would have been bored. The talk now is exclusively about Giacometti; even Chagall is scarcely mentioned.

We saw Nuria Schoenberg; Brainerd is madly in love with her, but she is still flirting with Bob, as is Augusta [McLane] who stuffs little notes into Bob's pocket.

Johnny Walsh gave a very nice dinner with presents for everybody. I received an antique snuffbox and Bob a tie. Catherine gave me a Venetian necklace with pink tourmalines. She gave an enormous cocktail party where I saw Varishkina, last seen in Paris thirty years ago.

I received a charming letter from Berman, who insists that I should have my own exhibition, which, he says, is a very important personal experience. "It may be a hard examination, but it is also a useful one." Yesterday I went to Father McLane's

---

[6] Mrs. Stravinsky noted that the opera was four hours long, but Stravinsky insisted on leaving after Act One.

[7] Huxley's mother-in-law.

[8] Conducted by Safford Cape. Stravinsky heard the contralto Jeanne Deroubaix on this occasion and later invited her to sing in his *Threni*.

[9] To discuss the staging of *Les Noces*.

126 November 1953. Los Angeles. Rehearsing the Los Angeles
Philharmonic.

midnight Mass with Beata, who was very eager to come, and Laure, who annoys Bob with her chatter. I was sorry for Beata, who now seems so old and who is really touching. She brought me a present, a box with a silver flower in it, which was much better than Dahl's present, a flat stone with some paint dribbled on it and a dry twig glued to it. The Babitzes sent a basket with pastries, fruit, and stuffed crab, and an apron for me, and music for you. Very generous. They have an open house today, but I doubt that I will go since I want to put my studio in order and think about my painting.

How is the cold affecting you and Andre? How are the rehearsals and concerts going? Madubo has not yet received a letter from Milene, but I said that one is on the way. Kiss Milene and Andre, remember me to our friends, and greet wonderful New York for me. It is hot here, but the nights are very cold. I embrace you with all my heart. May God bless you. I kiss you very, very hard. Your Vera.

PS You received a letter from a magazine editor who is preparing a memorial issue on Dylan Thomas. I advise you either to give them one of Thomas's letters to you or to write an article. (Bob could write it, and I could send it to you.)

A check for $1,843.20 and an award of $150 came from ASCAP and I will deposit both in the bank.

A check for $21.50 came from Mercury Music Corporation. I will deposit it and forward to you the letter that was with it. I am forwarding a letter from the Société des Auteurs et Compositeurs with a Christmas present of 55,000 francs, and I'm also sending you a letter from the US Department of Justice about Alien Property—since I don't know whether or not I should send it to Sapiro.

I asked Bob to send on to you a wire from Serge Lifar. How will you answer him? A kiss, Vera.

Vera to Igor
(Original in Russian)

Mr Igor Stravinsky
Gladstone Hotel
East 52nd Street
New York City, NY

1260 North Wetherly Drive
Hollywood 46, California
December 28, 1953

My dearest, All is well here. Yesterday, *everybody* came to see me: the McLanes, Paco Lagerstrom,[1] Morton, *et al.* I had let Evgenia go to Balboa for two days, and I did the cooking myself. Bill Brown[2] is coming tomorrow for two days. I continue to receive a tremendous number of Christmas cards, and I spend all my time reading and answering them. Now I am going to Madubo. A big kiss. Greetings from all of us to all of you. Vera, Silly, Pinky, Vaska, Michael,[3] Bob, Evgenia.

Vera to Igor
(Original in Russian)

Igor Stravinsky
Gladstone Hotel
East 52nd Street
New York City

1260 North Wetherly Drive
Hollywood 46, California
December 31, 1953

Dear Bubushkin, Happy New Year, and, please, without doctors; it is terrible to have a new doctor in every city. I am sending papers about the income tax to Andre in Philadelphia, also a clipping about the Cantata, sent by Fedya. Bill Brown was here and he gave me many suggestions about my painting. I hope you do not have any interruptions about business affairs. Did you hear about the fire in the Mount Wilson Observatory? I embrace you with much love, my dearest, your Vera.

1954

Vera to Igor
(Original in Russian)

Igor Stravinsky
Gladstone Hotel
East 52nd Street
New York City

1260 North Wetherly Drive
Hollywood 46, California
January 4, 1954

Dear Bubushkinsky, I hope all is well and that all of you are well. What did the doctor find out about Milene? Lately she has seemed to me to be anemic. I think that she has not been eating the right things. Edel was very displeased because you had the flu again. He is very pleased with me. I feel well and am getting thin slowly, which is the best way.

Hormel's New Year's party was fantastic. First, the house is very impressive. Second, everything was catered from Romanoff's, and one felt as if one were sitting in a restaurant: eating, drinking, and observing. Bob calculated that with the orchestra and with champagne flowing for the 100 people, the party must have cost at least 10,000 dollars. (He alone must have eaten fifty dollars' worth.) I went to bed at 3 a.m. and didn't have a hangover, since everything there was first-rate. Madubo had made me an enchanting dress, and I had the gloves that Milene gave me. As usual, January 1 was full of resolutions for me, one hour of walking and five hours of painting a day. I hope to do this during the whole year. Then, as an aftermath of the holidays, telephone calls, congratulations, visits, so that I did not walk at all the next day, but I have worked a great deal since then. Bill Brown stimulated me by giving me a lot of advice. At Hormel's I met a woman[4] who has a sort of painter's workshop. She is said to be a good teacher. I decided to go twice a week to her lectures. I kiss and embrace you with all my heart.

Vera to Igor
(Original in Russian)

Igor Stravinsky
Gladstone Hotel
East 52nd Street
New York City

1260 North Wetherly Drive
Hollywood 46, California
January 8, 1954

My dearest, I've been in a terrible hurry since this morning and have had no time for my own work. The telephone calls have not stopped, though none of them is important: Beata wants to see me; I have to invite Edith Sitwell; the Victor Babins are here and will

---

[1] A professor at the California Institute of Technology in Pasadena, a passionate lover of music and a friend of Alma Mahler's and of the Stravinskys'.

[2] William Theophilus Brown (b. 1919), descendant of H.D. Thoreau, painter, musician and pianist (pupil of Hindemith at Yale), mathematician, writer, was a member of the Stravinskys' inner sanctum in the California years, with Isherwood, Lawrence Morton, and, from May 1969, Ed Allen. Bill Brown had the keenest and least sparing wit of all of the Stravinskys' friends. (The cruellest joke ever made about R.C., at least of which he is aware, was Brown's remark, "Madame, your problem is that you have *two* geniuses to take care of." Mrs. Stravinsky entered this in her diary.) He was introduced to the Stravinskys by Mirandi in Santa Fe, February 11, 1951. In June 1952 he spent ten days with them in Holland. His name appears in all of her diaries thereafter, but with greatest frequency in 1964–69. He wrote to Mrs. Stravinsky in July 1971, three months after her husband's death:

"Chère madame, A few nights ago I had dinner with Christopher Isherwood and we both loudly lamented your absence in our lives. He said you were the best woman he'd ever known! I wanted to ask him who the best man was but restrained myself. Then next day your card came, saying how sad Venice has become. As for the tourists, I thought they were all here in California, as they pass by in an endless stream in their campers and trailers, hauling motor boats, motor cycles, dogs, ladies in hair curlers, etc. ¶My old (92) dad died just three weeks after my mother. I'm quite sure he wanted to, and he was ill only a few hours. But I had to go back East again and face another bunch of relatives. ¶Maybe you will paint when you get back to the apartment? I wish you would. To hell with lawyers . . ."

[3] Silly (Celeste), Pinky, Vaska, and Michael were the Stravinskys' cats.

[4] Mary Vartikian (Mrs. George Harris), a pupil of Rico Lebrun.

lunch with me. Yesterday when I could not find my best diamond brooch, I looked through all of the drawers with Evgenia Petrovna. This morning I found it fastened to one of my old dresses. A problem with the cats: they have started to do their business inside the house and, by preference, in my clothes closet. I had to wash the wall and the floor with eau-de-cologne. The reason for this is that they are terrified of an opossum that seems to inhabit our garden, and they are afraid to go out.

Huxley (we were there for dinner on January 5) gave me a book that will interest you, though it is not very well written and is not strictly scientific. I remember how you always blamed the weather for everything. In the book, *Today's Revolution in Weather*, by William Baxter, you will find justifications for your beliefs, as well as what weather means to your business, your health, your stocks, and your real estate. It is published by the International Economic Research Bureau in New York. You can find it everywhere. It costs one dollar.

Thank you so much for the birthday telegram. I was touched that you did not forget. I was also touched by Evgenia Petrovna, who sent me flowers from herself and from you. Yesterday I took Edel and his girlfriend to a good dinner in a restaurant called Luau (in the style of the Beachcomber). Also David Gray and Jack Cole[1] invited Bob and me to Perino's afterwards and to Agnes de Mille's ballet, a dinner *formidable* and a very entertaining ballet.

I work during the day and go out at night. Catherine has not yet had her eye operation, is terribly nervous, and does not want to be alone. We often dine with her, and Bob reads to her a lot.

I have been sketching at the workshop and find that my drawing reminds me of Rico Lebrun, but since I am aware of it, I have nothing to fear. As you see, my life is very active. Thank Milene for her letters. I am very skeptical of the thyroxin that Dr. Paine gives her. As a rule, tubercular people are not allowed to take thyroid medicines, besides which thyroxin always affects the nervous system. But perhaps he knows best.

I had a nice letter from Françoise which I have not had time to answer. I was hoping to write letters today but Brainerd invited me to a guitar recital. I kiss you from my heart. Please kiss the family for me. I embrace you with all my heart. Your Vera.

You received an ASCAP bonus check:	733.10
Also, Pure Oil	62.50
Crown Zellerbach	111.60
	907.20

The weather here continues to be sunny but cold. The Huxleys returned from Ojai and came to see me. Maria looks much better. Next week I'll arrange a dinner for the Sitwells.

Vaska disappeared this morning and we were very upset, especially Evgenia Petrovna, but he returned around 10 p.m. I think he has begun to court. Celeste is becoming fat and greedy; I will have to ask the veterinarian what to do about her. I close my letter with many kisses to all of you. Especially thank Milene for her charming and detailed letters. I embrace you with all my heart. Your Vera.

Vera to Igor
(Original in Russian)

Igor Stravinsky
Gladstone Hotel
East 52nd Street
New York City

1260 North Wetherly Drive
Hollywood 46, California
January 10, 1954

Dearest Bubushkin, I am so sorry to have missed you on the telephone, especially since it was so late, 1 a.m. your time. But I am glad to have talked at least with Andre and Milene. How can you stand such an amount of work? Everyone is astounded. What did [Drs.] Rinkel and Pierre[2] say?

This house is like a hospital. Evgenia Petrovna is sick again and complaining all the time. I took her to Dr. Knauer today. Bob has either an intestinal flu or food poisoning; he had a high fever for two days, but I cured him without drugs. Edel gave advice over the phone. It has been pouring for three days, but the roof leaked only slightly.

Did you see interesting things in New York? According to *The New Yorker*, there are lots of good plays, exhibitions, ballets. What about Balanchine's last ballet? How did your recording go? Milene must have seen many new things, since she did not go with you to Washington.

I took Madubo to a good restaurant, where she ate so prodigiously that I fear she has been starving for some time. I see the Huxleys quite often—I was dining with them when you telephoned. The call could easily have been transferred, but you hung up just as Evgenia Petrovna was going to tell you I was at the Huxleys'.

As for the witholding taxes, I asked Mrs. Feeney,[3] who said not to worry, and that you had a similar paper from the City Center about the ballet. I am looking forward impatiently to your arrival. You will have a good rest at home. I kiss you with all my heart. Vera.

January

13 To the Babin and Vronsky concert. **14** Babin and Vronsky for dinner. Bob goes to a rehearsal. **16** Bob to a rehearsal. **17** Tea at Huxleys'. Take Maria Huxley to visit the Baroness in the hospital. **18** Bob's Evenings on the Roof Concert. **19** Telephone call from Igor in New York. **23** A visit at the Schoenbergs'. Dinner at Huxleys'.

February

3 I meet Igor's airplane at 6. **8** Bob's Evenings on the Roof concert: Couperin and Webern. Afterward here: Huxley and Morton. **10** Dinner at Huxleys'. Aldous is in bed. **15** Visit from Witter Bynner, Isherwood, and Don Bachardy, Isherwood's new friend. **24** Igor flies to Portland.[4]

March

3 Telephone from Igor in Portland: he says we have to leave for Italy on the 25th. **6** Huxley for tea. [On this date Stravinsky wrote to Vera from the Hotel Olympic in Seattle: "Verushkinsky, Please give the enclosed to Grace-Lynn[5] in memory of the premiere. Thank you for the few lines and for forwarding the letters. Embraces, I."] **7** Santa Barbara. Bob's concert. **8** Bob's Monday Evening Concert. **9** Jack Cole with Morton and Bob to discuss *Apollo* at Ojai. **10** Igor arrives from Seattle at 4. **12** Party at Isherwood's. **14** The Huxleys go to New York. Here for dinner: Auden, Isherwood, us. **18** Bob goes to New York. **25** Igor and I fly to New York, but because of bad weather we land in Washington and complete the trip by train. **27** To T.S. Eliot's *The Confidential Clerk*. **31** To *Tea and Sympathy*.

April

1 To Jack Cole's *Kismet*. **2** At 6 p.m. we fly to Rome. **3** In Paris for 3

---

[1] Dance director and choreographer for many films and musicals, of which *Kismet* may have been the best known. David Gray, photographer, was Cole's constant companion.

[2] Dr. Jules Pierre of New York City. See *A Stravinsky Scrapbook*, op. cit.

[3] Assistant to the Stravinskys' lawyer, Aaron Sapiro.

[4] With Andre Marion, for concerts there and in Seattle.

[5] Grace-Lynn Martin sang the first performance of Stravinsky's "Three Songs from William Shakespeare."

hours, Rome at 7 p.m.   **4** Drive to Castel Gandolfo and Frascati. To a concert at 5:30, then a reception at the American Academy (Nabokov). **5** Lunch at Viterbo. Ville Lante. Bomarzo.   **7** Gertrud and Nuria Schoenberg arrive. A fight in the lobby of the Rome Opera.[1]   **8** Drive to Tivoli. I send my *Apollo* drawings to Morton through the Galleria Obelisco.   **9** Bob rehearses the whole day. To the Villa Giulia.   **14** Igor's first Rome concert.   **15** Bob goes to Naples. We go to the Vatican Museum.   **17** Lunch at Bassiano (Prince Caetani). Igor's RAI concert. **19** Igor and Andre leave for Torino.   **21** Leave for Orvieto (lunch) and Siena by car with Milene and Bob. The hotel in Siena is terrible. **22** Siena (marvels!) and Arezzo.   **23** Pisa, San Gimignano.   **24** Lucca and Florence (Grand Hotel). Call Igor in Lugano.   **25** Russian Easter. What a wonderful city! To the Mostra of the Four Masters (Piero, Uccello, Andrea del Castagno, Domenico Veneziano).   **26** To the Medici Chapel. **27** Santa Maria Novella, Santa Maria del Carmine, and the Bargello. **28** Train to Milan and car to Lugano.   **29** To the Thyssen collection. Igor's concert: tremendous success.   **30** Car to Stresa, followed by photographers from *Paris Match*. Train to Geneva.

May

---

1 Lunch and dinner with Ansermet.   **2** To Baden-Baden via Lausanne and Basel.[2]   **3** Bob has three rehearsals: 9:30–12; 4–6:30; 8–10.

Vera to Igor
(Original in Russian)

Monsieur Igor Stravinsky   Brenner's Park Hotel
Hôtel des Bergues   May 3, 1954
Genève
Suisse

Dearest one, I was so sorry to hear that you had to stay on in Geneva. Otherwise you could have rested here for three days before going to Cologne. It is wonderfully beautiful here in the spring. The park is so rich and elegant. I could recognize the trees that I sketched three years ago. The restaurant is superb; the waiters remembered me [from October 1951] and the dreadful cold that you had and how you lost your voice. I told them that you will be coming in ten days and that they should take good care of you. Andre will have to order à la carte.

The train trip is very tiring. If possible, you should fly to Cologne. The train is very shaky, the conductor asks to see your tickets every half-hour, the stops at the frontier to check passports are endless, and the restaurant car is hooked on for only one hour. We ate sandwiches, which were brought through the cars. Eight hours from Geneva to Baden-Baden is really too long, and from Cologne it would be even longer. We were met by Frau Strobel,[3] who is nice and thoughtful, and who was very helpful to Bob. He asked me to translate some of his remarks to the orchestra into German, but I do not know any of the musical expressions.

Frau Strobel and I have been chatting quite a lot so I now know all of the gossip about Rosbaud and his lady pianist.[4]

I now have all of the information about the airplane. It leaves from Frankfurt at 2:30 p.m., which means that Thursday morning is lost for Bob. He has three rehearsals a day, which is tiring. He started with *Norwegian Moods* and was slightly depressed, since he could not express himself in German. The orchestra seems heavy, and he remembered what you said about their habit of 'dragging.'

I will write again to Cologne and also wire there about my arrival in California. I kiss you with all my heart. Your Vera.

Vera to Igor
(Original in Russian)

Monsieur Igor Stravinsky   Brenner's Park Hotel
Hôtel des Bergues   May 4, 1954
Genève
Suisse

Dearest Bubushkinsky, Welcome to Baden-Baden! Get a good rest here if you can and walk in the park, enjoy the flowers, the trees, and the air. The Strobels were very nice. I had dinner with them once and invited them once to the hotel. I am leaving an interesting book for you, but if you do not want it, throw it away. I wanted to phone you last night but did not know where you would be. God bless you. Your Vera.

Vera to Igor
(Original in Russian)

Monsieur Igor Stravinsky   Brenner's Park Hotel
Excelsior Hotel   May 5, 1954
Cologne
[The letter was forwarded to Stravinsky at the Hôtel des Bergues, Geneva, and received there on May 5.]

My dear one, the train trip from Baden-Baden (Baden-Oos) to Frankfurt was very tiring. It stops at every station for just two minutes, and there is no one to help with the baggage. At Frankfurt, the Pan American Airway office is across from the railroad station, and an autobus takes you to the airport. We had only five minutes in which to do this. I was relieved to board the airplane at last, but in Düsseldorf we had to get off, have our passports checked, and show our money. There were only nine people on the plane. I am writing this letter in the waiting lounge at the Düsseldorf airport. I embrace and kiss you with all my heart. Your Vera.

Igor to Vera
(Original in English)

Vera Stravinsky   Excelsior Hotel
Pan American Airlines   Cologne
London International Airport   May 6, 1954
                                                 [Cable]

Please deliver on board to Mrs. Igor Stravinsky, passenger in transit from Frankfurt to New York, Flight #101, May 6: Violent throat inflammation[5] now fortunately under control prevents Cologne concert. Staying here another week before going directly to Baden-Baden. Please wire me Hôtel Bergues. Bon voyage from all. Love, Igor.

Vera to Igor
(Original in English)

Monsieur Igor Stravinsky   New York
Hôtel des Bergues   May 7, 1954
Genève   [Cable]
Suisse

Hope throat better. Leaving for Hollywood as scheduled. Love Vera.

---

[1] Before the premiere of Henze's *Boulevard Solitude*. See *A Stravinsky Scrapbook*, op. cit.

[2] In Baden-Baden, Vera sent a telegram to Stravinsky at the Bergues Hotel in Geneva: ''Tiring trip and train. Hotel marvelous. Miss you. Love, Vera.''

[3] Hilde Strobel, wife of the music critic Heinrich Strobel, who was director of

music at the Südwestfunk in Baden-Baden and editor of *Melos*.

[4] Hans Rosbaud, the conductor, and Maria Bergmann, the pianist.

[5] Stravinsky had accidentally gargled with Lysol and severely burned his throat. His Cologne concert was cancelled and his Baden-Baden concert was postponed.

Vera to Igor
(Original in English)

Monsieur Igor Stravinsky
Hôtel des Bergues
Geneva

1260 North Wetherly Drive
Hollywood 46, California
May 8, 1954
[Cable]

Terribly bumpy flight from New York but happy to be home wish you could be here and rest love Vera.

Vera to Igor
(Original in English)

Monsieur Igor Stravinsky
Hôtel des Bergues
Geneva

1260 North Wetherly Drive
Hollywood 46, California
May 11, 1954
[Cable]

Please cable further news of illness nothing since Milene's letter love Vera.

Igor to Vera
(Original in English)

Mrs. Igor Stravinsky
1260 North Wetherly Drive
Hollywood 46, California

Hôtel des Bergues
Geneva
May 12, 1954
[Cable]

Fully recovered flying Frankfurt then drive Baden-Baden Friday hope you are rested now love from all Igor.

Vera to Igor
(Original in Russian)

Mr. Igor Stravinsky
Brenner's Park Hotel
Baden-Baden
Germany

1260 North Wetherly Drive
Hollywood 46, California
Wednesday morning, May 12, 1954

My poor, poor Bubushkin, I know how you must have suffered from that burning throat. After my operation I used to drink buttermilk to assuage the burning sensation. I was especially worried, since I had no more news after Milene's letter until this morning. I sent a cable Monday morning and received the reply only today. I hope the letter that I sent you in Cologne will be forwarded, also Bob's letter from Baden-Baden. Thank you for the cable. I advise you to rest in New York, unless you have had a very smooth flight. Ours was terrible, extremely bumpy from Frankfurt to Shannon, and just before London we flew into a storm so terrible that I thought the end was near.

It was calmer over the ocean but took a very long time. Alyosha Haieff came to the airport and spent four hours with us.

On arriving in New York, Bob received a message from his father to telephone him immediately, which he did and learned that his grandmother on his mother's side had died. He loved her very much and was very upset. She was a good and kind woman, and the whole town came to her funeral. Bob wanted to stay over one day for his mother's sake, but he had a rehearsal and a radio talk the next day in Hollywood and could not do it. Moreover, he was exhausted himself.

We took a DC7 non-stop flight to California, thinking that we would be there in seven hours. I sent a wire to John Walsh to ask him to come with Catherine d'Erlanger to meet us, which he did. We had such a terrible flight that one stewardess and several men were sick. I took Dramamine and became very sleepy, but the way we were tossed around sleep was impossible. Only when the plane gained altitude did the flight become calmer. I don't know why this wasn't done sooner, but perhaps there was a storm. In

any case, we were two hours late, and Hollywood looked very gloomy under a pouring rain, the rain that has pursued us since Rome.

The very first evening I received bad news. *Apollo* had to be cancelled because Jack Cole fell at one of the rehearsals, injured himself, and must have an operation. It seems that a substitute could not be found. Morton[1] and I are convinced that Cole was simply frightened, since he had never directed a classical ballet before. Morton was in despair, because *Apollo* was the main attraction. Finally he hired Lichine, who cannot present *Apollo* but will give a ballet that he has done before, on Bach's B minor flute suite. I am very, very disappointed, having so looked forward to *Apollo*. Cole supposedly has a hernia, but since he did not intend to dance himself, this should not have prevented him from finishing the rehearsals.

The other troubles are with our cats. It seems that a man who lives above us on the hill and who hates cats took shots at them, hitting Pinky's skin, blinding Vaska[2] in one eye, and striking Michael near the ear. You can imagine Evgenia Petrovna's reaction. She searched the neighborhood, but without finding who did it. Vaska was in a hospital for three weeks, but he still bleeds from the eye. I take him to the veterinarian for penicillin injections. He is just as beautiful as ever, and his only good eye seems even more expressive.

Feeling terribly tired, I went to Edel. I am better now but still cannot adjust to the nine-hour time difference, waking up and wanting coffee at 5 a.m. Bob is working hard, and the rehearsals are going full steam. I started to work in my studio and am very pleased. Something seems to be happening already.

With what did you accidentally gargle, Lysol or formaldehyde? I want to mail this letter as soon as possible. I kiss you and ask you please not to leave me without news of yourself. I kiss you again from all my heart. God bless you. Your Vera.

A kiss to Andre and Milene, especially if they have taken good care of you. Regards to the Strobels.

Vera to Igor
(Original in Russian)

Herr Igor Stravinsky
Brenner's Park Hotel
Baden-Baden

Hollywood
May 17, 1954

Dearest one, Now you are in Baden-Baden, and I know exactly what you saw from the windows of the train and how annoyed you were by the conductors. The Strobels met you at the station, which must have been nice, since he is always so full of enthusiasm. I hope that the weather is good and that Fedya[3] will admire the trees in the park.

The weather here is bad. Smog and rain are the norm, and this after I had been dreaming of sunny California and of swimming in the pool. I have been working a lot and have come to the conclusion that I should not be too enraptured by Giotto and Piero della Francesca, since their influence can confuse my struggle to find my own way—which I thought I had begun to do about two months ago.

Bob is working terribly hard. He has three rehearsals a day, starting at 9:30 a.m. and finishing at 11 p.m. The Festival in Ojai begins on Thursday this week with three concerts in Ventura on the first day, at 11 a.m. and 4 p.m. for the school audience, and in the evening for the grown-ups. If he had realized how much work was entailed, he would not have accepted the contract. Of your

---

[1] Lawrence Morton was director of the Ojai Festivals, which had programmed *Apollo*. Cole was actually quite ill, underwent an operation on May 31, and did not live very long.

[2] The cat's name in full was Vassili Vassilievitch Yetchkin.

[3] Andre Marion was ill in Geneva and Theodore accompanied his father.

music there will be: the Piano Concerto (Foss[1] is playing very well), and the *Symphonies of Wind Instruments*. Morton also works like an ox and sometimes does not sleep for 48 hours. Is such an uninteresting public worth it?

I phoned Miss Rothman.[2] ASCAP sent a sum that matches your birthdate, $1,882. The check from the Société des Auteurs Dramatiques was $660.96.

Vaska is at the veterinarian again. He has diarrhea from the streptomycin and swollen paws from the penicillin.

Not being able to get into any of my dresses, I have gone on a strict diet. I have been gaining weight for two reasons: the removal of my thyroid gland and my resolve to stop smoking. But I do not eat much. Dr. Edel is waiting for me to rest from the trip before he starts giving me injections. Darling Milene sent me two letters, telling me in one of them that Dr. Gilbert told her to eat everything. Why do doctors give such contradictory opinions? I put that question to Edel and got a flood of explanations.

Guess who appeared all of a sudden? Edward James. He looks thinner and older. He came into the house and resumed talking exactly as if he had left off only yesterday.

I hope that this letter will be forwarded if it does not reach you in time in Baden-Baden. I'll go to the post office to inquire, then perhaps send it to Geneva. Denise wrote me a long letter. I embrace you with all my heart. Your Vera.

Igor to Vera
(Original in Russian)

Mrs. Igor Stravinsky
Hollywood

Baden-Baden
May 18, 1954

Verushkinsky dearest, Here we are, Fedya and I. Andre is better, though he has had a temperature constantly. He telephoned this morning from Geneva. Gilbert has not found anything serious, only this lengthy bronchitis, which kept me an extra week in Geneva and caused me to miss the Cologne concert. Here, as in Geneva, the spring is gray and rainy, but the air is very good.

Your letter describing problems in Hollywood upset me. Is it possible that *Apollo* frightened Jack Cole to the extent that he ruptured himself and required an operation? Whatever the truth, the cancellation is terrible and very annoying. Was it worth it for you, all the trouble and anxieties, and to be in a hurry all the time when you were in Rome? What an absurdity. I'm in a rage, in fact, and since last night think about it all the time and cannot reconcile myself. Also about our cats, and our utter helplessness in the matter. What the devil!

This morning, at Rosbaud's rehearsal,[3] I sat in a room with a radio and listened to the Symphony in Three Movements, which was very clear in his performance but somewhat mathematical and lifeless. Tomorrow I start my rehearsals, *Jeu de cartes*, *Symphonies of Wind Instruments*, and, in the evening, the Symphony in Three Movements. I have two more rehearsals on Thursday and the concert is on Friday at 8 p.m.
(Later)
After the concert we had a cold banquet at the hotel, exactly like the last time,[4] and with all the "big shots." Adenauer is also staying in our hotel, going daily to Strasbourg for Atlantic Pact conferences. Are we not lucky with the great ones of the world? Only yesterday at the Hôtel des Bergues, I saw an Arab Emir in full regalia. What beauty! I wonder who and what I will see in London?[5]

I am returning to Geneva and will spend the night at Fedya's. On Monday, Andre and I will fly to London (Swissair, two-and-a-half hours). On the 28th, we return to Geneva, pick up Milene, and on the 29th, at 6 p.m., fly non-stop to Lisbon,[6] where we should arrive in four hours.

Are you still going to Edel for the injections? Let me know. I will be at the Savoy Hotel in London.

Bob made a very good impression on everybody here and Strobel definitely wants him back. Rosbaud also praised Bob very much. Tell Bob I will bring his recordings of the Septet and of Webern's Variations Op. 30, but on tape, not on discs; the tape, they say, will not be difficult to transfer to discs in the USA. Embraces, embraces, I.

Igor to Vera
(Original in Russian)

Mrs. Igor Stravinsky
Hollywood, California

Lisbon
Aviz Hotel
May 31, 1954

Hello Verushkinsky! Here we are in Lisbon, and you have probably received our cable. I will not describe anything: all will be in person, which is better and more amusing.

Andre, though back to normal, was so frightened by his bronchitis that he falls into a depression as soon as he hears a gurgle in his bronchial tubes. He is still afraid of a relapse. Gilbert assured him that the lungs are well, but Andre does not seem convinced because he knows by experience that his form of bronchitis is particularly insidious. He is cheerful for a few hours, then melancholy again for several more. Milene and I are constantly trying to cheer him up.

We were sad leaving the Geneva airport, where we were seen off by Dr. Gilbert and his small (very nice) son [Luc Gilbert], as well as by Fedya, Denise, Kitty, Madubo (who came to London with Fedya, when I was there, to see me and Milene).

The flight to Lisbon, four hours and twenty minutes on the gigantic Swedish plane, was wonderful. It was not yet dark when we landed at 9:30 p.m. over beautiful Lisbon. I am enclosing my photograph.[7]

I suffered from dizziness for three days, but it finally stopped today. I'm resting a lot. I rehearse on Thursday (twice), Friday (twice), then once on Saturday morning, with the first concert that evening. The second concert is on Tuesday the 8th. We leave on the 10th at 6 p.m.

Tell Bob that I was very, very glad to have his letter of the 26th and am most impatient to see him. I'll tell him about many interesting things and impressions. He's very much loved in Baden-Baden.

This is all for today. The food is very good here, the hotel small and old-fashioned but very elegant. The air is exceptionally clear, the colors of the sky and of the streets are extraordinary, as if they had swallowed lots of mescalin—unbelievable! Embraces, embraces. Your Bubushkinsky.

Vera to Igor

Mr. Igor Stravinsky
Aviz Hotel
Lisbon
Portugal

1260 North Wetherly Drive
Hollywood 46, California

---

[1] Lukas Foss, teaching at UCLA at the time.

[2] Stravinsky's tax accountant and an assistant to Aaron Sapiro.

[3] Hans Rosbaud rehearsed Stravinsky's Baden-Baden radio concert for him.

[4] The reference is to a post-concert reception for the Stravinskys in October 1951.

[5] Stravinsky conducted a Royal Philharmonic concert and received the Orchestra's

gold medal. He had balked at going, since he considered the fee too low and felt that the British press was hostile to his music, but he was persuaded to accept by his London publishers, Boosey & Hawkes.

[6] Stravinsky conducted two concerts in Lisbon.

[7] A front-page newspaper picture (*O Seculo*, May 30) of Stravinsky leaving the airplane, with a caption: "The great composer will conduct two concerts at Tivoli Hall," and the identification, "the author of *Passaro de Foyo*."

My dearest, I am so glad that this is your last stop. I can imagine how you are longing to get home. Milene has written me about it. The weather here is improving—less fog and more sun—and the Baroness is now giving swimming parties on Sundays, though Johnny Walsh really organizes them and she simply puts in a "Madwoman of Chaillot" appearance, wearing a raspberry house-dress and lots of jewelry, and with her red hair disheveled. When she emerges on her balcony, all conversation stops for a minute or two; I suppose that those who have never seen her before spend the rest of the week describing her to friends.

Now I must give you sad news. We have lost our two cats, Pinkie and Vaska. Pinkie had to be put to sleep, and Vaska expired at the veterinarian's, who could not extract the gunshot. We are very upset about it.

Evgenia Petrovna and I are working in the garden trying to get it in order for your arrival. Since Dmitri Stepanovich has been looking forward to his retirement, he has become arrogant and lazy. I will be relieved when he goes, since he does no work. I have another gardener, a Mexican, in view.

I am painting and working very hard at it. For eight hours yesterday I did not even come home to eat. Slowly but surely, I am getting thin. I have already lost five pounds. Taking thyroxin seems to help. A test was done, the results indicating a very low iodine level in my blood, which means that I have lacked thyroxin since the operation.

On Sunday I had the McLanes for dinner, partly in order to be rid of the invitation before your arrival. It was noisy and animated, what with my talk about the Rome festival and the museums, and Bob's about Ojai and Europe. Giacometti and various events at the Pierre Matisse Gallery were the main subjects at their house.

Imagine, Evenings on the Roof no longer exists! Morton is forming another organization, which Mr. Moss[1] has promised to support. It will probably be called Monday Evening Concerts, and Morton and Bob are already working on the programs. My painting class has been suspended, but Howard Warshaw and a painter called Finch have opened a new school on La Cienega. On Friday they had a great opening, but I did not join because Mary Vartikian will not be teaching there, and drawing from models will take place only in the evenings and under Warshaw's instruction.

This is my last letter. If you want to communicate, please send a cable. If you are tired, I advise you to rest in New York. Kiss Andre and Milene for me. I am waiting for you impatiently. Your Vera.

Thank you for the cable from Lisbon.

Igor to Vera
(Original in Russian)

1260 North Wetherly Drive   Aviz Hotel
Hollywood 46, California   Lisbon

Verushkinsky, The concert, Divertimento, *Scènes de ballet*, *Jeu de cartes* and *Petrushka*, went brilliantly, but in the sense of the

mercilessly bright ceiling lights. The orchestra tried hard, but the players are quite mediocre. The public came in droves, but the audience level is mediocre, too.

Yesterday, Pentecost, we went to Fatima, which is 150 kilometers north of here. Some new friends here telephoned and the whole seminary was awaiting us. I will describe this to you, and all that we saw on the roads there, at length. On the way back—unbelievable!—but I will not write anymore about it now.

Tell Bob that I received his second letter[2] (and with it the article by Arthur Berger), and that I am very grateful.

I received your letter with the sad news about the death of our cats.

Today the sky is clouded over and it's cold. Yesterday was depressing. But what a trip!

This is all for now: I am not going to write any more. Tomorrow I am conducting *Apollo*, *Scènes de ballet*, *Petrushka*, *Firebird*, and I can imagine how the audience will shout (ovation). But I could not care less. I know that you spoke on television, and how you worried, and all the effort over the make-up.[3] I embrace you.

July

6 Balanchine arrives.   **9** Balanchine for dinner.   **11** Lunch at Bel Air after Gerald Heard's lecture. Bob has a rehearsal. I make a cheesecake for Balanchine.   **12** To Balanchine's ballet at the Greek Theater.
17 Balanchine.   **25** Tea at Gerald Heard's.   **28** 3 p.m.: we go to Gerald Heard's lecture at UCLA.

August

19 Drive to Las Vegas with Edel.   **22** Back from Las Vegas.

September

5 Two rehearsals of *In Memoriam Dylan Thomas*.[4] Visit at Schoenberg's.
6 Rehearsal here of Gesualdo madrigals, 1 to 3. At night Bob reads D.H. Lawrence's Introduction to the memoirs of Maurice Magnus to me and Igor.   **7** Bob's Webern rehearsal here from 9 to 11.   **9** Lunch at the Huxleys'.[5] Rehearsal at our house from 9:30 a.m. At night Bob records Webern.   **18** Rehearsal of Gesualdo madrigals at our house, then late dinner (9 p.m.) here with Huxleys and Morton.   **20** Bob's Monday Evening Concert. Premiere of *In Memoriam Dylan Thomas*.   **21** Visit at 4 from Irene Brin and Gasparo del Corso.[6]   **23** Del Corso comes at 4 to discuss my show. The Huxleys at 5:30.[7]

October

2 Bob and Igor translate *Mavra*.   **3** More translating.   **4** The *Mavra* translation is finished.   **5** A boring party at Huxleys' for Julian.   **16** To Julian's lecture (dull).   **22** Igor goes to Chicago.[8]

Vera to Igor
(Original in Russian)

Igor Stravinsky   1260 North Wetherly Drive
Chicago   Hollywood 46, California
                                   October 23, 1954, 11 a.m.

---

[1] Oscar Moss, a Los Angeles attorney.

[2] This talks about the death of Charles Ives and about R.C.'s forthcoming concert (June 27) at the Los Angeles County Museum of Stravinsky's Cantata, Septet, and Shakespeare songs.

[3] On June 2, Mrs. Stravinsky had appeared on an educational television program with Lawrence Morton, William Russell of Pomona College, and R.C.

[4] These took place in the Stravinsky home. On January 2, 1954, R.C. had written from Hollywood to Stravinsky in New York: "I do hope you will set one of his poems during the twenty days you will have in February . . . for string quartet . . . and bass voice: 'Do not go gentle into that Good Night.'"

[5] On this visit Aldous Huxley gave Mrs. Stravinsky a copy of *The Doors of Perception*, inscribing it: "For Vera, whose paintings prove that she sees some of these things even without mescalin. Aldous. 1954."

[6] Signor and Signora del Corso, of the Galleria Obelisco in Rome, came to invite Mrs. Stravinsky to exhibit her paintings there in April 1955.

[7] The Huxleys, who spoke impeccable Italian, were regularly invited to the Stravinskys when they had Italian guests.

[8] With Andre Marion, by train, to conduct a ballet performance of *Petrushka*. For a description of Stravinsky during this event, see *Encounters With Stravinsky* by Paul Horgan, 1972.

Balanchine and myself at the Greek Theatre Hollywood July 1954

127 July 1954. Hollywood. The Greek Theater. With George Balanchine.

Dear One, I hope that you had a good trip and that you rested and stayed in your compartment reading. I am forwarding some letters but not one from Sapiro thanking you for Fedya's book. All is well here. I miss you. Your Vera.

29 Igor is back from Chicago. **30** With Igor to *Fidelio* at 2 p.m., then to *Tosca* at 8:30. Between the two performances Igor left a note for Monteux at his hotel, congratulating him on the Beethoven.

November

8 Bob rehearses. I see the *Barefoot Contessa* with Igor. **9** Bob and I start to write a short story about the pirates.[1] **25** At the Huxleys'. **27** Auden, Isherwood, and Don for dinner.

December

5 Igor and I go to a cocktail party at Isherwood's for Anna Magnani and Tennessee Williams. **6** Bob's rehearsal. After Bob's Monday Evening Concert (Schütz's *Christmas Oratorio*), we fly to San Francisco (at 11:45 p.m.). **7** Not enough sleep. Igor rehearses at 10:30 a.m. In the evening Igor conducts *Petrushka*.[2] **11** Igor conducts the second performance of *Petrushka*. **12** We fly to Los Angeles at 12:55, and are met at the airport by Maria Huxley and her mother. **16** For dinner: the Huxleys, Gerald Heard and Michael.[3] **25** Igor conducts *Petrushka* in the Shrine Auditorium. **31** Igor conducts *Petrushka* in the Shrine Auditorium.

1955

January

1 Igor and I relax the whole day with a jigsaw puzzle. Bob reads us 200 pages of *The First Night of "Twelfth Night."* **2** (Sunday) A criticism in the *Los Angeles Times* by Albert Goldberg: too much Stravinsky, Schoenberg, and eighteenth-century music at the Monday Evening Concerts. **3** To *Romeo and Juliet*.[4] **5** Fly at noon to Portland, Oregon (the Hotel Multnomah). **6** Igor rehearses the Portland Symphony 6 to 9 p.m. **9** Igor has rehearsals from 9:30 to 12:30 and from 6 to 9. I spend the time reading Herbert Read's *Meaning of Art*. Bob telephones after his Arizona concert.[5] **10** Igor's concert in Portland. **11** Bob arrives for breakfast. Igor's concert in Salem. **12** We leave on the 5:30 train for Chicago. **13** Marvelous trip, relaxing. Read Freud's *Moses and Monotheism*. **14** Chicago, the Blackstone Hotel. **15** Bob leaves for Albany (Kingston) on the 1:40 train. Igor and I in the museum 2 to 5. Reading Brill's *Psychoanalytic Psychiatry*. **16** Nini comes at 10; lunch with him. Igor and I take the train to Birmingham, Alabama, at 4:30. **17** The Hotel Tutweiler, Birmingham. Igor rehearses in the evening. **18** Igor rehearses 7:15 to 10:15. **19** Lunch with Lipkin, conductor of the orchestra. Igor rehearses at night. **20** Igor's Birmingham concert. **21** Fly to New York through Pittsburgh at 10:30. In New York at 4: Alexis. **22** To the Ben Shahn and Picasso exhibits in the morning. Matinée: *The Pajama Game*. At 5, see Berman's new apartment. Visit from Claudio Spies. To the theater in the evening, *The Bad Seed*. **23** For lunch: Alexis and Phyllis [Crawford] and her family. At 4 to Balanchine's rehearsal. Spies. **24** For lunch: Balanchine and Lincoln Kirstein. In the

---

evening: *House of Flowers*. **25** To the Museum of Modern Art for the Cone Collection. Lucia Davidova for tea. For dinner: Auden, Kallman, and Protetch. In the evening: Menotti. **26** Fly to Atlanta, the Biltmore Hotel. Igor rehearses 4 to 6:30. **27** Igor's rehearsal. **28** Igor rehearses 4 to 6. Dinner with Sopkin (conductor of the orchestra). **29** 9:30 a.m. rehearsal. **31** Igor's Atlanta concert.

February

1 Fly to New Orleans, the St. Charles Hotel. Wonderful city, but the climate . . . **3** On the Southern Pacific railroad. **4** Home at 4:30. **6** To Gerald Heard's at 5:30 for tea. Very bad news about Maria Huxley.[6] **10** Bob's rehearsal here: 15 musicians in the living room. **11** Ona Munson's suicide. I call Genia. **12** Maria Huxley died at 6 a.m. **13** Gerald's lecture in the morning. Afterwards Peggy comes to tell us the details of the illness and death. **14** To Maria Huxley's funeral at Father McLane's.[7] **15** Bob's Webern recording. **16** Aldous for dinner. **17** Igor and Bob edit the records. **21** Bob's concert. After it, here: 19 people, including Křenek. **22** Bob's Webern rehearsal. **23** Chorus rehearsal (Webern) at our house, 10 to 1. **25** Bob records. **27** To Gerald's lecture. **28** For dinner: Isherwood and Don.

March

2 For dinner: Aldous and Gerald. **5** 4:30 train to Pittsburgh. **7** Pittsburgh, the Shenley Park Hotel. **8** Igor rehearses the Pittsburgh Symphony at 10:30 a.m. In the museum: terrific dinosaurs and terrible pictures. **9** Igor's 9:30 rehearsal. **10** Igor's 9:30 rehearsal. **11** 8:40 p.m.: Igor's concert. **13** (Sunday) 3:10: Igor's second concert. I go ahead to the airport to organize the departure. We fly to New York at 5:45. At La Guardia airport: Bob, Phyllis, Jack. Berman is waiting at the hotel. **14** For lunch: Alexis and Claudio Spies. We fly to Lisbon at 2 p.m. Land in the Azores at midnight and meet Bill Congdon, who is on the same plane. **15** Heavy landing at Lisbon, 9:30. Met by Constantin Varela Cid, the Aviz Hotel. Drive after lunch to Belem (the museum, the cathedral), Sintra, Cascais, Estoril. **16** Drive to Evora. Dinner at the hotel with Congdon. **17** After lunch, drive to the north. The Sibelius prize?[8] **18** Drive to Seville via Badajoz. The Alfonso XIII Hotel. We go to the cathedral and are followed by a musical priest, rather stupid and sticky. **19** To Cordoba and Granada (the Alhambra Palace). **20** To Madrid: marvelous landscape. **21** Igor rehearses at 3:30. **23** To Illescas—the El Greco church—and Toledo. **25** Igor's concert. **26** To the Escorial in two cars, with Prince Eugenio, Antonio de las Heras, Felicitas Keller, ourselves, and a photographer. Lunch there and back at the Ritz at 4:30. In the evening: Ortega y Gasset and the Marquesa de Slauzol. **27** Fly to Rome at 12:40. **29** Opening of my show at the Obelisco. Dinner at Orso after.

April

1 Drive to Palestrina. At 5:30 to Segovia's concert. Then to Obelisco with Igor and photographers. I sell the picture *Verklärte Nacht*. **6** Igor's concert with Nabokov. Supper after at the Fontanella Borghese. **9** Lunch in Ostia Antiqua with the Pannis, Vlad, and the Peragallos. **12** Igor is ill, doctor early in the morning. **15** Igor's rehearsal 4 to 7. **16** We go to Bob's concert at 5:15. **17** Train to Venice at 1:05. Venezia! **18** Test the acoustics in the Salute and the Frari.[9] Lunch with Count Alessi and Piovesan. **19** To Verona. Igor must be in Baden-Baden. **20** Milan, the Ambassador Hotel. At 6, the opening of my show. Dinner at Biffi's with

---

[1] Based on Mrs. Stravinsky's experience in May 1920 on the French ship, the S.S. *Souhira*, after leaving Trebizond for Constantinople. At this coaling stop, Georgian pirates had come aboard pretending to be passengers and had robbed everyone of all valuables, except the future Mrs. Stravinsky.

[2] Danced by Anton Dolin. This was the same company for whom Stravinsky had conducted the piece in Chicago in October, and with whom he would conduct it in Los Angeles. Nijinsky's daughter Kyra was present and talked to the Stravinskys at intermission and after the performance.

[3] Michael Barrie was Heard's constant companion, but the Stravinskys had not invited him before.

[4] The Italian film with music by Roman Vlad.

[5] At the University of Arizona in Tempe. R.C. had conducted a Los Angeles ensemble in pieces by Mozart and Beethoven, then flown from Phoenix to Los

Angeles, and the next day (January 10), taken the night train to Portland.

[6] While the Stravinskys were at Heard's, Aldous telephoned and said she was dying (of cancer), whereupon Gerald exclaimed: "Oh what bliss to have the mask off at last."

[7] Mrs. Huxley, a lapsed Roman Catholic, asked for a church service. She was buried in the cemetery at St. Matthias.

[8] When the Stravinskys returned to their hotel, the concierge told Stravinsky that announcements had been made on the radio and in the press that he had been awarded the Sibelius prize (about $50,000), but he never had any confirmation.

[9] Stravinsky listened to a small brass ensemble play in both churches, in the event that the Basilica of San Marco would not be available for the concert being planned for the premiere of the *Canticum Sacrum*.

128 1955. Galleria Obelisco, Rome.

Michelangelo Spanio.[1]   **21** Train to Bern, Schweizerhof Hotel.   **22** Spend a very emotional day with Madubo.[2] Igor's concert in Baden-Baden.   **23** Train to Innsbruck (8 hours from Bern), Hotel Europe.   **25** *Mittersill, das grab von Anton Webern.*   **26** Third day in Innsbruck, *sehr langweilig.*   **27** 11 a.m. to 8:23, Innsbruck to Milan.   **28** Lugano, the Grand Hotel Palace. Igor's Lugano concert.   **29** To Zurich by train, then to Stuttgart, the Park Hotel.   **30** Stuttgart is terribly dull.

May

1[3] Help Bob by translating phrases to the orchestra: "don't anticipate," "pitch," "smooth."   **3** By car to Mannheim, Park Hotel (paid by the Rundfunk so I must not be critical). Concert with Cherkassky [Stravinsky's Piano Concerto]: a big success.   **4** To Frankfurt by car. Fly to Copenhagen. Dozens of photographers and reporters. We meet Frederick Ashton and Vera Volkova in the lobby of our hotel.   **5** Lunch at Krug's restaurant in the fish market. We leave on SAS at 8:10 for Los Angeles.   **6** Over Greenland and Labrador. In Los Angeles, television, photographers, reporters.   **19** Bob's two concerts for children in Ventura. Back to Los Angeles for a rehearsal (I drive). Mirandi arrives.   **20** The Ojai Festival.   **21** Endless rehearsals, concerts, parties. Edward James arrives.   **22** (Sunday) The last concert. We drive to Santa Barbara.   **24** Home.   **25** Igor has sciatic pains.   **28** Dr. Engleman for Igor.   **29** Bob's Mozart concert.[4] For dinner: the Kreneks and Morton.   **31** To the Klee exhibition—the Galka Scheyer Collection—in Pasadena: marvelous!

June

5 To Gerald's lecture. Bob's museum concert.   **7** To the Pasadena Art Museum with Igor, Bob, Sabine Ricard.[5]   **17** Dinner at Isherwood's with Gerald and Tony Duquette.[6]   **18** Igor's birthday. Big dinner at Bel Air.   **27** Bob records.   **29** Dinner here for Gerald and Michael, Christopher and Don, and James.   **30** Bob edits the recording all afternoon.

July

3 Igor and I go to Gerald Heard's lecture.   **19** Andre brings Michael and shows him all of the work: Igor is furious.[7]   **21** Dinner at Isherwood's: we are drunk.   **23** Dinner at Krenek's.   **28** Rehearsals the whole day. Igor and Bob record in the evening.   **31** Party here for Isherwood.

August

2 We leave for Carmel at 3 and spend the night in Paso Robles (hot and noisy).   **3** Carmel, the Torres Inn. Cold.   **4** Yosemite. Spend the night in Fresno: terrible.   **5** Home.   **26** Christopher Isherwood's birthday: surprise party at Tony Duquette's (enchanting).   **30** Dinner at Szigeti's in Palos Verdes.

September

2 Aldous comes back. Dinner at Luau.   **3** Dinner at Bel Air with Aldous.   **5** Madrigal rehearsal at our house. For dinner: Lucia Davidova and Aldous. Lucia buys my picture *Pink Houses* for $50.   **16** Dinner with Aldous at Bel Air.   **21** For dinner here: Aldous, Gerald, and Michael.   **25** To Gerald's lecture.   **26** Aldous for lunch.

October

1 We go to Bob's rehearsal in the hall.   **2** The opening of the Monday Evening Concerts. Aldous, *et al.*   **4** Duquette's Mexican dinner with Isherwood and Gerald, beautiful house.   **5** Dinner with Aldous at The Captain's Table.   **9** To Gerald's lecture.   **10** Isherwood, Don, and Michael for dinner.   **11** Igor has the flu.   **15** Bob has the flu.   **16** Concert at Santa Barbara with Aldous.[8]   **17** Bob's Monday Evening Concert.   **27** To a film with Igor, *The Big Knife.*   **28** Dinner at Bel Air, then the movie *The Wages of Fear.*[9]   **30** Do a puzzle with Igor. We have a late supper after Bob's rehearsal.   **31** We go to Bob's Gesualdo recording at 8:30.

November

1 With Aldous to the Shrine Auditorium for Verdi's *Macbeth* (a bore, stupid).   **3** [Isherwood writes from Naples: "We reached Naples yesterday in a rainstorm and, obeying Bob's instructions, went straight to the Galleria, drank 3 grappas, and then had supper at the Pappagallo. The proprietor sends you his respects. Am writing this on the boat to Ischia to see Chester. Love, Christopher."]   **4** To the opera, Walton's *Troilus and Cressida.* We leave and eat dinner in the Statler during the third act.   **5** Willy Strecker for lunch. To *Don Giovanni* (good).   **15** Igor goes with Bob to his rehearsal of *Renard.*   **16** Igor and Bob working on *The Nightingale* translation.   **20** Igor's concert at UCLA. Here afterwards for supper: Jerry Robbins, *et al.*   **28** To Bob's Monday Evening Concert.   **30** Dinner at Morton's with Aldous, listen to recordings.

December

1 Bob worked all day and all night with Jackie Horne. At 8 we leave for New Orleans and New York by train.   **2** Sunset Limited: a wonderful train.   **3** Landscape: swamps. At 4 change in New Orleans for the train to Chicago (not good).   **4** Change in Chicago for Cleveland. Mr. Pitcock meets us in Cleveland with a car at 7 p.m.   **5** Igor rehearses 12:30 to 3.   **6** Igor rehearses 12:30 to 3. We go to the Museum. Read *Le Naïf.*   **7** Igor rehearses 10 to 12:30. Museum with Igor.   **8** Igor rehearses 10 to 12:30. The Samples.[10] Elden Gatwood.[11] Igor's concert.   **10** A tape-recorded interview with Igor is broadcast at 11 a.m. Igor's second concert.   **11** Igor records *Le Baiser de la fée.* At 9 p.m., train to New York.   **12** NEW YORK! To the theater: *Witness for the Prosecution.*   **14** Alexis Haieff at 6. To the theater: Pirandello's *Six Characters in Search of an Author.*   **19** Dinner at Lieberson's.   **20** Igor sick. To the theater: *The Chalk Garden* with Gladys Cooper.   **21** Dinner with Aldous. To the theater: *Bus Stop.*   **22** To the theater: *Rock Hunter.*   **23** Lunch with Auden and Kallman. Ben Shahn comes for tea.   **24** Dinner at Lucia Davidova's.   **27** To the theater: *A View from the Bridge.*   **28** To the theater: *Silk Stockings.*   **29** Cocktail party at Fizdale's and Gold's, with Alexis. Very, very nice.   **30** Diane for 24 hours.[12]   **31** To the theater: *Plain and Fancy.*

January

5 Dinner at Lucia Davidova's with Joseph Cotton, then to *King Lear* with Orson Welles.   **7** Birthday party at Auden's for Chester and me.   **8** Igor

---

[1] The second husband of Stephanie Guerzoni, mother of Denise (Mrs. Theodore) Stravinsky. After dinner he drove Mrs. Stravinsky and R.C. to the Villa d'Este Hotel at Como and confessed that he could no longer endure his marriage. He committed suicide a few years later. Denise shared Vera Stravinsky's Milan hotel suite with her.

[2] This was the last time that either Mrs. Stravinsky or R.C. saw her.

[3] Stravinsky rehearsed the *Symphony of Psalms* on May 1 in the broadcasting studio of the Villa Berg, and a tape was made both of the music and of his conversation.

[4] In the Los Angeles County Museum. R.C. played the "glass harmonica" piece on the celesta, and conducted.

[5] A relative of the Baroness d'Erlanger's.

[6] Stage designer, most notably of the San Francisco Opera's *Rosenkavalier.*

[7] Michael Barrie had considered working for Stravinsky as a secretary, but Stravinsky had not agreed.

[8] R.C. accompanied Marilyn Horne at the keyboard.

[9] The Stravinskys were deeply impressed by this film. Six years later they met its director, Henri-Georges Clouzot, in Tahiti.

[10] James Sample had conducted the premiere of Stravinsky's version of *The Star-Spangled Banner.*

[11] Elden Gatwood, oboist in the Cleveland Orchestra, had been a student at Juilliard at the same time as R.C., who introduced him to the Stravinskys in August 1951.

[12] R.C.'s niece had come to stay for one day; she slept in the twin bed in Mrs. Stravinsky's room. The Stravinskys took her to see *Oklahoma.*

sick. Dinner with David Protetch (alone). **9** Dr. Pierre comes for Igor. **11** Visit from Ansermet. Leave for Los Angeles, *hélas*. **12** We are three hours in Chicago at the station. **14** Morton meets us with the Buick at the Los Angeles station. **15** Igor and Bob go to the Marions' to see *The Magic Flute*[1] on TV. **16** A man to see Igor about televising a short animated cartoon film of *Petrushka*. Bob started rehearsing for his concert. **22** [Sunday] We go to Gerald Heard's lecture. **23** Go to Bob's concert.

February

4 Dinner with Aldous and Morton at Bel Air. **5** To Gerald Heard's lecture on tragedy and in the afternoon Bob's concert in the Los Angeles County Museum. **9** Bob's recording. **11** Igor, Bob, and I for dinner at the Bel Air. **12** Bob and I bring my paintings to Santa Barbara. Dinner with Igor at Luau. **19** To Gerald's lecture on laughter. Dinner with Aldous. **20** David Raksin for lunch. Bob's Monday Evening Concert. **21** Hitchcock movie, *Psycho*. **22** Prince Pierre of Monaco visits us at 5:30, tells us about the engagement of Rainier to Grace Kelly. **28** We go to Santa Barbara. The opening of my show at the Museum.

March

1 The recording of the *Petrushka* music for the film. **8** Bob's final Webern recording.

April

6 Dinner here for Aldous and his new wife, with Christopher Isherwood and Gerald.

May

3 Dinner with Maurice Chevalier at Ciro's. **12** Huxleys here for dinner. **21** Igor's *Noces* rehearsal. **27** Ojai rehearsal 11–3, then the concert (*Noces*). Dinner in the Ojai Inn, then drive to Santa Barbara. **28** Home.

June

1 [On this date Igor wrote to Theodore describing an attack of arthritis in his left leg that had tortured him for ten days but did not stop him from conducting in Ojai on May 22 and that, "thanks to an excellent orthopedist, is much better."] **7** The Huxleys and Gerald for dinner. **10** Gerald's lecture on creation coincides with my dream. **16** Train—City of Los Angeles—to New York. **18** Chicago. Lunch in the Pump Room with the Phil Harts. **19** New York. Bob goes to Kingston. **22** Dinner at Lucia's. **23** Lunch with Brainerd at the Museum of Modern Art. Dinner with David Protetch. **24** Spend the day at Alice de la Mar's with Balanchine, Lucia Davidova, Berman. **25** Lunch with Lieberson, dinner with Debbie Ishlon [of Columbia Records], and to the theater: *My Fair Lady*. **26** Visits from Elliott Carter, Milton Babbitt, and Ingolf Dahl. Dinner at Maria's with Protetch, who takes us to a horrible musical, *Most Happy Fella* (we leave). **27** Sail at noon on the *Vulcania*. **29** Cable: Madubo died.

July

2 See the Azores. **4** Lisbon. Car to the Aviz Hotel. Trip to Mafra, Sintra, Queluz. Marvelous. **6** Barcelona. Dinner with Eduardo Toldra. **8** Naples. In two automobiles to Gesualdo with Adriana Panni and

Loredana Franceschini. **9** Palermo. **10** Patras, the Cecil Hotel. At customs: a mess, bedlam. **11** At 8 a.m.: ferry to the north side of the Gulf. Dinner at Delphi. **12** Athens. **14** Lunch with Iolas and the painter Ghika, dinner with the Dushkins. **16** Igor in bed. Bob and Morton go to Nauplia alone. **17** Igor still sick. Dr. Doxiades (rue Homer 50) comes. **19** Flight to Istanbul (Hilton Hotel) on TAE at 2 p.m. View of the Bosphorus. Ourselves, and Mr. and Mrs. V. de Bosset.[2] **23** Motorboat to the Black Sea with Mildred and Robert Bliss, Mrs. Carp (US Consulate). Later, back at the hotel: Dr. Farouk. **24** Kariye Camii, mosaics and frescoes. *Scandale* in hotel about bedbugs. **27** Fly to Athens for one night. Dr. Doxiades comes to the hotel. **28** At 10:30 a.m., Igor's interview is broadcast on the Athens radio. At 3 p.m. leave for Venice on the *Mediterranean*, a miserable boat. **30** Venice: unload in the canal of the Giudecca. Piovesan at the dock. Bauer Grünwald. The *bonheur* to be in Venice!

August

3 Dinner with the Soulimas. **4** To an outdoor performance of *Tosca* in the Campo S. Angelo. **5** To the Biennale: 25 Mondrians. To *Trovatore* in the Campo S. Angelo. **10** To Torcello for dinner with Piovesan, in the Biennale motoscaffo. The lagoons—marvelous. **12** Lunch at Carletto (Treviso), then to Villa Manin, Grado, Aquilea. **15** Deaths in the last few days: Bert Brecht, Jackson Pollock, John Latouche, Alice Bouverie, Frieda Lawrence. **20**[3] We go to Stra, Pisani, Piazzolo, Villa Contarini, Barberigo, Valsanzibio, and Petrarca's house. **30** First rehearsal for *Canticum Sacrum*.

September

2 (Sunday) To Urbino and back with Lucia Davidova, tiring but marvelous. **4** Lunch with Luigi Nono and Nuria Schoenberg. In the evening Igor and I and the Artur Rubinsteins go to Segovia's concert in the Conservatorio Benedetto Marcello: beautiful sound, breathtaking technique, but too precious. **13** Igor's dress rehearsal in San Marco. The performance in San Marco. Taverna La Fenice afterward. **14** Party with Artur Rubinstein at the Villa Volpi. **18** Attend the opening of the New York City Ballet. Dinner at Martini's with Ambassador Charles E. Bohlen and Ambassador Thompson. **20** Igor leaves for Montreux in the car of Theodore and Denise. **22** Leave for Torino, awful train. Il Principe di Piemonte Hotel. **25** Train to Milan, plane to Berlin (Kempinski Hotel). **29** Lunch at the Von Westermanns'. **30** Lunch at the Aben Restaurant (Kurfürstendamm) with Senator Bach and the Von Bendas.

October

2 Igor's Berlin concert. He is very nervous. The performance is bad. Thunderstorm. **3** Igor stays in bed. He comes downstairs at night to see Scherchen after his performance of *König Hirsch*. **4** Fly to Munich. Met by Karl Amadeus Hartmann. At the Vier Jahreszeiten Hotel. Professor Dr. Diehl. **10** At 5, Igor goes to the Rote Kreuz clinic, Bob and I come at 7. **12** At 10 a.m. Hartmann takes us to the hospital, then to Wies and other examples of Bavarian baroque. Back to the hospital. Klemperer arrives in the hotel: his wife has had a heart attack. **22**[4] Hospital. Jackie Horne is typing for Bob in my room. **23** Igor is fully aware that he has had a major stroke. With Bob and Jackie to an Italian restaurant. **24** Hospital. **28** Maurice Gilbert is at the hospital all day. **30** Morning in the Pinakothek. Lunch with Lotte Klemperer. Boris Blacher and Hartmann after dinner. The Russians are in Hungary! War?

[1] In the Auden-Kallman translation.

[2] This cryptic remark might refer to Mrs. Stravinsky's stay here in May 1920 with Serge Sudeikin, who could have been traveling under her name.

[3] On August 19, Aldous Huxley wrote to the Stravinskys from Los Angeles: "Dear friends, I hope you are now safely in Venice. Your postcards from Greece were rather disquieting—so much heat, with all the attendant ills that flesh is heir to: what one has to suffer in the name of Culture! My nearest approach to Greece this summer has been in a fascinating book by Professor Dodds of Oxford, called *The Greeks and the Irrational*. Immensely learned, but lively and very enlightening. Greece seems to have been rational for about 150 years, from 350 to 200 BC. Before and after, what extraordinary manifestations (in spite of the Parthenon and Socrates, in spite of Roman efficiency and engineering) of the irrational. Read this book if you can get hold of it.
"Bob's letter about your visit to Gesualdo was very interesting. I hope the locked chamber [in the castle] will finally be opened. What bliss if it contains an archicembalo! Count Chigi has written to thank me for the record, and says he is

making the pupils of his Academy listen to it as a perfect example of madrigal singing. Why not pop in to see him at Siena? Meanwhile I hope all goes well with St. Mark and rehearsals. . . . Work continues. The play will go on, I hope and believe, as soon as De Liagre can find a goddess. But the species is scantily represented in New York. . . ."

[4] On October 13, Aldous Huxley wrote to the Stravinskys in Munich: "Morton has just given me your very sad news. I hope that everything is now as much better as possible and that Igor will take the rest that is so necessary in his condition. Will you return directly to California? I hope so. But if the trip is too long, make a sojourn in Sicily or even Menton—no matter where so long as it is not cold and there are no concerts.
"We leave the day after tomorrow for New York where I must speak before the Academy of Sciences—*quelle blague!* We will be back here by the end of the month, if all goes well. The staging of my play is becoming a little less problematical, but nothing in the theater is certain. Meanwhile I am working too much at too many things at a time. With all my thoughts for you and for Igor and love to Bob. Your friend Aldous." [Original in French.]

129

130

129–130 June 1956. Weston, Connecticut. At Alice de la Mar's, with Balanchine.

131

132

131 July 1956. Shopping in Athens.

132 1956. Athens airport.

133 July 1956. On the S.S. *Vulcania.*

134 1956. Venice. By the Scuola di San Fantin.

133

134

November

1 Everyone in the hotel lobby is reading the newspapers. Lotte Klemperer comes to talk to us: her mother is dying. **3** Bob left for Paris on the 12:47 "Mozart-Zug." Frau Klemperer died. **7** Jean Rouvier [art dealer] for lunch. **10** Bob's concert in Paris. **11** Bob arrives at 10 a.m., room 417. **16** Nicolas Nabokov comes. **17** Igor is discharged from the hospital, back to the hotel at 6! **18** Bob goes to Vienna on the 1:15 train. **19** Bob phones from Vienna. **20** Schwester Dagmar, Igor, and I go to the movies. **22** We leave on the 10:30 train to Rome. **23** Rome at 2:30 p.m. Vlad, Berman, and Alexis are at the station. Bob arrives from Vienna at 8 p.m. and goes directly to a rehearsal at 9. **24** Beautiful Rome, bad political news. **27** Mondrian show. Consultations (Gozzano and Gilbert). Igor *triste* afterward. Lunch with Berman (Bob is at Vlad's). Igor's rehearsal 9 to 11 in the evening, conducted by Bob. **28** Igor's rehearsal. **29** Igor's Rome concert.

December

2 Doctor Gozzano in the morning. Leave for Paris at 1:30. **3** 9 a.m. Paris. Taxi strike: Georges Sachs comes to the station with a Cadillac; also Boulez with a car; also Françoise and Zizi with a car. Igor goes with Bob to a recording session of the *Canticum Sacrum* and Bach Variations. We leave on the night train for London. **5** Savoy Hotel, London, 9 a.m. **7** Igor's right side is stiff. Consultation. Igor has a blood-letting. In the evening to the musical *The Boy Friend* (poor). **8** Car to the Tower of London in the morning. Then Igor has a blood-letting (Dr. Stoddart). Lunch with Boulez and Jean-Louis Barrault. Drive to Hampton Court. At 5, tea in the Savoy Grill with T.S. Eliot. After dinner to *Cymbeline* at the Old Vic. **9** Bob rehearses until 5 p.m., then Igor has a blood-letting. In the evening we go to the movie *Bus Stop* with Kitty.[1] **10** Lunch with Isaiah Berlin and Nabokov. Bob's rehearsal in St. Martin-in-the-Fields. Dr. Stoddart. I visit Salome[2] and Sir Gerard d'Erlanger.[3] **11** The last consultation for Igor. Bob's concert,[4] then a party at the IMA at 14 South Audley Street.[5] **12** We are supposed to sail on the *Flandre* but it is cancelled because of a strike. **14** We sail from Southampton on the *Mauretania*. **21** New York. **24** Party at Lucia Davidova's with Lincoln Kirstein, Baron Raffaello de Banfield, and Moore Crosthwaite. **29** To the movie *War and Peace*. **30** Isherwood comes at noon, then Arthur Berger and Milton Babbitt. **31** To Dr. Pierre. New Year's party at Lucia's.

1957

January

1 Lincoln Kirstein for lunch. He takes us to the Balthus show at the Museum of Modern Art. To Eugene O'Neill's boring play *Long Day's Journey Into Night*. **2** To see Judy Holliday in the play *Bells are Ringing*: cheap and vulgar. **3** To *Happy Hunting* with Ethel Merman. **10**[6] Igor's first concert with the New York Philharmonic: big success.[7] **11** Igor's second Philharmonic concert. **13** (Sunday) Igor's third concert: he receives a scroll, honorary membership of the Philharmonic. **14** Igor records *Perséphone*. **15** My show at Iolas opens at 5. Afterward to Menotti's ballet-opera, *The Unicorn*, etc. **16** Igor and Bob lunch in the Pavillon with Arthur Judson, who tells them about the death of Toscanini. To Terence Rattigan's play *Separate Tables*. **17** Bob and Igor lunch with people from *Time*. In the evening to [Anouilh's] *Waltz of the Toreadors*. **21**[8] With Liebersons to *Waiting for Godot*. **22** See Graham Greene at the

---

[1] Stravinsky's granddaughter was boarding in London.

[2] Princess Salomeya Andronikov, Mrs. Stravinsky's friend since Tiflis in 1919.

[3] Son of the Baroness and director of BOAC. Three years later he sent an airplane to take his mother from Hollywood to Paris, where she died.

[4] In St. Martin-in-the-Fields. Stravinsky sat in the first pew next to Ralph Vaughan Williams.

[5] The guests included Michael Tippett, Peter Heyworth, Spender, William Glock, Edward Clark.

[6] On January 9, Catherine d'Erlanger wrote to Mrs. Stravinsky: "The cook, the masseuse, everyone has news of you, and me, nothing. . . . It might interest Igor to write music for the film *Atlantide* with Jean-Pierre Aumont. . . . When are you coming back?"

[7] Stravinsky's stroke had been publicized and the greenroom and stage-door

---

preview of his play *The Potting Shed*. **23** Leave for Los Angeles on the 6 p.m. train.

February

4 We go to Bob's Monday Evening Concert. **18** Bob's Monday Evening Concert (Schoenberg's Serenade): party here. **19** At 5:30, Peter Brook for tea.

March

2 Dr. Knauer. Igor has a fit. Boulez for dinner. **3** Boulez for lunch. **8** Boulez's lecture at UCLA: very impressive. **11** Boulez's concert. He invites us to dinner at Bel Air. **18** Igor and Boulez go to Bob's recording session of Schoenberg's Serenade. **19** Bob edits the Serenade tape. Dinner with Gerald: interesting conversation.

April

17 Herr Joseph Rufer and Frau Schoenberg for tea. **28** To Gerald Heard's lecture.

May

11 Isherwood and Don come for dinner. **15** Dinner with Gerald. **16** Lunch with Christopher Isherwood and Don at MGM Studios. **17** Bob records Gesualdo 2 to 5. **19** Aaron Copland for dinner. **22** Bob records. **24** For dinner here: Isherwood and Don. **29** Lunch at Bel Air. The whole day with Robert Graff (NBC Television): I am going mad. Bob rehearses for his recording.

June

12 The whole house is upside down with 20 NBC television people.[9] **13** NBC film. **14** Film until afternoon. Then to Bob's rehearsal of *Agon*. **15** Igor's rehearsals. **16** Igor's rehearsals. **17** Igor's concert. Eisenhower message is read. Aldous gives a speech. World premiere of *Agon* conducted by Bob. **18** Recording *Agon* and Bob records Schoenberg's Variations on leftover time.[10] **20** Bob takes the "Super Chief" to Boston.

July

3 Visit from Křenek. **6** Good-bye party: Christopher, Don, Gerald, Michael. **7** 8 p.m.: leave for Santa Fe on the "Super Chief." **14** From 5 to 7, cocktail party: the boring "beau monde" of Santa Fe. Dinner at Brink Jackson's with Mirandi and Paul Horgan. Very nice. **15** Opening of my show at 4: *tout* Santa Fe. Dinner at Dr. Hausner's: 6 to 10. Dress rehearsal of *Rake*: cold wind. **18** The premiere of the *Rake* (postponed from yesterday). **19** Isherwood and Don arrive; dine with them at Babin's and Vronsky's. *Rake* second performance. **21** At 1:30, train from Lamy. **22** Cross the Mississippi at 9 a.m.: green, marvelous country. Do not leave the train in Chicago. **23** New York at 8:30. **25** Dinner at Lucia Davidova's with Mrs. Harkness. **31** Pavlik Tchelichev died.

August

1 At 11:30 we sail on the S.S. *Liberté*. **7** At 6:30 a.m., arrival at Plymouth.

---

crowds were larger than ever before in New York. Leonard Bernstein brought Maria Callas, who had seen Stravinsky many times in Venice during the summer of 1956, but had not yet been introduced to him.

[8] On January 20, Catherine d'Erlanger wrote to Mrs. Stravinsky: "Nothing from you since London. I know that you are in New York but I would like to know about Igor's health and your exhibition. There are many letters here for Bob and I don't know whether or not to forward them."

[9] For the half-hour film of Stravinsky (*Wisdom* series). The Stravinsky house was blanketed and insulated and Wetherly Drive was closed off against street noise. All electricity came from a mobile generator. Since television at that date could not show Stravinsky moving from one room to another, two sets had to be prepared, one at his piano and one at a table in his living room. See *A Stravinsky Scrapbook*, op. cit.

[10] On this date, Stravinsky noted, "I gave the Sibelius medal to Balanchine to the National Foundation for Infantile Paralysis, Greater New York Chapter, in the name of Tanaquil LeClercq. IStr."

135 January 1957. Carnegie Hall. Listening to a rehearsal of *Perséphone*.

136

136 January 1957. During a concert with the New York Philharmonic.

137 1957. 1260 North Wetherly Drive.

138 Spring 1957. 1260 North Wetherly Drive. Composing *Agon*.

139

140

73 ✗ " II (R.H.) last note of first group (D) is C♯ in full sc.

76 ✗ " II (L.H.) fourth note (D) is E in Full sc.

89 ✗ " I (R) the first two quavers' worth in Full sc. is

this is right [musical notation] must be wrong, as it equals only one quaver.

97 ✗ Piano II (R.H.) - last note of 3rd beat, Full sc. has C (not E♭)
    " " (L H) " " " " " " [musical notation] (not ♮)

129 ✗ " I (R.H.) - last beat - The lower notes F, E are not in the Full sc. (see also bars 261 and 394)

148 ✗ " II (R.H.) 3rd beat - The # to F is missing from Trombone I in Full sc. *You are right!*

156 ✗ " II (L.H.) 1st note. In Full sc. Bass Trombone has F. Is G♯ correct?

261 ✗ (same as bar 129)

289 ✗ Piano II (L.H.) Full sc. has C# [crossed out] *must be* D♮

[crossed out]

336 ✗ et seq. Barring differs in Full sc. (This has been noted in your set of proofs). *I know. Piano score barring is right, although different from full score.*

394 ✗ (same as for bar 129)

466 ✗ et seq. Barring differs from F. sc. *Yes, I did it intentionally*

487 ✗ Piano I. - Full score has [musical notation] not [musical notation]

565 ✗ In Full score is the rhythm of Trumpet II wrong? *Yes - wrong.*

Taken ashore on a tender. We lose two suitcases and acquire one by mistake but eventually everything is sorted out. Bob and I rent a car in Torquay. **8** Drive to Exeter cathedral. Hear Julian Bream's lute concert at Dartington Hall. **9** To London by train, Dorchester Hotel (excellent). **10** With Igor to the Victoria and Albert Museum (marvels), and to the National Gallery. **11** With Igor to the British Museum. **12** Bob records at the BBC from 9:30 a.m. At 11, a BBC car takes us to hear his tapes. **17** Drive across Dartmoor to Tintagel. **18** Lunch at Lord Chaplin's. **19** Lunch at a hotel in Bath with H.D.F Kitto (author of *The Greeks*). Return via Wells and Glastonbury Abbey. **20** *Un jour très rempli pour Bob.* Igor is photographed by Gjon Mili (*Life*). **21** To London in a Rolls Royce (paid for by *Life*). Stop at Stonehenge and Salisbury. **22** To the Tate: Turners!!! To the theater: *The Mousetrap*. **24** The night train to Paris. **25** Paris, 9:10 a.m.: Nabokov and Boulez at the station. **28** Venezia!

September

4 Igor in bed all day (diarrhea). Bill Congdon comes at 6. **8** Lunch with Chirico, then in the evening to a René Clair film at the Lido festival. **10** Bob drives us to Mantua and Sabbioneta. **12** Lunch with Nabokov and Rolf Liebermann. Take the Biennale motorboat to Malamocco. **14** The big event: yesterday Nabokov and Liebermann decided to bring the Hamburg orchestra to Venice. Afterward to the Fenice: Werner Egk's *Der Revisor*. **15** To Bologna for photographs by Mili. **17** Igor photographed in San Marco. **18** Second concert: Hindemith with Von Benda conducting. *Raté*: nobody wants to hear such a bore. **19** To the Bassano exposition. Bill Congdon sends a gondola at 6 and we go to his studio (we buy his painting Piazza 12), then to dinner in the Colombo. **22** To Palladio's Villa Barbaro in Maser, then to Asolo to see Malipiero. **23** To Torcello: Congdon, Piovesan, us. **26** To Peggy Guggenheim's. Dinner with Congdon. **30** To Munich by car over the Grossglockner (snow and fog). See the Hindemiths in the Vier Jahreszeiten.

October

4 Igor's Munich concert: tremendous success. **5** Car to Baden-Baden: Count Salm,[1] Strobels, Rosbauds. **7** Igor's rehearsal at 4. **8** Igor's rehearsal. Boulez for lunch. **10** Arrive in Paris on the night train. **11** Igor's Paris concert. Nabokov's party: Cocteau, Mary McCarthy, Giacometti, *et al.* **12** Dinner with Giacometti. **13** Giacometti draws Igor in our rooms at the Berkeley. **14** Party at the American Embassy, 6:30 to 8 (Florent Schmitt). Dinner at La Bourgogne. **15** I and Suvchinsky and Igor go with Bob to the train for Rome. **16** Dinner at Henri Monnet's[2]— *bourgeois* and *langweilig*. Telephone from Bob in Rome. **17** We take the 10 p.m. train to Zurich. **18** At 8 a.m.: Zurich. Car to Donaueschingen. "Family" dinner for 30 at Prince Fürstenberg's, with Schwarzenbergs and other nobility. Very nice. **19** Igor's concert at 5 in Donaueschingen. Car to Zurich. **20** Fly from Zurich to Rome in a terrible fog. Vlad picks us up at the airport. Bob comes after his rehearsal to eat in our salon—his birthday. Our rooms: 520, 519, Hotel Hassler. **21** To Bob's concert. **23** Igor's concert, a big success. Party at Panni's with Chirico, Carlo Levi, Moravia, the English Ambassador. **25** The 1:50 train to Paris. **26** Paris at 9 a.m. Doctor for Igor. We go to see Jean-Louis Barrault's production of Kafka's *Castle*. **27** Dinner at the Berkeley with Boulez, Suvchinsky, and Giacometti. Strange appearance of Judith. Stupid situation. **29** We sail from Le Havre on the S.S. *Liberté*.

November

6 New York. To *Look Back in Anger*, interesting play and good actors, very good direction. Dr. Protetch for Igor. **10** We go with Lucia Davidova to Balanchine's rehearsal of *Agon*. Talk to Aldous on the telephone. **15** Los Angeles. Morton meets us with our car. **30** Bob rehearses in our house.

December

4 Bob's rehearsal at our house. **7** Jazz and poetry. Babitz. Kenneth Rexroth. **9** Work hard for the party after Bob's Monday Evening concert; Kreneks, Huxleys, *et al.* **22** (Sunday) To Gerald's lecture. **26** Dinner at Romanoff's with the Huxleys. **29** Igor and Edward James go to dinner and the movies.

---

1 The Matthias Grünewald expert. The Stravinskys had met him in October 1951.

2 See the chapter "Cher père, chère Véra" in *Present Perspectives*, op. cit.

January

1 No resolutions. Yesterday was the best New Year's Eve: Huxleys, Gerald Heard with Michael, and us. Music, champagne, and good conversation. **2** We leave the house at 12:30 and are in the Rice Hotel, Houston, at 11:30 p.m., which is too long. Catherine d'Erlanger took a chair and sat in the driveway to see us pass by. Touching! Poor old fat lump. In the plane I work on my rug and read Baron Corvo (marvelous). **3** Friday. Igor has a rehearsal. Paul Horgan arrives in the morning and Mirandi at 4. **4** Peggy Kiskadden is here: her husband's operation lasted 3 hours (it was 8 hours five years ago). We will soon be toys, all organs replaced by nylon tubes. Dinner party for 35 at Cushmans'. **5** Igor's rehearsal 2–5. At 5 I go with Mirandi to the reception for the opening of my show. 500 people, terrible noise. Igor and Paul come later. **6** To Igor's concert. The Cushman Gallery has sold my *Christmas in California*. **7** We go for a ride in a tugboat along the waterfront. To Igor's concert, then dinner in the Shamrock. **8** Fly to Los Angeles, an endless trip, arriving at 11:30 p.m. Bob has a rehearsal and comes home at 12:30. **26** Dinner with the Huxleys at the Bel Air Hotel.

February

3 Bob records *Le Marteau sans maître*. **13** Dr. Knauer at 12. For dinner (bouillabaisse): Christopher Isherwood, Don Bachardy. **22** At 5, Karl Böhm [conductor]. **23** Bob's Vivaldi rehearsal (Concerto for 2 mandolins) here, also rehearsal here with five singers. **24** We go to Bob's concert. **25** Igor and I drive Bob to the airport. **26** Bob telephones from New York with bad news: Piovesan died. How terrible! Venice without Piovesan!

March

8 9:30 a.m.: Igor and I go to Union Station to meet Bob's train.[3] **10** To Bob's Monday Evening Concert.

April

7 Igor and Milton Babbitt go to Bob's Stockhausen recording (*Zeitmasse*: 6 hours). **10** We leave for San Francisco, stopping in Torres Inn in Carmel. **11** Carmel. Wonderful air, landscape, flowers. **12** San Francisco. **13** Igor's first rehearsal with the San Francisco Symphony. Bill Brown comes. **17** At 4:30 Igor and I go with Bill and Bob to the Afro show in Mills College. Dr. Neumeier, Director of the Art Department. **18** Last San Francisco concert in the afternoon, after which we drive to Carmel. **19** Leave Carmel, home late in the evening. **28** I start yoga classes with Indra Devi.

May

17 Dinner party with Aaron Copland, Dahls, Fosses, Alexis Haieff. **19** Igor has a sleepless night and he feels sick and weak. Rehearsal here for the Schütz singers. **20** To Bob's concert at the County Museum. **22** The Kreneks for dinner. **29** Igor, in the Cedars of Lebanon Hospital, has his first tranfusion and already looks better. **30** Igor's second transfusion.

June

7 I bring Igor back from the hospital. **10** Igor's *Mavra* rehearsal at UCLA. **16** Igor's concert at UCLA. **18** Igor's birthday dinner at the Beverly Hills Hotel. **19** Alexis for dinner, then to Bob's Gesualdo recording. **20** A brilliant opening (Comara Gallery), 600–800 people, six paintings sold. **30** Igor at Dr. Schiff's. Last day of my show.

July

2 Igor has his second radio-phosphorus injection at Cedars of Lebanon. **3** Isherwood and Don for dinner. **20** At 9 p.m. we leave on the "Super

---

3 Stravinsky was in a state of deep depression because of the death of Willy Strecker.

141 1958. 1260 North Wetherly Drive.

142 November 22, 1958. Rome. Exhibition of Vera's paintings at the Galleria Obelisco.

143 1958. New York. The Museum of Modern Art. With Dr. David Protetch.

Chief." **22** Chicago. Lunch with Paul Fromm in the Gold Lion on Union Street. The "Broadway Limited," a good train, to New York. **29** Sail on the S.S. *Cristoforo Colombo* at 4 p.m. **31** We are surrounded in the dining room by rather uninteresting people, old, self-satisfied, eating and drinking with appetites that are dangerous at their ages. One table of eight people laughs loudly at every triviality (unfortunately we hear their conversation). All of the young, pretty girls are in tourist class. I see them in the swimming pool, young, fresh bodies in bikinis. The first-class passengers look at them enviously.

August

8 Genoa. Lunch at Portofino. To the Campo Santo. **9** Lunch at Piacenza, dinner in Venice. **17** 4:30: motoscaffo to S. Lazzaro degli Armeni, S. Francesco del Deserto, Torcello. Marvelous day. **25** By car to Ferrara. **26** Dinner with Nina Kandinsky. Nathan Milstein joins us afterward. **29** At the Villa Cipriani in Stella Adler's apartment. **30** Bob goes to Hamburg. Letter from Catherine d'Erlanger: we are furious.[1]

September

1 Lunch with Artur Rubinstein. **4** Send books home: Tocqueville, Antonello da Messina, Wittgenstein's *Blue and Brown Notebooks*, Rilke, etc. **7** Lunch at the Villa Malcontenta with the Landsbergs.[2] Back in Venice we watch the regatta from Peggy Guggenheim's. **16** Bob comes back. My show at the Cavallino Gallery opens at 6. **23** The premiere of *Threni* in the Scuola di San Rocco. **24** Igor leaves for Zurich, by car. **27** Send our books to California: Auden's *Poets of the English Language*, Hutton's *Naples and Campania*, Pound's *Cantos*, Eliot, *Zen Archery*, Berlitz Italian, Darwin, *Musical Diction*, *Mycenae*, *Morea*, *Mannerism*, Biennale catalog, *The Last of the Medici*.

October

1 Igor comes back from Switzerland. Bob leaves by train for Brussels.[3] **6** Bob's concert in Brussels.[4] **7** Igor and I leave for Hamburg by car, spending the first night in Munich. **8** Stay in Frankfurt, where Bob joins us. **9** Arrival in Hamburg. **10** Bob has two rehearsals daily. **11** Igor and Bob go to Lübeck with Rolf Liebermann. **13** We listen to tapes of Schoenberg in Liebermann's office. Igor's concert tonight is the biggest success. Supper afterward superbly organized by Liebermann: Nabokov, a senator, the Von Westermanns, Philip Jarnach.[5] **15** Car to Baden-Baden; Brenner's Park Hotel, the best in Europe. **16** Stockhausen and Boulez for dinner. **18** To Donaueschingen. **19** Boulez's concert. Drive to Zurich; dinner there with Hansi Lambert.[6] **20** Bob's birthday. Doctor for Igor. Lunch with the Lamberts. **21** Doctor for Igor. Night train to Florence. **22** Florence. The Grand Hotel has a bad restaurant and mediocre rooms, but what a view of the Arno! **24** Bob goes to Rome and flies back to Hamburg—very reluctantly. **26**[7] At 5, Igor's first concert in Florence. **30** Igor's second Florence concert. **31** Car to Venice and 5:30 train from there to Vienna. During our two hours in Venice, the bells of the city ring for the new Pope, Giovanni XXIII.

November

1 Vienna. I hate it. I write to Frau Heinrich Strobel: "Chère Hilde, I am

sorry that we left Donaueschingen without saying *au revoir*, but it was a *hetze*, as always. How I hate these concert tours. Now we are in Vienna which, in spite of its name 'little Paris,' I find very boring. Now I know the meaning of the phrase 'house arrest.' . . . Also, I have had to take care of Bob who was very ill in Hamburg. . . . The doctor here says an appendectomy is necessary, but Bob wants to do it in New York, and stay on antibiotics until then. He must cancel his recording in Baden-Baden, but he might do half of the concert in Paris with my husband, although I doubt it. . . . I hope to see you in Paris." **4** Igor conducts *Oedipus Rex* at the Vienna Opera. **7** Igor's concert.[8] **8** At 9 p.m., the night train to Paris.

1959

January

4 New York. Town Hall. Bob's concert. *Threni*, Berg's *Altenberg Lieder*: biggest success, very select audience. **7** Party at Auden's for Kallman and me (his birthday as well as mine), with Lotte Lenya, *et al.* Cassoulet.

February

26 Igor is sick. **27** Gerald Heard and Bob have a televised conversation on CBS.

March

1 (Sunday) We go to Gerald's lecture. **6** Dinner at Isherwood's. Igor buys Don's drawing of Isherwood. **12** Dinner here: Isherwood, Don. **13** Igor and I to the Festival Ball in the Beverly Hills Hotel. I dance a solo waltz with Vincent Price. **15** At 4: Igor and I go to Milene's to see the televised conversation between Gerald and Bob. Very good! **18** Dinner here with Gerald and Michael. **23** Bob's Monday Evening Concert. Here afterward: the Kreneks and Lieberson. **25** Fly to Honolulu at 9. Arrive at 4, Princess Kaiulani Hotel. Swim on Waikiki Beach. Beautiful young Hawaiian girls; ugly, fat, and old US businessmen. **28** Fly to Wake Island, crushed coral. **30** Babies crying all night; impossible to sleep on the plane. Land in Manila at 5:30. Morris from the US Embassy picks us up. Mrs. Charles Bohlen comes to the hotel at 9 a.m. Dinner at the US Embassy. **31** Party at the Embassy with Philippine musicians. Quiet dinner with the Bohlens.

April

1 Fly at 12:30 to Hong Kong. **5** Japan. Very bumpy arrival. *20* photographers. **7** 1 p.m. press conference for Igor. Dinner with the Frank Korns at Fukidaya's. **8** Kabuki. **9** Gasparo del Corso for dinner. **12** Dr. Rosenberg for Igor at 7:30 a.m. The 9 a.m. train for Kyoto: shaking. The Hotel Miyako in Kyoto is not perfect. **19** With Nabokov to Osaka. Noh plays. Dinner in Kobé with Michi Muriyama and Pringsheim.[9] **20** Osaka. Bunraku. **21** Kobé. Lunch at Muriyama's. Back to Kyoto at 6. **22** Bob went alone to Nara. I read *Sayonara*. **23** I send home books: Huizinga's *Homo Ludens*, Haiku, *Japanese Conversation*, *Gardens of Kyoto*, *Japanalia*, Donald Richie's novel, catalogs, art books. Igor sick. We return to Tokyo by train. **24** My show at the Matsuya Store in the Ginza opens at 11. At 3 we go to Suma's with Hans Popper. **25** At 3:30 to the court dances: Gagaku. Marvelous music. **30** Back to Osaka.

---

[1] She had written that the studio which Mrs. Stravinsky rented from her would have to be vacated because someone else was going to live there. Later she quarreled with this person and wrote to Mrs. Stravinsky, November 8: "Perhaps some good news for you. I don't need the cottage—I can no longer walk and I can't go through the trouble of installing someone else there. It is six months since I have been able to go anywhere. My [helper] Katherine has disappeared—dead or married, I don't know. . . . I miss the sight of Igor walking up or down our street. Pray for me."

[2] The Baroness d'Erlanger had owned Palladio's masterpiece on the Brenta for fifty years. After the visit, Mrs. Stravinsky sent her a photograph of her husband with Bertie Landsberg and a letter saying: "I understand very well that you need the apartment, and the only difficulty is that your request to us to vacate was occurred during our absence. To move now during our concert trip in Europe will be very complicated. I propose to have Varzhensky come with his helpers and put all of my furniture and Bob's in my studio, except for the piano which will not fit. As for the move from my studio, this must wait until my return."

[3] R.C. stayed in the Square de Meeus home of the Baroness Hansi Lambert on this visit and wrote to the Stravinskys on October 5 (they preserved the letter): "The rich life would kill me in a week, and it is so good for me to see how fresh and stimulating our lives are compared to bankers' lives. How lucky I am to have been

with you these ten years. . . ." (Igor Markevitch was living in the Lambert house at the same time, and R.C. had many interesting conversations with him.)

[4] A Stravinsky-Webern program in the World's Fair.

[5] Composer, best known for having completed Busoni's *Doktor Faust*.

[6] Mrs. Stravinsky does not say that Suvchinsky and the Baroness Lambert were also in their car.

[7] Mrs. Stravinsky kept a letter with this date from R.C., then in Hamburg: "I did the rehearsal yesterday, but I could not rehearse today so Krenek did it for me. . . . Glenn Gould calls me on the telephone. He has been flat in bed for two weeks but is better now and might do the Vienna concert after all. I will fly to Vienna on Wednesday and stay at the Sacher. Let me know *there* when your train arrives Saturday. . . . Why do I do these silly concerts?"

[8] Stravinsky conducted *Apollo* and the *Pulcinella* Suite, and R.C. conducted Haydn's Symphony No. 101 and Schoenberg's Five Pieces.

[9] A nephew of Mrs. Thomas Mann.

May

1 Igor's concert in Osaka. **2** Back to Tokyo. **3** Igor's first Tokyo concert. **5** To Kabuki at 4:30. **7** Igor's second Tokyo concert. **8** Flying back to the USA!!! **9** Arrive in Los Angeles from Seattle with one motor dead, the runway covered with foam. **21** Igor and I fly to Copenhagen. **25** Igor's Copenhagen concert. **26** Fly to Los Angeles.

June

8 To Waxman's concert: Shostakovich: bore, bore, bore. After the concert, a party at Lytton's: Los Angeles society is dull and primitive. **15** Igor's and Bob's concert at UCLA. Party here afterward: 20 people. **17** Bob records. **27** Isherwood and Don at 5. **28** We leave for Santa Fe on the 9 p.m. train. **29** Arrive Lamy at 2:30. **30** Go every day to the hospital to see Bob, who has a dislocated elbow.

July

24 Hollywood. **25** Lunch at Huxleys' with Romain Gary and his wife, Leslie Blanche. **26** Dinner at Christopher Isherwood's.

August

12 Dinner with Gerald and Michael. **13** Dinner with Christopher and Don.

September

5 Drive to Windsor Castle with Bill Brown. Later Bill says that when he was walking with Igor and an airplane flew overhead, Igor observed that the noise consisted of seven distinct pitches. **9** Train from London to Edinburgh. At 8 to Fischer-Dieskau's Schubert recital. **13** Train to London (Claridge's). Doctor for Igor. Dinner with Stephen Spender, who introduces us to Ralph Richardson. **14** Train to Paris. **15** Beautiful Paris. The Berkeley Hotel is like home. **16** Lunch with François Michel[1] at Calvet. Leave on the 9 p.m. Simplon Orient Express for Venice. **17** *Bella Venezia!* **18** Dinner with Lucia Davidova, Berman, and Bob Sandbach. **26** Leonard Bernstein's concert in La Fenice.[2] **30** My name day. To Torcello.

October

1 With Berman to Udine and Duino. **12** Igor and Bob fly to Rome. I go with them to the Treviso airport. **18** (Sunday) Igor's Naples concert. **20** Join Igor in Bologna. Bob's birthday. **21** Rehearsal. Then to Giorgio Morandi's studio. He gives us a painting. Shy, gentle man. **22** Igor's Bologna concert. **23** By car to the Este Library in Modena, then Parma and up the winding, unpaved, mountain road to Canossa. Reach Milan for dinner in the Biffi with Leonard Elmhirst [from Dartington], then the night train to Paris. **25** To the matinée of Jean-Louis Barrault's performance of Claudel's *Tête d'or*. Bob flies from Paris to Hamburg. **31** Bob arrives in London from Hamburg.

December

31 [New York] The last day of the year was not a very happy one. Coming back to the hotel from the Ambassador restaurant, we found the Lillian Libmans sitting in the lobby and waiting for us. Nobody had told me about their intention to come and wish us a happy New Year, so I was again unhappy. The only cheerfulness was brought by Max Edel who had just arrived from Los Angeles. I wanted to talk to the Edels alone and I left everybody in the living room and closed the door until Debbie came in saying that everybody was furious. What an end to 1959.

---

[1] A cultural official of the French Government, assistant to Malraux, François Michel had been a friend of the Stravinskys from 1957.

[2] *Age of Anxiety* and Shostakovich's Fifth Symphony. Stravinsky left after a few minutes.

[3] In Town Hall. Matinée. Stravinsky conducted the premiere of his Movements for Piano and Orchestra.

January

10 Concert.[3] **19** At 8 to Balanchine's ballet. **21** At 10 p.m., leave for Los Angeles by train. **24** 8 a.m. Arrive home.

February

7 Dinner at Christopher Isherwood's in his new house. **11** Isherwood for dinner at our house. Christopher borrowed 3 books: Eric Ambler, Leavis's *Lawrence*, and Lawrence's "Maurice Magnus." **12** Igor records *Petrushka* at night.[4] **28** Bob rehearses *Histoire du soldat*. Fred for dinner with us. **29** Bob's Monday Evening concert.

March

4 Lillian Libman comes from New York. **10** To Christopher Isherwood's lecture on Kipling at the State College in East Los Angeles. He is a marvelous lecturer. We lunch with him afterward at Lacey's restaurant. **11** Bob reads Isherwood's unpublished diary to us: wonderful! **18** Dinner at Isherwood's. **22** For lunch here: Virgil Thomson. He is very brilliant, but it is like a lecture, without our participation in the conversation.

April

4 We go to Bob's Monday Evening Concert. **8** Party at the Beverly Hills Hotel. Leslie Blanche calls me every hour. **17** A nice Easter lunch at our house: Isherwood and Don, *et al.* **24** At 12:01 p.m. I bring Bob to Union Station to go to Toronto.[5] He is *triste*. Edel starts to sculpt Igor's head.

May

2 Christopher, Don, and Mirandi for dinner here. **6** Dinner at Isherwood's with Gerald Heard. **10** Bob will arrive from New York.[6] **31** Rehearsal for Igor's concert (Waxman) in Royce Hall.

June

6 Rehearsals: 3–6, 6–7, 8:30–10. **7** Igor's concert in Royce Hall. **17** Dinner at Isherwood's for Igor's birthday. **18** Dinner at Perino for Igor's birthday. **20** Opening of my show at the Comara Gallery. **23** Cocktail party to celebrate completion of our new room: 3 architects with wives, and 19 others. **26** Downtown Los Angeles for Bob's concert in the Museum. **30** Bob records Mozart's Serenade K.361.

July

1 Igor goes to three doctors—*wenn das nicht hilft!* **5** Take the "Super Chief" to Santa Fe.

August

1 At 10 a.m., fly to Mexico, arrive at 4:40. A colossal reception at the airport: crowds of schoolchildren, newspaper people. The Hotel Bamer is good but not as promised "the best in the world" (Villa Cipriani, Villa d'Este, Baden-Baden), and the restaurant is very mediocre and noisy. **2** Rehearsal ridiculously early (7 a.m. Los Angeles time), exhausting for poor Bob. Press conference: stupid questions; it was better organized in Tokyo. To the Ambassador restaurant—in a separate room because of impossibly loud music. **4** Dress rehearsal, Igor and Bob. Lunch and

---

[4] In the American Legion Hall, the first session.

[5] R.C. conducted Tchaikovsky's Second Symphony there, the Monn Cello Concerto (Schoenberg's basso continuo realization), etc.

[6] During this trip, R.C. convinced Balanchine to choreograph the *Monumentum*. As a card to Stravinsky postmarked May 4 indicates, Balanchine was attracted by Stravinsky's treatment of the orchestra in groups or blocks.

144 April 1959. Tokyo.

145 April 1959. Tokyo.

146 1959. In her studio.

147

147 May 1959. Copenhagen. With the Baroness Blixen (Isak Dinesen).

148 September 1959. Torcello.

148

149 1959. Copenhagen Zoo.

150 September 1959. New York. With Aldous Huxley. Photo by Arnold Weissberger.

149

150

151

151 November 1960. Rome. Photo by Casamento.

152 1960s. Beverly Hills. Photo by William Claxton.

152

dinner—bad—in our rooms. *Scandale* with Libman about money. Concert in the Bellas Artes: great success.   **5** Igor's rehearsal at 10 a.m. Reception at Mme Castillo-Ledon's at 6. Dinner at Villaseñors': very charming.   **6** Too much trouble with Libman, Alcazar. I go to the rehearsal 2–5.   **7** Morning concert in the amphitheater. Lunch at Morley Webb's, a nice house opposite Chapultepec Park.   **8** The Bal y Gays and Laura Villaseñor come to the airport for our 8 a.m. flight. Land at Panama at 3 p.m. and transfer to a jet to Bogotá, arriving there at 9:39, the Hotel Tequendama: dinner in our rooms.   **10** See the pre-Columbian gold collection in the basement of a bank.   **12** 6:30: concert in Bogotá. Dinner at 9 with Olav Roots.[1]   **13** At the Bucholz bookshop, we buy books about Klee. Second Bogotá concert.   **14** We go to the cathedral in a saltmine, but the altitude bothers us. For dinner: Roots, Alcazar.   **15** Depart 10:45, arrive Lima 5:20. Our hotel, the Country Club, is too far from the center and we change to the Bolivar.   **16** A very Italian city, crowded, lively. Bob's rehearsal. He said it is the worst orchestra ever.   **17** After the rehearsal, Bob and I go to a cemetery and look for the grave of my uncle, the Marquis Theodore de Bosset.   **18** Rehearsal. Bob and Igor are annoyed and afraid of the bad orchestra. Drive to the ruins of Pachacamac.   **19** Rehearsal. Two doctors for Igor. Lima concert.   **20** Depart at 10:20, arrive Santiago at 5:25, the Hotel Carrera. A very difficult landing. Claudio Spies waiting for us. A lot of insistent, almost arrogant photographers and newspapermen, almost a battle to avoid interviews.   **21** A drive in 2 cars to the country and go to a house where 20 composers and a lot of *inutile* people are gathered; but finally they are kind and nice. We thought it was a trap.   **23** At 11, I go with Fyodor Vadim Konstantinovich to the cemetery to look for my father's grave. Telephone from Juanita de Gandarillas.[2] Dinner at Spies's.   **24** The Santiago concert, but I do not go. Big dinner afterward in the hotel with Letellier and others.   **25** Depart at 7 p.m., arrive Buenos Aires 10:35, Hotel Plaza—the worst hotel I saw in my life and terribly expensive.   **27** Tea with Irena de Mella[3] and the Mestcherskys.[4]   **29** The Buenos Aires concert: biggest success. I wear my white ball gown.   **30** Lunch at Victoria Ocampo's in San Isidro. At 5 p.m. 20 composers and others come. At 8:30, back in Buenos Aires, dinner with people from the Mozarteum in an ugly, tasteless house.   **31** Lunch at Angelica Ocampo's apartment with Jorge Luis Borges, who inscribes one of his books for Bob. Afterward I go with Victoria to look at galleries. We receive Aller, a dancer we knew in Biarritz.

September

1 4–6: tea with Irena and Mestcherskys. Igor kindly accepts an invitation to dinner with the Mestcherskys.   **2** Tea with Irena in the American Club for Women. Almost a fight with Alcazar.   **3** At noon, Igor receives a decoration from the Argentine government. I was not even invited—what polite people! At 5: the Mozarteum concert. I do not go because I do not want to have a heart attack. Afterward the Mestcherskys come to say good-bye, and the secretary of the Minister of Culture comes to apologize.   **4** Fly to Rio de Janeiro, the Hotel Ouro Verde.   **5** We decide to cancel all concerts here and elsewhere in South America.   **6** Buy André Levinson's book on the ballet at a bookstore.   **7** At 8 in the morning, Igor gives me two aquamarines. Leave for Brasilia at 9:45, then a jet to Port of Spain and New York!   **17** We fly to Rome.   **18** Arrive in Rome and are met by a car and chauffeur from Venice. Drive to Perugia and spend the night there.   **19** Lunch in Borgo San Sepolcro; Piero della Francesca. Drive to Gubbio, then to Predappio, Ravenna, and Venice. In the Hotel Bauer-Grünwald at 9 p.m.   **22** With Lucia Davidova.   **23** Igor's first two rehearsals.   **27** Concert in the Palazzo Ducale. The audience in Venice is always stupid and the press nasty.

October

3 Igor has a temperature.   **7** To a Goldoni play at La Fenice.   **15** A flood! We watch from our balcony as the water comes in. The lobby and the restaurant are completely submerged.   **20** Bob's birthday.   **24** Sent today to Los Angeles: books on Umbrian and Pre-Incan art, Herbert Read's *The Forms of Things Unknown*, Adorno's *Philosophie der neuen Musik*, Mann's *Doktor Faustus*, Italian Touring Club books, book of Emilio Vedova's paintings, Agatha Christie's *Cat Among the Pigeons*, the Biennale catalog, Berensons, Sitwell, Kenneth Clark, *The Cathedrals of Apulia*.   **27** Igor has a temperature (38°). Doctor Pesenti comes at 10:30.

November

5 Car to Genoa.   **13** At 6, Igor's Genoa concert. Dinner with the Lanfrancos.   **14** Train to Rome. The first minutes in Rome are marvelous, then troubles start.   **18** Berman's dinner at Ranieri's (though actually the son of Paul Getty pays). Bob meets Signora Crespi: *coup de foudre*.   **23** Mirandi arrives. Party at Adriana's.   **24** Igor's Rome concert.   **25** At 4:20, train to Paris.   **27** From 1 to 5, lunch at the Boule d'Or with François Michel and Suvchinsky. At 5 we have a meeting with Rolf Liebermann and Chagall at Nicolas Nabokov's, but everybody is so drunk (1 bottle vodka, 3 of burgundy, 4 of champagne) that I had to go alone. Liebermann laughed terribly, for which I will always love him, but Chagall was disapproving and pompous. Returning to the hotel, I found Igor asleep and Suvchinsky applying cold compresses to Bob's forehead.   **30** 8:30 a.m., train to Le Havre and board the *Rotterdam* for Hoboken.

December

3 It is a bore to be on the boat. The upper rooms are good, but the cabins are too small and not very cozy, and, if you are spoiled, the restaurant is not as good as on the *Liberté*.   **7** The arrival in Hoboken at 6 a.m. Paul Horgan with a Rolls Royce, Debbie Ishlon with a Cadillac. The rooms in the St. Regis are small. I am happy in New York.   **14** Igor has a mild flu. Milene tells me Father McLane died yesterday.   **16** Bob has six hours of recording (*Lulu* suite, *Der Wein*, *Sieben Frühe Lieder*).   **31** New Year's Eve party at George Balanchine's.

January

3 Igor very sick, from oysters.   **5** Igor records the Octet. Paul, Bob, and I go to hear T.S. Eliot read his poetry at the 92nd Street YMHA.[5]   **6** Lucia Davidova helps out: she is so kind and does everything at the right moment. Lunch with Wystan. Go again to *Beckett*, this time for Igor.   **7** To Brigitta's [Mrs. Lieberson's] to look at my pictures for *Perséphone* and her costume. She is not wearing make-up, and is beautiful like ivory. Igor goes to the electronic-music studio at Columbia University with Milton Babbitt and Debbie, but he suddenly felt badly and Debbie took him to David Protetch who gave him an injection. David for dinner.   **9** We have a smooth, on-time flight to Los Angeles.   **13**[6]   **18** Bob flies to Toronto.   **21** Goddard Lieberson for dinner. Bob arrives from Toronto at 9:30.   **23** Igor records *Firebird*.

February

1 Igor and Bob recording: Symphony in Three Movements.   **10** Igor and Bob recording.   **11** Invite Edels to Perino's.   **12** John Crosby comes to discuss Santa Fe Opera projects. I work with him the whole morning. He likes my drawings for *Perséphone*—I hope so. Recording: bad, bad.   **13** We buy a Jaguar. More recording.   **26** (Sunday) We go to Edel's to watch Leonard Bernstein's very good TV presentation of *Oedipus Rex* and Stravinsky. Afterward Bob brings me to the hospital, then leaves on the "Super Chief" for New York. Igor stays for dinner with the Edels.   **27** My operation at 12. I wake up at 5.

---

[1] The Russian-speaking conductor of the Bogotá orchestra.

[2] The niece of Mme Eugenia Errazuriz.

[3] Mrs. Stravinsky's stepmother.

[4] Last seen in France more than twenty years earlier.

[5] The Stravinskys had been invited by Robert Lowell to E.E. Cummings's, where Eliot went after the reading, but Mrs. Stravinsky decided not to go without her husband, and went instead to his recording session.

[6] On this date, Stravinsky sent the following telegram to Kay Halle, 3001 Dent Place NW, Washington, DC: "My most grateful thanks to President elect and Mrs. Kennedy for their invitation and though regretfully I cannot attend I wish success to the first United States Administration to make such a gesture to its artists."

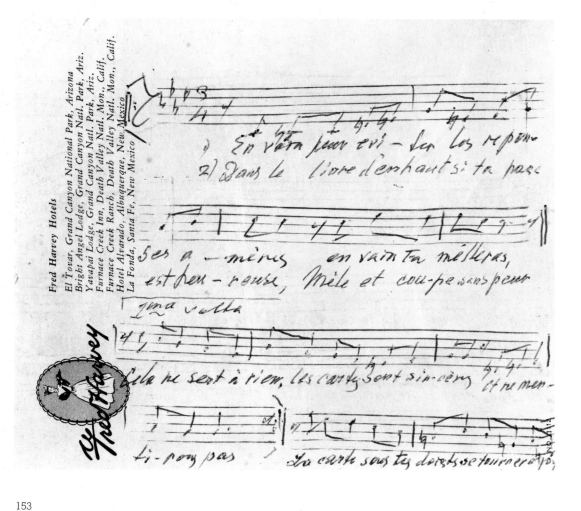

153

154

155

153–155 July 1961. Santa Fe, New Mexico. With Paul Hindemith. The German composer was in Santa Fe to conduct his opera *Neues vom Tage*, Stravinsky to conduct his *Oedipus* and *Perséphone*. Stravinsky was impressed by *Carmen*, which he had not heard in many years. He and Hindemith attended the premiere, and during the last intermission Stravinsky wrote down his favorite music from the opera.

156 September 1961. Stockholm. Talking to Swedish musicians. On September 22, H.M. King Gustav VI Adolf bestowed the Order of Vasa on Stravinsky.

March

2 Igor takes me home from the hospital in a taxi. Bob calls from New York. **30** Death of Olga Sallard. Igor, Bob, and I fly to Mexico City. **31** To Taxco.

April

1 To Acapulco. **3** Back to Mexico City. **4** "Selected Opening" of my exhibition for photographers. Dinner at the Villaseñors'. **7** Igor's and Bob's concert in the Bellas Artes. **8** With Laura Villaseñor and Bob to Topoztlán: at last I found *my* church. **9** Concert in the auditorium at 11 a.m. Go to a *corrida* with Prieto's sons, then dinner with them at La Cava. **10** Fly to Los Angeles. **25** With Igor and Bob to Glenn Gould's concert in the Wilshire Ebell. **26** Bob flies to New York.

May

3 Igor and I go to the airfield to pick up Bob. **12** To the movie, *Virgin Spring*—in order to know Ingmar Bergman.[1] Hollywood fire! **13** Aldous Huxley's house burned down. The whole morning telephoning. Nobody knows where the Huxleys are. **18** The Huxleys for dinner. **23** Birthday dinner for Edel (b. 1906) at our house. **28** Bob has two rehearsals.

June

4 Bob and Igor recording all day. **5** UCLA concert: Bob: *Die glückliche Hand*; Igor: *Psalms*. **8** At 5 the Russian composers come here: Khrennikov, Kara Karaya (champagne, caviar, foie gras). Dinner here at 7 with Aldous and Gerald. **10** To a ball in Bart Lytton's "backyard" for the "First International Music Festival." **11** We go to the concert by the Russians. **12** Bring Igor to Dr. Jaffe at Cedars of Lebanon. **17** An avalanche of telegrams, congratulations, also from Moscow. Visit from Knauer and Indra Devi. **18** 5 to 6:30 Babin and Vronsky at Mirandi's. **28** Bob records Varèse's *Arcana*, Igor in the control booth. **29** Igor records his Violin Concerto with Isaac Stern. **30** Igor recording: 3–6.

July

1 Train to Santa Fe at 9 p.m.

August

24 We arrive in New York, the Hotel Pierre.

September

1 Leave for Göteborg on the S.S. *Kungsholm*. **12** The Helsinki concert. **24** The Stockholm concert. **25** Fly to Berlin. **30** Fly to Belgrade, Hotel Majestic. My name day: very *triste*.

October

3 Reception by George Kennan, American Ambassador. **19** London, Savoy Hotel.

November

7[2] **17**[3] **25** Melbourne. The Menzies Hotel. If you want to commit suicide you have to come to New Zealand or Australia. People are very nice and Nature is beautiful—the trees are big and happy-looking and flowers are everywhere in profusion, but the cities are terribly provincial, and in Wellington between Friday evening and Monday you will be arrested for drinking whiskey. The hotels are miserable, especially Wellington, where it is cold, windy and we have no heat, sitting here all day surrounded by poor furniture (no table on which to write). You have to eat at a fixed hour, and if you want tea after dinner you must have it back in your room. Coffee is not served in the restaurant but in a lounge. The food is much worse than terrible: it is impossible to swallow, all covered with greasy gravy. I asked Bob what kind of exercises Trotsky did in prison, and in my little room I walked ten feet from one wall to the other and back and forth. To have some heat, I filled the bathtub with hot water. Sydney was livelier, but the air-conditioning in the Hilton Hotel was so strong that I put a newspaper in the vent. At Lady Lloyd-Jones's house we at last have some comfortable rooms with fireplaces, some good food, and nice people like Patrick White.

December

6 10 a.m. Leave Tahiti. Arrive Los Angeles 8:30. Dreadful Customs, but happy to be in Los Angeles.

January

6 Igor's concert in the Wilshire Ebell. **7** Up at 6, to the airport. Dreadful flight to Toronto. The Chicago airport is snowbound, we are rerouted to New York, where we change planes and land at a different-than-expected time in Toronto, therefore missing a welcoming committee, as well as ending up in a different-than-scheduled hotel, the Park Plaza. **8** Our baggage, which was not on the plane with us, is delivered at noon. In the afternoon Igor is recorded reading.[4] **9** Film with Nadia (touching!).[5] **10** Taped interview with me in my hotel room, for which Bob and I work from 10 to 6. **13** Limousine to Buffalo and flight from there to Washington at 9:35 p.m. **15** Lunch at Mildred Bliss's where we are charmed by Saint-John Perse. Igor receives a Key to the City of Washington, and the State Department's medal from Dean Rusk. **18** Dinner at the White House. **19** Lunch at Saint-John Perse's with Auden. First performance.[6] Reception at the Austrian Embassy. Nicolas Nabokov. **21** Second performance at 5:30. Reception, but Igor goes to bed. **22** Igor sick. Telephones, doctors. Third performance. I do not go. **23** At 11:45 a.m.: train to New York, Gladstone Hotel. **26** Igor records *Renard* and Ragtime. **29** We go to the theater.

February

1 We go to the ballet. Party at Lucia Davidova's afterward. **2** To the Galérie Internationale, the theater, and the Russian Tea Room afterward

---

[1] The Stravinskys were already planning to see his production of *The Rake's Progress* in Stockholm.

[2] On November 7, Isaiah Berlin wrote from Oxford to R.C.: "Herewith the text. I have adopted a fairly home-made method of transcription and there are no mysterious Orientalisms of pronunciation etc.—nothing that cannot be comfortably pronounced by anyone we know. My system is: 1. To put in apostrophes between vowels where two vowels come together and are not a diphthong, say as in the name Jeal or Joel where each vowel is given its full value. So far as other vowel sounds are concerned, they are pronounced as they would be in German or Russian: 'a' as in 'father', 'e' as in 'bed' or the German 'mehl', 'ei' like the 'a' in 'bake', 'ai' like the 'i' in 'like', 'i' like 'ee' in 'keen', 'o' as 'aw' in 'bawl', 'u' as 'oo' in 'soon', and 'y' is simply used like a German 'j'—'ya' instead of 'a', 'ye' instead of 'e', etc. As for consonants, that is slightly more tricky because the apostrophes between them indicate some kind of gap which could, for singing purposes, best be replaced by a very short 'e'. V'lekh should be pronounced ideally as a 'v' held for a second and then 'lekh', ('kh' is of course the Russian 'x' or the 'ch' in the Scottish 'loch') but quite often it is transliterated as 'velekh' where the first 'e' is extremely short and this is what I recommend. I didn't put in 'e's simply in order to avoid the trouble of putting squiggles for shortness above them which would give the whole thing a Czech look. But whenever you see an apostrophe between consonants, a short 'e' may and should perhaps be substituted. I have also accented the thing as best I could, and I think both pieces—both the first Seven Days of Creation and the (non-) Sacrifice of Isaac—are now in order. So, for

example, the complicated Hebrew pronunciaton of the equivalent of Isaac—Yitzhak is most comfortably pronounced Yitzekhak, if the 'e' is not lingered on. What more have I to tell you? I was sorry that I wasn't able to come to the concert in London. I enjoyed your visit very, very much indeed. I send my warmest love and affection to the Stravinskys and in five minutes I must go to India. And that will be that. Do let me know what is happening. The fee for the composition will present no difficulties, I gather. I long to be secretly immortalized by the purely simple little piece of work that I have done with great hope and devotion. If you really want a tape recording, I could send you even that, it would not make me self-conscious, but I should send it even if it did."

[3] On this date, the Huxleys and Isaiah Berlins sent the Stravinskys the following postcard from Agra, India: "I am not as impressed as *Sadko*: the famous song does *exact* justice to the qualities of Sadko's hosts."

[4] Actually he was recording a conversation with R.C.

[5] A brief excerpt from an interview with Nadia Boulanger was included in Franz Kramer's documentary film for Stravinsky's 80th birthday. Auden, Cocteau, and Balanchine were also interviewed, and Stravinsky conducted parts of *Histoire du Soldat* and *Agon*.

[6] Stravinsky conducted *Oedipus Rex*, R.C. *L'Heure espagnole*, for the Washington Opera Society in Lisner Auditorium.

157–159 January 1962. New York. Stravinsky and Edgard Varèse during the recording of Stravinsky's *Renard*.

160

160 March 1962. Self-portrait.

161 May 1962. Paris.

162 September 1962. Moscow. With Ekaterina Furtseva (Minister of Culture), Mr. and Mrs. Dmitri Shostakovich, Kyril Kondrashin, Karen Khatchaturian, and Mr. and Mrs. Aram Khatchaturian (foreheads only).

163 October 8, 1962. Conducting in the Great Hall of the Leningrad Philharmonic.

(caviar *blini*). **3** Fly to Los Angeles. **19** To Bob's Monday Evening Concert. Party at our house afterward: Stephen Spender, Elliott Carter. **22** Spenders for dinner.

March

2 Dinner at Chris Isherwood's. **14** George Balanchine arrives. **15** Dinner with Balanchine at Luau. **16** Dinner at home with Balanchine. **26** To Bob's concert with Brigitta.[1] **27** Meetings with Balanchine.[2] **29** Brigitta went home. **30** Recording *The Flood* and meetings. **31** Recording *The Flood*. For dinner: Graff, Ter-Arutunian. The last day of the dreadful week.

April

1 Dinner at Jerry Lewis's.[3] **6** Yellow fever shots for Africa. Bob edits *The Flood* recording until 12 p.m. Igor and I eat at 10 p.m. **18** We fly to Seattle: Olympic Hotel, room 824. **19** Automobile tour of the World's Fair grounds and of Seattle. **20** Rehearsals.[4] **21** Concert in Seattle.[5] **22** Train to Vancouver and from there to Toronto. **25** Arrive in Toronto at 5 p.m. **30** Since the fog has canceled all flights, we take a limousine from Toronto to the Pierre Hotel, New York, arriving at 5:30 a.m.

May

1 My vernissage at Galérie Internationale. **2** Dinner at the Houghtons, 3 Sutton Place, with Leonard Bernstein, *et al.*, then to the opening of the Wildenstein Gallery of the exhibition "Stravinsky and the Dance." **5** We lunch at the Four Seasons with Leonard and Felicia Bernstein, after seeing a screening of his film of *Oedipus Rex*. Balanchine with us. **6** Dinner in the Oak Room (Plaza Hotel) with the Elliott Carters. **8** I sold till now five paintings: Leonard Bernstein, Carter, Dushkin, Graff,[6] Bobsy [Goodspeed Chapman]. Sail on the S.S. *Flandre* for Le Havre. **15** Arrive at Le Havre. Because of a railroad strike, François Michel meets us at the dock with three cars.[7] Dinner at Beatrice Rothschild's.[8] **16** Nabokov's dinner at the Laurent, with Simone Signoret, Boulez, *et al.* **18** We fly to Nice, the Congo, Rhodesia, and Johannesburg. Pay $300 baggage overweight. **20** Native dances. **22** First concert in Johannesburg. **25** Second concert in Johannesburg. **26** To a Bantu village near Pretoria, then the Union Hotel, Pretoria. **27** Concert in Springs for the Bantu. **29** Drive to Kruger Park. **30** Kruger Park. **31** Kruger Park back to Pretoria.

June

1 Fly to Capetown. **3** Tea with the Prime Minister at his country home. **5** We fly to Rome. **6** Check in at the Hassler Hotel, Rome, at 4 a.m. In the afternoon Adriana Panni takes us for a drive to Tivoli. **17** Fly to Hamburg. Tremendous welcome at the airport and hotel. **18** Celebrations and hundreds of telegrams and letters for Igor's 80th birthday.[9] **29** Marvelous Lufthansa flight to New York, Hotel Pierre.

July

6 To the film *Last Year at Marienbad* with Debbie: she and I like it, Igor

and Bob don't. Dinner at the Russian Tea Room. **12** Probably the sun had a lot of dark spots today: everything went wrong. On the way to Lewisohn Stadium we decided that it would rain and that the concert would be cancelled. During and after the four-hour rehearsal there, big mistakes, quarrels, fights, offenses. Lucia [Davidova] arrived rather late and told me that someone she knew in City Hall remarked on the failure of New York City to celebrate Stravinsky's 80th birthday, while the rest of the world has big festivals. Lucia repeated this in our limousine on the way back to the hotel, and Libman, sitting with the driver, started to cry. Stravinsky said he neither needed nor wanted this kind of recognition. After lunch in the hotel, Libman stayed the whole afternoon in my room, lying about everything and complaining that she had not received money from her husband: Igor gave her a check immediately. The evening began in a very bad humor, but the concert[10] was better than I expected. I sat with Hurok, Natasha, Lucia, Protetch. The audience was enthusiastic and there was no rain. I wanted supper after the concert but forgot to telephone the maître d'hotel at the Russian Tea Room. "Don't worry, I'll call the restaurant and everything will be marvelously prepared," Libman said, and I heard her say on the telephone: "Darling Sidney, please prepare the best supper in the little room in the back." After the concert we stopped for a moment at the hotel because Igor had to change. The telephone rang from the Russian Tea Room, and Balanchine said, "A crowd is waiting for you. When are you coming?" "A crowd? But we want only a very few friends." [Libman had told everybody.] We saw the crowd, but went to the back room—where nothing had been prepared. Anatole, the maître d'hotel, said that Sidney, the owner, had not given the order to prepare anything. Furious, we went to the main dining room and spoke to Balanchine, who left saying, "Maybe I am the hair in the soup." **17** Very shaky night train to Chicago. The Ambassador East. **19** Igor's rehearsal in Ravinia. **20** Rehearsal in Ravinia. **21** Concert in Chicago. **22** Train to Los Angeles. **23** Arrive in Los Angeles. **26** Igor's concert in Hollywood Bowl. **27** Train to Lamy. **28** Arrive in Santa Fe four hours late.

August

8 To Carlos Chavez's lecture at 4, and at 8:30 to *Oedipus* and *Perséphone*, conducted by Igor and Bob, respectively. **10** *Oedipus* and *Perséphone*, the second time. **12** Concert in the Museum: Bob conducts *The Flood* twice. **21** By car to Albuquerque and by plane from there to New York. **22** Hotel Pierre. The air-conditioning is such a relief! **26** Dinner at Lucia Davidova's with Balanchine. **28** *Scandale* with Protetch.[11] Dinner in the Russian Tea Room with Goddard Lieberson and Milton Babbitt. **29** 14-hour flight to Israel, the Dan Hotel, Tel Aviv.

September

2 Igor's concert[12] in Haifa, in unbearable heat. **4** 8:30: the concert in Jerusalem. **5** To Hebrew University (Dead Sea Scrolls), then to President Ben Zvi's (we speak Russian) and back to Tel Aviv. At 5, the opening of my exhibition: speeches and 500 people. A party at the American Embassy. If I were Jewish I would immediately give up California and come here to live. One can do this without being Jewish, but I do not like to live in a country without speaking the language. Not that I speak good

---

[1] Mrs. Lieberson performed Hindemith's *Hérodiade* (Mallarmé) and Debussy's *Chansons de Bilitis* (Pierre Loüys) at the Monday Evening Concerts and recorded both pieces.

[2] To discuss the staging of *The Flood* for television.

[3] The comedian-entertainer owned a restaurant on Sunset Boulevard near Holloway Drive, and hence not far from the Stravinsky home. At this time, the Lewis ate there every Thursday with Gerald Heard and Isherwood. Lewis used to attend Stravinsky's recording sessions incognito (dark glasses, etc.) and take photographs, an album of which Lewis once showed to the composer.

[4] Danny Kaye attended these and carried Stravinsky's scores.

[5] The program for this opening concert of the Seattle Fair included Beethoven's *Leonora* Overture No. 3 and Rachmaninov's Third Piano Concerto (Van Cliburn), Stravinsky's Symphony in Three Movements (conducted by R.C.), *Firebird* Suite (conducted by Stravinsky).

[6] Robert Graff was the producer of *The Flood*.

[7] One car was for the Stravinskys' twenty bags, the second was for Russian-speaking passengers—Suvchinsky had come from Paris—the third was for R.C. and the French. After a stop at Rouen, we reached Paris, Berkeley Hotel, in late afternoon.

[8] In the great house near the Rond-Point des Champs-Elysées. Giacometti was among the guests.

[9] On June 20, Nicolas Nabokov, in Paris, wrote to Vera, in Hamburg, advising the Stravinskys not to go to the USSR, pointing out that the Russians had been so awful about Stravinsky for so long and that they would simply use him now to show how "liberal" they had become. Moreover, if Stravinsky should say something critical of America, as he always did about his taxes, there would be problems on the other side. Nabokov asked them to postpone the trip for a year when he could go with them.

[10] Stravinsky was to have concluded the program with *Firebird*, but because of threatening rain, he began the concert with it, and R.C. concluded with *Sacre*. The mistakes referred to in Mrs. Stravinsky's note were managerial, not musical.

[11] Dr. Protetch had wanted to accompany Stravinsky to the USSR, as his personal physician and also to study drug abuse in Russia. The composer did not agree and never saw Protetch again.

[12] Stravinsky conducted *Firebird*, R.C. the Symphony in Three Movements and Violin Concerto (Zvi Zeitlin).

English. Also, in Israel almost everyone speaks another language besides Hebrew—French, Russian, English.   **6** Last concert: Tel Aviv. Big supper party at the Dan Hotel given by Abba Eban.   **7** Fly to Rome, change airplanes there, and to Venice, reaching the Bauer-Grünwald Hotel at 11 p.m. Marvelous.   **8** Lunch with Adriana Panni, Bogiankino and his wife.[1]
16 Fly to Paris, Berkeley Hotel.   **21** Fly to Moscow.   **22** *Boris Godunov* at the Bolshoi Theater.   **23** Ekaterina Furtseva invites me for tea, but I do not go, partly because I have no time, partly because I feel indifferent to the past.[2] I ran into Alice Kooner, and we embraced and she said I was as beautiful as ever. I did not feel moved by this, however, took the compliment as matter-of-fact, and went on with the banal conversation.
30 My name day: everybody comes with gifts.

October

4 Fly to Leningrad, Hotel Europa.   **8** Igor's Leningrad concert.   **9** Igor's second Leningrad concert. Midnight train to Moscow.   **10** Beautiful countryside. Suddenly I remember the name of our gardener at Gorky, Alexander Kalistratovich, and the flower present that he had created for the leader of the nobility in our region—strange that I cannot remember *his* name! I remember how Father and Mother left for this presentation in a horse and carriage, early in the morning, and that I was sent on later by boat. The present was a pillow of moss on a wire frame, with a design and initials made of flowers. 8 a.m. arrive in Moscow. Dinner with Shostakovich and others.   **11** Paris dinner with François Michel and Suvchinsky at Fouquet's.   **15** We fly to Rome.   **18** Igor's concert at the Teatro Eliseo. Lunch with Bill Congdon in the Piazza Navona. Dinner after the concert at Gigi Fazzi with Henze and Vlad.[3]   **20** Concert in Perugia.[4]
21 Return to Rome via Assisi and Spoleto.   **23** Fly to New York.   **28** At 9 a.m. fly to Caracas. Stay in the Circo Militar.[5] *Affreux.*

November

1 First concert.   **2** Second concert.   **5** 9:15 a.m. fly KLM to New York. What a relief!   **8** To *Don Giovanni* at the Met, invited by Berman [who designed the production].   **11** Balanchine comes from Russia for a few days.[6]   **12** Rehearsals start for the *Rake*.[7]   **19** *Rake* rehearsal at 5. Afterward Oxenberg comes to our hotel for discussions.   **20** Rehearsal. Performance of the *Rake* in Carnegie Hall.   **21** Igor decides to go to Toronto.   **22** Bob goes to Toronto ahead of us, to rehearse.

December

3 Toronto. Igor's last recording, until 1 a.m.   **4** After a bad flight, changing planes in Chicago, during which my mink coat is lost, we arrive in Los Angeles at 7 p.m.   **10** Dinner at Christopher Isherwood's with the Huxleys and Gavin Lambert.[8] Letter from A.E. Golumb in Kharkov, saying that Goddard Lieberson sent him some Stravinsky recordings on request,

---

[1] Massimo Bogiankino, now (1985) the director of the Paris Opéra, and his wife, a professional translator at high-level political meetings.

[2] The tea party would have taken place in Mme Furtseva's apartment, which had been Vera's apartment fifty years earlier.

[3] Mrs. Stravinsky does not mention that Henze was with his librettist, Ingeborg Bachmann, perhaps the most gifted German poet of her time.

[4] The Stravinskys went to Perugia by car, lunched at the home of the Perugina (chocolates) family, and rested only a short while before the concert.

[5] The "hotel," and Army Officers' club, was totally unoccupied except for the Stravinskys and R.C.

[6] The Stravinskys had seen Balanchine in Moscow for only a brief meeting, since he and his dancers were arriving as the Stravinskys were leaving.

[7] A semi-staged—orchestra on stage— performance by the American Opera Society, in Carnegie Hall, conducted by R.C. Allan Oxenberg was the very gifted director of the company, but Stravinsky insisted on certain changes.

[8] Author of *The Slide Area*, famous for its fictionalized portrait of the Baroness d'Erlanger.

[9] Aaron Propes, director of the Festival of Israel.

[10] The sound track for this film consisted of Stravinsky's Octet and *Soldat*, recorded by R.C.

[11] To narrate the part of Perséphone in performances conducted by Zubin Mehta with the Los Angeles Philharmonic.

---

but that a Soviet citizen has no right to receive recordings from abroad and consequently these were confiscated; and asking Stravinsky to send some scores and some of his books in German or English.   **13** Igor records a speech for Japan. Propes[9] for dinner.   **15** Christopher and Don for dinner.   **18** Joseph Strick, director of the movie *The Balcony* (Jean Genet).[10]   **28** Dinner at Christopher Isherwood's. Igor gets drunk.
31 New Year's Eve: Mirandi and Ralph Levy at 9:30, then Christopher and Don.

January

7 Dinner at Luau with Brigitta; she came for *Perséphone*.[11]   **10** Dinner at the Huxleys' with George Cukor.   **12** Dinner at Perino with Brigitta.   **29** I buy a television set for Evgenia Petrovna.   **31** Dinner with Chris and Don at Jerry Lewis's.

February

1 Dinner at George Cukor's. "Star" company. Not for us; we feel *déplacés*.[12]   **2** Balanchine comes for one day.   **8** Dinner at Bernard's[13] with Gerald and Michael.   **12** Joseph Strick for dinner.[14]   **21** Gerald, Michael, and Christopher Wood here for dinner.

March

1 Dinner with the Huxleys at Trader Vic's.[15]   **2** Mirandi, John Crosby, and John Moriarty come for lunch to discuss the production of *Lulu* at the Santa Fe Opera.   **5** Dinner at Perino.   **7** Bob and Edel went to the Mahler concert.[16]   **10**[17]   **21** Igor's Oberlin concert.[18]   **22** Fly to New York at 12 a.m. Dinner at Liebersons' with John Gunther.   **23** To *Othello* at the Met.   **24** Dinner at the St. Regis with Paul Horgan.   **25** Dinner at the Pavillon with Hurok. To Ustinov's play.   **27** The "boys"[19] went to Toronto.   **31** Igor back from Toronto.

April

1 Bob back from Toronto. Dinner in the Russian Tea Room.   **5** Igor has a blood-letting. We go to Balanchine's ballet rehearsal.   **6** Bad news about Igor's blood. A film about the Blaue Reiter in the museum.   **8** We sail at noon on the S.S. *Bremen* for Hamburg (Bremerhaven).   **11** The passengers are dull. Igor stays in bed, reads, and eats in his cabin.
12 The Canadian film people annoy us.[20]   **16** We reach Bremen five hours late. Rolf Liebermann and about 20 reporters come aboard from a small boat: interviews, photographs, films.   **17** Bob has two rehearsals

---

[12] Cukor lived only a few houses away from the Stravinskys. The "stars" to whom Mrs. Stravinsky is referring were Groucho Marx and Bette Davis (both remarkably foul-mouthed). Katharine Hepburn was there, too, but the Stravinskys already knew her. Apart from Hepburn and Cukor himself, the quality of the conversation was certainly well below that of an evening with Huxley, Isherwood, and Gerald Heard.

[13] A Latinist who lived in Santa Monica and who was correcting the text of Stravinsky's *Oedipus Rex* with its composer.

[14] Strick had finished his film of Genet's *The Balcony*.

[15] This was the last time that the Stravinskys saw Aldous Huxley.

[16] The Seventh Symphony, William Steinberg conducting the Los Angeles Philharmonic. This was the last time R.C. saw Anna Mahler.

[17] On March 10, Stravinsky had written to Theodore: "A week ago I finished *Abraham and Isaac* for baritone and chamber orchestra to be sung in Hebrew. . . . I am so relieved to have completed it before our long trip. If I feel well enough I will go to Israel to conduct it."

[18] Stravinsky conducted the *Psalms* and R.C. conducted the Symphony in C and the two orchestral movements from *The Flood*.

[19] Stravinsky and R.C. went alone.

[20] The Canadian National Film board had begun a documentary of Stravinsky recording the *Psalms* in Massey Hall, in Toronto, and the film crew—Roman Kroiter, Wolf König—accompanied the Stravinskys on the boat to Bremen and Hamburg, photographing the final scene of *The Flood* in the Hamburg Opera.

164 1963. 1260 North Wetherly Drive. One of Stravinsky's bookshelves with the drawing of himself by Don Bachardy and a reproduction of Yves Klein's portrait of Nijinsky.

165 November 1963. Rome.

and is unhappy with the results.[1] Gunther Rennert comes to the hotel at 5:15.[2]   **23** At 6, the eye doctor for Igor. Very bad rehearsal. To hell with the Boches.   **25** To *Hamlet* by Gründgens[3] with Maximilian Schell.   **28** In the evening to *Don Carlos*.   **29** At 11 a.m., the dress rehearsal for *The Flood*. In the evening, *Wozzeck*. Dinner at Lemke's afterward with Nabokov and Liebermanns.   **30** *The Flood*. Party afterward at the hotel.

May

2 To *Der Rosenkavalier*.   **3** To *Ballo in Maschera*.   **4** Last performance of *The Flood*. Dinner at Lemke's. In the morning I visit my relatives in Bielefeld and am horrified by their dullness.[4]   **5** To Budapest via Amsterdam and Prague.   **7** Lunch at Totti del Monte's.[5]   **8** The concert. After it, Igor, Bob, and I go to a café and hear tziganes played by a cimbalom, clarinet, and violin.   **9** By car to Zagreb, arriving at 7 in the evening.   **11** Rehearsals. People from the Union of Composers in Moscow come from 5 to 10, bringing gifts and drinking Scotch.   **12** The Zagreb concert.   **13** Lunching at the Mayor's, Igor got drunk.   **14** To the Hamburg Opera's *Lulu*. To hell with all traveling, and especially in Mitteleuropa. Here in Zagreb are more enemies than friends, and to avoid everybody we have our meals in our rooms. For me it is an extreme bore. Shopping is impossible, combining German, English, and Russian words being too complicated. Besides, nothing is available, not even aspirin, which I need for my daily headaches. I asked about a delicatessen, since the food here is inedible. They do not have black bread and the only caviar is from Iceland, which is horrible. There is even no halvah. There are two Russian shops across the street from our hotel, but no one understands our pronunciation. Last night I forgot to draw the curtain and I saw the large blue letters of "PRVOMAJSKA." How long would it take to commit suicide here? All specialists are dull and now I am a specialist in boredom.   **15** Fly to Munich and Paris, Berkeley Hotel. Dinner at Ami Louis restaurant with François Michel and Suvchinsky.   **16** Dinner with Ionesco, Nathalie Sarraute, Michel Butor.   **17** Lunch at the American Embassy with the Bohlens. At Nabokov's, hear a tape of his *Rasputin*.   **18** At the Musée Cluny. Dinner with Michel Butor. After all of Igor's refusals to go to Bergen, Bob has to go as substitute.   **19** Bob left for Bergen! Poor boy. A big meeting with Nabokov at 6.   **24** Igor has the flu. We do not go to the *Rake's Progress* at the Opéra Comique.   **25** Fly to London, Savoy Hotel (marvelous). Bob arrives from Bergen late at night.   **27** To the Tate Gallery.   **28** The T.S. Eliots for dinner.   **29** Oxford. Lunch at Isaiah Berlin's. In the evening we go to one act of *Figaro* at Covent Garden, then Part Two of the *Sacre* 50th jubilee in Albert Hall. Afterward, turn down a party at Ian Fleming's and go to T.S. Eliot's.   **30** To the National Gallery.   **31** Lunch at Kenneth Clark's castle, dinner at the Garrick Club with Henry Moore and the Spenders.

June

1 Spenders for lunch. Visit David Jones at Harrow at 3.   **2** Fly to Dublin, the Russell Hotel.   **3–4** Two beautiful days in the country. Clonmacnoise.   **5** Rehearsals.   **6** Rehearsal.   **7** Rehearsal. We visit the President of Ireland. Lunch at the American Embassy.   **8** Rehearsals. **9** The dress rehearsal and concert.   **10** Fly to Hamburg.   **12** Igor conducts *Oedipus Rex* at the Hamburg Opera.   **13** Fly to Stockholm. **14** Dinner for us by the Swedish Radio.   **19** The Stockholm concert. Bob conducts *Capriccio* with Ingmar Bergman's ex-wife Keti Larabei as pianist. Reception afterward.   **20** Fly to Milan, the Grand Hotel—bad hotel, bad service. The Milanese are conceited and rude, and their city is noisy.   **22** First rehearsal.   **23** I hope never to be in Milan again. After the evening rehearsal, dinner at Biffi Scala with Luciano Berio and Umberto Eco.   **24** First performance of *The Flood* and *Oedipus*. **26** Dinner at Berio's.   **27** Second performance at La Scala.   **28** Third performance at La Scala.   **29** We fly to New York, the Pierre Hotel.

July

1 We fly to Los Angeles.   **4** Dinner at Perino's for Hurok.   **11** Igor and

Bob fly to Chicago for the Ravinia concert.   **13** Bill Brown and I drive to Santa Fe. It was 115° in Needles. We spend the night in the Thunderbird Inn in Williams, Arizona—very good.   **14** Bill and I arrive in Santa Fe at 6. La Posada is a big disaster: no mirror, no table, no anything. I cry. **21** Ed[6] and Bill have supper with us.   **22** Igor stays in bed.   **25** Igor's x-rays are good. Dinner at the Palace.   **29** Igor goes to Bob's *Lulu* rehearsal.

August

1 First dress rehearsal of *Lulu*.   **2** We go to *Madama Butterfly*.   **7** *Lulu* premiere.   **9** Second *Lulu*.   **17** Edwin helps a lot.   **18** "Coronation" in the Cathedral: Igor becomes a Commander of St. Sylvestre. We drive to Albuquerque and spend the night there.   **19** Sleep at Williams'. **20** Home at 5:30 p.m.   **25** 10:20 a.m. American Airlines flight to New York.   **29** 8:30 p.m.: flight 351 to Rio de Janeiro, after a stop in Trinidad. **30** To Copacabana. Visit the botanical gardens.   **31** To the zoo.

September

1 Rio is a big bore. Visit from Carlos Chavez.   **2** Rehearsals. **3** Rehearsals. The Rio concert.   **6** Macumba and other boring events. **8** Concert in the Candelaria. Igor receives a medal.   **9** We rush to the airport. New York: how marvelous!   **13** Dr. Lewithin helps a lot.   **14** To live in New York at the Pierre is my dream.   **17** Fly to Los Angeles. **25** Heatwave.   **29** Four doctors for Igor. His white count is bad. X-rays. **30** Flowers. My name day. Poor Bob conducts a Monday Evening Concert and is exhausted.

October

10 Jean Cocteau died.   **28** For dinner at our house: Christopher, Don, Bill Brown.

November

2 Dinner at Christopher's with Don, Bill Brown, Paul Bonner.[7]   **4** Gerald brings his book and gives us bad news about Aldous.   **5** Fly at 9:45 to New York, the Hotel Pierre. Dinner in the Russian Tea Room with Aaron Propes.   **6** To Osborne's boring play, *Luther*.   **11** At 7:30 p.m. fly to Rome on Pan American.   **13** Lunch at Ranieri with Berman.   **16** Fly to Palermo in a small bumpy plane. The Villa Igiea: dirty and dull. The weather in Palermo is like the weather in Los Angeles, hot until three o'clock, then very cold at night. We are all dreaming of New York—five days left, four days left. Dinner at the Jockey Club with Barone Agnello. **17** Visit decayed palazzi with Berman, and he, Bob, and I go to Cefalù. **19** Archeological Museum. We go to see the widow Lampedusa. The first half-hour is very impressive. She is a Balt and speaks Russian, but she is also a fat, dirty-looking woman, with a resonant, bossy voice and decayed looking, like her palazzo, though in Palermo it is called a villa instead, because it is not fortified. She talks only about her late husband and how difficult it was to find a publisher for his book. Berman and Bob go to Segesta.   **20** Two rehearsals. Bill Congdon comes for 24 hours. **21** The Palermo concert.   **22** Igor and I go by train to Catania, Berman and Bob by car via Noto, etc. President Kennedy is assassinated.   **23** Bob and Berman to Syracuse. At 6: the concert in Catania. Afterward the night train to Rome.   **24** Rome. Dinner at Adriana's with twenty people, Carlo Levi, Nabokov, *et al*.   **25** Igor's concert in Santa Maria Sopra Minerva. Bad organization in the church and we are all furious. Supper afterward with Berman and Nabokov at Ranieri. Berman very offended.   **26** Fly to New York. *Bella Roma*, but *vecchio* and all ruins. New York, *moderno, nuovo*. Marvelous apartment in the Pierre.

December

5 The opening of my exhibition at the Galérie Internationale. Dinner

---

[1] The Oberlin orchestra had performed the same *Flood* excerpts, apparently without effort, that the orchestra of the Hamburg Opera declared unplayable.

[2] The stage director. On April 26, Stravinsky wrote to Theodore: "We have started rehearsals. One could say a lot about the staging of this version of *The Flood*, which was not conceived as an opera."

[3] One of the great stage directors of his time, Gustaf Gründgens was married for a time to Erika Mann.

[4] Emilie Thiele (Aunt Mila) and her daughters, Gretchen, Olga, and Alice. Their actual address was in Hasenheeke über Kassel.

[5] Concert agent. The Stravinskys had known her in the 1930s.

[6] Edwin Allen, librarian, a later friend of the Stravinskys.

[7] Painter, Bill Brown's long-time companion.

afterward at La Caravelle. **12** Dinner at the Pavillon with the T.S. Eliots. **18** Elliott Carter for lunch. **23** Isaiah Berlin at 6. **24** We go to Balanchine's at 9 p.m. **31** Lunch at the Carlyle with Isaiah Berlin and Allen Pryce-Jones, editor of the TLS. New Year's party here: Lucia Davidova, Bob Sandbach, us.

1964

January

5 The "boys"[1] go by car to Philadelphia. **8** The "boys" come back for 1 day. Dinner at La Caravelle. **10** Igor's matinée concert in Philadelphia. **11** Igor's evening concert in Philadelphia. **12** Igor and Bob come home for 1 day. **13** Blizzard. Concert in Philadelphia, coming home the same night.[2] **14** Concert in New York, Lincoln Center. **20** Concert in Washington with the Philadelphia Orchestra. **21** Auden for dinner. He drank everything we had. **24** To Arthur Miller's play.[3] **25** Go to the ballet matinée. Stephen Spender comes. **26** Ballet matinée. Dinner in the Russian Tea Room. **28** Igor and I go to Menotti's opera[4] at the Met. **29** Igor records *Apollo*.[5] **31** Bob goes to Toronto.[6]

February

5 At 6 p.m. leave on the train for Chicago. **6** Dreadful train. **8** Arrive in Los Angeles. **9** Igor has the flu. **20** Chris Isherwood, Don, and Bill Brown for dinner.

March

3 We buy the Baroness's house, putting $5000 in escrow. **8** Fly to Cleveland, Wade Park Manor Hotel. **9** The dullest place. **12** First concert. **13** Recording.[7] **14** Second concert. **15** By car to Cincinnati, the Netherlands Hotel. **16** Opening of my exhibition in Cincinnati, brilliant—flowers, telegrams. **18** Fly to Los Angeles.

April

11 Dinner at Chasen's with Luciano Berio. **29** Fly to Detroit and go from there by car to Ann Arbor. The hotel is terrible, but after two hours we find a motel de luxe.

---

[1] Stravinsky and R.C. went to Philadelphia for a week of rehearsing the orchestra in a program of *Perséphone*, conducted by Stravinsky with Mrs. Lieberson as narrator, and the Stravinsky Symphony in C and Schoenberg Five Pieces for Orchestra conducted by R.C.

[2] Mrs. Stravinsky does not say that she made the trip with her husband and R.C.; that they waited three hours in Pennsylvania Station for trains that failed to come; that they finally hired a daredevil limousine driver who negotiated the scarcely passable roads and delivered them at the Academy of Music at two minutes before curtain time; and that the concert took place for an audience of fewer than ten people (one of them Eugene Ormandy), though every member of the orchestra was present.

[3] *A View from the Bridge.*

[4] *The Last Savage.* R.C. had seen it the night before. Stravinsky thought he was the target of its satire on "modern music."

[5] In Manhattan Center, West 34th Street.

[6] R.C. had a conducting engagement in Toronto after which he went by taxi to Buffalo and joined the Stravinskys' train to Chicago in the middle of the night.

[7] Stravinsky recorded *Jeu de cartes* and *Ode*; R.C. recorded Schoenberg's Five Pieces for Orchestra.

[8] With the Philadelphia Orchestra, the same program as in January.

[9] Actually in two cars, the Stravinskys in a limousine, Professor Glenn Watkins and R.C. in the Professor's car.

[10] With Richard Burton as the Prince of Denmark. The Broadway area near the theater was blocked off because of crowds seeking a glimpse of Elizabeth Taylor, and the Stravinskys' car could not fetch them after the performance.

[11] This was one of the most difficult recordings R.C. ever made. The Royal

May

1 Igor was drunk—and how! **2** Soulimas arrive. **3** Concert in Ann Arbor.[8] By car to Toronto.[9] **8** Fly from Toronto to New York. **12** *Hamlet*.[10] **19** Fly to Los Angeles, arriving at 5 p.m.

June

11 Fly to Denver. **13** Denver concert, not in Red Rocks but in the Coliseum, because of rain. **14** Fly to New York. **15** Fly to London, Savoy Hotel. **16** Igor's first recording session of *The Rake's Progress*. **17** Igor's second recording. **18** Igor's third recording. **23** Last recording session of *The Rake*. **24** We go to Olivier's *Othello*. **25** Bob nervous, recording *Von Heute auf Morgen*.[11] **26** Bob in a state with two big recording sessions. **27** Lunch in the Savoy Grill with the ex-Queen of Italy, Maria José.[12] **28** Rehearsal for the Oxford concert. **29** Two rehearsals in Oxford, concert in Oxford. **30** Fly to New York at 3 p.m.

July

5[13] At 2 p.m., American Airlines flight to Los Angeles. **14** Dinner with Paul Kohner.[14] **16** Luciano Berio for lunch. Later Igor and Bob fly to Chicago. **18** Igor's and Bob's Ravinia concert. **20** Igor comes back.[15]

August

6 Dinner with Balanchine at the Beverly Wilshire Hotel. **12** Bob's *Lulu* performance in Santa Fe. **14** Igor and I fly to New York. Bob's second *Lulu* performance. **15** Pierre Hotel. Dinner with Lieberson and Edwin; Bob arrives. **17** Fly to Paris.[16] **20** Fly to Israel. Met by Isaiah Berlin, Kollek, Propes. Bob goes directly from the Jerusalem airport to rehearse *Abraham and Isaac*. **23** The Jerusalem concert,[17] very nice dinner. **24** Leave for Caesarea at 11:30, but the car breaks down and we continue by taxi. Concert in Caesarea. **25** Up at 5 a.m. for a 9 a.m. flight to New York.[18] **27** Igor and I to a film and dinner in the Russian Tea Room. **31** Fly to Hollywood.

September

8 First night in the new house! **13** Fly to New York. **16** Fly to Paris. **17** Fly to Berlin. **21** Nadia Boulanger arrives. **22** The Berlin concert. **24** Big *scandale*: Nabokov–Dagmar–Bob.[19] Return to Paris. **26** With Bob to Amiens, Beauvais, Chantilly. **27** At 5 p.m., Air France to New York, the Drake Hotel. **30** My name day. Igor gives me beautiful lilies in a silver vase.

Philharmonic was sight-reading, and the allotted time was cruelly inadequate.

[12] She was musical, like her mother, the Queen of Belgium, and had written about Stravinsky.

[13] In his medical diaries—see *A Stravinsky Scrapbook*, op. cit.—Stravinsky did not enter a visit on July 5 to his skin doctor Anderson, but one took place at 3 p.m., and Stravinsky made a note to procure Erytromycin.

[14] Film agent. The dinner was in connection with an unrealizable project to use Stravinsky's music in Dino de Laurentiis' film, *The Bible*.

[15] R.C. flew from Chicago to Albuquerque and Santa Fe to conduct two performances of *Lulu*.

[16] Theodore wrote to his father shortly after: "I am sorry not to have known about your stop in Paris on your way to Israel. It would have made me very happy to come and embrace you. I wouldn't have taken much of your time. The flight from Geneva to Paris is only 15 minutes. But I understand that with all your work you did not have the time to let me know." Stravinsky also seems to have kept secret from Theodore the trip to Paris in September.

[17] Stravinsky conducted the *Psalms* (sung in Hebrew, not Latin) and *Vom Himmel hoch* (sung in Hebrew, not German), and R.C. conducted the *Capriccio* and *Abraham and Isaac*.

[18] The Stravinskys stayed in the Regency Hotel, which was inconvenient because Burton and Taylor were in the adjoining penthouse apartment and the Beatles were in Delmonico's, thereby blocking Park Avenue most of the time.

[19] Dagmar Hader, a young, very beautiful painter, had been Nicolas Nabokov's secretary during the Berlin Festival. Angry with her for going to East Berlin with R.C., Nicolas attacked her in the lobby of the Kempinski Hotel, had to be restrained by porters and the police, and later suffered a thrombosis in the Stravinskys' rooms.

166 September 24, 1964. Berlin. Following the score of *Abraham and Isaac*, with Elliott Carter (on Stravinsky's right), at a rehearsal. The pianist Nikita Magaloff is seated behind Stravinsky, Gilbert Amy behind Carter. Peter Heyworth is in the last row, left. In front of him are Mrs. Stravinsky, Nicolas Nabokov, Hans Werner Henze. The young woman on the other side of the aisle is Dagmar Hader.

October

4 Johnny [Stravinsky] for lunch. To the Ballet. Peter Nabokov.[1] **5** Fly to Hollywood at 6 p.m. Edwin comes to the airfield.

November

2 Monday Evening Concert. Bill Brown and Gavin Lambert afterward. **6** Bill Brown brings pictures. **7** The lady from San Francisco, Irena Arn. Dinner at the Wilshire Ebell with her. **9** Igor in bed. **22** Fly to New York. **30** Rehearsal.

December

6 Concert in Lincoln Center.[2] **7** Igor and Bob go to Washington. **8** Igor and Bob back from Washington. **9** We go by limousine to Boston. Concert there. **10** Back to New York. **11** Recording all day. Igor sick. **31** Igor has been sick already for two days. I drink champagne with Bob, watching television.

January

11 American Airlines to Los Angeles at 4 p.m. **23** Sarah Robin, caterer, begins to work for us.

February

3 Dinner at Laura Huxley's with Dr. Volf. He demonstrates his resonator. **5** Dinner at Chasen's with David Oppenheim. **6** Sarah makes dinner for Christopher, Gerald, Michael, Edwin, and us. **13** Dinner at Chasen's with Rolf Liebermann, who proposes a television documentary to Igor. **14** Liebermann for lunch; he flies back to Hamburg at 4. Morton and Edwin for dinner. **15** Balanchine at 4. **19** Bill Brown helps me with my studio. **20** For dinner, made by Sarah, Bill Brown, Morton, Edwin. **21** Edwin comes, last day before he leaves. **27** Dinner at Chasen's with Isaac Stern, Kollek, Gregor Piatigorsky.

March

2 With Bill Brown to the gallery. **3** Bill Brown for dinner. **6** For dinner here (Sarah): Christopher Isherwood, Gerald, Michael. **8** Dinner at Bill Brown's house in Malibu. **16** Liebermann's filming begins. **17** The cameraman Richard Leacock brings a young girl assistant, Sarah Hudson. **20** Farewell dinner by Liebermann at Chasen's. **24** Dinner for Boulez at Morton's. **25** Boulez's dress rehearsal (*Éclats*). Bob, Edw., Igor, and I. **31** Fly to Dallas and Austin (Commodore Perry Hotel). CBS films our arrival.

April

1 Dinner at Robert Tobin's house. **2** Igor has a temperature, but he is filmed with students. **3** 11:30: Igor filmed with students. University reception. Brother of George Kennan. **4** Concert.[3] We go by car to San Antonio[4] and fly home from there. **5** Edw. for dinner. **14** Concert in the evening. **15** We fly to Chicago. CBS films continuously. **16** Claudio Spies and Glenn Watkins arrive. Filming. In "Old Chicago." Concert.[5] **18** Spenders for lunch. Afterward to the Chicago Art Museum. **19** We see Jerome Robbins's *Les Noces*. Big discussion afterward. **20** Fly to New York. **21** Doctor Lewithin at 4: Igor's cardiogram is bad. **27** Igor's recording at 2: *Ebony Concerto* with Benny Goodman, Preludium. **29** Film in the Park, at Balanchine's rehearsal, and at Café Chauveron.[6] **30** Filming Igor at night in the Guggenheim Museum, with the choir of St. Thomas Church.

May

1 We sail on the *Kungsholm* to Göteborg with Oppenheim, Haskell Wexler, and CBS television crew. **2** The boat is the biggest bore. **3** Rough seas. **10** After landing in Göteborg, we fly to Copenhagen, rest in a motel near the airport, then fly to Paris, Plaza Athénée Hotel. Dinner in our rooms. **11** Go with Bob to Fontainebleau—Barbizon. Dinner in the Closerie des Lilas. **12** Too many people are here. We are exhausted. Big dinner in the hotel restaurant. **13** Igor is filmed in the Théâtre des Champs-Élysées. He must stay in bed: all visitors refused. Bob goes to Chambord and back by car. **14** Henri Michaux for lunch, Giacometti afterward. Filming. **15** Go by car to Vevey. Marvelous lunch in Saulieu. Arrive exhausted, but Theo and Denise arrive. **16** Kitty comes from 12 to 4, Theo and Denise from 4 to 10. Filming in Clarens. **17** Theo and Denise. Filming in Clarens. To Basel by car and stay in the *Drei Königen*. **19** To Paris by car. Lunch in Strasbourg. **20** Doctor for Igor. **21** Analysis of Igor's blood. **23** Bob and Oppenheim fly to Warsaw at 7 a.m. Igor gives an interview. **25** Igor and I fly to Warsaw, Hotel Europejski: awful, cold, no hot water. **27** I think only of the day of departure. **28** A telephone call from the Vatican asks us to come to Rome. Concert at 7:30[7] **29** Concert at 6. **31** Filming. Lunch at the Jablonna Palace.

June

1 Fly to Amsterdam and Paris. The Hotel Lotti—excellent. **5** The Paris Opéra: 3 Stravinsky ballets, *Renard*, *Noces*, *Sacre*. Returning to the hotel, Suvchinsky tells me that he has had a big telephone conversation with the Soulimas about Johnny. **6** Lunch with Boulez and the Suvchinskys. Leave by train for Rome. **12** Concert at the Vatican. Very boring dinner at the Hilton Hotel. **13** We fly to New York. **18** American Airlines to Hollywood. Our gardens are *formidable*. **25** Isherwood and Mirandi for dinner. **28** We fly to Indianapolis and go from there by car to Muncie. **29** I give an interview. **30** Dress rehearsal.

July

1 Concert in Muncie. **2** Chicago. **7** Rehearsal in Ravinia. **8** Rehearsal and Ravinia concert. **9** Fly to Seattle and Vancouver. **12** Very successful concert in Vancouver. **13** Second concert in Vancouver. **14** Fly to Los Angeles. **26** Dinner at Isherwood's.

August

10 Igor has phlebotomy at 5:30. **13** Kitty arrives from Geneva. **14** Goddard comes with Simone Signoret. **19** Recording session (Bob and Igor). **20** Igor has two recording sessions. **26** Igor records the Variations (Bob helps).

September

1 Igor and Bob: concert in Hollywood Bowl. **3** We fly to New York. **6** 8 p.m. Lufthansa flight to Hamburg, not direct, as promised, but changing in Frankfurt. Vier Jahreszeiten Hotel. **10** Fly to London with Leacock and Sarah Hudson. **12** First London rehearsal at 2:30. **13** Second rehearsal at 10. **14** Third rehearsal and concert, Festival Hall; see Julian Huxley. **15** Fly to New York, with a delay at Boston. **22** We go to Prokofiev's *Flaming Angel* at the City Center Opera. **23** See the CBS film rushes. Spenders for dinner. **24** Cocktail party in our rooms: Isaiah Berlins, Spenders, Robert Lowell. **30** We go to Nabokov's ballet: *Don Quichotte*.

October

7 See the CBS film of Igor. Dinner at Oppenheim's. Jean Stein. **8** Lunch

---

[1] Son of Nicolas and a gifted writer, especially about American Indians.

[2] *Bourgeois Gentilhomme* Suite and *Abraham and Isaac* conducted by R.C., *Pulcinella*, *In Memoriam JFK*, *Berceuses du chat*, *Pribaoutki*, and Pastorale (Isaac Stern) conducted by Stravinsky.

[3] R.C. conducted the concert with the University of Texas Orchestra (*Orpheus*, etc.).

[4] The Stravinskys were accompanied to San Antonio by Professor Lothar Klein.

[5] The first performance of Stravinsky's Variations.

[6] The Stravinskys were filmed in one of the Central Park horse hansoms on the 72nd Street Bridge, at the north end of the Mall; with Balanchine and Suzanne Farrell on the stage of the New York State Theater; and dining with David Oppenheim and his wife (Ellen Adler) at the Chauveron.

[7] Stravinsky conducted *Firebird* and R.C. conducted the Variations, etc.

167 1965. 1218 North Wetherly Drive. The photograph is of Nietzsche.

168 Spring 1965. 1218
North Wetherly Drive.

218

with Weissberger and Cornelia Otis Skinner.   **9** Igor works with Gregg Smith and Alicia Adler on the translation of *Les Noces*.   **10** Fly to Cincinnati. Max Rudolph.   **13** Two rehearsals. Lecture in the evening: Igor talks. Afterward to a very good restaurant, Pigalle.   **14** Two rehearsals. Our 25th wedding anniversary, celebrated in the Pigalle.   **15** Cincinnati concert.   **16** Cincinnati concert.   **17** Fly to Los Angeles. Ed comes to the airfield.

November

2 Dinner here with Mrs. Schoenberg[1] and Bill Brown.   **9** Dinner at Christopher Isherwood's.   **13** Bill Brown for dinner.   **23** Bob and I go to the wedding reception for Ronald Schoenberg and Barbara Zeisl.   **27** Recording Stravinsky.   **28** Bob's concert in the Los Angeles County Museum: Schütz: *Christmas Oratorio*.   **29** Recording Bob, recording Stravinsky.   **30** Recording Bob (Schoenberg's Septet Suite).

December

10 Fly to New York at 11 a.m.   **13** Igor has a temperature. Dr. Lewithin.   **14** Strong diet for Igor. Nabokov comes.   **16** Igor has temperature. Dr. Lewithin. Nabokov.   **20** 12 to 7: Bob records *Les Noces*. Igor is there.   **26** Soulimas for dinner.   **27** Igor has a bleeding. Go to the theater in the evening.   **29** Bleeding no. 2. Theater in the evening.   **30** Visit from Soulimas.   **31** Bleeding no. 3. New Year's Eve: oatmeal and Dom Perignon with the Liebersons and Ed.

1966

January

2 Igor was ill: champagne, probably.   **3** Laboratory for Igor: not perfect. To the theater, *Cactus Flower*.   **11** George Balanchine comes, and Nicolas Nabokov (back from Europe). Giacometti died.   **13** NET, channel 13: film of the Boston concert of December 1964.   **15** To a screening of the CBS film. Dinner at Oppenheim's: 1st-class intellectuals.[2]   **17** Laboratory for Igor. To Leacock's film: big dispute afterward.   **18** Fly to Minneapolis, the Sheraton Ritz Hotel.   **19** Bob rehearses.[3]   **20** Bob rehearses.   **21** Dress rehearsal. Concert. Dinner afterward with Elliott Carter.   **22** Fly to Los Angeles, Western Airlines flight 63.   **27** Concert[4] with the Los Angeles Philharmonic.   **28** Los Angeles concert no. 2.   **30** Bob's new beauty is pretty, stupid, pretentious, and vulgar: *les hommes intellectuels aiment ça.*

February

1 At 4:40 Igor and Bob go to St. Louis.   **5** The St. Louis concert takes place without me.   **6** Igor and Bob come back from St. Louis.   **9** We decide to make an apartment out of the garage, since the cooks complain about the small room.   **11** I finally pass my driver's test and receive my license.   **12** Mirandi and Bill Brown for lunch.   **18** Fly to San Francisco at

5:35.   **19** Ernie's restaurant: excellent.   **23** Bob very sick (flu), with high temperature. The doctor gives him a morphine injection to enable him to conduct.[5] 8:30: first San Francisco concert.[6]   **24** Second concert.   **25** Doctor for Bob. Third concert.   **26** Return from San Francisco.

March

3 The Montaperts[7] and Marion come in the afternoon for a meeting about taxes and Verigor.[8]   **6** We fly to Rochester, New York, changing planes in Chicago.   **7** Press conference. Go to a concert for Stravinsky by the Eastman students.   **8** A symposium at 1 p.m.: I am on the stage with Igor.   **9** A performance for the maestro at 3:15. Family dinner at Walter Hendl's.   **10** 1:30: another symposium for composers.   **11** Final rehearsal. Concert (Igor and Bob) at 8:15. Reception afterward.   **12** New York!   **17** Nabokov and Dominique Cibiel for dinner.   **18** We see the BBC film of Auden at a studio in Rockefeller Center.   **19** Fly to Los Angeles.   **20** Claudio Spies for dinner in our house.   **27** Irena Arn for dinner. I swim[9] and feel slightly ill afterward.   **28** Milene for lunch.   **31** Igor and Bob go to a concert.[10]

April

4 Dr. Corday at 3:30. Babin and Vronsky at 5.   **5** Bill Brown for dinner.   **18** Monday Evening Concert. Bob conducts Bach.   **21** The Francis Steegmullers for dinner.

May

4 Igor has a blood-letting. Igor goes to the dentist.   **5** Igor's concert at Royce Hall. Here after the concert: Brigitta, Bob, Karen Armstrong.   **6** Igor has a blood-letting.   **8** We fly to New York at 1 p.m.   **12** Fly to Paris, Hotel Lotti.   **13** Dinner at the Closerie des Lilas (excellent) with Suvchinsky.   **14** To the Balthus exhibition with Bob. Dinner at Prunier with Suvchinsky.   **20** Two doctors come for Igor.   **22** Bob and I go to the Vallée de Chevreuse, Rambouillet, Maintenon, and Chartres—back in time for dinner with Suvchinsky and Mario Bois.   **23** Dr. Thiroloix for Igor. Fly to Athens.   **25** Bob and I drive to Corinth and back.   **26** The Athens concert.[11]   **27** A difficult trip to Lisbon because Alitalia is on strike, therefore our plane is overcrowded. Bob rehearses from 9 to 12 midnight.   **28** Bob rehearses from 3:30 to 6 and from 9 to 12.   **29** Igor not well.   **30** Igor rehearses for only one hour, 10:30–11:30, Bob the rest of the time and from 3:30 to 6.   **31** Two rehearsals.

June

1 The Lisbon concert.[12]   **2** Fly to Paris. Dinner at the Boule d'Or with Bois and Suvchinsky.   **6** Lunch at Le Grand Vefour with Cartier-Bresson and Mme Lazare (*New York Times*, Paris bureau). I visit Irene Dana.   **7** I have a long talk with Carl Flinker.[13] Dinner at Vilette with Suvchinsky.   **8** In the morning, the Montaperts.[14] Carl Flinker again.   **10** Kitty comes for two days.[15]   **11** The CBS film shown.[16] Bob has a fever.[17]   **12** Igor, Bob sick in bed. Doctors, tests, x-rays.   **18** All concerts cancelled.   **21** Fly to

---

[1] On this occasion she gave Stravinsky a facsimile of the score of *Jacobsleiter*.

[2] Meyer Schapiro, Lionel Abel, the widow of Noah Greenberg.

[3] Stravinsky was so intent on finishing Capote's *In Cold Blood* that he took no interest in the rehearsals.

[4] R.C. conducted Schoenberg's orchestration of Bach's E flat Fugue, Stravinsky's *Zvezdoliki* and Symphony in C. Stravinsky conducted the *Psalms*.

[5] R.C. incurred permanent heart damage by conducting the San Francisco rehearsals and concerts; a cardiogram, taken immediately afterward, showed that from that time he had a "split beat" and infarction in the aortic valve.

[6] R.C. conducted the Variations and *Sacre*, Stravinsky conducted *Psalms*.

[7] William D. Montapert and his wife Armine were graduates of the University of Southern California Law School. Mrs. Montapert's mother, Marie Tchanguian, was the sister-in-law of Mrs. Harold English. Mrs. Montapert died August 4, 1970.

[8] The "true gold" of this klutzy pun proved to be a cost of $100,000 to the Stravinskys. See the essay "Cher père, chère Véra" in *Present Perspectives*, op. cit.

[9] The Baroness d'Erlanger's pool had been cut in half when she sold a portion of her property. The Stravinskys constructed a new pool.

[10] The Los Angeles Philharmonic. Zubin Mehta conducted Schoenberg's Orchestra Variations.

[11] Stravinsky conducted *Oedipus Rex* and R.C. conducted the Symphony in Three Movements.

[12] Stravinsky conducted *Oedipus Rex* and R.C. conducted the *Sacre*.

[13] See "Cher père, chère Véra," op. cit.

[14] The Stravinskys' suspicions about Montapert's connections with Andre Marion were aroused from this date, because of Montapert's unannounced appearance in a hotel adjoining that of the Stravinskys and because he was coming from and returning to the Banque Suisse in Basel.

[15] See "Cher père, chère Véra," op. cit.

[16] Accompanied by Mrs. Stravinsky, R.C., Adriana Panni, Xenakis, and Maurice Béjart, Stravinsky was taken to an already crowded screening room. The CBS film of Stravinsky was screened, then another film of Mehta conducting the *Sacre*. Suddenly Stravinsky erupted, jumping from his seat, shouting at the producers that they should know better than to expose such a *connerie* to him, that not a single tempo, or anything else, was right.

[17] Brucellosis, which R.C. had contracted from goat cheese eaten in Lisbon.

169 December 1966. Hollywood. Recording session.

170 The last page of Stravinsky's last complete composition, *The Owl and the Pussycat*, 1966. Inscribed by Stravinsky March 31, 1968.

New York.   **30** Opening of the Stravinsky Festival in Philharmonic Hall.[1]

July

1 We fly to Los Angeles at 2 p.m., American Airlines.   **5** Concert (Igor and Bob) in Hollywood Bowl. Dinner with Hurok at Chasen's.   **9** Bob goes to Santa Fe by train.   **11** Grigorevitch[2] for dinner.   **12** Christopher Isherwood and Don for dinner.   **14** At 11 a.m. fly to New York, Pierre Hotel.   **15** Go to Stravinsky Festival in Lincoln Center: Balanchine's *Ragtime* and *Histoire du soldat* with Elliott Carter as the Soldier, John Cage as the Devil, and Aaron Copland as the Narrator.   **16** Ed for lunch. To Kyril Kondrashin's concert in the evening.   **17** Much work to arrange Bob's travel here: all kinds of combinations.[3]   **18** Dinner with the Elliott Carters in the Côte Basque.[4]   **19** Igor goes to the *Oedipus Rex* rehearsal.   **20** Igor to the *Oedipus* rehearsal. Three telephone calls to Bob: very complicated air travel.   **25** Back to Hollywood.   **28** Igor and I go to the film *Khartoum: formidable!*   **29** Bill Brown for dinner.

August

3 Dinner and *Khartoum* second time with Bill Brown.   **18** Bill Brown for dinner.   **19** Bob's performance of *Wozzeck* in Santa Fe. For dinner here: Isherwood, Don, Mirandi, Morton.   **24** Bob's last performance of *Wozzeck*.   **25** Bob will come home.   **26** Dinner (Sarah) ourselves and Bob alone.   **28** Igor and I to *Khartoum* for the third time, with Bob and Morton.

September

7 Igor has blood-letting at 10. Bill Brown for dinner with William Inge.[5]   **8** Igor is all right.   **14** We fly to Louisville, Hotel Brown.   **15** Fred comes[6] (boring). Bob rehearses twice. In the evening we are part of an audience for a screening of Liebermann's film.   **16** Overtime rehearsal. Dinner at a country club on the Ohio River.   **17** Concert in Louisville.[7] Reception at the Brown Hotel afterward.   **18** Fly to New York.   **20** Bob works all day with Spies.[8]   **29** Little by little I am going mad: telephone calls, business conversations, meetings with Krebs.[9]   **30** My name day. Goddard and Brigitta for lunch. In the evening to Albee's *A Delicate Balance*, then supper at L'Etoile.

October

1 Bill Brown and Spies for lunch. At 5, Arnold Newman to photograph Igor.   **3** Bob rehearses 2:30–6:30. Bob, Ed, and [Linda Anderson] go out.   **5** Rehearsals.   **6** Two rehearsals. For dinner: Morton, Glenn Watkins, Ed, Spies.   **8** To Princeton. Premiere of *Requiem Canticles*. Home (Pierre) at 3 a.m.   **11** Igor has x-rays and blood-letting. Isaiah Berlin comes after lunch. Bob records from 4 to 11. Ed and I come with Igor, but I am furious and I make a speech.[10]   **12** We fly at noon to Los Angeles.   **13** Igor is sick (flu). I cook the whole day.   **20** Bob's birthday. Soulima arrives and we have a family dinner at the Marions'.   **24** Igor's blood analysis is good!   **30** Bill Brown and Don Bachardy for dinner. Evening rehearsal (bad) in our basement of *The Owl and the Pussycat*.   **31** Monday Evening Concert: premiere of *The Owl and the Pussycat*.

November

5 Igor and Bob to Bob's rehearsal in Pasadena.   **6** Rehearsal in Pasadena.   **7** The Pasadena concert goes very well.[11]   **12** We fly to Honolulu.   **14** First rehearsal.   **17** Third rehearsal. I go to hear it: the orchestra is the worst we've had.   **18** Orchestra party for Igor on the other side of the island. Igor drunk.   **20** The Honolulu concert.[12] Reception afterward by the beau monde of Honolulu who did not attend the concert.   **22** Second Honolulu concert.   **23** Fly to Los Angeles.   **25** At 4 p.m. fly to Columbus, Ohio, Hotel Sheraton Plaza.   **26** Rehearsal (Bob).   **29** Concert in Columbus.   **30** Bob's lecture (*Sacre*) at Ohio State University. Performance of *Histoire du soldat*. At 4 p.m. we fly to Chicago, change planes for Seattle, and change there for Portland.

December

1 (Thursday) Portland. We arrive in the middle of the night Wednesday–Thursday, and I sleep in my dress. Our baggage comes at noon. Rehearsal (Bob alone). Igor says: "Each time I sit down to compose I have new problems, which require a new approach on my part. The public, on the other hand, has habits. The public is already familiar with my old works, and when a new one is played the public cannot tell whether it is a bad work or a new approach. That it could be a new approach to a new problem does not enter the public's mind."   **4** Rehearsals: 12:30–3:00, 5:30–8:00.   **5** Portland concert.[13]   **6** Second concert in Portland.   **9** Hollywood. Laboratory tests for Igor. To the Chianti restaurant.   **10** To the Ukrainian Ballet, supper afterward at the Music Center Pavilion.   **15** At 2, Bob makes the United Airlines recording, later rehearses Schütz's *Christmas Oratorio*.   **17** Bob's Schütz rehearsal.   **18** Bob's Schütz rehearsal.   **19** At 9 p.m. Igor and I go to the second performance of Schütz's *Christmas Oratorio* in the Los Angeles Museum, afterwards to Luau with Newman.   **23** 1 p.m. American Airlines flight 194 to Chicago (the Drake Hotel: very elegant suite).   **24** Buy a mink coat. To the theater: *The Odd Couple*.   **27** Bob rehearses 1–3:30.   **28** Rehearsal. 3 Soulimas arrive. Chicago concert: big success, bad reviews.   **29** Lunch with Soulimas; they go home. Go to the Art Institute. Dinner with Krebs, Bernal, Ray, very lively and informal.   **30** Lunch with Glenn Watkins and friend. Glenn Watkins' dinner.

January

1 Second Chicago concert at 3:30. At 7 p.m. fly to New York.   **3** Igor's analysis is very bad. He has a blood-letting.   **4** A second blood-letting. Consultations with the doctors.   **6** Igor's first treatment.   **7** My real birthday. Dinner with William and Jean Vanden Heuvel at the Pavillon, then to Pinter's play, *The Homecoming*.   **8** Arnold Newman photographs Igor and Balanchine. Go to a marvelous film by Antonioni: *Blow-Up*.   **9** Igor's second treatment. Dinner at Newman's with Marcel Duchamp.   **10** Bob flies to Los Angeles to start rehearsals.   **11** Igor's third treatment.   **12** We fly to Hollywood.   **13** I cook and clean. Bob will have a nervous breakdown: too much work.   **15** Go to Inglewood for Bob's

---

[1] Leonard Bernstein conducted the *Sacre*, provoking the loudest applause imaginable, until Stravinsky bowed from his loge a minute later, and "brought the house down."

[2] Director of the Russian ballet company that Hurok was presenting in Los Angeles.

[3] R.C. was flown in a Piper Cub from Santa Fe to El Paso, where he joined a midnight flight, stopping there en route from Mexico City, to New York.

[4] Mrs Stravinsky does not say that Frank Sinatra and Mia Farrow came to Stravinsky's table and asked for his autograph and that neither of the Stravinskys, unlike the Carters, recognized them. The next day Sinatra eloped with Miss Farrow to Honolulu.

[5] The author of *Picnic*, *Bus Stop*, *Come Back Little Sheba*, lived near the Stravinskys on the same Hollywood hill. Mrs Stravinsky wrote to him the next day: "Dear Mr. Inge, Your flowers are delightful and I thank you very much for thinking of me in such a charming way. I could write you a ten-inch long letter but my English is not expressive enough. I hope we will see you soon. Sincerely, Vera Stravinsky." The Stravinskys did not see Inge again, and not long after, Bill Brown wrote to Vera in New York: "Did you see that Bill Inge killed himself? Tomorrow we go to see his last play, about three men on death row, called, appropriately, *The Last Pad*."

[6] From Lexington, Kentucky.

[7] Stravinsky conducted *Firebird*, R.C. conducted *Sacre*.

[8] Preparing for the premiere of *Requiem Canticles* at Princeton.

[9] Clyde Krebs, of Chicago, wanted to use Stravinsky music for a commercial travelog for United Airlines. The film was already made and the music had to be fitted to it. This was done by Bill Bernal, after much listening to Stravinsky's recordings. Then R.C. recorded the excerpts and Burgess Meredith the narration. In Chicago, in December, Bernal completed the splicing. The film was shown in movie theaters throughout the country but neither R.C. nor the Stravinskys ever saw it.

[10] See *Stravinsky in Pictures and Documents*, op. cit.

[11] Stravinsky conducted *Danses concertantes* and Act I, Scene III from *The Rake's Progress*, R.C. Beethoven's First Symphony and the *Dumbarton Oaks* Concerto.

[12] Stravinsky conducted *Firebird*, R.C. the Symphony in Three Movements and the Violin Concerto (with Itzhak Perlman).

[13] Stravinsky conducted the *Pulcinella* and *Firebird* Suites, R.C. Schoenberg's Five Pieces and Beethoven's First Symphony.

concert: Beethoven's Seventh Symphony.   **16** Bob's Monday Evening Concert of Monteverdi's *Vespers*.   **18** Bob records 9–12 and 7–10 at night.   **19** 9 a.m.: Bob records the *Vespers*.   **20** Bob records *Danses concertantes*.   **22** Bill Brown for lunch. I took the whole day to translate Russian letters for Bob.   **23** Bob records.   **24** Bob's last recordings, *Abraham and Isaac*,[1] *Japanese Lyrics*.   **25** Bill Brown for lunch. Go to an Egon Schiele exhibition.   **29** Isherwood's dinner.   **30** Dinner at Jean Stein's.

February

10 Igor and I to the dentist. Photos taken for Ross of the Seattle Opera, for the *Histoire du soldat* performance.   **12** Just the three of us, Igor, me, Bob, for dinner at Perino's.   **15** Igor's second bleeding. Gertrud Schoenberg died.   **19** At 1 p.m. fly to Miami, Eden Roc Hotel. Calling Nabokov in New York, we learn that Robert Oppenheimer died.[2]   **20** Press conference, very vulgar.   **21** First rehearsal.   **24** The Miami concert.   **25** We arrive in Los Angeles absolutely exhausted. In Princeton today, a memorial concert for R. Oppenheimer: the recording of the *Requiem Canticles* was played because he left a note requesting it.   **26** Bob's two rehearsals, 10:30–12:30, 2–5.   **27** Concert in the Beverly Hills Hilton Hotel: boudoir pink, and the people drinking martinis.   **28** We fly to Seattle, the Benjamin Franklin Hotel.

March

1 Bob rehearses *Histoire du soldat*.   **2** Return to Los Angeles.   **17** To Chaplin's film *The Countess From Hong Kong* at the Pantages Theater, for Italian flood relief.   **18** The three of us dine alone at Perino's.   **20** Bob flies to Boston.[3]   **21** Theodore will come (!).   **22** Two doctors for Igor: he is better!   **23** Luau with the Marions and Theodore.   **28** Theodore leaves.   **29** Doctors for Igor. Bob telephones after *The Rake* in Boston.   **31** Second performance of *The Rake*.

April

2 Third performance of *Rake*.   **7** Bob arrives in Lexington, Kentucky.   **8** Bill Brown and Mirandi for lunch.   **12** Bob will come from Lexington via Cincinnati.   **14** Christopher and Don for dinner (Sarah).   **29** I go with Bob to the Russian Easter midnight mass.   **30** A Japanese boy, Hideki Takami, will be our new cook.

May

12 We fly to Toronto via Cleveland. Igor is tired and Bob arrives absolutely sick.[4]   **15** Rehearsals of *Pulcinella* and *Oedipus Rex*.[5]   **16** At 10 a.m., Igor is televised rehearsing *Pulcinella*.   **17** The concert and reception.   **18** Fly to New York, the Pierre Hotel. Dr. Lewithin comes.   **22** Igor to Dr. Temple at 3:30.   **24** Igor to Dr. Donald Simon for an electroencephalogram, a three-hour visit.   **25** Rain and cold (40°). Igor has a phlebotomy at 12. Buy a wedding gift for Diane.[6] Visit Lucia Davidova.   **26** Igor to Dr. Temple at 3:30. Bob and I go to dinner at Francis Steegmuller's.   **27** Ed comes.   **30** For dinner: Spies and Jean.   **31** Fly to Los Angeles.

June

15 Bill Brown for lunch. Dinner at Chasen's with Bill Brown and Mirandi.

---

[1] Sound track, no singer.

[2] The Stravinskys were deeply moved by Oppenheimer's death. They had chatted with him during the intermission of the Princeton concert on October 8, and he had been the first to stand and applaud Stravinsky after the performance of the *Requiem Canticles*. When the Stravinskys called on him in August 1959, he was barefoot. Later Stravinsky said: "Even his feet were intelligent."

[3] To conduct *The Rake's Progress* with Sarah Caldwell's Boston Opera Company.

[4] R.C. was suffering from calcium deposits in the kidneys, discovered a week later in New York. Meanwhile he was able to work by taking Gantrisin.

[5] Stravinsky conducted the *Pulcinella* Suite, the last time he was to conduct. R.C. conducted *Oedipus* with Marilyn Horne as Jocasta.

[6] R.C.'s niece, a mathematician, who was marrying a fellow graduate from Cornell, a physicist.

16 At 3:30 we drive to the Coronado Hotel. The Marions come late at night.   **17** San Diego.   **18** The birthday is successful.[7]   **19** Back from Coronado. Flowers, stacks of telegrams. I swim in our pool.   **21** Beata Bolm died this morning.   **23** Dinner with Christopher and Bill Brown at La Chaumière, then the cinema.   **25** Dinner at Christopher Isherwood's.   **28** *Panikhida* for Beata.

July

1 For dinner: Christopher and Don.   **2** Bob goes to Santa Fe.[8]   **4** Rather gloomy and sad.   **7** Bob comes back for the weekend.   **9** Bob sad to go back to Santa Fe.   **10** Cartier-Bresson for lunch, photographs us. In the evening to *Barefoot in the Park*.   **14** Bob comes back for the weekend.   **15** At 5: Nureyev and Fonteyn to visit Igor.   **16** I start to translate my diaries. Bob goes back to Santa Fe. Sad.   **21** Bob comes for the weekend.   **24** Bob goes back to Santa Fe.   **26** The Santa Fe Opera House burns to the ground in the middle of the night, after the performance of *Cardillac*.   **27** Bob is back.

August

4 To the movie *Ulysses*[9] with Edels.   **15** Bob flies to New York at 11 a.m.[10]   **16** Isherwood for a drink.   **20** Igor not well, pain.   **21** Igor has inner bleeding (from aspirin?) and is sent to the hospital, Cedars of Lebanon.[11] I go there, 3–6, with Milene.   **22** To the hospital. Bob returns from New York.   **23** To the hospital with Bob, and again at 6–7: a 45-minute drive each way in traffic and heat.   **24** It is 90°–95° all the time. Igor is taken in an ambulance to Mount Sinai.[12] In the hospital from 2 to 6.   **25** Bill Brown for lunch. Hospital.   **26** Hospital from 2 to 5.   **27** Christopher and Don for dinner.   **28** A very good concert in the museum for I. Stravinsky's 85 years.[13]

September

1 Hospital from 4 to 7. Marilyn and Adriana[14] come back from their vacations. I will not be so alone.   **4** Igor comes back from the hospital.   **7** Bill Brown.   **8** Igor goes for x-rays at 2.   **9** Igor is low all day.   **16** Consultation: Drs. Pincus, Carpenter, Edel. Goddard sees Igor. Dinner: Bill Brown, Jean.   **18** Igor sounds better.   **19** For dinner: Bill Brown, Christopher Isherwood.   **21** Igor very nervous; the gout is unbearable.   **25** Balanchine comes for dinner and sleeps here.   **27** Two doctors (Pincus and Edel). Balanchine goes back to New York.   **29** Igor has a terrible pain. Dr. Pincus gives him an injection of Demerol.   **30** My name day. Flowers from: Liebersons, Morton, Spies, Arn, McClure. Igor takes 3 colchicin tablets.

October

1 Christopher Isherwood, Don, Bill Brown for dinner with nice gifts. Sarah cooks.   **3** Very late and emotional conversation with Bob.[15]   **4** I take Igor for a drive. After five days the colchicin produces only nausea and diarrhea.   **5** Drive with Igor in the car but he is full of pain.   **6** The pain is terrible. Nurse Wilma Walling.   **7** Consultation: 3 doctors.   **9** At 4 p.m. Igor feels terrible. Suddenly at night he has a temperature. I sleep on the sofa next to him.   **10** No temperature (*no gout!*), but weakness.   **11** X-rays for Igor. Disappointment: his ulcer has not healed.   **12** Take Igor for a drive, 3 to 4.   **13** X-rays (spine) done here. Drs. Rothenberg and Edel. The gout is back.   **14** Yom Kippur. Consultation: 3 doctors. All

---

[7] The Stravinskys had gone to Coronado Beach in order to avoid the publicity and telephone calls for his 85th birthday.

[8] R.C. conducted a performance there of Hindemith's *Cardillac*.

[9] Directed by Joseph Strick.

[10] R.C. had to complete some recordings.

[11] Mrs. Stravinsky telephoned R.C. at the St. Moritz in New York to say that her husband was in Edel's office when a hematologist came in and noticed that Stravinsky was very pale. He had lost half of his blood.

[12] On Melrose Boulevard, not far from the Stravinsky home.

[13] R.C. conducted the *Requiem Canticles*, *Movements* (with Karl Kohn), etc.

[14] The Stravinskys' secretary and cleaning woman, respectively.

[15] R.C. was alarmed by the lack of improvement in Stravinsky's condition.

171 1967. In the patio, 1218 North Wetherly Drive.

172 March 1968. 1218 North Wetherly Drive. With Theodore Stravinsky, and Mr. and Mrs. Andre Marion.

medications are changed: now benamid, elavit, codeine, suppositories for sleeping. **20** Bob's birthday. Edel invites us to Le Bistro. **21** Isherwood and Don for dinner, made by Sarah. Igor has terrible pains at 10 p.m. These two days without help from Milene are difficult for me. **25** Bad days for Igor. We now have a nurse in the evening. **26** Not a good day for Igor. **27** Suvchinsky arrives at 6:40 p.m. Pick him up at the airport. **31** Igor is bad. A consultation at 4.

November

1 Igor is bad. A consultation at 5. **2** I telephone Lewithin who tells me to call a specialist for gout. A consultation at 8 a.m. with a new doctor, Marcus, who says it is not gout but a thrombosis. At 3, take Igor to the hospital. Igor has a novocaine treatment.[1] **3** Igor has two novocaine treatments. I am very upset. **4** Igor has a novocaine treatment in the morning, also intravenous alcohol, sugar, and vitamins. Dinner here (Sarah) with Suvchinsky and Bill Brown. I go with Bob to the hospital. **5** Igor is given Scotch in milk (!) to enlarge the arteries. Dr. Lewithin calls me. **6** We go to the Monday Evening Concert.[2] **7** He is better. We are three times in the hospital, 11 to 1, 5 to 7, 9 to 11. The fourth intravenous injection. **8** P. Suvchinsky goes back to Paris. **9** An x-ray shows that the ulcer is almost healed, but why is the radioactive phosphorus always postponed? **13** Igor's finger is again black. **14** Igor is finally given radio phosphate and three injections of heparin. **16** Edel calls me at 12 with the result of the visit with Dr. Windsor.[3] Hospital 4 to 7.[4] **17** To the hospital at 12. Igor's explosion, fury, and complaints.[5] **18** Hospital with Bob from 11 to 1, and 5 to 7. Telephone call from Balanchine **20** Igor has 24-hour intravenous medication and feeding. **21** Igor better. I am in bed all day exhausted. **22** Igor better. 5 to 7 in the hospital: Igor much better. **23** Igor very restless and capricious. **24** Igor not so good, 5 to 7. He is restless, waiting for me in the evening, but I am so tired I go to bed. **25** This is Igor's second day without intravenous. **26** To the hospital 4 to 7 and again after dinner. **28** *Igor comes home*! **29** A French night nurse, Eliane.

December

1 Platelets 950,000, white corpuscles 17,000. Igor listens to music for the first time. **2** Dr. Rothenberg with news about Igor's eyes. We listen to music, Schütz and Beethoven. **6** Bob went to New York and Ithaca. X-rays at home for Igor. Marcus and Pincus. **7** Bob calls from Ithaca. Lawrence Morton brings beef Burgundy. Bad day for Igor. Charcoal.[6] **8** Igor's last heparin injection. He takes charcoal and camomile tea. **11** Igor is better. Calcium shot (Igor). Igor's pain starts at 5 o'clock. **12** Igor better. **13** Igor better, but moody. **15** The French girl [nurse] is fired: she was *emmerdante*. I go for dinner with Christopher, Don, Gavin Lambert. We come home and spend a half-hour entertaining Igor. **16** Bob will come from New York: we are happy. Bob and Igor listen to music in the evening. **19** Igor freezing, has a temperature. Edel comes at 8:30 p.m. and gives antibiotics. **20** Igor's temperature is gone, but he is very weak. **21** Igor's last antibiotic. **22** Igor is very weak. Dr. Marcus gives him a shot. The finger is warm for eight hours. I buy a canary. **23** Igor is sleepy, drugged. We are all worried. **24** What a *triste* day. I call Lewithin. Igor sleeps until 11. Dr. Pincus comes. **27** Nika Nabokov calls from New York. Consultation here: Carpenter, Pincus, Edel. Edel, furious that I called Lewithin, ignores me.[7] **28** Bill Brown for dinner (Sarah). **31** Dr. Marcus comes. For New Year's Eve: Igor and Bob listen to Beethoven quartets and Schumann. Bill Brown, the Stalveys. Only champagne.

[1] To increase the circulation.

[2] Michael Tilson Thomas and another pianist played the four-hand version of the *Sacre*.

[3] The gout specialist, who finally visited Stravinsky in the hospital.

[4] On this date Darius Milhaud wrote to Stravinsky: "I have just heard the *Requiem Canticles* played by the new and admirable Orchestre de Paris. We adored your work, were taken, gripped by this music from the first note to the last. A great masterpiece."

[5] About the mis-diagnosis of gout.

[6] Stravinsky had always swallowed charcoal before drinking champagne, to absorb or counteract the acidity.

[7] Mrs. Stravinsky discharged Edel after this incident and never spoke to him again.

January

3 Igor has minor surgery (removal of skin) in Dr. Marcus's office. **4** At 9:15 a.m. Igor has x-rays. The ulcer has healed! **7** My Russian birthday. Dinner at Chasen's. Igor goes out for the first time since his illness. **10** Igor practices conducting (2 minutes).[8] **16** The BBC records Igor's talk (in Russian) about writers in Russia.[9] **18** Igor lost some papers: we look in vain through all of his files.[10] To Chasen's with Christopher Isherwood and Don. **19** Dr. Rothenberg comes, very happy about Igor's recovery. **20** Igor's morale very low. I take him for a drive. Dr. Pincus comes. **22** I read my diary of the Russian Revolution to Bob, who says it is very good. **25** Go with Igor to the Jules Stein Eye Clinic at UCLA. **26** Igor to UCLA again. **31** Two people from Fratelli Fabri, Marina Penesatti and Ettore Proserpio, are here most of the afternoon. They want to publish six illustrated books about Stravinsky.

February

1 The Italians are here choosing objects to photograph. **3** The Italians with photographer. **4** We go to dinner at Chasen's with Bill Brown. **7** Bob flies to San Francisco. **8** Bob returns from San Francisco at 1:30 a.m., after his Oakland rehearsal. **9** Dr. Rothenberg at 1:30. **10** We fly to San Francisco, the St. Francis Hotel: Igor's first trip. **13** The first Oakland concert: Igor bows from the stage. **14** The second concert: Igor bows from the stage. **15** The third concert. We fly home after it, at midnight. **19** Bob goes to New York (recording), calls me twice. Debbie Ishlon here for lunch. **21** Milene's attitude upsets us; she complains that Andre is moody and dislikes not only music and art but also movies and books. **22** Maybe Bob will come back tomorrow. **23** Bob arrives at 6 p.m. **26** Bill Brown for dinner.

March

2 We go to *The Graduate* for the second time, with Bob. Igor is recognized by a fan.[11] **5** Film: *Bonnie and Clyde* with Bob and Libman. **8** Dr. Rothenberg at 1, Pincus later. **9** Bob flies to Boston. **11** Heparin for Igor two times a day. Igor's platelets have started to go up. **14** Bob comes back at 10 p.m. **17** Bob flies to Phoenix at 10 p.m. **19** We fly to Phoenix at 3 p.m. for the *Rake*. The Casa Blanca: a nice place but awful food. **20** *Rake* rehearsal from 10 to 2. **21** We go to the *Rake* performance in Phoenix.[12] **22** 10 a.m.: fly back home. Goddard Lieberson for dinner. **25** Igor to the optician at 3. **27** We go to the *Rake* in the Los Angeles Music Center. **28** Dr. Rothenberg at 5:30. **30** Anniversary dinner: Bob is with us 20 years tomorrow. **31** Very dull dinner at Chasen's with Sarah Caldwell and Libman.

April

2 We go to the *Rake* at the Music Center, but Igor is bad-humored. Nowadays even to go to the cinema requires a plan and involves a discussion; often we think that it may be better to stay at home and watch television. **4** At 9:30 to Dr. Weinstein.[13] **7** Business visit from Marions and Montapert. When Milene kisses her father, he is happy that someone shows him tenderness and consecrates a moment to him. But she and Andre look in only rarely any more, and only for a short time. **10** Heat wave. Igor to Weinstein at 11:30. **11** At 9:15 Igor has x-rays at Pincus's. **17** Igor to Weinstein at 11:30. **24** To Dr. Weinstein at 11:30. **28** With Bill

[8] Before his illness, Stravinsky had accepted a conducting engagement in Oakland. He practiced with the Octet and marked in red some of the meters in R.C.'s score of the piece.

[9] In response to a request from Isaiah Berlin and Stephen Spender, Stravinsky joined the protest against the imprisonment of Andrei Sinyavsky and Yuri Daniel.

[10] The files of the Swiss Bank account and of other accounts had disappeared: this was the first time that Stravinsky began to suspect Andre Marion. See the chapter "Cher père, chère Véra," in *Present Perspectives*, op. cit.

[11] Dael Klippensteen, who had actually painted a portrait of Stravinsky and who wrote to him the next day offering to send it as a gift.

[12] Vaslav Nijinsky's granddaughter—daughter of Tamara Nijinsky-Weninger—met Stravinsky after this performance, with a letter of introduction from her mother. The girl was a music student at the University of Arizona.

[13] Dr. Weinstein, hematologist, found the formula of medications that finally succeeded in regulating Stravinsky's blood.

173 1968. 1218 North Wetherly Drive. Stravinsky is wearing hippie beads in protest against the Vietnam war.

Brown to *The Producers*, a vulgar and overplayed film. Then Chasen's with Bill and Morton.[1]

May

1 Igor to Weinstein at 11:30: good news. Igor is very hardy in spite of all his illnesses, but I have an enlarged aorta and high blood pressure. What will happen to him if I have a heart attack? And I am tired from trying to be diplomatic, trying to create a pleasant atmosphere at home, to protect Igor from balletomanes, and from business complications. **2** I call Lucia Davidova [for a report on] Balanchine's ballet in memory of Martin Luther King. **3** George Balanchine comes with a film of his ballet on the *Requiem Canticles*. **4** Dinner with Balanchine at Chasen's. **5** Balanchine goes to Tucson. **7** I call the Soulimas. **8** To Weinstein at 11:30. **9** Igor at the UCLA eye clinic. **14** We fly to San Francisco. Bob has six hours of rehearsal.[2] **16** Dr. Wallerstein for Igor. **17** Drive to Muir Woods with Igor. Dinner at Ernie's.[3] **21** First concert: *Oedipus* and *Psalms*. Bill Brown comes. **22** Second concert. Dr. Wallerstein at 3. **24** Rehearsal of the *Soldat* until 12. **25** Concert of Octet, *Soldat*, and *Noces*. Party after in Robert Tobin's suite in the St. Francis Hotel. **26** Last concert. 11:55 p.m. flight to Los Angeles. **27** Igor has lumbago, severe pains. Dr. Pincus. **29** Dr. Ilfeld for Igor. **30** Alberto Moravia and wife come at 6. **31** X-rays for Igor (spine).

June

1 Bill Brown for dinner (Sarah). **3** Igor in traction. Dr. Knauer. **4** Robert Kennedy shot at 1:25 a.m. Wednesday. **5** Watching television for five hours. Kennedy died. **10** Igor starts to move and to listen to music. **12** A Miss Bergman from CBS in New York comes to sort our photographs and to have them copied. **18** Party for Igor's birthday. **20** Dr. Knauer for Igor at 11 a.m. Weinstein for Igor at 1:30. **21** We dine with Goddard at Chasen's. **24** Bob is very depressed about Igor. **25** Christopher and Don for drinks. **26** Weinstein for Igor. **27** Igor very slow. Morton for dinner. I bring pills for Igor from Knauer. **28** X-rays of Igor show that he has a broken or displaced vertebra. **29** Maya Plisetskaya comes to see Igor at 5. **30** Plisetskaya comes again.

July

2 A corset for Igor (Krüger). **3** Weinstein for Igor, 11:30. **6** [Draft of a letter to Petya Suvchinsky: "All was well in May and we went to San Francisco for two weeks. Bob conducted at the University in Berkeley. Igor was in good shape and he talked to the students. But the day after our return he had lumbago. X-rays found that one vertebra had been damaged, and he had to wear a corset. The trip to Europe has been postponed until September. Bob has a contract with Harvard to lecture and give concerts but he cancelled in order not to leave Igor and myself alone. Every evening Bob plays recordings of Beethoven quartets (*Grosse Fuge*) for Igor."] **7** Isherwood, Don and Bill Brown for dinner (Sarah). **9** Dr. Rothenberg for Igor at 1:30. **10** Igor to Weinstein 11:30. **12** Igor, Bob, and I to Chasen's with Bill Brown. **17** Igor to Weinstein at 11:30. Later Dr. Barton. **24** Drs. Weinstein and Gabor. **25** Igor and I to the movie *Rosemary's Baby* (very disturbing). **26** Dinner at Chasen's with Marions, Johnny (grandson), and Libman. **28** With Igor and Bob to *The Thomas Crown Affair*, very good movie. **31** Bill Brown gives me some advice for my painting and invites us to the Beachcomber.

August

7 Igor to Weinstein at 11:30. To the movie *The Detective*. **11** Take Igor for a 2-hour drive through Topanga Canyon. **12** Bill Brown for dinner. **13** Igor for a drive in Griffith Park. **17** Drive Igor through Griffith Park with Valerie Ossin[4] and daughter. **19** Igor to Dr. Weinstein. **25** At Chasen's: birthday dinner for Christopher Isherwood.[5] **28** Igor to Weinstein at 11:30.

September

2 Ronnie Knox drives our Cadillac to New York.[6] Bob's rehearsals start. **5** Igor to Weinstein at 2. **6** Television concert: *hommage à Stravinsky*. He receives an ovation.[7] **8** We fly to New York at 1 p.m. **9** Dr. Lewithin at 4. **13** Claudio Spies visits Igor. **15** Ed comes, then Libman. **18** Igor and I go to the theater: *Plaza Suite*. **19** We lunch at La Grenouille with Weissberger. Dinner at the Passy with Lucia Davidova and Natasha Nabokov. **20** Igor very bad after all these parties. **24** We fly to Zurich. **25** The Dolder Hotel is marvelous, in the forest, air *formidable*. Igor said: "I don't want to go back to California." **27** Dr. Probst (shots for osteoporosis). **28** Dr. Probst. **29** Church bells. No rooms in the hotel for Theodore and Ampenova.[8] **30** My name day. Theodore.

October

2 Suvchinsky arrives at Mrs. Anda's.[9] She is nice. **5** Nabokov and Dominique Cibiel come from Berlin. **7** Drive to Basel, 1 to 3, then 1½ hours in the bank. **8** Blood test for Igor. Visit from Lina Lalandi. **11** Theodore, Denise, and the dog. **12** Theo and Denise leave: we are finally alone. **13** Big drive in the forest. **15** Laboratory tests for Igor. **17** Anda comes to see our Picassos. **20** Bob's birthday. **22** Frau Anda brings Mr. Larese from the St. Gall Museum to see my pictures and to appraise our Picassos. **23** Fly to Paris (the Ritz). Suvchinsky and Morton for dinner. **30** Mme Christian Zervos at 4 to see the Picassos. **31** We go to Chantilly. On our return Igor has a piano in his room.

November

1 By car to Versailles for lunch in the Trianon Palace Hotel. Return to Paris via Saint-Germain-en-Laye (to see Debussy's house). Nadia Boulanger comes to tell me that Georges Sachs died from cancer. **4** Drive with Igor in the Bois de Boulogne. **6** Telephone to Ira in Marrakesh. **7** Telegram from Ira, explaining that the Hotel Mamounia in Marrakesh is full, but asking us to telephone the Countess de Breteuil, Villa Taylor in Marrakesh. We decide not to go and instead to return to California. **8** We go to the Opéra for *Le Sacre de printemps* (ballet), eat in our rooms afterward. **9** Kitty comes with Svetlana, her daughter. **11** I visit Madeleine Malraux, 20 avenue Foch. **13** Igor's platelets are too low (65,000): no more Milleran. **14** We fly to New York, but the Pierre Hotel is Nixon's headquarters and in a terrible mess. **18** We fly to Los Angeles—seven hours in the plane—but do not land there, because of fog. We complete the trip in a car. **26** Bob has rehearsals every day.[10] **27** Take Igor to the doctor. Bill Brown for lunch.

December

4 Rita[11] goes to San Francisco. **6** Valerie Ossin from 10 to 2. Igor to the

---

[1] Edward G. Robinson was dining at Chasen's when the Stravinskys entered. Mrs. Stravinsky stopped to talk to him. As she moved on, Robinson said: "Now she is going to remind her husband who I am."

[2] For two concerts to inaugurate Zellerbach Hall in Berkeley—except that the students objected to the name, which was then changed.

[3] On the 15th, 16th, and 17th, Stravinsky made his arrangements of the Wolf Songs.

[4] Russian-speaking nurse, who stayed with Stravinsky until he left Hollywood a year later.

[5] Mrs. Stravinsky does not say that Dr. Edel and his wife were sitting in the next booth. No greetings were exchanged, but when the Edels left, Stravinsky shook hands with the doctor.

[6] Knox was a friend of Isherwood's. The Stravinskys thought that they might need the car in New York.

[7] The 1917, 1919, and 1923 versions of *Les Noces* were performed in this Los Angeles Museum concert, the 1920 and 1947 versions of the *Symphonies of Winds*, and the premiere of Stravinsky's arrangements of the Wolf Songs. The audience was aware that Stravinsky had been gravely ill and he was applauded warmly on entering the hall as at the end of the concert. He never saw the National Educational Television film.

[8] Rufina Ampenova, of Boosey & Hawkes in London. See "Cher père, chère Véra" in *Present Perspectives*, op. cit.

[9] Ex-wife of the pianist Geza Anda.

[10] For a concert of *Pierrot Lunaire* and Messiaen's *Couleurs de la Cité Céleste*.

[11] Rita Christiansen, employed as a nurse by the Stravinskys since their second day in Paris, remained with the composer until his death, except between July and November 1969. She was Danish but spoke both French and English.

dentist. Rita comes back at 1 a.m. **8** Bob has had many rehearsals this week. **9** Igor has herpes zoster (shingles). Dr. Anderson. Bob's Monday Evening Concert. Bill Brown after. **11** Igor to Weinstein at 11:30. **27** Dr. Rothenberg for Igor. **28** Marions go to Cambria for five days. Bob sleeps in Igor's studio. **29** Drive with Igor. **30** Disagreeable conversation with Nini. **31** Bill Brown for lunch. We spend New Year's Eve alone, drink champagne and go to bed early. Rita goes to parties with Jack Quinn.

January

1 Dr. Gabor came for a social call: very nice. Morton brought dinner (paella) to our house. **2** I start to work on my painting, first with the poem of Mandelstamm. **3** Dr. Pincus comes for Igor. **4** To Chasen's with Morton and the Marions, but Igor keeps asking me in Russian: "When are we going home?" **5** Take Igor for a drive. He and Bob listen to music in the evening. **7** Isherwood and Don for dinner. Rita goes to Carmel for three days. **8** Take Igor to the dentist at 11:30. **9** Milene brings couscous which we eat here. **10** Dr. Weinstein comes. Bill Brown for dinner. **11** Dr. Weinstein gives Igor a blood-letting. **13** At 2:30 Igor to the dentist. Igor tired but listens to music in the evening with Bob. **14** Igor better. **15** At 11:30 take Igor to Dr. Weinstein: good results of the blood analysis. **18** Dr. Marcus comes at 5 to give Priscolin and Heparin injections. At 8, while sitting at the dinner table, Igor feels ill, goes to the landing bathroom, and for a second or two loses consciousness. Rita calls Dr. Pincus, who comes quickly. We stay with Igor in his room until midnight. **19** Drs. Marcus and Corday. **20** Dr. Marcus at 6. **21** At 6, Dr. Marcus gives Igor the fifth injection. **23** Bill Brown for lunch. Dinner at Chasen's after Dr. Marcus's visit at 8:30. **24** Rita's birthday. Soulima arrives at the Marions'. **25** Dinner here with Soulima and Marions. Afterwards Igor and Bob listen to music. **26** Hideki's day off. Soulima leaves. Letter to Ira. **27** Igor calls me twice in the night.

February

1 Bob and I go to Morton's, 5 to 6, to see Boulez. **5** A business meeting with Montapert: Igor is present. Dinner afterward at Le Bistro. **6** Rain. I struggle with leaks during the night, and a hangover from yesterday's dinner. Igor is very low. **7** Marcus gives Igor an injection. Pat Cosby [physical therapist] comes for two hours during which Bill Brown takes Bob and me to the Brown Derby. **9** Hideki's day off; he tells me that he will leave on March 1. **10** Up at 7 helping Igor. **12** Igor wakes me at 6:30. **13** Dr. Pincus comes. **14** Dr. Pincus here. **21** We take Igor for a promenade. I drive. **24** Dinner at Le Bistro with Bob and Donald Mitchell [of Faber & Faber]. **25** Mitchell at 9 p.m. for drinks. **26** Igor is better. Bill Brown comes for lunch.

March

1 New cook, Jean-François. Visit from Dr. Pincus. Rita goes to Mexico. **5** Dinner here with the Liebersons. Jean-François did it well. **6** Dr. Marcus. **7** With Isherwood, Don, and Chris Wood for dinner. **9** Rita came back.[1] I cook the whole day to make dinner for seven. **12** At 9:30: Dr. Knauer. **13** Dr. Weinstein. **17** Take Igor to the dentist at 12. **19** Dr. Weinstein for Igor. **20** To dinner at Morton's with Igor. **21** Dr. Knauer at 9. **22** Alexis Haieff comes from Salt Lake City. **23** Alexis and Bill Brown for lunch. **24** Igor to the dentist. Dr. Marcus. **26** At 3, take Igor to the dentist (new dentures). At 4 take him to Dr. Marcus. **27** Igor to the dentist. **28** Bill Brown for lunch. **31** Igor watches Eisenhower's funeral on television.

April

1 Meeting with Montapert at 5. **2** Another Montapert meeting. Isherwood and Don for dinner, after which we drive downtown with them to see Christopher's dramatization of Shaw's *Black Girl in Her Search for God*. **5** Bill Brown for dinner. **7** Igor and I go to a Diaghilev show at the Los Angeles County Museum. **8** Go to Marcus's office for Igor's toe. A screen and sound equipment are set up in our hallway and we see Rolf Liebermann's film portrait of Igor. **10** Igor's white count is better. At 3, Dr. Marcus operates on Igor's toe. **13** Sunday. Marcus tells us that we can go to New York. Bob leaves today for Florida. I write to Ira: "I have been silent for so long because things were going so badly. Igor's left leg was ice cold and the circulation was blocked. The doctors even mentioned the word 'amputation.' But injections of an anticoagulant directly into the artery seem to have helped. The doctors call it a 'miracle.'" **15** At 3:15 to Dr. Marcus. **16** At Dr. Weinstein's at 11:30. **17** To the dentist, the safe-deposit box in the bank, and Bekin's Storage. **18** Montapert at 10. At 3:30 to Marcus. **20** We fly to New York, the Pierre Hotel. **21** Visits from Berman and Nabokov. **22** Everything is better. **23** Bob works like hell.[2] **24** Lunch with Goddard. Visits from Dushkin, Rieti, Nabokov. Good new night nurse, Ruby. **25** Flowers from Kirstein. **26** Dinner at the Quo Vadis with Berman. Igor in a bad mood. **27** A marvelous day. Trip to, and a concert in, Stony Brook. Excellent.[3] **28** At 5, a consultation with Drs. Lewithin and La Due.

May

1 Nicolas and Dominique for dinner. **2** Igor to New York Hospital for examination. Dr. Block decides to operate immediately to remove a clot from the left leg. **3** I am in the hospital from 1 to 5. Bob calls me all the time, comes with Phyllis, who sleeps in Igor's room. Second operation for removal of a second clot and to cut the sympathetic nerve. **4** Three hours in the hospital, then lunch, then in the hospital until 8. Telephone calls every 5 minutes. **5** At 8 p.m. Igor is taken from Intensive Care to his room.[4] **6** Marilyn Stalvey arrives from Los Angeles to help. **9** Dinner with Bob, Marilyn, and Ed[5] at La Côte Basque. **11** In the hospital in the afternoon. **13** Bob very nervous. **14** Telephone Paris for Montapert. Igor is x-rayed (the old ulcer). John Stravinsky came to the hospital but Igor was reluctant to see him, and did not let him in. **15** Bob and I go to Dr. Lewithin, then twice to the hospital. **17** Soulima comes for 45 minutes. Igor terribly weak. I am worried. Ed starts to help for $20 a day. I am six hours in the hospital. **18** Disagreeable telephone call with Milene. **20** Suddenly Igor has a 39° temperature and the shivers. The doctors are certain it is pneumonia, but they say that it is *not*. X-rays at night. Bob telephones Milene to tell her to be prepared for the worst. **23** Ballet matinée: *Rubies* (marvelous), to Igor's *Capriccio*. **24** The Marions telephone to say that Jean-François must return to Paris. **25** Igor is better. **26** In the hospital. **27** To *Hamlet*, directed by Gielgud. See Ricky Leacock and Sarah Hudson there. **29** Dr. La Due orders me to bed for three days. **30** Dr. Lewithin. **31** Read Salka Viertel's autobiography.

June

1 Dr. Lewithin at 11. I go to the hospital. **2** Elliott Carter at 11. Dinner in Lucia Davidova's garden. **3** Alexis Haieff comes. **4** I have a visit from Johnny who looks like a hippie, but nice. **12** I now expect a check from ASCAP, a check from Boosey & Hawkes, and the Boosey & Hawkes surplus check. I call the Marions. **13** Ed goes home. Dinner at Passy with Rita and Bob. **17** To the Stuttgart Ballet at the Met to see *Jeu de cartes*. **18** IGOR IS BACK FROM THE HOSPITAL. **20** Laboratory for Igor and me. At 2:30 I go to see Brinn, a new lawyer. **21** Igor receives David Adams on a business visit. **22** Ed goes home. **27** Mimi Pollock (RN).[6] **28** Drs. Lewithin and La Due. Dinner with Goddard.

---

[1] A letter from the Suvchinskys, dated March 12, inquires whether Rita has returned from Mexico, and adds that "we are glad that Rita turned out to be so suitable and nice." The Suvchinskys had met her in Paris.

[2] Rehearsing for a concert in Stony Brook on the 27th.

[3] This all-Stravinsky concert began with the *Three Sacred Choruses* and included the *Dumbarton Oaks* Concerto, the Wolf Songs, and *Les Noces* in three versions. Stravinsky received a standing ovation.

[4] On May 5, Suvchinsky wrote that he "read in the newspapers and heard on the radio that Igor Fyodorovich had surgery but expected to return home soon."

[5] Allen had been studying librarianship in London, and this was his first contact with the Stravinskys since September 1968.

[6] Ms. Pollock had been Stravinsky's nurse in the New York Hospital.

174 April 30, 1969. New York. Pierre Hotel. Photo by Dominique Cibiel.

1 Take Igor for a drive. Dr. La Due writes to Dr. Clarence Agress, 465 North Roxbury Drive, Beverly Hills, describing Igor's "broad range of interests" and "charm," but also his medical history, which is alarming: four days before Igor entered New York Hospital, a thrombosis occurred in the left femoral artery. In the hospital, the arterial thrombosis was excised with a Fogarty catheter and a left lumbar sympathectomy was performed— the latter after a re-extraction of a thrombus that had formed after the first operation. . . . There is a necrosis in the right great toe, and he had a severe post-operative Monilia infection and some mild pneumonia. But strength has increased and he can walk with help. He is still composing—which means the Bach arrangements. **2** Igor has a sudden chill and a temperature of 103°. Dr. Lewithin comes. **7** Igor's last blood analysis in New York: hemoglobin 103%, platelets 230,000, prothrombin time 20 seconds. Rita goes home to Denmark and we weep. **8** Dr. Lewithin at 3. **9** We fly to Hollywood. **11** Bill Brown for lunch, Morton for dinner, after which Igor has a 103° temperature. Bob drives him to the UCLA emergency room. **12** Igor is brought home in an ambulance at 6 p.m. He has a temperature again in the night, but he stays home and it is normal in the morning. **13** I call Lewithin. Dr. Bernstein looks for a room for Igor but everything is taken and there is a nurses' strike. **14** Igor has a good night. **15** I do not know why everybody is glad to be home. It is not comfortable. We have no cook and we must run up and down two flights of stairs. Of course, Igor is better, but someone who had not seen him in some years would be shocked: he is 87 and weighs only 87 pounds. He hardly talks. Sometimes all of a sudden, he says: "Where is Bob? I want music." Now I will have three helpers, Bob, our secretary Marilyn, and Ed Allen, who is a librarian and who took a long leave of absence to be able to help me. After two operations Igor cannot get well very quickly. Sometimes it seems as if we pass the time expecting death, and when we realize that this is true we want to cry. I am hoping still that Igor will feel better. **16** Igor goes in an ambulance to Cedars of Lebanon, room 318. **17** To the hospital, 4 to 6. Igor has a lung scan. Ed arrives from New York with our car. **18** Dr. Bernstein says that all of Igor's tests are good and that he will come home tomorrow. Montapert comes: a big *scandale* with the Louriés.[1] **19** Igor home at noon. He listens to music with Bob. **20** Watch the man on the moon on television.

August

7 Montapert does not answer as promised. *Que faire?* **8** Montapert comes. **9** Conversation all night and morning about the securities which Montapert says he sold. **13** Dinner with Montapert at Perino's. **16** Drs. Corday and Bernstein. **17** A visit from Soulima, Françoise, and, later, Michel Yellachich. **18** Weissberger here for lunch. Meets with Montapert. **19** Dr. Harris and Dr. Bernstein. Igor is much better. Christopher Isherwood for dinner. **21** Bill Brown for dinner. **22** Milene's outburst.[2] **25** Anna Hodek is impossible, stubborn and stupid.[3] Morton for dinner. Igor again has temperature for 6 hours.[4] **26** Two doctors, Bernstein and Harris. Isherwood comes for his birthday dinner (Sarah). **30/31** Spend two days throwing out old letters.

September

2 Go with Ed at 10 a.m. to Beverly Hills Storage. **3** Igor comes with us to dinner at Morton's. **7** Packing, packing. **9** At 8 a.m. the storage company takes all of our books. **10** For dinner: Christopher Isherwood, Don, Bill Brown. **11** Goddard Lieberson comes at 5. **15** After driving us to the airport Ed leaves for New York in our car. At 12:30 we fly American Airlines to Newark, limousine to the Plaza Hotel. **16** Dr.

---

[1] See "Cher père, chère Véra" in *Present Perspectives*, op. cit.

[2] When Vera Stravinsky asked Milene why no one had thanked her father for the gift of the Stravinskys' orange groves in Yuma, Arizona, Milene ran from the room screaming: "Ask Andre." Writing on February 28, 1970, Ira asks Vera why "neither Fedya nor Svetik had complained about Andre Marion since the Stravinsky brothers were also cheated [out of their share of the properties in Arizona]. Since Fedya is not too bright, Denise must be managing their affairs."

[3] The Stravinskys' cook. A Czechoslovakian national, she did not adapt to Stravinsky's capitalist, authoritarian manners. She continued to live in the Stravinsky house until December 15, 1969.

[4] In a draft of a letter on this date to an unidentified correspondent, Mrs.

Lewithin. **17** Visit from the Dushkins. **18** Lewithin, Weissberger. **19** Meeting of Weissberger, Montapert, Bob, and me. Dinner at Côte Basque with Weissberger, Milton Goldman, Bob, and me. **20** Montapert comes for a half-hour. I write a document dictated by him. He says that Marion called him at night to ask about the meeting. Visit by Dushkins. **22** Yom Kippur. Card from Nika Nabokov saying he has heard that Igor has tuberculosis. Write to Nabokov. **26** I look for an apartment in the Essex House. I write to Milene. **27** Visits from Balanchine, Lucia Davidova, Dushkin. **28** Balanchine and Lucia come. Bob went to Berlin, very sad. **30** My name day. Flowers from Lucia.

October

2 Bob's Berlin concert. Call Bob in Basel, telling him about the decision to move to the Essex House.[5] **4** Bob arrives exhausted from Berlin and Basel, with bad news about Berlin. (Igor's Bach arrangements could not be performed because more editing is needed.) **12**[6] Igor goes for a promenade in Central Park. Write to Isherwood. **14** We move to the Essex House, Mimi Pollock taking Igor, while I go in the car with Bob. **15** Two doctors, Lewithin and Riley, for a consultation. Ampenova arrives. **21** At noon, Archbishop John comes with Svetlana Stalin Alleluyeva; Igor talks to her. **22** Nabokov at noon. **24** Lunch with Dushkin. We go to the theater in the evening: *Butterflies Are Free*. **25** Ampenova and Bill Brown for dinner. **28** I send a nice letter to Milene. **29** Riley and Lewithin consultation for Igor. **30** Igor signs the contract for the archives with Ampenova. **31** Lunch with the Dushkins.

November

2 Isherwood writes: "Dear Vera, please forgive my delay in answering your sweet letter. I have written to no one for weeks because we have been toiling away at the screenplay of *I, Claudius* for Tony Richardson. I never thought it would end—but it's ready at last. We send it to England tomorrow! If we shall follow it soon, I don't know. It's possible—if Tony likes it and wants more work done on it. Also we have to make up our minds about our play *A Meeting by the River*. There's a possibility of getting it done in London in January.

"You *must* take care of yourself and not be 'The Slave of the Slaves'— that was what they called one of the saints, Pedro Claver. If we can manage, we'll stop in New York either coming to or back from England. We miss you terribly and talk about you often. Many embraces and love to Igor, Bob, Ed, from your always loving Christopher." **3** Igor signs a new will, witnessed by Bill Brown, Dushkin, Mimi Pollock. **4** Igor goes for a ride in the Park. Nicolas and Dominique for dinner with Igor. **9** Aaron Propes and wife Mara for dinner with Igor in our rooms. **12** Igor and I go to Dr. Riley. **18** Theodore arrives from Geneva and Dushkin picks him up at the airport. **21** Lucia Davidova for dinner. **22** Nabokov for dinner. The story of Igor's suit to recover his manuscripts from Marion and Montapert is in all of the newspapers. **23** Theodore goes to Urbana. Nabokov and Dominique for dinner. **29** For dinner: Nabokov and Dominique, Lucia, Ed.

December

1 Big conversation with Theodore. He is incomprehensible. Why does he refuse to help? **3** Theodore goes home. **4** Consultation with Lewithin and La Due. **5** Trial [hearing of the charges against Marion] is postponed. **6** Igor has x-rays. Everything—heart, blood pressure, laboratory—is marvelous!! **8** Lieberson's son Peter comes. He tells Stravinsky that he wants to be a composer. Stravinsky says, "That is not enough, my dear." **11** House call from Dr. La Due. **12** Take Igor to the dentist. Call from Haieff. The Marion hearing is again postponed. **13** At 6

Stravinsky writes: "Igor feels much better, eats well and has gained two pounds. The doctors finally found the reason for the sudden temperature elevations: it is tuberculosis, which can be cured, it seems, by streptomycin injections."

[5] On October 10, the Elliott Carters wrote to Mrs. Stravinsky: "It was lovely to be with you and Mr. Stravinsky the other day. [We] only hope your move to the Essex will be a smooth one."

[6] On October 12, Bill Brown wrote to the Stravinskys from the MacDowell Colony in Petersborough, NH: "Hello! Welcome to the Essex House!? Will give you a full report on New England when I see you—on the 25th? Meanwhile the recent photo [actually of a very bald Roger Sessions] will show you I've become mature here, like the autumn leaves."

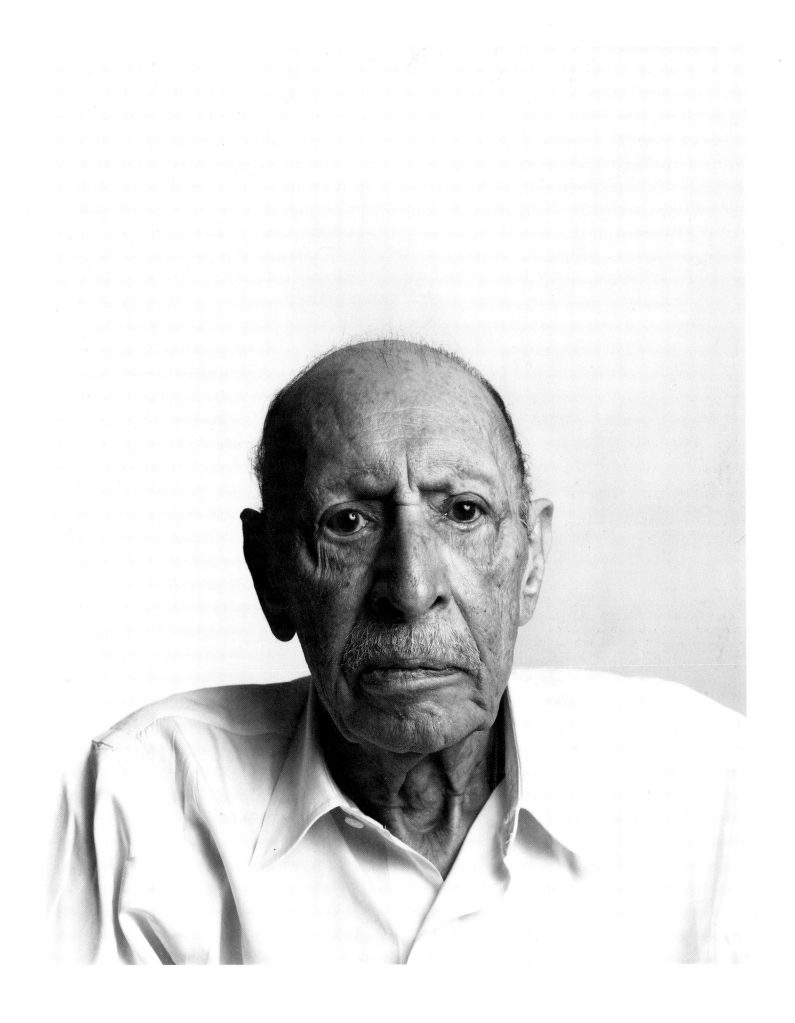

175 November 3, 1969. Photo by Richard Avedon.

176 December 1969. New York. With Balanchine.

the Lieberson family here for drinks.   **16** Harold Spivacke[1] here with Igor.   **18** For dinner here: Auden, Balanchine, Kirstein.[2] I now have Bombay Gin, since martini lovers recommend it, but since Auden drinks about 15 martinis and does not know exactly what he is drinking, I bought Gordon's Gin for him. My God how drunk he was, and how dirty. His face is covered with dirty rills. Finally, he could not pronounce words, and when he went to the toilet I had to watch to be certain that he did not miss the room. Igor is definitely better and he wants to have conversations with his friends. Naturally, he is soon tired but so are we all.   **22** The court order is effective and the manuscripts are free.   **24** A very nice evening with Rita and Ed, but Igor is sad.   **25** Lots of visitors and telegrams. Snowstorm.   **31** Finally we have the manuscripts, though even now I do not understand how the whole affair started and how stupid we were not to notice that money was disappearing. For New Year's Eve in our living room: Lucia, Bob Sandbach, Balanchine, Mme Malraux, Jean Stein, Miss Gillian Walker, Igor, Bob, and I.

1970

January

1 The *Los Angeles Times* reports that the manuscripts have been recovered from Marion and Montapert and that the suit has been dropped.   **2** We go down to the restaurant with Igor for dinner.   **5** Dr. La Due. Igor starts to have a cold leg, which Rita notices. I call Nabokov to ask him to get his doctor, Henry Lax. Two absolutely incompetent appraisers come to look at the manuscripts, and the qualifications of one of them was that he had appraised some music by Kostelanetz.   **6** Dr. Lax comes.   **7** Nabokov and Dominique for dinner. A bad night for Igor. **8** Igor is better.   **9** Dr. Lax for Igor.   **10** Nabokov and Dominique for dinner before they go to a Russian concert. We drink a lot.   **11** A walk with Igor in Central Park.   **13** Cold and windy. We decide to send Libman to liquidate our Hollywood house.   **14** Dr. Lax comes.   **16** Big surprise: Hideki comes. Igor not very good. Ed arrives.   **17** Hideki will work for us, cooking lunches. I work on the inventory of the house.[3] Dr. Maurice Gilbert visits us on his way to Manila.   **18** Rather *triste* day. Bob nervous, insists on more attention to Igor from doctors, consultations. **19** Maurice Gilbert eats lunch with us (Hideki cooking).   **23** Libman to Hollywood.   **24** Rita's birthday. Igor eats dinner with us in the restaurant downstairs.   **25** Elliott Carter at 5.   **27** At 3, two men from Sotheby[4] and an appraiser.   **28** Igor goes to Dr. Lax.   **29** The Sotheby people again. Stephen Spender and Mirandi come at 5.   **30** I take Igor for a drive. **31** Libman arrives from Hollywood with packages.

February

1 Opening the packages from Hollywood makes me nostalgic. Christopher Isherwood and Don see Igor from 5 to 7.   **4** Rickless[5] comes; he has already been to the Basel Bank.   **8** Letter from Bill Brown in Santa Barbara describing the disposal of the contents of our Hollywood house

and my studio.[6]   **9** Dinner with the Liebersons, and a film at CBS. **14** Snowstorm. Bob and I dine at Francis Steegmuller's with the Elliott Carters and Muriel Spark.   **15** Igor has a temperature. I telephone Dr. Lax.   **17** Bob and Elliott Carter to Luciano Berio's concert in Carnegie Hall.   **18** Nicolas for lunch.   **19** The Steegmullers come at 4:30.   **20** Dr. Lax.   **21** Dinner at the Côte Basque with the Steegmullers.

March

1 At 11 p.m. with Bob to Rumpelmeyer's for an ice-cream soda.   **3** Dr. Lax. Very bad day. Igor is weak and I am desperate.   **5** At 9:15 Dr. Riley.   **6** Dr. Lax comes twice—Igor has a temperature—and Virginia Rice[7] and Peggy Brook at 4.   **7** Dr. Lax from 12 to 1.   **12** Bob goes to *Petrushka*.[8]   **14** Igor is excellent and I make a good dinner.   **16** Bob and I go to Sviatoslav Richter's recital in Carnegie Hall.   **17** To the theater with Bob, *Child's Play*, very bad.   **18** Dr. Lax at 3. To a film with Liebersons in a CBS screening room, *Easy Rider*.   **19** Paul Horgan for dinner.   **21** At 6 to a cocktail party for Alexis Haieff, and at 7 to a Danish pornographic film, *Without a Stitch*, with the Lieberson family at CBS. **25** Weissberger and Milton Goldman to see Igor.   **26** Nabokov for Igor at 4, Dushkin at 5.   **27** Our Hollywood house is sold and I am very sad. **28** Visit from Babin and Vronsky.

April

1 Dr. Lax.   **3** Our passports arrive. Visits from David Adams[9] and Lou Feldman (manuscripts).[10]   **5** Igor sick again.   **6** Igor goes to Lenox Hill Hospital.   **7** Igor is better.   **9** Dr. Lax goes on vacation.   **10** Go twice to the hospital.   **11** Dinner at La Côte Basque with the Elliott Carters. **12** Igor is silent and does not smile.   **13** In the hospital from 3 to 6. **14** Igor: danger of uremic poisoning. He is taken back to special care. **15** Igor is better. Bob and I go to Carter's concert.   **16** Theodore and Denise arrive.   **17** Dinner at the Plaza with the Theodores, Bob, and Ed: expensive and bad.   **18** Go to the hospital with Theodore.   **20** Igor is back in his own room at the hospital. Dinner at the Pavillon with Iannis Xenakis and Nicolas and Dominique—to celebrate their marriage. **21** Dinner at La Croisette with Rita and the Theodores.   **22** Igor is taken off intravenous feeding and decatheterized.   **23** (Saturday) Leave the Theodores with Igor, and Bob drives me to New Paltz for dinner at Phyllis's. Walk in the forest.[11] Superb.   **26** Russian Easter. Igor restless the whole day.   **28**[12]   **29** Igor comes back to the hotel at 4, but he says, ''This is not home.''

May

1 Bob and I take Theodore and Denise to the airfield in a limousine. **2** Send a limousine to the airport for Bob Cunningham,[13] who brings the *Sacre* score.   **4** Dr. Lax returns from his vacation. We have new nurses. **6** To the Parke-Bernet auction of our Cocteau drawings and the Chagall portrait of Igor, 2–6.   **7** Spend a very interesting afternoon with Professor Malmstad from Columbia University, apropos Kusmin.[14]   **8** The Elliott

---

[1] Chief of the Music Division of the Library of Congress. Stravinsky wanted him to take two manuscripts, the piano scores of *Mavra* and of the Piano Concerto, for a tax deduction in 1969.

[2] See the photograph in *Stravinsky in Pictures and Documents*, op. cit.

[3] i.e., what should be sent to New York and what should be sold in Los Angeles.

[4] Thilo von Watzdorf and Gabriel Austin. The Stravinskys had decided to auction some Cocteau drawings, the Chagall portrait, and some of the manuscripts of the Stravinsky-Dushkin transcriptions. The Cocteau and Chagall sold but not the manuscripts.

[5] Elwood Rickless, attorney, retained by Weissberger to repatriate the Stravinskys' money from their Swiss bank. Rickless had double (Swiss and American) citizenship. He had married Regina Sarfaty, mezzo-soprano, whom the Stravinskys had known since 1957.

[6] Mrs. Stravinsky had asked him to choose the best of her paintings to send to New York and to destroy the others. Brown wrote that the ''inbetweens'' had presented the problems, and that he gave half of them to Libman, half to Mrs. Stalvey. He said that he had taken the brass stand in the hallway as a souvenir, but that it had lost its glamor in his house, and taken ''several bottles of Scotch, which, fortunately, retained their magic. . . . You are sorely missed, but I won't go on about it, or I'll begin to sound like Paderewski's parrot who is supposed to have sat on his foot when he practiced, and kept saying, 'Ach Gott, wunderschön.'''

[7] Stravinsky's literary agent since 1957. She was related to Judge Morris Lasker who, after her death, gave R.C. her Stravinsky files.

[8] Performed by the Ballet Theater in the 55th Street City Center.

[9] Of Boosey & Hawkes.

[10] Weissberger was trying to sell Stravinsky's manuscripts through Feldman, who had sold the T.S. Eliot and Evelyn Waugh libraries to the Houghton Library at Harvard and to the University of Texas.

[11] Anasting Falls, which, Mrs. Stravinsky said, made her think of Russia.

[12] On this date, Michael Barrie, Gerald Heard's friend, wrote from Santa Monica to the Stravinskys in New York: ''The night before last I had such a vivid dream of being with you three. We were all happy, chatting away as we used to do, and it has left me with such a feeling of nostalgia and such a realization of how much I have missed seeing you. . . . Poor Gerald has now survived fourteen strokes of varying degrees of intensity.''

[13] Lawrence Morton's brother-in-law. On May 1, Morton and Marilyn Stalvey removed the *Sacre* score from a vault in the Union Bank, Los Angeles. Morton kept the manuscript overnight, and Cunningham brought it to the Stravinsky apartment in the Essex House the next day.

[14] One of the Russian poet's most important poems is dedicated to Vera Sudeikina.

Carters come, Ed later. **13** Dr. Lax. Dinner at Pavillon with Donald Mitchell from London. **15** Lax from 12 to 1. Ed comes. **16** Igor not brilliant, restless and complaining. He resents his old age, especially that it prevents him from hearing everything and taking part in discussions, especially when they are in English and about abstract subjects. He keeps asking me in Russian for help—it is strange that he reads almost exclusively in Russian now, and speaks Russian only with me. **17** Laura Villaseñor at 5. **18** 1:30: Bob and I lunch with Laura. Paul Horgan for dinner. **19** Lax says Igor is better and asks me why I am so disturbed. **22** Theodore sends an idiotic letter. **23** Dinner at La Côte Basque with the Carters and Steegmullers. **28** With Igor for a promenade in Central Park. Visit from Dushkin. **29** Igor receives a letter from a Professor Ilya Friedman of the Glinka Conservatory in the city of Gorky, USSR, describing the great interest in Stravinsky's music there, and their pride in Russia "for having reared such a great composer." **30** No wonder people are horrified at the thought of giving someone a power of attorney. Now we know that a power of attorney can bankrupt us. Both the lawyer and Andre had our power of attorney and full access to our money. We were not checking on them, and it is especially difficult for us to verify the securities and the amounts of money in different banks.

June

1 Bob comes back with six cases of books and photographs. Stay up late sorting the photos. **4** Nicolas and Dominique for lunch. **5** Dr. Lax. Look for a coat for Igor. Rita returns from Mexico. **6** Lucia, the Dushkins. **9** I begin to pack for Europe. **11** We, Rita, Libman fly to Geneva at 7:10 p.m. **12** Evian, the Hotel Royal, Dr. Thaon. **13** Dr. René Della Santa comes from Geneva. Dinner in the terrace restaurant with Arnold Weissberger and Milton Goldman. **15** Ampenova comes. **16** Lunch outside with Igor. Denise brings a new nurse. Kitty comes. **18** Igor's 88th birthday: big lunch with Theodore and Denise. **19** Our car arrives.[1] Take Igor for a drive. **21** Take Igor for a drive. **22** Laboratory tests for Igor. Take him for a drive. **23** Dr. Della Santa. **24** Dr. Della Santa. **25** Big drive with Igor. **27** Take Igor to the hospital in Thonon for x-rays, cardiogram, and a transfusion (11–4). Libman to New York. **28** Dr. Della Santa. **30** Theodore and Denise here for a visit. Igor is bad.

July

2 Dr. Della Santa. **3** Meet Suvchinsky's train from Paris at 5:22. **4** Bob drives Suvchinsky, Igor, and me to Montreux and Clarens, where I photograph the house in which *Sacre* was composed. **5** Dr. Della Santa. Suvchinsky returns to Paris. I drive Igor for 45 minutes. **7** Eat in the bar with Igor. **8** Theodore and Denise. **10** Drive with Igor to the Château de Ripaille. **11** Big drive with Igor through the forest. Theodore and Denise bring Maurice Gilbert for dinner. **12** Drive Igor from 12 to 1. **13** Bill from Mme H. Maurin, nurse, 1201 Geneva, for 1000 Swiss francs, June 23–26: four days of work, forty days of *scandale*. **14** Theodore, Denise for dinner. **15** I walk with Bob. His sister, her husband, and their daughter are staying at a nearby hotel. I receive a letter from Christopher Isherwood: "Dear Vera, We have just found out where you are! At the time of Igor's birthday we called you three times at the Essex House, first calling your private number and then the hotel number, but we couldn't reach you or anyone else, except the hotel operator! Have just been looking up Evian-les-Bains on the map. I am so ignorant that I didn't even know, until this moment, that part of Lake Geneva is in France!

"If I had written earlier, it would have been to tell you that we were returning to England and might get over to see you. Alas, that's no longer probable. The would-be producers of our play had decided to give it a try-out at a theater called the Phoenix at Leicester, without star actors, which was what we had wanted all along. But then they discovered that it wouldn't be a good idea because the College would be down and so we wouldn't have much of an audience. (I should have

thought they might have known this in advance!) Anyhow, that puts an end to the whole scheme, because Robert Chetwyn, our director, has to go to New York quite soon, to direct a new play by Tom Stoppard. So now the play will hardly be produced this year.

"However, we are not in utter despair! We are both very busy. I am making a great effort to finish my big book about my parents. In my mother's diary I found a sort of prophetic entry which seems to refer to this book. It was written when I was five: 'Christopher dictated a story called The Adventures of Mummy and Daddy, chiefly about himself!'

"The weather is beautiful and hot but there is awful smog in town. There are still hippies on the Strip, though not as many as in the old days. Now one of the oil companies is threatening to drill some wells on Santa Monica Bay and even right in our canyon. There is a hearing about it today and a big crowd of protesting residents appeared.

"Do please write and tell us how you are and who you are seeing and how you spend your time. Very much love, as always, to you all."
16 Dr. Della Santa. **18** Xenia[2] arrives on the train from Paris at 5:22. **19** Lucia Davidova and Bob Sandbach come for lunch. **21** Xenia returns to Paris. **22** I go to see Château Allinges and the farm. Nurse, Madame G. Fedya and Denise for dinner. **23**[3] Dr. Della Santa. I take Igor for a drive. **24** Drive with Igor. **25** Letters from Nicolas Nabokov in Aspen (asking for the Evian telephone number, since he will soon be in Monte Carlo and will call) and Bill Brown in Santa Barbara: "Chère Madame, It's good to think of you surrounded by crystal air and quiet. It *is* quiet, isn't it? Here I've taken to wearing earplugs most of the time to shut out freeway noises, dogs barking, and the neighbor's hi-fi. California is grimmer than ever. I hope you don't consider coming back to the USA. I picture you for the winter either in Paris or in a house in Southern France—where we are (in this fantasy) all out on the terrace having drinks: you, white wine, your husband, Scotch, Bob, champagne. In the distance we see the lights of Cannes. A black and white cat, immaculately dressed, announces dinner. Dinner lasts three hours and has 23 courses. Afterwards we proceed to the casino where you win at craps.

"Yes, where were we?

"Took Chris and Don last week to a stage adaptation of 8 of Grimm's fairy tales, a lot of amateurs running around trying to be dogs, cats, roosters, and hens, and only succeeding in being asses.

"I bought the records of the *Requiem Canticles*, *Variations*, etc.: very beautiful. Do you have records to hear in the evening? It must be good to drive around in that countryside, or does it make you long for the city?

"As we passed by Wetherly Drive on Sunset Boulevard the other night with Chris and Don, we all groaned. When will *I* make 'my escape into the beautiful'? (Emily Dickinson)." **26** Igor complains all the time. The doctor wants him to go to a clinic in Geneva. **28** Igor has a transfusion (500 cc) from 10 to 3. **29** Dr. Della Santa, the Theodores. Igor looks very well. I won: we are *not* going to the clinic in Geneva. **30** To Thonon to take the letter to Dr. Blanc. Bouillabaisse in the hotel restaurant.

August

1 Dinner with the Theodores and Maurice Gilbert. Igor is in a nasty mood. **3** I go to Geneva to repair the car. Denise helps me a lot: lunch, library. Mirandi arrives at 5:30. Nabokov telephones from Monte Carlo. **4** Drive Igor to Thonon for another transfusion. **5** Mirandi is very entertaining and gives good advice. Struggle with decisions. The Theodores for dinner. Mirandi leaves for London. **6** Dr. Della Santa comes very late. **7** Theodore and Denise bring a dentist for Igor. **8** Drive Igor to Thonon for a transfusion. **9** Dr. Della Santa. **11** Natasha Nabokov comes. **12** Igor to Thonon for a transfusion. **14** With Natasha to Geneva and Coppet for lunch with Nikita Magalov and wife, then Bob drives us around the lake to Evian. **15** Sol and Mae Babitz come to see us in the morning, on their way to Italy. Robert and Sybil Paterson here from London for lunch and dinner. **18** Magalovs for dinner. Igor very nervous. **19** Igor has another transfusion at Thonon. The Theodores come again: Igor is very irritated. What a life! **20** Dr. Della Santa.

---

[1] The Stravinskys' Lincoln Continental had been shipped from New York and Libman went to Le Havre (June 16–19) to bring it to Evian. Mrs. Stravinsky was afraid to drive any car except her own, and her pre-war French driving license was still good in France (!). The car was shipped to New York from Le Havre on the S.S. *Atlantic Crown* on August 28, driven to the port by M. François, husband of the nurse mentioned under June 16.

[2] Xenia Yurievna, the daughter of Stravinsky's elder brother, Yuri, had come from Leningrad in the hope of convincing Mrs. Stravinsky that her husband should be buried in his native city. She had written to "Uncle Igor and Vierochka," March 5, 1970, saying that she had news of the European trip from Fedya, and that she

would come via Paris where she would stay with Natasha Yellachich. On July 16, 1970, Ira wrote to Vera: "Xenia sounds nice in her letter, but we have nothing in common. I hope that her visit to Stravinsky will not last long. I am glad that you can live in some comfort now. Uncle Igor worked hard, did a lot for his children, and should be able to spend his money on himself now. I feel that only Uncle Igor and Fedya are my relatives now. Milene and Svetik are totally antipathetic to me."

[3] On this date, Victoria Ocampo wrote to the Stravinskys from Buenos Aires: "Graham Greene just spent several weeks with me, and we were very pleased to be able to go together to the beach at Mar del Plata."

177

177 September 1970. New York.

178 1972. At home, 920 Fifth Avenue.

François Michel and his friend André take us to La Bourgogne, a good restaurant in the town of Evian. **21** Lord Snowdon wants to take photographs of Igor. Again the Theodores. **23** The Patersons return from London. **24** Dinner with Lord Snowdon and his friend. The Theodores dine with Igor in his room. **25**[1] Snowdon[2] photographs Igor. **26** Lunch at La Bourgogne, then drive to Geneva and fly to New York at 6 p.m. **27** Dr. Howard (Lax's substitute) for Igor. Hideki comes to make lunch. Ed and I shop. **28** Dinner with the Elliott Carters.

September

1 Laboratory tests. Lunch with Tom Messer.[3] **2** Therapist for Igor: Amy Levin. Paul Horgan for dinner. **3** Igor to the dentist at 11 a.m. Levin at 4:15. **5** Phone Geneva, 470577, for medications: Nervifene, Bisolvon, Resyl, Eucalyptine. I decide to rent an apartment and buy a country house. **7** Promenade in the Park with Igor. **8** Dr. Lax. **11** Nabokovs for dinner: we play records, Igor, Bob, Nicolas listen to *Sacre* following the original manuscript. **12** Nicolas calls: "How marvelous it was yesterday." **13** Nabokovs for dinner. **14** Lucia brought a cake— mistakenly thinking it was my name day. **15** Dinner at Pavillon with Nabokovs. **16** Dr. Lax. **17** Paul Horgan, with limousine, takes us to the Côte Basque, then to film with Liebersons at CBS. **18** At noon: Drs. Lax and Wasserman. With Steegmullers to dinner at the Pavillon. **19** Ed comes. **20** Visit from Balanchine and Nabokov. **21** Igor is in a nasty mood. **22** Nicolas tries to talk to Igor and is badly received. **23** Look for an apartment. With Bob to a party to celebrate the publication of Steegmuller's *Cocteau*. The Founders Room at the Museum of Modern Art. **25** At 4 I go to talk to Andre Meyer,[4] Apt. 33A, 35 E. 76th.

October

3 I go to Tiffany to buy a silver cup for John McClure's baby. **5** Dinner at Pavillon with Weissberger and Milton Goldman. **6** Bob and I look at a penthouse apartment in the Mayfair Hotel: NO! Dinner in New Paltz at Phyllis's: very nice. **11** The Dushkins at 5. **13** Dinner at Steegmullers'. **16** Ed comes late. **18** Ed went back. At 5, go to Sylvia Marlowe's cocktail party. **19** Bill Brown arrives. **20** Bob's birthday. Dinner at the Pavillon with Bill Brown. Bob and I look at an apartment on Park Avenue; not bad, but Bob disagrees: no view. **21** The Steegmullers come to discuss the question of Francis writing Igor's biography.[5] **24** Dr. Lax says he is satisfied with both of us. **25** Bill Brown for dinner, the Nabokovs later. **28** Life in the Essex House is so expensive that I do not know how to manage. Also, it is uncomfortable, noisy, with a bad kitchen, and our furniture and our library are in storage. **29** Aaron Propes [Director of the Festival of Israel] visits us. Dinner with Liebersons at the Ground Floor (CBS building), then to a pornographic film, *Vixen*. **30** Nabokovs for dinner.

November

2 Leonard Lyons writes something bad in his column that Igor is supposed to have said about Russia, that we received an invitation to go to Moscow and turned it down with an insulting remark. **6** Baron Fred

for dinner, but it is boring to talk only about the past. Dr. Lax. **8** Ed helps with books and goes back at 5. **13** Igor has a transfusion. At noon I see a marvelous apartment. At 2:30 to the eye doctor. At 5, David Adams from London. Lawrence Morton for dinner. **14** Show Bob the apartment.[6] Big dinner for Copland,[7] but we do not go. **15** Dr. Lax. The Elliott Carters at 5. **16** To the theater: *Sleuth*. **17** To the theater: *Home*, with Ralph Richardson and Gielgud. Dinner at the Pavillon. Delightful evening. **19/20** The apartment will be mine, if we can get rid of the Essex House lease. **21** Dinner at Nabokov's: very cozy, nice, and touching. **24** To the theater, *Promises, Promises*. **26** Hideki cooks a marvelous turkey. Ed arrives. **28** Lunch with Steegmullers. Dinner at the Pavillon with Nabokovs, Alain Daniélou, and friend.[8] **29** Nabokovs with Russian friends, Petrovsky. **30** Dr. Lax. Cocktails at Nabokovs'. Alexander Schneider visits and wants to see Igor, but his door is closed and he is playing the piano. Schneider says it is enough to hear his piano.

December

1 Dr. Lax. A big day. We want to sign the contract for the apartment but change the date to February 1. **2** I sign the escrow agreement for the apartment ($27,000). Auden for dinner. **3** Dr. Lax. **5** Visit from Foldi.[9] Fizdale and Gold invite me to a musical tea but I do not go because of the taxi strike. **9** Dr. Lax for Igor. **13** The Elliott Carters for dinner. **14** Dr. Lax at 4. Bob and I go to Weissberger at 5:30 because of a bad letter from Theodore. **15** Nabokovs for dinner. **16** I lunch with Shirley Hazzard [Mrs. Steegmuller]. **17** Dr. Lax. **19** Nicolas is supposed to play his opera[10] for Igor, but there are too many people. **20** Rita discovers the supposedly stolen things under her bed, which means that a hotel employee must have returned them, since the police made a search of the room. **21** Dr. Lax. Dinner at La Grenouille with Paul Horgan. **23** Ed arrives. **25** See *The Twelve Chairs* with Ed—very funny. **31** The Dushkins come. Ed comes late. Champagne.

1971

January

2 A visit from Kyriena. **6** Bob comes back from Florida. Igor happy to see him. They listen to music (*Apollo*). **7** Russian Christmas and my birthday. **8** Ed comes very late. **9** Dr. Lax comes with skin doctor. Bob and Igor play music all evening. **10** Sonya Kroyt comes at 4 and proposes an exhibition for me in the Chelsea Bank (825 Seventh Avenue).[11] Ed goes home. **11** Go to the apartment. Mrs. Howard has not even started to move. **12** Buy a gift for Lillian Libman in Lord & Taylor, and a canary cage for Igor. **13** Dinner at the Pavillon with Carters. **16** Ed comes. **19** Buy linen for Igor's bed. **20** Big supper at Pavillon after Peter Brooks' *A Midsummer Night's Dream*: Liebersons, Horgan, Dominique. Natasha stays with Igor. **21** Buy an armchair and card table for the apartment. **22** With Bob to buy a desk for the apartment. In the evening to the ballet to see Igor's *Concerto per due pianoforti soli*, choreographed by Massine Jr.: *comme çi, comme ça*. **23** With

[1] On this date, Victoria Ocampo wrote to Mrs. Stravinsky from Argentina referring to Greene's *Travels with My Aunt* and saying that "Borges has become a great world star, but he has not had any luck with his wife. At this moment they are divorcing. She has behaved in an abominable manner, and I think he has suffered greatly, and no one understands why he married her in the first place. She doesn't allow him to see his old friends, and she thinks only about pocketing the money that he earns (which at present is not bad). In short, a disaster."

[2] Snowdon wrote to Mrs. Stravinsky: "It was so kind of you to allow me to spend so long photographing your husband. I am sure we were right to stop when we did, as I would have hated the thought of having tired him before your journey to New York."

[3] Director of the Guggenheim Museum, which had purchased one of Mrs. Stravinsky's paintings for its permanent collection.

[4] The banker (Lazare Frères), a patient of Dr. Lax, had agreed to give Mrs. Stravinsky financial advice, but he did not know that she was almost without money.

[5] The Stravinskys agreed, but Ampenova, of Boosey & Hawkes, would not give Steegmuller permission to use Stravinsky's archives. Meanwhile, in mid-November, Steegmuller rented room 921 in the Essex House, and took the archives there for study, carton by carton, from the Stravinskys' room 928, an office adjoining their suite.

[6] At 920 Fifth Avenue. Mrs. Stravinsky purchased it December 1 from the widow of a renowned scientist, Frank Howard, founder of the Sloan-Kettering Institute for Cancer Research. His widow, the former Duchess of Leeds, wished to live in her native Paris, but she was slow in vacating the apartment, and when the moving began, Mrs. Stravinsky wrote: "I am spending a lot of money to redecorate the place. The previous owner was a very untidy woman. How could she, elegant and rich, have tolerated such a shabby place? Will Igor like the place?" Mrs. Stravinsky was to live there for twelve and a half years.

[7] His seventieth birthday.

[8] One of the great authorities on ragas, Daniélou had retired to Venice. He was the brother of Cardinal Daniélou, who translated the Cocteau-Stravinsky *Oedipus Rex* from French to Latin.

[9] Andrew Foldi, the Metropolitan Opera basso, had known the Stravinskys since 1957 in Santa Fe. Foldi's daughter brought the Stravinskys' Picassos and other paintings from a bank vault in Paris to New York, where the Stravinskys sold them to meet medical and hotel expenses.

[10] *Love's Labour's Lost*.

[11] This exhibition took place months after Stravinsky's death.

Liebersons, Avedons, and Leonard Bernsteins to see a film in the CBS screening room: Ken Russell's *Delius* (which makes me cry).   **24** I cook for six and am very tired. At 6, go with Rita to a big cocktail party for Peter Brooks: Nabokovs, Bob Silvers, *et al*.   **25** At 4, two lawyers, representing the Stravinsky children, meet with Weissberger. At 6 we go to the Béjart Ballet in Brooklyn. Disastrous. Supper afterward at Pavillon.   **29** Buy a bed for the new apartment, for Bob.   **30** Ed, sick, will not come.   **31** Carlos Chavez sees Igor, goes on his knees and kisses his hands.

February

2 Dinner here for Nabokovs.   **3** Igor goes to the dentist and has one tooth extracted. Lillian Libman comes from Baltimore and agrees to work for us beginning February 8.   **4** Dr. Lax 3 to 4. Erminia.[1]   **10** I go with Natasha to a Stravinsky concert at Columbia University, McMillan Theater.   **12** Go to the apartment: terrible disappointment; so dirty and run down. Dr. Lax.   **16** Talks with the painter, carpenter, electrician.   **18** Dinner at the Pavillon with the Robert Patersons and David Frost, who wants to interview Igor on television.

March

5 Dr. Lax.   **6** To the Carters', from whom I buy curtains and a mirror. Ed comes and we drink a lot and it is a little more gay.   **7** Rieti: dull conversation. He is disappointed that Igor does not see him.   **11** Nikita Magalov invites us to lunch at the Pavillon.   **12** Go to Third and Second Avenue antique stores.   **18** Khrennikov calls me from Moscow to invite us to live in a home on the Black Sea in the summer. Two hours later Igor goes to the Lenox Hill Hospital.   **19** Hospital. Ed comes.   **22** Igor is bad. Dinner at Pavillon.   **23** Five men, movers, from Beverly Mayflower. At six to the hospital. Igor much better.   **24** Finish packing.   **27** I buy a canary for Igor.   **28** Our last night in the Essex House.   **29** We move to the new apartment. Igor comes there directly from the hospital.

April

4 Igor very sick. Madeleine Malraux's concert: I did not go, but Dr. Lax did.   **5** We do not sleep. Crying and waiting for the end. Dr. Lax three times. Dr. Brown, Dr. M. at night.   **6** IGOR DIES AT 5:20 A.M.

Un Couple de Légende

Depuis 1971, dès que les premiers jours de printemps arrivent à Venise, on voit débarquer une grande dame distinguée, qui aussitôt descendue sur les quais, se dirige vers San Michele. . . .
  Madame Vera STRAVINSKY vient régulièrement se recueillir sur la tombe de son mari. . . .
  Dans les allées, sous les cyprès, se perpétue une belle légende d'un couple hors de destin; d'un couple qui a trouvé son oasis, sa paix sous le ciel de Venise, d'un couple de créateurs; lui, musicien, et elle, peintre, dont toutes les oeuvres sont inspirées d'un air étrange, féerique, d'une Venise d'un autre monde. . . .
  (*San Michele* by Charles Maray)

[1] Erminia Tomici was Mrs. Stravinsky's dressmaker for the next ten years.

179 December 1978. New York. Vera's ninetieth birthday party, at the home of L. Arnold Weissberger, who took the photograph.

180 May 1982. At "The Beachcomber," Pompano Beach, Florida.

181–182 September 24, 1983. Venice. San Michele. Photos by Eva Resnikova.

Brenners Park-Hotel in Baden-Baden

-2-

нашёл Radio и слушал Symph.
in 3 movements от Бюро (и нес-
колько математически безупреч-
нично) исполненную имъ.

Завтра начну свои репетиции:
Jeu de Cartes, Symph d'instr. à vents, ~~[illegible]~~, вечером
Capriccio и Symph in 3 M^{ts}.

Въ четв. вечеръ ~~[illegible]~~ репетиция
и въ пятн. въ 8 веч. - концертъ
Послѣ концерта холодный банкетъ

CASINO · THEATER · KONZERTE
18 L. GOLF · TENNIS · REITEN · SCHWIMMBAD · THERMALBÄDER
GANZJÄHRIGER KURBETRIEB